D0072058

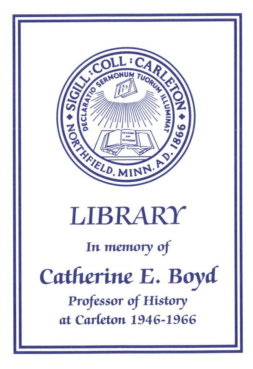

LIBRARY

In memory of

Catherine E. Boyd

Professor of History
at Carleton 1946-1966

THE REALM
OF ST STEPHEN

THE REALM
OF ST STEPHEN

A HISTORY OF
MEDIEVAL HUNGARY, 895–1526

PÁL ENGEL
Translated by Tamás Pálosfalvi
English edition edited by
ANDREW AYTON

I.B. Tauris *Publishers*
LONDON • NEW YORK

Published in 2001 by I.B.Tauris & Co Ltd
6 Salem Road, London W2 4BU
175 Fifth Avenue, New York NY 10010
www.ibtauris.com

In the United States and Canada distributed by St. Martin's Press
175 Fifth Avenue, New York NY10010

Copyright © Pál Engel, 2001

All rights reserved. Except for brief quotations in a review, this book, or any part thereof,
may not be reproduced, stored in or introduced into a retrieval system, or transmitted, in
any form or by any means, electronic, mechanical, photocopying, recording or otherwise, without the prior written permission of the publisher.

This book has been published with the support of the
Hungarian Ministry of Cultural Heritage and the Frankfurt '99 Kht.

ISBN 1-86064-061-3

A full CIP record for this book is available from the British Library
A full CIP record for this book is available from the Library of Congress

Library of Congress catalog card: available

Typeset by The Midlands Book Typesetting Co, Loughborough, Leicestershire
Printed and bound in Great Britain by MPG Books Ltd, Bodmin

Contents

DB
929
.E545
2001

092302 - 6116 H6

Foreword

In 1993 I approached Pál Engel with an ambitious publication proposal: that he should write a new history of medieval Hungary for an English-language readership and that I could provide substantial assistance in bringing the project to realisation. Just how substantial my role was to be was only to become apparent some years later, when portions of the draft text began to appear on my desk; but from the outset it was clear what sort of book was needed. It was to be the first comprehensive survey of its subject in English, and rather than being merely a translation of an existing work, it was to be written afresh by one of Hungary's leading medievalists and with the non-Hungarian reader in mind.

As someone who had recently become interested in the medieval history of east-central Europe – seeking to develop a research interest for myself as well as endeavouring to introduce medieval Hungary to undergraduate students – I was only too well aware of the serious shortage of historical literature on the subject in English. (There was a good deal more in German, but a reading knowledge of that language is not possessed by many history undergraduates in Britain, nor I suspect in the USA.) There were, of course, general surveys of Hungarian history, from the classic volume by C.A. Macartney to the then recently published *A History of Hungary*, edited by Peter Sugar and Péter Hanák; but treatment of the Middle Ages in these books, though expertly handled, is necessarily brief and selective. Also available was a range of specialised works (now more numerous), some translated from Hungarian, some written by scholars based in the West; and a useful selection of primary sources in modern editions. I can well remember the excitement with which I read these works, and the genuine enthusiasm with which my students took to the subject, despite the difficulties involved in bridging the chasm between concise historical surveys and demanding monographs and articles. It was, however, undoubtedly the case that, for newcomers to this field, the accessible historical literature was patchy in coverage and uneven in quality. The bulk of the most important writing on medieval Hungary was available only to those able to read Hungarian. What was urgently needed was a volume conceived on a large scale that combined a detailed narrative with a broad-based thematic coverage; which synthesised the most up-to-date research by Hungarian (and other) scholars; and which presented it in an accessible, readable fashion for a non-Hungarian audience. It was with these needs in mind that this book was written.

Naturally, we hope that the publication of this book, happily coinciding as it does with the thousandth anniversary of St Stephen's coronation, will serve also to bring the medieval history of the Carpathian basin to the attention of a wider academic and general readership. The importance and distinctiveness of this region's history are matched only by the degree to which it has been neglected by the academic community of western Europe and the USA. Yet the region, and the realm of St Stephen within it, that bore the brunt of the Mongols' onslaught on Europe in the 1240s, that became Europe's leading producer of gold in the fourteenth century and that stoutly resisted the advance of the Ottoman Turks (whilst, under Matthias Corvinus, witnessing the first flowering of the Renaissance north of the Alps) in the fifteenth, surely deserves more attention than it has hitherto received. Such attention would be amply rewarded. For beyond gaining an understanding of the internal life and external relations of one of the major kingdoms of Christendom, an examination of medieval Hungarian history presents opportunities for fruitful comparisons with the familiar themes, social groups and institutions of western Europe. For example, while an English medievalist may be as intrigued by the 'honours' of Angevin Hungary as the Florentine chronicler Matteo Villani appears to have been, he will also find in *familiaritas*, the relationship between lord and retainer (*familiaris*), a close resemblance to 'bastard feudalism'.

What tends to emerge from such comparisons is the strong impression that St Stephen's realm was at once part of the mainstream of Christendom, yet in some respects different, enduringly influenced by the cultural and social legacies of its pagan past and by its geographical location on the frontier of Christian Europe. This is an impression that is vividly conveyed by the numerous miniatures, nearly 150 of them, which decorate the text of the Illuminated Chronicle of *c.* 1360. Most striking in this respect is the symbolic depiction of Louis the Great's cosmopolitan court, but also notable are the miniatures that offer glimpses of Louis's armies, which are shown as consisting of western-style knightly warriors, supported by lightly equipped mounted archers, apparently of Cumanian or Iasian origin, wielding composite bows. And this is surely the impression of Angevin Hungary that would have been carried home by western-European visitors – by men like the Dominican friar, Walter atte More, who in April 1346 arrived in Hungary on a diplomatic mission from England. His expenses account shows that he met the queen-mother at Visegrád, then travelled to Zagreb, where the royal army was mobilising, for discussions with King Louis himself. The English Dominican would, therefore, have seen at first hand the workings of the royal court and the distinctive features of Hungarian military organisation; and he may well have formed judgements about the character of the political elite and the capabilities of the king's army. Like other travellers in the region, he would no doubt have been struck by the comparative sparseness of the population. And he may also have gained some appreciation of the mineral wealth of Hungary and the advantages that it gave a young king with military ambitions. Thus, whatever the outcome of his negotiations, we can be fairly certain that the Dominican friar would have conveyed to his political masters in England a view of mid-fourteenth-century Hungary likely to arouse both intense interest and a certain amount of envy.

Whilst further specialist works on particular aspects of the Hungarian Middle Ages written in western-European languages are greatly to be welcomed (as, for example, Martyn Rady's forthcoming study of the *Nobility, Land and Service in Medieval Hungary*), what we may also hope for in the future are, on the one hand, comparative works involving Hungarian history and, on the other, the integration of the medieval experience of the peoples of the Carpathian basin into studies with a coverage that is truly European – studies of, for example, kingship and representative assemblies, the nobility and peasantry, the ecclesiastical hierarchy and monastic orders, or warfare and military institutions. To take the last subject as an example, imagine a work like Philippe Contamine's magisterial *La guerre au moyen âge*, yet with a purview stretching as far as eastern Europe and the Balkans. In this respect, there have indeed been some promising publications in recent years: witness, for example, the scope of David Nicolle's *Arms and Armour of the Crusading Era, 1050–1350*, 2 vols (White Plains, New York, 1988). But a good deal more comparative work needs to be done in the field of medieval military institutions. As the present volume shows, the military role of the nobility – their theoretical obligations as well as the role they actually performed – is one of the central threads of Hungarian history; but how does this role compare with the martial activities of the nobility elsewhere in Christendom? The study of Hungarian armies needs also to be set within a wider context. For example, it would be appropriate, indeed illuminating, to view the armies raised by the Angevin kings as but one further facet of the general development of contractual military service in medieval

Europe, whilst any study of the emergence of standing armies in the fifteenth century should not fail to take account of Matthias Corvinus's mercenary army, not to mention the permanent garrisons installed in Hungary's southern frontier fortresses.

It is, therefore, my hope that this book, which itself is the result of Anglo-Hungarian collaboration, may contribute in some small measure to the broadening of medievalists' horizons, and to the further integration of St Stephen's realm into the mainstream of historical research and teaching in western Europe and the USA.

Andrew Ayton

Preface

This book was written for the non-Hungarian reader who wishes to discover what happened in the Carpathian basin during the Middle Ages. It is to be hoped that nobody living in that region who has strong national feelings will find comfort in it. Each of the nations of the region has its own vision of the past, incompatible with that of the others, and it was my firm intention that none of these visions should be represented in this volume.

Throughout this book are to be found topics which do not sit comfortably with particular national perspectives on the past. Many Slovakians do not like to read, for instance, that their country was once merely part of Hungary. Similarly, many Romanians prefer not to be reminded that in the Middle Ages Transylvania was a Hungarian province, for they would like to believe that it was in fact a Romanian principality, only loosely attached to a foreign power. All Croatians know well that Croatia as a kingdom was older than Hungary, but many of them would prefer to forget that this kingdom was much smaller than modern Croatia and that their modern capital, Zagreb, lay in Hungary. As for Hungarians, they still cling on to the fiction that there has only ever been one Hungary: the one that was founded by St Stephen in 1000 AD, and which still survives after a thousand years, even if it happens to be much smaller now than it once was. They will never accept the obvious fact that the republic of Hungary is not identical to the ancient kingdom of Hungary; that, as political entities, these are as different as are Turkey and the Ottoman Empire.

A particular area of sensitivity where national feelings are concerned is the use of personal names and place names. There are as many name forms as there are languages in the region, but there is no rule to determine which form is correct when the language of communication is English. Košice in modern Slovakia can be called Kassa, for it was, after all, a town in Hungary; but it was also known as Kaschau, for at that time it was inhabited by Germans, and also Cassovia, for this was the Latinised name of the town, used in contemporary records. To make things easier, and also for the convenience of the reader, the *modern names of localities*, the names which can be found on a modern map, have been used in this book. (References to other names can be found in the index.) The only exceptions to this rule are recently created names, use of which would have involved obvious anachronisms. One should not refer to Budapest before 1873 when the three cities of Buda, Óbuda and Pest were administratively united to form the modern capital. Also inappropriate in this book would be Bratislava or Cluj-Napoca, since both names were created in recent times.

Most persons who appear in this book have also had different names in the vernacular languages of the region, while bearing a Latinised name in contemporary records. It is often impossible to say which of these names is historically 'correct'. Johannes de Hunyad may equally be called Iancu de Hunedoara (Romanian) or János Hunyadi (Hungarian), because he was born a Romanian, but became a Hungarian nobleman and also regent of Hungary. The lords de Gara were Hungarian lords and can be referred to as Garai (Hungarian); but they had many Croatian subjects who probably called them Gorjanski (Croatian). However, it would have been nonsensical to differentiate between Hungarian lords according to their 'modern nationality'; nor would it have been meaningful to use their Latinised names, for these people were not Romans. They were or became Hungarians, so in each case the name that has been accepted in Hungarian historiography has been used in this book, apart from their Christian names, which are always given in the English form.

In preparing the manuscript I have very much profited from the comments of Jörg K. Hoensch (Saarbrücken), Martyn Rady (London), János M. Bak, Enikő Csukovits, Zsuzsanna Hermann, András Kubinyi, István Tringli and Attila Zsoldos (Budapest). I am peculiarly indebted to Tamás Pálosfalvi for the vast amount of work that he put into preparing the rough English version of my Hungarian text; and to Andrew Ayton, who expended no less effort going through the text meticulously word by word, making many suggestions and reworking the prose extensively, thereby shaping the text into its now readable form. I am also grateful to Béla Nagy for drawing the maps. But, in the first place, I am indebted to my wife for supporting me with infinite patience while I was writing this book.

Pál Engel

Introduction

Hungary is now one of the smallest countries of Europe. This book, however, is concerned with the medieval period, and here the name 'Hungary' will refer to the former kingdom of Hungary, which (even without the kingdom of Croatia which was once united with it) was more than three times larger than the present-day republic, and also somewhat larger than the combined area of Great Britain and Ireland. It extended over the whole of the Carpathian basin, including not only present-day Slovakia, but also considerable parts of Romania, Ukraine, Austria, Yugoslavia and Croatia. Although the kingdom of Hungary ceased to exist as an independent country at the end of the Middle Ages, politically it survived as an autonomous part of the Habsburg Empire until the end of the First World War in 1918.

LANDSCAPE AND HISTORY

The medieval kingdom of Hungary was born in a geographically well-defined region that is usually called the Carpathian basin. This is the drainage-area of the middle Danube valley, and is named after those mountain ranges with 2000 metre peaks that border it to the north, the east and the south. It is divided by the Danube into two parts of unequal proportions, and its centre is surrounded by mountain ranges of medium height. The region to the west of the Danube has been called Transdanubia since the period of the Ottoman occupation when the capital of the country was temporarily moved from Buda to Pressburg, on the northern bank of the river. The climate here is predominantly temperate, with a relatively heavy rainfall. This is a fertile landscape with hills of modest elevation interrupted by valleys and basins, and with the Balaton, the largest warm-water lake in Europe, at its heart. There are also mountain ranges – the Mecsek in the south-east, the Bakony and the Vértes north of the Balaton – but none rises higher than 600 metres. The landscape east of the Danube is profoundly different. The Great Hungarian Plain, which stretches without a single hill from Budapest to Oradea in the east and Belgrade in the south, can be regarded as a kind of appendix to the Eurasian steppe. The climate is rather more extreme here, with hot, dry summers, but the region is abundantly supplied with water by its main river, the Tisza, and its tributaries, which, before the nineteenth-century regulation works, meandered across the Great Plain. These rivers were flanked by marshlands, swamps and inundation forests, and also by fertile pastures and meadows, offering favourable conditions for fishing and livestock breeding. To the north, east and south-east of the Great Plain, in present-day Slovakia and Romania, there are mountain ranges that become progressively higher as one travels outwards from the Plain. They were formerly extremely rich in minerals; but, with the exception of the valleys, they have never been propitious to human settlement. Consequently, until the late Middle Ages these mountains were covered by forests and largely uninhabited, and colonization of them continued into the early modern period.

When, in the ninth century, the Hungarians emerged from the obscurity of prehistoric times they were living as nomadic horsemen on the steppe along the Black Sea. They spoke a language of Finno-Ugric origin, but their culture in general resembled that of the Turkic peoples of the steppe. In 895 they moved into the Carpathian basin under the leadership of their pagan prince, Árpád. Here they soon became notorious through their plundering raids into Western Europe in the tenth century. But Hungary as a political unit can only be spoken of from the year 1000, when Stephen I, a descendant of Árpád and later to be known as Saint Stephen, converted to Christianity and was crowned king. The kingdom founded by him became one of the great powers of the region and remained so for 500 years, until the sixteenth century, when it was crushed by the expanding Ottoman Empire. 1526, the year of the battle of Mohács, where King Louis II himself was killed, constitutes the traditional closing date of the history of medieval Hungary. The central part of the kingdom, including Buda, the capital, was soon overrun by the Turks and incorporated into their empire. In the east, Transylvania became an autonomous principality under Ottoman control, while the rest of the kingdom, which was defensible against the Turks, was to be governed by kings from the Habsburg dynasty until 1918. The latter, who were at the same time rulers of Austria and Bohemia and also Holy Roman Emperors, consistently regarded Hungary as one of their hereditary dominions. Between 1683 and 1699 they finally expelled the Turks from Hungary, annexing Transylvania in 1690, but the integrity of medieval Hungary was only restored in 1867, when the Austro-Hungarian monarchy was founded. However, the end of the First World War brought about the total dismemberment of this short-lived empire, and the Treaties of Trianon and Versailles allotted more than two thirds of the former kingdom of Hungary to the newly born national states of Czechoslovakia, Austria, Romania and Yugoslavia.

The medieval history of Hungary can be divided into three periods. The age of the rulers of Árpád's dynasty (1000–1301), at least during the first two centuries, still recalls in some respects the barbarian kingdoms of the Dark Ages. The thirteenth century, when Hungary had to face, if only for a moment, the invasion of Dzinghis Khan's successors (1241), witnessed spectacular changes in the structure of both society and the economy. From this time on, by its outlook as well as by the nature of its institutions, Hungary increasingly resembled the older kingdoms of Christian Europe, although, lying on the periphery of Christendom, it quite naturally preserved a number of features peculiar to itself. The period of the Angevin rulers (1301–1382) and King Sigismund of Luxembourg (1387–1437) can be described as the apogee of medieval Hungary. It is marked by strong royal power, an aggressive foreign policy and, somewhat in contrast to the manifold crisis that was then gripping the West, dynamic economic development. The main feature of the last century of medieval Hungary (1437–1526) was the defence against the increasing Ottoman threat. This was accompanied by the decline of royal power, which was naturally not unconnected with the growing importance of the Estates. The two personalities who dominated this period were the regent, John Hunyadi (d. 1456), hero of the Ottoman wars, and his son, King Matthias Corvinus (1458–1490), who is remembered less as the conqueror of Vienna than as a generous patron of Renaissance art and humanism. The union with Bohemia under the feeble Jagiellonian kings (1490–1526) was merely a prelude to the fall of the medieval kingdom.

SOURCES

The history of Hungary is poorly endowed with narrative sources. Even those that we have are not very informative. There are almost no monastic annals and no family chronicles. Diaries, memoirs and other genres of historical literature are also unavailable. Up to the end of the fifteenth century, no period is illuminated by more than a single account, with the exception of one decade (1345–1355), which is covered by two works. Moreover, there are certain periods, such as that between 1150 and 1270, for which there is no narrative source at all, but only short chronological notices marking the dates of accession and death of successive rulers. The oldest texts can only be reconstructed from later redactions, and there will always remain a good deal of uncertainty around them. An example is the putative 'Primeval gesta', now lost but usually dated to the eleventh century. Those works that have survived, like the *Gesta* of Simon Kézai (*c.* 1285), the Illuminated Chronicle (*c.* 1360) or the Chronicle of John Thuróczy (1488) give only a brief and fairly terse report of events. The longest, Thuróczy's Chronicle, which covers the period from Attila to Corvinus, could be published quite comfortably in a single volume of modest size.

The Hungarian narrative sources do not, therefore, provide sufficient detail for the proper reconstruction of events, a fact that explains why contemporary foreign sources are often of great importance. For the first centuries of Hungarian history the annals of certain German and Russian monasteries, as well as Byzantine, Dalmatian, Austrian and Bohemian chronicles, are especially rich in information concerning Hungary. Equally indispensable are the writings of some later authors, like the chronicle of the Florentine Villani brothers for the Angevin period or that of the Polish Jan Długosz for the age of the Hunyadis. As regards the political situation in the decades immediately preceding the battle of Mohács, particularly informative are the diplomatic correspondence and reports of foreign (Venetian, Papal, Austrian, and Polish) envoys. From the beginning of the thirteenth century the relative insignificance of the narrative sources is somewhat counterbalanced by a distinctively Hungarian type of source, namely the narratives incorporated in royal grants of privileges. These documents provide valuable information on the 'meritorious deeds' performed by the grantee in the campaigns of the king. Some of these accounts are quite lengthy, covering several years, and often illuminate events for which no other sources are available.

Unlike the narrative sources, the archival material of medieval Hungary is, with the exception of the earliest period, relatively extensive. From the eleventh and twelfth centuries, apart from some important collections of laws, only a handful of charters, issued in favour of ecclesiastical institutions, have been preserved; but the number of documents increases rapidly from around 1200 when the laity began to feel the necessity of putting down their property (and other) rights in a written form. As a result, roughly 10,000 documents have survived from the thirteenth century and about 300,000 from the period between 1301 and 1526. About half of this corpus is now preserved in the Hungarian National Archives at Budapest, the rest being scattered in collections within Hungary and abroad, mostly in Vienna, Bratislava, Cluj and Zagreb. (Photographic copies of all of them are available in the Hungarian National Archives.) Most of these documents are unpublished, and at least half have not been inventoried. Of the other archives where sources concerning the history of medieval Hungary are to be found, the most important are those of the Vatican, which still cannot be said to have been fully exploited.

The documents in question were partly the products of central administration and jurisdiction, and partly records of legal transactions between private persons and institutions. The use of written administrative documents, in the first place the issue of royal writs, began sporadically under the last Árpádians and became a daily routine under the Angevins. By that time the central courts had also adopted the methods employed by the chancellery and began to produce thousands of letters ordering inquiries, prorogations and compensations, or pronouncing final decisions for the interested parties. The orders issued by the chancellery and the courts were carried out by local ecclesiastical institutions, called 'places of authentication' (*loca credibilia*), which at the same time performed a notary office function, drawing up contracts between individual parties.

The documents that have come down to us represent only one or two per cent of those that were once issued. Private collections that had never been accessible to scholars were destroyed as late as the Second World War. Many documents, judged irrelevant for one reason or another, have been thrown away during the course of the centuries, among them the bulk of private letters and papers concerning manorial administration. But the greatest destruction of all seems to have been caused by the Ottoman conquest in the sixteenth century. All the archives that were not removed in time from the path of the invading army disappeared without trace. This is what happened to the most important and probably greatest collection of the realm, namely the documents of central administration that had previously been preserved at Buda. This lost collection included the private and diplomatic correspondence of kings (only some letters of Matthias Corvinus have survived in a codex), the volumes in which charters and writs issued by the chancellery had been registered since the Angevin period (the Hungarian equivalent of the English chancery rolls), and the whole of the chamber's administrative records, including tax assessment lists. (Although certain sections of the archives were probably only burned during the siege of Buda in 1686, they had remained inaccessible under Ottoman rule.) Most of the material that has survived, therefore, consists of the private archives of magnate and gentry families, and, to a certain extent, those of ecclesiastical institutions and municipalities. The majority of the documents concern western and northern Hungary, Slavonia (part of modern Croatia) and Transylvania. They are for the most part legal documents issued by places of authentication, the chancellery or the courts, and are generally written in Latin, the official language of multinational Hungary until 1844. It was only in a few cities, like Sopron or Pressburg (Bratislava), that German was used for internal affairs from the fourteenth century. As for Hungarian, it did not emerge as an instrument of written communication before the early modern period, and even then only as the language of private correspondence and local administration.

LIMITS OF MODERN RESEARCH

The possibilities of modern historical research are, therefore, fairly limited. It is as if the history of medieval England had to be written without access to the Public Record Office or the archives of the southern counties. Compared to Russia or the Balkan states, however, where medieval documents are counted in hundreds, Hungary is well endowed with records and the predicament of a historian unquestionably advantageous. The source material is particularly suitable for historical research focusing on government or the land-owning classes. We have relatively abundant chronological, archontological and prosopographical information from the thirteenth century onwards, and the picture we can draw becomes still more detailed from the Angevin period, when the great majority of documents were already being dated by the day of issue. (Between 1308 and 1323, for example, only one document in fourteen was issued without indication of the day.) Lists of prelates and principal lay officeholders can be established relatively fully from 1190 onwards with the help of the names of dignitaries included in royal grants. The reconstruction of royal itineraries, the main source of late medieval political history, is only made possible from 1310 by the increasing number of royal charters. The genealogy of many noble families can be pieced together from the thirteenth century, but only in the male line, since daughters are rarely mentioned before the fifteenth century. From the late medieval period we have scattered biographical data concerning several thousand people belonging to the elite, but exact dates of birth and death can rarely be established outside the royal family before the end of the Middle Ages.

In contrast to the history of administration and of the nobility, the economic and demographic conditions of the medieval period remain obscure. No comprehensive register of the taxpayers or the settlements of the medieval kingdom is known to exist. The only surviving source of this kind are the lists, drawn up by the papal tax collectors sent from Avignon between 1332 and 1337, of the parishes of the Hungarian bishoprics and of the tax paid by them. However, the historical importance of these lists lies primarily in the sphere of ecclesiastical geography. Moreover, they do not cover all bishoprics. Rolls enumerating all the landowners of the country and their peasant households by counties and villages are supposed to have been drawn up regularly for military or fiscal purposes since the reign of Sigismund of Luxembourg (1387–1437), but only a few pieces have survived before 1531. As for the revenues of the kingdom, a rough estimate can be made for the last years of Sigismund's reign, but the earliest detailed evidence comes from the accounts of the treasurer Sigismund Ernuszt, bishop of Pécs, concerning the years 1494–95. They contain, among other things, the number of peasant holdings in the kingdom and their distribution by counties. What of local economic conditions? The recording of seigneurial revenues in written form was exceptional before the end of the fifteenth century, and even thereafter few lords kept regular accounts. This fact enhances the value of the accounts that were prepared for Cardinal Ippolito d'Este, archbishop of Esztergom and bishop of Eger (d. 1520), by his Italian stewards in Hungary. For the everyday life of the peasantry we have innumerable allusions scattered among the archives of noble families, due to the fact that every lord went to law personally in cases of damage done to, or caused by, his peasants. What we lack in this respect is documentary evidence of a more coherent nature, such as records of lawsuits pursued before the seigneurial courts. Records of this kind do not seem to have been produced. Much more is known about urban life, thanks to some carefully preserved archives. From the reign of Louis the Great (1342–1382) onwards, municipal tax assessment lists, accounts, wills and other documents have survived in increasing numbers and for the most part remain unpublished.

Given the particular nature of the written sources, the evidence provided by other disciplines is indispensable, especially for the tenth to twelfth centuries. Archaeology has developed rapidly since the 1940s, producing important results, despite being forced until the end of the Communist era to dispense with its most effective tool, aerial photography, because of its political and military implications. Another related discipline is linguistics, or more exactly toponymy, whose evidence is simply indispensable for the reconstruction of the topography and ethnic structure of medieval Hungary. The memory of thousands of vanished settlements and other place names has been preserved in medieval and early modern documents, and most of them can be localised by reference to modern maps and by collecting still surviving toponyms. Although the ancient network of settlement in the southern regions had been practically destroyed by the end of the Ottoman occupation, the tax assessments from the first period of Ottoman rule (1540–1590) help us to reconstruct late medieval conditions.

Chapter 1

The Carpathian Basin before the Hungarians

The central areas of the Carpathian basin have been quite densely inhabited since Neolithic times. Its earliest known inhabitants were Indo-Europeans, and it was they who named the Carpathians, the Danube and most of its main tributaries, like the Tisza, Maros/Mureş, Körös/Criş, Dráva/Drava. There were Illyrians in Transdanubia during the Bronze Age and they were joined by Celts in the Iron Age. The Great Plain was occupied from at least the seventh century BC by Iranian horsemen, such as the Scythians, Sarmatians and Alans. For nomadic people coming from the East, this was the last region where they could pursue their traditional way of life relatively undisturbed. The eastern part of the Carpathian basin, later called Transylvania, which was rich in salt and gold, was the territory of the Dacians, another Indo-European people who were probably of Thracian origin. The plains and valleys of Slovakia, where settlement was possible, were inhabited by Germans, among them the Markomanns and Quads, who are known from their wars against Emperor Marcus Aurelius (161–180 AD). Their memory has also been preserved by a few toponyms, such as the Váh, the main river of Slovakia.

ROMANS, HUNS AND AVARS

The territory of Transdanubia was conquered by the Romans in the time of Augustus (d. 14 AD) and became part of their province of Pannonia. The Dacians, led by their king, Decebalus, were subdued by Emperor Trajan in 106 AD, and from their lands another province with the name Dacia was formed. Roman rule in Dacia lasted for only 165 years, for in 271 the Emperor Aurelian was forced by the frequent attacks of the Goths to withdraw the Roman legions. Pannonia, on the other hand, remained part of the Empire for more than four centuries,

1

and this seems to have resulted in the complete romanisation of the province. Evidence of the high standard of living of its inhabitants is to be found in the ruins of numerous *civitates* and *muncipia*, like the legionary camp Aquincum in present-day Budapest, and also in *villae* of the Late Empire, such as that of Balácapuszta, near Lake Balaton, which is famous for its mosaic. The line of the Danube, which constituted the frontier of the Empire, was flanked by the watch-towers and *castella* of the *limes*, the remnants of one of which can still be seen in the very centre of Budapest.

Roman rule proved to be a short-lived episode even in the history of Transdanubia. From the third century onwards its cities were devastated by repeated Sarmatian and German invasions, and what remained of them was completely destroyed around 430 by the nomadic Huns. The whole of the Carpathian basin became part of their short-lived empire. From here, King Attila launched fierce attacks against Constantinople, Italy and Gaul until his death in 453; and it might have also been here, somewhere in the Great Plain, that he was visited by the envoy of Emperor Theodosius II, the *rhetor* Priscus, who has left us a vivid description of the king and his court.

Whereas the memory of the Romans and of the Germanic peoples has only been preserved by archaeological sites, that of the Huns was to play an important role in medieval and even modern Hungarian historical thinking. Medieval clerics from Hungary, learning of the Huns in Western chronicles, promptly recognised that their fierceness and bellicosity were not unlike the mentality of their Hungarian contemporaries. Developed and reinforced over many generations, the theory that the Huns and Hungarians were of common origin, even identical, has remained part of national mythology until recent times. The theory has, of course, been refuted by modern scholarship. The possibility that the Árpádian kings of Hungary may have been Attila's descendants cannot be wholly excluded, and it is more than probable that the ancestors of the Hungarians, who themselves appear as late as around 830, had once lived under the rule of the Huns, together with a number of other Turkic, Germanic and Iranian peoples. The Huns were, however, an Asian people whose empire disappeared without trace before the end of the fifth century, and whose language, apparently a Turkic one, had certainly nothing to do with that of the Hungarians.

Shortly after the death of Attila, the Hun empire was swept away by the revolt of German peoples. One of these, the Gepids, established themselves east of the Tisza, while the Transdanubian region was soon occupied by the Langobards. Around 567 or 568, the Avars, another nomadic people from the East, invaded the Carpathian basin. They decimated and subdued the Gepids, while the Langobards, wishing to avoid the same fate, moved to the valley of the River Po and founded a new kingdom there. Like the Huns, the Avars were nomadic horsemen of the steppe. At the time of their arrival in the Carpathian basin they lived off livestock breeding and plundering. At first they launched devastating attacks against the Byzantine Empire and the Merovingians. In 626, allied to the Sassanid rulers of Iran, they almost succeeded in capturing Constantinople. From this time on, however, they occur less and less frequently in the sources. Their power diminished, finally being confined to the Carpathian basin, where they were subjugated between 791 and 803 by Charlemagne and his lieutenants in a series of three bloody campaigns. By that time they seem to have abandoned nomadic life in favour of settled agriculture.

References to the Avars in the laconic Byzantine and Frankish sources seem to suggest the continued existence of a single people. Yet the archaeological evidence of the Carpathian basin, based on thousands of burials, clearly demonstrates that there was an important change in the ethnic structure during this period. Around 700, another people moved into the region. Archaeologists have given them the name 'late Avars', because their material heritage is neatly distinguishable from that of the Avars proper. In fact, they seem to have belonged to the Onogurs, a Turkic people. The Onogurs, also called Bulgars, had lived in the seventh century in the region between the Rivers Don and Volga. Their name, meaning 'ten Ogurs' in Turkic, is one of those denoting the political union of a certain number of tribes. The short-lived Onogur-Bulgar empire was destroyed around 680 by the Turks of Inner Asia, later to be known as the Khazars. Some Onogur tribes then moved to the Balkan peninsula where they founded the Bulgar khanate, predecessor of present-day Bulgaria. The 'late Avars' who occupied the Carpathian basin can be identified with another Onogur group, those who are known to have fled from Ukraine towards the West.

One of the most important developments of the Avar age was the Slav migration in the seventh century, which completely transformed the ethnic patterns of central Europe and the Balkans. It might have been at that time, or even earlier, that they infiltrated those peripheries of the Carpathian basin that had been left unoccupied by the Avars. Their presence in some regions of Transdanubia, modern Slovakia and Transylvania is clearly attested by ninth-century sources, and also by a multitude of Slavonic toponyms in Hungarian documents of the earliest period.

In the ninth century, which began with the fall of the Avars and ended with the Hungarian conquest, the Carpathian basin was in the sphere of influence of three political powers. Ancient Pannonia, up to the Danube, had been part of the Carolingian Empire since the time of

Charlemagne. By its repeated divisions (817, 843) this province, called *Oriens*, was allotted to Louis 'the German' (843–876) and his successors, including Emperor Arnulf (887–899), who was the last king of the eastern Franks to possess some kind of control over this far-eastern part of his realm. The Carolingians were represented either by vassal princes, like the Slav Pribina (c.840–860) and his son Kocel (c.861–870), who had their residence at Mosaburg (modern Zalavár), or by governors, such as Arnulf's lieutenant, Duke (*dux*) Braslav, who may have been the founder of Pressburg (originally *Brezalauspurc*, 'Braslav's castle').

North of the Danube a new political entity, Moravia, was being formed around 830 under the Slav prince Moimir. He and his successors tried, through constant warfare with the Carolingians, to preserve their independent status. Prince Svatopluk I (870–894), an outstanding figure of the dynasty, seems to have controlled a vast region from Moravia to the heart of the Great Plain. He even attempted to conquer Pannonia and proved a dangerous rival to Emperor Arnulf.

The third important power in the region was the Danubian Khanate of the Bulgarians, which reached its apogee under the reign of Krum (803–814), Boris (852–889) and his son, Tsar Simeon (893–927). They ruled over the greater part of the Balkans, and were powerful enough to pose a serious threat to the Byzantine Empire. They were also neighbours to the Franks between the Rivers Drava and Sava, which resulted in frequent clashes between the two powers. An important stronghold of the khanate to the north-west was modern Belgrade, which retained its epithet 'Bulgarian' (*Alba Bulgarica*, Hung. *Nándorfehérvár*, 'white castle of the Bulgarians') under Serbian and/or Hungarian rule until the end of the Middle Ages. Archaeological evidence shows that the southern part of both Transylvania and the Hungarian Plain also belonged to the Bulgarian empire. The Bulgarian territories in Transylvania were controlled from another 'white castle', built on the River Mureş (originally Belgrade, now Alba Iulia, Hung. *Gyulafehérvár*).

An important development of this period was the reappearance of Christianity. It is unlikely that early Christian communities from the Roman period could have survived the Hun and Avar invasions; but from the ninth century we have plenty of information relating to Christians in Pannonia and Moravia. Our most important source is the *Conversio Bagoariorum et Carantanorum*, which was written around 870. As a consequence of the Frankish conquest, Pannonia adopted the Latin rite, and its ecclesiastical government was disputed, even after the arrival of the Hungarians, between the dioceses of Salzburg and Passau. On the other hand, the Bulgarians converted to Orthodoxy in 864, while the conversion of the Moravians led to a political rivalry between Rome and Constantinople. An important role in this was given to the Greek 'apostles of the Slavs', Cyril and his brother Methodius, who was consecrated archbishop of Sirmium (now Sremska Mitrovica) by the Pope. In Moravia it was the German church that finally gained the upper hand, but the consequences of its victory were soon swept away by the Hungarian conquest.

PROBLEMS OF CONTINUITY

When the Avars arrived in Pannonia the only remnants of Roman rule were uninhabited ruins. The destruction caused by the invasions – mainly those of the Huns – seems to have been more brutal here than in the West. Not only was life in the towns interrupted for centuries, or indeed permanently, but judging from the evidence of toponymy the indigenous population also disappeared, and with it all traces of romanisation. The only place that preserved its ancient name was *Sabaria* (now Szombathely), the first Roman colony founded by Emperor Claudius in 50 AD; but even this name was used only in medieval Latin documents and not in the vernacular. On the site of Pécs, the centre of southern Transdanubia, there had also been a Roman town, *Sopianae*, but its medieval Latin name was *Quinqueecclesiae* ('five churches', German *Fünfkirchen*), which may have derived from an early Christian community. These are almost the only signs of the survival of Roman civilisation in medieval Hungary. In the Middle Ages, Transdanubia was certainly more developed than the eastern part of the kingdom, but this fact can hardly be attributed to its different roots. The Pressburg region had never been exposed to Roman influence, yet as early as the twelfth or thirteenth centuries it was, in terms of its level of civilisation, not unlike Transdanubia.

The impact of the Dark Ages on the later development of Hungary has also been considered insignificant. There is hardly a single aspect of that development where modern historiography has taken account of Avar, Frankish, Bulgarian or even Slav antecedents. Everything reported by written sources since the eleventh century is thought to have been an autochthonous development, created *ex nihilo* after the conquest. If there were earlier influences, they would have come from the pagan traditions of the steppe. The organisation of the kingdom, the conversion to Christianity and the birth of settlements have all been presented according to this interpretation. It is as if the nomadic newcomers of about 895 found an uninhabited land, a *tabula rasa* in every respect.

The evidence furnished by archaeology and linguistics seems to fit into this picture. The 'late Avar' finds cannot be dated to a period much later than the reign of Charlemagne, when the Avar empire was destroyed. The next layer of finds belongs to the Hungarian conquerors. No other archaeological evidence has been connected with the ninth century, thereby filling the yawning archaeological gulf between the Avars of 800 and the Hungarians of 900. Only in some parts of Transdanubia, in Transylvania and Slovakia are there cemeteries attributed to a Slav population. The results furnished by toponymy seem to be in perfect accordance with the archaeological evidence. Most of the early place-names in the region are thought to be of Hungarian origin. Slavonic toponyms appear only in the peripheries of the Carpathian basin. This suggests that the genesis of the network of settlement cannot be dated to a period earlier than the arrival of the Hungarians.

A book such as this may not be the best place for a critical reassessment of accepted views. However, it must be stated clearly that the picture outlined above is far from being wholly convincing. First, it is hardly conceivable that the central part of Hungary could have been left uninhabited throughout the ninth century. In the case of the Great Plain, we can do no more than draw attention to the problem; where Transdanubia is concerned, the doubts have some evidential foundation. The earliest charters of about the year 1000 show a dense network of well established villages in the region of Pécs and elsewhere. It is not easy to visualise how they could have come into being in a matter of a few years. We ought, therefore, to suppose the presence there of a ninth-century population. If so, they could only be 'late Avars', for all the archaeological finds in the area preceding the Hungarian conquest belong to this ethnic group. Indeed, certain sites attest the biological coexistence of Avar and early Hungarian populations. These facts may suggest that the dating of the Avar cemeteries of the latest period should be re-examined.

The language of the 'late Avars' (that is, the Onogurs) is not known but it is generally supposed to have been Turkic, for this was the language of the early Bulgarians who belonged to the same people. We must take into account, however, that the name Onogur, in the form *ongri*, was the early Slavonic name of the Hungarians, and that this was what became known in all European languages through its Latin form *Hungari*. It is first mentioned, many years before the conquest, by a Frankish source that speaks about the *Wangariorum marca*, the 'Hungarian frontier', somewhere in present-day western Hungary or Austria.[1] It seems to refer to a surviving 'late Avar' population. It is not, therefore, impossible that those Onogurs who arrived in the seventh century could have been a Finno-Ugric (that is, Hungarian) speaking population. In other words, one might suppose that the 'late Avars' were in fact Hungarians.

This hypothesis, first articulated a number of years ago by the archaeologist Gyula László, could account for a large number of hitherto unexplained phenomena. It involves, however, a reinterpretation of the whole of tenth- and eleventh-century Hungarian history and the revision of many questions upon which scholarly consensus has hitherto existed. Since even the preparatory works, which would be indispensable for a proper evaluation of the evidence, are still lacking, we shall have to set aside this hypothesis in this book.

Chapter 2

The Pagan Hungarians

The first, rather scattered historical data concerning the Hungarians come from the ninth century. However, they did not make themselves known to Christian Europe before the end of the century when, having occupied the Carpathian basin, they began to launch their devastating raids against the West.

THE ORIGIN OF THE HUNGARIANS

Although it is believed that the pagan Hungarians knew a version of the runic alphabet, probably of Turkic origin, they have left no written sources. Everything we know about them comes from their literate neighbours. The first detailed description of them derives from Muslim merchants who visited the land of the Hungarians around 870. The information that they provided was incorporated into the geographical work of Jayhani, who was working in the Samanid court of Bukhara around 920. This compilation was lost, but later Persian and Arab works (for example, Ibn Rusta, Gardizi and the *Hudud al-Alam*) preserved certain sections of it. After the conquest, the Hungarians disappeared from the horizon of the Muslim writers, but at the same time Byzantine and Western authors began to provide information about them. The Emperor Leo VI (886–912) concentrated on their warfare in his *Tactics*, only occasionally including details of their everyday life; but his son, Constantine Porphyrogenitus (913–959), wrote in detail about their past and their political organisation in his *De administrando imperio* from around 950. This work is a most valuable source of contemporary Hungarian history, but also a most problematic one, since the account contains obvious errors and misinterpretations. Reporting on the Hungarian raids, Western chronicles, annals and hagiographic sources sometimes give precious data on

8

the way of life of the invaders. To all this can be added some obscure, though sometimes valuable, pieces of information that have been preserved in later Hungarian chronicles.

Not surprisingly, a leading role in the study of this period is played by archaeology. This has been developing quite rapidly for several decades, adding immensely to our knowledge of tenth-century society, though few traces have as yet been found of Hungarians living before the conquest in what is today Romania and Ukraine. Also of great importance to the study of tenth-century conditions is linguistics. Within the rich toponymic heritage of the Middle Ages can clearly be distinguished different place name types, and those formed from a noun without a suffix – from the name of an ethnic group, an occupation, or a person – clearly belong to the oldest type. Although the misuse of toponymic evidence can result in hazardous and unjustifiable hypotheses, when used with caution, place names are most helpful in the reconstruction of post-conquest (or later) settlement patterns.

Although the earliest mention of the Hungarians comes from about 830, as a people they are obviously much older. Their language belongs to the eastern – that is, Ugric – branch of the Finno-Ugric family of languages, its closest relatives being Vogul and Ostyak, spoken by two small peoples who until recently lived off fishing and hunting in the north-western corner of Siberia. Their relationship with Hungarian, however, is not much closer, and no more evident for non-experts, than that between, say, English and Welsh.

The name 'Hungarian' comes, as we have seen, from the Turkic word 'Onogur'. Some Byzantine chroniclers called the Hungarians 'Turks', just as they had with the Khazars before them, while Western writers often referred to them as 'Huns' or 'Avars', for their way of life was similar to what they knew about these earlier peoples. When archaisms came into fashion in twelfth-century Byzantium, the Hungarians were called 'Pannons' or 'Scythians'. They have always called themselves 'Magyar'. As early as the ninth century this name occurs in Muslim sources (*m.j.gh.r*) and it is at least partly of Finno-Ugric origin.

The Hungarians had detached themselves from the main body of the Finno-Ugric peoples very early, presumably during the first millennium BC. They then wandered on the Eurasian steppe in the company of Iranian, and later, Turkic horsemen. Their linguistic unity remained essentially intact during these two thousand years: even today, with respect to its grammatical structure and basic vocabulary, the Hungarian language clearly shows its Finno-Ugric origin; but it had, of course, been exposed to a number of foreign influences.

At the time of their emergence the Hungarians no longer resembled their distant relatives in the north. Their culture had in the meantime been adapted to the culture of nomadic horsemen. In this respect they came closest to the Turks, which explains why the Byzantine authors called them by this name, while the Muslims thought that the Hungarians were but 'a branch of the Turks'.[1] The strongest influence might have come from the Onogurs who spoke that version of Turkic which, with the exception of Chuvash (spoken in certain parts of Russia), is now extinct. The Hungarian language contains some 300 words of Turkic origin, which bear witness to the considerable linguistic and cultural influence of the Onogurs.

Besides, and also certainly preceding, the Turkic influence, the culture of the ancient Hungarians must have been shaped by the old Iranian peoples, such as the Scythians and the Sarmatians, but we know very little about this. The linguistic influence of the Alans, who were related to the Sarmatians, has been examined more thoroughly, but the results are not as rich as might have been expected. The number of Hungarian words borrowed from Iranian languages is still disputed; what is clear is that it is far smaller than the quantity of words of Turkic origin. This suggests that future research will have to take other possible approaches into consideration.

The Hungarians are first mentioned, as the allies of the Bulgarians in the time of Emperor Theophilus (829–842), by the tenth-century Byzantine chronicle of *Georgius Monachus Continuatus*. Around 860 Saint Cyril, returning from the Khazars, met the Hungarians in the region of the Crimea, while his brother, Methodius, was allegedly received in 882 by a Hungarian 'king' somewhere in the lower Danube valley. All this is confirmed by the information, furnished by Muslim authors, that around 870 the 'country' of the Hungarians bordered upon the land of the Bulgarians along the lower Danube, while in the east, along the River *Atil*, it had the Pechenegs and the Khazars as neighbours. *Atil* was the usual Turkic name for the Volga, but in this case it may have referred to the Don. The Hungarians later told the Emperor Constantine that they had called their land Etelköz (*Etilkuzu*), which meant in old Hungarian something like 'the land near the Atil'. In the north their territory extended into the zone of the deciduous forests and it is known from Muslim sources that they regularly attacked and ransomed the Slav tribes living there.

THE CONQUEST

The *Annales Bertiniani* report for the year 862 that the Eastern Franks were attacked by the *Ungri*, an enemy not known to them before. This is the first piece of information concerning the Hungarians in Western sources. The next comes from 881, when they fought the Franks in two battles as the allies of Svatopluk of Moravia. In 892, however, they changed sides and fought with the Frankish king, Arnulf, against Svatopluk. The Hungarians are mentioned more frequently from 894 onwards, when the event that we generally call the Hungarian conquest, that is the occupation of the Carpathian basin, took place.

This event had a profound impact on the collective memory of the Hungarians, but precise details of what happened are lacking. Around 1200 a Hungarian cleric, a former notary of King Béla III (1172–96), who called himself Master P. and had studied in Paris, related in a novelistic form what he thought had happened at the time of the conquest. The 'Anonymus', as he is known in Hungarian historiography, depicted the move into the Carpathian basin as a series of victorious exploits. He described in minute detail how the princes and their peoples whom the Hungarians found in their future homeland were subdued one after another. However, it is evident that Anonymus did not have the faintest idea about the real state of affairs in the Carpathian basin at the time of the Conquest. He was consequently forced to rely on his own imagination. Instead of Simeon of Bulgaria, Arnulf and Svatopluk, of whom he had no knowledge, he invented imaginary figures as enemies of the Hungarians. In the construction of his stories, he sometimes drew on legendary elements, but more frequently he worked with toponyms. His method can be illustrated by the example of one of the enemy princes, Zobor. According to Anonymus, Zobor 'had become *dux* of Nitra by the grace of the prince of the Bohemians, but the Hungarians took him to the top of a high mountain and hanged him.'[2] The name Zobor is a derivative of the Slavonic word *sobor* ('gathering', 'church'), and was the name of a hill not far from Nitra where, before the time of Anonymus, a Benedictine monastery had been founded. The legendary character of all the other enemies of Árpád, the Bulgarian *Salan* who is said to have held his court at Titel, the Khazar *Menumorout*, lord of Bihor, or the Wallachian prince, *Gelou* of Transylvania, is no less probable.

Such is the scarcity of the historical facts concerning the Conquest, that they can be pieced together in more than one way. The version of events presented below is only one of the possible interpretations. It seems that within the process of what is called the conquest, two phases can be distinguished: first, the occupation of the Great Plain and Transylvania; and second, the evacuation of Etelköz. The first was the result of a victorious war against Moravia and Bulgaria, while the second was a flight caused by the attack of another Turkic people, the Pechenegs.

The Conquest proper seems to have taken place in 894 as the result of a military intervention in support of Byzantium and the Franks against Moravia and Bulgaria. The Bulgaro-Frankish alliance, still in force in 892, broke up shortly after the accession of Khan Simeon in Bulgaria in 893. It was replaced by active Bulgaro-Moravian co-operation. In 894, while Simeon attacked the Byzantine empire, Svatopluk simultaneously challenged Arnulf by invading Pannonia. It was only natural that both Leo VI and Arnulf would seek help from the Hungarians, who were well placed to attack the Bulgarians and Moravians from the rear. This was, according to the *Annales Fuldenses*, the first large-scale Hungarian attack against the West. Svatopluk himself 'finished his days unhappily' in that year,[3] and later Hungarian tradition held that he lost his life whilst fighting them somewhere near the Danube. At the same time another Hungarian army, which had been carried across the lower Danube by Byzantine ships, defeated the Bulgarians. These victories seem to have resulted in the Hungarian occupation of Transylvania and the Great Plain. It was not without reason, therefore, that Arnulf was blamed, many years later, for having opened up Europe to the Hungarian raids, for it was certainly he who had invited the Hungarians to occupy Svatopluk's lands east of the Danube. Arnulf maintained the alliance with the Hungarians until his death in 899, and Pannonia, which formed part of his empire, was consequently spared from Hungarian attacks during this period.

The evacuation of Etelköz was brought about, not much later, by a formidable attack from the east. The Pechenegs, nomadising in the area beyond the Volga, were forced by the Uzes, another Turkic people, to quit their homeland, while the migration of the Uzes was itself probably provoked by a campaign mounted in 893 by Ismail, the Samanid emir of Bukhara, against the Turks of Inner-Asia. Whatever the cause, the fact remains that the Pechenegs surged into the land of the Hungarians between the Don and the Danube with irresistible vehemence. Simeon, who was at the point of asking for peace, immediately took advantage of this unexpected change of circumstances. He interrupted negotiations with Byzantium and attacked the Hungarians, defeating them in a bloody battle. This double attack, which seems to have taken place in 895 or early 896, put an end to Hungarian rule in Etelköz, which was occupied by Pecheneg tribes. The survivors fled into the Carpathian basin, and the horror inspired by these events long persisted among them. It was not defeat by the Bulgarians but the massacre committed by the Pechenegs that haunted the imagination of the Hungarians in the tenth century, leaving lasting traces in their later traditions.

THE RAIDS

The Hungarians did not occupy the whole of the Carpathian basin in 894. Pannonia remained a Frankish possession until the death of Arnulf and only passed under Hungarian rule, with the eastern part of

Bavaria, in 900. What was left of Moravia after 894 was probably destroyed in 902, with the fall of Svatopluk's dynasty and their kingdom. In the meantime the Hungarians began to launch destructive attacks against the Christian kingdoms of the West. Initially, these raids took place almost every year; then, after the Hungarians had suffered their first defeats, they became more sporadic. But they were only stopped altogether by the memorable catastrophe at Augsburg in 955. Although the Western annals apparently report an enormous number of Hungarian raids, in reality there must have been far fewer of them, since many entries from different years seem to refer to the same event. Hence we shall content ourselves with enumerating the most important campaigns, whose date can be determined with relative certainty.

It was Italy that initially gained first-hand knowledge of nomadic warfare and of the destructive spirit of the ancient Hungarians. They arrived in the peninsula as the allies of Arnulf in 899 and defeated his rival, King Berengar I, in September near the River Brenta. Since Berengar undertook to pay them an annual tax in order to spare his kingdom, the Hungarians now turned their attention towards Germany. In November 900 the Bavarians halted them at the River Enns, but the great Bavarian counter-attack, launched in 907, collapsed at Pressburg on 5 July, where even the leaders – Duke Liutpold, the archbishop of Salzburg, and several bishops – were killed. This victory opened up the whole of Germany to the Hungarians. In 908, in alliance with the Daleminci, a Slav tribe living near the River Elbe, they defeated the duke of Thuringia and pillaged Saxony. In 909 they visited Swabia, and although on the way back, on 11 August, they were beaten at the River Rott by the new duke of Bavaria, Arnulf, they found ample compensation in a great victory that they won over the Frankish and Swabian army of King Louis IV not far from the border of Franconia (12 June 910). This was to be the last attempt to stop them for a long time. Henceforward, they were free to pillage the whole of Germany, from Bremen to Aargau, virtually without resistance, and sometimes even spent the winter there. On 21 January 917, they destroyed Basle, then crossed the frozen Rhine and appeared in Alsace and Lorraine.

Arnulf of Bavaria, who had fled from his enemies to the Hungarians, won back his duchy around 919 and remained their ally until his death in 937. Bavaria was thus spared for quite a long time, but the Hungarians found more distant regions to terrorise. In 922 they helped their ally, Berengar I of Italy, against the king of Burgundy, Rudolf, and pillaged the peninsula. In 924 they were called upon again by Berengar, this time to suppress his own rebellious subjects. In the course of this campaign the Hungarians burnt Pavia. On 2 May 925

(926 is less likely) they sacked Sankt Gallen, one of the richest Benedictine monasteries in Europe. In 926 they crossed the Rhine, marched through France and reached the Atlantic. In 935 they pillaged Burgundy. Their longest campaign seems to have taken place in 937, when, having sacked Franconia and Swabia, they crossed the Rhine at Worms in February, wandered all over France and as far as the Atlantic, then crossed the Alps and went down to Capua before returning home. In the spring of 942 they visited their ally, Hugh, king of Italy, who, having paid his tax, advised them to visit Spain. There they laid siege to Lérida, and the news of their arrival aroused terror even in the court of the caliph of Córdoba. In 947 they went to tax the new king of Italy, Berengar II, then once again pillaged the peninsula, this time advancing as far as Otranto. In 951 they crossed Lombardy and the Alps before reaching Aquitaine, but on the way back they seem to have been defeated at the River Ticino by the troops of Otto I, king of Germany, who had just secured his rule over Italy.

In fact, the main obstacle to the Hungarian attacks against Germany had long been the increasing power of the kings of the Saxon dynasty. The first failure had occurred in 924, when King Henry I bought nine years of peace in return for the liberation of a captive Hungarian chief. In this way he gained enough time to prepare against them; and when the peace expired and the Hungarians renewed their attacks, he halted them at an unknown place called *Riade*, and defeated them in battle on 15 March 933. His son, Otto I (936–973) soon extended his rule over southern Germany, thus further restricting the range of the Hungarian raids. In 938 the Hungarians were beaten in Saxony and thereafter avoided this province. On 10 August 944 (or 943) they suffered another defeat near Wels, on the River Traun, this time at the hands of Duke Berthold of Bavaria. The new duke, Henry, drove them back in 948 in the Nordgau, then attacked himself two years later.

The last successful western raid of the Hungarians, in 954, was made possible by a revolt against Otto. They were received in Worms by the leader of the rebels, Conrad, duke of Franconia, and, having crossed the Rhine, they pillaged the eastern regions of France as far as Laon and Reims, before returning home, as usual, across Lombardy.

The Hungarian raids against the West came to an abrupt and dramatic end in 955. In the summer of this year they launched a major attack against Germany, but Otto was waiting for them near Augsburg, by the River Lech, and on 10 August he crushed them in battle. This victory not only meant that the West had no longer to fear the deadly arrows of the Hungarians; it also left indelible traces in the collective memory of the Hungarians. Popular legends lived on for centuries about the seven 'miserable Hungarians' who alone escaped from the battle, thereafter living as despised beggars.[4] The fate that awaited the captured leaders, Bulcsú, Lél and Súr, impaled (or hanged) by Duke Henry in Regensburg, had an even greater impact on posterity. According to pagan beliefs, their execution meant that they would serve their enemies in the other world. Therefore, a legend was created that held that it was Lél who made the 'Emperor Conrad' his servant by striking him with his horn before his own death. 'Lehel's' horn, decorated with ivory carvings, possibly of tenth-century Byzantine origin, can still be seen in the museum of Jászberény.

Although the defeat at Augsburg brought the period of Hungarian raids against the West to a close, it did not immediately bring about the end of those directed against other peoples. It is almost certain that the neighbouring Slav peoples had been ransomed as frequently as the western Europeans, since this had already been the case in Etelköz; but, understandably, only those raids that were directed against the Byzantine empire are documented. It seems, however, that the Hungarian raids never played a significant role within the complex network of imperial foreign policy. In the time of Emperor Romanus I, first in 934 and then in 943, plundering armies approached Constantinople, but were neutralised by shrewd Byzantine diplomacy offering small concessions. Other attacks are mentioned after the defeat of Augsburg, as in 959 and 961, but the empire, which was recovering its former strength, had no difficulty in checking them. In fact, these two events mark the end of the period of plundering raids, although in 970 Hungarian troops did participate in the campaign against the Byzantine empire that was led by Svjatoslav, duke of Kiev and which ended in his defeat at Arcadiopolis.

PAGAN SOCIETY

Muslim, Byzantine and Western contemporaries were almost unanimous in describing the Hungarians as nomadic horsemen, who in their habits were practically identical with such well-known enemies of earlier times as the Huns and the Avars. In their eyes, the Hungarians were essentially nomads whose main occupations were war, plundering and destruction. Around 900, Regino, abbot of Prüm, the first to write about them in the West, was content to depict them with phrases taken from a description of the ancient Scythians: 'They spend all their time on horseback; they travel, rest, think and talk on their horses; they are extremely careful in teaching their children and servants the art of riding and using the bow.'[5] And when, about the same time, Emperor Leo VI described Hungarian warfare, he was satisfied with an old description of the Avars from about 600 AD, seeing no reason to make more than minor corrections to it. According to him, the Hungarians grew up on horseback and were actually unable to fight on foot. They had an immense number of horses, which they grazed both in winter and summer. For their campaigns they took more horses than they needed, 'partly as a source of food and milk, partly to make the enemy believe that they are more numerous.' They were well prepared to resist the extremes of weather. They normally wore a leather hauberk, carried a sabre, a spear and, of course, a bow, which they handled with outstanding skill, taking aim with it even from horseback. The main elements of their warfare were long-distance shooting and surprise. Their favourite trick was to send part of their army into battle, enticing the enemy to pursue them with a feigned flight, while the remainder lay in ambush and penetrated the rear of the pursuing enemy. 'Then, when the signal is given, those pretending to flee turn back and outflank the enemy troops.'[6]

Foreign observers conveyed a stark impression of the cruelty of the Hungarians and there is no reason to doubt their testimony. For whilst the Germans and Vikings plundered and burnt villages, the Hungarians seem to have derived pleasure from slaughtering people and destroying all signs of human activity. Contemporary accounts speak of piles of corpses and smouldering ruins throughout Europe in the wake of the Hungarian hordes. They set fire to every town or village they encountered and massacred all the adults they could find, carrying away as captives only young women and children. It is clear that the destruction caused by the Hungarian raids was much more substantial than that brought about by the normal wars of the period. All this seems to bear witness to a distinctive mentality that was typical among nomad warriors. The Hungarians themselves were to meet such a mentality when, in later centuries, they experienced invasions by the Mongols and Crimean Tatars. In view of the demographic catastrophes that these later incursions are known to have brought about in Hungary, we have no reason to reject as a mere exaggeration the laments of Western contemporaries of the Hungarian raids.

Archaeological evidence of nomad warriors living at that time in the Carpathian basin is relatively plentiful. About one thousand burials that can safely be linked to such warriors or their families have so far been recorded. These burials are marked by characteristic weapons (sabres, arrow-heads etc.), ornaments and jewels. A good many people, men and women alike, were buried with their horse or with artefacts symbolising it. In a few burial-places hoards of gold objects have been found that must have belonged to persons of princely status. Several other burials, though more modest, were also decorated with splendid objects, among which the silver sabretache seems to have been a 'status symbol' of unknown significance. We may assume that the men and women buried in this way were 'notables', living in separate residences, surrounded by their studs, flocks, and slaves. The simple warriors, who formed a sort of 'middle class', were often buried in groups, each with 25 to 30 graves. One hundred and eight of the burials, including all of the types described, can be dated by the presence of coins. Most were issued by Western rulers during the first half of the tenth century, among whom the kings of Italy from Berengar I (888–924) to Berengar II (950–961) are especially well represented. There are also many contemporary dirhems of Samanid emirs that seem to have arrived in Hungary not as booty but through commercial activity.

It is clear, however, that not all Hungarians of this time were warriors, nor even nomads. Many men who are thought to have been 'warriors' have been found buried in great cemeteries amidst crowds of poor people who seem to have been of markedly inferior social status. In fact, the overwhelmingly preponderant part of the archaeological heritage of this period consists of such cemeteries where many hundreds of poor 'commoners', all of them buried without warrior attributes, were buried alongside a handful of distinguished men. A mass of poor people, then, certainly formed part of tenth-century Hungarian society; and they seem to have been unarmed peasants. On one or two occasions, the village where they lived has been found in the proximity of the cemetery. Their culture, typical of the tenth and eleventh centuries and called Bijelo Brdo (a locality on the River Drava east of Osijek) by archaeologists, was for a long time ascribed to the subjugated Slav population, for scholars, Hungarian or otherwise, could not imagine Hungarians without arms and jewels. However, the region where these cemeteries have been found was later inhabited by a Hungarian-speaking population, so nowadays it is generally supposed that most the 'commoners' buried in this simple way must have been Hungarians, mingled with Slavs and other ethnic groups who had survived the Conquest.

Within Hungarian society of the pagan period we may thus speak of a three-level hierarchical order. The mass of the population consisted of commoners who seem to have been governed by a small class of warriors. Both were dominated by an even smaller elite of nobles. It must have been the members of the elite that Muslim writers were speaking of when they described the Hungarians of Etelköz: good-looking people, 'their clothes are of brocade and their weapons are [made] of silver and are gold-plated.'[7] Those Hungarians who 'have tents and travel about following the herbage and lush vegetation' and 'have extensive plough lands' may also have been nobles and warriors, while the men who tilled these lands and were left unmentioned by contemporaries were most probably settled peasants or serfs.[8]

This conclusion is confirmed by a number of old Hungarian words that refer to different forms of agricultural activity and which were borrowed, at a time certainly earlier than the tenth century, from a

Turkic language. The prevalence of stock-breeding, a fact to be expected with a nomadic people, is proven by the multitude of words that concern the breeding of cattle, sheep and goats (ox, bull, steer, calf, sheep, ram, wool, goat), dairy farming (cottage cheese, buttermilk, churn) or animal husbandry in general (sty, pen, trough). However, another group of loan-words seem to refer quite definitely to a settled way of life. The rearing of pigs, incompatible with continuous wandering, is attested by several words (pig, barrow, bristle). The basic vocabulary of arable farming is equally of Turkic origin (harvest, wheat, barley, tailings, hop, hemp, plough, sickle, grind, stubble, barn), and the same applies certainly to viticulture (grape, wine, filter, lees) and possibly also to the elements of horticulture (fruit, apple, pear, nut).

THE POLITICAL ORDER

Fragments of information concerning the political order of the pagan era are scarce and contradictory. According to the earliest piece of evidence, deriving from Muslim authors and referring to the ninth century, the Hungarians were ruled conjointly by two 'kings'. The major one, called *kende* (or *künde*), enjoyed nominal leadership, while effective power was exercised by his colleague, inferior in rank, called the *gyula*. The Hungarians, so we are told, 'obey the *gyula* in war and defence as well as in their other affairs'.[9] This peculiar form of government is generally supposed to have been imitative of the Khazar Khanate, which did indeed have a similar organisation. Many scholars assume, therefore, that the position of the *kende* was more or less identical to that of the Khan, and that he could even serve, at a given moment, as an object of ritual sacrifice.

At the time of the conquest, the Hungarians still seem to have had their two princes. In 894, according to a contemporary Byzantine chronicle, these were Árpád and a mysterious person with the name 'Kusanes'. He is obviously identical to the Hungarian 'king' Cussal, who was killed by the Bavarians at a common banquet in 902 (or 904). The humanist Aventinus (1477–1534) depicted him ('Cusala') as the person leading the Hungarians during the Conquest; but we are not certain whether he had access to authentic sources that have since disappeared, or whether what he wrote was based on no more information than is known to us. It has also been much disputed whether Kusanes (Cussal) may, or may not, be identified with Curzan, son of Cundu, who, according to much later Hungarian tradition, was one of the seven leaders of the Conquest. For those who accept this identification, the name Cundu is considered to be proof that Curzan held the dignity of *kende* and his colleague Árpád that of the *gyula*.

Although, in contrast to Cussal, the name of Árpád cannot be found in any contemporary Western text, he is well recorded in early Byzantine and later Hungarian ones. His father, Álmos, was the son of a certain Ügyek, but in the Hungarian chronicles we find that Álmos was conceived through intercourse between his mother Emese (Hung. *emse*, 'sow') and a bird of prey called *turul* in Old Hungarian (from Turkic *toghrul*, 'hawk'). The story is thought to be based on a totemistic myth concerning the origin of the kings of Hungary, although this theory is far from consistent, since it was undoubtedly Árpád, and not Álmos, who was later considered to be the ancestor of the dynasty that ruled Hungary until 1301.

No trace of the 'double kingship' can be found in Hungarian chronicles. Anonymus claimed that the first ruler of the Hungarians was Álmos, whom he presented as an offspring of Attila. The Hungarians, Anonymus says, knew nothing of princely power until the eve of the Conquest, when the seven chiefs (*dux*) of the people, called the 'seven Hungarians' (*Hetumoger*), 'elected of their free will Álmos as their prince'. They also ratified the election, 'following their heathen customs', with an oath, 'pouring their blood into a vessel'.[10] By that act they are reported to have agreed on five basic principles: that the princely honour would always be held by the descendants of Álmos; that all the wealth collectively acquired by the leaders should be distributed among them; that the leaders and their descendants should always have a place in the prince's council and should always participate 'in the honour of the realm'; that those breaking their faith to the prince or fomenting strife should be put to death; and, finally, that whoever might seek to break the agreement should be punished by eternal malediction. This famous 'treaty of blood' clearly reflected the political ideas of the author, who was writing around 1200. Nonetheless, before the Second World War it was often presented by Hungarian historians as the very first manifestation of modern parliamentary thinking in Europe.

Later tradition also held that Álmos 'was killed in Transylvania for he was not allowed to enter Pannonia'.[11] This somewhat obscure reference in the Illuminated Chronicle to the death of Álmos is often thought to have preserved the memory of a ritual murder of a *kende*. In that case both Álmos and Árpád must have held that dignity, and this would imply that Kusanes was the *gyula*. At any rate, Hungarian chroniclers are unanimous in reporting that the Conquest was directed by 'Duke' Árpád. They believed that he died in 907 and was buried in the area of present-day Budapest. They also claimed that the princely dignity belonged henceforth to his dynasty in the direct male line, Árpád being followed first by his son, Zoltan, then by his grandson, Taksony, in 947, and finally by Géza, the son of Taksony, in 972.

This tradition is, however, wholly contradicted by what was told to Constantine Porphyrogenitus by his 'friend' Tormás, a grandson of Árpád, in about 948 and by other princes from Hungary who visited the Emperor in the following years. They summarised for him what seemed important to them concerning the origin of their political order and its actual state. Their first prince, so they said, had been Árpád who was elected, at some time before the Conquest, on the recommendation of a certain Voivode Levedi. They emphasised that Árpád, 'being more respected', was chosen in preference to his father Álmos; and the Hungarians 'made him prince according to the custom... of the Khazars, by lifting him upon a shield'.[12] Árpád had four sons, none of whom was alive in about 950, but through them there were five living grandsons. The dignity of Grand Duke, the visitors went on, was being held by Phalitzes (Fajsz) who was the son of Árpád's third son, Jutas. This seems to imply that the succession at this time was governed by the principle of seniority, traces of which could still be detected for a long time after the foundation of the Christian kingdom.

From everything else that the emperor was told it becomes clear, however, that the Grand Duke's authority over Hungary was hardly more than nominal. Besides him the Hungarians still had the *gyula* as their second prince, and they had also a third one, called *karkhas* (in Hungarian *harka*), this dignity being held by Bulcsú (one of the 'kings' who were to be put to death by King Otto in 955). Each of the seven 'tribes' also had its own chief (*archon*), but the Hungarians, so Constantine was informed, 'do not obey their own particular princes, but have a joint agreement to fight together ... upon the rivers (i.e. on the frontiers) wherever war breaks out.'[13] All this is in perfect accordance with what we know of the nature of Hungarian leadership from other sources. The Hungarian raids, unlike those of the Huns or the Avars, do not seem to have been organised by a central authority, but rather by a number of autonomous chieftains, normally titled 'kings' in Western sources. We have also seen that the memory of the seven 'dukes' was still living in later tradition. Their contemporary title may have been *úr*, a Hungarian equivalent of the word 'duke' (*dux*). (Its original meaning was to be devalued to 'lord' in the Middle Ages and to 'mister' in modern Hungarian.) The word *ország* ('realm', from *úr-ság*, 'dukedom, duchy'), meaning a country in modern Hungarian (cf. *Magyarország*, 'Hungary'), seems to have originally referred to a well-defined territory ruled by an *úr* (cf. Hung. *uralkodik*, 'to rule'). It was apparently only after 955 that these local powers were broken, thereby allowing a political unity to be established that formed the basis of the future kingdom of Hungary.

THE TRIBES

Constantine is the only author to inform us that the Magyar people were organised into seven 'tribes' (*genea*). Yet we have no reason to doubt him, for his report is well supported by later tradition and even more substantially by toponymic evidence. The distant memory of the tribes has been preserved in the name *Hetumoger* ('seven Magyars'), which was used by Anonymus to denote the seven 'dukes'. Evidently, the word has the same form as the name Onogur ('ten Ogurs') and other similar compounds that were used by nomads to denote their tribal alliances. There is hardly any doubt, therefore, that *Hetumoger* was originally the collective name of the seven Magyar tribes. Moreover, the names of these tribes, which we also know from the emperor, have been preserved in toponyms in the Carpathian basin. In fact there were eight such names (*Nyék, Megyer, Kürt, Gyarmat, Tarján, Jenő, Kér, Keszi*), for one of the tribes, called *Kurtugermatu* by Constantine, was seemingly born from the union of the tribes *Kürt* and *Gyarmat*. Like other toponyms of ancient origin, these eight are to be found scattered throughout the whole area later inhabited by Hungarians (the only exception being Transylvania, for which see below), but they form a special group in view of their apparent frequency. All told, more than three hundred localities are known to have borne a 'tribal' name. In the territory of present-day Budapest there were four of them. Nyék (in the garden suburb of Buda) and *Jenő* (at the end of the Margaret Bridge in Pest) disappeared before the beginning of the modern period, while two others have continued to live on as the suburban districts of *Békásmegyer* ('Megyer of Frogs') and *Káposztásmegyer* ('Megyer of Cabbages').

Thus the fact that some sort of tribal organisation existed in the tenth century cannot be questioned. However, it is impossible as yet to explain its exact nature. All that can be said with some certainty is what a 'tribe' was *not* like. We know from Constantine that a link existed between 'tribes' and 'dukes', and we have good reason to think that each of the seven 'dukes' was in fact the leader of a 'tribe'. Also the fact that the dukes had their own 'realms' can be taken as almost certain. But, curiously enough, we may not go a step further and draw what might seem an unexceptionable conclusion. The link between 'tribes' and 'duchies' in Hungary seems to have been quite different from that between, for example, Anglo-Saxon tribes and kingdoms in early England. Whatever their original nature might have been, the Magyar tribes of the tenth century certainly no longer formed ethnic groups; nor can they be placed in discrete dwelling areas. All available evidence points to a very different conclusion: that medieval Hungary, unlike early medieval England, was surprisingly homogeneous in every respect – its archaeological heritage, its language, its legal and other customs. All scholarly efforts to allot a 'duchy' to a tribe have been unsuccessful; nor has it been possible to find an area with characteristic features that could convincingly be attributed to a separate ethnic group. The haphazard way in which 'tribal' place names are scattered throughout the Carpathian basin only serves to confirm these conclusions.

According to Constantine, the Hungarian people came into being from the union of the seven Magyar tribes with the three tribes of the Kavars (*Kabaroi*). The fact that a people of that name did exist is confirmed by an entry of a Bavarian annalist who, speaking about an incursion of the Hungarians (*Ungri*) in 881, refers to a fight against the *Cowari*. Many scholars believe that the memory of the Kavars has also been preserved by Anonymus who tells us that the Hungarians were helped in their conquest by the 'Cumans', another people who were subjected to the rule of Árpád but led by their own seven chiefs. Constantine was told that the Kavars were in fact a part of the Khazars, who joined the Magyars after a war within the Khanate. Thus the Kavars had originally spoken 'the language of the Khazars', but both they and the Hungarians had become bilingual by the Emperor Constantine's time, having learned each other's language. It is evident that the Kavars were an ethnic group of Turkic origin. However, linguists emphasise that, besides its Turkic loan-words, the Hungarian language does not show any trace of a bilingual coexistence with a Turkic dialect; indeed, in view of its uniform Finno-Ugric character this possibility can be discounted. Neither is it possible to identify, with the help of toponyms, a dwelling area in the Carpathian basin where a Turkic-speaking population may have lived as late as in the tenth century. With regard to archaeological evidence, no special objects or burial habits have been found that might point to the existence of a different culture in the region.

Taking all this into account, it is unlikely that the Hungarians and Kavars of the tenth century still formed two distinct peoples. Rather, it seems almost certain that, by the time of the Conquest, they had long melted together. We are led to the conclusion that the emperor misunderstood his guide on more than one issue. Since he was told that the Kavars joined the Magyars 'on the land of the Pechenegs',[14] a phrase that apparently refers to some region east of the Volga, it would appear that their union had taken place long before they first appeared in Etelköz in about 830. Yet there must have been a reason why the visitors thought it important to relate this old story to the emperor. It is possible that they wanted to give him a summary of the origins of the Hungarian people. It should be remembered that the word 'Hungarian' is a modern version of the ethnic name 'Onogur', meaning 'ten Ogur' tribes. It was just such an alliance of ten tribes that came into being when seven Magyar and three Kavar tribes were united.

SETTLEMENT

Burials of Hungarian warriors and toponyms bearing the name of a 'tribe' clearly mark off the territory where the conquerors settled in the early tenth century. If we put all these data on the map, what we find emerging is a coherent territory which comprised the central part of the Carpathian basin with its plains and hills, and surrounded by mountain ranges. Within this area, a substantial number of toponyms refer to the existence of isolated ethnic groups of non-Hungarian origin. *Varsány* (originally *Vosian*), for example, was the original Iranian name of the Alans (*As-yan*), while *Oszlár* was a derivative of their Turkic name (*As-lar*). The occasional presence of Choresmians, also called *Hvalis* (Old Hung. *Káliz*), is attested by toponyms like *Koromszó*, *Káloz* or *Kalász*. *Var-khun*, the name for the early Avars, has been preserved in villages called *Várkony*. The ancient Hungarian name for the Bulgarians, *Nándor*, which is a derivative of the Turkic *Onogundur*, can also be found in several place names (cf. Hung. *Nándorfehérvár*, Belgrade). *Bercel* preserved the memory of the *Barsil*, a tribe of the Volga Bulgars, while toponyms like *Besenyő*, *Talmács* and *Kölpi* (*Kölpény*) hint at the existence of scattered Pecheneg groups.

The names of tenth-century Árpádians and other notables have also survived in more than one place name. A former village called Árpád now forms a suburb of Pécs; another of the same name still exists in Bihor (Arpăşel, Romania). Localities bearing the names of Taksony and Fajsz can be found along the Danube south of Budapest as well as elsewhere, while a Bulcsú (now Búcsú) lies near Szombathely and a Lél just upstream of Komárno (now part of Vel'ké Kosihy). It is generally believed that some at least of these place names commemorate persons well known from history. It has even been suggested that they mark the location of winter or summer quarters of princes or notables between which they were still migrating, as nomads, during the tenth century. This interpretation has, however, been strongly disputed.

In the course of the Hungarian conquest considerable numbers of Slavs may have passed under Hungarian rule. Their old Hungarian name seems to have been *tót*, a name that is supposed to derive from the German word *theud* ('people') and which may have entered Hungarian through the Avars. It was later applied to southern (Slovenian, Serbian) and northern (Slovakian) Slavs alike. In many instances, as in certain parts of Transdanubia, the Slav toponyms seem to be considerably older than the surrounding Hungarian villages. It seems, therefore, that the population there was already Slav-speaking when the Hungarians arrived.

With regard to settlement, special attention must be given to Transylvania. The Latin name is a literal translation of the Hungarian word *Erdély* (originally *Erdő-elve*), which denoted a land lying 'over the forest'. It was composed in the same way as the medieval Hungarian name of Wallachia (*Havas-elve*, 'the land beyond the snowy mountains' i.e. the Carpathians), and seems to have indicated that, right from the beginning, Transylvania was regarded as forming a separate geographical and political unit within the Hungarian settlement area. Archaeological finds that can be ascribed to Hungarian warriors have come to light in sufficient numbers to confirm the fact, known from other sources, that Transylvania was under Hungarian rule in the tenth century. Nevertheless, the almost total absence of 'tribal' toponyms, which is conspicuous as compared with Hungary proper, argues against regarding Transylvania as a mere fringe region of the kingdom. A particularly important Slav substratum is present in the toponymic evidence. Over nine per cent of the toponyms that occur in written sources up to 1400 (104 out of 1119) have a Slav etymology, including the names of important localities that are thought to have an ancient origin (Bistriţa, Bălgrad, original Romanian name of Alba Iulia, etc.) and some important rivers (Târnava).

In fact, Transylvania in the tenth century seems to have been an independent principality. It was not ruled by the successors of Árpád, but was governed by a line of princes who were invariably called *Gyula* (as a proper name) by contemporaries. Evidently, they were the successors, and perhaps also the descendants, of the *gyula* of Etelköz. The *gyula* who reigned around 952 is reported to have made peace with Emperor Constantine, from whom he received the title of *patricius*; and he also had himself baptised in Constantinople. Indeed, he seems to have taken his new religion seriously. The Greek Hierotheus, who followed him to Transylvania with the title of 'bishop of Turkia', is said to have 'shown the way to a great many people out of their barbarian superstitions'.[15] It was probably the same *gyula* who later gave his daughter Sarolt to Prince Géza. The very fact of this marriage hints at the more or less equal status of the dynasty of the *gyula* with that of Árpád. It is no less curious that the *gyula* gave Turkic names to both his daughters (*šar-oldu*, 'white weasel' and *qar-oldu*, 'black weasel'), a fact that suggests that he and his court still spoke a Turkic dialect.

Chapter 3

The First Century of the Christian Kingdom

At the time of the Hungarian invasions, Christian civilisation, even in its broadest sense, hardly extended beyond the River Elbe in the north and the Danube in the south. Beyond these frontiers lay the land of the barbarian peoples, who held on to their pagan beliefs and lacked any form of stable political organisation. By far the most important, and most surprising, development of the decades around 1000 was the sudden expansion of Christian Europe. The Scandinavians, the Czechs, the Poles, the Russians and the Hungarians, independently of one another, but at almost the same time, embarked on a course that was to take them from their barbarian origins towards the establishment of a Christian kingdom. As a result, by the middle of the eleventh century the greater part of present-day Europe had become, both politically and spiritually, part of the Christian commonwealth.

PRINCE GÉZA

Although local motives may have varied, this transformation was carried out everywhere according to a similar pattern. One member of the princely family monopolised power, forced his subjects to convert to Christianity, set up the organisation of the Christian Church, and then, usually, used its authority to legalise his rule by taking the title of king. As a result of this transformation a completely new political system, the Christian monarchy, was born. It was to remain a long-lasting reality. Nevertheless, the adoption of Christianity, even if motivated by personal conviction, was not an aim in itself, but a method for founding a new political order. Consequently, it was followed by measures that were intended to consolidate the new order but were not directly connected to the conversion. In historiographies of central Europe the whole process of this transformation is often called the 'foundation of the state'; but this is surely anachronistic, bearing in mind that the regime that was born around 1000 would not deserve the designation 'state' for centuries.

Such a profound change could rarely be carried out by one generation. In Hungary the transformation began under the rule of Géza (d. 997) and was completed by his son, Stephen (997–1038). Since it was Stephen who had himself crowned king, his name was later, especially after his canonisation, to outshine that of his father. For later generations he was the author of all the innovations that had somehow contributed to the emergence of the new order. It seems probable, however, that at least some of these changes had been introduced during the reign of his father.

The radical transformation of the regime must have been a consequence of the defeat of Augsburg in 955, but the details of this process of change are as obscure as the exact nature of the political order that preceded it. As early as 972, a single prince, Géza, who was a great-grandson of Árpád, governed the Hungarians. No other descendant of Árpád is ever referred to later, and the simplest explanation for this is that they had all been killed at some time before 972. A large-scale purge seems to have been carried out by Géza, who was stigmatised by the chronicles as a rabid, 'cruel' ruler, whose 'hands were soiled with human blood'.[1] The only other survivor of the dynasty seems to have been Koppány, son of Zerind 'the Bald', who in Géza's time ruled part of Transdanubia as duke of Somogy. He must have been a close kinsman of the prince, so perhaps he was a nephew of Taksony. The principle of seniority was, however, no longer invoked: Géza wished to be followed by his elder son, Stephen.

Since Géza's foremost aim was the consolidation of his recently acquired authority, he tried to maintain peaceful relations with all of his neighbours, but above all with the Holy Roman Empire. At Easter in 973 he sent envoys to Otto I in Quedlinburg and renounced his claim to those parts of Bavaria and Moravia that had hitherto been occupied by the Hungarians. Although he later fell into conflict with Otto's nephew, Henry II, duke of Bavaria, in 996 he made peace with the latter's son and heir, the future Emperor Henry II. Géza's son, Stephen, married Henry's sister Gisela, and Géza also renounced Vienna and the neighbouring territories. Henceforth until 1918, with only a short interruption between 1030 and 1043, the western frontier of Hungary was to be marked by the Rivers Morava and Leitha.

The first, and decisive, steps towards the adoption of Christianity were also taken by Géza. In 972, Emperor Otto, probably at Géza's request, ordered the consecration of Brun (or Brunward), a monk from Sankt Gallen, as 'bishop of the Hungarians', and sent him to Hungary. Géza then had himself baptised, together with several thousands of 'nobler'

Hungarians, and 'engaged himself to convert all of his subjects to Christianity'.[2] Although he kept his promise, doing his best to 'eradicate the blasphemous rites',[3] and punishing rebels ruthlessly, he continued to adhere to the heathen customs of his ancestors and never became a wholehearted Christian. In this he seems to have been followed by Sarolt, his Transylvanian wife, who, it seems, did not persist in her father's Greek Christianity and was notorious for her manly fierceness and cruelty.

KING STEPHEN I

In 997 Géza was succeeded by his son, Vajk, who had borne the name Stephen since his baptism. He seems to have inherited a strong, princely power from his father and easily overcame the initial difficulties of his reign. Yet the lion's share of the work was still to be done, for he had to make all of his subjects recognise his authority unconditionally, and he had also to establish the organisation of the Christian Church. It was then that the new political system upon which the power of the Árpádians was to rest until the thirteenth century was created, although it is not clear how much of the work had already been done by Géza and what remained to be done by Stephen. What is beyond question is that the formal foundation of the Christian kingdom was Stephen's achievement. This is sufficient to justify both his canonisation in 1083 and his status, in the eyes of posterity, as the founder of the kingdom of Hungary.

His first task was the unification of the Hungarian territories. An opportunity was provided by the revolt of Koppány who, on the basis of the principle of seniority, claimed the succession and – probably invoking the pagan custom of levirate – wanted to marry Géza's widow. In 998 Stephen defeated Koppány in a battle near Veszprém, and, having had his body quartered, ordered that its parts be hung over the gates of Veszprém, Győr and Esztergom as tangible signs of his unquestioned authority. The fourth part of Koppány's corpse was sent to the *gyula* as a clear warning that his rule would soon come to an end. Indeed, Stephen occupied Transylvania as early as 1003 and entrusted its government to one of his own men. The *gyula* was pardoned, however, and his descendants were later to be found among the Hungarian aristocracy.

Henceforth, Stephen's authority extended over all the lands inhabited by Hungarians. Meanwhile, in order to legitimise his power, he took the most decisive and (in its long-term consequences) enduring step of his rule. At Esztergom at Christmas 1000 or on 1 January 1001, he was solemnly crowned king. Thereafter he counted the years of his rule from the date of his coronation and assumed the title of 'king of the Hungarians' (*rex Ungrorum*), the Hungarian equivalent of which was *király*. This word was actually the Slav name for Charlemagne and thus duly expressed Stephen's exceptional authority. The queen was for a time addressed as *asszony*, a word of Iranian origin. It seems formerly to have been the title of the prince's wife, and it gave birth to the Hungarian name for the Holy Virgin (*Boldogasszony*, 'Holy Queen'). Nor was the title *úr* forgotten: from now on it was applied to the princes of the royal family.

It must be noted that the Holy Crown, which today can be seen in Budapest, is not Saint Stephen's crown. It consists of two diadems that were fitted together at some time under the Árpádians. Its lower part is of Byzantine origin; judging from its figures and Greek inscriptions, it was sent to King Géza I (1074–1077) by the Emperor Michael VII Ducas (1071–1078). The upper part may also have been prepared in the eleventh century, but the text on it is in Latin. Although it is generally supposed that the two parts were put together during the second half of the twelfth century, the first undisputed reference to the Holy Crown comes from as late as 1304.

The political background of the coronation is one of the hotly disputed issues of early Hungarian history. Early tradition from around 1100 held that Pope Sylvester II sent the crown to Stephen. Thietmar of Merseburg, a reliable contemporary, says somewhat obscurely that both 'crown and benediction' were given to Stephen 'by the grace and upon the encouragement' of Emperor Otto III (983–1002).[4] Thietmar's statement seems to imply that Stephen became in some way the vassal of the emperor, and this hypothesis is supported by the fact that it was the royal lance (*lancea regis*), given by Otto III to Géza, that Stephen used as a symbol of his authority. It was not the crown but the lance that could be seen on his coins, and we also find it on the coronation mantle, which showed the figure of the king and was made on his wife's orders in 1031. It is a fact, however, that we can find no trace of vassal status in Stephen's relationship with the empire. Indeed, he took every opportunity to stress his sovereignty.

Theoretical subordination to the empire, even if it did exist for a time, did not bring about any practical consequences for Hungary. In 1018 Stephen provided help to Emperor Basil II against the Bulgarians. The other emperor, Henry II (1002–1024), was his brother-in-law and friend. When Henry died, Stephen asserted his claim to the inheritance, demanding for his son a share of the duchy of Bavaria. This led to a war with the new emperor, Conrad II, who in 1030 tried to invade Hungary. He was defeated, however, and temporarily forced to renounce Vienna and its region.

The most serious problem facing Stephen concerned the succession. In 1031, his son, Emeric, who was reputed to live a holy life, died in a hunting accident. The obvious heir would have been Stephen's cousin, Vazul (Basil), the son of Géza's brother, Michael, but the king judged him to be wholly unsuitable to rule the kingdom. Instead he designated his nephew, Peter Orseolo, son of the duke of Venice, as his successor. Vazul was blinded and his three sons fled to Poland. Stephen died on 15 August 1038, aged about sixty, and was buried, together with his son, in the church of Székesfehérvár, which had been founded by him.

STEPHEN'S SUCCESSORS

Peter was the only foreign ruler of the country before the Angevin period. Not surprisingly, the Hungarian nobles were unwilling to accept him as their king. They took it amiss that he cheated the widow of Stephen out of her fortune and had her arrested, and that he filled his entourage with 'shouting Germans' and 'chattering Italians'.[5] In 1041 he was driven out of the country, and the nobles elected a new king, Aba, whose Christian name was Samuel (1041–1044). Aba was the head of an illustrious Hungarian kindred and also a relative, possibly a nephew through his mother (*sororius*), of Stephen. Although he was a faithful adherent to Christianity, his violent and ruthless rule alienated his subjects, none of whom was able any longer to feel secure. In 1042, after the Emperor Henry III had provided shelter for Peter, Aba laid waste Austria as an act of retaliation. But in 1043 the emperor advanced at the head of his troops as far as Győr and Aba was forced to sue for peace and renounce the Bavarian territories once acquired by Stephen. In 1044, when Henry III made another attempt to win back the Hungarian throne for his protégé, he was welcomed by most of the leading nobles. On 5 June Aba was defeated in a battle at Ménfő, near Győr, and executed soon afterwards. His kinsmen buried him in his 'own monastery' of Sár (today Abasár) near Eger.[6]

Aba's fall led to the restoration of Peter, who was determined to govern with the emperor's support. In 1045 he called Henry to Székesfehérvár, where on Whit Sunday (26 May) he solemnly handed over to him the royal lance, thereby declaring his kingdom to be an imperial fief. Moreover, it is possible that he wanted to introduce Bavarian law into Hungary. These measures enraged not only the adherents of dormant paganism, but also those of the new order. In 1046 the Christian nobles and prelates, putting their hope in the dynasty of Árpád, recalled Vazul's sons from Poland. Meanwhile the pagans considered that the time was ripe for the restoration of the ancient order and began to slaughter clerics and monks throughout the kingdom. It was at this time that the Venetian Gerald (Hung. Gellért), bishop of Cenad and former tutor of Prince Emeric, was killed together with two of his fellow bishops at the ferry of Budapest, under the hill that now bears his name.

Stephen's kingdom proved to be sufficiently robust to survive the crisis. As most of the leading men still wanted a Christian king, instead of electing the eldest of Vazul's sons, Levente, who was notorious for his pagan inclinations, they threw in their lot with the second son, Andrew. His election brought the Árpádians to power once again and they were to maintain their grip on it until the extinction of the dynasty in 1301. Andrew I (1046–1060), having adroitly taken advantage of the pagan revolt to defeat his rival, declared the restoration of the Christian order and promptly forced the pagans to obedience. Peter, who was captured by Andrew's faithful supporters at Székesfehérvár, was blinded and castrated, and died soon afterwards.

Henry III was unwilling to resign the overlordship that had been conceded to him by Peter. In 1051 he led his army deep into Hungary, but when the Hungarians cut his lines of communication and deprived him of supplies, he was forced to turn back without fighting a battle. The emperor's withdrawal amounted to a defeat, and later tradition held that the small range of hills called the Vértes, west of Budapest, were named after the armour (Hung. *vért*) that the retreating Germans discarded there. In 1052 Henry tried to take Pressburg, but this campaign also ended in failure. Andrew was consequently able to maintain his independent status and only made peace with the Empire a few years later, when the situation in Hungary made it necessary for him to seek help from abroad.

Andrew's anxieties at that time were caused by the problem of the succession, which was to be a constant cause for concern throughout the history of the Árpádians. It was possible to interpret the restoration of the dynasty in 1046 as a return to the ancient principle of seniority, which meant that, after the Levente's death, the lawful heir to the throne would be Béla, the third of Vazul's sons. Béla returned home not long after Andrew's election to the kingship. The new king gave Béla the eastern part of the kingdom, together with the title of 'duke'.

The ducal institution involved the territorial division of the government between the king and his closest kinsman, the 'duke', and functioned until 1107. It seems probable that the origins of this practice should be sought in tenth-century dynastic partitions about which we know very little. We do know that Koppány was 'duke' of Somogy under Géza. Peter might also have borne that title, for Stephen appointed him 'leader of his army'. Yet it is only from the time of Andrew I that the real nature of this institution becomes visible. The area governed by the duke was the country east of the Tisza and the region of Nitra, the centre of his power probably being in Bihor.

The duke exercised a range of royal privileges within his province, including coinage, and his sovereignty was only restricted in the field of foreign policy.

Andrew and Béla co-operated without incident until 1053, when a son, Solomon, was born to Andrew. Thereafter, the king was determined to secure the succession for his son. He had him crowned king in his own lifetime, an act that was followed in 1058 by Solomon's betrothal to Judith, daughter of the late Emperor Henry III. At the same time Andrew tried to persuade his brother to renounce his right to the succession. Tradition holds that he invited Béla to a meeting at Várkony (modern Tiszavárkony), a village on the frontier of their respective territories, and, putting the symbols of royal and ducal power – the crown and the sword – before him, he let him choose one of them. The duke, we are told, was well aware that choosing the crown would cost him his life. He therefore contented himself with the sword, but fled to Poland and quickly returned with troops of his own. Andrew was defeated and died soon after from his wounds. He was buried in his monastery of Tihany, where the lower part of the church and a gravestone made of red marble still preserve his memory. His adherents took Solomon to Germany, while Béla was crowned king on 6 December 1060.

The most memorable event of the short reign of Béla I (1060–1063) was the last outburst of paganism. In 1061, when the king was sitting in judgement at Székesfehérvár, a great crowd of ordinary people gathered and came forward with embarrassing demands. They wanted the ruler's authorisation for the slaughter – by stoning and impaling – of all the priests in the kingdom. Béla asked for three days for reflection, collected his army and routed the pagans. This time the triumph of Christianity was definitive.

In 1063 the Emperor Henry IV launched a large-scale attack with the aim of securing the Hungarian throne for his brother-in-law, Solomon. Béla, who seems to have been ready to abdicate in exchange for the ducal honour, met an accidental death on the eve of the invasion. His sons, Géza, Ladislaus and Lambert fled to Poland. Consequently, Solomon had no difficulty in taking possession of the kingdom. He soon made peace with his cousins, making over to Géza the duchy that had formerly been held by the latter's father. For a time, Solomon and Géza appeared to rule harmoniously. In 1068 they co-operated to halt a Pecheneg raid at Chiraleş in Transylvania; then, in 1071, they together attacked Belgrade, defended by the Byzantines, whom they accused of having helped the Pechenegs. Fraternal strife is said to have been revived by the division of the booty acquired during the siege. Géza and his brothers hired Czech auxiliary troops, while a German army backed Solomon. On 14 March 1074 Solomon was defeated at Mogyoród, near Pest, and fled to the West. Although Emperor Henry IV did everything to help him win back his throne, and invaded the kingdom as far as Vác, the only result was that he secured for Solomon the castles of Pressburg and Moson. The greater part of the country went over to the new king, who now bestowed the ducal authority upon his younger brother, Ladislaus.

Since Solomon had taken the treasury with him, Géza I (1074–1077) asked the Pope for a new crown. Initially, Gregory VII regarded the expelled king, Solomon, as the lawful ruler of the kingdom; then, the Pope demanded Géza's recognition of papal overlordship in exchange for his official acknowledgement. Instead of obeying the Pope, Géza made peace with the Byzantine empire and contented himself with a crown sent by the Emperor Michael VII. When Géza died on 25 April 1077, none of his sons was of age, and his brother Ladislaus had no difficulty in securing his own succession.

KING LADISLAUS I

Ladislaus I (1077–1095) is, alongside Stephen, one of the outstanding figures of early Hungarian history. It is not his deeds that make him shine brightly against the obscure and dim background of the first centuries of the kingdom, for we know no more about him than we do about Stephen. Although he obviously played an important role in the final consolidation of the Christian order, his work was not comparable to that of his great predecessor, and his heroic image was moulded by posterity. Indeed, his posthumous popularity exceeded that enjoyed by Stephen, although the reasons for this are not altogether clear. A generous patron of the Church, he too was canonised in 1192, and in the later Middle Ages he became the most popular Hungarian saint. While Stephen lived on in the collective memory as a pious but stern old man, the creator and ultimate source of law and order, Ladislaus was remembered as a young and valiant knight. Not much was said about his pious deeds, but his most memorable act, that of defeating a Cuman warrior in a duel to set free an abducted Hungarian girl, could be seen centuries later in frescos in the remotest parish churches of the kingdom. For the court and the military elite, Ladislaus I came to embody the ideal Hungarian knight, although, at so early a time, he could hardly have been imbued with the ideas of Christian chivalry. It gradually became a tradition that every ruler would follow up his coronation by making a pilgrimage to Ladislaus's tomb. Charles I gave Ladislaus's name to his second son, who died prematurely; Louis the Great put his effigy on his coins; and Sigismund of Luxembourg wanted to be buried next to him.

32

Ladislaus spent the first years of his reign settling the affair with Solomon. He succeeded in persuading the expelled former king to renounce his claims to the throne and return to Hungary; but Solomon's incessant intrigues soon forced the king to lock him up. He was kept as a prisoner at Visegrád, where a tower, which was actually built in the thirteenth century, was later said to have been his prison. On the occasion of the canonisation of Stephen, Solomon was set free and sought refuge among the Pechenegs living along the Lower Danube. With their help he led a last and unsuccessful attack against his former kingdom, and ended his adventurous life in 1087 while fighting the Byzantines somewhere in the Balkans. Later he became the hero of popular legends, and was even rumoured to have lived on as a hermit. A tomb alleged to be his at Pula (in Istria) has continued to be displayed until the present day.

At the opposite extreme from Ladislaus's lenient treatment of his most obstinate enemy was the cruelty with which he crushed all those who posed a threat to the new order. Virtually all of his efforts were aimed at the consolidation of the social and political system founded by Stephen. It was in order to achieve this that he promulgated his draconian laws and persuaded Pope Gregory VII to canonise Stephen, his son Emeric and Bishop Gerald. This step did not lack magnanimity, given that Vazul, who had been blinded by Stephen, was Ladislaus's own grandfather. The person of Stephen, however, symbolised everything that was new and, therefore, to be preserved in contemporary Hungary. The translation of Stephen's body from his tomb at Székesfehérvár took place on 20 August 1083. Although his right arm was missing, it was soon found intact, and an abbey (Sâniob, near Oradea in Romania, from Hung. *Szentjobb*, 'holy right hand') was consecrated to it. 'The Holy Dexter', now in Budapest, has since been the object of a special cult.

One of Ladislaus's most significant achievements was the occupation of Hungary's southern neighbour, Croatia. This was in fact the beginning of a new period in Hungarian foreign policy. The small kingdom, born in the tenth century, stretched from the Kapela mountains to the Adriatic sea, its centre being Biograd, located on the coast. Its inhabitants belonged to the Latin Church, whereas the Serbs, who spoke the same language, lived under Byzantine rule and followed Orthodoxy. King Demetrius Zvonimir, who, not being a member of the ruling dynasty, obtained his throne through election, asked Pope Gregory VII for a crown in 1075, and, in return, declared his kingdom a papal fief. After his death, Ladislaus laid claim to his realm by the right of his sister, Zvonimir's widow, and had no difficulty in taking possession of Croatia in 1091. He bestowed the new kingdom, together with the royal title, on his nephew, Álmos, son of Géza I, and when Pope Urban

II, as overlord of the kingdom, expressed his indignation at Ladislaus's action, the latter changed sides and went over to Urban's rival, the Emperor Henry IV.

It was during the invasion of Croatia that the area between the River Drava and the Kapela mountains, called Slavonia, was integrated into Hungary. Shortly before 1091 Ladislaus founded the ninth Hungarian bishopric at Zagreb as a symbol of his authority. We do not know what the former status of Slavonia had been. To judge from its name, the Hungarians regarded it as a region inhabited by Slavs, and so not belonging to their own land. A thirteenth-century source suggests that it had been part of the kingdom of Croatia, but this is hardly credible in view of the later relationship between Hungary and Slavonia. In contrast to Croatia, which always remained a separate realm (*regnum*), Slavonia's status within the kingdom much resembled that of Transylvania. It formed a separate diocese, but the bishop of Zagreb, like that of Transylvania, was the suffragan of the archbishop of Kalocsa, while the Croatian bishops belonged to the metropolitan provinces of Split and (from 1154) Zadar. It is this special status of Slavonia that must lie behind the *marturina*, that peculiar and apparently archaic tax that was due from its inhabitants. As its name indicates, the *marturina* was originally a tax payable in the form of marten fur, but King Coloman (1095–1116) converted it into a money tax. Taxes of this kind, normally paid in the form of some kind of fur, could be found throughout eastern Europe, where nomadic princes imposed taxes on the Slavs of the neighbouring forests. We may assume, therefore, that *marturina* was originally a special tax that the Slavs of Slavonia had to pay to their Hungarian overlord. It seems that Slavonia, before becoming effectively incorporated into Hungary, had already been attached to it in some way.

KING COLOMAN

Ladislaus, like Stephen, did not have a male heir. He designated as his successor his younger nephew, Álmos, whom he found more suited to the requirements of kingship. Nevertheless, when Ladislaus died on 29 July 1095, Coloman, the elder brother of Álmos, succeeded him. Coloman seems to have had a good education but an unprepossessing appearance. He was, if we are to believe his contemporaries, 'half blind, hunchbacked, lame and stammering',[7] and because of these handicaps was originally destined for an ecclesiastical career; but now he exchanged the bishop's seat for the royal throne. A contemporary Polish chronicler says that 'in the art of writing he was the most skilful'[8] of all rulers of his time,[8] and in Hungary he was later given the epithet 'the Learned'. Coloman tried to appease Álmos by appointing him duke, but the latter could not acquiesce in being set aside. From 1098 Álmos revolted against his brother on no fewer than five occasions, generally with German and Polish help. Finally, he was even prepared to become the vassal of Emperor Henry V if the latter could secure the Hungarian throne for him. Although for some time willing to pardon his brother, Coloman eventually lost patience and around 1113 ordered the blinding of both Álmos and his son, Béla. With the fall of Álmos the duchy as an institution fell into abeyance. Hungary proper was no longer to be divided between king and duke, and the younger members of the royal family normally governed Croatia and Dalmatia or, in the thirteenth century, Transylvania.

It was early in Coloman's reign that the first crusaders marched through Hungary. The country had been much favoured by those going to the Holy Land ever since Stephen had opened his kingdom to pilgrims in 1018 and had founded a hostelry in Jerusalem. The crusaders arrived in several waves between May and September 1096, led by Walter 'Sans-avoir', Peter of Amiens and Godfrey of Bouillon. Although the only troops to maintain proper discipline were Godfrey's, the crossing of all of them was carried out without serious conflict. It was King Coloman himself who received Godfrey at Sopron, and escorted him along the left bank of the Danube to the border castle of Zemun, opposite Belgrade, while keeping his brother, Baldwin, the future king of Jerusalem, as a hostage. A few crusader bands that tried to engage in plundering were prevented from crossing the kingdom. A marauding war-band led by a Frenchman called Foucher was routed by the king himself near Nitra, while that of the German priest Gottschalk was dispersed at Székesfehérvár. Coloman also drove back the troops of Emich of Leiningen from the Hungarian border at the castle of Moson. As far as we know, the crusaders were not joined by any Hungarians. The first known pilgrim to go to Jerusalem was Duke Álmos, who undertook this long and tiring journey around 1107, between two of his revolts.

It was Coloman who took the final steps towards the definitive attachment of Croatia to the Crown of Hungary. In 1097 he defeated a certain King Peter, who had emerged as a rival; then in 1102 had himself crowned king at Biograd. According to a fourteenth-century forgery, he also made a convention (*pacta conventa*) with the heads of the Croatian clans, in which he supposedly recognised their autonomy and specific privileges. Curiously enough, the content of the alleged *pacta* is concordant with reality in more than one respect. Croatia was henceforth to be ruled by the kings of Hungary, but it was given an associate status and was not incorporated into Hungary. Although, with the exception of Coloman, none of the kings was crowned in Croatia, its separate status as a kingdom (*regnum*) was expressed in the royal title (*rex Croatiae*). Moreover, Croatia was not governed by counts (*ispánok*), as in Hungary proper, but by a governor who exercised vice-regal authority and bore the special title of ban (*banus*). Apart from the fact that both the ban and the members of his following were normally Hungarians, there was nothing that made Hungarian rule seem over-bearing. The Croatian nobility continued to live according to their own laws and customs, and were only required to perform military service within the boundaries of their country. Although, on occasion, Hungarian noblemen were given lands in Croatia, during the later Middle Ages the contrary occurred more frequently. It is probably this particular situation that explains the absence of any serious form of Croatian separatism until the end of the Middle Ages.

Coloman wished to extend a similar status to Dalmatia, his other acquisition, but this region, in contrast to Croatia, did not become a permanent part of the Hungarian Crown. Medieval Dalmatia did not constitute a country in the normal sense of the word, for the name stood not for a contiguous territory but a collection of scattered spots on the eastern coast of the Adriatic, including a few fortified towns and a number of nearby islands. Dalmatia was clearly distinguishable from Croatia by its government, its Mediterranean climate and its different culture. The towns, among which Zadar (Zara), Trogir (Trau), Šibenik (Sebenico) and Split (Spalato) were the most important, formed part of the Byzantine empire, enjoyed a broad autonomy and were governed by civic oligarchies with the archbishop or the bishop at their head. Unlike those in Croatia, the cities of Dalmatia were Italian in their outlook, and their population still spoke a Latin dialect.

Coloman invaded Dalmatia in 1105, his expedition meeting with rapid success. The Emperor Alexius Comnenus, who had just asked Ladislaus's daughter, Prisca, to be the wife of his son, the future John II, did not object to Coloman's action, a favour that the Hungarian king later returned by helping Alexius against his Norman enemy, Bohemund. Coloman forced Zadar to surrender after a brief siege, and this resulted in all the other cities recognising his rule as well. The conditions offered by the king seem to have been acceptable. As a symbol of their recognition of his authority, Coloman demanded two-thirds of their customs revenues, but he left intact the autonomy of the cities and in 1108 confirmed their former privileges.

From the time of the conquest of the Adriatic coast Coloman titled himself 'king of Hungary, Croatia and Dalmatia' (1108), in contrast to his predecessors who had been 'kings of the Hungarians' (or of the 'Pannons').[9] This modification of the royal title reflected important conceptual changes. On the one hand, the pagan notion of the 'people' (*gens*) was beginning to be replaced by the 'realm' (*regnum*) as the object of royal authority, which meant that the rule over persons was giving way to the rule over a territory. On the other hand, and no less importantly, the territories themselves began to be institutionalised. The annexed regions were neither actually nor conceptually incorporated into the Hungarian kingdom, but continued to be regarded as separate countries. They were politically united to Hungary first by the person, and later on by the crown, of a common king. All this meant that the *regnum Hungariae* was now beginning to have clear notional and territorial outlines. As in the other countries of Latin Europe, this came to be the guarantee of political stability, in contrast to other regions, where the absence of the notion of *regnum* resulted in less clearly defined and less durable political formations.

The conquest of Croatia and Dalmatia opened a new, expansionist period in Hungarian foreign policy that was to last for about three hundred years. During the eleventh century, as we have already seen, Hungary had to face the expansionist ambitions of the Holy Roman Empire on several occasions, although these attempts never represented a real threat to the independent status of the kingdom. The country was also exposed to attacks by the nomadic tribes of the neighbouring steppe, like the Pechenegs or the Cumans. But the last raid from the east took place in 1091. Henceforth, Hungary was not to be a target of foreign invasions until the arrival of the Mongols. On the contrary, the reigns of Ladislaus and Coloman mark the beginning of a period of Hungarian expansionism that was to last until the first Ottoman incursion in 1390. During this period the Hungarian kingdom was a leading power of central Europe, which meant that, while not having to fear external attacks, it continually harassed its neighbours. Expansion was therefore the dominant feature of this period, even if it did not manifest itself in actual conquests, but rather in incessant campaigning, nominal annexations and, by these means, the continuous enlargement of the royal title. By the end of the thirteenth century the Árpádians were able to call themselves king of no fewer than eight neighbouring countries, all of which were to remain nominal parts of the Crown of Hungary until as late as 1918.

THE CHRISTIAN MONARCHY

Looking back to the eleventh century, it is clear that the most spectacular development of the period was the adoption of Christianity, together with its institutions, and the establishment of the Christian monarchy on this foundation. These two phenomena were closely intertwined. On the one hand, the new order was not sustainable without a strong royal power; on the other, it was the Christian religion that gave the kingship an authority never possessed by pagan rulers. The new power, now bestowed upon the king 'by the grace of God', was not only more substantial than the one that preceded it; it was also fundamentally different in character. The Christian ruler could derive from religion an authority that could not be imagined by a pagan prince. At the same time, however, he was expected to use this authority to maintain peace and order, and to consolidate the Christian faith. Consequently, Christian kingship meant a social and political system that was in many ways different from what preceded it. The collective sacrality of the dynasty of Árpád, upon which the tenth-century order appears to have been based, was now replaced by the single and unquestionable authority of a Christian king.

The basic principles of the new order and of just government were summarised in a small work called *Libellus de institutione morum*. Although the authorship was attributed to Stephen, it seems in fact to have been written by a well-educated prelate, possibly Archbishop Asrik, around 1015. However, the author must surely have taken into consideration the remarks of the king, whom we know to have acquired a certain skill in the *ars grammatica* during his education. The work, while resembling the Carolingian 'mirrors', was an original composition as regards structure, style and conception, and contained the moral 'admonitions' of Stephen for his son. It focused upon the exercise of the Christian virtues, but laid a special emphasis on two requirements whose importance was justified by the 'immature and weak' state of the Hungarian kingdom. On the one hand, it strongly recommended the invitation of 'guests', that is foreign knights and priests, 'for the country that has only one language and one custom is weak and fragile' *(nam unius lingue uniusque moris regnum imbecille est et fragile)*. On the other hand, it underlined the importance of respect for ancient traditions, without which, said the king to his son, and certainly not without reason, 'it would be difficult for you to govern this part of the world.'[10]

The 'Admonitions' clearly reflected the dual – secular and temporal – character of early medieval royal power. According to the well-known concept of the tenth century, the Christian king (*rex*) was not only the worldly ruler of his people, but also their religious leader (*sacerdos*). Although the expression *rex et sacerdos* does not occur in the text itself, the whole structure of the work shows that Stephen conceived his royal authority in terms of this dualism. The king's office was not limited to the direction of politics; he also had to establish the organisation of the Church, and his laws accordingly paid equal attention to lay and ecclesiastical matters.

The process of the foundation and organisation of the kingdom can best be reconstructed with the help of the eleventh-century law-codes.

From Stephen himself we have two such codes, with 56 articles (35 and 21 respectively). Two further codes are attributed to Ladislaus, the so-called 'second' and 'third' law-codes, which contain 47 articles (18 and 29). It is the 'third' law-code that is the older, and some scholars think that it was in fact compiled before the reign of Ladislaus, probably in the time of Solomon. From Coloman's reign we have only one collection but, containing 84 articles, it is much longer than any of the other four. To the information furnished by these codes can be added the canons of the council of Szabolcs of 1092, formerly known as the first law-code of Ladislaus, and those of Esztergom of about 1100. These canons contain many prescriptions concerning the laity, in the same way as some of the secular laws laid down rules that affected the life of the Church.

The small number of charters that have been handed down to us from this early period were, with a few exceptions, issued by rulers. The earliest of them, which bears the date 1001, is a charter of Stephen confirming the privileges of the abbey of Pannonhalma, but it has only been preserved in a twelfth-century interpolated form. Perhaps older is an undated charter of Stephen, which was issued for a nunnery near Veszprém and has survived in a transcription of King Coloman's reign. It is notable for being the only extant charter written in Greek. The first charter whose original has survived was issued in 1055 by Andrew I for his monastery at Tihany. This document is also remarkable from another point of view, for it contains, in the description of the domains given to the monastery, the words *Feheruuaru rea meneh hodu utu rea* ('on the military road which leads to Fehérvár'), which is the oldest known phrase written in Hungarian.[11] The earliest, non-royal charters were issued by Count Otto in 1061 and Count Peter in about 1067, in favour of their respective monasteries.

THE ORGANISATION OF GOVERNMENT

To construct his new regime, Stephen needed the help of foreign knights, most of whom came to him from Germany in the company of Queen Gisela. The extent of their support is shown by the fact that contemporaries regarded the battle against Koppány as a fight between 'Germans' and 'Hungarians'.[12] Among the foreign knights one should mention the brothers Hont and Pázmány, who were later remembered as having girded Stephen with his sword before the campaign against Koppány; and Vecelin of Swabia, who is said to have killed Koppány in the battle. They were each given a prominent role in government, and their descendants were to form some of the most illustrious kindreds of the Árpádian period. We should not, however, overemphasise the influence enjoyed by foreigners. It is beyond doubt that Stephen's rule was, above all, founded on indigenous Hungarian leaders whose support he and his father had managed to secure. Their number must have been quite considerable, for most of the thirteenth-century Hungarian nobles claimed descent – and certainly not without reason – from persons who had once taken part in the conquest and the raids. One of them, and not the least illustrious, must have been Aba, whose father was distinguished enough to secure the king's sister as his wife.

The leaders, be they of foreign or Hungarian birth, all bore the Hungarian title *ispán*, which was normally translated into Latin as 'count' (*comes*). The word *ispán* was the Hungarian equivalent of the southern Slav *župan*, and was used to denote the head of a kindred or the chief of a district and, in Hungary, the royal governor of a fortress or a county. The counts were the most important lay office-holders of the kingdom from the eleventh century onwards. In their totality they constituted the 'order of the counts' (*ordo comitum*). Together with the bishops, they were regarded by the 'Admonitions' as the principal supports of kingship. It was the counts and bishops who composed the royal council (*senatus*), the consent of which was more than once referred to in the laws of Stephen. From the beginning, the most prominent among the counts was the palatine (*palatinus*, originally *comes palatinus*, Hung. *nádor*), an office that was held by Aba in Stephen's time.

The new royal authority rested upon a number of newly erected fortresses. Although Anonymus stated that many 'castles' (*castrum*) had been occupied or constructed by the invading Hungarians, archaeological evidence seems to prove that no such places existed in Hungary before the last quarter of the tenth century, the earliest fortresses being erected by Géza and Stephen. Esztergom, Székesfehérvár and Veszprém were intended to be the residences of the king or the queen and were built of stone. In several places the ruins of a late Roman *castellum* were transformed into a fortress. But the normal royal 'cities' of the eleventh and twelfth centuries were simple earthworks crowned by a wooden wall and surrounded by a ditch and bank. While they normally extended over an area of about five to twelve acres, Sopron, a border fortress watching the main route from the West, was as large as 21.5 acres.

These early fortresses, which in Latin documents were termed 'cities' (*civitas*) or 'towns' (*urbs*) until the twelfth century and 'castles' (*castrum*) thereafter, were all in the hands of the king and were to serve as the local centres of royal government. To most – or maybe all – of them a district (*parochia, provincia*) was allotted. This was something similar to an Anglo-Saxon shire and was called the 'county' (*comitatus*) of the castle. To such a district the Hungarians gave the name *megye*, also a

Slav word with the original meaning of 'border', and they probably did so because, from the beginning, all the counties had well defined boundaries. The counties could, therefore, serve as the bases of ecclesiastical organisation as well. According to a royal charter from 1009, the diocese of Veszprém comprised four 'cities' (*civitas*),[13] by which was certainly meant the four counties belonging to these fortresses.

The castles, together with their counties, were from the outset entrusted to counts. The relation between the count and his 'city' was so close that many fortresses, like Hont or Abaújvár ('the new castle of Aba'), were apparently named after their first governor. Most of the modern counties go back to those founded by Stephen and his successors, and even their boundaries seem often to have remained unaltered until the twentieth century. The counties of Hont and Abaúj were cut into two by the Treaty of Trianon in 1920, but the halves that remained with Hungary continued to survive as administrative units until 1950.

Stephen may have established as many as 40 or 45 counties, but we may assume that a count normally had more than one county under his command and that he governed them individually through deputies. It is unlikely, for example, that the authority of Count Hont extended no further than the small county that was later named after him; and the idea that Aba's power might have been restricted merely to the district of his 'new castle' seems no less improbable. In our sources the counts appear as persons having the same prestige and authority as a bishop, and hence we must conclude that the territory entrusted to them, as far as its size is concerned, was probably comparable to that of a diocese. The counts of Stephen's time can therefore be regarded, with some justification, as the Hungarian counterparts of the Anglo-Saxon ealdormen; and this would also account for the fact that contemporary sources sometimes refer to Hont and other counts as 'princes' or 'dukes'.

The way in which the building up of the kingdom proceeded may be inferred from the legend of Saint Gerald, which tells us how the county and bishopric of Cenad were founded. The town of Cenad, on the River Mureş, was at that time called Marosvár (*urbs Morisena*) and was the residence of a certain 'Prince' Ajtony, whose province extended from the River Körös to the Danube. Ajtony seems to have embraced Byzantine Orthodoxy and founded a Greek monastery near his residence, but otherwise he was 'very imperfect in the Christian faith', having as many as seven wives.[14] He also had vast studs of wild horses, innumerable cattle and so many warriors that he even dared, so we are told, to oppose Stephen and to levy a tax upon the king's salt as it was being transported from Transylvania. Around 1030 the king, being tired of all this, declared him an enemy and sent Cenad (Csanád) against him. Anonymus states that Cenad was Stephen's nephew, while, according to the legend, he was a pagan in the service of Ajtony who deserted him for the king. In any case, Ajtony was defeated and killed, and Cenad became his successor as the 'prince of the king and of the house of Ajtony'.[15] At Marosvár, which was later given the name of Cenad, a bishopric was immediately founded, and Gerald, who had hitherto lived as a hermit in the forest of the Bakony, was invited by the king to be its first bishop. The region that is said to have belonged to Ajtony was henceforth to form the diocese of Cenad.

In modern historiography Ajtony is usually presented as an independent prince, similar to the *gyula* of Transylvania, but this view is probably erroneous. The defeat of Ajtony, in contrast to that of Koppány and the *gyula*, is not mentioned by the chronicles, which seems to show that it was not considered by contemporaries to be an event of importance. The existence for several decades of an independent principality in the very heart of the kingdom is hardly credible. It is much more probable that Ajtony had something of the status of Aba or Hont, that is that he governed, hereditarily or not, a part of the kingdom in the name of the king. But, in contrast to Aba and others, Ajtony seems to have been unable to tame his pagan sympathies, and had therefore to be broken by force.

THE NEW HUNGARIAN CHURCH

The rule of Christianity was to be secured by the organised Church. For the descendants of the pagan warriors of the Conquest this must have been the most intolerable of the changes that they had to endure. The introduction of the ecclesiastical hierarchy and of legislation meant not only that the leaders were thereafter forced to share power with the bishops, who were their new peers, but also that the warriors and common folk had to accept new lords who, besides propagating ideas completely alien to their traditional beliefs, sought to impose these upon them in a foreign language. The earliest priests in Hungary, who we know by name, were, of course, foreigners – mainly Germans, Italians and Frenchmen. The first prelate born in Hungary seems to have been Maurus, bishop of Pécs, who was appointed by Stephen not long before his death.

Although some scholars think that the bishopric of Veszprém was actually founded by Géza, it remains the case that the establishment of the ecclesiastical organisation as such was carried out by Stephen. He is reported to have founded ten dioceses with two archbishops at their head. The see of the royal residence at Esztergom was consecrated to Saint Adalbert, who had visited the court of Géza in 995 and who later was held to be Stephen's godfather. The archbishop of Esztergom was from the beginning the highest ranking prelate of the Hungarian Church. His most important prerogative was his exclusive right to crown the kings of Hungary. Esztergom had five suffragans, the bishops of Eger, Pécs, Veszprém, Győr and Vác, and we happen to know that the boundaries of their dioceses, at least in Transdanubia, were drawn in 1009. Around 1100, a sixth, Nitra, was added by King Coloman. The other archbishopric was established at Kalocsa and was later to be united with the Orthodox metropolis of Bač, the origins of which are unknown. The first suffragans of Kalocsa were the bishops of Cenad and Bihor, and also a third, the bishop of Transylvania, whose see was at Alba Iulia. From about 1100, the diocese of Bihor was named after its new seat, Oradea. The see of Zagreb, founded by Ladislaus I in about 1090, was also subordinated to Kalocsa, the suffragans of which were supplemented in the thirteenth century by the two missionary bishoprics of Syrmia (Srem) and Bosnia. Henceforth the Hungarian Church comprised fourteen bishops but was divided into twelve dioceses, for the missionary bishoprics had no jurisdiction outside their estates.

Cathedral chapters appear in the sources from the end of the eleventh century, but they had not become separate bodies with property of their own before 1150. At about that time the wealth of a cathedral began to be divided between the bishop and his chapter. At the head of a chapter stood the provost, its principal dignitaries being the *custos*, the *lector*, the *cantor* and the archdeacons, whose authority normally extended over a county. The earliest collegiate chapters also traced their origins back to the reign of Stephen. The most illustrious, and the richest among them, was that of Székesfehérvár, dedicated to the Holy Virgin. Stephen, who transferred his seat there from Esztergom, was buried in its church, followed by fourteen other kings, including Béla III, Louis the Great and Matthias Corvinus. It was at Székesfehérvár that the kings and queens were crowned from 1038 onwards, and the custos of the local chapter was in charge of the most precious treasures of the dynasty, including the royal crown. The Holy Crown was also kept there until the beginning of the fifteenth century, when it was taken to the castle of Visegrád.

It was in these early times that the Benedictine order appeared in Hungary. Its first and richest monastery was at Pannonhalma, which has preserved much of its ancient form to the present day. Dedicated to Saint Martin of Tours, it was founded in 996 by Géza, but owed its lavish endowment to his son. The monasteries of Pécsvárad, Zalavár, Bakonybél and Zobor (near Nitra) were also founded by Stephen and these were followed by other monastic foundations under his successors (Tihany in 1055, Szekszárd in 1061, Hronský Beňadik in 1075, etc). The example set by the rulers was soon imitated by leading nobles, and the monastery of Zselicszentjakab (near Kaposvár), founded by Count Otto in 1061, was as generously endowed as any of the royal monasteries.

In the eleventh and twelfth centuries there still existed a few monasteries that followed the Orthodox rite, such as the convent founded by Stephen for Greek nuns who had settled in a valley near Veszprém. The Slavs must have played a very important role in the evangelising process, for nearly all the basic terms of the new religion in Hungarian (Christian, pagan, baptise, confirm, bishop, priest, monk, saint, angel, altar, idol) were adopted from them. The names of four days of the week are also of Slavonic origin.

The material foundations and spiritual authority of the Church had to be strengthened in every possible way. Clerics were, in Hungary as elsewhere, exempt from the jurisdiction of the secular courts, whereas ecclesiastical courts could judge laymen in certain cases, such as marriage disputes. Although the wind of the Gregorian reform reached Hungary at the end of the eleventh century, the problems there were obviously different from those to be found elsewhere, and it would have been unwise to enforce the new ideas without respect for local custom. It was laid down that 'no one shall presume to buy and sell a church',[16] yet the institution of the 'private church' (*Eigenkirche*) still existed in the thirteenth century. Not even celibacy could be unconditionally imposed upon the early clergy. A synod held in the time of Coloman accepted the fact that 'in consideration of human frailty', bishops and priests lived with their wives. It only prescribed that they should do it 'with moderation',[17] and prohibited remarriage, concubinage and, of course, bigamy.

One of the most important of the Church's resources was the tithe. Stephen had ordered its general imposition upon the population, but the exact details of how it was to be collected were not regulated before the end of the century. It was always levied on wine and grain, sometimes also on other crops, and up to the thirteenth century it was mostly collected in kind. Yet the authority of the Church rested from the outset on its huge estates. Ecclesiastical property enjoyed the special protection of the king. Donations once promised could not be revoked. As elsewhere in Europe, the establishment of the Church's authority manifested itself above all in its taking possession of extensive landed estates. Stephen gave 1136 households in 41 villages to the abbey of Pécsvárad, while the monastery of Pannonhalma possessed as many as 2200 households at the beginning of the thirteenth century. The bishoprics were not so lavishly endowed with land, for they received the lion's share of the tithe. The bishopric of Eger, for example, received only ten villages from its founder. It should be added, however, that most ecclesiastical establishments steadily increased the extent of their property until at least the thirteenth century. By that time, some of the prelates, such as the two archbishops or the bishops of Pécs and Oradea, were to hold enormous domains.

THE DESTRUCTION OF PAGANISM

An important prerequisite to the consolidation of the new order was, as the example of Ajtony shows, the destruction of pagan institutions. In order to establish the lasting rule of Christianity, everything that could somehow recall the memory of pagan rites had to be eradicated. It took at least a century for this purgation to be carried out, but it was ultimately done so thoroughly that almost nothing of the heritage of the previous epoch survived. This fact poses a serious problem for modern research, for it is now extremely difficult to establish which institutions of the first Christian centuries were new creations and which had antecedents in the tenth century. Paganism could be represented not only by religious beliefs; it also seemed to be inherent in all kinds of ethnic customs and institutions. Even an army crossing a river on goatskins was something that Anonymus thought to be 'pagan' (*paganismus*).[18] The conversion to Christianity required, therefore, much more than a simple acceptance of new religious dogmas; it also required an outward adaptation to the normal way of life of Christian peoples. Those who were not willing to change their habits demonstrated thereby that they remained pagans in their souls. Vata, a pagan nobleman and an instigator of the rebellion of 1046, 'consecrated himself to the demons, had his hair shaved off, leaving only three braids according to the pagan custom', while his followers 'began to eat horse meat'.[19] It is clear that they did so in order to express their pagan preferences.

Pagan beliefs and habits were bound together very strongly, for they reflected the lay and spiritual side of the same ethnic identity. All those who bore the name Magyar had in common the same customs and the same religious ideas. Indeed, it was through these customs and ideas that they differed from other people. We may suppose, therefore, that the most characteristic of pagan institutions was the 'tribe'. In whatever way the seven tribes might have functioned, there is no doubt that they comprised the totality of the pagan Hungarian people. This could explain why all traces of the tribal organisation disappeared during the foundation of the kingdom, with not even its memory surviving. If our reasoning is correct, the destruction of tribal identity must have been regarded as the first thing to be done when the Christian faith was being established.

The observance of Christian rules, which had replaced pagan ritual, was guaranteed by the force of new laws. The first of these, issued by

Stephen, ordered the observance of Sunday, fasting days, Friday fast and confession before death. They also ordained that everyone should go to church 'with the exception of those who guard the fire',[20] and prescribed the punishment of those who 'mutter among themselves and disturb others by relating idle tales during the celebration of mass'. The old were only to be driven out of church, but the young and the common people were to be punished 'by whipping and by the shearing off of their hair'.[21] Under Ladislaus at the latest, the observance of Lent was made obligatory, though still according to the Byzantine style (that is, beginning on the Sunday before Shrove Tuesday), and the other obligatory ecclesiastical feasts – nearly 40 in number – were also laid down officially. The second law-code of Stephen ordered that 'ten villages shall build a church and endow it with two manses and two serfs, a horse and a mare, six oxen, two cows, and 30 small animals. The king shall provide vestments and altar cloths, and the bishop the priests and books.'[22] Those who lived far from a church were later given the right to send representatives, that is, says the law, 'one among them on behalf of all shall come to the church with a staff and shall offer at the altar three loaves and a candle.'[23] The earliest churches were in all probability built of wood, and by the end of the century some of them were already 'ruined by age'.[24]

In response to the polygamy and patriarchal traditions of the pagans, the laws paid special attention to the fundamental institution of Christian marriage and to the protection of women in general. These measures were amply justified. He who killed a man had invariably to pay 110 steers, which included a fine to the king and the blood money due to the victim's kin; but the killing of one's wife was expressly excluded from the category of homicide. A husband who committed such a deed had to pay to the kinsmen of his wife a wergild that could amount to 50, 10 or 5 steers, with the sum dependent on his and not her status. Even centuries later, a wife caught *in flagrante delicto* could be killed by her husband without legal consequences. On the other hand, the king extended his protection to orphans, prohibited the nomadic custom of compelling widows to get married against their wish, and condemned the tradition of abducting women. Measures were also taken against those who 'flee their wives by leaving the country',[25] and against the husband who, 'because of the hatred he bears towards his wife', sells himself as a slave.[26]

TRACES OF PAGAN BELIEF

As a result of persecution, pagan religion disappeared without leaving any written traces. All that we know is that it was closely connected to the nomadic way of life, and that sacrifices offered to the gods in sacred places and the cult of ancestors each had important parts to play in it. The horse was also the object of a special cult. Some notions of pagan belief, like the patriarchal 'Godfather' (*isten*) or the supreme devil (*ördög*), could be incorporated into Christian vocabulary. The old word *igy* ('sacred'), surely a central concept of pagan belief, disappeared, but can be detected by linguists as a forgotten adjective in Hungarian words like *egyház* ('sacred house', today 'church'), *ünnep* ('sacred day', today 'feast') and probably *üdvösség* ('being sacred', today 'salvation').

Some elements of pagan mythology, distorted into superstitions or sublimated into tales, continued to live on in the folklore of isolated peasant communities throughout the Carpathian basin and could still be recorded as late as this century. One such idea was the 'tree reaching the sky', which by means of its branches connects the three worlds on, under and above the earth. Another was the 'dual soul', one part of which stayed continuously in the body till the moment of death, while the other, the 'free soul', left it regularly and only returned to sleep. These pagan beliefs must have been of very ancient origin, for their closest parallels can be found among the religious concepts of Siberian peoples. Moreover, they are closely connected to shamanism, which is sometimes thought to have been the essence of the religion of the pagan Hungarians. The shaman (Hung. *táltos*) was a person with superhuman power who, by virtue of certain clearly discernible corporal signs (e.g. six fingers, more teeth than normal) was predestined to communicate with the transcendental world. Communication was made while in a state of ecstasy, brought about by rhythmic music and dance. The chief instrument of the shaman was his magic drum, which was brought down from the top of the world-tree and with which he could heal and also tell the future and make rain if necessary.

In spite of the obvious difficulties involved, we may say that the triumph of Christianity was relatively easily achieved. After the suppression of the second pagan uprising in 1061, the dominance of Christianity was never again to be questioned, although thirty years later it was still deemed necessary to legislate against those who 'make a sacrifice next to wells or give offerings to trees, fountains and stones according to pagan rites'. Stephen had already prohibited the activity of witches, wizards and fortune-tellers. By the end of the century the situation had improved to such an extent that King Coloman could put an end to the persecution of 'vampires' (*strigae*), 'who do not exist'.[27] It was also Coloman who ordered that 'no Christian should be buried outside churchyards'.[28] That his order brought about the desired result is proven by the absence of either heathen burials or the usual grave objects. The synod of Esztergom around 1100 merely imposed fasting upon those who 'celebrate anything taken from heathen rituals'.[29] This is a sure indication of the definitive triumph of Christianity in Hungary.

The earliest written sources, while providing much valuable information about the pagan order of the tenth century, mainly shed light on the enormous transformation which took place during the period that ran from the reign of Saint Stephen to the time of Coloman. The historical importance of this period can hardly be overestimated. Although the social and political order that came into being during the first century of the Christian kingdom broke up two centuries later and, consequently, many important features of it remain unknown to us, Stephen's achievement as a whole proved to be lasting. He was remembered for centuries as the ultimate source of all manner of rights. Not only the nobility but also other social groups strove to derive their privileges from a concession of the Holy King. As late as in 1437 the leaders of the peasant revolt of Transylvania sent envoys to Buda in the hope of finding there the charter of Saint Stephen in which, they thought, the 'liberties' of peasant tenants were laid down.[30] More than one institution founded by him – including the dioceses and the counties – has continued to exist until the present day. Yet by far the most significant step at that time was the decision to join the Roman Church. As a result of this, Hungary remained a part of Latin Christendom, and the cultural and political implications of this fact can hardly be overestimated.

Chapter 4

The Twelfth Century

The kingdom of Hungary, which had been founded by Stephen I and enlarged by Ladislaus I and Coloman, appears to have survived the twelfth century without major changes. It is important to note that the sources at our disposal for this period are much poorer than for the previous century. We have more charters, and an increasing number of them are of private origin; but law codes, which would be of particular value for the historian, are completely missing. Nevertheless, the overall picture that can be drawn of this century is more vivid than that of the eleventh, due to three foreign authors, all of whom wrote around 1150. Idrisi, the famous Arab geographer of King Roger II of Sicily, worked from indirect sources, but Bishop Otto of Freising, a crusader, and Abu Hamid, a Muslim traveller from Andalusia, saw Hungary with their own eyes and were consequently in a position to provide first-hand information.

COLOMAN'S SUCCESSORS

Coloman died on 3 February 1116, and his successor was his only son, Stephen II (1116–1131), who was aged fifteen. This ailing but quarrelsome and aggressive young man went to war in neighbouring territories in almost every year of his reign. Yet it is not easy to discern a coherent strategy underlying his actions, nor were they in any respect successful. In 1116 he was heavily defeated in battle by the Bohemians, and in 1123 was forced by his grumbling counts to return from an expedition to Galicia. In 1124 Stephen recovered Dalmatia, which had been taken by Venice immediately after the death of Coloman; but he lost it the following year. In 1127, after the Emperor John II had given refuge to Álmos, Stephen attacked the Byzantine Empire, advancing as far as Plovdiv, but this led to a retaliatory attack by the emperor in

1128. By this time it had become evident that Stephen would not have an heir of his own body. Consequently, when he was told that his cousin, Béla – who, as a child, had been blinded at the same time as his father, Álmos – was being kept hidden in an Hungarian monastery, he sent for him, placed him in a more suitable residence and married him to the daughter of the grand župan of Serbia. Stephen died soon afterwards (1 March 1131), and the throne passed to Béla.

In reality, it was not Béla II (1131–1141) himself who took over the reins of power but his wife, Helena, whose first action was to take vengeance upon those whom she held responsible for the blinding of her husband. During an assembly at Arad she ordered the massacre of those leading men who were considered to have been adherents of Coloman and his son. The survivors turned for help to Boris, an Árpádian bastard living in Russia. Boris was the son of Euphemia, sister of the Grand Duke Vladimir Monomachus of Kiev and Coloman's second wife, who had been discovered in an adulterous relationship by her husband and driven home. In 1132 Boris attempted an invasion with the help of Boleslaw III of Poland. Although on this occasion defeated near the River Sajó, he was to remain in the forefront of Hungarian politics as a pretender for several decades.

The joint rule of Béla and Helena may also be remembered for a territorial acquisition. In 1136 they recovered part of Dalmatia from Venice, and in the next year a Hungarian army penetrated into the wild mountains of Bosnia. It seems to have returned home without gaining an inch of land; but the king nevertheless appointed one of his sons duke of Bosnia, and presented himself with the title of 'king of Rama'. Curiously enough, a country of that name has never existed. Rama was, in fact, a small tributary of the River Neretva, the valley of which was later to form a remote county of Bosnia. So it seems to have been due to some kind of misunderstanding that Rama became incorporated into the royal title. Nevertheless, all the kings of Hungary were to bear that title until 1918, and it was to provide a legal basis for their pretence of supremacy over Bosnia.

The unfortunate King Béla, who was said to have turned to drink, was hardly more than thirty years of age when he died (13 February 1141). He was followed on the throne by his eldest son, Géza II (1141–1162), who, being a minor, ruled for several years under the guardianship of his Serbian maternal uncle, Beloš. Boris tried in vain to enforce his claim to the throne, first with German, then with Byzantine support. For his part, Géza intervened in the internal strife of the Empire on behalf of the Welfs, and in 1146 defeated Henry, margrave of Austria, a supporter of the Stauf party, near the River Leitha. In 1147, when the Second Crusade began, Géza's relations with Germany were still so strained that Conrad III marched through Hungary as an enemy. With King Louis VII, the leader of the French crusaders, Géza was on friendly terms, the only source of tension between them being that Louis refused to deliver Boris, who had joined his army, to the Hungarian king. Instead, he was taken unharmed to Constantinople.

The events of the following decades were shaped by a new constellation of powers within international diplomacy. Hungary found herself caught between the ambitions of the Emperors Manuel Comnenus and Frederick I, and this made co-operation with every potential enemy of Byzantium or Germany advisable. By the end of the 1140s a coalition had begun to take shape, its axis running from Sicily to Kiev with the court of Hungary in its centre. This did not mean, however, that Hungary was forced to adopt a defensive policy, for the king's authority was exceptional and his resources not inferior to those of his rivals. Otto of Freising noted, with obvious envy, that the Hungarian notables 'obey their prince so unconditionally that they would consider it a crime not only to rouse his anger with open resistance, but even to offend him with hidden whispering.'[1] Not much later, Abu Hamid found that the 'empire' of the king of Hungary 'is many times more powerful than that of the Byzantine ruler and his troops are innumerable.' He added that 'every nation fears his attack because of his valour and the number of his army.'[2]

Even if such a judgement should be read with caution, it remains the case that Géza's foreign policy does not suggest that he was intimidated. Between 1148 and 1152 he sent, or led personally, no fewer than six armies to Russia in support of his brother-in-law Izjaslav, Grand Duke of Kiev, against his rivals. Besides these campaigns, he had sufficient strength to attack the Byzantine empire in 1149 after entering into an alliance with the grand župan of Serbia. Although the war with Byzantium went on intermittently until 1155, Manuel finally turned out to be too powerful an enemy. After the Serbs had been suppressed, Géza decided not to wage war without his allies and made peace with the emperor.

Despite, or because of, his incessant activity, Géza's reign ended with the collapse of internal order. For nearly a decade, one conflict after another occurred among the ruling elite, and this weakened royal authority considerably. The reasons for these upheavals are not altogether clear, but it seems that one aristocratic faction did not approve of the king's policy and wanted to pursue a pro-Byzantine course. They intended to elect Stephen, a younger brother of Géza, as king. Stephen left the country in 1157, asked first Frederick and then Manuel for help, and was later joined by his elder brother Ladislaus. At first Géza was successful in putting off the German emperor: he sent auxiliary troops to assist the emperor in Lombardy in 1158 and asked him to arbitrate in the fraternal conflict within the Hungarian royal family. In

1159, however, when a dispute between Pope Alexander III and Frederick broke out, the co-operation between Géza and Germany came to an abrupt end. This change in Hungary's political orientation was due to Luke, the new archbishop of Esztergom and former classmate of Thomas Becket. He may have been the first Hungarian bishop to study in Paris, and his erudition was accompanied by a profound knowledge of European affairs and an unyielding attachment to the Holy See. He sympathised with the reformist wing in Rome and played a key role in bringing Hungary into Pope Alexander III's camp.

THE AGE OF BÉLA III

Géza II died on 31 March 1162. He was the sixth Hungarian king not to reach the age of 40. He was followed on the throne by his eldest son, Stephen III. Within six weeks, the new king was forced by his uncles, backed by Byzantine troops, to seek refuge in Austria with Duke Henry, one of his father's former enemies. The crown passed to Géza's brothers, first to Ladislaus II, then, after his premature death on 14 January 1163, to Stephen IV. Since Archbishop Luke refused to accept either of them as king, and even put them under anathema, he was imprisoned and the archbishop of Kalocsa carried out both coronations.

Stephen IV followed Emperor Manuel's instructions in a subservient way, and this made him so unpopular that within a couple of months his nephew had no difficulty in overthrowing him. In the spring of 1163, hardly a year after his flight, Stephen III invaded the kingdom with an army, defeated the usurper near Székesfehérvár and took back his throne. Although Manuel advanced with his troops as far as the Hungarian border, he soon realised that he had no choice but to abandon his protégé. He soon found another, however, in the person of Béla, brother of Stephen III and duke of Dalmatia and Croatia. In return for his being recognised by the emperor as king of Hungary, Stephen III allowed Manuel to take the young Béla under his guardianship and bring him to Constantinople to be educated there. This bargain opened up interesting possibilities. The emperor, to whom no son had yet been born, gave the boy the name Alexius, treated him as his own heir and, after betrothing him to his daughter, invested him with the new title of despot. Consequently, in the event of Stephen's death, there was the real possibility of Hungary being united with the Byzantine empire under the rule of an 'emperor and king' of Hungarian birth.

For the time being, however, the new situation, instead of normalising Hungaro–Byzantine relations, actually made them more strained than ever. The Hungarian king was not willing to hand over Dalmatia, Béla's duchy, to the emperor, and this resulted in a war of fluctuating fortunes that lasted until 1167. Manuel twice took the field in person, once advancing as far as Bač. As a consequence of this military action, the district of Srem and the Dalmatian cities passed under Byzantine rule, as parts of Béla's heritage. Manuel seems to have been satisfied with this and henceforward withdrew from Hungarian affairs. The stormy period of clashes between Hungary and the Byzantine empire, which had lasted since 1149, was thus brought to a close. Moreover, Béla's position also changed, after the emperor had a son of his own in 1169. Manuel immediately withdrew the privileges that Béla had enjoyed as the heir of the throne, and married him, not to his daughter, but to his niece, Agnes (in Greek, Anna), whose father was Renauld of Châtillon, the adventurous prince of Antioch.

Stephen III died childless on 4 March 1172, and was succeeded by Béla. Manuel did not object to his return to Hungary, but the accession of the new king was nevertheless far from smooth. Archbishop Luke, defying the order of Pope Alexander III, refused to crown him. He feared, so we are told, that Béla, educated as he had been in Constantinople, might allow the Orthodox Church to grow in influence. The coronation was ultimately carried out by the archbishop of Kalocsa (13 January 1173), while Luke received a papal rebuke for his inflexibility. His anxiety proved to be wholly unjustified. For, while remaining loyal to Manuel until the emperor's death, Béla III (1172–1196) governed his kingdom from the outset as an independent ruler and a faithful son of the Roman Church.

The death of Manuel in 1180 brought the great period of Byzantine expansion to a close and profoundly changed the international position of Hungary. Serbia became an independent country under the rule of the grand župan, Stephen Nemanja, and his dynasty, while in 1186 Bulgaria also threw off Byzantine rule and became an important power under the Cuman Asenid brothers. The Hungarian king was not long in taking advantage of the new situation in the Balkans. Immediately after the death of Manuel he recovered Dalmatia and Srem and in 1182 he launched a devastating attack against the Balkan provinces of the empire. He only returned to a Byzantine alliance after the fall of the dynasty of the Comneni in 1185, marrying his daughter to the new emperor, Isaac Angelus. At about the same time, Béla himself, having lost his first wife, married Marguerite, the daughter of Louis VII of France and widow of Prince Henry of England. It was in her company that in 1189 he received the Emperor Frederick who was marching at the head of his army to the Third Crusade. Their meeting took place in Béla's palace at Esztergom, which had just been rebuilt on the castle hill by French masons and was one of the first major buildings in early

Gothic style to be erected in central Europe. It was at the emperor's request that Béla set free his younger brother, Géza, who had been arrested and imprisoned some years previously after a failed conspiracy. Géza left with Frederick at the head of a small Hungarian contingent and found shelter in Byzantium, where his sons were still living during Andrew II's reign.

During these years Béla concentrated his attention upon Galicia. This small, western principality of Russia had on several occasions since the reign of Coloman been the scene of Hungarian armed intervention (1099, 1123, 1150–52), but annexation was not considered until Béla III's reign. In 1188, taking advantage of a disputed succession in Galicia, Béla had his younger son, Andrew, recognised as duke. Although the attempt turned out badly, it set off a memorable sequence of events. The young prince, whose troops desecrated Orthodox churches, was expelled by his Russian subjects within two years. But after his accession to the Hungarian throne, Andrew renewed the fight for Galicia and obstinately continued with it for almost thirty years.

Béla III died on 23 April 1196 and was buried next to his first wife in the cathedral of Székesfehérvár. Although the royal tombs there were dispersed during the Ottoman occupation, Béla's was somehow left intact. (It can now be seen in the Matthias church in Budapest.) His skeleton, 190 centimetres long, shows that he would have been a giant in his time, and it is clear that in other respects too he was the most outstanding king of Hungary since Coloman. However, his rule not only represented the apogee of the kingdom of the Árpádians, but also marked the end of an epoch. From the 1190s onwards there are many indications that the kingdom was going through a profound transformation. During the century that followed the death of Béla III, the political and social system upon which the rule of Stephen and his successors had been based broke up with surprising rapidity. Hungary in the decades around 1300 bore little resemblance to the kingdom under Béla III. Yet in order to appreciate the importance of the transformations that occurred, we must first examine the internal state of the kingdom during the eleventh and twelfth centuries.

ANIMAL HUSBANDRY

For visitors to Hungary the most striking feature of the country seems to have been the great number of livestock that were to be found there. They were unanimous in praising the 'fat and lush' pastures and the 'incredibly fertile land', where immense herds of animals wandered.[3] By far the most important animal was the horse, which retained its dominant role even after the nomadic era had ended. Right up to the eleventh century the horse had probably been an attribute of the free status of both warriors and commoners. Stephen prescribed that anyone working with his horse on Sunday should be deprived of it, and when saying this he was obviously thinking of peasants. When the tribal organisation was dissolved and new conditions of dependence emerged, the horse slowly became a symbol of distinguished status. As early as the twelfth century, those who 'served with a horse' represented a privileged class within the peasantry, their duties consisting of services that could be accomplished on horseback, or at least – as in the case of transport – by means of horses. During the thirteenth century this group of peasants disappeared, and the horse became one of the distinguishing features of noble life. Noblemen would do their utmost to have a stud. The enormous number of horses that this might involve is well illustrated by the fact that in 1212 the small monastery of Baracska (near Budapest) received 130 mares from its founder.

Since the possession of horses reminded the nobility of their belligerent pagan ancestors, it was important that breeding should follow ancient traditions. Wild horses, called 'horses of the stud' (*equi equatiales*), occur frequently in medieval records. They were kept in the open throughout the year and were consequently exposed to all kinds of weather. Stables were reserved for those animals that were tamed by their owners for private use, but these were already kept 'in houses' as early as Ajtony's time.[4] It goes without saying that horses of this period were not yet the substantial mounts of the later Middle Ages, but smaller horses, of the tarpan type, with which the raiding Hungarians had wandered all over Europe. The sturdy war-horse, which was a necessary instrument of the new chivalric warfare, began to be used by Hungarian noblemen no earlier than about 1200.

By the twelfth century, the rearing of cattle, sheep and pigs had come to play a dominant role in animal husbandry. Judging from the evidence furnished by bones, three-quarters of the entire stock were made up of these greater animals, although the consumption of poultry was also considerable. Cattle, like horses, were generally kept outdoors, especially by the nobility, and the herds were watched over by shepherds of servile status. This type of wild herding survived in some areas of the Great Plain until the first half of the twentieth century. The peasantry, who did not have immense pasturelands at their disposal, used the common waste of the village in the summer, while during the winter they locked up their animals in pens. Parcels of land, which were thereby thoroughly manured during the winter, were highly valued. Pigs were generally fed on mast, chiefly on the Great Plain, where the flood areas of the meandering rivers were covered by extensive oak forests. We know from later evidence that pigs were often driven a considerable distance, involving several days' journey, in order to be put to masting in the forests of another lord to whom a fee was due for the use of his woods.

Despite the predominant role of animal husbandry, fishing also retained its economic importance throughout the Middle Ages and even beyond it. Lakes as well as rivers were proverbially rich in fish; only Norway was rumoured to offer a greater abundance. Landowners set up fisheries, mainly in the form of underwater traps, and these were regarded as an important source of revenue. A speciality of the Danube was the sturgeon, which could grow up to seven metres long. During the spawning period it appeared in the Danube and Tisza, swimming upstream from the Black Sea as far as Pressburg and Tokaj respectively. Only after the water regulation works of the nineteenth century was it lost from the Carpathian basin.

In contrast to fishing, which was always important in the everyday nourishment of the common people, hunting seems to have been a markedly noble activity from the beginning. Unlike some other countries of Europe, medieval peasants in Hungary were allowed to hunt, but there were always forests reserved for the king and his lords, and the number of restrictions on peasant hunting tended to grow in later centuries. A considerable part of the country must have been covered by forests, for the envoy of the lord of Mantua, visiting Hungary as late as 1395, remembered seeing nothing but woodland between Zagreb and Buda. Despite his testimony, it is clear that the densely forested area had already retreated to the highland region by the twelfth century.

The medieval forests of the Carpathian basin were rich in bears and bison, but the admiration of Abu Hamid was above all aroused by the 'cow that resembles an elephant'.[5] This strange animal might have been the *urus* (German *Auerochs*), which was to die out in the early modern period and is generally thought to have been the ancestor of the robust Hungarian cattle. The huge forests also offered favourable conditions for fur hunting and apiculture. Some of the early villages paid taxes in ermine or beaver furs, others having to furnish honey, mead and wax.

ARABLE FARMING

Medieval descriptions of Hungary, in this period as in later centuries, depict it as a real Canaan. Abu Hamid, who had visited many foreign lands before spending three years in Hungary, suggested in all seriousness that 'this is one of the countries where life is the easiest and most comfortable.'[6] Evoking the fertility of its land had become a commonplace; almost all foreign visitors mentioned it. Wheat was cheap, wrote Idrisi, 'since they have plenty of it',[7] and a Frenchman asserted in 1308 that the name of Pannonia was due to the abundance of bread (*panis*).[8] And there was also plenty of meat. Although arable farming had become the main pillar of economic life by the twelfth century at the latest, stock-breeding retained an important role throughout the Middle Ages, partly because of the force of tradition, partly because there were huge pasture lands all over the country. Consequently, to a much greater extent than elsewhere, nourishment depended upon meat and fish; and it seems, therefore, that the majority of the population consumed protein in sufficient quantities throughout the Middle Ages. The silence of the sources suggests that famine, which was a not infrequent visitor to other parts of Europe, was almost unknown in Hungary.

The Hungarians seem to have learned a good deal about arable farming from the Slavs whom they found in the Carpathian basin. That their rather primitive agriculture gave way to more developed methods is indicated by the rich stratum of Slavonic words – much larger than the Turkic group – in the Hungarian language. The Hungarian vocabulary of horticulture is predominantly of Slavonic origin (beans, lentil, cabbage, carrot, radish, cucumber, dill, poppy), as are the names of almost all the garden fruits (plum, apricot, cherry, strawberry, raspberry, melon). Several other important plants (rye, oat, flax), as well as agricultural techniques (hoe, fallow, waste, straw, hay, stack [of corn], crib) and tools (yoke, oxbow, scythe, hay fork, harrow, rake, shovel, flail, barrow, coulter) also have names of Slavonic origin.

Arable farming had become the dominant form of agricultural activity and the chief occupation of the great majority of the population by the twelfth century. The two principal crops continued to be wheat and barley, the latter basically as the raw material for beer brewing. Rye was much less important economically, while millet and oats mainly served as fodder. Vines were cultivated all over the country, even in areas where climatic conditions were not at all favourable, for after the adoption of Christianity wine became an everyday drink. Horse-milk, which had been quite common in the pagan era, disappeared so completely that even its Hungarian name has been forgotten. From the middle of the twelfth century our sources regularly mention the wine of Srem, which was to remain the most famous and most expensive variety until the Ottoman occupation. Tokaji only became well known during the early modern period.

The dominant method of cultivation until the thirteenth century was quite different from the later open-field system. It merely involved the periodic changing of the land that was tilled. Given the abundance of available land, only the best parts of it were cultivated, and when one piece of land had been exhausted, another was sought for cultivation. Ploughing was done with those relatively small oxen that were also commonly used in western Europe. Eight were needed to move a plough, which seems to have been of the symmetrical, heavy type. Iron parts from such ploughs have been found throughout the country and it was in use up to the thirteenth century. The light plough of the Slavs, which could be operated with a single pair of oxen, was also known. The principal instrument of harvesting was the sickle, which was not to be replaced by the scythe before the end of the Middle Ages. (During the medieval period the scythe was only used for cutting hay). The crop was normally ground in hand mills, but water mills are also mentioned from the middle of the eleventh century.

The method of arable farming based on the periodic changing of the land under tillage entailed the frequent movement of whole communities. In some places, archaeologists have found traces of villages from this period in such density that an explanation can only be found by reference to this technique of arable farming. This is normally thought to account for a prescription of the synod of 1092, which ordered that 'if villagers abandon their own church and wander away', they must return to their former place.[9] Somewhat later, the synod of Esztergom decided that 'a village in which there is a church shall not move far from it', and urged the communities that had already moved to return.[10]

POPULATION AND SETTLEMENT

Otto of Freising was so much impressed by the beauty and the fertility of what he saw in Hungary that he was reminded of Paradise. At the same time, he was very disappointed with its inhabitants, for 'they are ugly, with their eyes seated deep in their face, of rather small stature, and barbarous and savage as regards both their customs and their language.' So, he added maliciously, 'we should blame our bad fortune, or rather admire God's endless patience, that he had given such a beautiful country to these monsters who hardly deserve the name of man.'[11] The bishop, being a member of the ruling dynasty of Austria, might have felt some antipathy towards the Hungarians, for his anthropological description cannot be supported by archaeological evidence. Analysis of about 2100 skeletons from the eleventh to the thirteenth centuries has clearly shown that 95 to 97 per cent of the population had Europid features by this time.

As regards the size of the population in the eleventh and twelfth centuries, the available evidence is hardly sufficient for even the wildest estimate. Since large areas on the peripheries of the Carpathian basin were still completely uninhabited, the average density of the population, if calculated for the entire basin, cannot have been more than four or five people per square kilometre. The central part of the basin, and especially the Transdanubian region, was evidently much more densely populated, but it remains true that there was much available land everywhere, and most of the villages had large areas of pasture and woodland at their disposal.

Despite the continuing importance of semi-nomadic animal husbandry, the greater part of the population pursued a sedentary way of life almost from the beginning. So settled a manner of living may appear inconceivable where the Hungarians of the conquest period are concerned, their great mobility being demonstrated by the conquest itself. How it was that their lifestyle changed in two or three generations is not clear; but it is beyond doubt that by the year 1000 the village (*villa*) had already become the dominant form of settlement for the common people. This is borne out not only by archaeological evidence and by several of Stephen's laws, but also by his charters, which yield information about villages granted to churches. Since most of the localities mentioned at that time still existed many centuries later, and many of them can even be found today, we have good reason to suppose that they were in fact real villages and not simply nomadic dwellings in the process of becoming permanent settlements.

The villages of the twelfth and thirteenth centuries were relatively populous. The first of Stephen's charters makes reference to 52 and 54 households respectively in two villages; an average village seems to have consisted of about 30 to 40 families. Most of the villages were situated in the vicinity of water, the individual houses scattered in a disorderly fashion at some distance from one another. Each was surrounded by a yard, pens and stables. Otto of Freising found that the Hungarians 'have rather flimsy houses, made of reeds, sometimes of wood, and only exceptionally of stone, and they spend the summer and the autumn in their tents.'[12] His account can be confirmed on many points. Archaeologists have uncovered in early villages the remnants of huts, which were built 60 to 100 centimetres deep in the ground and consisted of one or two rooms with floors made of levelled earth. As far as one can judge from the traces of piles, they were timber-framed houses without windows, and the roof seems to have been made of reeds. The hearth was set up in a corner, but there was no chimney and so the smoke went out through the hole that served as a door. It is, therefore, understandable that the family would live in a tent erected next to the house, for as long as the weather would allow. Excavations have shown that the Cumans on the Great Plain were living in the same way at the end of the Middle Ages. The only stone buildings appear to have been churches, but in this early period most of these would also have been simple wooden structures.

Among the thousands of settlements, there were some that our sources call 'suburbs' of a fortress, 'cities' or 'towns' (*civitas, urbs*). Idrisi mentions a good number of them, but it is not easy to visualise them. It is certain that most did not have stone walls or houses. We should imagine relatively populous, pre-urban settlements, little different from villages, which were situated in the immediate neighbourhood of a comital or episcopal castle. Their most important characteristic seems to have been the market that was always held on the same day of the week. At first, this day was Sunday: this is shown by the etymology of the Hungarian word *vasárnap* ('Sunday'), which meant literally 'the day of the market'. During Géza I's reign (1074–1077), pressure from the Church caused the Sunday markets to be moved to Saturdays. Besides these pre-urban centres, new markets were created in many other localities, where they could be held on other days of the week. Some villages even acquired their name from that day: for example, *Szombathely* ('Saturday market') and *Szerdahely* ('Wednesday market'). One hundred and twelve place names of this type, datable to the eleventh and twelfth centuries, have been preserved on maps or in medieval records, but many of these markets had ceased to function by the late Middle Ages and only a handful were to develop into towns or boroughs.

It was in the twelfth century that Western settlers began to migrate in great numbers to the East. There was still more than enough room for them in Hungary, Bohemia, Moravia and Poland, and particularly in the uninhabited areas of Transylvania and present-day Slovakia. In the first phase of migration, which began in the late eleventh century, most of the immigrants were Walloons, called by the Hungarians *olasz* ('Italian' in modern Hungarian), a Slavonic loan-word that, in this early period, was applied to any people speaking a Latin language. The Walloon settlers seem to have favoured the episcopal residences, such as Pécs, Eger or Oradea, where their memory has been preserved in the name *Olaszi* given to a suburb or a street. A number of other toponyms are also of Walloon origin: for example, *Tállya* from *taille* and *Gyán* from *Jean*. They also settled in great numbers in the south, in the region of Srem, where the town *Nagyolaszi* ('Great Wallonian village', now Mandjelos) and possibly also the mountain range called Fruška Gora (originally *Franska Gora*, 'French Hill') are testimony to their past settlement. Yet their two largest centres seem to have been formed at the royal residences of Esztergom and Székesfehérvár, where they established themselves in a way that came very close to the Western patterns of urban development. They built a wall around their quarter and, possibly at some time during the reign of Stephen III (1162–72), they were granted extensive privileges. These were the first nuclei of urban development of the Western type in Hungary.

In the long run, however, the immigration of Germans into the whole central European region turned out to be much more important. In Transylvania and Spis, where they were invariably called Saxons, their settlements formed large and contiguous blocks, which guaranteed the survival of their language and urbanised culture. German immigration, like the Wallonian settlement, began in the eleventh century, when localities called *Német(i)* ('Germans') and *Szász(i)* ('Saxons'), which are scattered throughout the whole kingdom, are thought to have come into existence. One of them, Lompértszásza ('the Saxons of Lambert', now Beregove in Ukraine), owed its name in all probability to the younger brother of Ladislaus I. Yet the large-scale immigration of German settlers only began in the twelfth century. The first groups of those who later came to be called Saxons arrived in Transylvania from Flanders in around 1150, in the time of Géza II, and were followed later by another German group that settled in Spis. As we shall see later, the German immigrants were to play an outstanding role in urban development in Hungary from the thirteenth century onwards.

ROYAL REVENUES

The immigration of the eleventh and twelfth centuries profoundly modified the ethnic and economic outlook of the country. Areas that had hitherto remained uninhabited were now given over to the plough, thereby increasing the resources of the kingdom considerably. There is a unique document that throws some light on the economic conditions of Hungary at the end of our period. It is a brief account, found in a codex in Paris, of the revenues that were due to King Béla III from different sources. Some scholars have suggested that it was drawn up for the English court, on Béla's orders, before his second marriage in 1185, whilst others suppose that it was produced for the court of Barcelona before the marriage of Béla's heir, Prince Emeric, with Constance of Aragon in about 1195.

According to our document, the royal revenues, converted to money, amounted to 166,000 marks, to which different services in kind were to be added. This sum is incredibly large, being double that which Sigismund of Luxembourg is generally thought to have had at his disposal at the apogee of his reign, 250 years later. Most scholars agree, therefore, that whatever its purpose, the document did not depict reality. Nevertheless, we may perhaps suppose that the categories of royal revenue, and their proportions, are correctly given, and this at least can provide valuable information about the structure of the economy.

More than one third (36 per cent) of all the revenues sprang from the coinage (*de redditu monete*), which had been in continuous use in Hungary since around 1000. The silver coins of Saint Stephen, weighing 0.75 to 0.8 g, were made after Bavarian patterns and are supposed to have been halfpennies (*obulus*). His successors continued to issue high-quality coins, although of even smaller size (0.4 to 0.7 g). The period of Stephen II's reign (1116–1131) witnessed in Hungary, as in most parts of Europe, the practice of large-scale devaluation, and with it the appearance of very small coins, weighing only 0.2 g. The absolute nadir was reached during the reign of Béla II (1131–1141), some of whose coins contained nothing but copper. Monetary affairs began to be normalised during Géza II's reign when lightweight coins of a much better quality were issued. (Bracteates occur sporadically only under Béla III.)

By the end of the eleventh century, the characteristic Hungarian money of account, the *pensa*, which was to remain in use until about 1400, had become widespread. It was equivalent to 40 pence; for, according to the chronicles, under Béla I (1060–1063) one Byzantine *solidus* was worth 40 coins issued by the Hungarian king. The mark, the usual unit of silver weight (and also of money) in central Europe, was also in use by 1146 at the latest, but its weight varied a good deal according to local custom. The two most widespread weights were the 'Hungarian' mark (233.8 g), identical to that of Cologne, and the mark of Buda (245.6 g), which was the same as that used in Regensburg and Paris. But there were local differences in their value, for their silver content varied from mine to mine, and there existed other weights. The Saxons of Transylvania, for example, used their own mark of Bruges, weighing 206.7 g, throughout the whole of the Middle Ages. It is also worth noting that the mark in Hungary was not divided into *lotones* or ounces, but into *fertones* (1/4 mark) and *pondera* (1/48 mark). These and other peculiarities of accounting money in Hungary were later to drive papal tax collectors to despair.

Coinage remained a royal privilege and one of the main sources of the treasury. It seems to have been based from the beginning upon domestic silver, the export of which is already mentioned around 970. According to Abu Hamid, the mountains of the country 'contain lots of silver and gold'[13] and other sources also offer information about the continuous export of precious metals to both East and West. It seems probable that, while gold was still only being panned out of the rivers of Transylvania, silver mining was already being pursued extensively. Its earliest centre, possibly from the eleventh century, was Banská Štiavnica, which, in this early period, is simply referred to as 'the Mine' (1217) or 'Silver Mine' (1228). The other important mining town was Rodna in Transylvania, which had been founded by German settlers and flourished until the Mongol invasion. Up to the fourteenth century, all the mines were in royal hands, and the most important ones continued to be so even later. In the fourteenth century, and probably before, a certain part of the extracted metal, the so-called *urbura*, representing an eighth of the yield in silver and a tenth of that in gold, went to the king.

The most important source of revenue was, as everywhere else, the regular renewal of money (*renovatio monete*), the yield of which in Hungary was called 'the chamber's profit' (*lucrum camerae*). The practice of coinage renewal seems to have been introduced by Andrew I (1046–1060). Initially it took place every two years; then, from the time of Béla II, it became an annual event. Its tariff seems to have been very high. In the thirteenth and fourteenth centuries, when we begin to have information about it, the tariff invariably amounted to 33 per cent; that is, the treasury always gave two pennies for three at the time of the exchange. Therefore, if we are to believe the account of the revenues of Béla III, an annual income of 60,000 marks from coinage renewal would imply that 180,000 marks (42 tons) of silver were used to strike coins every year. This is an incredibly large amount, and the most that we may infer from it is that silver was being mined on a large scale at that time.

Compared with its later importance, the salt monopoly was as yet relatively insignificant. In the time of Béla III, only ten per cent of royal revenue originated from this source. From the outset until the end of the Middle Ages both the mining of salt and its trade were in the hands of the king. Until the thirteenth century the only source of salt was Transylvania, where rich mines stretched from Dej through Cojocna and Turda to Ocna Sibiului. From Transylvania the extracted salt was carried to the two main centres of distribution, namely by boat on the River Mureş to Szeged and by wagon overland to Sălacea in Bihor. It was put into circulation in the form of cubes and evidently in enormous quantities, since its normal measure of account was the *tumen*, meaning ten thousand cubes. In Hungary, perhaps even more than in other countries, the salt cube was used as a form of currency until the early modern period. It was in salt, for example, that the treasury of Andrew II (1205–35) paid the annual allowance due to those monasteries that had been founded by the king. Later, soldiers also frequently received their pay in this form.

More than half (54 per cent) of royal revenue came from a number of further sources: from the tolls, ferries and markets (18 per cent); from that part of the tax of the 72 counties which was due to the king (15 per cent); from the annual obligatory 'gift' of the counts (six per cent); and, finally, from the money tax paid by Slavonia (six per cent) and the Saxons of Transylvania (nine per cent). If all this were in fact paid in silver, it would mean that a considerable proportion of royal income must have come directly or indirectly from commerce. This process did not necessarily entail the circulation of coins, however, since silver bars were more common in Hungary than pennies until the thirteenth century. It is, therefore, certain that the revenues of Béla III, whatever they amounted to, were to a great extent collected in the form of silver bars and other silver objects.

NATURE OF THE ECONOMY

All this information is hardly sufficient to provide a convincing picture of the Hungarian economy in the eleventh and twelfth centuries. What is clear is that, by comparison with the later Middle Ages, commercial relations with the East and the Balkans were much more important than they were to be later. The two main international routes led towards Kiev and Constantinople, the principal economic centres of eastern Europe, while the most important route towards the West was that which linked the Carpathian basin through Vienna with Regensburg. Imported goods consisted principally of luxury objects, and their main consumers, at this time as indeed later, must have been the king and his court.

Consequently, from the outset, the centre of gravity of the Hungarian economy was Esztergom, which lay at the junction of the three main trade routes. Esztergom was a typical pre-urban settlement, having several nuclei in the vicinity of the royal castle. Besides the fact that the kingdom's only mint was located here, its growth was given further momentum at the end of the eleventh century by the prescription of an obligatory itinerary for merchants, which later developed into a staple right. However, because of the importance of eastern commercial relations, the most substantial market places were as yet in the eastern part of the country. One of the important centres was Bač, where Greek scholars are reported to have lived around 1150; another was Kovin at the main crossing of the lower Danube. A further important settlement in the time of Idrisi, somewhat surprisingly, was Užhorod, its significance apparently being due to its being a station on the route to Kiev.

Trade, together with the administration of royal finance, was for the most part in the hands of experts from the Orient. The role of Muslims, often called Ismaelites in Hungary, was especially important in these early centuries. Abu Hamid discovered, with obvious pleasure, that there were 'innumerable' Muslims there, even if some of them 'pretend to be Christians'.[14] According to his report, many of them were warriors, and Géza II is known to have had Muslim soldiers recruited from among the Alans of the steppe. Muslim and Jewish merchants are frequently mentioned from the tenth century onwards. As far as we can judge, coinage and the administration of the royal revenues in general were in the hands of Choresmians and other Muslims.

In several respects, the economic structure of the country must have been similar to that of later centuries. The most frequently mentioned export commodity was the horse, though its trade was sometimes limited because of its strategic importance. The export of cattle, copper, silver and gold are also referred to at an early period, and there is plenty of evidence concerning the sale of slaves until as late as the beginning of the thirteenth century. King Coloman prohibited Jews from taking abroad Hungarian-born slaves, and ordered them to put down in writing the contracts they made with Christians. Although this demand might seem ambitious, even absurd, for so early a period, there is one piece of evidence showing that around 1135 such contracts were far from exceptional. This fact alone demonstrates just how limited our knowledge of the period is. While the structure of long-distance trade can be reconstructed with some certainty, the functioning of the internal market remains one of the mysteries of early Hungarian history. All that we know about this period suggests the existence of an economy in which money and trade in general can only have played an insignificant role. We shall see, however, that around 1100 all 'freemen' were expected to pay an annual tax of eight pence. And even if we doubt that Béla III could have drawn 30,000 marks from tolls, ferries and markets, toponymic evidence shows the existence of a large number of market places in the twelfth century.

Sometime before 1150 the king granted to the abbey of Tihany his part of the market toll of Veszprém, which was due to him from the sale of 'cooking utensils, iron ploughs, buckets and all sorts of ironware'.[15] Who bought these goods and with what did they pay? Where, indeed, did the 'freemen' get the money to pay their annual tax? Such questions spring to mind, but for the time being there is no way of providing answers to them.

Chapter 5

Early Hungarian Society

In trying to provide an outline of the social structure of this period we are bound to encounter many difficulties. What is certain is that its features differed profoundly from those that were to be dominant in later centuries. Perhaps the most important development in the history of medieval Hungarian society was its fundamental transformation between 1200 and 1350. In the course of this transformation the social order, which had been formed in the eleventh century, was dissolved and replaced by a profoundly different one, which in its turn remained intact in many respects until the early modern period. The structures that emerged from this transformation are, of course, quite well known, but those that preceded it are not easy to describe, for the real nature of the social categories that we find in our sources is usually obscure. Such is the case, above all, with the meaning of 'freedom' and 'serfdom'.

FREEMEN AND SERFS

By the thirteenth century the essence of freedom in Hungary, as elsewhere, was seen in one's right to move freely. People who had the right to choose their lord without hindrance, and who could consequently change their residence at will, were considered completely free. They enjoyed what was then termed 'golden liberty' (*aurea libertas*). This was the kind of liberty that nobles and burghers possessed, along with those groups of peasants who had the privilege of moving freely for some special reason. Others who were obliged to do perpetual service to a lord and who were consequently bound to their domicile, were considered serfs or bondsmen. Their state was, therefore, just the opposite of those who were held to be free. The vast majority of the population, including almost all categories of peasants, belonged to this class – that is, they were of unfree status.

In modern Hungarian historiography it is taken as an accepted fact that the notions of medieval 'freedom' and 'serfdom' cannot be interpreted otherwise. People who are termed 'free' in eleventh-century documents are thought to have enjoyed the liberty of free movement, while all those who owed hereditary service to a person or institution are thought to be *ipso facto* of servile status. As 'free' status seemed to be much more widespread originally than it was later, when it became an exception, it has also been supposed that most of those who were originally 'free' had gradually lost their liberty by being expelled from their home or by being degraded to hereditary bondage in some other way. So the essence of the social history of peasantry between 1000 and 1200 could be defined as the transformation of a homogeneous class of 'free' peasants into a much differentiated class of 'serfs', although it is generally believed that some remnants of the class of 'freemen' continued to exist well into the thirteenth century. It would seem, however, that this interpretation of eleventh-century sources can no longer be accepted. The most conspicuous social cleavage that existed at that time did indeed separate 'freemen' (*liber*) and 'serfs' (*servus*); but in order to understand these terms correctly we need to recognise that the notions of serfdom and liberty changed radically between 1000 and 1200, and that both terms had a meaning in the time of Stephen I quite different from that of two hundred years later. Lexicography seems to support this hypothesis, for the original Hungarian words denoting 'free' and 'serf' had disappeared perhaps as early as the thirteenth century, to be replaced by new words of Slav origin (*svobod* becomes Hung. *szabad*; *sluga* becomes Hung. *szolga*). It can be supposed that the disappearance of ancient Hungarian terminology was a natural consequence of the fact that both words had lost their original meaning.

It has never been difficult to determine the status of a 'serf'. He was not much more than a piece of property, a 'thing' (*res*), whom his master could treat, almost like his animals, according to his own will. Naturally, he could be alienated, like any other piece of property, and no wergild was due for him: that is, the killer of a serf had only to compensate his master for the material loss. Marriage and even fornication between freemen and serfs were for a long time forbidden. If a freeman had sexual intercourse with a person of servile status, he became a serf himself, 'in order that freemen preserve their liberty undefiled'.[1] Yet it would be an exaggeration to say that serfs were simply treated as 'speaking animals'. Their life was regulated, not by the 'law of the freemen' (*lex liberorum*), but by other rules that were collectively called the 'law of the serfs' (*lex servorum*).[2] So, there were 'laws' for them; indeed, that a serf was a kind of 'person' had already been recognised by the laws of Stephen. If he committed theft, punishment was directed against him and not against his master. The murderer of a serf, besides paying compensation, had to do penance, and a serf who killed another of his kind had to do the same.

The serf, in the original sense, belonged to his master's household. He normally worked around the house or tilled the demesne. In the latter case, he was inventoried along with draught animals and ploughs. Occasionally, we find that he had property of his own, and so it was possible for him to convert his punishment into a payment in cattle, even if the things he was allowed to have were not his property in the legal sense of the word. From the time of Ladislaus I onwards it is with growing frequency that our sources mention serfs who had been granted as much as a peasant holding for their own use, thereby becoming the Hungarian counterparts of the Western *servi casati*. They were allowed to maintain a family, lived in their own dwelling, worked with their own animals on the demesne of their lord, and retained enough of the crop to pay the tithe. And, of course, from the beginning there were serfs who, having been granted 'eternal freedom' by their lord, henceforth belonged to the order of the free.

In spite of these important changes, there remained the ultimate and indelible difference between servile and free status, which was due, it seems, to their different origins. The serf might be *allowed* to do more than one thing, but he could not transform what he was allowed into his right. In contrast to freemen, the main feature of servile status seems to have been the total absence of a legal personality. The serf could not represent himself in court, nor could he possess any right, for he was not a person. Whatever degree of alleviation he obtained from his master, he was to remain, from the legal point of view, the property of his owner – that is, he was to remain a 'thing'.

A freeman, by contrast, was considered to be a fully privileged member of the community, one of 'the people of this kingdom' (*gens huius monarchie*), from whom the serfs were naturally excluded.[3] Freedom manifested itself above all in the legal capacity of the freeman, that is, in his being able to attend a court both as accuser and witness. Although, as we shall see, the social status of the freemen was not uniform, in the eleventh century his wergild invariably amounted to 110 steers, 50 of which went to the dead man's kin, another 50 to the king and the remaining ten to the mediators.

In the eleventh century free status was perfectly compatible with what was later to be defined as hereditary bondage. It seems that from the beginning some kind of hereditary service was the normal status of 'freemen', with the exception of the counts and those few who were considered nobles. The bondage of a warrior consisted of performing military service, while the commoner was obliged to do manual labour. So it must have been quite normal for a freeman to be bound hereditarily to a lord and to perform some sort of service for him. Indeed, independent status – a person without bondage to anyone – may well have been inconceivable. The service required from a freeman could be burdensome or even humiliating, but in one respect it differed fundamentally from that of a serf. The amount of service that a serf could be compelled to perform was not limited, either in its nature or in its extent; he was, after all, a kind of animal. The nature of the service required from a freemen was always determined by his status, the extent of that service always limited by custom. He had legal status and so possessed rights that were inalienable, even if they were usually minimal.

There was a special category of freemen who enjoyed liberty in the later, or modern, sense of the word. These were the groups of foreign settlers who came to the kingdom as merchants or peasants. From the eleventh century at the latest, their communities are found in all parts of the kingdom, on the lands belonging to a castle, to the king, to counts or bishops. Provided they were allowed to settle there, which must normally have been the case, they could enjoy the peculiar status of 'guests' (*hospites*). This allowed them to retain their ethnic customs and to live according to their own laws, whether they be Wallonian, German or Czech. As a consequence, these communities were named after the ethnic groups to which their inhabitants belonged. They were to pay a money-rent for using the land they were given to live on, but they also had the right of free movement, which was otherwise unknown among freemen: 'They shall leave for wherever they like,' as the synod of Szabolcs decreed in 1092.[4] It was a status which was defined later as 'totally free' (*omnino liber*), and which was to be the model of peasant liberty in general from the thirteenth century.

THE ORGANISATION OF FREEMEN

Apart from a small elite of counts and nobles, we can detect within the order of freemen the existence of two classes, which were always sharply distinguished from each other. The laws of Stephen show the community of freemen to have been made up of 'rich' and 'poor'. The social gap between them was expressed not by the wergild, which in Hungary was, as we have seen, the same for all freemen, but by the different amounts of compensation that they were required to pay. The punishment that was due for oath-breaking, or for the manumission of someone else's serf, could be converted to a payment of 50 steers by a rich man, whereas a poor man had only to pay twelve. For murdering his wife, for abducting a girl or for attacking a house, the count had to pay a compensation of 50 steers to the offended party, while a warrior or a 'man of wealth' paid ten steers and a 'commoner' (*vulgaris*) only five.[5] It is more or less clear that the terms 'rich' and 'warrior' referred to the same social category.

The terms 'warrior' and 'commoner' seem to have referred to hereditary classes. The most conspicuous feature of early Hungarian society was that it was founded on differences of birth. The exact structure of this society only becomes visible through the records of the early thirteenth century, and it was apparently much more complicated then than it had been two centuries earlier. Its main feature must, however, have been of very ancient origin. Even after 1200, everybody knew his exact social rank, and the smallest differences of hereditary status were observed in a pedantic way. It was generally held that status was hereditary: in other words, that it was inherited from one's ancestors, who had naturally belonged to the same class. The line between 'rich' and 'poor' in the time of Stephen seems to have been drawn in the same way. It was undoubtedly a very clear line, dividing the mass of freemen into two distinct classes. It could not, therefore, have been drawn according to a concept as relative as wealth. The difference between classes must have been founded upon something fundamental and easy to define, and this could hardly have been anything other than birth.

The descendants of the free warriors and free commoners of Stephen's time are later found organised in communities belonging to royal castles. They consisted of two classes, called 'castle warriors' (*iobagiones castri*) and 'castle folk' (*cives, civiles, castrenses*). The gulf between them was unbridgeable, just as we may assume was the gulf between warriors and 'commoners' in the eleventh century. Both warriors and common folk were hereditarily bound, probably from the beginning, to the service of a castle; they could not be regarded as free in the new sense of liberty that was being born around 1200. So there was a natural tendency to regard them as the king's bondsmen and they have been considered as such in modern historiography.

Although both 'castle folk' and 'castle warriors' were bound to their service hereditarily, there is hardly any doubt that they were free in the traditional sense of the word. They were in possession of all the rights that were the original attributes of free status. They could appear in court, give testimony there and engage in lawsuits. They could bear arms; indeed, they had to go to war in the king's army. Moreover, they paid the 'pennies of freemen' (*denarii liberorum*, later *liberi denarii*), a royal tax which was originally due, as the name itself shows, from all people enjoying free status. It seems that it was only from King Coloman's time that its payment was limited to peasants.

The 'castle folk' lived in their own villages, used the land collectively and were mainly engaged in agricultural activities. For administrative purposes their villages were grouped into hundreds (*centurionatus*), but these, unlike their English counterparts, were not to survive the thirteenth century. The land that these peasants occupied was theirs, in as much as they could not be expelled from it, but it was called 'castle land' (*terra castri*) and was regarded as the property òf the castle. The 'castle folk' were subjected to the rule of both the castle and the count who governed it in the king's name. They were bound to their state and were not allowed to leave it, for it was their hereditary duty to maintain the count and his retinue, the class of warriors, and also the king or his agents whenever they happened to appear among them. Hence, the characteristic and most general imposition upon the castle folk was a food-rent, very similar in nature to that which had been called the king's feorm in Anglo-Saxon England. In Hungary its name was 'lodging' (*descensus*), the most natural – and not in the least humiliating – service that anybody could provide for his superiors. By the time that it appears in the sources it had already been transformed into a regular payment in kind.

The castle warriors, on the other hand, formed a sort of upper class. In the thirteenth century they claimed that their 'freedom' had been established by Saint Stephen, referring to themselves as 'the freemen of the Holy King' (*liberi Sancti Regis*). In all likelihood this group did indeed originate in Stephen's time. That the network of royal castles was founded by him has never been disputed by scholars, and it is difficult to imagine how these castles could function without warriors attached to them. In fact, in one of his laws, Stephen ordered that 'each lord shall have his own warriors',[6] and the warrior who left his lord was regarded as a fugitive in the same way as a runaway serf. Nonetheless, the warrior was obviously thought to be a free man, for it was possible for him to make an appeal to the king against the judgement of his count, though such an action was not necessarily approved of. Naturally, there were warriors whose lord was the king himself, and it was to him that they owed hereditary service. Stephen regarded them, like his serfs, as part of his property, but at the same time he was inclined to refer to them as the buttresses of his kingdom. In his 'Admonitions' he exhorted his son to hold them in high esteem, since 'they fight for you and are not your servants'.[7]

The castle warriors formed a privileged, elite class that ruled over the mass of castle folk. By the time that we begin to know more about them, all had landed estates that they owned in a hereditary way like any nobleman. Even the king was not allowed to deprive them of their land. In fact they were considered to be nobles, in sharp contrast to the castle folk, who certainly were not. The most important privilege of the castle warriors seems to have been their general exemption from taxation. So, in perfect accordance with their noble status, they had to pay neither the 'pennies of freemen' nor the food-rent. However, they were as hereditarily attached to their duties as anybody at this time, even though these were honourable duties, consisting of military service and governing the castle folk. They could be compelled to fight by their count and there was no limit to their military obligation, in contrast to real nobles whose service was voluntary. It was from their ranks that the subaltern officers of the count were chosen, the most distinguished among them being those who stood at the head of the hundreds (*centurio*), and those who commanded the military contingent of the castle (*maior exercitus*) or the castle itself (*maior castri*).

THE CASTLE AND ITS COUNT

The castle warriors formed an elite that was insufficiently numerous to make up an army. A small section of the common folk were also expected to do regular military service. Otto of Freising observed that in Hungary 'of the peasants who live in villages, nine equip the tenth or the seven the eighth, and send him to war, or even more of them if necessary, while the rest remain at home to till the land.'[8] It seems that the bishop was well informed. To send to war one person out of eight was a speciality of the castle folk, while the equipping of one person out of ten was, as we shall see, an obligation of another class of freemen. It would seem logical to equate these 'seven people' remaining home with those who were called *hebdomadarii* ('seven-men') in the time of Coloman,[9] and further to assume that the few who went to war formed a separate class. In fact, we find in thirteenth-century documents that some of the 'castle folk' were assigned to military service hereditarily. They had some land and their only duty was to fight. To that extent they were almost identical with the castle warriors; indeed, they were given that name. Yet they continued to be sharply distinguished from the 'noble' castle warriors – those who belonged to this class by birth. They were permanently taken out of the class of unarmed peasants – hence their official name, *iobagiones de castrensibus exempti* – but they could never attain the social status nor acquire the rights that were the attributes of 'noble' warriors. It was an indelible mark of their peasant origin that they continued to pay the food-rent like the rest of the castle folk; and neither they nor their descendants could in any sense become owners of their land. They were allowed to live on its revenue, but the land allotted to them remained inseparable from the other castle properties, and was as easily alienated by the king as any other piece of 'castle land'.

The contingents mustered by the castles and consisting of 'noble' and 'non-noble' warriors made up the bulk of Hungarian armies during the first centuries of the kingdom. Each contingent will have consisted of hundreds of soldiers, the number varying from castle to castle according to the number of subjects belonging to each. Muslim, Russian, Byzantine and Dalmatian sources from the period 1150 to 1241 referred to these contingents as 'banners', 'battalions' or 'counties' (*comitatus*); and their total number was invariably put at 72. We arrive at the same number if, using thirteenth-century records, we draw up a list of the castles that had a social organisation consisting of warriors and castle folk.

The link between castles and counties is far from clear. The castle served as a basis of military organisation and its authority extended only to those persons – warriors and castle folk – who were expressly subjected to it. The county was quite different in its nature. It was an administrative unit consisting of a well-defined part of the kingdom. Around 1200 there were about fifty counties and they all had fixed boundaries, within which the count exerted supreme authority as the king's immediate representative. This authority extended to all people living in the county, even if it was limited by the different liberties these people enjoyed. There is no doubt that, as in the time of Stephen, most counts had more than one county under their command. For example, the count of Bihor governed the counties of Bihor, Békés and Zărand; in each he was represented by a deputy who bore the title of 'curial count' (*curialis comes*).

The counts might be termed the tenants-in-chief of the realm, though it should be noted that their rank was not hereditary, for they were appointed and replaced by the king at his will. At the same time, the count was a person of the highest standing who had a part in the 'honour of the realm' (*honor regni*). His office, which itself was called an 'honour', was something of a temporary fief, and its revenues – the 'pennies of freemen', tolls and fines – were divided between the king and himself. Two thirds, called 'the king's two parts' (*királyketteje*), went to the king and one third remained with the count. But the count's high esteem was due first and foremost to the fact that he was a military commander. The most obvious sign of his rank was a banner, decorated with his own badge. Along with other people, he had the castle warriors of his province under his command, and it was his honour and duty to lead them to war under his banner. He commanded as many 'banners', or contingents, as there were castles entrusted to him.

The most important castles lay in the frontier regions (*confinia*) and were organised in a special way. In the early period, their counts are sometimes called 'margraves' (*marchio*), and the province entrusted to them was a 'march' (*marchia*). It included a special defensive system called *indagines* (Hung. *gyepű*), consisting of logs, ditches and hedges blocking the routes leading into the kingdom. Beyond the *indagines* was a large frontier zone called *gyepűelve* ('the land over the *gyepű*'), originally a no-man's-land that was only gradually populated. Its defence was entrusted to light mounted archers (*sagittarii*, Hung. *lövő*), mostly of Székely and Pecheneg origin, and to a group of castle folk called 'guards' (*speculatores*, Hung. *őr*), whose main task was probably reconnaissance. Traces of this complex defensive system can still be found in toponyms, especially in the west of the kingdom. The town of Kapuvár ('gate castle') still marks the site of an early frontier station, while the villages of Őr (today Oberwart and Unterwart in Austria) were inhabited by 'guards'. The district of the Őrség ('guardsmen') along the Hungaro–Slovenian border, originally consisting of eighteen small villages inhabited by 'guards', maintained its ethnographic peculiarity until recent times.

THE HALF-FREE CLASSES

From the beginning we find an intermediate group between the freemen and the serfs: the class of the *udvornici*. Since the name itself is evidently of Slav origin, the ancestors of the *udvornici* can perhaps be traced to those groups of the indigenous Slav population that had collectively been subjected to the lordship of the Árpádians. What is certain is that their original lord was the king himself, and they can perhaps be regarded as the descendants of royal 'serfs'. However, by the time that we begin to have information about their social rank, we find it to be almost equal to that of the castle folk.

The intermediate status of the *udvornici* was clearly defined in one of Stephen's laws. It prescribed that if one of them 'commits a theft, he shall be judged according to the law of the free, but his testimony shall not be accepted among freemen'.[10] In other words, the *udvornici* were held to be free in every respect, excepting only that they were not allowed to attend a court. Since, however, this was the principal characteristic of free status, the *udvornici*, when compared with such free people as the 'castle folk', were always considered to be serfs. Their servile origin was common knowledge to such an extent that it was remembered long after the ancient difference between free and serf had disappeared. As late as about 1400, villages that were known to have once been inhabited by *udvornici* were still exempted from royal taxation on the grounds that this was only to be paid by freemen. (It is worth noting that, in this respect at least, the free origin of the 'castle folk' was never questioned.)

Within the order of serfs the *udvornici* enjoyed a highly privileged status. The services they were required to do were unquestionably heavy, but they were fixed as were those of the freemen. While we do not, of course, hear of villages inhabited by mere serfs, the *udvornici* lived, like the castle folk, in their own villages, which could be found throughout the country, here and there forming contiguous groups. They were governed by a privileged class, probably of free origin, who bore the collective name 'the free of the *udvornici*' (*liberi udvornicorum*). These freemen did military service just as the non-noble castle warriors did, with the slight difference that nine rather than seven of them were required to equip one warrior – a fact, as we have seen, that was also recorded by Bishop Otto. If we set aside the stigma of the servile origin of the *udvornici*, their social position differed little from that of the castle folk.

It is evident that the great majority of peasants were either free commoners (including castle folk) or *udvornici*, and this seems to have been the case as late as the early thirteenth century. There were, however, a sizeable number of other groups that cannot easily be placed in either of these categories, for they owed special services after which they were named. Their collective Latin name was later to be *conditionarii*, for it was their 'condition' that determined their social status. However, in the eleventh and twelfth centuries they are referred to by the type of service that they were required to perform.

This group must have been of early origin. The memory of special services due from a village has been preserved by hundreds of toponyms that consist of a name of an occupation in the singular, sometimes completed by the old suffix -i. They belong to that type of Hungarian place name that is thought to be the most ancient. Several such names occur in the charters of Stephen, showing that there must have been villages named in this way as early as the tenth century. Some of these occupations, like carpenter, potter, fisherman, black-smith, stableman, cook, carter, furrier or hunter were to exist until recent times; others have disappeared in the meantime. Several names are of Hungarian origin, such as *Szántó* (ploughman), *Födémes* (beekeeper), *Hódász* (beaver hunter), *Hőgyész* (ermine hunter) and *Horó* (cook), while others have a Slav etymology, like *Bocsár* (cooper), *Csitár/ Csatár* (armourer), *Esztergár* (turner), *Gerencsér* (potter), *Peszér* (hound-keeper) and *Taszár/Teszér* (carpenter).

In spite of their name and the burden that it implied, the inhabitants of such villages were peasants. They earned their living from agricul-ture, as did the simple castle folk or the *udvornici*. Their particular name referred to the fact that their obligation was distinctive. Either they had to pay their tax in a particular product, or they were compelled to do a certain kind of service. Both kinds of obligations were, needless to say, hereditary, but they were imposed not upon indi-vidual households but collectively upon the village community. None of the duties made it necessary for whole villages to engage continu-ously in the same occupation.

With regard to social status, the group of *conditionarii* could not have been homogeneous, for there was enormous disparity in the levels of prestige attaching to particular obligations. The 'ploughmen' and the 'vine-growers' were almost despised, while the *tovarnici* and 'stablemen', who were responsible for the goods and chattels of the king, seem to have enjoyed a special esteem. The 'jesters' (*joculatores*, Hung. *igric*, from Slav *igra*, 'play'), whose service involved the entertainment of the royal court, were surely of inferior rank. In the absence of research on the subject, it is not yet clear which of these groups were freemen by origin and which were considered 'half-free', like the *udvornici*. One thing is certain, namely that the burdens of each category were fixed minutely, so in the beginning at least there were probably no real serfs among them.

Most of these categories disappeared in the thirteenth century at the latest, but in a few villages they were to survive. The inhabitants of Szakácsi ('cook', today Nagyszakácsi near Nagykanizsa), petty nobles in the late Middle Ages, went on to furnish cooks for the royal kitchen until about 1541, while the doorkeepers of the royal palace, who were of about the same rank as the cooks, were drawn from the village of Oroszi (today Nagyoroszi near Vác). The word *orosz* (from 'Rus') means 'Russian' in Hungarian, but earlier it had also been used as a noun, meaning 'janitor'. It is thought that the earliest bodyguards of the king in the eleventh century were of 'Russian' – that is, Scandinavian – origin.

THE BIRTH OF LORDSHIP

Some forms of private property certainly had existed in pagan times, though we have no clear idea about their nature. By the time of Stephen's reign, the boundaries of villages, whether inhabited by freemen, *udvornici* or *conditionarii*, were well defined. Noble kindreds must have owned vast lands and pastures in order to maintain their horses, cattle and serfs. But whatever might have been the case before, that form of private authority over subjects, which would later be called seigneury or lordship, clearly emerges in the time of Stephen and his successors, when churches, and without doubt other people too, were endowed with lands.

The nature of private lordship, as distinct from the authority of a count over freemen, is well explained in the laws of Stephen. One of these ordered that 'everyone during his lifetime shall have mastery over his own property and over grants of the king, *except for that which belongs to a bishopric or a county*, and upon his death his sons shall succeed to a similar mastery.'[11] It was also allowed 'that anyone shall be free to divide his property, to assign it to his wife, his sons and daughters, his

76

relatives or to the church.' Moreover, Stephen did not fail to stipulate that 'just as we have given others the opportunity to master their own possessions', so the king should have the right to secure possession of everything that belongs to him.[12]

In Hungary as elsewhere, much more is known about the lands given to monasteries than about those owned by the king or by laymen, for only the churches insisted that their property rights should be put down in writing. The nunnery of Veszprém was given nine villages by Stephen, while the abbey of Tihany received from Andrew I certain lands whose boundaries were carefully described. The bishopric of Eger traced ten of its villages back to grants by Stephen and eleven to those of Ladislaus I. A good many early toponyms, like Püspöki ('bishop's' [property]) or Apáti ('abbot's') also bear testimony to early donations, and most of these are still to be found in the hands of a church many centuries later.

We have detailed knowledge of the 1116 men, living in 41 villages, who were given by Stephen to the abbey of Pécsvárad in 1015. There were 22 categories of *conditionarii* among them, including 110 'vine-growers', 36 ploughmen, 50 fishermen, ten blacksmiths, 12 turners, eight carpenters and many others. Twenty of them were 'iron-givers' (*tributarii ferri*), that is, they had to pay their tax in blocks of iron. It was obviously from them that the name of the nearby village of Vasas (from *vas*, 'iron'), now a suburb of Pécs, was derived. The grant also included two hundred warriors, who were said to be 'free' and whose duty was 'to hurry in arms to the defence of the monastery if there would be a revolt in the region', as well as to give an escort of twelve mounted knights to the abbot 'whenever he goes to the king's presence'. There were also many 'servants' (*ministri*), clearly of free origin, 156 of whom were to serve the lord 'with horses' and 409 who did the same 'with horses and carts'.[13]

The list of people granted to the abbey reflects the social structure of the time, and even hints at the proportions of its various classes. It seems as a whole that 18 per cent of the households belonged to the class of warriors, 51 per cent were free commoners of the status of the simple castle folk and 31 per cent were of a half-free status, similar to that of the *udvornici*. There were no serfs among them, for all the people granted to the abbey lived in villages and the services they were to perform seem to have been exactly defined.

It is clear that, at this time, the king had the right to dispose of his free subjects, be they warriors or commoners, in the same way as he could with his unfree tenants. Being granted to a monastery did not at first bring about a radical change, because the free status of those involved was to remain intact. It was not the village inhabitants themselves who became private property, but the land on which they lived. For the freemen it did not involve an immediate change in their status and duties, for both were regulated by ancient custom, and no new lord was allowed to modify them arbitrarily. As we have seen, the charters laid down the extent and nature of the services that could be required from the persons whose land was granted away, and the same must have been the rule in the case of a verbal agreement. The boundary between 'freedom' and 'serfdom' was not to be obscured. As late as 1138, the provost of Dömös was prohibited from raising any of his subjects 'from among the serfs into the order of the free' or, conversely, relegating them.[14] Yet the change must have been deeply distressing. Many communities, which had hitherto considered themselves free and bound only to serve the king, found themselves in the service of new lords. Whereas in the past only serfs had been regarded as pieces of property, now it looked as if 'freemen' too had been put in a similar position by virtue of grants: firstly, because the land on which they lived was in no respect any longer theirs; and secondly, because their judge was henceforth not an agent of the king but that of their lord.

At first, the freemen who wished to escape this fate had no choice but to move away, and many of them did so. When giving the Greek nuns the village of Kenese (now Balatonkenese), Stephen ordered that 'those who do not want to live under the authority of the monastery... shall be driven out of that place against their wish and will.'[15] Count Peter handed over one of his villages to the abbey of Százd with the condition that 'everyone who lays claim to the status of freedom shall depart from there with the exception of the family (i.e. the serfs) of the church'.[16] By the middle of the eleventh century the kingdom was full of fugitive freemen, who posed a constant threat to public order. It became the duty of special royal agents to round them up like stray animals. The problem was still an issue in the time of Coloman, who ordered that the 'dispossessed former peasants shall, if they have no land elsewhere, return to their own place.'[17]

The large-scale transformation accompanying the emergence of private lordship overturned the traditional order of society, and the accepted norms of property were thrown into question. The protection of property was plainly the central problem of the time: more than half of the laws of Ladislaus I were concerned with this issue. 'The magnates of Hungary have taken an oath neither to be lenient to a thief nor to hide him' – so ran the very first decree;[18] and a long series of prescriptions of almost inhuman cruelty was directed against thieves, regardless of their social standing. Hitherto, the crime of theft could be bought off; but Ladislaus I's laws ordered that all cases should be punished with exemplary severity, a severity that later was increased still further, probably because the measures had not yielded the expected results quickly enough. Anyone caught in the act of stealing was hanged; if he sought refuge in a church, he could get away with being blinded, but his children over the age of ten were sold as slaves. Anyone found guilty of stealing a goose or a hen lost one of his eyes, but if the object stolen was more valuable, the punishment was to be hanging. Forms of mutilation, like cutting off an arm or the nose and tearing out the tongue, were also often applied. Anyone merely suspected of a crime was allowed to cleanse himself by way of ordeal – by taking a red-hot iron or being immersed in water. However, the judge was not encouraged to be lenient. If he allowed the offender to go free, he was deprived of his property and sold as a slave, whilst if he happened to hang an innocent man he had only to pay the wergild of his victim. The persecution of thieves became somewhat less severe under Coloman. The crime of theft came to be confined to the stealing of four-footed animals, and the punishment was simple blinding. Moreover, only the adult children of the guilty person were sold as slaves. Mere suspicion was no longer sufficient to launch a criminal procedure. Indeed, it could now lead to the punishment of the slanderer. Since fugitives are no longer mentioned in the sources, it seems that the social crisis that accompanied the emergence of private property was over.

The traditional conceptions of 'freedom' and 'serfdom' had been profoundly modified during the course of this social transformation. We can observe some of the stages in this process, before new notions were crystallised in their fully developed form in the thirteenth century. Since Coloman's time only those common 'freemen' who had a plough as a minimum of property were allowed legal status, 'so that there shall be a warrant for true testimony'[19] (that is, the person who gives testimony should be able to pay a fine). A completely new idea was gradually to emerge, according to which only those people who were in full command of themselves – free to choose their place of residence and their lord – could be regarded as free. All those who were bound by a form of perpetual service were excluded from this freedom, however high-born they might otherwise have been. Their burdens, whether involving some kind of humiliating work or consisting of a military obligation, were connected by the fact that they were meant to be perpetual, their bearers being subjected to the 'yoke of servitude'. By virtue of this new conception, every form of hereditary service became incompatible with freedom, since each was but a different degree of servitude, strictly distinguishable from the status of those who enjoyed 'golden' – that is, real – freedom.

FORMS OF PRIVATE PROPERTY

Royal castles, along with the land and people attached to them, are generally considered to form one part of the royal demesne. Most scholars believe that 'castle lands' were royal estates reserved for military purposes, just as the people subjected to a castle were but one class among the king's bondsmen, whose special duty was to perform military service. This view, however widely held it might be, cannot be accepted, for it is clear that royal castles had nothing to do with seigneury. 'Castle land' appears to be quite different from 'private property', royal or otherwise, whilst the castle folk seem to have comprised those categories of the population who managed to preserve their free status and did not come under private lordship. Their overlord was, of course, the king and as time went on his authority over them was more and more comparable to that of a private lord. However, not even in the thirteenth century were the castle folk deprived of such basic rights of free people as attending a court and bearing arms. Confusing 'castle land' with the royal demesne makes it extremely difficult to understand the essence of landed property.

There were no fiefs in Hungary, neither at this time nor later. A landed estate was always an absolute property, that is, an *allodium* (*praedium*). It was marked off by well-defined boundaries, within which the owner enjoyed unrestricted property rights. Royal demesne and ecclesiastical domains were often referred to as *allodia*, but lands belonging to laymen were also almost invariably so called – or termed simply 'land' (*terra*) – until the thirteenth century. They were called 'possessions' thereafter.

As for what is termed the royal demesne, it is beyond doubt that in Stephen's time the king and his family became by far the greatest landowners of the kingdom. They retained for their own use huge and contiguous domains, as well as many villages dispersed throughout the country. These belonged to the royal family collectively, and some parts of them were usually given to the queen or other members of the dynasty for the use of their households. The whole demesne seems to have been organised into administrative units, each centring on a royal manor (*curtis*). The great island of Csepel near Budapest, for example, was an important part of the demesne and is said to have served as pasture for the royal stud. The village of Lórév ('horsesford'), a locality at the southern end of the island, still evokes the memory of this fact.

Much of the royal demesne consisted of forest. In Hungary, as in England, a forest was a well-defined district which comprised both the land (open territory as well as woodland) and all those who inhabited it. Besides the Bakony and the Pilis, which lay in the centre of the kingdom, the king owned immense territories, often as large as a county, in the sparsely inhabited mountain regions. There was an almost continuous expanse of woodland in the north-east, including the districts of Ugoča, Bereg, Sárospatak, Šariš, Turna and Zvolen, each of them being organised into a royal forest. Zvolen, in the central part of modern Slovakia, was the greatest among them, comprising the territory of four later counties. All the forests, like other parts of the royal demesne, were regarded as the personal property (*praedium*) of the king. They did not form part of any county and were guarded by a special staff, consisting of royal foresters (*custodes silvarum*) and of *draucarii*, the nature of whose service is unknown. Like other groups who owed a special form of service, both the foresters and the *draucarii* lived in villages of their own, many of which bore their vernacular name *Ardó* and *Daróc*. At their head was a royal keeper (*procurator*), who had acquired the title 'count' by the thirteenth century. He was, however, in the private service of the king and his social rank was much inferior to that of the counts proper. Nor did he have a castle under his command, for no castles could be built on private property until the middle of the thirteenth century, the royal demesne being no exception.

Ecclesiastical estates continued to grow steadily in the course of the twelfth century, not least as a consequence of the establishment of new monastic and military orders. The Premonstratensian canons arrived in Hungary in the early phase of their history; their first monastery is said to have been founded by Stephen II (1116–31) on a 'promontory' near Oradea. Somewhat later their protection and enrichment was taken up by lay lords, whilst the Cistercians became the new favourite of the dynasty. After they had been settled by Géza II at Cikádor (1142), Béla III showered them with grants. The rich monasteries of Igriş, Zirc, Pilis and Szentgotthárd were all his foundations. Géza II (1141–62) founded a hospital in Esztergom in honour of St Stephen and organised an order of 'hospitallers' around it that existed until about 1440. It was in Géza's time that the military orders began to establish themselves in Hungary. The greatest convent of the Knights of St John was generously endowed by his widow. The Knights Templar, first settled at Csurgó, had come to form a separate province by 1194, the centre of which became the castle of Vrana near Zadar in Dalmatia. The appearance of the new orders did not diminish the role of the Benedictines, although their monasteries in the twelfth century were for the most part private and not royal foundations.

We have very little information about the lands given to, or inherited by, the nobility, for until around 1200 lay landowners contented themselves with verbal agreements. There can be no doubt that all the counts and their kindred owned considerable lands, but the extent of this property only becomes visible when one of them endowed a monastery. In 1061 Otto, count of Somogy and later palatine, disposed of no fewer than 360 households in favour of his abbey of Zselicszentjakab. He may have retained even more for himself, for the kindred that descended from him was to be among the richest in Transdanubia.

Around 1067 Count Peter, probably a kinsman of King Aba, bestowed nineteen estates upon the monastery of Százd. On one of these estates there were 140 households. We also have a glimpse of how extensive the property of Count Hont might have been through a donation that was made by one of his descendants. In 1132, he gave estates and serfs in 23 localities to the monastery of Bzovík (in modern Slovakia), evidently without ruining his family.

The *allodium* generally served as the permanent residence of its owner. This is shown by its Hungarian equivalent, *lak,* which meant a house or the 'home' of a person. It was the place where the lord lived and kept his valuables. All those living in or around the house were considered to be part of his property; hence on most of the *allodia* there were only serfs, who cultivated the lord's demesne with his own ploughs, or worked as craftsmen in the workshops around the house. They belonged, together with the women and children, to the 'family' of the lord, who had almost unlimited authority over them. The notion of the word *čeljad,* borrowed from the Slavs, comprised both the family in its narrow sense (Hung. *család,* 'family') and the servants and serfs belonging to the house (Hung. *cseléd,* 'servant').

Twelfth-century Hungary was still archaic in both its culture and its social structure. At the end of the period, we can observe the rapid expansion of Western ideas, institutions, technology, and customs. Its agents were foreign knights, merchants and peasants, who came to Hungary, but also Hungarians who had visited the West. It is from around 1150 that we begin to hear about Hungarian clerics, who, having studied in Paris, were subsequently given important posts within the ecclesiastical hierarchy of the kingdom. Their number would increase from the early years of the thirteenth century when Italy, and more particularly the faculty of law at the university of Bologna, replaced Paris as the most popular destination for students. Western impact upon Hungary, massive and multifarious, brought about a process of transformation that was to reshape the kingdom in almost every respect during the following century.

Chapter 6

The Age of the Golden Bulls

The mist that shrouds the early history of Hungary disperses quite suddenly around 1200. That we know much more about the following period than about the twelfth century is because of an abrupt proliferation of records. From the time of Géza II, there is a slight increase in the number of surviving charters, but these still total no more than a couple of dozen items. Around 1200 the situation changes rapidly, and the number of charters issued per year can soon be counted in hundreds and even thousands. Overall, we have about ten thousand documents from the period before 1300. Equally important is that it was at this time, during the pontificate of Innocent III (1198–1216), that relations between the kingdom of Hungary and the Holy See became much closer than before. The Papacy, especially in the first decades of the century, not only followed events in Hungary with constant attention but on several occasions actively intervened in them. The diplomatic correspondence between the Pope and the king is, therefore, a first-class source of information on both Hungarian foreign policy and the internal affairs of the realm.

THE ORIGINS OF THE NOBILITY

The most important development of this period was the emergence of the nobility as both a class and an active political force. In Hungary the term 'nobility' did not denote the same social phenomenon as elsewhere. In most European countries the class of nobles grew out of knighthood, and was an aristocracy distinguished from the rest of society by birth and wealth, with an accompanying mentality and lifestyle that were particular to those who called themselves 'noble'. The Hungarian nobility, which emerged as a class during the thirteenth century, was of a quite different nature. It was sharply separated from the peasantry, possibly even more sharply than elsewhere, but the key to its separate status was the allodial nature of its property and the privileges that were attached to it. The nobility comprised all those who possessed a *praedium*, that is, an *allodium*. As to its extent, there was no minimum qualification and, as a consequence, an enormous number of persons, who would have been regarded as peasants in other parts of Europe, were considered to be nobles in Hungary. Their status had nothing to do with chivalry, which was an idea that was hardly known. The Hungarian nobleman was noble not because he was an offspring of knights or because he lived and thought as a knight, but simply because the land he lived on was his own, as opposed to the peasant who lived on someone else's land.

The lowest stratum of those who were held to be 'noble' was formed by those who continued to be subjects of a lord and owed him hereditary service. By the early thirteenth century the ancient dividing line between 'freemen' and 'serfs' had become obscure, and a new distinction arose that was no less sharp. This separated those who did peasant work from those who 'used to go to war' (*populi exercituantes*). From about 1200, this was to be the basic criterion of noble status in the widest sense. Those classes of freemen whose inherited duty had been fighting and the supervision of the lord's domains detached themselves more or less completely from the mass of the simple peasants. This elite was numerous, consisting of noble castle warriors, the freemen of the *udvornici* and the warrior class of the great ecclesiastical estates. They were all considered nobles but did not possess the privileges by which the 'real nobles of the realm' (*veri nobiles regni*) were distinguished. Several communities enjoying this half-noble status, like those subjected to the archbishopric of Esztergom, were to survive until the nineteenth century.

The 'real nobles of the realm' formed what is known as the Hungarian nobility proper. Consisting of many thousands of kindreds, it came into being through the union of social components of different origin. The majority seems to have come from those who were called 'royal servants' (*servientes regis*) in the time of Andrew II. Many nobles, most of them very poor, were to rise from the class of castle warriors or even from among peasants who were granted land and noble status by royal charter. The elite of the nobility consisted, however, of those who claimed descent from an illustrious ancestor, like King Aba or the counts Hont and Pázmány. By the end of the century all these groups were to form, in spite of their very different origins, a more or less homogeneous class, bound together by the liberties common to all 'real nobles', which were put down for the first time, but not the last, in the Golden Bull of 1222.

Undoubtedly the most numerous section of this class were those who are referred to as 'royal servants' in the first half of the thirteenth century. In the medium size county of Hont alone we find at least forty villages in the thirteenth century that were owned, partly or entirely, by petty nobles whose ancestors seem to have been royal servants. In greater counties like Bihor there must have been hundreds of them. The status of 'royal servants' appears similar to that of Anglo-Saxon thegns: namely, that they served not a bishop or a count, but the king himself. Little is known about their origins. Many of them seem to have owed their lands to a royal grant. We have scattered evidence of such grants from the middle of the twelfth century, and after 1200 it became a widespread phenomenon. The grantee could be a foreign knight or 'guest', or a native Hungarian who had been raised by the king from the status of bondman. He received an allodium from the king and became a member of the royal household. In other words, he became one of the king's warriors. But certainly there were also many who were descended from the free warriors of the eleventh century and who had been owners of their land ever since that time.

THE HIGH-BORN KINDREDS

Originally, however, the term noble referred only to persons who belonged to a noble kindred (*genus*): that is, those who were the male descendants of the 'order of the counts' of the eleventh and twelfth centuries. According to Simon Kézai, around 1285, there were 108 such kindreds. Interpretation of this number has given rise to dispute; but if we try to draw up a list of the kindreds that might have been of ancient origin we arrive at about the same figure. Around 1300 this group was still distinguishable from the mass of the nobility by its greater wealth and elevated origins. Many of the high-born kindreds claimed that their ancestor had been a 'duke' or a chieftain of the pagan era. The powerful Csák and Bár-Kalán kindreds, as well as much poorer ones like the Szemere and the Lád, claimed descent from one of the legendary seven leaders of the Conquest. The Kán kindred held the *gyula* to have been its ancestor, and often used the 'Christian' name Gyula as late as the early fourteenth century. The ancestor of the Tomaj kindred was allegedly Tonuzoba, a Pecheneg chief who came to Hungary around 950 and was – or had himself – buried alive in King Stephen's time. The person from whom a kindred took its name was not its earliest known member but the best known one. The Aba kindred, for instance, claimed descent from Ed and Edumen, two of the 'Kavar' leaders, but they took their name from King Samuel. The supposed ancestor of the Csák was Szabolcs, son of Előd, but the person whose name they took probably lived in the time of Saint Stephen.

By the early thirteenth century the name of the ancestor became the common name of his kindred and was often used to indicate noble origin. The descendants would remember their distinguished birth for many generations: for example, the nobles who claimed to be descended from King Samuel called themselves 'from the kindred of Aba (*de genere Aba*)', even if the exact line of their descent was not known. It is worth noting, however, that the richer and more illustrious a family happened to be the less its members needed to emphasise their descent. Indeed, some renowned families that had not been split up into branches never referred to themselves as 'kindreds'. To belong to a notable kindred was particularly important for those who had sunk into poverty, for without the emphasis on their distinguished origin they would pass unnoticed in the anonymous mass of the lesser nobility.

Descent from pagan Hungarian ancestors was thought to be important as late as about 1270. Kindreds that descended from foreigners who had settled in Hungary at a later time were still carefully distinguished as 'newcomers' (*advena*), however illustrious they might be. Among a long list of such 'newcomers' we find the Hont-Pázmány kindred, which descended from Count Hont and his brother, or the much less illustrious Bogát-Radvány, the progeny of Bogat's son Radovan, a knight from Bohemia who was palatine in the time of King Solomon.

Besides the common name, a common coat of arms could also symbolise a noble kindred. It must have been the presence and influence of foreign knights that encouraged the growing attachment of the Hungarian nobility to Christian chivalry, especially to its outward signs. Such was the influence of fashionable chivalric romances, that names like Alexander, Paris, Hector, Lancelot, Tristan and Iseult became popular for a time. The use of coats of arms also appeared at the end of the twelfth century, initially on the coins and seals of the king. The double cross as a symbol of the Crown was introduced by Béla III, probably after the Byzantine pattern. The red and silver bars, which came to represent the dynasty, appeared in the time of his son, and were possibly inspired by the Aragonese coat of arms of Queen Constance. The royal example was soon followed by nobles who, transforming the ancient badge of their kindred into a coat of arms, put it on their seals and probably also on their shields. Families having a common ancestor can normally be found centuries later with identical or similar coats of arms. The descendants of Aba had an eagle on theirs, those of Csák a lion. That some of these symbols must have been used as far back as the eleventh century is proved by the example of a certain Beche and his brother Drusba, who occur in a charter of King Géza I in 1075. Beche was the ancestor of the noble kindred

Becse-Gergely, while from his brother another kindred, called Dorozsma and including the illustrious family Garai, descended. The families that belonged to each of these kindreds were later unaware of their common origin, but as late as the fifteenth century they all had a snake in their arms. It is clear that the snake had once been a common badge of Beche and Drusba, and was later to be transformed into the coat of arms of their descendants.

The term 'kindred' served as a reminder of common birth but it did not in any sense imply community of property. From the time of Saint Stephen everybody could freely dispose of his fortune; that which remained was divided between his sons or his grandsons. According to the rule of inheritance in Hungary, each son was given an equal share of the patrimony. The division was meant to be definitive and eternal; henceforth each of the branches lived its life independently from the others. The ancestral monastery, which had been used as a burial place for his progenitors, was left undivided. As long as the institution of 'private churches' (*Eigenkirche*) existed, the monastery was considered to be the common property of the kindred, but by the end of the thirteenth century co-ownership had been replaced by patronage. The monastery of Zselicszentjakab, founded in 1061 by Count Otto, was initially the property of the Győr kindred, and was then jointly patronised by families of the same kindred until as late as the fifteenth century.

The rule of equal division meant that considerable fortunes could, and did, break up into petty estates in a few generations. By about 1230, the Bogát-Radvány kindred had split into six branches, each of them possessing no more than several thousand acres. Throughout the remainder of the Middle Ages they were all to belong to the lesser nobility, and it was by pure chance that one of these insignificant families, the Rákóczi, was to acquire a fortune and take the throne of Transylvania in the seventeenth century. Much richer than the progeny of Radvány were the nobles who were descended from Hont and Pázmány. They had a good many estates of varying size dispersed all over the kingdom: for example, around 1300 there were at least 50 in the county of Hont alone. But this kindred also split up into many branches. In the fifteenth century there still existed 29 noble families who could claim descent from them, but by then many of these possessed no more than a single hamlet.

It was on behalf of a neglected group of these kindreds that Anonymus spoke in his *Gesta Hungarorum* around 1200 or 1210. Although he was a cleric, his entire work is a panegyric of pagan warriors, for what he wanted to prove was that rule over Hungary ought to be the inheritance of their descendants. The core of his ideology seems to be the 'treaty sealed by blood', by which government was to be divided hereditarily among the seven 'dukes'. From this it followed that counties and bishoprics should be held by their descendants by right of birth. These were not, however, the barons of his own time, for the then powerful kindreds were passed over by him in silence. It may have been due to this that his work was soon forgotten and only a single copy, discovered in Vienna in the eighteenth century, has survived. Later historians were not aware of Anonymus, so he cannot have exerted any influence on them. Nevertheless, he was the first exponent of that aristocratic attitude towards history that was to characterise Hungarian historiography for many centuries.

KING EMERIC

Emeric (1196–1204), the elder son of Béla III, was the first king of Hungary to show a lively interest in the Balkans, something which was to remain a constant element of Hungarian foreign policy until the Ottoman conquest. This new departure was closely linked to the initiatives of Pope Innocent III (1198–1216), who strove for the extension of Catholicism not only by peaceful evangelising, but even more by means of diplomacy and armed force. Located on the margins of Latin Christendom and bordering enemies of the Roman Church to the east and to the south, Hungary was to play an important role in these ambitions. Serbia and Bulgaria were inhabited by Orthodox 'schismatics', the Cumans were still pagans, while Bosnia was held to be a hotbed of Patarene heresy. Against these Balkan neighbours, the Hungarian kingdom could pose as a protagonist of the Catholic faith, and consequently enjoyed not only the approval of the Papacy but also its active support. The expansion of Hungary and that of Rome would thus become inextricably linked for more than two centuries.

Emeric was the first Hungarian ruler to consider the conquest of Serbia. He intervened in the internal strife of the Nemanja dynasty on behalf of Grand Župan Vukan, his protégé, whom he helped to power against Vukan's brother, Stephen. The Hungarian intervention had no tangible consequences, for as early as 1204 Stephen regained his throne with Bulgarian support, and later (in about 1217) he even obtained a royal crown from Pope Honorius III. Serbia thus preserved its independence from Hungary under the rule of the Nemanjids, and was to remain her powerful rival in the south until the fourteenth century. Nevertheless, Emeric added 'king of Serbia' to his titles, and all of his successors until 1918 retained it.

Conquest of Bulgaria was not yet contemplated. She grew to become an important power under the Asen dynasty, and it was during Emeric's reign that she established direct contacts with the Papacy. Tzar Kalojan (1197–1207) asked Innocent III to send him a crown.

Emeric detained the papal legate on his way to Bulgaria for some time, but was finally unable to prevent the tzar from being crowned.

The smallest and weakest of the southern neighbours was Bosnia and it was there that Hungarian expansion met with the most success. It seems probable that Bosnia had been under Hungarian influence since the time of Béla III, an influence that was to increase steadily during the course of the thirteenth century. In 1200, Emeric was called upon by the Pope to take measures against the Patarenes, and in 1203 the Hungarian king induced Ban Kulin of Bosnia, who was his vassal, to take measures to liquidate the heretics.

Power relations in the Balkans were modified decisively by the sack of Constantinople in April 1204. However, from Hungary's point of view the only memorable event of the Fourth Crusade was that the crusaders, en route for the East, had taken the Dalmatian city of Zadar, which was then under Hungarian rule. The attack had been instigated by the Doge of Venice, Enrico Dandolo. Having received Emeric's protest, the Pope excommunicated the Venetians and obliged the crusaders to pay for the damage, but he was unable to do more. Completely destroyed as it was, the city was later ceded to the Republic by Andrew II, Emeric's successor.

King Emeric died in September 1204. Shortly before, on 26 August, he had his three-year-old son, Ladislaus III, crowned king and appointed his brother, Duke Andrew, as regent. Andrew seems to have inherited the restless nature of Duke Álmos, who was his great-great-grandfather. Although he had been given a large sum of money by Béla III for the purpose of leading a crusade to the Holy Land, he instead turned against his brother from whom he secured the cession of Croatia and Dalmatia. On two occasions he even revolted against Emeric in order to acquire the royal crown. As soon as he became regent, Andrew began to regard himself as king and counted his regnal years from Emeric's death. It is by no means surprising, therefore, that Emeric's widow, Constance of Aragon, felt insecure and fled with her son to Austria. The child king died on 7 May 1205. After he had been buried at Székesfehérvár, Andrew had himself crowned king on 29 May. As for Constance, the Pope soon made her marry his protégé, Frederick of Sicily, the future Emperor Frederick II.

KING ANDREW II

Andrew II's foreign policy was given a distinctive character by his repeated attacks on Galicia. Between 1205 and 1233, 14 campaigns were launched against Russian territories, on four occasions (1205, 1212, 1226, 1231) under the personal leadership of the king. Although

Andrew took the title of 'king of Galicia and Lodomeria' as early as 1205, he initially acted merely as the protector of the young Daniel Romanovič, a member of the Rurik dynasty. This was partly against the local nobility and partly against other claimants from Russia. Since Andrew was unable the consolidate Daniel's rule, in 1214 he bestowed the duchy upon his second son, Coloman, whom he had crowned king in 1217. When Coloman was expelled in 1219, the king tried to secure the throne of Galicia for his third son, Andrew. This he succeeded in doing in 1227, but the rule of the young duke remained unstable until his death in 1234. Although Daniel then recovered Galicia, acknowledging temporarily the overlordship of Hungary, Galicia ceased henceforth to be the object of Hungarian expansion.

A new element in Hungarian foreign policy was introduced by the appearance of the Cumans, a Turkic people who since the eleventh century had pursued their nomadic life in the ancient homeland of the Hungarians between the Lower Danube and the Don. For the Hungarians, therefore, 'Cumania' meant the land beyond the Carpathians, where in the fourteenth century the Romanian principalities of Moldavia and Wallachia were to be established. It was Andrew II who first considered expanding Hungarian dominance in this direction. In 1211 the Teutonic Knights, who were returning from the Holy Land, were settled by the king in the region of Braşov in the south-eastern corner of Transylvania. The main duty of the knights was to be the conversion of the Cumans, and they were given all the territory they could conquer beyond the Carpathians as a fief to be held from the king of Hungary. With admirable energy, the knights set about colonising this largely uninhabited marcher region. They built castles and established villages, but these promising efforts were soon brought to an end by their growing ambitions. Beginning to regard themselves as independent, they sought the Holy See's protection for their land. Andrew lost patience and in 1225, at the head of an army, drove them out. The Pope made protests for some years, but to no avail, and the state of independence that the Teutonic Order aimed at was only to be realised in the Baltic region several years later.

Andrew II's reign was, however, to be marked more by internal conflicts than by external ambitions. One of the principal issues was the irritating presence of 'foreigners'. The king's first wife, Gertrud, had come from the dynasty of the margraves of Andechs-Meran, and while she lived she held Andrew firmly under her influence. She was reported to be 'generous and friendly towards the Germans, wherever they came from, and tried to help them in every possible way'.[1] Her relatives and favourites were indeed showered with offices and grants. This included her brother, Berthold, who though young and uneducated was appointed archbishop of Kalocsa. He also held the office of ban of Croatia and then the voivodate of Transylvania. Two of the queen's other brothers, who had been accused of having taken part in the murder of Philip of Swabia in 1208, were for a while given shelter in the Hungarian court. Hungarian lords found the German presence so unacceptable that in 1213, while the king was heading for Galicia, they slaughtered the queen and her entourage in the forest of Pilis. Later tradition held that the sanguinary deed was conceived by Ban Bánk, whose wife was said to have been raped by one of Gertrud's brothers. The king had no choice but to be indulgent, for he had the support of no more than a handful of barons. One of the conspirators, Count Peter – to whom Petrovaradin, now a suburb of Novi Sad, owes its name – was impaled. All the others survived with impunity, though some of them were to be sentenced to loss of property by Gertrud's son, Béla, in 1228.

In the meantime, Andrew had been under pressure from the Pope to keep his childhood promise and thereby fulfil his father's crusading vow. After 20 years of reluctance, he took up the cross, apparently unperturbed by internal problems that were growing steadily worse and worse. He was to be the only Hungarian ruler to lead a crusade to the Holy Land. In the autumn of 1217 he departed from Split with a substantial army, which included many prelates and barons of his realm. He was also accompanied by his cousin, Leopold VI, duke of Austria, while Hugh of Lusignan, king of Cyprus, joined them *en route*. The enterprise proved to be a signal failure. In spite of their considerable military resources, the allies were unable to mount a decisive operation, and Andrew, probably bored, left for home three months later. On his way back, however, he visited all the princes from Asia Minor to the Balkans in order to establish new diplomatic relations. It was at that time that he obtained the daughter of Theodore I Lascaris, emperor of Nicea, as a wife for his heir, Béla; and he betrothed his own eldest child, Maria, to Ivan Asen II, who had recently acceded to the throne of Bulgaria. A third betrothal between the Andrew's third son and the daughter of Leo II of Armenia also took place, but was later broken in favour of a more advantageous Russian match.

THE 'NEW INSTITUTIONS'

Immediately after his accession Andrew II introduced what he called 'new institutions' (*novae institutiones*), the basic idea of which was the distribution of land among his adherents. Giving land as a 'perpetual' (or inheritable) grant must have been a mark of royal favour since the time of Saint Stephen, but it had probably been exceptional and had only involved escheated lands or the king's demesne. The measures that followed now were new in two respects. First, the lands that Andrew distributed were of enormous extent; second, they included not only uninhabited woodland, which would have been acceptable, but also villages of the castle folk and of *udvornici*. Giving away 'castle lands' in such quantities, if at all, was unheard of. Moreover, the king's generosity was wholly excessive: 'the best measure of a royal grant', he declared with obvious satisfaction, 'is its being immeasurable.'[2] Only a few of the charters issued at that time have come down to us, but later evidence suggests that something of a landslide occurred. Immense fortunes were created overnight, and many of the great domains of late medieval Hungary, at least in their nuclei, seem to have been formed during these decades. The grants were large enough to allow the foundation of new monasteries. The most impressive monuments of this period are those abbey churches that were built by newly enriched barons, such as that of Palatine Pat at Lébény or that of Count Martin at Ják.

The greatest acquisitions of land were made by 'the barons of the realm' (*barones regni*) and their relatives, all of whom belonged to powerful kindreds of noble descent. It was in 1217 that the new term 'baron', denoting the highest office-holders of the kingdom, emerged, a term that was to remain in use until the end of the Middle Ages. (Such men had been called 'count' in the eleventh century and '*iobagio*' in the twelfth.) The barons were appointed and replaced by the king, but if superseded they expected to be compensated with another office, and so a normal career for a baron lasted until his death. Nor was the king absolutely free in making his choice. It was prescribed by unwritten custom that he should select his barons from among the 'nobles', that is, from the members of the most illustrious kindreds.

At the head of the barons, who numbered around 20 in all, we find the palatine and the judge royal (*curialis comes*, called *iudex curiae* from 1230), the two justiciars whose competence extended over Hungary proper. Equal to them in rank were the ban of Croatia (which sometimes included Dalmatia and Slavonia) and the voivode of Transylvania, both of whom exercised similar authority, judicial as well as military, in their respective provinces and were to represent the king there. Immediately after the first four barons there followed the 'count' (*curialis comes*), i.e. the head, of the queen's household, and the *magister tavarnicorum* of the king, who was in charge of the royal chamber, a new dignity recorded from 1214. From about 1220 the officers standing at the head of the royal household also appear among the barons. They were the Master of the Horse (*magister agazonum*), the Master of the Table (*magister dapiferorum*) and the Master of the Cup-bearers (*magister pincernarum*). Each of the nine highest dignitaries also held a county. The rest of the counties were governed by mere counts, but until the early fourteenth century the most powerful among them were also considered to be barons.

The aim of the 'new institutions' seems to have been the modernisation of the army. It is generally believed that Andrew tried in this way to introduce a form of feudal service in order to create for himself a body of effective mounted knights, something that he had been in need of before. Indeed, we find that those who were given 'much land' in these years were expected to be at the king's disposal whenever necessary. This short-lived feudalism was not, however, to survive. All kings of Hungary, including Andrew II himself, granted lands that were (to use Western terminology) not fiefs but allodia. The grantee was given an estate 'forever' (*perpetuo iure*) and unconditionally, in the form of an allodium (*haereditas*). It was not given, as would be normal in the case of a fief, for certain services to be rendered in the future, but for services that had already been done and were now to be rewarded. Hence none of the charters of grant contained any stipulations concerning feudal service. Instead, they narrated at length the 'merits' that the grantee had acquired in the king's service and had made him worthy of remuneration. This is a curious literary genre, very similar to a family chronicle, somewhat profusely written but containing many episodes that provide invaluable help to the historian seeking to reconstruct political events.

Andrew's reforms shook the ancient regime to its very foundations. Giving away castle lands on a large scale undermined the social and military organisation upon which the prestige of the counts and castle warriors rested. Moreover, the royal grants overturned the relative equilibrium within the nobility and increased the wealth of a small group in a way that could not be endured. It is small wonder that the 'new institutions' provoked general indignation and discontent, and that they were soon followed by a major reaction.

THE GOLDEN BULL OF 1222

Before his departure for the crusade, the king had appointed John, archbishop of Esztergom to be governor in his absence. The archbishop had been the principal opponent to Andrew's previous policy; but even this step turned out to be ineffective. On his return from the Holy Land, Andrew found his kingdom (as he wrote to Honorius III) in a 'miserable and destroyed state, deprived of all of its revenues' and also 'full of discord'.[3] In fact he had run up enormous debts in preparing for his crusade, and had resorted to coinage debasement, along with the imposition of an extraordinary tax, a measure that had never occurred before. However, there were also deep-rooted social conflicts, which were more difficult for Andrew to pacify. Some 'perverts' (*perversi*) soon set the king's eldest son, Béla, against him. Béla had been crowned in 1214 but not given a province to govern. In 1220 Andrew was forced to cede Croatia and Slavonia to his son, that is, the province between the River Drava and the Adriatic.

This was the prelude to the revolt of 1222. As the Pope was informed, 'an immense crowd' gathered together and, 'forgetful of wise moderation, demanded grave and unjust things' from the king.[4] They forced him to dismiss his barons and appoint new ones, and a charter of liberties, known as the Golden Bull, was issued. In its preamble the king stated that 'the liberties established by Saint Stephen in favour of the nobles of our realm as well as of other persons have been diminished in many respects by the violence of certain kings', and that this 'has often led to not inconsiderable bitterness between them and us'. In the bull the king sought to assure everyone of 'the liberties given by the holy king', and adopted further measures with a view 'to the reformation of the state of our kingdom'.[5]

Most of the 30 paragraphs of the Golden Bull were directed in some way against the encroachments committed by the king and his adherents, and described the harmful practices that were to be avoided in the future. They prohibited the granting away of 'whole counties', and tried to set a limit on the influence of foreigners. Yet, for posterity, by far the most important statutes were those that laid down the privileges of the 'royal servants' – that is, the nobility. It was stipulated for the first time that nobles were exempt from any kind of royal tax, including 'lodging'; that they were not obliged to go to war *gratis*, not even with the king, save in the case of a foreign invasion; that they were not to be subject to the count's jurisdiction, their cases only being judged by the king or the palatine; and that they could not be arrested without a valid indictment. All of these privileges conclusively distinguished the 'royal servants' from all other social groups, and in particular from the noble castle warriors and other nobles living on ecclesiastical domains, who continued to be required to do unlimited military service and remained subject to the law court of their lord.

The last clause of the famous Golden Bull, often referred to as 'the thirty-first paragraph', contained a memorable sanction. In the event of a king encroaching upon the prescriptions of the Bull, 'the bishops as well as the other barons and nobles of the realm, singularly and in common' were authorised 'to resist and speak against us and our successors without incurring the charge of high treason'.[6] It is worth noting, however, that this clause was hardly ever invoked throughout the rest of the Middle Ages. It was only to acquire importance much later when used as a weapon by the Estates during their clashes with the Habsburg kings.

In Hungarian historiography the Golden Bull has often been compared to Magna Carta. It was once thought to be proof of parallel processes in the constitutional history of England and Hungary. Such a view can no longer be sustained, for it is clear that the two privileges were, in origin and character, as far from each other as were the kingdoms of the Árpádians and the Angevins. Could the Golden Bull have been influenced in some way by Magna Carta? In spite of some similarities this does not seem probable. We cannot suppose that more than a handful of well informed clerics in Hungary had any idea of what was going on in contemporary England, and such men do not seem to have had much influence on events in any case. The movement that brought about the issue of the Golden Bull was clearly led not by bishops but by laymen, and their purposes were entirely different from those of the barons of King John's realm.

The upheaval that led to the issue of the Golden Bull was soon brought under control, and the barons who had been replaced recovered their offices within a few months. The afterlife of the document was more important than the role it played in its own time. In 1318 King Charles of Anjou was put under pressure to renew it, though in vain, and it was King Louis I who was finally willing to confirm it, in a slightly modified form, in 1351. Henceforth the original charter lost its value and, although it had been issued in seven copies, not one of these has survived. The document issued by Louis was to be the fundamental law of the kingdom and the very summary of noble privileges from the fifteenth century to the birth of the modern state.

ANDREW II AND HIS SONS

During the last years of Andrew II's reign, the kingdom's foreign policy was directed by Béla, the younger king. He was duke of Transylvania from 1226, and led the expansion towards the south and the east, which was strongly supported by the Dominicans. The Cumans, who from 1223 were exposed to the increasing pressure of the Mongols, had become willing to adopt Christianity. As early as 1227 one of their princes subjected himself and his people to Béla, converted to Christianity and agreed to pay an annual tax and the tithe. In about 1232 the missionary bishopric of Milcovia was established in southern Moldavia. At the same time, the south-western part of Cumania was put under the authority of a Hungarian governor, who received the title of ban and set up his residence in Turnu Severin on the lower Danube. As a result, in 1233 the young king adopted the title of 'king of Cumania'. After his accession to the throne, this dignity became attached to the royal title, though Cumania itself was to soon to disappear in the storm of the Mongol invasion.

Béla enjoyed the support of his brother, Coloman, who governed Slavonia and bore the title of 'king of Russia' as a result of his short-lived rule in Galicia. Coloman's main interest lay in the evangelisation of Bosnia. In 1233, Pope Gregory IX entrusted this work to the Dominicans, to whom from 1234 Coloman gave armed support. The evangelisation of the province was directed by a missionary bishop, who had hitherto been subjected, at least nominally, to the see of Dubrovnik. He was now subordinated at first to the Holy See; then, in 1247, he became, as 'bishop of Bosnia', a suffragan of Kalocsa and a member of the Hungarian episcopate with his residence at Đakovo in Hungary. In 1232 another missionary bishopric was created at Srem. Also subordinated to the see of Kalocsa, this bishopric was to lead the conversion of the Serbs. One of the residences of the new 'bishop of Srem' was at St Irineus on the River Sava (a part of modern Sremska Mitrovica), the other being at Banoštor.

Meanwhile the Church appeared in the political arena as a new and independent force. It objected on moral grounds to the administration of finance by non-Christians. At the same time it feared that its revenues would suffer as a consequence of the king's fiscal measures. In 1231 the prelates forced the king to issue another Golden Bull, which while reiterating the most important points of the previous one, was completed by paragraphs favouring the Church. Instead of the clause concerned with the right of general resistance, the new document authorised the archbishop of Esztergom to enforce the king's observance of the bull by means of excommunication. In the event, the archbishop soon had occasion to make use of his privilege. Andrew disregarded the provisions of the bull and Archbishop Robert consequently put the whole country under interdiction in 1232 and excommunicated Andrew's leading barons. In this awkward situation Pope Gregory IX sent Jacopo Pecorari, cardinal–bishop of Palestrina, to restore order. In 1233 the legate forced Andrew to accept the Treaty of Bereg, which amounted to the fulfilment of almost all the demands of the Church. It laid down the fundamental privileges of the Church, persons and institutions alike, forbade the employment of Jews and Muslims in financial administration, and regulated the salt monopoly, with particular regard to the share due to the royal monasteries.

Spiritual influence from the West grew at this time through the expansion of the mendicant orders. The Dominicans arrived in 1221 under the direction of Paulus Hungarus, an expert in canon law who was well known in his time. By 1233 they had established a Hungarian province, and had twelve friaries by the time of the Mongol invasion. The Franciscans were for a time less numerous, but they too had their own province from 1238. The influence of the mendicant orders on the royal house soon became evident. Elizabeth, a daughter of Andrew II, became a paragon of humility and charity. She was given in marriage to Louis IV, margrave of Thuringia, died a widow in Germany at the age of 24 in 1231, and was canonised four years later. Two of Béla IV's daughters soon followed in her footsteps. One of them, Kunigunda (1224–1292), lived for many decades in chaste marriage with Duke Boleslaw of Cracow. The youngest daughter, Marguerite, born at the time of the Mongol invasion in 1242, was offered to God by her parents and was brought up on Rabbit's Island (now Marguerite Island) near Buda in a Dominican friary, the ruins of which still survive. When Béla wanted to her to marry, Marguerite defied him (in the process, bringing the wrath of the king upon the Dominicans) and remained a nun until her death in 1270. Her life, spent in humility and mortification, gave birth to legends even in her lifetime, and immediately after her death the Hungarian court took steps to promote her canonisation. The records of her first process, which followed in 1276, provide a unique source for the cultural history of the time, but her beatification was not to come until 1943.

Until this time the presence of Muslim merchants and Byzantine monks had given Hungarian culture a special oriental flavour. It was in Aleppo in the 1220s that Yakut, an Arab geographer, was told by students coming from Hungary that Muslim communities were living there in 30 villages. The influence of Orthodoxy must also have been considerable. Around 1150, as we have seen, Greek scholars worked at Bač, and it was at about the same time that Cerbanus of Venice, working on Greek manuscripts found at Pásztó, produced Latin translations of the works of Maximus Confessor, and perhaps also of those of Johannes Damascenus. In modern Dunaújváros, in the very heart of the kingdom, there existed a Greek monastery as late as 1238. It was dedicated to St Pantaleon and had a certain Andronicus, evidently himself a Greek, as its patron.

The growing influence of the papacy and the zeal of the mendicant orders put an end to the religious tolerance of the royal court that had been one of its characteristics. The peaceful life of Oriental communities was brutally interrupted. With the fourth Lateran Council in 1215 signalling the beginning of religious intolerance, a steady accumulation of disturbing news about Hungary reached Rome. Both Innocent III and Honorius III were stupefied to hear that large numbers of Muslims were living unharassed in Hungary. Even worse, there were Christians who had found it advantageous to convert to Islam. On the orders of Honorius III, the Greek monastery of Visegrád – one of greatest – was handed over to the Benedictines as early as 1221. The Holy See emphatically demanded that Jews should be compelled to wear the distinctive signs prescribed by the Lateran Council, and that they, as well as Muslims, should be excluded from the administration of royal finance. These steps were evidently followed by harsher measures, for we hear no more of either Greek monks or Muslim communities during the period after the Mongol invasion.

THE MONGOL INVASION

Andrew II died on 21 September 1235. Two years earlier he had lost his second wife, Yolande de Courtenay, sister of Robert and Baldwin II, Latin emperors of Constantinople. Although nearing sixty, he contracted a third marriage with Beatrice, the young daughter of the marquis of Este. Upon Andrew's death, the widow, who was already pregnant, considered it advisable to flee the country, and it was abroad that she gave birth to a son, Stephen, father of Andrew III, the last king of the dynasty.

Béla IV (1235–1270) had already become known for his conservative views. Between 1228 and 1231, as a younger king, he had taken serious measures to reverse his father's 'useless and superfluous perpetual grants'; but at that time his father had often prevented his decisions from being put into effect. Now, as king, he began his reign by expelling or imprisoning his father's principal counsellors and confiscating their estates. Palatine Denis, who was held to be more responsible than anyone else for what had happened during Andrew II's reign, was blinded. Béla also made efforts to restore the kingdom to the state it had been during the time of his revered grandfather. As a first step he ordered that the barons should henceforth stand during meetings of the royal council, having their seats burnt as a symbolic act. He also ordered that all those with grievances should submit these, by written petition, to the office of the judge royal in order that their cases might be examined. Only the most important cases would be placed before the council. However, Béla's foremost aim was to put an end to the dissolution of the kingdom's castle organisation, so he ordered a careful census of what remained of it and, in order to swell the dangerously diminished stock of royal estates, he resorted once again to the rescinding of his father's land grants. All these measures bore witness to the king's determination to interpret royal power as being almost absolute; and, indeed, they seemed to reinforce royal authority for a short time. The Italian Rogerius, canon of Oradea and later archbishop of Split, an astute contemporary who described in his *Carmen miserabile* the story of the Mongol invasion, was of another opinion. He thought that Béla's actions had provoked 'hatred' between the king and his subjects, leading to a level of tension that he saw as the main reason for the catastrophe that was to follow.

It was at this time that the mysterious 'eastern' Hungarians became involved for a moment in the history of their western relatives. In the tenth century it was still recalled that the Hungarians had been cut into two by the attack of the Pechenegs in about 895 and that one part of them had remained in the East. This episode seems later to have been forgotten, and the existence of these distant relatives only became known again via the conversion of Cumania. Prompted by hints provided by a missionary, a Friar Julian and three other Dominicans left for the East in 1235 in order to find the lost Hungarians. Following the instruction of the chronicles, the Dominicans looked for them first in 'Scythia', that is, around the sea of Azov, but the eastern Hungarians were finally found in Bashkiria, along the River Volga, in a land called *Magna Hungaria* by Friar Julian. By the time he encountered them, all his companions had died. It was there that Julian realised the danger posed by the Mongol expansion, and as soon as he had arrived home he informed his king of it. In 1237 a new mission was dispatched, this time with the aim of converting the pagan Hungarians, but it had to stop at Suzdal, for in the meantime Khan Batu's troops had begun their westward movement and had swept away the Hungarians' eastern relatives for ever.

Mongol pressure led to the first migration of the Cumans into Hungary. In 1237 Prince Kuthen asked for his people's admission, promising that they would become good Hungarian subjects and adopt the Roman Catholic faith. Regarding the Cumans as potentially useful allies against the Mongols, as well as against his own subjects, Béla settled them on the Great Plain, but their arrival only deepened the crisis in Hungary. The king was overwhelmed with complaints that the Cumans had violated women and disregarded property rights. There was little he could do to prevent these transgressions, but was nevertheless accused of bias in favour of 'his Cumans'.

In the meantime the Mongols arrived on the scene. Kiev fell in December 1240 and in the spring of 1241 the Mongol armies set out for Hungary. The right wing crossed Poland and, having defeated Henry, duke of Silesia at Legnica on 9 April, invaded the kingdom of Hungary from the north. The left wing pushed through the passes of the Carpathians from the south. The main army, led by Batu in person, aimed the very heart of the kingdom. On 12 March they broke through the defensive works of the pass of Vorota and defeated Palatine Denis Tomaj. Five days later Vác was plundered by their vanguard.

Few realised the seriousness of the danger. While the royal army was gathering near Pest and the Mongols were advancing with a speed that only nomadic horsemen could attain, a riot broke out against the Cumans who were accused of complicity with the enemy. The crowd slaughtered Kuthen and his retinue, while his enraged people left the royal camp and marched away, doing as much damage as they could. Nevertheless, even without the Cumans, the Mongols still thought that the Hungarian army outnumbered them. Béla confidently marched eastwards and met Batu near Muhi on the River Sajó. It was there that took place the battle which was to be greatest military catastrophe experienced by medieval Hungary prior to 1526.

The Hungarian troops took position on the plain, surrounded by their carts. According to Batu, they 'closed themselves in a narrow pen in the manner of sheep',[7] which made effective defence impossible. By dawn the Mongols had crossed the river above and below the Hungarian camp, encircled it and killed by archery all those who could not escape. The very best of the Hungarian army perished, including the palatine, the judge royal and both archbishops along with other bishops and barons. Béla's brother, Coloman, was severely wounded and died soon after in Slavonia. Although the Mongols did their best to catch him, Béla managed to escape, and a number of nobles were later rewarded for helping him with fresh horses. He asked Frederick of Austria for help, but the duke preferred to take advantage of the situation and forced Béla to cede three counties. From Austria the king fled to Slavonia, and continued to send letters to the West asking for help. But all was in vain, for Gregory IX and Frederick II, whose support he might have hoped for, were heavily engaged in fighting each other.

In fact the help could not have arrived in time, for the Mongol storm subsided as quickly as it had arrived. In the beginning of 1242 the invaders crossed the frozen Danube and took Esztergom with the exception of the castle. They chased Béla as far as Trogir in Dalmatia, but did not have time to lay siege to the city. The news came that the Great Khan, Ögödey, had died at the end of 1241, and Batu wanted to be present at the election of his successor. In March the Mongol army withdrew from the country, killing and taking thousands of captives en route. 'In this year', noted an Austrian annalist under the year 1241, 'the kingdom of Hungary, which had existed for 350 years, was destroyed by the army of the Tatars.'[8]

Chapter 7

The Last Árpádians

Internal development and the Mongol invasion brought about notable changes during second half of the thirteenth century. Some of them turned out to be decisive. By about 1270 political events had led to a rapid decline of central power and brought about an anarchy that culminated in 1301 with the dying out of the Árpádian dynasty. But this was also a period of major social and economic changes, unparalleled since the eleventh and until the nineteenth centuries. Ancient forms of serfdom began to disappear, and wide regions of what is today Slovakia, as well as of Transylvania, which had been almost uninhabited before, began to be settled with increasing density during these decades. Special attention must be given to the emergence of the diet (or parliament) and of local autonomies, preparing the way for the growing influence of the nobility as an 'estate' in the following period.

THE EFFECTS OF THE MONGOL INVASION

The destruction caused by the Mongols during the course of a single year is hardly imaginable. They carried off thousands of captives, and what they left behind was vividly described by Rogerius, who had been a captive of theirs but managed to escape with some of his companions. For a week they wandered in Transylvania from village to village 'without meeting anyone', guided by church towers and living on roots. When they finally arrived in Alba Iulia 'they found nothing but the corpses and skulls of those slaughtered by the invaders'.[1] The spectacle must have been the same wherever the enemy had passed, and even many decades later villages throughout the kingdom were found to have been uninhabited 'since the time of the Mongols'. The fields could not be tilled while the enemy was there and the unburied corpses caused the spread of epidemics. Consequently, there followed in 1243 a horrible famine, which 'took more victims than the pagans before', according to an Austrian contemporary.[2]

The number of casualties has been disputed, but there is no doubt that the invasion led to something of a demographic catastrophe. Some scholars put the loss, probably with exaggeration, at about 50 per cent of the population (Gy. Györffy), but even the most prudent estimates do not go below 15 or 20 per cent (J. Szücs). The disaster can certainly be compared to the Black Death, which was to strike the West a century later, and its consequences were of the same importance. The trauma caused by the Mongol attack itself prompted a series of comprehensive political reforms, but its indirect social effects were even more significant. Strange as it may seem, the cataclysm speeded up the process of transformation that had begun in the reign of Andrew II. The next few decades saw spectacular changes that transformed the general outlook and social structure of the kingdom profoundly and enduringly.

The Transdanubian region where the invaders spent only a couple of months was relatively spared, but the Great Plain, which had borne the Mongol presence for a whole year, was devastated. Archaeological excavations have shown that in the region of Orosháza, east of Szeged, 31 out of 43 villages disappeared for ever. In the immediate outskirts of Cegléd, eight ruined churches were in later centuries to serve as reminders of the villages that must once have stood around them. In the late Middle Ages many deserted places still bore the name of a patron saint, showing that they had been inhabited in earlier times. It has been demonstrated that medieval place names ending with the word *egyház* ('church', as in the names of the modern towns Nyíregyháza and Kiskunfélegyháza) also referred to an abandoned church. Obviously not all the deserted localities should be attributed to the Mongol destruction. The abandonment of settlements must have been as common in Hungary as elsewhere in Europe, and the apparent disappearance of many villages that had been mentioned before 1241 was probably due to a change of name. Nevertheless, it is clear that the consequences of the Mongol invasion were grave indeed. It is a significant fact that all of the 40 Hungarian monasteries that are known to have disappeared at this time lay in the area that was affected by the invaders, 35 being on the Great Plain and the remainder in the adjacent part of Fejér county.

The profound transformation in the network of settlements on the Great Plain should be seen, on the whole, as a consequence of the Mongol invasion. Even today this part of Hungary is characterised by towns and large villages, with each having an extensive area belonging to it, while a dense network of much smaller settlements is more typical elsewhere. The lands belonging to the abandoned settlements on the

Great Plain were taken over by the survivors and used as pastures. In this way, the general destruction in the thirteenth century can be seen as a prerequisite for the spectacular boom in horse and cattle breeding in the following period.

No less fatal for the whole of eastern Hungary was the simultaneous collapse of eastern European commerce. An initial blow had been dealt by the sack of Constantinople in 1204, for as a consequence the main commercial route that led through the Balkans lost its importance. Flourishing towns like Bač and Kovin, which had hitherto lived off the trade along this route, soon declined to the status of insignificant villages. However, the final blow was brought about by the Mongol destruction of Kiev in 1240.

It seems that, until that date, eastern Hungary had been a flourishing region. It was not, of course, more civilised than the western half of the kingdom, but it had certainly developed dynamically. Among the evidence for this are thousands of pennies of Friesach dating from Andrew II's reign that have been found along the route leading to Kiev, but not elsewhere. They were probably buried at the time of the Mongol attack. The earliest known royal privilege that contained liberties for a community of peasant settlers was granted in 1201 by King Emeric to Walloons who came to the royal forest of Sárospatak. The village they founded, later to be called Olaszi (now Bodrogolaszi), lay along the route towards Kiev. The earliest urban privilege we know of was accorded by Andrew II in 1230 to the German 'guests' (*hospites*) of Satu Mare. The fact that Galicia remained a target of Hungarian foreign policy until about the same time was probably not unrelated to its economic importance. The route to Galicia led through the passes of the north-eastern Carpathians, so the king and his court must have been frequent visitors to the region. After the destruction of Kiev, commerce with the East virtually ceased to exist and the region quickly became marginalised, from the economic as well as the political point of view. Užhorod, a 'great and flourishing town' in the time of Idrisi,[3] was not to recover from the blow until modern times. The same could be said of many other centres in the region, which henceforth would experience a royal visit no more than once a century.

MILITARY REFORMS

The military defeat brought about a radical change in Béla IV's political outlook. In the first place, it clearly indicated the necessity of constructing strong fortresses. Many of the early earth and timber castles had probably been abandoned by the time of the invasion, while those still in use were destroyed by the invaders. Apart from the walled cities of Esztergom and Székesfehérvár, there were only a few fortified monasteries and stone castles that were able to resist the Mongols. The most spectacular change of the years following the invasion was, therefore, the rapid spread of stone-built castles.

Béla completely abandoned the old principle according to which the erection and administration of fortresses was a royal prerogative. Immediately after the Mongols had left the country he initiated a large-scale programme with the aim of adopting the type of stone castle that had already become common in the West. The policy of lavish land-grants was renewed. Béla, as he himself put it, was prompted by his royal office 'not to reduce but to enlarge' his grants.[4] Both the castle-building programme and the creation of a knightly army were dependent on the lords receiving huge parcels of land, from the revenues of which they could construct and maintain castles. The king himself began such construction on the royal demesne, and simultaneously permitted others to do the same on their own estates. The first known authorisation for a private person to build a castle was issued in 1247, and by the time of Béla's death about a hundred new fortifications stood throughout the kingdom, ready to face a new invasion. They were held by bishops, lay lords, as well as the king and the queen.

The most important new castles lay mainly in the royal forests and were erected by the king himself. Good examples are Spišský hrad and Šarišský hrad. The castle of Visegrád, perched on a hill above the great bend of the Danube north of Budapest, was built by Queen Mary to be the centre of the forest of Pilis. The fortifications erected by nobles, often called 'towers', were more modest constructions. They normally consisted of a massive tower, sometimes supplemented by a palace and a chapel, and surrounded by a stone wall, the whole site occupying no more than an acre. During the first decades they were usually built on inaccessible peaks, often in a remote mountain region, clearly indicating that they were intended to serve not as residences but as refuges for the owner and his family in case of danger. The outcome of the programme set in motion by Béla and continued by his immediate successors can still be seen. All over the Carpathian basin there are hundreds of castles great and small, often rebuilt or enlarged later and now lying mostly in ruins, that have nuclei dating back to the second half of the thirteenth century.

Another military implication of the invasion was that there was a pressing need to modernise the army. The bulk of the king's army continued to consist of the castle warriors serving as light cavalry. Although they were unable to afford more than the traditional leather armour, the king tried to increase their number and modernise their equipment. From the 1240s onwards he began to grant small parcels of land in the uninhabited royal forests upon the condition that the grantees equipped a certain number of heavily armoured cavalrymen for the royal army. It was the descendants of these settlers who, by the end of the Middle Ages, had come to form the lesser nobility of the basin of Turc and of the district of the 'ten-lanced' (*decemlanceatus*) nobles of Spis. The king also wanted to increase the number of heavily armoured Western-style knights, and proved to be as generous as his father had been in distributing enormous landed estates among his barons and followers.

In view of the Mongol menace, mounted archers skilled in nomadic warfare were also needed. This military element had hitherto been furnished by the Székely and the Pechenegs, but after the invasion the role of the latter was taken over by the Cumans, whom Béla managed to lure back into his kingdom in 1246. In order to bind them closely to his dynasty, he made his eldest son marry Elisabeth, the daughter of the Cuman prince. He assigned them a territory of their own in those regions of the Great Plain that had recently become uninhabited. One of their groups, later called 'Major Cumans', settled east of Szolnok, while the 'Minor Cumans' occupied the sandy area between the Danube and the Tisza. It might have been about the same time that a group of nomadic Alans, called *jász* in Hungarian and, for an unknown reason, Philistines in some Latin sources, also appeared in Hungary. In the early fourteenth century they were allotted a district of their own in Heves county, in the region now called Jászság.

The extensive pastures that the Cumans and Alans found on the Great Plain enabled them to pursue their traditional nomadic life for some time, but within two or three centuries they had become assimilated into the surrounding population. By then their temporary nomadic 'dwellings' (*descensus*) had been transformed into villages, and they had also abandoned their original languages. That of the Cumans, a Turkic language, left no written traces, while that of the Alans is represented by a list of 38 Iranian words scrawled on the back of a legal document from 1422. Both the Cumans and the Alans were directly subjected to the king and, like the Székely or the castle warriors, were expected to perform unlimited military service. Their constant presence in the Hungarian army in all of its wars gave it a peculiarly exotic flavour.

BÉLA IV AND STEPHEN V

In Hungary, the years following 1242 were spent feverishly preparing to face a new Mongol attack. The fear finally turned out to be unjustified, for the Mongol empire had broken into parts in the meantime, and the aggressive energies of the Golden Horde, founded by Batu, were directed towards other ends. A second Mongol invasion did take place in 1285, but it only affected eastern Hungary and its consequences were hardly comparable to those of the first incursion.

After the withdrawal of the Mongols, Béla revived his predecessors' aggressive foreign policy in the Balkans. Through two rapid campaigns in 1244 and 1253, he reinforced his influence in Bosnia. Around 1254 he entrusted the protection of his Balkan interests to Rostislav Mihailovič, prince of Černigov, who had sought refuge with him from the advancing Mongols. Béla made him marry his own daughter, Anne, and appointed him duke of Bosnia and Mačva. With the active support of his father-in-law, Rostislav managed to enlarge the Hungarian sphere of influence significantly and built up a sizeable principality that stretched from Bosnia to Braničevo. After the extinction of the Asenids, he intervened in Bulgaria, occupied Vidin at the beginning of 1257 and took the title of tzar. After his death in 1262 his lands passed to his sons, who were minors and ruled as vassals of Hungary under the guardianship of their mother.

In 1246 the Babenbergs, the ruling dynasty of Austria and Styria, became extinct through the death of Duke Frederick II, who was killed by the Hungarians in a battle on the River Leitha. Seeking to gain control of these lands, Béla took the field in 1250 against the husband of Frederick's sister, Otakar Přemysl, first heir and then king of Bohemia (1253–1278). In 1254, after four years of war, Béla and Otakar came to an agreement and divided the disputed provinces. The Hungarian king was given the greater part of Styria in the south, which in 1258 he granted to his elder son, Stephen, with the title of duke. The Styrian lords soon revolted, however, and sought help from Otakar. The king of Bohemia defeated the Hungarians near Kroissenbrunn in 1260, and in the following year forced them to sign a peace in Vienna. Béla gave up his claim to the Babenberg inheritance and even entered into an alliance with his former enemy, giving him his granddaughter, Rostislav's daughter, as a wife.

The defeat of 1260 led to a serious crisis in Hungary. Duke Stephen, who as compensation for the loss of Styria was given the government of Transylvania, was not content with his share of power and revolted. In 1262 the king was forced to confer on his son the title of 'younger king' and to concede to him the government of that part of the kingdom lying east of the Danube. The situation remained unstable, however, the political atmosphere being contaminated by 'calumniators and tattlers' on both sides. Defections from each camp were commonplace. To put an end to this undesirable state of affairs, Béla took the field against his son in 1264 and chased him as far as the eastern corner of Transylvania. However, the king's army was beaten by the ducal troops at the siege of Codlea (Feketehalom), near Braşov. Stephen launched a counter-attack during the winter and in March 1265 inflicted another defeat on his father's army at Isaszeg. In 1266 Béla and his son finally met on Marguerite Island and made peace on the basis of the partition of 1262.

During Béla's last years, the foreign policy of the kingdom was directed mainly by his son. As lord of Transylvania, Stephen's main interest lay in consolidating Hungarian supremacy in the Balkans. Through a series of three campaigns (1261, 1263, 1266), he reinforced his authority over Vidin. He made Jakov Svetoslav, one of the princes of Bulgaria, his vassal, and took the title of 'king of Bulgaria'. Yet in terms of its long-term consequences, Stephen's most important step was the alliance that he formed in 1269 with Charles I of Anjou, who had recently come to power in Naples and Sicily. Stephen had his seven-year-old son, Ladislaus, marry Elizabeth (Isabelle), Charles's granddaughter, while his own daughter, Mary, became the wife of the future King Charles II. This marriage was later to be the legal basis of the Angevin claim to the Hungarian throne.

Béla was 64 years old when he died on 3 May 1270, surpassing in age all the members of his dynasty, with the possible exception of Stephen I. In accordance with his will, he was buried in the Franciscan friary of Esztergom, and was followed on the throne by his son as Stephen V (1270–1272). Some of his barons in the western counties, fearing retribution from the new king, looked to Otakar for support and acknowledged him as their overlord. Anne, Rostislav's widow, also fled to her son-in-law in Prague, taking with her the royal treasury. Otakar marched deep into Hungarian territory, but in 1271 at Pressburg he made peace with Stephen, by which agreement he retained Béla's treasury, but gave up his conquests and promised not to assist his Hungarian partisans against Stephen's rule.

The short reign of Stephen V was overshadowed by struggles between the baronial parties that would lead to open fighting after his death. In 1272 the short-lived order was disturbed by the revolt of Joachim Gútkeled, ban of Slavonia, who captured Ladislaus, Stephen V's infant son, and imprisoned him in his castle of Koprivnica. He seems to have wanted to use the young prince as a hostage to enforce a new division of the kingdom between Ladislaus and his father. Stephen tried in vain to liberate his son, a failure that is said to have hastened his premature death on 6 August 1272. He was buried next to his sister in the Dominican convent on Marguerite Island.

LADISLAUS IV AND ANDREW III

Up to that point the kingdom had enjoyed relative stability. In spite of the internal struggles, Charles of Anjou's envoy could still report in

1269 that 'the king of Hungary has incredibly great power and such a military force that there is no one in the east and in the north who would dare to move if the glorious king mobilised his enormous army'.[5] Now the situation suddenly changed. The death of Stephen V introduced a long era of instability. The crown passed to the ten-year-old Ladislaus IV (1272–1290) under the nominal regency of his Cuman mother, Elizabeth; but the political agenda was set by the rivalry of baronial groups, the Csák and the Héder, and their conflict brought about civil war and chaos.

As soon as Stephen died, Henry Héder (also called 'of Kőszeg' or 'of Güssing'), ban of Slavonia and the most powerful lord in western Hungary, had Béla, Rostislav's son, killed and divided Béla's principality among his own adherents. Braničevo, Kučevo, Mačva, Sol, Usora and Bosnia became separate provinces for nearly a decade, each of them governed by a Hungarian lord with the title of ban. In 1274 Henry captured Ladislaus's younger brother, Andrew, but was killed by Peter Csák in a battle at Föveny (near Székesfehérvár). Henry's power passed to his four sons, and it was during the war against them in 1276 that Peter destroyed Veszprém so thoroughly that all the treasures of the cathedral chapter including the library of its school were burnt. Early in 1277, the Saxons of Transylvania, who were engaged in a local conflict with their bishop, took Alba Iulia and set fire to the cathedral. Many of the canons and two thousand inhabitants were consumed in the flames.

With the kingdom on the verge of anarchy, it was the Church that tried to find a remedy. The bishops had for many years demanded moral support from the Holy See, but without response. In May 1277 they summoned an assembly to meet on the plain of Rákos near Pest. In addition to some of the barons, the envoys of the nobles and those of the Cumans were also invited, so the assembly could be regarded as something approaching a diet, the first in Hungarian history. The assembly declared the fifteen-year-old king to be of age, and called on him to proceed with all possible means against the 'pestilences of the kingdom', in order that peace and order should be restored.[6]

At first the young king did achieve some success. He suppressed the brothers Geregye, lords of Bihor, occupied their castles and had one of them beheaded. He entered into an alliance with Rudolf of Habsburg, king of Germany against the brothers Héder. Rudolf was at that time fighting with Otakar for the possession of Austria and Styria. Ladislaus was still able to muster a considerable army, at the head of which he played a decisive role in Rudolf's victory. On 26 August 1278, in the memorable battle on the Marchfeld, Otakar was killed and the short-lived hegemony of the Přemysl dynasty came to an end. Henceforth, the western neighbours of Hungary were to be the Habsburg dukes of Austria and Styria.

At the beginning of 1279, Philip, bishop of Fermo, the long-awaited papal legate, arrived in Hungary. After a short inquiry he declared that the most important thing to be done was the regulation of the Cumans, for he found it absurd that, in the very heart of a Catholic kingdom, there should be 'insubordinate' pagans 'shedding Christian blood' day by day.[7] Urged by the legate, the assembly of Tétény (now a district of Budapest) accepted a statute in June 1279 that was intended to resolve the problem of the Cumans once and for all. It prescribed that they should join the Catholic faith: they were to 'abandon idolatry and reject all the pagan customs', and all those who had hitherto remained pagans were to be baptised. It also laid down that 'from now on [the Cumans] shall settle down and leave their tents and houses made of felt. They shall reside and remain in villages of the Christian sort with buildings and houses attached to the ground.'[8] All that the unyielding legate was willing to tolerate was the Cumans' hair, beard and dress worn in the accustomed way.

The 'Cuman question' set the king against his barons and led to an unprecedented level of anarchy. Ladislaus, a Cuman himself through his mother, showed sympathy towards them. He tried to prevent the implementation of the decree that had been brought against them, and when the Cumans revolted he went over to them. It was probably at the king's order that the legate was seized and suffered a spell of captivity in Cuman hands. Having been freed, the legate was able to leave the kingdom in the summer of 1281. He declared, so we are told, that he would never return, 'not even for the sake of the Holy Father'.[9] In the meantime, the king once again took the side of his barons and personally led the army that defeated the Cumans at Lake Hód (near modern Hódmezővásárhely). In 1284, however, he abruptly refused to obey the bishops, broke with his Neapolitan wife, whom he hated, and re-joined the Cumans, this time for good. The barons and prelates, with Archbishop Lodomer of Esztergom at their head, henceforth governed the rest of the kingdom for themselves. They held assemblies without the king, who spent most of his time in the company of his Cumans on the Great Plain. He wore their clothes, adopted pagan customs, took Cuman warriors to form his retinue and Cuman girls as his concubines. One after another his Hungarian followers deserted him. Common opinion of him was so unfavourable that when in 1285 he succeeded in driving back the second Mongol invasion, he was accused of having invited them in himself. In 1287 he was excommunicated by Lodomer. In response, he said that he would 'kill and drive the whole brood' – that is, the Christian clergy – 'with Mongol swords as far as Rome.'[10] The kingdom was on the edge of collapse when, on 10 July 1290, the king was assassinated by a group of Cumans near Cheresig, in Bihor.

Ladislaus left no children, but there was a living Árpádian prince: Andrew, grandson of Andrew II. He had been brought up in Venice by his mother, Tomasina, who belonged to the well-known family of the Morosini. Although the legitimacy of his descent had earlier been questioned, the majority of the lords were now willing to accept him as king and Lodomer crowned him on 23 July 1290. The church and the nobility expected Andrew III (1290–1301) to restore public order and to govern with their consent. At the diet of Buda in September 1290 the new king issued a decree in which he promised to do these things and which contained a number of paragraphs intended to put an end to anarchy. They ordained, among other things, that the fortresses that had recently been built without royal permission should be destroyed; that all estates occupied unjustly should be restored to their rightful owners; and that stability should henceforth be guaranteed by the diet, which was to be held every year and was authorised to examine and remedy the barons' trespasses. An unheard-of innovation, inspired by up-to-date political ideas, was the election of noble assessors onto the royal council.

Andrew was well intentioned but lacked the means to carry out his programme. Although it seems that the majority of his subjects longed for peace, he was unable to unite and mobilise them. Thus, in spite of his efforts, he was powerless against the barons and could not prevent them from building local centres of power. Hardly a year would pass without an open rebellion. Although it was usually Andrew who gained the upper hand, his victories had little if any practical effect. During his campaign of 1294 he took the castles of the Borsa, a kindred that had governed Bihor since the fall of the Geregye, but he pardoned them as soon as they had surrendered. The same was to happen in the west when the Héder bluntly refused to acknowledge his authority. Andrew defeated them with the help of Albert of Habsburg, his father-in-law, but then let them go unharmed. In 1297 Matthew Csák, the son of Peter, who had control of the north-western counties, revolted and successfully defied the king. It was not without reason that the diet of 1298, while renewing the decisions taken eight years before, also referred to 'the laxity of the lord king'.[11] Some castles were indeed destroyed, but royal authority remained as weak as it had been under Ladislaus.

Croatia and Dalmatia had been detached from Hungary proper since 1290 when the Ban Paul Šubić and his kinsmen acknowledged Charles Martell of Anjou as king of Hungary. Queen Mary of Naples, wife of Charles II, was at that time of the opinion that the male line of the Árpádians had died out with Ladislaus and that the crown of Hungary should pass to her family. When Charles Martell died in 1295 he was succeeded as a pretender by his seven-year-old son Charles, called Caroberto. At the invitation of the Šubić and other lords of Croatia, Charles disembarked in Dalmatia in August 1300. Soon afterwards, on 14 January 1301, Andrew III died without male offspring, leaving Hungary in a critical situation.

SETTLEMENT AND URBANISATION

The growing importance of western Hungary from this period onwards paralleled the decline of the eastern regions. From the beginning of the thirteenth century the links tying Hungary to Germany and Italy had become ever closer. In addition to the route that led through Vienna to the West, those towards Venice and Prague (via Brno) also grew in importance. Venetian merchants were accorded commercial privileges by Andrew II as early as in 1217, while a new town in the north-west, Trnava, received a charter from Béla IV in 1238 and was to remain the main station of the trade route to Moravia throughout the Middle Ages.

An important aspect of Hungary's economic development was the adoption of new agricultural techniques. Here, too, the western part of the kingdom was most favoured, for the innovations appeared first in the western counties and from there slowly spread eastwards. The earliest example of an asymmetric heavy plough was found near Zemendorf in modern Burgenland, whilst the distinctive type of independent peasant holding that was to become dominant by the later Middle Ages also reached Hungary from Austria. It is first to be found in Burgenland in 1214 and was initially known by the German word 'Lehen' (*laneus*).

As a consequence of the Mongol invasion the peasantry seems to undergone a profound transformation. The general disorder that followed in the wake of the destruction did not favour the survival of traditional social bonds. After 1242 there were widespread complaints about serfs and bondsmen leaving their lords without permission. It was strictly prohibited to give them shelter, and there were attempts to hunt them down, but it is small wonder that most of these efforts were in vain. There are growing numbers of charters mentioning lands that had become uninhabited, mostly *praedia*, that is allodia previously inhabited by serfs. This process was so general that by 1300 the meaning of the word *praedium* itself had changed. It came to refer to the *puszta*, that is, an 'uninhabited estate' (*possessio habitatoribus destituta*) with fixed boundaries but no remaining tenants.

The scale of population movement that took place at this time was not to be surpassed before the eighteenth century. The runaways were mostly absorbed by the emerging seigneuries. The great domains lying in recently depopulated lands or uninhabited woodlands were urgently in need of manpower and consequently were bound to profit from the general flight of bondsmen. Royal grants were followed everywhere by an industrious 'gathering of people' (*congregatio populorum*), to use a contemporary phrase. The settlers who came from abroad or from those regions that had been spared by the Mongols were attracted by particularly favourable conditions: by the promise of personal freedom and of relatively light burdens. This process could not fail also to affect those peasants who had not abandoned their lords, for it was almost imperative to reduce their burdens in order to prevent their flight. Gradually all landowners seem to have been forced to join the process, which within a couple of decades had led to the birth of a new class of free peasant tenants.

It was during the reigns of Béla IV and Stephen V that a conscious policy of urbanisation appeared in Hungary. Their efforts to increase the number of towns were originally part of the programme of military reforms, but the wider implications turned out to be of much greater importance. The walled towns were to serve as fortresses, while the urban communities were required to equip a fixed number of warriors and to send them to the royal army. Yet the social and economic aspects of the process were much more important than its immediate military purpose, for it resulted in the spread of urban municipalities of the Western type.

The model, here as elsewhere in central Europe, was furnished by those towns that had been founded during the twelfth century in the northern and eastern marches of Germany. The settlers were mostly German knights and merchants who, having been granted the privileges of a prestigious mother-town by the ruler, followed its laws and traditions thereafter. The extent of German immigration was so considerable that most Hungarian towns remained German enclaves in a predominantly foreign environment throughout the Middle Ages and even beyond. But whereas in Bohemia and Poland the laws of Nuremberg, Magdeburg and Lübeck were most common, in Hungary the ancient usage of the Walloon citizens of Székesfehérvár was adopted as the model to be followed. Their privileges, referred to as 'the law of Fehérvár' in modern historiography, were granted by Béla to Trnava in 1238, to the German burghers of Pest in 1244, and later to other localities.

The most memorable of Béla's foundations was the city of Buda. In about 1247 he ordered the burghers of Pest to move to the largely uninhabited hill on the opposite side of the Danube and to found a new fortified town there. This was at first called 'the city on the new hill of Pest' (*Civitas Novi Montis Pestiensis*), but soon it became known as Buda, and the ancient settlement near the Roman ruins of Aquincum, which already bore that name, was henceforth called 'Old Buda' (*Vetus Buda*, Hung. Óbuda, now a district of Budapest).

Although the towns founded in the thirteenth century were not necessarily surrounded by walls, the 'law of Fehérvár' was comprehensive even by European standards. A locality that was declared a royal 'city' was removed from the authority of the count and accorded the full rights of self-government. It was henceforth to be governed by an elected magistracy, consisting of a 'judge' and twelve jurors, who had the right to judge both the major and the minor cases and – a specific Hungarian feature – the right to elect their parish priest. The citizens were exempted from paying tolls within a defined territory, which could be one county or two, or even the kingdom as a whole. The most important and almost only duty of the community was to pay to the royal chamber an annual tax of fixed amount, the burden of which was distributed by the magistracy among the burghers in proportion to their wealth.

The speed and scale of the changes in both the life of the peasantry and the field of urban development can be illustrated by the example of the enormous royal forest of Zvolen, which comprised the districts, later counties, of Zvolen, Turc, Liptov and Orava. In spite of the importance of the silver mines of Banská Štiavnica, this part of modern Slovakia seems to have been sparsely inhabited before the Mongol invasion. After it, Béla IV built a stone castle in each district, and in 1252 founded a Premonstratensian monastery in Turc. Most of the basin of Turc and Liptov was distributed among small landholders who, in return for their noble liberties, were required to do military service. As a result of this process, in the single county of Turc 28 small villages were created in the course of a century. Moreover, no fewer than seven localities were accorded communal rights within two decades: Zvolen (1243), Krupina (1244), Dobrá Niva and Babiná (1254), Banská Bystrica (1255), Partizánska Ľupča (1263) and Hybe (1265). Between 1257 and 1270, the inhabitants of the forest were also given privileges by Béla, 'since many of them wandered away and settled on the estates of others.'[12] The king moderated their burdens and authorised them to move freely within the forest of Zvolen. He gave them the right to elect their reeve and to dispose freely of their property with the exception of a small part called 'one thing' (*una res*, Germ. *Besthaupt*), which was due to the forest count.

THE SAXONS OF TRANSYLVANIA

The largest-scale colonisation movement of the time was that of the Germans in Transylvania. The first group of Flemish settlers had arrived in about 1150. During the thirteenth century, they were followed by numerous waves of 'Saxons' from the region of the Rhine and the Mosel. Despite the heavy losses caused by the Mongol invasion, their numbers and the territory they occupied increased considerably. By around 1300 three great blocks of Saxon settlements had come into existence, all of them in the southern and eastern marches of Transylvania. The natural centres of the two southern blocks were the towns of Sibiu (Ger. Hermannstadt) and Braşov (Ger. Kronstadt). They guarded the only routes that led towards the Black Sea through the otherwise impassable southern Carpathians, so their burghers could control all trading activity in this direction. By the fourteenth century both of these towns had been enclosed by walls, and they were among the most important trading centres not only of Transylvania but also of Hungary.

Sibiu was to remain the first in rank of the Saxon settlements. According to a plausible hypothesis, its original German name was Cibinburg, which was soon deformed into Siebenbürgen (Lat. *Septem Castra*) and became the German name for Transylvania in the modern period. It was in Sibiu that German settlement in Transylvania began. Around 1190 a collegiate church was founded there. It was taken out of the authority of the bishop of Transylvania and subjected directly to the archbishop of Esztergom. şThe Saxons of Sibiu, whose territory had by that time spread from Orăştie in the west to Baraolt in the east, were given wide-ranging privileges by Andrew II in 1224. In the document, later referred to as the *Andreanum*, the king engaged himself not to grant away any part of their land, which as a consequence practically became the property of the Saxon community. Their judge remained the count of Sibiu, appointed by the king, but the minor cases were to be judged by their own magistrates, whom (along with their priests) they had the right to elect. They were to pay to the royal chamber an annual tax of 500 Hungarian silver marks, and were expected to host the king three times a year and the voivode of Transylvania twice. As military obligation, they were to equip 500 warriors for campaigning within the kingdom and 100 for foreign wars. In exchange for all these duties they were allowed to trade freely throughout the realm.

By the fourteenth century the Saxons of Sibiu had grouped into eight autonomous districts, called 'seats' (*sedes*), with their centres at Sibiu, Orăştie, Sebeş, Miercurea Sibiului, Nocrich, Cincu, Rupea and Sighişoara. At the end of the Middle Ages these were called collectively the 'Seven Seats'. In 1402 King Sigismund attached to them the districts of Mediaş and Şeica Mare, which were also inhabited by Saxons but had hitherto been subjected to royal lordship. These two districts later came to form the so-called 'Two Seats'. The greater part of the Saxon territory acquired ecclesiastical autonomy, its churches being subjected directly to the archbishop of Esztergom and organised into deaneries instead of archdeaconries.

The colonisation of the region around Braşov, called Burzenland, was initiated by the Teutonic Knights but was not interrupted after their expulsion in 1225. This region constituted an autonomous Saxon region independent from Sibiu just as did the three districts of Bistriţa, Rodna and Kyralia in eastern Transylvania, which together came to form a third unit. There were many other Saxons who settled on noble estates, but they became subject to private lordship and were assimilated. Overall, German immigration into Transylvania appears to have been very considerable, for in the modern period there were 242 localities with a German speaking population, and the Saxon autonomies extended over an area of about 11,000 square kilometres.

THE SZÉKELY

It was also during the thirteenth century that the Székely (Lat. *Siculi*) occupied the territory that they currently live in as the largest Hungarian-speaking ethnic group in Romania. From the beginning until as late as 1876, the Székely enjoyed territorial autonomy that extended over an area of 12,710 square kilometres, including the towns of Târgu Mureş, Odorheiu Secuiesc, Sfântu Gheorghe and Şumuleu-Ciuc (now part of Miercurea-Ciuc). Their area was divided into seven districts, called 'seats' (*sedes*, Hung. *szék*), six of which formed a coherent block in the south-eastern end of Transylvania, while the seventh seat, Aranyosszék, (of only 345 sq. km) lay apart in the proximity of Turda. From the thirteenth century the whole community was governed by a count (*comes Siculorum*) who was a Hungarian lord. He was appointed by the king and governed the Székely independently from the voivode of Transylvania, with whom he was more or less equal in rank. From 1462 his dignity was united, with short interruptions, with that of the voivode who thereby became the governor of the Székely.

The Székely of the Middle Ages were a well organised community of warriors living off cattle breeding. Their main duty was to perform military service whenever required. They served as light horsemen in the royal army and throughout the centuries preserved elements of nomadic warfare. They did not pay tax, but they owed the king a gift, called 'ox-branding', at the time of his coronation, his wedding and the birth of his heir. On these three occasions each household was to give the king an ox marked with his sign. The political and social order of the Székely, threefold in its nature, was also quite different from that in any other part of the kingdom. The 'seats' were the territorial units of jurisdiction and administration. From the social point of view, the whole people were divided into three 'orders': the 'notables' (*primores*), the *lófő* (*primipili*; a class of subaltern officers) and the 'community' of ordinary people. From a military point of view, all were organised into six 'tribes', each consisting of four 'branches'. Neither of these forms of classification were ethnically or territorially based; rather, they provided the framework for Székely military and political organisation. In the event of war, each 'branch' had to equip one hundred horsemen. All Székely being freemen, there were no tenants among them and the institution of seigneury was unknown. Fields under cultivation were divided equally among the 'branches', all other land remaining the undivided property of a 'tribe'. Neither pasture nor arable was allowed to become individual property, but was drawn by the members of the community for a year or more by means of bow shots. All these details are known from records that date from no earlier than the end of the Middle Ages, for the Székely community functioned verbally and had little need for writing. Yet their social organisation was obviously archaic in nature and must have been of very ancient origin. Indeed, it could be held to be a copy of the tenth-century organisation of the pagan Hungarians.

The origins of the Székely are a mystery and have been an object of endless scholarly debate. The only point on which there is general agreement is that they were a separate ethnic group, that is, a people. They were mentioned as such for the first time in 1116 when they fought along with the Pechenegs in the army of Stephen II. It has often been supposed that they could have been a Turkic tribe that had once joined the Magyars, but no evidence has been found to support this view. The language of the Székely is purely Hungarian, coloured by Romanian loan-words but without any trace of a Turkic substratum. Moreover, apart from a small Slav group, the toponyms of the Székely lands are also Hungarian. Yet it is evident that the Székely were not Magyars. Not only did the Hungarians hold them to be a foreign people, the Székely had their own ethnic identity as well. They held themselves to be the descendants of the Huns and thus related to the Magyars, but they bore the conviction that their ancestors had already been living in the Carpathian basin when the Hungarians arrived. They had a runic alphabet, probably of Turk origin, as early as the thirteenth century. It was thought to be a Székely speciality and remained in use until the early modern period.

Originally the Székely, like the Pechenegs, lived in widely dispersed groups throughout Hungary. Small districts inhabited by them existed in the west, on the River Morava, in the south around Nagyváty (in Baranya), in the east around Tileagd (in Bihor), while a large group lived, until the arrival of the Saxons, in southern Transylvania around

Sebeş, Gârbova (Orbó) and Saschiz (Kézd). At some time during the twelfth and thirteenth centuries most of these communities were transferred, clearly by royal initiative and probably not by a single act, into the area that was to be their permanent home. It was an area that had only a sparse Hungarian and Slav population. Those who came from the land taken by the Saxons named their seats of Sebes, Orbó and Kézd after their previous settlements. That the Székely had been gathered from different regions of the kingdom is shown by their dialects, which show curious resemblances with certain idioms spoken in distant parts of Hungary.

THE ROMANIANS

The Romanians who now form the great majority of the population in Transylvania are first mentioned by Anonymus. According to him, Transylvania was inhabited by 'Vlachs' and Slavs at the time of the Conquest and was ruled by the Vlach prince, Gelou. After Gelou was killed by the Hungarians in a battle near the River Someş, his subjects elected Tuhutum, one of the 'seven dukes', as their prince. The great-grandson of Tuhutum was 'Gyula minor', whose land was then conquered by King Stephen.[13] The problems that arise from Anonymus's story are of a different nature from those that concern the origin of the Székely, but they are equally difficult to resolve.

On the one hand, Anonymus's statement that 'Vlachs' (whom we must take to be Romanians) inhabited Transylvania before the arrival of the Hungarians appears convincing for several reasons and has, indeed, been widely accepted. First, a great part of Transylvania, including the region of Cluj, where Gelou is said to have been killed, had once formed part of the Roman province of Dacia, and it seems reasonable to suppose that the Romanians of Transylvania were the descendants of the Roman or romanised population of Dacia. Second, Romanians living in Transylvania occur as early as about 1200 in the very first surviving documents that concern Transylvania. Third, Romanians, as well as localities inhabited by them, are mentioned in hundreds of instances throughout eastern Hungary from the fourteenth century onwards, when written documents become abundant. Finally, with the exception of the Székely area and of some ethnic islands elsewhere, Hungarians were clearly outnumbered by Romanians in the modern period when we first possess reliable data concerning population and its ethnic distribution, and it seems reasonable to suppose that this had always been the case.

On the other hand, accepting this hypothesis raises serious difficulties. First, while all other inhabitants of the region were Roman

Catholic before the Reformation, the Romanians were of the Orthodox faith. They followed the Old Slavonic rite and had the patriarch of Ohrid (in Macedonia) as their spiritual head until the late fourteenth century. In order to explain the striking difference of faith between ethnic groups we have to suppose that all Romanians had been converted to Orthodoxy by the time that the Catholic mission or the Hungarian immigration began. Yet no early traces of Orthodoxy can be found in the region. Early Romanian churches are known in the region of Hunedoara, and some of them date back to the thirteenth century, but no other Romanian churches or monasteries of ancient origin are known to have existed elsewhere. At the same time hundreds of Catholic parishes were recorded throughout Transylvania by the papal tax-collectors between 1332 and 1337, and many of their churches have survived.

It is even more difficult to harmonise the evidence of Anonymus with toponyms. Firstly, Romanian place names abound, and are in fact dominant, in all those parts of eastern Hungary which were, and partly still are, covered with forests and were thus areas of secondary human settlement. All these regions, mostly lying in the mountains, seem to have been colonised during the later Middle Ages. On many occasions even the time and circumstances of the original settlement can be established by written sources. Secondly, Romanian toponyms are missing in all those regions where early settlement could be expected and where, indeed, in many cases it can be verified by archaeological evidence. Hence the names of all important localities in Transylvania seem to have been taken over by the Romanians from another language.

A good many rivers and localities, some of them important, have an evidently Slav name, like the River Târnava or the towns of Bǎlgrad (now Alba Iulia) and Bistriţa. A much larger number of toponyms are obviously Hungarian, like the towns of Sebeş (Szászsebes), Mediaş (Medgyes), Sighişoara (Segesvár), Hunedoara (Hunyadvár), Haţeg (Hátszeg) or Orǎştie (Szászváros), along with dozens of villages. There are toponyms that are known to have been old Hungarian personal names like Dǎbâca (Doboka), Turda (Torda) or Dej (Dés). There are even place names that were borrowed by the Romanians from the Saxons, such as Nocrich (Neukirch, later Leschkirch) or Viscri (Weißkirch), while the name of Saschiz must have come from the Hungarian Szászkézd. This Hungarian name, meaning 'Kézd of the Saxons', must have been born well after the German colonisation. There are hundreds of other toponyms that Hungarian linguists regard as being of Hungarian origin. Even if some may be doubtful, hardly any of these names can be explained by reference to Romanian. Hence, if any weight is to be given to toponymic evidence, it can be stated with certainty that in all parts of Transylvania that seem to have been inhabited before the thirteenth century, Romanian presence was always preceded by Slav, Hungarian and even Saxon settlement. This is true, for example, of the region of Cluj, where according to Anonymus, Wallachians were living in about 900.

It is not easy to reconcile such contradictory evidence. There must have been a Romanian population in Transylvania well before the time of Anonymus, and since he thought them to be the native population there their number cannot have been wholly insignificant. However, their early presence in the central and northern counties is highly improbable. When they appear about 1200 they are living in the south-ernmost regions of Transylvania, on and below the slopes of the southern Carpathians, their land (*terra Blacorum*) bordering upon the territory of the Teutonic Knights in the east and that of the Saxons of Sibiu in the west. This land, later called Făgăraş, was to remain until the end of the Middle Ages a separate Romanian district, not melting into the Saxon lands nor becoming a county of Transylvania. There must have been many Romanians in the county of Hunedoara, a region where they are in evidence as early as about 1250, and maybe also in the mountains south of Caransebeş. In other parts of Transylvania their numbers may have been small at this time, for in 1293 King Andrew III thought it possible to gather 'all the Wallachians living on the estates of the nobles and of anyone else' on the royal domain of Armeni (near Alba Iulia).[14]

For a long time the main occupation of the Romanians was sheep-breeding. Just like the Székely and the Pechenegs, their service during this early period seems to have involved guarding the frontiers. Being Orthodox, they were exempt from the ecclesiastical tithe, but they paid the king of Hungary a special tax in sheep, called 'the fiftieth' (*quin-quagesima*), which was to remain typical of the Romanian population throughout the Middle Ages. They grazed their livestock in the mountains in summer and in the valleys in winter, and their name became so closely attached to this form of sheep-breeding that all those who lived in this way in the Carpathian basin, even in Slovakia, were later referred to as 'Vlachs' regardless of their language.

THE ORDER OF NOBLES

One of the important developments of these decades seems to have been the increasing political influence of the nobility as a social class. It is shown, in the first place, by the diet, a new institution inspired by corporative thinking imported from the West. At the same time local autonomies of the nobility were also taking shape, while the exact nature of noble status and the basic privileges of the noble order were definitively laid down. Lastly, the central ideas that were to dominate the mentality of the noble class for centuries were first formulated during these decades.

After 1260 there is clear evidence of the new-found identity of the nobles as a separate order within society. In 1267, during the course of an otherwise little-known assembly at Esztergom, 'the nobles of all Hungary, who are called royal servants' forced Béla IV and his son to issue a charter confirming their most important liberties, which were in fact almost identical to those laid down in different words by the Golden Bull of 1222.[15] The confirmation of noble liberties was soon followed by the demand that the nobility as a whole should be given a role in the government of the kingdom. Accordingly, from 1277, their delegates can be found at the parliaments that were convened with growing frequency, and in 1290 their elected representatives were admitted for the first time, if only temporarily, into the royal council, hitherto reserved for the prelates and the barons. The emergence of parliamentary ideas is known to have been a general phenomenon in Latin Europe in the thirteenth century. That they came to Hungary at a relatively early stage was certainly due to the influence of a clerical elite whose members are known to have studied law in Bologna, where they were imbued with the most advanced political ideas of the age.

The beginnings of local autonomies of the nobility, each organised within a royal county, seem to go back to the time of the Golden Bull. As early as 1232 'the royal servants living on both sides of the River Zala' held an assembly at Kehida (north of Nagykanizsa).[16] It seems that they represented a social group that was later to form the nobility of Zala county. We may assume that there were similar events in other counties at this time or even earlier, but they have left no written traces. Immediately after the assembly of 1267, four 'judges' chosen from among the local nobility were at work in several counties of Transdanubia, their duty being to revise existing property rights under the direction of the count. It is disputed whether these committees, appointed by the king, could be regarded as the origins of future noble self-government, but they certainly had a very similar constitution.

The corporative body of a 'noble county' in its classic form occurs for the first time in Bodrog county in 1280. It consisted of magistrates called 'the judges of the nobles' (*iudices nobilium*), with the representative of the count at their head. The 'judges of the nobles' were elected, at least in the fifteenth century and later, by the community of nobles of the county. Their number was four as a rule, with the exception of Transylvania, Slavonia and some other counties, where there were only two. The head of the body was appointed by the count from among his retainers, and was titled 'curial count' in the beginning and 'deputy count' (*vicecomes*) from the mid-fourteenth century. Fifty-one counties in Hungary proper and six in Transylvania are known to have had this sort of autonomy before 1350 (their number being about twenty in 1300).

The ideas concerning the origin and nature of noble status were developed by Simon Kézai, chaplain of King Ladislaus IV, who wrote a 'History of the Hungarians' (*Gesta Ungarorum*) between 1282 and 1285. It seems that he was not a university graduate and it was probably during his travels as a diplomat in Italy and France that he became acquainted with modern political ideas.

As a historian, Kézai was able to draw information from his predecessors whose works have been lost. When these were composed and what they contained can only be deduced, with much uncertainty, from the collation of Kézai's text with the fourteenth-century Illuminated Chronicle and its variants, which drew on the same sources. Philological analysis has shown that the earliest piece of work on Hungarian history must have been written at some time in the late eleventh century by a cleric of a sharply anti-pagan disposition. This early composition, called the 'primeval gesta' by modern philologists, seems to have been continued by other authors until 1167. Around 1270 a new version of these texts was prepared, markedly aristocratic in its tone and generally attributed to 'Master' Ákos, a high-born prelate and chancellor of Queen Mary under Béla IV. Kézai seems to have relied on this version when composing his own work.

As regards Hungarian history proper, Kézai did not add much to his sources except a narrative of the events of his own time. Much more important were the additions that he made for ideological reasons. It was Kézai who first formulated the idea of a common origin and ethnic identity of the Huns and the Hungarians. He could find plenty of allusions to this identity in the works of Western authors, but whereas they referred to this relationship as something shameful, Kézai made it a source of glory and derived historical rights from it. According to him, the ancestors of the two peoples were Hunor and Magor, sons of Nimrod in the Old Testament, and their descendants 'differed from each other in their language only, like the Saxons and the Thuringians'.[17] At the beginning of his work he inserted a long history of Attila and the Huns, meant as the first and glorious chapter of early Hungarian history. To build up his story he drew on the works of classical authors, as well as on his own imagination. What he wanted to emphasise was that the Hungarians had gained a right to their homeland through Attila; that the warriors of Árpád had in fact taken back what already belonged to them.

Although probably of servile birth himself, Kézai was much concerned with the origins of the nobility. He was keen to emphasise that the 'pure Hungarian people' consisted only of the offspring of those who had come from Scythia, while the others, who later mingled with them, were 'foreigners or descended from prisoners of war'.[18] To his work he annexed a list of forty or so illustrious kindreds that he considered to be of foreign origin. He also explained how the noble caste had come into being. In the pagan era, he argued, those who absented themselves from the army without good reason were executed, exiled or sentenced to eternal serfdom on the basis of the 'Scythian law'. This is the reason why 'although all the Hungarians were begot by the same father and mother, some of them are now called noble, and the others ignoble.'[19] According to his conception, the Hungarian 'people' was identical to the 'community' of the nobility. Its members constituted the 'nation' and were linked to one another not only by common law and language but also by blood relationship. We shall see that these ideas were to exert a lasting influence upon political thinking in Hungary.

THE EXPANSION OF WRITTEN RECORDS

The second half of the thirteenth century saw the rapid expansion of written records, a development that was partly due to the exigencies of government, but even more to the growing demands of the nobility.

The initiative came from the royal chancellery, which began to acquire the form of a writing office in the late twelfth century. From the time of Andrew II it had become customary for royal grants and judicial decisions to be recorded in writing. It was Béla IV who took the first steps in using written records for administrative purposes. From about 1250 it became usual practice for the king to send writs to the counts and other dignitaries, expecting written reports from them confirming that his orders had been duly carried out. At the same time the activity of the judicial courts became increasingly professional, which further increased the production of official documents. From the years after 1260 the judge royal and his deputy acted, in the name of the king, as the royal 'personal presence'. They held their court at Buda, which thus began to function for the first time as the kingdom's capital.

Documents issued by the chancellery and central courts were supplemented by those produced by the 'places of authentication' (*loca credibilia*), a legal institution peculiar to Hungary. A 'place of authentication' was a cathedral chapter or monastery that was obliged to take part in royal administration and to offer notarial services for laymen. The beginnings of the institution can be traced back to the eleventh century. In lawsuits between laymen it became customary for oaths to be taken and ordeals to be administered by a chapter. In about 1200 at the latest, the chapters began to keep written records of the cases that came before them, the earliest and most outstanding example of this being the *Regestrum Varadinense*, which contains the minutes of 389 ordeals held at the chapter of Oradea between 1208 and 1235.

About the middle of the thirteenth century it had become customary for nobles to turn to the nearest chapter or monastery as a place of authentication in order to have their cases put down in writing. In return for a fee, the clerics were expected to prepare the document required and even to store it securely in their sacristy. They drew up contracts that later came to be referred to as 'confessions' (*fassio*), and they were also authorised to issue authentic copies (*transsumptum*) of any document kept by or presented to them. Yet the most burdensome of their duties was to bear witness to the scene of any sort of legal act. They were to attest to how estates were divided or their boundaries fixed. In the case of a royal grant, a writ ordered them to witness the investiture. They would then draw up a record of it for the grantee and send a report to the chancellery. Many of their activities arose from lawsuits. They had to be present when plaints were examined, summonses handed over, witnesses questioned or a judgement carried out, and it was also before them that one could announce a protest, make an oath and give powers of attorney.

The places of authentication left no room for the institution of notaries. When they appeared in Hungary, after 1300, their activity was restricted to the field of canon law. Private charters soon fell out of use, being replaced during the thirteenth century by the notion of the 'authentic record'. This was the collective name for documents that the courts were willing to accept as written proof. Besides charters issued by the king and the judges of the realm, such legal force was especially attached to documents drawn up by a place of authentication.

As to the number of places of authentication, the activity of some 20 minor convents was stopped by law in 1351, and until the Turkish occupation 38 chapters and convents (34 in Hungary proper, two in Transylvania and two in Slavonia) functioned as such. They included all fifteen cathedral chapters (the 'canonically united' archbishopric of Kalocsa-Bač having two seats and, thus two chapters), nine of the collegiate churches (Arad, Buda, Čazma, Požega, Pressburg, Spišská Kapitula, Székesfehérvár, Titel, Vasvár), eight major Benedictine abbeys (Cluj-Mănăştur, Hronský Beňadik, Pannonhalma, Pécsvárad, Somogyvár, Szekszárd, Zalavár, Zobor), five Premonstratensian monasteries (Csorna, Jasov, Kláštor pod Znievom, Leleś, Šahy) and the house of the Knights Hospitaller at Székesfehérvár. The last of these, as well as the chapters of Székesfehérvár, Buda and (from 1498) Bosnia had a competence extending throughout the kingdom, while the activity of the rest was restricted to one, two or three counties.

Chapter 8

Charles I of Anjou (1301–1342)

The two centuries that followed the extinction of the Árpádians have long been referred to as the age of the 'kings of various dynasties'. The period was shaped by four outstanding rulers, and the significance of each has been fully appreciated by modern historical writing. In the past, however, the notion of glory was attached only to the reigns of the truly 'national' kings, Louis the Great and Matthias Corvinus. The importance of Charles I of Anjou and Sigismund of Luxembourg, both of them regarded as 'foreigners', was only to be discovered by twentieth-century historiography.

THE 'OLIGARCHS'

With the death of Andrew III 'the last golden branch' broke off from the tree of Saint Stephen's family, as a contemporary put it.[1] The extinction of the dynasty came at a time of serious crisis for royal authority. In the midst of the anarchic conditions that prevailed during the reigns of the last Árpádians, huge territories slipped from the ruler's effective control and were appropriated by certain barons to form semi-independent provinces. Although most of them recognised Andrew III's nominal authority, his death unleashed centrifugal forces. Central power practically ceased to exist. That the kingdom might fragment into several independent provinces became a real possibility. These years are often referred to as the *interregnum*, yet this word is not really appropriate, for the realm did have kings – indeed, more than were needed.

Each of the baronial 'provinces' consisted in fact of a number of neighbouring counties over which a high dignitary exerted royal prerogatives. There was nothing unusual in this, for the kingdom had been governed in this way since its very foundation. What was new was that the authority of the baron was supported by his private lands, which were often of enormous extent. His authority tended, therefore, to become gradually more permanent and irrevocable. As long as the old regime functioned, the king was able to replace any governor or count at any time according to his will. In the years after 1272 he became less and less able to do this, and many counties became practically, if not legally, the hereditary provinces of a baron.

The nuclei of these provinces were almost everywhere the private domains of a noble kindred. Ever since the barons had been permitted to construct castles on their own estates, they had had the opportunity openly to oppose royal power whenever the occasion arose. In this they could naturally count on the support of their kinsmen, and their growing power lured many of the local nobility into their service. From the moment they received the legal authorisation to govern the county where their estates were dominant, their private lordship was combined with an official power and with the judicial authority that went with it. From this moment on they had under their command not only their private followers, but also the royal castles together with the associated military force of the castle warriors.

Although the available evidence does not allow us to form a clear picture of how each of these provinces was established and grew, the main lines of the process are more or less clear. One of the mightiest local powers, centred in Vas county, was founded by Henry Héder, palatine of Béla IV. By 1270 he already had the castle of Kőszeg and three other fortresses by hereditary right, and it was due to them that he was an important player in the war between Stephen V and Otakar Přemysl II. His sons continued to enhance the family patrimony by means of purchases and exchanges. They soon managed to subdue all the other local powers in their region and they also secured a firm foothold in Slavonia. In 1284 Ladislaus IV tried to drive them out of their castles, but to no avail. In 1289 Albert of Habsburg, duke of Austria, launched a large-scale attack against them, took some of their fortresses, but was unable to break them completely. Immediately after his accession, Andrew III tried to find a *modus vivendi* with them. He gave them the offices of the palatine, the *magister tavarnicorum* and the ban of Slavonia, but even this liberality failed to satisfy them. In 1291 they went over to the Angevin party and overtly opposed the king. By then John Héder virtually owned the county of Vas, and held a regular judicial court at Sárvár. Andrew marched against him several times and was able to prevent him from expanding his power, but that was all he could do. The part of the realm that was in the hands of the Héder brothers was practically lost to him.

By the time of the extinction of the Árpádian dynasty a number of local powers similar to that of the Héder had emerged throughout the realm. Matthew Csák, son of Peter the palatine, who chose the castle of Trenčín as his residence, ruled over the valley of the River Váh with the title of palatine. Stephen Ákos, another 'palatine', had a castle built for himself at Diósgyőr (today part of Miskolc), whence he governed the counties of Borsod and Gemer. The north-eastern counties from the Polish frontier to the Tisza were ruled by 'Palatine' Amadeus Aba. Beyond the Tisza, in Bihor and the neighbouring counties, the 'voivode', Roland Borsa, and his brothers built up their province. From the end of the thirteenth century, Transylvania was governed by the voivode, Ladislaus Kán. Authority over Srem between the Rivers Drava and Sava was in the hands of Ugrinus, another member of the Csák kindred, who had begun his career under Béla IV and was now *magister tavarnicorum*. Somogy together with other counties formed the province of Ban Henry Héder junior, who also controlled northern Slavonia. Southern Slavonia was in the hands of the Croatian Babonić brothers, while Croatia and the cities of Dalmatia were governed by Count Paul Šubić.

FAMILIARITAS

The power of the 'oligarchs' was, in essence, based upon their castles and their armed retinues. In the thirteenth century those who entered the service of a baron, prelate or other illustrious person were called 'servants' (*servientes*). In the later Middle Ages such a man became known as a *familiaris*, and thus the relationship itself has been termed *familiaritas* in modern historiography.

The armed retinue itself must have been as long-established in Hungary as it was elsewhere. The laws of Saint Stephen had already taken it for granted that all counts should have their own warriors, and it is difficult to imagine the other high office-holders of the kingdom being without them. Thirteenth-century evidence suggests that the followings of great men were still largely made up of kinsmen (*fratres et proximi*). The Hungarian nobility attributed particular importance to ties based on blood relationship. It was, therefore, not at all surprising that the members of a comital kindred should most willingly serve the person who had emerged from among them to become a baron; and it was equally natural that a baron should look among his own kin for his trusted followers rather than among strangers. Besides relatives, there must have been persons of servile status in the following right from the beginning, since, as one of Stephen's laws shows, the king himself had the right to put a serf at the head of a county.

By the time that the evidence becomes more abundant in the fourteenth-century, it is clear that the armed following was no longer restricted to a great man's own kinsmen. For the most part it was composed of lesser noblemen who entered the service of a greater lord not because of kinship, but in search of advancement. Their service usually lasted until the death of one of the parties. Once engaged, the retainer became a member of his lord's household, ate at the latter's table, was given full supplies and other benefits, in return for which he owed unconditional fidelity to his lord and had constantly to be at his disposal.

The essence of this relationship was well expressed by the word *cseléd*, the Hungarian counterpart of *familiaris*. Until quite recently, this was the name given to 'non-noble' (*ignobilis*) servants, who lived in their master's dwelling and did all kinds of service in and around the house. Until the end of the Middle Ages it also referred to the noble-born servant, who was equally a member of his lord's household, but whose service had to be compatible with his social standing. This service was above all, but not exclusively, of a military character. The noble retainers made up the lord's armed following and fought in his contingent in the event of war. But they also gave him counsel in times of peace; governed his castles, estates and people; collected his revenues; administered justice in his place; and, at least those who had the necessary qualifications, drafted his letters or represented him before the law. Naturally, the advantages of the service were proportional to the lord's social status. If he became a baron, his leading retainers themselves moved into higher positions, their task being to govern in his name the castles and estates that pertained to his office. Far from being a private affair between lord and servant, *familiaritas* had, therefore, assumed a clear political nature.

With the emergence of the baronial 'provinces', the value of these retainers increased, but the nature of the relationship itself also changed. In the counties that were appropriated by one of the barons, the local nobility entered his service as a matter of course. But, whereas the engagement had hitherto been strictly voluntary, now in many cases it became obligatory. The lord of the province would expect at least the wealthier noblemen to join his following, and would in any case try to prevent their entering another lord's service, even that of the king. In 1311, when by chance we are allowed a glimpse of the 46 most important followers of Amadeus Aba, we find in the list almost all the illustrious noblemen of the counties of Abaúj, Šariš, Zemplín and Ung. Many of them owned a castle and they would also have had their own armed retinues.

Familiaritas is sometimes referred to as the Hungarian counterpart of vassalage, but this comparison is in several respects misleading. The *familiaris* was not a vassal, since he did not have a fief. His engagement did not involve his land, only his person. His hereditary land was not in any way affected by his service. He was to account for his deeds not before the court of his lord but before that of the king. It was often the case that the sons of one and the same father served different lords. Their legal status was the same as that of other noblemen who did not engage themselves. It should also be noted that the kind of social equality of lord and vassal that was expressed in the ceremony of homage was missing in the case of *familiaritas*. In the eyes of a lord his *familiaris* was not a companion but a servant, a person of a rank much inferior to himself.

Although the territorial power of the barons paralysed government, it did not pose a direct threat to the survival of kingship. The notion that their provinces were parts of the realm was so deeply rooted in their minds that they did not for a moment consider leaving the throne vacant. Yet the extinction of the dynasty presented the ecclesiastical and lay lords with an unusual dilemma: is the throne in a case like this heritable or elective? It was at this time that this question first emerged, and it was to remain a constant political problem thereafter.

THE ACCESSION OF CHARLES I

By right of inheritance the primary candidate was Charles of Anjou. At first he had very few supporters apart from the Šubić in Croatia and Ugrinus Csák, but he could count on the whole-hearted backing of Pope Boniface VIII. The Pope, overlord of the kingdom of Naples, hoped that the accession of the Angevins to the throne of Hungary would lead to the expansion of papal influence. In the spring of 1301, while the leading barons were still hesitating, Charles suddenly entered Esztergom with a tiny escort. The archbishop-elect, Gregory, who was a partisan of the Pope's, promptly crowned Charles with a provisional crown. Henceforth Charles regarded himself as the lawful lord of the kingdom and always counted his regnal years from this event.

In the eyes of most of the barons papal support was by no means a good recommendation. They did not accept Charles's coronation, pointing out that it had not been properly carried out. The principle according to which a valid coronation must involve the Holy Crown and take place in the church of Székesfehérvár was first formulated during these years, and was to be frequently invoked in the future. Accordingly, the leading barons insisted that the throne should be filled by election, and they chose not Charles, but Wenceslas, son and heir of Wenceslas II of Bohemia. They could argue that the young prince had some Árpádian blood in his veins, his great-grandmother being Béla IV's daughter, and that he was betrothed to Elizabeth, Andrew III's daughter, even if the marriage did not finally take place.

Yet the strongest argument in his favour must have been that he, like Charles, was still a minor. Consequently, the barons, at least for the time being, had no reason to be anxious about their power. On 27 August 1301, after his father had escorted him to Hungary, the young Wenceslas was crowned with the Holy Crown by the archbishop of Kalocsa at Székesfehérvár.

Wenceslas, who as king of Hungary used the name Ladislaus, set up his residence at Buda. His rule was strictly nominal, his actions being limited to the rewarding of his partisans. 'The barons,' says the chronicle, 'did not concede him a single castle, nor any sort of power or office, not even a parcel of royal authority.'[2] Charles retired to the 'province' of Ugrinus Csák in southern Hungary and spent the following years there. The war between him and Wenceslas broke out immediately and led to ever growing anarchy. The Héder, who had been Charles's supporters before 1301, now went over to Wenceslas and had conquered almost the whole of Transdanubia by 1304. In 1302 Matthew Csák persuaded Wenceslas to give him the counties of Trenčín and Nitra as a perpetual grant, and soon occupied the counties of Hont, Bars and Komárno as well. A clear sign of the prevailing anarchy is that no fewer than seven barons used the title of palatine during these years, and that at least four of them exercised effective palatine authority in their own provinces. Central government was virtually non-existent, and it seems that most of the offices, among them that of the judge royal, remained vacant.

It was Charles who gradually gained the upper hand. As early as the autumn of 1301, at the council of Buda, the papal legate, Nicholas, bishop of Ostia, had persuaded most of the bishops to go over to Charles. Even more decisive was the intervention of Charles's maternal uncles, Albert of Habsburg, king of Germany and his brother, Rudolf, duke of Austria. As a result of this, most of the barons had joined the Angevin party by the beginning of 1304. In the summer of the same year Wenceslas's situation seemed so hopeless that his father came to take him, together with the Holy Crown, back to Bohemia; and in the autumn of 1304 it was Charles and Albert who conducted a campaign into the very heart of Bohemia. When in 1305 the young Wenceslas acceded to the Bohemian throne, he abandoned his claims in Hungary, transferring them, together with the regalia, to his relative, Otto, duke of Bavaria.

Otto, being Béla IV's grandson through his mother, had indeed some right to the Hungarian throne, but he had little chance of securing it. Although the Héder and the Saxons of Transylvania went over to him, that was all the support he could muster. He managed to find two bishops to crown him at Székesfehérvár on 6 December 1305, and then wandered aimlessly throughout the country. Finally, in the spring of 1307, Ladislaus Kán, with whom Otto was seeking to establish a family tie, arrested him in Transylvania, deprived him of the Crown and sent him home. Otto continued to use the Hungarian royal title until his death in 1312, but he made no further attempts to recover his kingdom.

With Otto's departure, Charles was unrivalled on the battlefield. He occupied Esztergom in 1306 and took Buda a year later. Being a determined supporter of Wenceslas, the city had been under interdiction since 1302, but some 'false priests' continued to administer the sacraments and, 'adding insult to injury', went as far as to excommunicate the Pope and all the prelates who adhered to Charles.[3] In June 1307 Charles's followers took the city through treason, tortured two councillors to death and let the rebellious priests perish in prison. The judge was replaced by a royal governor, called a *rector*, and Buda was not to recover its self-governing status until 1346. This last victory was followed by a diet on 10 October 1307 on the field of Rákos, where Amadeus Aba, James Borsa, Ugrinus Csák and some other lords solemnly declared Charles the lawful ruler of the kingdom.

In stabilising his rule Charles could rely on further papal assistance. In the spring of 1308, Cardinal Gentile da Montefiore, the legate of Clement V, arrived in Hungary and, combining pleas with threats, persuaded Matthew Csák and the Héder to submit. At the same time he found himself confronted by the cult of the Holy Crown. He was unable to gain acceptance for the validity of Charles's first coronation; and a second ceremony, in 1309 in the church of Our Lady at Buda in which the cardinal officiated using a crown that he had consecrated himself, also proved ineffective. 'Public opinion' insisted, as the cardinal was forced to realise, that a valid coronation could only be performed with the Holy Crown. The question of legitimacy was only settled when the legate managed to persuade Ladislaus Kán to restore the holy diadem, with which a third and final coronation, faultless in every respect, was carried out 'with great solemnity and joy' on 27 August 1310.[4] With the kingdom now having a legitimate ruler, recognised by everybody, the period of the 'interregnum' was over. The only question was whether or not the formal restoration of the monarchy would be followed by the effective restoration of royal authority.

WAR AGAINST THE OLIGARCHY

Initially obliged to adapt to the existing situation, Charles tried to govern in co-operation with the oligarchs. He distributed the offices of state among them, being at pains not to offend any of them. But also from the outset, he was determined to make full use of his royal prerogatives. He insisted on the restoration of all the estates and revenues usurped from the royal demesne and the Church, and that the barons should give up the practice of forcing the nobility of their provinces to enter their service. This led to a long and desperate war that lasted until 1323. During the conflict the new foundations of royal authority were laid down, and by the time the fighting ended the Angevin monarchy had been born.

The long series of conflicts began with the war against Matthew Csák. The former palatine had submitted himself to the king with much reluctance and did not attend his coronation. He later refused to comply with the king's demands. In the spring of 1311 Charles deprived Matthew of the office of *magister tavarnicorum*, had him excommunicated by Cardinal Gentile, and then took the field against him. The scene of the war soon shifted to north-eastern Hungary, where Amadeus Aba happened to die in a revolt that had broken out at Košice in September 1311. Charles saw the opportunity to profit from the event to subdue Amadeus's province, but the latter's sons turned to Matthew Csák for help. Matthew sent a large army to lay siege to Košice, and it was against this army that Charles had to fight his first major battle at Rozhanovce (Hung. Rozgony, east of Košice) on 15 June 1312. According to a contemporary, no battle as bloody as this had taken place in the kingdom 'since the time of the Mongols', and 'although more men fell on the king's side, it was he who won a glorious victory.'[5] The battle is often seen as a decisive turning point in the long fight against the oligarchs. In fact, it meant no more than that the monarchy had stood the first test. The most difficult phase of the war lay in the future.

In 1313 Charles was able to take Trnava from Matthew, but he had soon to realise that he could not rely on his barons' support. In order to encircle Matthew he renewed the alliance with his cousin, Frederick III of Austria, in the summer of 1314. He also made contact with John of Luxembourg, the new king of Bohemia. A joint campaign was arranged for the next year, but Charles was unable to take part, for at the diet held in August 1314 the oligarchs openly refused to support him. Determined to accept the challenge, the king declared his opponents rebels, deprived them of their offices and set up a new government, recruited from among his knights. At the same time he began a war against the recalcitrant barons and in the spring of 1315 transferred his residence from the centre of the kingdom to Timişoara.

The long series of victories that followed during the next few years is difficult to explain, bearing in mind that virtually the whole kingdom was aligned against Charles. The only territory firmly held by him was the former province of Ugrinus, who had died in 1311 leaving a young son as heir. It was from this region that the king recruited most of his first followers. In addition, he could count on the support of the prelates, whom he had bought off with major concessions in 1313. He could also rely on the devotion of those members of the lesser nobility who were seeking refuge under the royal banner against the oligarchs, and on the towns, although these were of limited importance at this time. Charles's final victory seems to have been the result of the coincidence of favourable circumstances. The barons were apparently reluctant to unite their forces and oppose the legitimate ruler in open rebellion. This gave the king the opportunity of suppressing them one by one. Each victory was to increase the king's prestige and at the same time attracted new followers to his camp. The help that came from Austria should also not be underestimated.

Charles achieved his first major success in the north, where Donch, lord of Zvolen, joined him as early as 1314. In the winter of 1314–15 he restored order in the region of Spis and Šaríš, then moved swiftly against the Borsa and the Kán, both of whom he forced to sign a truce. Having thus secured his back, in the spring of 1316 he turned against the Héder. It now became clear how fragile a base the seemingly solid lordships of the oligarchs had been built upon. When the king appeared on the scene, the province of John Héder in southern Transdanubia collapsed within a couple of weeks. The nobility of the counties of Baranya, Somogy and Tolna welcomed the king as liberator. Many castles surrendered without resistance, while the remaining ones were taken one by one by a royal army that became stronger by the day.

THE YEARS OF DECISION

The decisive phase of the war came in 1317. Fighting was still going on in the west against the Héder, when Palatine James Borsa, alias Kopasz, and his brothers denounced the treaty that had been signed in 1315, and entered into an alliance with Peter, son of Petenye, upon whom Charles himself had conferred the government of Abaúj and Zemplín. It was said that they planned to give the throne to one of the Russian princes of Galicia. Meanwhile Stephen Uroš II, king of Serbia, attacked the region of Srem. Charles himself turned against Uroš, and, having crossed the frozen Sava, took the castle of Mačva. By the time of his return, his lieutenants had already routed Kopasz near Debrecen around March 1317 and occupied the rebels' fortresses in northern and eastern Hungary. In June Charles personally directed the siege of Adrian, Kopasz's residence. After its fall, Kopasz shut himself in his castle of Şoimi, deep in the forests, but the royal army starved him into surrender and led him to the king in irons.

After the suppression of the revolt in the east the king marched against Matthew Csák. While his lieutenants laid siege to Visegrád, he himself took Komárno in October 1317, with the help of Frederick of Austria. Having lost two important strongholds, Matthew accepted a truce. At the same time, Frederick's intervention exposed the vulnerability of Andrew Héder, lord of western Transdanubia, and he consequently came to the royal camp at Komárno to surrender. He was allowed to retain the county of Vas, but was forced to hand over all of his other castles.

The war was still far from over, however. John Héder continued to resist in Slavonia for several years and was joined by Andrew in 1319. They did not lay down their arms until 1321, and even then managed to preserve much of their power. The situation in Transylvania was also undecided for some years. Here the resistance was led by Moses Ákos, Kopasz's son-in-law. Although Dózsa of Debrecen, Charles's voivode, marched triumphantly into Cluj during the summer of 1318, he only managed to defeat Moses in 1320. The decisive pacification of the province was carried out in 1321 when the new voivode, Thomas Szécsényi, deprived the sons of Ladislaus Kán of their castles. Meanwhile, as the truce expired, the war with Matthew Csák and his allies flared up again. In 1319 the royal army laid siege to Diósgyőr, which was the residence of the sons of Stephen Ákos; then, in 1320, the fortresses in the counties of Gemer, Heves and Nógrád were wrested from the hands of Matthew's partisans. The last obstacle to the final restoration of peace and order was Matthew himself, who still had firm control of a number of almost impregnable castles along the River Váh. Charles hesitated to launch an attack against him, but was assisted by fortune. In March 1321 Matthew died without a male heir, and his province immediately broke up. The royal army occupied it virtually without resistance, and in July 1321 Trenčín was forced to surrender by Charles himself.

The exhausting war had come to an end. In order to complete the work of consolidation, Charles went to Slavonia in the autumn of 1322. He took the office of ban from his former supporter, John Babonić, and conferred it upon Nicholas Gútkeled. In the summer of 1323 he left Timişoara and moved his court back to the heart of the kingdom, thereby demonstrating that the long war had been triumphantly concluded. Ill-disposed as he was towards the citizens of Buda, Charles chose instead the picturesque location of Visegrád as his residence. At the same time he ordered the manufacture of a new royal seal, and revoked all the grants that he had hitherto made – a clear indication of his intention to begin a new chapter in the history of Hungary.

Charles's victory over the oligarchy was so complete that for the remainder of his reign he had no difficulty in sustaining his authority. The former oligarchs either died or went into exile, their castles being in the hands of the king's followers. Only two families, the Héder and the Babonić had sufficient power to stir up trouble, but their movements were easily checked by the king's lieutenants. Their first revolt was put down in 1327 by the ban of Slavonia, Mikcs Ákos, and the judge royal, Alexander Köcski. Some castles were confiscated and the Héder lost their last counties of Vas and Varaždin. In 1336 the two kindreds rebelled again, this time with Austrian support, but their revolt was once again suppressed. In 1339 one branch of the Héder emigrated to Austria, while the rest of the kindred surrendered to the king and thereafter remained, with their wealth considerably diminished, the obedient subjects of the Angevin monarchy.

The internal peace of the kingdom was not again to be threatened for several decades. The new regime, constructed by Charles on the ruins of the provinces of the oligarchy, turned out to be exceptionally solid. Both Charles and his son, Louis, derived an unusual degree of power from it. The bitter fight for every inch of land had not been in vain. As tiring it had been to secure overall authority, it proved to be easy to sustain it, and the political edifice erected by Charles was to survive until the death of Louis the Great.

ASPIRATIONS IN THE BALKANS

With the fall of the oligarchs the kingdom was restored and became more powerful than before. No king of Hungary since the time of Béla III had been able to draw on the resources of his kingdom to the extent that Charles I could. There remained but one thing to do in order to revive the ancient splendour of Saint Stephen's crown, and that was to recover the hegemony of the Balkans. It was to this end that Charles devoted, with varying success, most of the nineteen remaining years of his reign.

His main objective seems to have been to win back the Serbian marches. Rostislav's ancient duchy of Mačva and Bosnia had slipped out of Hungarian control in the turmoil of the years following 1280. Mačva itself had been governed since 1284 by the dethroned king of Serbia, Stephen Dragutin, whose wife was a sister of Ladislaus IV. After his death in 1316, his province was annexed by his brother, King Stephen Uroš II, and this led, as we have already seen, to a counterattack by Charles, who took the castle of Mačva early in 1317. This success was followed up by another campaign in the autumn of 1319, which seems to have brought about the occupation of Belgrade.

The possession of Mačva dragged Charles into an endless conflict with the kings of Serbia, Stephen Dečanski (1321–1331) and Stephen Dušan (1331–1355). Charles led at least two (and perhaps more) campaigns in person into Serbia. In 1329 he relieved Belgrade, then in 1334 responded to an earlier attack by Dušan by annexing the castle of Golubac. There are signs that at this time a large number of Walla-chians under the leadership of the voivode, Bogdan, moved from Serbia to the region between the River Maros (Mureş) and the Danube. Golubac became attached to the county of Caraşova and was governed by Hungarian castellans until 1390. Towards the end of Charles's reign Mačva was exposed to increasing Serbian pressure. Dušan devastated Srem and around 1340 he seems to have recaptured Belgrade.

Throughout the wars against Serbia, the Angevin kings could count on the support of Bosnia. Until 1322 Bosnia was controlled by the Šubić of Croatia and then by the Kotromanić until 1463. Ban Stephen Kotromanić, the founder of the new dynasty, always looked to the Angevins for protection against Serbia and remained a loyal vassal of Charles. Around 1340, he was rewarded for his services by the comital honour of the Hungarian counties of Fejér and Tolna, which he was to hold until his death in 1353.

While obstinately clinging onto Mačva, Charles resigned himself to the loss of Croatia and Dalmatia. Here Paul Šubić was followed in 1312 by his brother Mladen, who governed in the name of Charles but enjoyed effective independence. In 1322, during the pacification of Slavonia, Charles made a brief visit to Croatia and, with the aid of the local magnates, removed Mladen, taking him as a prisoner to Hungary. However, this step did not bring about Hungarian hegemony. The power of the Šubić was indeed irreparably weakened, but it was not the rule of the Angevin king that followed in its wake. The cities of Dalmatia placed themselves under Venetian protection, while the castles of the Šubić were shared out by the victorious Croatian lords. In 1326 Ban Mikcs tried to enforce obedience from them but was defeated, and no Hungarian army was to appear again in Croatia in Charles's lifetime. Only the counts of Modruš in northern Croatia, known later as Counts Frankopan, remained faithful to Charles. As lords of the town of Senj, they gave him access to the Adriatic Sea.

Hungarian expansion was also renewed towards ancient 'Cumania' in the south-east. From the later Middle Ages this region was generally called Wallachia, while its Hungarian name was 'the parts over the snowy mountains' (partes Transalpinae), that is, the land lying beyond the range of the southern Carpathians. It was mostly inhabited by Romanians and was organised into a principality in the first decades of the fourteenth century by Voivode Basarab, who was of Cumanian origin. Basarab was at first willing to recognise Charles's suzerainty, but he later changed his mind and placed himself under the protection of Bulgaria. In 1330 Charles led a punitive expedition against him, but was forced to turn back and became trapped in the narrow pass of

Turnu Roşu (south of Sibiu). In four days, from 9 to 12 November, the cream of the Hungarian army perished, and Charles only escaped through the self-sacrifice of one of his barons.

As a consequence, the conquest of Wallachia was for a long time removed from the political agenda. Nor was an attack against Bulgaria, which since 1323 had been governed by the dynasty of Šisman, seriously contemplated. Nevertheless, from 1322 the Hungarian zone of influence along the lower Danube spread beyond Orşova, and Charles thought it appropriate in 1335 to revive the office of the ban of Severin, which had ceased to exist around 1280. This did not involve the annexation of Turnu Severin, however. Under the Angevins a ban of Severin occurs only temporarily (1335–1359, 1376), and his authority seems to have been restricted to the control of Mehadia, Orşova and some other border castles.

RELATIONS WITH AUSTRIA, BOHEMIA AND POLAND

Charles's friendship with his Habsburg cousins was for a while undisturbed. At the battle of Mühldorf in 1322 a Hungarian contingent assisted Frederick III in his struggle for Germany against Louis of Bavaria, a favour that the dukes of Austria returned in 1323 by handing back Pressburg, which had fallen into Habsburg hands in 1301 as the dower of Agnes of Austria, widow of Andrew III. However, from that time on relations between Charles and the Habsburgs deteriorated rapidly. In 1328 it was only at the point of the sword that Charles could secure the restitution of the Medjumurje – the border region between the Rivers Drava and Mura, occupied by the Austrians in Otakar's time. Then, in 1336 the duke gave armed support to the rebellious Héder and went as far as to receive homage from them. In 1337 Charles launched a retaliatory attack against Austria, while his captains devastated the southern Habsburg provinces as far as Ljubljana. Although peace was soon restored, mutual hostility persisted until Charles's death. In 1339 it was Duke Albert II who gave shelter to that branch of the Héder which had refused to surrender to the king.

In fact, it was in the north that Charles found constant allies: in Poland, ruled by the Piast dynasty, and in Bohemia, governed by the Luxembourgs. As early as 1306, despite his own problems with the oligarchs, Charles provided armed support for the future King of Poland, Wladislas Łokietek (1320–1333). From then on the Polish-Hungarian alliance remained one of the strongest pillars of Angevin foreign policy. On several occasions during the reigns of Wladislas and his son, Casimir III, 'the Great' (1333–1370), Charles sent auxiliary troops to support the Poles against the Teutonic Order, the Golden

Horde and the Lithuanians. This political alliance was given additional force by a matrimonial tie. Charles had lost his first three wives, princesses of Galicia, Silesia and Bohemia respectively, and was still childless when in 1320 he married Elizabeth, a daughter of Wladislas. Elizabeth bore him five sons, three of whom – Louis, Andrew and Stephen – survived. It was thanks to this relationship that in 1339 Casimir decided that, in the case of his dying without a legitimate heir, his kingdom should pass to the king of Hungary and his successors.

Angevin-Luxembourg relations, though not reaching the intensity of the friendship with Poland, were nevertheless cordial. We have seen that King John (1310–1346) had aided Charles against Matthew Csák. Their alliance was given additional strength by the deterioration of Austro-Hungarian relations, for the relationship between the Luxembourgs and the Habsburgs was consistently far from friendly. Yet to maintain a simultaneous friendship with both Poland and Bohemia was by no means easy, since these countries were rivals for several decades. Whereas the Luxembourgs claimed Poland as the inheritance of Wenceslas III (d. 1306), the Piast rulers were intent on recovering Silesia, which had once belonged to their dynasty.

It was surely Charles's most outstanding diplomatic achievement that he was able to bring lasting stability to the relations between Bohemia and Poland. In August 1335 the envoys of John and Casimir met in Trenčín in Hungary, and agreed on a number of issues, including the abandonment of their respective claims that had hitherto made any rapprochement impossible. In November of the same year, the rulers met in person at Visegrád, where they had been invited by Charles. There they celebrated the settlement of their long dispute, and at the same time entered into a triple alliance, which was basically directed against the dukes of Austria. A commercial agreement between Bohemia and Hungary was also concluded. This was intended to neutralise the staple right of Vienna and favour another route from Hungary to Germany – that which went via Prague.

In the meantime the Angevins, who already had the prospect of acceding one day to the throne of Poland, seemed to be given a new hope of securing the kingdom of Naples as well. This throne had been allotted by means of a papal judgement to King Robert (1309–1343), third son of Charles II, but Charles of Hungary had never acquiesced in this decision, referring to the fact that his father was Charles II's eldest son and thus the crown of 'Sicily' was due to him by the right of primogeniture. Moreover, he laid claim to the principality of Salerno and the 'honour' of Monte Sant' Angelo, which he claimed was his part of the Angevin inheritance in Italy. In 1333 Charles was invited to Naples and the family dispute was settled by an agreement. Robert, who had only two grand-daughters, betrothed one of them, Joan, his prospective heir, to the six-year-old second son of Charles, Andrew. Since it seemed absurd, at least in Hungary, that a woman could accede to the throne in her own right, Charles might reasonably hope that his son would one day become king of Sicily.

THE DEATH AND REPUTATION OF CHARLES I

After ruling Hungary for 41 years, Charles died at Visegrád on 16 July 1342, at the age of 54. He was buried a month later at Székesfehérvár. It is an indication of the prestige that he had acquired that the ceremony was attended by the king of Poland and by the heir to Bohemia, the future Emperor Charles IV. Yet the achievements of his reign later fell into oblivion, to be given due weight only in modern historiography. Indeed, in the eyes of contemporaries his reputation was outshone by that of his son, and it was easily forgotten that Louis's kingdom rested upon that of his father, unified with the sword and resolutely reformed.

Oblivion was partly due to the fact that Charles's deeds did not find a suitable chronicler. The decisive years of his rule were narrated by a Franciscan friar, who has with some certainty been identified by modern research as John, the minister provincial of Hungary. His narrative is accurate and respectful, but he can hardly conceal his profound antipathy towards the king. He devotes no more than a few lines to the dramatic struggle against the oligarchs, but describes, with some relish, the sad episodes of the reign. He relates in detail the king's revenge, disproportionate in its cruelty, for an assassination attempt on his family; and proceeds to show how Charles was himself soon punished, no less cruelly, by God during his campaign in Wallachia. And so the 'Záh affair' has come to be remembered by posterity as the most memorable episode of Charles's reign.

Felician Záh was a member of an ancient kindred and a knight of some wealth. He had formerly been one of Matthew Csák's leading followers, then went over to the king and for a time was royal castellan of Šintava (near Trnava). On 17 April 1330, having just returned from a diplomatic mission to Prague, Felician attacked the royal family with a sword as they dined in the palace of Visegrád. He wounded the queen on her hand, but was promptly cut to pieces by the guards. 'His head was sent to Buda, and his two legs and two arms to other towns...'.[6] The vengeance that followed was cruel in the extreme. The assailant's children were immediately tortured to death, and the final verdict, brought by 24 barons on 15 May, declared all his relatives to be guilty. His sons-in-law, grand-children and sisters, along with their offspring and all members of the kindred 'within the third degree of kinship' were to be punished with death, those within the seventh degree with loss of their property and eternal serfdom. The pursuit of those suspected of any relation with the Záh was to continue for years. The fact that neither the chronicler nor the barons who sat in judgement offered a motive for the assassination attempt has given rise to a good deal of conjecture over the centuries. The explanation given by an Italian contemporary would seem to be the only credible one. According to him, Felician was seeking revenge for his maiden daughter, Claire, who as a lady-in-waiting to Queen Elizabeth had been seduced by the queen's brother, the future King Casimir III.

Chapter 9

The New Monarchy

From our perspective, it is clear that the accession of the Angevins brought a change of dynasty, but what contemporaries emphasised was continuity. Charles derived his right from neither election nor his having been crowned with the Holy Crown. Rather, he considered it to be the lawful inheritance of the Árpádians, his 'pious ancestors of holy memory', that devolved upon him 'by right of birth'. It was surely not by chance that two of his sons were given the names of Ladislaus and Stephen. The close connection with the former dynasty was also expressed by the coat of arms of the Angevins, which was divided into two fields, showing the lilies, their family symbol, on one, and the red and silver bars, used by their predecessors, on the other. The principle of inheritance was an important advantage in developing authoritarian forms of government.

THE PRINCIPLES

The programme of Charles and his supporters, as was that of any new regime in the Middle Ages, consisted of the restoration of the 'good state of the realm'. Whatever the ideas behind this slogan were, holding diets was obviously not one of them. During the years of civil war, Charles had been forced to hold a diet almost every year, though it seems that he disliked them from the beginning. The last diet we know of was convened in 1320. After his victory the king saw no further reason to respect his subjects' expectations. As they complained later, 'he prohibited their traditional assemblies'.[1] Indeed, he did not even hold the annual public courts, prescribed by the Golden Bull.

Instead of the holding of diets, the idea that the king should rule 'with the plenitude of power' (*plenitudine potestatis*) prevailed, and some went as far as to declare that 'his word has the force of law'.[2] Indeed, he adopted the habit of granting privileges 'out of his special grace' (*de speciali gratia*), with no regard to the customs of his realm. Although this broad interpretation of royal authority was by no means alien to the Árpádians, its first sophisticated exposition emerged during Charles's reign, and probably derived from the political traditions of the kingdom of Sicily.

In theory at least, decision-making was shared by the monarch and his council, the latter consisting of the 'prelates and barons', that is, the ecclesiastical and lay dignitaries of the kingdom. The list of barons, which had been included in all royal grants since about 1190, went through important modifications after 1323. (It should be noted that in Hungary these lists were purely formal, and are not to be confused with the lists of witnesses that were much in use elsewhere.) Under the late Árpádians most counts still had the rank and privileges of a baron. By 1333 this status was maintained only by the count of Pressburg, the other counts having been gradually omitted from the lists of dignitaries. They were soon to lose the baronial privileges of having a banner and using a distinctive seal. Neither were the office-holders of the queen's court counted among the barons after 1354. The number of the lay barons of the realm was thus established at around twelve, including the Master of the Doorkeepers (*magister ianitorum*), a new dignitary who became a member of the council in 1350. Since he was in charge of the royal palace, from 1380 onwards he was also called, though unofficially, 'Master of the Court' (*magister curiae*). The ecclesiastical barons comprised, as earlier, fourteen prelates, that is, the two archbishops and twelve bishops.

In the absence of a diet, the barons, together with other high dignitaries, were to represent 'the *universitas* of the realm', that is, the Estates. If the king sat in judgement himself, he did this together with members of his council. When making a 'perpetual' (that is, inheritable) grant of an estate or any other privilege he always referred to the counsel (*consilium*) of prelates and barons. His acts became valid only with their formal consent. In 1330, as we have seen, 24 barons and counts pronounced the final verdict against Felician Záh, who had dared to raise his hand against the royal family. As for foreign affairs, in 1328 three prelates and 29 lay office-holders (barons, counts, and castellans) guaranteed in a separate charter, 'in the name of themselves, their descendants and heirs', the Treaty of Bruck, which Charles had signed with the dukes of Austria.[3] The peace treaty with the Republic of Venice in 1348 was also confirmed by 20 ecclesiastical and lay office-holders.

As early as 1318 Charles had refused to confirm the Golden Bull and he was not inclined to respect it later. In sharp contrast to its provisions, he made it clear that 'whenever we take the field the nobles of our kingdom are obliged to join us, according to their customs, at their own expense.'[4] During the war against the oligarchs the king had become accustomed to proclaiming the general levy every year, and he had no intention of refraining from this practice later. Between 1316 and 1340 there were, as far as we know, only two years when no 'royal campaign' was proclaimed. In 1336 there were two within a single year. (Unfortunately we do not always know the destination of these expeditions.) In such cases it was usual to adjourn all lawsuits until the end of the campaign, which was officially called the 'day of the army's rest' (*dies residentiae exercitus*). From 1329, most expeditions were conducted abroad, and it is almost certain that the nobility was obliged to take part in them.

THE KING AND THE CHURCH

The king's autocratic views dominated his relations with the Church, despite the fact that he owed much to his prelates. At the time that Ladislaus Kán was still tyrannising the bishop of Transylvania and Matthew Csák occupied the estates of the sees of Nitra and Esztergom, it was from the Church that Charles found the support he needed for his survival. In 1313 he bestowed the county of Veszprém upon its bishop hereditarily, while in 1315 the archbishop of Esztergom was given the county of Komárno in a similar way, though it was actually still held by Matthew Csák. Problems began to arise in 1317, when Charles found himself less in need of his bishops. Their wrath was first roused by the treaty that Charles had signed with Matthew Csák, which left the usurped ecclesiastical domains in the hands of the oligarch without the Church's authorisation. In the spring of 1318 the bishops assembled at Kalocsa and allied themselves against 'everybody' trying to encroach upon any of the Church's privileges. They wanted to take measures in order 'to provide for the good state of the realm', and called upon the king to convene a diet where they could put forward their suggestions.[5] The bishop of Nitra went as far as to excommunicate Matthew and all of his followers, many of whom had gone over to the king's service in 1317.

Charles summoned the assembly as he had been required to do, but he was not a man to forget. As early as 1320 he took Komárno back from the archbishop and gave him the county of Bars instead: a grant of doubtful value, for Bars was still in Matthew Csák's possession. In 1323 he annulled his former grants concerning Veszprém and Bars, and made the prelates the obedient instruments of his power. Around 1338, one of them denounced the king to the Pope, requesting anonymity lest 'the king's wrath should fall upon' him. He briefly summarised the grievances of the nobility, but devoted most of his letter to the acts of injustice committed against the Church. The king, he claimed, had not permitted canonical elections for 23 years, appointing bishops himself, frequently in the lifetime of their predecessors. On the occasion of an investiture, he had demanded a fee, and at New Year a special gift; he imposed arbitrary taxes upon the people of the Church; he compelled the bishops to go to war every year or even more often; he confiscated the property of deceased prelates and laid his hand upon vacant sees; he granted away patronage rights; he had priests summoned before secular courts and even forced them to fight duels. As a result of all this, the anonymous author added, it was feared that 'a revolt of the whole Hungarian people' would break out.[6]

This was, of course, no more than a dream. Charles enjoyed the unqualified support of his barons and had a firm grip on the reins of power. Neither could the Hungarian Church hope for assistance from Avignon, for in the later part of his reign Charles received as much support from the Holy See as he had earlier. The greed of the cardinals not being aroused by this poor and distant land, they rarely demanded benefices there, and the Pope did not inquire about episcopal elections if he received, more or less, the payments that were due to him.

It was between 1281 and 1286 that the first papal tax collector, Gerardo da Modena, had been active in Hungary, presumably with limited success. In Charles's reign, the first collectors arrived with Gentile in 1308. From 1317 onwards it was the task of Rufinus de Civino, archdeacon of Tolna, to collect the annual income of all the vacant benefices and that part of Gentile's *procuratio* that had not been paid. All he managed to raise during his three-year stay were 2960 florins, 1744 of which were used to pay his own allowance. The next levy, which began in 1332 and lasted for six years, was more successful. It was aimed at collecting the papal tithe, that is, the tenth part of the income of all ecclesiastical benefices. The king gave his consent to this exaction upon the condition that one third of the income would be his. The tax collectors went through the kingdom twice a year, squeezed the tithe from every single cleric, and the results of their work were put down on a detailed roll that listed benefices and parishes by diocese and archdeaconry. The document is far from complete, for in some dioceses only four, five or even fewer years are covered, and Nitra and Győr dioceses are missing altogether. Nevertheless, although papal tax collectors were also to visit Hungary from 1350 to 1354 and from 1373 to 1375, this is the only document of its kind to have come down to us and so provides a unique historical source.

CHARLES I'S BARONS

The long civil war had led to the destruction of the old elite, and its place was occupied by a newly created one that owed its rise to the

Angevin dynasty. From 1315 onwards new men begin to appear in key positions, and by the time Charles had taken (to use his own words) 'full possession' of the kingdom,[7] they had come to monopolise the government. Their relationship to the dynasty was completely different from that between the king and the oligarchs. Whereas the latter were claiming to have a share in power by right of their descent, the 'new men' were all the king's own creations, and the power to choose them resided more or less exclusively in him. All that tradition prescribed was that the baron should be of noble birth and wealthy. If the king wanted to raise one of his poorer followers to the status of a baron, he was expected to provide him with suitable domains; but this was in fact the only expectation he had to meet.

The only foreigners upon whom Charles conferred considerable power were Philip Druget, a French knight from Naples, and his kinsmen. Philip had come to Hungary in Charles's company, had played an outstanding role in the suppression of the Aba and in 1317 was given the government of Spis and Újvár. In 1323 he was appointed palatine, and henceforth this office became, so to speak, hereditary in his family. When he died in 1327, he was succeeded by his brother John and then, in 1334, by his nephew William, the eldest son of John. From the outset, Philip had been supplied with lavish grants and when he died the king transferred all his lands to William, so that in 1342 the patrimony of this family comprised as many as nine seigneuries.

Another leading person in the government was Thomas Szécsényi, a nobleman of high birth but modest wealth from Nógrád county. Whereas his kinsmen had joined Matthew Csák, Thomas accompanied the king to the south. His foresight was to yield ample reward in due course. In 1313 he was still castellan of Ľubovňa, a castle taken from the Aba, but he was soon given important honours, and in 1321 was appointed voivode of Transylvania. He distinguished himself in the immediate and decisive pacification of this province and by the suppression of a Saxon revolt there in 1324. He governed Transylvania for 21 years with almost unrestricted power, and also Szolnok, a county that had been attached to the office of the voivode since about 1267, and Arad, which for the remainder of the fourteenth century was to be governed by the voivode. He was entrusted with the county of Nógrád in 1335 and that of Trenčín in 1338. His unwavering fidelity was amply rewarded by lands confiscated from his own kinsmen and other rebels. At the time of Charles's death, Thomas Szécsényi was, with his four castles, one of the greatest landowners in the kingdom.

Mikcs Ákos was the third pillar of the new regime. He was a descendant of an illustrious kindred, but inherited no more than a few villages and a small monastery near Pest. He first appears in Charles's service in 1308 as castellan of Óbuda, and was governor of Šariš and Zemplín from 1315 to 1327. He also governed Slavonia from 1325 until his death in 1343. As ban, he played a decisive role in the suppression of the successive revolts of the Babonić and Héder, and acquired a patrimony consisting of three castles and many villages in Šariš, Zemplín, Zala, Slavonia and elsewhere.

For a time, Donch of Zvolen was also a powerful figure in the government, but his career shows how little confidence the king had in those who had come from the other side. Donch's father, Count Dominic of Zvolen, had once supported King Wenceslas, while his uncle, Demetrius, held Šariš against Charles and fell fighting him at Rozhanovce in 1312. Donch, who 'inherited' Zvolen from his father, changed sides in 1314 and from that point on faithfully supported the new king in all his wars. Yet he was never able to dispel suspicion, and Charles slowly but surely deprived him of his power. In 1330 he took Orava from Donch by means of an exchange, then in 1338 removed him from his office. Charles even dismembered the county of Zvolen in 1339, its districts of Turc and Liptov being governed henceforth by counts of their own. Finally, in 1341, he seized Donch's private seigneuries in the north and gave him Vălcou in the distant Crasna county instead.

THE ROYAL HOUSEHOLD

The true nature of Angevin government is still somewhat elusive. Modern historians have devoted much time to the study of the law courts and chancellery, but almost none to that of government itself. That in the late Middle Ages the king's 'court' (*curia*) and his 'palace' (*aula*) were still carefully distinguished has so far escaped attention. There is good reason to believe that this distinction was crucial, but little is known about its real nature. It may be supposed that by *aula* was meant the 'private court' of the king (more or less the equivalent of what was called the royal household elsewhere), while the *curia* denoted the king's 'public court', and was more or less identical with his council where he was assisted by the prelates and barons. These definitions are, for the moment, hardly more than guesswork, but they are helpful in describing Angevin government at work.

The court, at least in theory, was open to every nobleman. When Charles made peace with the Héder in 1339, he explicitly permitted them 'to present themselves before him, at a convenient time, either in his court or anywhere else where he should stay, to remain in his company and render him proper services' in the manner of other faithful men.[8] In fact, only those persons who held offices or became paid members of the royal household were able to do so. The Héder were kept out of the court, together with all those whose past was not immaculate. They might enjoy their wealth peacefully, but they could not hope for offices as long as the Angevins reigned.

It is certain that an early form of the royal household had already existed under the Árpádians. From the twelfth century onwards we know about noblemen who were in, or were entering, the king's personal service. In the thirteenth century we often hear of 'youths of the household' (aulae iuvenes), who accomplished certain commissions on the king's behalf. Nevertheless, the royal household in its fully developed form appears in the time of Charles I. While 'household youths' occur as early as 1311, 'pages' (aulae parvuli) are mentioned from 1321 and 'knights' (aulae milites) from 1324. Within this hierarchy, which seems itself to be a new invention, the page clearly occupied the lowest and the knight the highest place, promotions being, of course, possible. We know of about ten 'youths' who were promoted to knights, and in one case we can follow a full career from the status of page to knighthood. As regards the 'youths', a study of individual careers proves that the term had nothing to do with age. We know of several members of the household who were referred to as 'youths' for many decades. In fact, the term seems to have been the equivalent of 'squire' (écuyer, Knappe); that is, the 'youths' were men-at-arms who had not, or not yet, been dubbed. Earlier the term must have had a different meaning, because, as mentioned above, in the Árpádian aula there had been 'youths' but no knights.

The first of Charles's knights were chosen from among his foreign followers. There were Austrians, Croats, Czechs and Poles, but no Hungarians before 1336. Up to 1342, 60 persons bearing one of the household titles are known (including not only the king's establishment, but also those of the queen and the dukes, Louis and Stephen), but since the references are casual there must have been many more of them. As regards their function, few differences between the three ranks (knights, youths and pages) can be discovered. Apart from constituting the king's permanent escort, they frequently acted as the ruler's personal deputies. They delivered written or verbal orders to the chancellery and to the provinces. The knights were also sent on diplomatic missions. On the whole it could be said that members of the household acted in the ruler's place whenever this was desirable, and that matters of little significance were not infrequently given special emphasis through the presence of a royal envoy. Later on they were to play an important role in the organisation of military campaigns. Nothing is known about their allowances apart from the fact that the knights were often given small honours to live on. Their expenses must have been met by the treasury, and they probably received some form of regular payment, but this is no more than conjecture.

The structured order of the household shows that in many respects Charles's 'palace' resembled its Western counterparts. The knightly way of life, the beginnings of which is evident during the Árpádian era, now became firmly rooted in Hungary. The first tournament is thought to have been held in 1318, and they became regular events thereafter. From 1324, the king granted 'coats of arms' (that is, helmet crests) to his knights, then in 1326 he founded the Order of Saint George, one of the earliest chivalric orders in Europe. We know nothing about it except for its statutes, but it was probably intended to bring together the barons and knights of the court. It was during the fourteenth century that the armoured figure of Saint Ladislaus, albeit anachronistically idealised, became the model of knighthood, and during Louis's reign his effigy was put upon the reverse of the king's coins. On the whole the court of Charles and his son can be regarded as the most specific manifestation of chivalrous culture in Hungary, in as far as such a culture can be spoken of there at all. If the spiritual values of chivalry are counted among its defining criteria, then it must be conceded that nothing of the sort can be found in the Angevin court, neither lay poetry nor any sort of chivalrous ethos. The members of the court may have lived according to chivalrous ceremonies, and they certainly had a markedly aristocratic view of the world; but they remained essentially Hungarian noblemen, belonging to an archaic world that was inextricably intertwined with pagan and patriarchal traditions.

THE ROYAL RESIDENCE

Up to the end of the fifteenth century the kings of Hungary spent most of their time on the move, not staying in one particular place for more than a few months. Within the realm, the most frequent destinations were the royal 'hunting places' (*loca venationis*) in the mountains, such as Damásd in the Börzsöny (from 1339), Zvolen (from 1340), Diósgyőr in the Bükk (from 1343), and Gerencsér in the Vértes (from 1362). There is no evidence that the ruler travelled through his kingdom regularly, nor was it customary, at least from the time of the Angevins, to visit the royal domains merely to live on their supplies. The king went abroad for meetings with neighbouring princes or, more often, for campaigns, which were traditionally led by him in person.

Although the king was normally on the move there had long existed a location that deserved the name of permanent residence in the 'middle of the kingdom' (*medium regni*). Such was the role of Esztergom during the early centuries and of Buda in the thirteenth. Visegrád was to fulfil this role from 1323, when Charles established his residence there, until around 1406, with a short interruption between 1346 and 1355 when Louis moved to Buda. It was at the foot of the castle hill at Visegrád, within the walls of the town, that a new palace was built. It was to here that the king regularly returned from his journeys; it witnessed Felician's assassination attempt in 1330; and in 1335 it was sufficiently splendid to serve as the scene of the memorable meeting between the rulers of Poland, Bohemia and Hungary. The royal treasury was also deposited here, while the regalia were guarded in the castle. The crown of Poland was brought here for a short time in 1370.

The queen also resided at Visegrád, together with her following. Although, as was later to become clear, Elizabeth was strongly inclined to exercise power herself, her husband did not allow her much opportunity to interfere in government. In accordance with custom he allowed her to have her own household, and allotted to her important parts of the royal demesne, including the counties and domains of Bereg, Csepel, Segesd and Virovitica, 'for her support' (*pro sustentatione*). The lords who directed the queen's household, like her *magister tavarnicorum* and her *iudex curiae*, belonged to the highest officeholders of the kingdom, but they were mostly chosen by Charles rather than by Elizabeth.

About 1330 registers began to be used for the recording of documents that were being issued by the chancellery. The inspiration probably came from Naples. About the same time the countersign of the keeper of the great seal (and later that of the keeper of the secret seal too) appears on documents issued by the chancellery and presented to the ruler for sealing. Meanwhile, as one by one the central organs of government and the judicial courts moved to Visegrád, the town began to play the role of a primitive capital. It was only natural that the prelates and barons would want to have a house or piece of land in the vicinity of Visegrád, in order to have a permanent residence near the king.

THE ROYAL DOMAIN

The authority of the Angevins was based upon an immense royal domain. At the time of his death, Louis still had at his disposal 23 per cent of the kingdom's land, not counting the free and mining towns, the lands of the Saxons, the Cumans, the Jász and the Székely. Including these, the king's direct lordship extended over as much as one third of the kingdom.

It was during the Angevin period that a new concept of royal property was developed. According to this, the king was to be considered the lord of all lands that were not owned by the nobility or the Church.

The former distinction, fundamental and quite clear, between the royal demesne and 'castle lands' disappeared. Every property that the king could dispose of at will was regarded as 'royal estate' (*possessio regalis*), regardless of its previous status. Its inhabitants came to be termed the 'king's tenants' (*iobagiones regales)* or the 'king's people' (*populi regales*), whatever their previous status had been, whether 'castle folk', *udvornici*, *tavernici*, tenants or serfs of the king.

Since the reign of Andrew II, there had been several attempts to track down those lands belonging to the king that had been unwarrantably alienated. After the consolidation of his rule Charles also sent out commissions in order to identify such property. From this the new idea of the 'king's right' (*jus regium*) was born under Louis I. This right was declared to be inherent in all lands for which the validity of another's rights could not be proved. It concerned above all those estates that had once been in royal hands and for which their granting away could not be documented. In such lands, so ran the argument, the king had 'latent' rights, and those who usurped them were termed 'concealers of royal rights' (*celatores iurium regalium*) and were to be punished with the full rigour of the law. It was also laid down as a principle that such lands could be reclaimed by the Crown regardless of the time that had elapsed since their alienation.

The principle of 'royal right' furnished legal grounds for the extension of the royal domain and proved to be a dangerous weapon in the hands of the king's skilled lawyers. From about 1370, when it was first applied, nobody could feel safe, not even families who had peacefully owned their land for several generations. The descendants of 'castle warriors' were especially threatened, for it was often easy to demonstrate that they were not 'real nobles' (*veri nobiles*), and that the land they thought to be their own in fact belonged to the king. The legal insecurity caused by the search for 'latent royal rights' only began to settle in about 1410, when charters transferring the royal rights 'which may possibly be hidden' in property became available.

The normal unit of the royal domain was a seigneury consisting of a castle and its appurtenances. The number of fortresses erected before 1320 can be put at between 360 and 400. Most of them had been held by the oligarchs or by noble kindreds allied to them, but many castles were destroyed during the civil war, and no more than 260 to 270 had a legalised status at the end of Charles's reign. It is likely that about 40 new castles were built between 1342 and 1382.

During the war and the years of the consolidation that followed many large estates and most castles changed hands. Nearly 50 castles were taken from Matthew Csák and his adherents between 1313 and 1321; about 40 were confiscated or acquired by way of exchange from the Héder before 1340; ten were seized from the Aba, ten from the

Babonić, ten from the Kán and nine from the Borsa, not to mention other rebels. Although, interestingly enough, no executions are mentioned during or after the war, loss of property was the usual punishment for everyone who had in some way been involved in the troubles on the wrong side. Retaliation was mainly directed against the oligarchs and their partisans, who as a matter of course lost everything they had. (The astonishing degree of patience that the king showed towards the Héder is hard to explain.) Even lands that had been seized by the oligarchs passed to the king rather than to their original owners. Charles seems to have attributed to their loss to carelessness and was reluctant to hand back such properties, even to his own partisans.

Charles was willing to divide a few of these acquisitions among his followers as perpetual grants, but he kept the lion's share for the Crown. At the time of his death there were at least 160 castles in royal hands, and Louis still had possession of 150 of them in 1382, not counting his castles in Croatia, Bosnia and Serbia. In every part of the kingdom there stood at least one royal castle to make the might of the Angevin monarchy tangible for everyone. In Transylvania and Slavonia, in the counties along the western frontier and around Timişoara all the important castles were governed by royal officers. Royal presence was even more manifest in the former province of Matthew Csák, where practically all of the 30 or so castles were in royal hands.

Charles was determined to increase this already immense network by every possible means. As early as 1323 he ordered the revision of all of his previous grants and rescinded those that he judged to have been inappropriate. An effective means of increasing royal lands were the exchanges that he imposed upon his own subjects. His method was quite simple: he took much and gave less in return. In 1326 he gave two castles to the Csák in place of four, then in 1327 John Babonić received one instead of two (or three), and in 1341 Donch of Zvolen was given one in exchange for at least two. It was also by means of exchanges that Charles liquidated the remnants of the territory of the Héder in 1339–40. They were forced to hand over their numerous castles along the western frontier and in return were given three in the heart of the kingdom where they could do less harm.

The appurtenances of a castle comprised a specified number of villages or hamlets together with all their revenues, including payments and services due from the tenants, incomes from fairs, markets, tolls, forests, fishing places or other seigneurial rights. An average seigneury might comprise 14 villages and extend to 44,000 acres, but there was naturally much disparity in size. For example, between 1387 and 1390 as many as 28 villages belonged to the castle of Neuhaus (Vas county) and 27 to that of Topol'čany (Nitra county), while only four were attached to Sirok castle (Heves county) and three to Somló (near Doba, Veszprém county).

THE HONOURS

Government of the kingdom was founded upon the royal castles, which were divided, as under the Árpádians, among the barons and counts. These men exerted authority of a general nature over a well defined territory, consisting of one or more counties, and were also in command of several castles, most of which were located within the province entrusted to them.

The barons and counts held their dignity in the form of a royal 'honour', which meant that they enjoyed all the royal revenues that went with their office. Among these revenues were the fines that were due to the lord of an honour in his capacity as judge, but it seems that most of his income came from the seigneuries of the royal castles held by him. As far as can be determined, none of the revenues of an honour ever reached the royal treasury. Rather, they served to maintain the royal dignitary: he paid his retinue from them and had to provide for the custody of his castles, but he was free to expend the rest as he pleased. A vivid example is provided by an account, covering two months in 1372, made by the receiver of Benedict Himfi, who at that time was count of Timiş. It is clear that Himfi enjoyed all the revenues that were due from Timişoara, a royal castle, and its numerous appurtenances, including peasant services, tolls and markets, as well as one part of the tax due from the royal towns of Timişoara and Şemlacu Mare. From all these sources he covered the daily expenses of his household, took a sum when he went to see the king, gave occasional allowances to his retainers, sent money to his wife, and held festivities on account of the name-day of his grandson. The accumulated evidence of many further documentary references demonstrates that Himfi's case was not exceptional, that all the lords who held a royal honour enjoyed its revenues in the same way.

Most of the counties and the greater part of the 150 to 160 royal castles were held by the greatest lords. The voivode of Transylvania and the bans of Slavonia and Mačva had their own provinces to govern, while the other counties and castles were divided among the palatine, the judge royal and other dignitaries according to the needs of the moment. They all governed their honours in more or less the same way. Most of their time was probably spent with the king. They visited their respective provinces only when their presence was needed for some reason. Each of them had a staff of retainers at his disposal, mostly noblemen of modest origin who would serve their particular lords through many decades. When a baron was appointed to an honour he sent his men to govern it in his name. He usually paid them by allowing them a share of its income. When he was replaced by another baron, he withdrew his personnel to give way to those of his successor, but he was normally given another honour and so was able to transfer his men there. In the eyes of foreigners the honours of the Angevin era could, therefore, appear to be temporary fiefs. This is what the Florentine, Matteo Villani, appears to have thought around 1350, when he stated that 'the baronies in Hungary are neither hereditary nor lifelong, but are given and taken back according to the ruler's will.'[9]

For such a 'barony', the honour of the voivode of Transylvania may serve as a model. It included judicial authority over the seven counties of the province and, under the Angevins, there was also the seigneurial rights over the eight castles and other domains in Transylvania that were at that time in royal hands. The voivode was represented by a count in each county and by a castellan at the head of each of his castles. Justice at the highest level was administered by the *vicevayvoda*, the voivode's general deputy. All his officers were chosen from among his retainers. When Thomas Szécsényi was voivode from 1321 to 1342, he brought ten of his men from Nógrád and Gemer counties where his family estates lay, seven were recruited from other counties in Hungary, and only five are known to have been nobles living in Transylvania. The authority of the ban in Slavonia was very similar. Like the voivode, he was usually sent from Hungary and brought most of his men from there. Supreme judicial authority was exercised by his deputy, called the *vicebanus*, while he governed his counties and his fourteen or fifteen castles through his counts and castellans.

In 1320 Charles I's new acquisitions south of the River Sava were conferred upon a baron who henceforth bore the title of 'ban of Mačva' (*banus Machoviensis*). He held not only Mačva proper, but also some neighbouring counties, such as Vukovar and Bodrog (from 1320), Srem (from 1323), Baranya (from 1328), Bač (from 1333) and Tolna (from about 1376). Within his province he exercised a military and judicial power similar to that enjoyed by the voivode, and he governed the counties entrusted to him through his deputies. His office was to survive the loss of Mačva proper in 1411 and only ceased to exist in 1479.

Besides being the supreme justice of the kingdom, the palatine had an honour in which he exercised powers similar to those of the voivode and the ban. He enjoyed its revenues, appointed his retainers as castellans and counts, and led the nobles of his province to the royal army in wartime. In contrast to Transylvania or Slavonia, however, the province entrusted to the palatine was not a fixed one. He was given counties that were available at a particular moment, and on more than one occasion these did not form a coherent block. From 1323 to 1342, when the dignity was borne by the Druget, the honour of the palatine was of very considerable extent. At the time of Palatine William's death, he had under his command no fewer than nine counties, covering the whole of north-eastern Hungary from Heves to Ung, with fourteen or fifteen royal castles. Nicholas Kont, who was palatine from 1356 to 1367, governed the counties of Bihor, Spis, Šaríš, Trenčín, Nitra, Sopron and Vas simultaneously. Although they lay dispersed in four blocks, in all parts of the kingdom, they comprised more than fifteen royal castles and so as a whole formed a rich honour of enormous extent.

It was something of a principle that all the barons should be given honours appropriate to their dignity. The judge royal held the region of Žilina, with six castles, for many decades. The counties of Trenčín, Bač and Bihor formed the honour of the *magister tavarnicorum*, Demetrius Nekcsei, until his death in 1338. The remaining counties and castles were similarly distributed among the less influential members of the king's retinue in the form of royal honours. Most of them had no more than a single castle to command, but there were counts and even castellans who were richly endowed with royal domains. To the honour of Pressburg, five castles were continually attached, while the count of Varaždin (also called the count of Zagorje) commanded over ten. Counties and castellanies were often united in one hand. The castellan of Drégely held as a rule the office of count in Hont, that of Levice was count of Bars, while the castellans of Adrian and Mukačeve were counts of Szabolcs and Bereg respectively. It was by allotting royal castles or comital dignities as honours that the king rewarded the services of his favourite knights: even the keeper of the secret seal was given a castellany of his own.

CHAMBERS AND FINANCES

In Hungary the royal revenues were covered by the general term of the 'chamber', which originally meant the king's treasure that was guarded at Esztergom. For a long time it was the only place where coins were struck and where all the royal revenues were collected. During the course of the thirteenth century the administration of the revenues was decentralised. Some of the provinces were given a chamber of their own, which collected local revenues and struck coins from them. Henceforth, the word 'chamber' referred to a number of financial institutions all over the kingdom, and the totality of them was identical to the royal treasury. The chamber of the diocese of Cenad, later transferred to

Lipova, is mentioned from 1221 onwards, that of Srem from 1253, that of Buda from 1255, and that of Slavonia (at Pakrac, then at Zagreb) from 1256. In the 1330s, further chambers were created at Kremnica, Smolník (later transferred to Košice), Satu Mare (later at Baia Mare), Oradea, Pécs and in Transylvania. Each was in charge of a certain number of counties and each was directed by an entrepreneur called a 'chamber count' (*comes camerae*). These men had been Jews and Muslims before 1270, then mainly German and Italian merchants, though Hungarian burghers were occasionally to be found among them. The chamber count had the right to administer the royal revenues of his chamber according to certain well-defined conditions and in return for a fixed sum. Although the kingdom was divided into ten chamber districts, a chamber count could farm more than one district at the same time. They were in charge of all those financial resources that were regarded as royal property: besides coinage and the gold mines, the most important were the salt monopoly, the tax of the towns and the 'free villages' and the toll on foreign trade called the 'thirtieth' (*tricesima*). Those parts of the royal domain that were governed as honours by barons, counts and castellans were, naturally, not included among the chambers' administrative responsibilities.

The chambers, and royal finances in general, formed part of the king's private sphere of activity and lay outside the competence of the royal council. That such matters were beyond the reach of the barons was perhaps fortunate since these men appear to have had difficulty with elementary arithmetic. The chamber counts had genuine expertise in financial affairs, but due to their particular situation they were private employees of the king of an inferior social status and they were, of course, excluded from the council. Only two of the barons had any involvement in finance. The *magister tavarnicorum* traditionally acted as the supreme judge of all people belonging to the chamber, including its count with his staff and the burghers of the royal towns. The archbishop of Esztergom had the right to control, in the name of the realm, the quality of coins and in return could collect the *pisetum*, which was one tenth of the income deriving from the coinage.

As regards the coinage, silver coins remained predominant until the 1320s, as indeed they did everywhere in Europe with the exception of Italy. Since 1255 the chamber of Slavonia, controlled by the ban, had minted 'banal pennies' (*denarii banales*, later simply *banales*), which were silver coins of high quality weighing 0.93 g and copying the pennies of Friesach. They remained common currency throughout the whole kingdom for many years, although their quality deteriorated during the troubled years after 1272. From 1323, Charles himself minted a variant of the banal penny, but before 1330 he had issued new coins that copied the Vienna pennies of the dukes of Austria. They were made of silver 'of the third combustion' (that is, of a fineness of 666/1000) and with a weight between 0.6 and 0.8 g, they were worth exactly half of a 'good' banal penny. Silver groats, somewhat lighter than those of Bohemia, were also struck between 1329 and 1337, but they disappeared after florins had come into general use.

There followed in 1336 a reform of the 'chamber's profit' and of the renewal of money. The compulsory exchange of money, while maintained for the towns, was abolished in the villages and replaced by an annual tax, also called 'the chamber's profit', which was levied on each free peasant holding. Sometime during the century, the towns were also exempted from the compulsory renewal of money; or, more exactly, the 'chamber's profit' paid by them was merged into the yearly tax that they paid to the treasury.

The most ambitious, though unsuccessful, monetary reform was put into effect in 1338. The idea was to abolish the renewal of money altogether and to issue a new penny, intended this time to be 'perpetual'. While its exchange was declared voluntary, a series of additional measures were to ensure that nothing other than the king's money should remain in circulation. The use of foreign currencies and silver bars was prohibited upon heavy penalties, and it was prescribed that all payments should be discharged in royal pennies. At the same time the royal monopoly of precious metals was strengthened. Every exploiter was to deliver his ore for 'combusting' – that is, refining – in one of the chambers, and what he received after the refinement he was to 'sell' there at a fixed price. In order to carry out this measure a 'royal house' (*domus regalis*) was to be built in every mining town. With a view to preventing the emergence of a black market, no one was permitted to arrive in a mining region with more than two marks (equalling about 800d) in his purse.[10]

THE GOLD OF HUNGARY

It was during Charles's reign, in the years after 1320, that the rich gold mines of Hungary were discovered. They were to have a decisive influence upon the economy of Europe. By far the most important mine was at Kremnica, where the king settled German miners from Kutná Hora in Bohemia and invested them with wide-ranging privileges in 1328. For several centuries it was to remain the main centre for coinage. Also renowned for their gold deposits were Baia Mare in eastern Hungary (first mentioned in 1329), Baia de Arieş in Transylvania (privileged in 1325) and Smolník in the north-east, which was founded in 1327.

It must have been these discoveries that prompted the government to loosen the royal monopoly of mining in order to stimulate the opening of new mines. Hitherto a piece of land where precious metals had been found had usually been expropriated by the chamber and its lord given land elsewhere in compensation. From 1327 onwards private landowners were also able to open mines. They were required to sell the precious metal to the chamber at a fixed price, in return for which they could retain one third of the *urbura*. However, although mines in private hands do appear after the reform, the most important ones remained royal property throughout the Middle Ages.

Part of the gold was put into circulation in the form of coins. Charles I was the first ruler north of the Alps to issue a gold coin – the florin (*florenus*). In their name, appearance and value they copied the *fiorini* of Florence, but they were 'somewhat heavier' than these (3.56g),[11] their fineness being less perfect (23.75 carat). Hungarian florins are first seen in Moravia in 1326, and were to be minted for several centuries in a weight and quality almost unaltered. It should also be noted that gold bars must have continued to play an important role in the export trade, although they were not used on the domestic market.

The exact volume of gold production is not known. It has been argued that before 1500 Hungary supplied from 75 to 80 per cent of the gold mined in Europe, this being one third of world production. This is merely conjecture; but it is clear that the amount of gold extracted in Hungary must have been very considerable. According to the only piece of evidence that we have, when visiting Naples in 1343, Elizabeth, the queen-mother, took 'for her expenses', as the chronicler put it, 27,000 marks (6628 kg) of silver, 21,000 marks (5150 kg) of pure gold (corresponding to 1,449,000 florins but presumably in bars) and half a cart (*garleta*) of florins.[12] This enormous quantity of gold must have amounted to several years' total yield, and we would probably be not too far from the truth in estimating the annual production of the Hungarian gold mines at from 1000 to 1500 kg.

Of the measures that were aimed at increasing the revenues of the treasury, the most important were doubtless those concerning the production of precious metals. But there were others that were also far from insignificant. It has been suggested that it was under the Angevins that the almost inexhaustible salt-mines in Maramureş were discovered. Thanks to their exploitation, the monopoly of salt was to become the most important source of royal revenue by the beginning of the fifteenth century. The new system of taxing external commerce, which involved the reorganisation, extension and increase of the toll called the 'thirtieth' (*tricesima*), must also have been an innovation of the Angevin kings. It should be noted, however, that it was only after a series of later reforms that the revenues from the thirtieth became really substantial.

Chapter 10

Louis the Great (1342–1382)

Charles's successor was his eldest son, the sixteen-year-old Louis. If we set to one side the details, his reign can be seen as the direct continuation of his father's. His rule was based upon the authority that had been created by Charles and which had proved so solid that it was not in the least shaken by the change of ruler. The young Louis was surrounded by his father's faithful and obedient barons and his lands and treasury seemed inexhaustible. He faced no serious opposition and consequently could rely on the resources of his kingdom virtually without restriction.

THE VALIANT KING

The times when royal authority had been constantly weakened by dynastic strife were over. Charles's second son, Andrew, had been brought up in Naples since 1333, and Andrew's brothers seem to have got along well with each other in Hungary. Louis and Stephen were given the titles of duke of Transylvania and duke of Slavonia respectively by their father, though this did not mean that they effectively governed their provinces. Stephen received a household of his own in 1349, when he was allotted a small region to govern with the title of 'duke of Spiš and Šariš'. In 1350, during Louis's second Italian campaign, he was appointed king's lieutenant jointly with his mother. After Louis's return, Stephen was first given the government of Transylvania; then, in 1351, he became duke of Croatia and Dalmatia and also that of Slavonia two years later. As far as we can judge, his political role was not significant. When he died in 1354, at the age of 22, his province passed to his son, John, who was under the guardianship of his mother, Marguerite, daughter of Emperor Louis of Bavaria. In the spring of 1356, when the war with Venice broke out, the court decided

157

to put an end to the autonomous status of the duchy. Slavonia was provisionally placed under the government of a lieutenant (*vicarius*), who recovered the title of ban when the little prince died in 1360. Croatia and Dalmatia were likewise taken from the hands of Duchess Marguerite and bestowed upon another ban in 1357. Henceforth Croatia and Slavonia were to have separate governments until 1476, although on occasion (as between 1397 and 1409) the same ban governed both provinces.

Leaving aside the legends of the holy kings, Louis is the first king of Hungary for whom something of a portrait has come down to us. John, archdeacon of Küküllő, one of Louis's clerics, wrote a biography of him around 1390, according to which Louis was 'a man of middling stature, with fleshy lips and slightly bent shoulders', whose 'proud regard' was the sign of his self-consciousness and authority.[1] In contrast to his mistrustful and stingy father, Louis was amiable, open-hearted and generous. And while Charles had distinguished himself more in the work of administration than on the battlefield, Louis strove to embody the somewhat outdated ideal of the chivalrous and bellicose king. What he liked most was to go to war, 'since it is not the kingship itself that is desirable but the fame that goes with it',[2] and to his search of glory he subordinated politics. Hardly a single year passed without his taking the field personally, but his expeditions often lacked a realistic goal and sometimes even a reasonable pretext. It seems that it was war itself that gave him pleasure; indeed, he could fall under its spell to such an extent that on more than one occasion he endangered his own life. When, during the siege of Canosa in Italy, he fell into the moat surrounding the castle, his barons 'rebuked him for meddling in something that is alien to his royal dignity'.[3]

His other favourite pastime was hunting, and in this activity he displayed no less courage than on the battlefield. Once he was attacked by a bear and his followers were hard pressed to save his life. He visited his 'hunting places' several times a year. He rebuilt the castle of Gesztes and constructed a magnificent palace at Diósgyőr, at the foot of the Bükk mountains. However, most of the time he spent in his immense forest of Zvolen, where three castles built by him (at Ľupča, Víglaš and Zvolen itself) still bear witness to his passion for hunting. Although Petrarch suggested that he should pay more attention to the style of his Latin letters than to his favourite greyhounds, Louis was not entirely devoid of a taste for erudition. After the occupation of Naples he had King Robert's library brought to Hungary, and he bought books himself. His copy of the pseudo-Aristotelian *Secretum Secretorum* can now be seen in the Bodleian Library. His liking for astrology was widely known, and he seems also to have loved history. It was upon his command that the Illuminated Chronicle, a piece of Angevin art unique in Hungary, was made. The codex, once preserved in Vienna and now kept in the National Library in Budapest, summarised Hungarian history up to 1330 on the basis of earlier chronicles. Since it has preserved texts that have disappeared in their original form, its historiographical value is inestimable. No less valuable are the 147 splendid miniatures that decorate the text. These can be attributed to a local artist of Italian education, who can possibly be identified as the German, Nicholas, son of Hertul.

THE NEAPOLITAN ADVENTURE

It is customary to characterise Louis's reign as Hungary's age as a European power. In contrast to many of his fellow rulers, he was not troubled by disobedient subjects: there is no evidence of serious internal problems and we may safely conclude that there were none. Although towards the end of his reign some cleavages did appear in the regime, these had remained under the surface during his life. On the whole, he left a strong impression with his contemporaries, both within his own kingdom and, as far as we can judge, abroad as well. His biographer, who seems to have admired him, thought that 'the perfection of his virtues made him beloved even among the barbarians and made his name seem glorious to many a nation.'[4] Even if this was an exaggeration, it was indeed a foreigner who first added the sobriquet 'Great' to his name, not long after his death.

Immediately after his accession to the throne, Louis focused all his attention upon the Neapolitan question. King Robert died on 20 January 1343 and in his testament he designated his grand-daughter, Joan, as his only heir. Her Hungarian husband had to content himself with the title 'duke of Calabria'. Louis and his mother did their utmost to have the decision annulled and to secure the crown for Andrew. They sent one embassy after another to the Pope and Elizabeth travelled to join her son, spending nearly a year in Italy. She brought with her an enormous amount of treasure to cover her 'expenses', with the evident aim of creating a favourable atmosphere for her son. It appears, however, that Andrew was treated as something of a barbarian in the fine court of Naples. Joan simply could not stand him and was having an almost open affair with Robert of Taranto, one of her cousins. All that Elizabeth was able to achieve was the Pope's consent to Andrew being crowned. However, before the papal bull containing this decision could be issued, the news arrived that the duke had been strangled at Aversa on the night of 18 September 1345.

Although the actual executants of the murder were found, the background to it was never cleared up. Suspicion fell on Joan herself and on her cousins, the princes of Taranto, especially after one of them, Louis, married Joan and was even accorded the royal title by the Pope. Unconcerned with the details, the king of Hungary held the Angevin kindred as a whole responsible for the murder. With increasing anger, Louis pressed the Pope to put Joan on trial, and at the same time demanded for himself the throne of Naples, which he considered now to be vacant. He was not satisfied with the inquisition that had been carried out by order of the Holy See, and, receiving but evasive answers from the Pope, he eventually decided to take personal revenge for his brother's death.

One and a half years after the murder, in the spring of 1347, Louis sent off an army and followed it himself in November. Since the Adriatic Sea was controlled by Venice, he marched through Italy, his army swelling with German mercenaries *en route*. He met virtually no resistance. By the time Louis reached Aversa, Joan and her husband had already fled to Provence. It was to Aversa, the very site of the murder, that he summoned his Angevin relatives, but once they had arrived, Louis promptly set aside his feigned welcoming sentiments and seized them. Charles, duke of Durazzo, was executed on the spot without any formality and the others were held as prisoners. This extreme harshness was to do irreparable damage to his cause, but in the short term Louis met no obstacle when on 24 January 1348 he marched into Naples, took the title 'king of Sicily and Jerusalem' and began his rule.

It soon became obvious, however, that the crown of Sicily was easier to obtain than to hold. Only three months had elapsed before Louis was forced to return to Hungary by the outbreak of the Black Death. Although he installed his mercenaries in several important castles, his rule collapsed immediately after he had left his new kingdom. Joan had returned as soon as September and somewhat later only a couple of strongholds remained in Hungarian hands. At the beginning of 1349, Stephen Lackfi, voivode of Transylvania, whom Louis had sent to Italy with a freshly-recruited army, launched a successful counter-attack, but was forced to withdraw when his mercenaries abandoned him. Louis then realised that his presence was needed in order to maintain his rule.

In the meantime a treaty signed with Venice had opened the route across the Adriatic, and so on 1 May 1350 Louis disembarked in Apulia. Having reduced the coastal fortresses he took Aversa after a month's siege. Joan sailed from Naples to Gaeta. Although the military victory was almost complete, it was impossible to exploit it, for Louis had become so unpopular by this time that he had to leave Naples in the autumn of the same year. He at first went on a pilgrimage to Rome, then returned to Hungary, completely disillusioned. Joan recovered her throne immediately and the remaining Hungarian garrisons found themselves hard pressed once again. By this time Louis was forced to realise that his plan for a union of the two kingdoms of Hungary and Naples was doomed to failure. A peace treaty was elaborated through papal mediation. Once it had been signed by his envoys on 23 March 1352, Louis recalled his remaining troops and set the Angevin princes free.

The Black Death, which struck the West between 1347 and 1352, had reached Hungary in 1349. In March Venice withheld her ambassadors because the plague had already broken out there. In the summer Louis informed the Republic that it was over, but it flared up again and carried off Queen Marguerite in September. Entire villages are known to have been depopulated around Oradea, and in Sopron the year of the plague was later referred to as 'the time of mortality';[5] but it seems that the plague was less devastating in Hungary than elsewhere. Indeed, a second wave that arrived in October 1359 and lasted through the winter might well have been more destructive. A contemporary from Poland claimed that the epidemic of 1349 had mostly taken its victims in the countryside, while that of 1359 decimated the towns and the nobility, and the evidence that we have seems to support this observation. In January 1360 the Venetian ambassador spoke of the deaths of 'many famous barons', and in February he mentioned the great number of victims in Buda and Visegrád.[6] The lists of office-holders show that the voivode of Transylvania, the Judge Royal, the *magister tavarnicorum* and the Master of the Cup-bearers all died during, and presumably as a consequence of, the plague, and the government had to be reorganised in the spring of 1360. Yet it is evident that neither of the two epidemics had disastrous demographic consequences for Hungary, probably because the population was sparse and much better nourished than in the West. Hungary was proverbially rich in food and, as far as we know, had been spared by the famines that had been regularly decimating the West since 1315.

DALMATIA, CROATIA AND BOSNIA

Unlike the Neapolitan adventure, which offered no real prospect of success, the acquisition of Croatia and Dalmatia was an altogether more realistic proposition. From the very beginning of his reign, Louis considered it one of his most important tasks to complete his father's work by forcing the 'provinces' that formerly had belonged to his crown to obedience. High on the agenda was the bringing to heel of the lords of Croatia. The first attempt by the ban of Slavonia in 1344 yielded no success. In the summer of 1345, following the summons of a general levy, Louis marched in person to Croatia and his campaign brought about the desired result. The Nelipčić, the Šubić and the counts of Corbavia all submitted to the king without resistance. The province was to be governed from Slavonia until 1357.

The expedition to Croatia led to a conflict with Venice, which was in any case unavoidable given the disputed possession of Dalmatia. When Louis arrived in Croatia the city of Zadar shook off Venetian rule, as a result of which the troops of the Republic began a prolonged siege. In 1346 Louis returned and attempted to relieve Zadar, but on 1 July suffered a serious defeat under the walls of the city. Zadar fell soon after and in 1348 the king was forced to make peace for eight years. However, on the expiry of the peace in 1356 he took the field once again. This time he was able to secure the moral support of both Pope Innocent VI and Emperor Charles IV, while the lords of Padua joined him with their own troops. At first Louis directed his attack against the Italian provinces of Venice, but his advance was halted under the walls of Treviso and he was obliged to sign a truce at the end of 1356. The struggle was, in the event, decided in Dalmatia, where in the course of 1357 the Republic suffered a series of defeats. The cities revolted one after the other, drove out the Venetian garrisons and acknowledged the Hungarian king as their ruler. By the time Louis arrived at the end of 1357, Zadar had fallen as well, with only the citadel offering resistance. The situation of the Signoria had became hopeless. On 18 February 1358 it signed a peace at Zadar, acknowledging Louis and his successors as the only rulers of Dalmatia. It renounced 'for ever' its claims to rule the cities and islands, assured free movement for their trading ships in the Adriatic Sea and even consented to the doge's abandonment of the title 'duke of Dalmatia and Croatia', which his predecessors had borne for centuries.[7] Louis's victory was complete. He relinquished his acquisitions in Italy, but was now able, unconditionally and durably, to incorporate the whole coast of Dalmatia from Dubrovnik to Rijeka into his kingdom.

Hungarian rule over Dalmatia was not to be challenged in Louis's lifetime, but the friendship established with Padua dragged the king into two further wars with Venice. In 1373 Hungarian troops helped Francesco da Carrara in his war against the Republic, but they were defeated and their commander, Stephen Lackfi junior, was taken prisoner. In 1378 Louis entered into the alliance that had been formed by Genoa with the aim of ruining Venice. In the ensuing war another Hungarian army fought in Italy for several months, again assisting the lord of Padua. The peace of Torino, signed on 24 August 1381 and intended to last 'for ever', confirmed the stipulations of the Treaty of Zadar concerning Hungary. In addition, Venice agreed to pay her northern rival an annual sum of 7000 florins.[8] At the time of Louis's death, Hungarian rule in Dalmatia appeared more solid than it had ever been.

By the time of the Peace of Zadar, Hungarian authority had also become firmly established in Croatia, and it had even come to spread over the western part of Bosnia. Louis had seen to it from the beginning that his rule did not become purely symbolic in these parts. During his Croatian campaign of 1345, he forced the Nelipčić to hand over to him Knin and three other castles. From the Šubić he acquired Ostrovica (near Nin) in exchange for lands in Slavonia in 1347, Omiš (Almissa) in 1355 and Klis and Skradin (Scardona) in 1356. All these castles were to be governed by the Hungarian retainers of the ban.

During the time of the war against Venice in 1356, Louis began to contemplate the occupation of the neighbouring parts of Bosnia. In 1353 he had married Elizabeth, daughter of the ban, Stephen Kotromanić, ruler of Bosnia. This marriage alliance could now serve as a pretext for a move against Bosnia. In 1357 he summoned Stephen's successor, Tvrtko I, his wife's cousin, to Požega and compelled him to hand over the region west of the Rivers Vrbas and Neretva as Elizabeth's dowry. The local lords, who passed under his rule as a result of the treaty, were forced to consent to an exchange of their castles. Louis took into his own hands Imotski, Livno, Glamoč and Greben, and compensated their lords with domains in Slavonia. Some lords, however, were reluctant to accept the proposed exchange and found support from Tvrtko. This was bound to lead to an armed conflict, and in the summer of 1363 two Hungarian armies marched into Bosnia. The palatine and the archbishop of Esztergom attacked Usora (Northern Bosnia), but at the siege of Srebrenik they were so hard pressed that the great seal of the kingdom was lost. (According to the official version it was stolen from the tent of the archbishop.) Louis himself advanced into the valley of the Vrbas, but was forced to turn back from Sokol and only acquired the castle of Ključ.

In spite of his success, Tvrtko was forced in 1366 to ask for Hungarian help against his rebellious brother, and in the winter of 1367–68 he was restored to his throne by a Hungarian army. Henceforth, as far as we can judge, relations between the two rulers were peaceful. In 1377 Tvrtko took the royal title, apparently with Louis's consent.

WARS IN THE BALKANS

During the reign of Louis I there were important changes in the Balkans. The Byzantine Empire was weakened by the civil war that had been sparked off in 1341. Serbia broke up after 1355, as did Bulgaria in 1365. Behind them appeared a new conqueror, the empire of the Ottoman Turks, which at the end of the Angevin period was threatening the southern frontiers of Hungary.

Ottoman expansion did not play a major part in the politics of Louis I. In 1364 he attended a congress in Cracow, along with Emperor Charles IV. At this meeting, Peter, king of Cyprus, tried to persuade his colleagues to join a crusade against the Turks; yet this campaign would have been directed against the emirates of Anatolia, which presented little threat in comparison to that offered by the Ottomans. The Byzantine emporer, John V, who came to Hungary for help in 1366 and spent several months at Louis's court, had a much clearer view of the danger. In return for effective support, he would have been prepared to go as far as to accept the union of the Greek Church with Rome. Louis seemed willing to take the field in person against the Turks, but made the unacceptable condition that the Greek Christians should be re-baptised in the way that the Hungarian Serbs had. The consequent cooling of relations was evident when the emperor left for home in the autumn of 1366. Louis escorted him for a short distance, but turned back before John had left the country: a chilly farewell, indeed, leaving the emperor to wait alone at Vidin until, in December, Šišman of Bulgaria finally allowed him to cross his realm.

The idea of Hungarian supremacy over Serbia had not been raised for a long time. Stephen Dušan (1331–1355) had transformed Serbia into a major power in the Balkans and throughout his life his state remained an effective rival to Hungary. Louis's aim in this period seems to have been to retain the footholds that had been secured by his father beyond the Danube and the Sava. Since these had come under serious threat in Charles's last years, Louis consolidated them by means of a brief campaign in the summer of 1343 and strength-ened Belgrade at the same time. In October 1346, on the eve of his Italian expedition, he concluded a peace with Dušan, based upon the *status quo* and pledged with a matrimonial alliance. Dušan's heir, Uroš, was betrothed to one of Louis's female relatives, presumably with a princess of Silesia. It seems, however, that the marriage never took place, and when Dušan attacked Bosnia in 1350, war broke out again. In the summer of 1354 Louis is found in Serbia at the head of his army.

The situation began to change with Dušan's death in December 1355. Within a couple of years Serbia had broken up into semi-inde-pendent provinces and was unable to put up any resistance. The Rastislalić, lords of Braničevo and Kučevo, were the first to acknowl-edge Hungarian suzerainty. In the summer of 1359, perhaps at their invitation, Louis marched deep into Serbia and defeated Tzar Uroš at Kruševac. The period of the Serbian wars was concluded by a new intervention by Louis in the spring of 1361, when Lazarus, lord of northern Serbia, acknowledged his overlordship. He remained hence-forth a vassal of Hungary, but in this capacity he seems to have acquired Mačva, and direct Hungarian rule in Serbia around 1380 was limited to Golubac and possibly to Belgrade.

As regards Wallachia, Charles' defeat in 1330 served as a deterrent for some years. Albeit unwillingly, Louis had to accept the practical independence of Basarab and his son, Alexander. It seems that personal relations between the rulers were only established at the end of 1359, when Louis led an army to Moldavia. Alexander considered it advisable to submit himself to Louis, who recognised him as lord of Severin, as a result of which the ban of Severin disappeared from the lists of Hungarian office-holders. However, 'following the wicked example of his father', Prince Vlaicu, who acceded in 1364, was reluctant to renew his allegiance to the Hungarian king.[9] Louis declared him his enemy, but before launching an attack against him he turned on Bulgaria to secure his flank. In May 1365 he invaded Bulgaria and took Vidin, the residence of Tzar Ivan Stracimir, whom he imprisoned in the fortress of Gomnec in Slavonia. Vidin was to be governed by a Hungarian captain, who received the title 'ban of Bulgaria' (*banus Bulgariae*) in 1366 and whose authority extended to the neighbouring Hungarian counties including Timişoara.

After the fall of Vidin, Vlaicu of Wallachia submitted himself to Louis, and received the district of Făgăraş in Transylvania as a fief, with the title of duke. Nevertheless, when Šišman, brother of Stracimir and ruler of Tirnovo, attacked Vidin, Vlaicu joined him. In the autumn of 1368 Louis launched a two-pronged attack against Wallachia: he marched in by way of the lower Danube valley, while Nicholas Lackfi, voivode of Transylvania, advanced with another army through the Carpathians. The king took Severin, but Lackfi met with disaster. 'Such a great number of Wallachians rushed upon him from the forests and the mountains' that he perished together with his army.[10] Now Vlaicu took the initiative and reduced Vidin in early 1369, thus forcing Louis to negotiate. In the autumn a treaty was agreed that put an end to the short-lived banate of Bulgaria, but allowed Louis to save face. Vlaicu submitted himself once again, in return for which he was given Severin and Făgăraş. Having promised to remain a Hungarian vassal, Stracimir recovered his freedom and Louis 'sent him back happily to Vidin', retaining his daughters as hostages.[11]

While the tzar, according to John of Küküllő, kept his promise and 'persevered in his fidelity and obedience to his Majesty', Wallachia was not to be held in dependency for long. It was rumoured that Vlaicu had defected to the Ottomans as early as 1374, and in the summer of 1375 Louis marched once more into Wallachia. Prince Radu, Vlaicu's successor, was supported by Turkish troops, but his army was defeated in battle. In memory of this victory, Louis founded a chapel at Mariazell in Styria. Also arising from this military success was a short-lived revival of the banate of Severin. However, Wallachia did not submit to Louis. In 1377 the king constructed the castle of Bran to protect one of the passes through the southern Carpathians. The castle of Tălmaciu had been built at the entry of the other pass in 1370, while Orşova, commanding the road to Bulgaria, was also reconstructed in 1373. All this strategic building activity indicates the extent to which the southern frontiers of the kingdom were not regarded as secure.

Important changes took place during Louis' reign along the eastern frontiers. This region had long been dominated by the Golden Horde, which had naturally been regarded by Hungary as an enemy. Charles's reign seems to have witnessed some Tatar incursions, but nothing is known about relations with the Horde before 1345. In this year, we are told, Andrew Lackfi, count of the Székely, led an army over the Carpathians, defeated the Tatars and placed part of their lands under Hungarian rule. Encouraged by this victory, Louis asked the Pope in 1347 to restore the bishopric of Milcovia, which had been destroyed during the Mongol invasion, and to put a Franciscan friar from Hungary at its head. Louis entrusted the government of the newly conquered territory, which was mostly inhabited by Romanians, to the local voivode, Dragoş. This event is generally regarded as the birth of Moldavia, another Romanian principality.

After the death of Khan Berdibek in 1359 the Horde rapidly dissolved and the Tatars ceased to be a significant element in political calculations. In the turmoil, Moldavia was snatched by another Romanian prince, Bogdan, voivode of Maramureş in Hungary, who expelled the grandsons of Dragoş from their principality. In January 1360, Louis marched against him and appears to have forced him into submission; but five years later, accusing Bogdan of rebellion, Louis deprived him of his possessions in Hungary. From this time on we have practically no information concerning Moldavia; but it was probably with good reason that John of Küküllő wrote that, besides the Serbs, it was against the Moldavians that Louis had to fight most frequently. There is no other evidence concerning these wars, however, and we can only surmise that they took place in 1366, 1368 and 1370, which according to Louis's itinerary were the years that he dwelled in the land of the Székely for several weeks at a time. From the silence of Hungarian sources we may infer that none of these campaigns was successful, but there is some evidence that the situation changed in the last years of Louis's reign. In 1374 Wladislas, duke of Opole and governor of Galicia, led an army to Moldavia and by 1377 he had apparently succeeded establishing Angevin authority there. At least this is what John of Küküllő seems to suggest when writing that around the time of Louis's death 'the voivodes chosen by the Romanians of this country [Moldavia] regard themselves as the vassals of the king of Hungary and are bound to pay their tax to him on time.'[12]

There are chapters of Louis' policy towards the Balkans that remain obscure. We do not know, for example, why and against whom a Hungarian army marched to Bosnia in 1372, to Serbia in 1378, or to Wallachia in 1382. The discovery of new sources may provide an explanation of these shadowy events.

UNION WITH POLAND

Louis's bellicose attitude towards his southern and eastern neighbours was counterbalanced by the continuation of his father's peaceful policy towards the north and the west. Polish-Hungarian co-operation became even closer than before. Not only did Casimir III visit Hungary several times, but Louis frequently helped his uncle who, as we have already seen, from 1339 regarded Louis as his heir. In addition to sending him troops against the Luxembourgs, Louis supported Casimir in his ambitions in Galicia and Volhynia. At least this is what seems to have happened in the autumn of 1349, when the king of Poland took Galicia from the Lithuanians. At this very time, Louis was staying in Transylvania, his task apparently being to keep the Tatars, Lithuania's allies, at bay. His intervention may explain the treaty concerning Galicia that was signed, after the conquest, in April 1350. It stipulated that, on Casimir's death, Galicia would become part of the Crown of Hungary. Louis agreed to assist his uncle in defending it until then. Before the treaty was realised, Louis had been required to keep his part of the agreement on a number of occasions. In the summer of 1351 and the spring of 1352 he personally joined two of Casimir's campaigns to Lithuania, while in 1353 and 1355 he sent troops.

Casimir died on 5 November 1370 and only twelve days later his crown was put upon his nephew's head. The union of the two kingdoms was realised without difficulty, and Louis henceforth ruled over a vast territory extending from Dalmatia to Warsaw and from Sopron to Lviv (in Ukraine). Hungarian historiography of the Romantic era tended to regard Angevin rule in Poland as a national achievement, when 'the falling stars of the north, the east and the south were all extinguished in Hungarian seas' (Petőfi, 1845). In fact the union did not bring about the annexation of Poland to Hungary, and Louis left even less room for his Hungarian subjects to interfere in Polish politics than he did for his Polish followers in Hungary. He entrusted the government of his new kingdom first to his mother, then, in 1376, to Duke Wladislas of Opole, his kinsman from Poland, who had been palatine of Hungary from 1367 to 1372.

There are indications that Louis regarded himself above all as king of Hungary. He visited Poland on no more than three occasions and the overall time that he spent there hardly exceeded a couple of months. If he wanted to negotiate with his Polish subjects he summoned them to Hungary. Moreover, he did not annex Galicia to Poland, but granted it first to Wladislas of Opole and then, in 1378, established an Hungarian administration there in accordance with the treaty of 1350. Until 1387, when it was occupied by Poland, the province was governed by a Hungarian governor who bore the title of 'voivode of the realm of Russia' (regni Rusciae vayvoda). The campaign against Lithuania in 1377, in which Louis led a great Hungarian army, also gave rise to disillusionment in Poland, for the captured castles of Bełz and Chelm were entrusted to Hungarian lords, and the Lithuanian princes of Łuck, Vladimir and Podolia became Hungarian vassals. In 1376 some 160 Hungarians belonging to the retinue of the queen-mother were massacred in Cracow – an unequivocal sign of their unpopularity.

The close ties that linked Louis to Poland did not prevent him from maintaining a friendly relationship with the Luxembourgs. In 1345 he gave Casimir military support against John of Bohemia, but later he tried instead to mediate between them. Indeed, it was surely to a great extent due to Louis's efforts that Polish-Bohemian relations were maintained on a more or less trouble-free footing. In 1343, when the problem of the Neapolitan inheritance arose, the first person to whom Louis turned for counsel and support was Margrave Charles at Prague. When, soon afterwards, Louis married, his young bride was Charles's daughter; then, in early 1345, Louis accompanied John and Charles on their crusade against the Lithuanians. In 1353 Charles (now Emperor Charles IV) celebrated his marriage at Buda with Anne of Schweidnitz, a Silesian princess and Louis's niece: a clear mark of excellent relations, which were maintained by four further visits to Hungary, in 1355, 1360, 1365 and 1366. This friendly atmosphere cooled only twice during Louis's reign: first in 1361, when the emperor was reported to have defamed the queen-mother Elizabeth 'with impudent words',[13] then in 1368, when Charles came into conflict with Casimir III because of his wife's inheritance in Silesia. In the course of both conflicts Hungarian troops marched into Moravia, but these proved to be no more than passing clouds in the generally clear sky of Angevin-Luxembourg relations.

Louis's relationship with the Habsburgs had even fewer blemishes. After his accession to the throne there were no signs of the hostility that had been evident during the latter part of Charles's reign. Louis established friendship and even a political alliance with both Duke Albert II and his sons, and their alliance was regularly renewed in the course of amicable meetings. The only shadow – and that a passing one – was cast upon their friendship in 1367, when Louis approached the dukes of Bavaria in response to Austria's alliance with Emperor Charles IV, who was at that time in dispute with the Hungarian king. No military activity took place, however, and from 1371 the good relationship was not to be disturbed again. It was only natural, therefore, that, when the time came, it was from among the Luxembourgs and the Habsburgs that Louis chose husbands for his daughters who were destined to inherit his kingdoms.

THE PROBLEM OF THE SUCCESSION

The problem of the succession weighed on Louis's mind for many years. Since Elizabeth of Bosnia bore him no children for seventeen years, the only solution appeared to be for Louis to recognise his brother, Stephen, as his heir. When Stephen died in 1354 his place was taken by his young son, John, who in 1355 at Louis's request was also adopted by Casimir III as heir to Poland. John's premature death in 1360 made the extinction of the Hungarian branch of the Angevins a real possibility. For a couple of years Stephen's daughter, Elizabeth, was promoted to heiress and in 1365 the Emperor Charles came to Buda to negotiate her marriage to his son and heir, Wenceslas. Circumstances suddenly changed, however, and the projected alliance came to nothing, for in 1370 a daughter, Catherine, was born to Louis, followed by two others, Mary in 1371 and Hedwig in 1374. Naturally, Louis intended that they should inherit his kingdoms, and as a consequence winning the hand of each of the princesses became a preoccupation of Europe's rival princely courts. The question of which dynasty would inherit the Angevin empire became crucially important, with the outcome likely to bring about a profound modification to the central European balance of power.

The crown of Sicily was also given a role in these political manoeuvrings. Louis had omitted 'Sicily and Jerusalem' from his royal title once the war for Naples had been concluded; but now, having so many daughters to provide for, he decided that he had in fact never renounced them. His barons reassured him that this was, indeed, the case, and when in 1374 his eldest daughter, Catherine, was betrothed to Louis of Orléans, the second son of Charles V of France, Louis promised Naples and Provence as her dowry. Yet Queen Joan, ailing and childless, was still alive when Catherine died at the end of 1378, and the problem of the Neapolitan succession was soon to be settled in a different way.

Charles 'the Small' of Durazzo, nephew of the duke who had been executed at Aversa, had been living in Hungary since 1364. In 1371 Louis invested him with the duchy of Croatia and Dalmatia. After 1373, when Emperor Philip of Taranto died, Charles was the only remaining male member of the Angevin dynasty, apart from Louis. He had a clear right to a part at least of the Angevin inheritance. When Pope Urban VI, who was in conflict with Joan, offered the kingdom of Naples to the king of Hungary, Louis sent Charles to Italy with a Hungarian army. The young prince invaded Naples in 1381, captured Joan and, having taken the crown as Charles III, had her strangled in her prison.

In the meantime the two young Angevin heiresses were married. As early as 1372, the Emperor Charles IV had secured the engagement of his second son, Sigismund, born in 1368, to the one-year-old Mary. Their betrothal was celebrated in 1379 in Trnava in the presence of Charles's successor, King Wenceslas. Sigismund was to live in Hungary in order to learn the language and customs of the land that he was destined to rule. In 1378, Hedwig, then four years old, was married to William, son of Duke Leopold of Austria.

The very idea that a woman, let alone an under-age girl, could wear the crown of Hungary flew in the face of custom. As was to become clear later, the bulk of the nobility were of the opinion that the kingdom, like any other estate, should be inherited in the male line, with Charles of Naples as the only possible candidate. This proposal was not, however, made while Louis was alive, and the king met with little difficulty in gaining acceptance for his ideas concerning the succession. Given the nature of the Angevin monarchy, it followed that his will would prevail, at least as far as Hungary was concerned.

In Poland the situation was different. Louis's efforts there were at first confined to persuading the Estates to accept Catherine's right to the succession. In order to achieve this, in September 1374 he issued his famous decree at Košice in which extensive privileges were granted to the Polish nobility. After Catherine's death, further bargaining with the Estates ensued, this time on Mary's behalf. He tolerated the prelates' overt criticism of his policy, and the only means by which he was able to extract the Estates' acknowledgement of Mary's succession was to shut them up in Košice until they yielded to his will. In the summer of 1382 he summoned the Polish lords to his palace of Zvolen, this time to make them swear an oath of fidelity to Sigismund. His Polish subjects thought that Sigismund and Mary would rule over them, while the crown of Hungary would go to Hedwig and William. But Louis wished to preserve the union of his kingdoms and left both crowns to Mary alone.

RELIGIOUS ZEAL

From the outset, the general atmosphere of the court was determined by an old-fashioned religious zeal, which was not common at this time. Although it is clear that Louis himself was inclined to fanaticism, that this became a predominant feature is clearly to be attributed to his mother. Elizabeth of Poland had to conceal her political ambitions during her husband's lifetime, but after Charles's death there was nothing to restrain her. Due to her influence over Louis, she gained the upper hand at court and for several decades acted as a sort of co-regent. The king clung to her with boyish affection; indeed, it was rumoured that in 1362 he took the field against the Emperor Charles IV merely because he had insulted the queen-mother with abusive words. Even the barons were afraid of her: on one occasion when they were sitting in judgement, they modified their verdict 'out of fear of the queen mother'.[14] For a long time she had no rival. Her first daughter-in-law, Marguerite of Luxembourg, died in 1349, a child of fourteen years; the second, Elizabeth of Bosnia, seems in all respects to have subjected herself to her mother-in-law. She may not even have had a court of her own, for later we find in her entourage the same persons who had formerly served the older Elizabeth. The queen-mother's direct influence prevailed until 1370, when she left Hungary to rule Poland in the name of her son.

Elizabeth seems to have been a fanatical Catholic and succeeded in imbuing her son with her religious zeal. Already in her husband's life-time her favourite pastime had been the founding of religious houses. When she finally secured the power that she had long desired, her passion became overwhelming. We know of 13 churches that, in the course of some 40 years, owed their existence to Elizabeth and Louis. It was at that time that the order of the Paulines – the only order to be founded in Hungary – began to flourish. Taking its name from Saint Paul the Hermit, its first communities were formed in the thirteenth century and had been living according to the rules of Saint Augustine since 1308. At that time the order had some 20 houses, but their number grew to 58 by the time of Louis's death and to 69 by the end of the Middle Ages. The king favoured them to such an extent that, through the peace treaty of Torino in 1381, he acquired from Venice the relics of Saint Paul for the Pauline cloister of St Lawrence near Buda. During Louis's reign in Poland the hermits settled in that country as well and in 1382 founded there the community of Częstochowa, which is now the centre of their order.

Since the Paulines lived a retired life, it was not they but the Franciscans who exerted a dominant influence on royal policy. Half of the some 20 Franciscan friaries created during Louis's reign were founded by the king and his mother. Her favourite was the convent of the Clares at Óbuda, to which she gave a lavish landed endowment, an act that was, by this time, no longer usual. It may have been for these nuns, who were unable to read Latin, that a translation of the life of Saint Francis was prepared shortly before or after Louis's death. It is the oldest known book written in Hungarian.

The religious intolerance that characterised much of Louis's reign can be attributed above all to the predominance of the Franciscans. According to John of Küküllő it was at this time that a decisive break-through was made in the conversion of the Cumans of the Great Plain. The conquest of Vidin in Bulgaria in 1365 presented an opportunity for the conversion of the Orthodox Christians, who since the suppression of the Muslims had been the largest religious minority in Hungary. Orthodox Serbs are supposed to have always lived along the southern frontier, and the number of Orthodox Christians had been much increased in the fourteenth century by the Romanian settlement in Transylvania and neighbouring areas. Like the papacy, the Hungarian Church had always regarded the Orthodox Christians as 'schismatics', but they had tolerated their existence. Now Louis wanted to convert to Catholicism not only the Bulgarians of Vidin, but also the Serbs and Romanians living in his kingdom. In 1366 he ordered the gathering of all Serbian priests, together with their wives, children and movable property, though 'without any sign of mistreatment'.[15] We are told that 'these headstrong people were converted and baptised'.[16] Here, as well as in Bulgaria, the work of conversion was undertaken by the Franciscans, who were given no fewer than seven new friaries between the Rivers Mureş and Danube at this time. In spite of their efforts, success proved to be ephemeral. No sooner had Louis died than the Orthodox population 'relapsed into their former erring and even became worse than ever before',[17] and indeed both the Serbs and the Romanians remained attached to the Orthodox Church. The mission of the Franciscans yielded more success in Bosnia, where they soon came to form a separate province of their own. Louis supported them with the full weight of his authority, while their spiritual direction was initially in the hands of the bishop of Bosnia, residing in Djakovo in Hungary.

It was also during these years that the only attempt was made to expel the Jews from Hungary. Jewish communities had been living in several towns of the kingdom since the early Árpádian era, and although their situation had worsened by the end of the thirteenth century it was still more favourable here than in most parts of Europe. In 1279 the council of Buda prescribed that Jews should bear distinctive signs on their clothes. It also forbade the entrusting of the administration of royal revenues to Jews, and in fact we find none at the head of the royal chambers after 1280. However, within the walls of towns they lived undisturbed in their own streets and enjoyed the same rights as Christians. Important changes in this respect were effected during Louis's reign. Although there were no hysterical persecutions like those in Germany, the Jews were expelled from the kingdom sometime around 1360. They were allowed to take their movable wealth with them, but their fixed property was lost. A couple of years later, around 1367, they were permitted to return, but they were obliged to buy new houses. It is probable that, henceforth, their number was considerably smaller. The Jews were denied civic rights, and the former regulation promulgated by Béla IV in 1251 came into force. According to this, they were to be regarded as 'serfs of the chamber' and only Christians could act as judges in their cases against Christians. They owed an annual tax to the treasury, and from 1371 their interests were entrusted to a 'judge of the Jews of the realm' (*iudex Iudaeorum regni*), an office occupied first by the *magister tavarnicorum*, then by the palatine or another baron. Later, from the 1470s onwards, the so-called *praefectus Iudaeorum* was put at their head. He was chosen by the king from among the members of the Jewish Mendel family, patricians of Buda.

Louis' staunch support of Catholicism did not, however, extend to his becoming an obedient instrument of the papacy. Throughout his reign he nurtured close relations with the Pope; but, as we have seen, his view of the Neapolitan question diverged strongly from that of the papacy. He also insisted upon the bishoprics being filled according to his own will, and would not tolerate the papal court's support for another candidate. On the other hand, the system of papal provisions, which was the source of so much conflict elsewhere, caused few problems in Hungary, for this was a land too distant and poor to arouse the greed of the court of Avignon. For example, the revenues of the provost of Székesfehérvár, who was almost equal in rank to a bishop, scarcely exceeded those of a canon of Lincoln. As a consequence, Hungarian benefices were not often reserved for or given to foreigners.

Suffering in his last years from an illness similar to leprosy, Louis's religious zeal became stronger than ever. 'He retired from the noise of the crowd and chose a life of pious contemplation in order to devote himself with all his heart and soul and with the utmost devotion to the accomplishment of pious deeds and continuous praying.'[18] He died on 11 September 1382 at Trnava, and his body was buried in the cathedral of Székesfehérvár in a splendid chapel that he had founded there.

Chapter 11

The Monarchy of Louis the Great

Once it had been restored, royal authority remained effective until the death of Louis the Great. His first thirty years were characterised by his liking for armed conflicts and expansionism, even more than by his religious zeal. As long as he pursued this political course the court was necessarily dominated by persons who shared his preferences and who had demonstrated their talents as military commanders. Times changed only when Louis, growing old and afflicted by illness, abandoned his warlike outlook and turned to prayer. By that time, it had become obvious that his successor would be an underage female. In order to overcome the opposition that was likely to arise and to assure continuity of government, a centralisation of power, more complete and more logically consistent than before, was needed. The result was the series of administrative reforms that took place between 1372 to 1382. Although they did not succeed in achieving their ultimate aim, they were important steps in the modernisation of government.

NOBLES AND TENANTS

Between 1300 and 1350 Hungarian society took on new forms. 'Castle folk', *udvornici* or *conditionarii* are no longer mentioned, except when the ruler sought to recover their former lands for himself. The last traces of slavery also disappeared: the few slaves who still happened to survive were mentioned mostly on the occasion of their manumission. The free and unfree groups of the Árpádian period were fused into the single category of *jobagiones*, which is the Latin plural of a Hungarian word that meant something like 'free peasant tenant'. From about 1300 until the dawn of the modern period this class was to constitute the vast majority of the rural population.

The social status of the *jobagio* was more or less the same everywhere throughout the kingdom. His services were many and various, and

174

often burdensome, but they were finite and attached to his holding rather than to his person. Like the 'guests' he enjoyed freedom of movement, a right that had been a privilege of free peasants and officially accepted as early as around 1270. 'They should have the right [it was declared at that time] to depart as freely as they had come.'[1] Departure was, of course, conditional upon the completion of certain requirements. The peasant had to obtain the permission of the village reeve, pay a movement fee (*terragium*) to his lord and discharge his debts. A charter of Charles I, from 1327, refers to these conditions as a long-established custom and it is beyond doubt that the right of free movement was generally accepted from the early fourteenth century and practised throughout the kingdom, with the exception of Slavonia where it was to remain unknown until about 1400.

By the end of the thirteenth century the 'order of warriors' had gone through a similar process of fusion. Henceforth the descendants of the noble kindreds, the royal servants and the noble castle-warriors were all considered to be equally noble. The regional differences that had separated the nobles of Liptov and Turc, and other particular groups, from 'true' nobles gradually disappeared. The nobles of Transylvania were privileged by Charles in 1324, and in 1351 Louis decreed that all the 'real' nobles of the kingdom, including those of Transylvania and Slavonia, should 'enjoy one and the same liberty' (*sub una eademque nobilitate gratulentur*) in the future.[2] It is this article that standardised the noble privileges of different origin and extent throughout the realm, thereby formally sanctioning the process of unification of the noble class that had been going on for many decades.

Henceforth Hungarian society consisted mainly of nobles and *jobagiones*. Only a small fraction of the population belonged to social groups (such as the burghers, the Cumans or the Székely) that did not fit into either of the two major categories. In contrast to conditions in several other European countries, in Hungary the gap between nobles and peasants was wide and almost unbridgeable. Their difference can be simply defined by reference to their relationship to land. Noble was the man who had a house and land of his own, 'in the way of nobles' (*more nobilium*). Those, on the other hand, who were not landowners and lived as 'tenants' or 'peasant people' (*more jobagionum* or *rusticorum*) on the estate of another person were considered 'ignobles' (*ignobilis*). The 'man of property' (*homo possessionatus*) was therefore a synonym of the nobleman, while anyone without a landed estate (*impossessionatus*) was by this very fact counted among the peasants. The only means of acquiring an estate were inheritance and royal grant, both unattainable for peasants. The kind of social mobility that sociologists term 'vertical' was practically non-existent: the great majority of the population never left the caste into which they had been born.

As for the noble family, it was in fact a kindred, a community of 'brothers' (*fratres*) that included all those who had a common ancestor in the male line and 'ate the same bread' – that is, had an interest in the common, undivided property. Until it was divided, the members of the kindred enjoyed the inheritance collectively and were bound together by an unconditional and unlimited solidarity. So strong was this bond that each 'brother' had to share his own acquisitions with his kinsmen. Division of the patrimony, which often occurred only in the second or third generation, was carried out according to strict rules. Every branch (*linea*) of the kindred – that is, every son of the ancestor along with his descendants – was entitled to an equal share of the inheritance. However, since the division broke the ties that had hitherto linked the 'brothers' to one another, henceforth, each branch was to form a new kindred, within which the same rules were again operative.

In a kindred of males, women naturally played a subordinate role. The Golden Bull of 1222 had prescribed that a daughter who had no brothers was entitled to a 'daughter's quarter' (*quarta filialis, quartalicium, ius quartale*), that is, to one quarter of her father's patrimony, and it was to be inherited by her sons. (If there was more than one daughter, the *quartalicium* was shared between them.) The consequential dismemberment of the patrimony was prevented by new rules from the early fourteenth century. Henceforth, a daughter was to receive the equivalent of her quarter in money or movable goods, the land itself remaining in the hands of her kinsmen. Exception was made only when the husband was of 'ignoble' birth and consequently did not have an estate of his own. In such cases, daughters were given a share in land, lest their descendants should be compelled to live 'under an alien roof' like peasants.

Daughters who did have brothers were not allotted a quarter, but could bring to their marriage their mother's jewellery and other movable goods. These objects were thus handed down in the female line, frequently through many generations. If the husband did not have a male heir, his widow became entitled to a dower (*dos*), to be paid in kind and inherited by her daughter if she had one. On the whole, a daughter brought little advantage and much inconvenience for her father and kinsmen. She was held in somewhat higher esteem as a wife, but still remained under the domination of her husband, could not have property of her own, and was not treated as having a legal personality.

THE COURT NOBILITY

Out of the many thousands of noblemen only a couple of hundred were fortunate enough to find a living at court. The barons, the members of the royal household and a few respectable baronial retainers may be counted among them. They were bound together by the king's service, by an unconditional loyalty towards him, and also by a number of advantages that went with their position. Admittedly, among them there were great differences in social standing and they were divided in many other respects, belonging to different cliques or having different political preferences. Yet all those who were linked to the court in some way differed so much from the rest of the nobility that it seems convenient to refer to them as a 'court nobility', while those who lived far from the court made up what may be termed the 'county gentry'.

Differences between these two groups arose from their respective positions and concerned mentality. Whether or not a courtier, every nobleman set out in life to increase the estates of his kindred, the quantity of land being the measure – practically the only measure – of social rank. Yet the court nobility had a view of family ties different from that of their provincial counterparts, and they also had more opportunities to acquire land and privileges. The conflicts that had decisively set the two groups against each other by the end of Louis's reign derived mainly from these differences.

An important issue in these conflicts was the problem of escheat. Since there were no fiefs in Hungary, the term referred in general to an estate of a person who died 'without an heir' (*sine haerede*). Under the last Árpádians escheat had practically ceased to exist. The fourth paragraph of the Golden Bull of 1222 ordained that those who 'should die without a son' should have the right to bequeath their property at will, with the exception of the quarter that was due to daughters. If they gave up this right for some reason, collateral inheritance came into force, that is, the property would pass to the closest kinsmen in the male line. The king was the heir only in those rare cases when the deceased had 'no kin at all'.[3]

Many cases prove that this rule remained in force until about 1320, but then a radical change occurred. King Charles took possession of every piece of property that could devolve to him, and it seems that after this time none of the lords or major nobles dared to dispose of his estates in the accustomed fashion of the late Árpádian period, though we do not know whether this was as yet formally forbidden. What is clear is that when Louis confirmed the Golden Bull in 1351, he invalidated the critical paragraph and explicitly forbade childless nobles bequeathing their property. 'They should in fact have no right at all to do so,' he ordained; instead their estates 'should descend to their brothers, cousins and kinsmen.'[4]

In Louis's time, the emphasis undoubtedly fell on the first part of the sentence. Later, from the fifteenth century onwards, it would fall on the second, and the statute, as cited above, would be the legal basis of collateral inheritance of the noble estate. The principle inherent in it was to be termed *aviticitas*, for the estate deriving from the ancestor (*avus*) of a kindred was regarded as the common property of all those who could claim descent from him in the male line. Under Louis, and also under Sigismund, the same statute was used in the interest of the Crown. For those who had no relatives, the law was unambiguous. Such a landowner was regarded as a 'unique person' (*unica persona*) and was not allowed to dispose of his wealth without the ruler's written consent (*consensus*). As for collateral branches, their right to the inheritance was at this time accepted only within the third degree, the claims of more distant relatives being rejected and the property confiscated. Whenever a piece of property became vacant, the Crown seized it immediately, and the claims of remaining kinsmen were examined by the royal court. The king's interests were defended by highly skilled lawyers. Their arguments do not always seem convincing, but they are not known to have lost a single case. When a substantial fortune was at stake the king, leaving nothing to chance, decided the case in person. The statute of 'aviticity', prohibiting alienation of property rights in a general way, could thus serve as a weapon of the Crown to expand its right to escheated lands. It was ruthlessly exploited under Louis, during whose reign 21 castles and many other large estates lacking heirs fell into Crown hands.

Charles I had already occasionally exempted some of his barons from the obligation of dividing their estates with their kinsmen, ordering that these lands should remain in the hands of their descendants on the male line, 'with the exclusion of their brothers, cousins or any other kinsmen.' In 1343, immediately after his accession, Louis introduced completely new principles – termed the 'new royal donation' – concerning the inheritance of royal grants. What had hitherto been the exception now became the rule. Estates were henceforth to be inherited only by the direct male descendants of those who were explicitly named in the letter of grant. If the male line died out 'by deficiency of seed' (*defectus seminis*), the estate was to revert to the Crown. The grant could be extended to brothers or other close relatives by having their names included in the document, and it was henceforth the grantee himself who could decide whether to ask for this favour or not. The Cudar brothers requested each of their estates in common, whereas Stephen Lackfi senior reserved most of his estates for his sons, and excluded his brothers.

Another legal device, invented in favour of the court nobility, was the 'promotion of a daughter to a son' (*praefectio in filium*). It also helped to moderate the legal disability of women, which in the eyes of the court was 'contradictory to natural law'.[5] 'Promotions' occurred occasionally under Charles I, but became an everyday practice during Louis's reign. The ruler, making use of 'the plenitude of his power', invested a daughter who did not have brothers with the rights of a son, conferring upon her the inheritance that she would have received if she had been born male. In most cases this form of royal favour was petitioned by the girl's bridegroom, a courtier as a rule, who thereby acquired his wife's landed property. In this way, for example, Louis promoted to heiresses each of the wives taken by the four Cudar brothers.

THE DECLINE OF THE COUNTY

The inherently unfavourable situation of the county nobility could not fail to have damaging consequences for the county, the organ of their self-government. During Charles I's reign, the county was still an institution of considerable authority. The king's count spent a lot of time in the province entrusted to him, and actively participated in its government. For its inhabitants 'of any rank and status', he held assemblies (*congregatio*), over which he presided in person. Since his seal was regarded as authentic, his charters were accepted as legal proofs by law courts all over the kingdom. He had the right of sitting in judgement not only over criminals but also in cases of disputed ownership between nobles. The noble magistrates who acted as his fellow judges came from respectable families within the county.

During Louis's reign the situation changed profoundly. The first to fall victim to the royal court's centralising efforts was the count, who around 1350 was denied the right of using an authenticating seal. Henceforth all cases concerning property rights were to be decided by the central law courts, a measure that drastically curtailed the authority of the county court. The suppression of the county assemblies followed as a second step: their competence was taken over by the general eyre of the palatine and his staff. From as early as 1342 it was the responsibility of the palatine to visit all counties regularly and to hold an assembly in each. His main duty was to ensure the maintenance of public order and to proscribe notorious malefactors, but he also sat in judgement in all cases concerning the nobility. His assembly became practically the only local forum where the county gentry could meet a person who represented supreme authority. In fact they rarely, if ever, had that opportunity, for the palatine was far too great a lord to waste his time dealing with the petty affairs of a county. His assemblies were normally held by his deputies, whom he entrusted with his seal to act in his name with full authority.

The judicial competence of the county was further limited by the granting of exemptions. This occurred sporadically under the

Árpádians, but under the Angevins became a fairly regular favour. The grantee was taken, together with his land and his people, out of the legal authority of the county, and subjected directly to the judgement of the baronial courts or the king himself.

An even heavier blow to the county's authority was the granting to landowners of the privilege called *ius gladii*. During Charles I's reign such a grant was exceptional; under his son it became habitual. In the past, the count and the noble magistrates had held the exclusive right to execute or mutilate criminals who had been caught within the boundaries of their county. Landlords could pronounce a sentence to this effect, but were required to deliver the convict to the count's men. The new privilege of *ius gladii* invested those who acquired it with the powers of the county magistrate within the boundaries of their estate, hence the privilege was called 'free county' (*szabadispánság*) in the vernacular.

All these developments undermined the county's prestige. Having no incentive to stay in his county, the count preferred to remain with the king. What was left of his duties was henceforth carried out by his deputy, whom he appointed from among his retainers or, less often, from the ranks of the county gentry. It was now the deputy count who presided at the law court of the county (*sedes iudiciaria*, later abbreviated as *sedria*). This was convened at two-week intervals but dealt only with local matters of no importance. As a natural consequence, the office of the noble magistrates lost most of its weight and from about 1360 only the poorest nobles were willing to undertake it.

The nobility had thus been split into two unequal parts. The small proportion of noblemen who lived at the royal court had easy access to offices, estates and privileges. They could contract profitable marriages and were in most cases able to bequeath their advantageous position to their sons. However, the overwhelming majority of noblemen were excluded from all the advantages that went with life at court. Those who reflected upon their predicament would have found it difficult to avoid the conclusion that they had been cast in the role of life's perpetual losers. Whereas his fellows in the king's entourage amassed enormous riches, the provincial nobleman saw his fortune melting away. Not only was he unable to acquire new land, he had also to fear for his ancestral estates. Land he believed to be the lawful property of his family was taken away from him by means of a 'promotion'; his brothers who had made their fortune cheated and defrauded him; and if he went to law, he was bound to lose. In addition to this, he had to acquiesce in the decline of the county's authority; and he was forced to tolerate the trampling of his liberties and also the arrogance and arbitrary methods of the barons and their retainers.

During the 40 years of Louis's reign there was but one occasion when the grievances of the counties were, if not redressed, then at least listened to. In November 1351 Louis convened a diet at Buda, and on 11 December he sanctioned a statute that was aimed at redressing some of the nobility's complaints. A number of paragraphs were directed against the king's towns or ecclesiastics, but no matters of real importance were touched upon, and the diet was only memorable because the king solemnly confirmed 'for all times' the Golden Bull of 1222, though with the explicit exception of the article, discussed above, concerning the bequest of property by childless nobles.

As a consequence of the opposition's temporary success, another diet was held at Székesfehérvár on 20 August (St Stephen's day) of the following year, in accordance with the Golden Bull. This was the last concession that the Estates were able to extort from Louis. No further diets were convened for 33 years, nor did those that had been held leave a lasting mark on political life. Royal authority was no less solid in the years after 1352 than it had been before 1351. The nobility was obliged, as before, to take up arms whenever required, despite the provisions to the contrary of the Golden Bull, which had just been confirmed.

A reflection of the resentment that must have been general among the county gentry may be found in a contemporary legend about Nicholas Toldi, a knight of exceptional physical strength. The story was first committed to writing in the sixteenth century and became widely known through János Arany's famous epic of 1847. According to his legend, Toldi was compelled by his brother George, one of Louis's courtiers, to live the life of a peasant; but he managed to take revenge and struggled his way up to become the king's favourite knight. In fact, both Nicholas and George were real people. As a lesser nobleman from Bihor county, Nicholas began his career in about 1350 in the service of Simon Meggyesi, assisting him as deputy count of Pressburg and following him to Italy in 1360 as a captain in his army. Nicholas remained there for five years as a mercenary captain. On his return home, he became a knight of the royal household and governed several counties successively. It is more than probable that the frustrated ambitions of the county gentry found a literary expression in Nicholas Toldi's story.

WARLIKE BARONS

Those who succeeded in making a court career were often able to found a 'dynasty' of courtiers. Their sons grew up in the royal household as a matter of course, and they could also gain admission for their brothers or other kinsmen to whom they were particularly attached. In this way, the court nobility formed a distinct social group, comprising a number of families that served the ruler from one generation to the next. Upward mobility within the group was possible, but a leading elite of 30 to 40 illustrious kindreds, who monopolised almost all the important offices, clearly stands out, as may be illustrated by several examples.

Among the leaders of Charles's government, Thomas Szécsényi was able to preserve and even extend his influence, being not only a favourite of the queen-mother, but also a relative of hers through his second marriage with a princess of Auschwitz (in Silesia). After the death of Palatine William Druget in September 1342, Szécsényi ousted William's brothers from power, having induced the king to confiscate most of the Druget lands, and died as judge royal in 1354. His son, Nicholas, held lesser dignities for a while and died as ban of Croatia in 1368. A much more important personality was Nicholas Szécsi, who was probably Thomas Szécsényi's son-in-law. Although not belonging to any baronial clique, he enjoyed Louis's special favour throughout his life. He held the office of judge royal on three occasions, and that of ban several times. After Louis's death he finished his career as palatine. Nicholas Szécsi's authority was accepted by everyone, and all the baronial parties seem to have turned to him whenever they were in disagreement as to the distribution of offices.

Of all the warlike barons of the age, the Lackfi were to enjoy the greatest fame. Their fortunes may be taken as illustrative of baronial dynasties of the Angevin era. Their ancestor, Ladislaus (also called Lack, a diminutive of Ladislaus), was a kinsman of Lambert Hermán (d. 1324), who was judge royal. Lack himself was count of the Székely from 1328. His eldest son, Stephen (d. 1353), was simultaneously Master of the Horse and governor of several counties, while another of Lack's sons, Denis, who joined the Franciscan order, became the future Louis I's tutor and died as archbishop of Kalocsa in 1355. The family's spectacular rise began after Louis's accession. Stephen himself, his three brothers and four sons remained in power continuously until 1376. Five members of the family – Stephen's brother, Andrew, and his four sons – succeeded one another in the office of voivode of Transylvania between 1356 and 1376; one of Stephen's sons, Emeric, was also palatine from 1372 to 1375. Younger brothers in the family held the office of Master of the Horse continuously until as late as 1395. During these years the Lackfi accumulated many estates, mainly through royal grants, so that at the time of Louis's death they were undoubtedly the wealthiest family in the kingdom.

All the Lackfi were soldiers, and their influence lasted as long as an aggressive foreign policy prevailed. Stephen senior was, at one stage, the king's lieutenant and commander of his troops in Naples. Of his brothers, Andrew led the campaigns against the Tatars in Moldavia, while Paul was in charge of the troops that were sent to Switzerland on behalf of the Habsburgs in 1355. Stephen's son, Denis, voivode of Transylvania, distinguished himself at the siege of Vidin in 1365 and became its first commander, while Denis's brother, Nicholas, as voivode, directed the invasion against Wallachia in 1368. The contingent that was dispatched in 1373 to relieve Padua was led by another Stephen, son of Denis and a nephew of Palatine Emeric. The fact that, for several decades, foreign policy was dominated by aggressive solutions seems in large part attributable to the Lackfi, who apparently derived considerable pleasure from military pursuits.

The careers of Peter Cudar and his brothers were in several respects similar to those of the Lackfi; but the Cudar were parvenus. Having in some way gained admittance to the royal court as a child, Peter soon became one of Louis's favourites. Beginning as a page, he was in no time made a squire and then a knight of the household; and, while receiving one privilege after the other, he managed to get each of his seven brothers into the court as well. Two of them entered the Church, Emeric finishing his career as a bishop and John dying as provost of Székesfehérvár. Peter himself was Master of the Cupbearers, and so a baron of the realm, from 1360. He was appointed ban of Slavonia in 1368, and found other baronial offices for two of his brothers. There was at least one year, 1376, when four of the Cudar brothers simultaneously held places on the royal council. The growth in their wealth was proportionate to their standing as office holders. While their father had no more than four villages, they owned 168, with the castle of Makovica, at the time of Louis's death.

The court was by no means free from the usual clashes between rival cliques, though we know very little about them. It is by pure chance that we learn that in 1366 the palatine, Nicholas Kont, 'blackened' Stephen Kanizsai, bishop of Zagreb and lieutenant of Slavonia, before the king, with the result that the prelate was deprived of his offices and exiled. He was unable to return before the palatine's death.[6]

THE ARMY

A baron's commission, under both the Árpádians and the Angevins, was above all military in its nature. In the event of war, it was his duty, and also his privilege, to lead the arms-bearing men of his province to the royal host. His authority was symbolised by his banner (*vexillum*), the usual attribute of military command, decorated with his own coat-of-arms. In the fourteenth century, under Italian influence, the banner began to be called *banderium* (from Ital. *bandiera*). Soon the term came to refer to the contingent that fought under the banner of a baron: the name of a symbol had thus become the name of a military institution. Misled by the emergence of the new term, the prevailing view of modern historiography has been that under Charles I an overall military reform took place that produced a new 'banderial organisation'. However, it seems that no such thing happened, and that the 'banderia' of the Angevins and the 'banners' of the Árpádians were essentially similar military contingents and commanded in the same way. The differences between them were of another kind. First, during Charles I's reign, as we have seen, the counts lost their right to have a banner; second, the class of 'castle warriors', who had disappeared in the meantime, was replaced by other types of arms-bearing men, including both nobles and peasants.

It seems that the general levy, which had been enforced by Charles, continued to be regularly summoned under Louis. As early as the spring of 1343 all the arms-bearing men of the counties were obliged to go to war against Serbia, and in the years that followed similar summonses were frequently issued. Some light is thrown on the composition of the army by a couple of summonses that have been preserved by chance. These were issued by Louis on 15 May 1362 at Zagreb, where preparations for a war, otherwise unknown but probably directed against Serbia, were being made. The surviving summonses were sent to the count of Satu Mare, Benedict Himfi, and to his colleague, the castellan of Şiria, who was ordered to join the Himfi's army. Such summonses were delivered to commanders by a squire of the king's household, along with instructions (unfortunately by word of mouth) as to the plan of operation they were to follow. The army that had to gather under Himfi's banner was surprisingly mixed in composition. Among those who were summoned – including both mounted soldiers and infantrymen – we find the entire nobility of the three counties governed by Himfi, namely Satu Mare, Ugoča and Maramureş; the burghers of the six royal 'free villages' in Maramureş; and the peasants from the seigneuries of the royal castles concerned, including 'all the Romanians' living in the domains of Şiria.[7] It is evident that this rabble of an army, though inexpensive to raise, had only limited military value. What seems to have counted was quantity, not quality, of personnel, so we have every reason to believe contemporary observers from Italy who put the effective strength of Angevin armies at several tens of thousand men.

Not all of Louis's armies were like this, however. It would seem that poor quality armed forces were employed for wars in the Balkans and, perhaps, against Lithuania, but that for campaigns elsewhere, especially those fought in Italy, there was a strong preference for paid troops. Among them were many mercenaries, Germans and other foreigners. Indeed, we happen to know that around 1380 English archers were guarding the castle of Bran in Southern Transylvania.[8] Yet most of the paid troops were undoubtedly Hungarian nobles. A contingent of such men consisted, as elsewhere, of a number of 'lances', that is of heavily armoured knights, to each of whom was attached several archers (*pharetrarii*), also mounted but lightly equipped. The recruitment of 'lances' was the duty of the king's knights who received a commission (*dispositio*) to equip and lead a certain number of men-of-arms, usually fifty to eighty. The sum that was necessary to hire them was supplied by the treasury.

It was these troops that made up the core of the royal army in wars where quality of manpower was thought to be important. The 'lances' mobilised through the household took the field most often under the king's own banner, but the royal army (or at least part of it) might also be placed under the command of a baron. An army organised in this way first made an appearance in Louis's wars in Naples and was later to be employed fairly regularly. Such an army, consisting of hired knights and under the command of the count of Pressburg, Simon Meggyesi, was sent by Louis in 1360 to help Pope Innocent VI against Bernabo Visconti. Simon himself returned to Hungary upon the expiry of his commission, but many of his soldiers remained in Italy. Forming a mercenary company called *Magna Societas Ungarorum*, they were to play an important role in the Italian wars during the following years. The army with which Charles of Durazzo set about the conquest of Naples in 1380 was probably similarly composed. It was led by two barons who apparently had fifteen royal knights as captains under their command.

Such an army must have cost a great deal of money. In the second half of the fourteenth century the monthly pay of a knight and his 'lance' was at least six florins. That of a captain was sixteen florins or more. These costs were for the most part met from the ordinary revenues of the treasury, but on some occasions a heavy subsidy (*collecta, subsidium*) was also levied. Evidence concerning subsidies is frustratingly scarce, and there can be no doubt that they were levied more frequently than surviving documentation would suggest. We do know that in 1323 a war tax of a half *ferto*, that is one eighth of a mark, was imposed on each peasant holding, while in 1332 the assessment amounted to one mark. A sum of one mark may seem remarkably high (it would have been four times higher than the usual seigneurial rent), but we have no reason to doubt it since in 1350 the tariff of the subsidy was no less than four gold florins per household, a sum equal to one silver mark.[9]

For a long time the usual problems of 'liquidity' that afflicted so many of the monarchies of this period did not arise in Hungary. This can be explained, on the one hand, by the archaic nature of Hungarian military organisation, and on the other by the vast resources of the treasury. Ordinary royal revenues, supplemented by special taxes if necessary, seem to have been sufficient for the mounting of campaigns, even on an annual basis. That until at least 1375 Louis encountered few difficulties in financing them can be deduced from scattered pieces of evidence. 'If the money you have is not enough [for paying the soldiers], tell us how much you want,' Louis wrote to Benedict Himfi, then ban of Bulgaria, in 1366.[10] When he dispatched auxiliary troops to the lord of Padua in 1373, he explicitly forbade his commanders to accept any pay from the prince, reminding them that they had all been given sufficient money.

FINANCES

In the early years of Louis's reign most of the chambers were still administered by German citizens from Buda, Kremnica and other towns, but soon the role of Italian financiers became dominant. From 1349, Jacopo and Giovanni Saraceno, two brothers from Padua, gradually extended their influence over one chamber after another. By the end of Louis's reign they controlled all of them, together with the gold and silver coinage. The memory of their activity has been preserved by a high-quality silver penny that was being struck from 1373 and which showed their family symbol, a 'Saracen' (that is, a Negro) head. The Saraceno were the first among the chamber counts to play a part in politics. Although they did not belong to the barons, and one cannot imagine that they were ever admitted to the royal council, their reputation was such that in Dubrovnik their influence was thought to be equal to that of the palatine or the chancellor. It was in their wake, about 1370, that the first entrepreneurs from Florence appeared in Buda. They had a brilliant future before them.

In the absence of data, it is impossible to estimate the scale of royal revenues under Louis I. However, the greatest contribution to them surely came from gold. Due to the incomparable richness of its gold mines, Hungary enjoyed the status of a producer with a near monopoly. As time went on the temptation to abuse this position was bound to arise. As early as 1337 the treasury resorted to a peculiar financial manoeuvre, which involved a radical increase in the price of gold in terms of silver. The new price, being 25 per cent higher than that on the market, prompted everyone to pay his tax in gold, and to exchange his stock of gold for silver in the chamber. After Louis's accession, it seems that this policy was abandoned for a while, but it was resumed in 1352 or 1353 and then lasted until the end of the reign. The price of gold was once again fixed at an artificially high level, and was then raised from time to time, always followed by a fall of the price of silver.

Consequently in every land where the gold of Hungary had any influence on economics the silver currencies began to sink. Apart from Hungary, those most concerned were Austria and Bohemia. Here the exchange rate between gold and silver, which was still 1:12.5 in about 1350, reached 1:14.5 in about 1360 and was as high as 1:16 in about 1375. Expressed in terms of gold florins, the penny of Vienna and the groat of Prague, just like the royal penny of Hungary, were simultaneously losing their value at exactly the same rate. This was not, as has been thought, the result of their debasement, for their mutual value did not change between 1350 and 1380, and the silver penny of Hungary is known to have preserved its weight and fineness throughout this time. Their 'devaluation' was a natural consequence of the manipulated gold price. The effect of this measure seems to have been restricted to the region where the florin of Hungary was in circulation, and was much less evident elsewhere. Whereas in central Europe over the course of three decades inflation reached the rate of 44 per cent, at Venice it amounted to only 25 per cent, and at Florence and on the markets dependent on her, one of them being England, it was hardly felt at all. Here the exchange rate between gold and silver remained stable throughout the whole period.

We may conclude that, for the royal treasury at least, the gain from the raised gold price was substantial enough to counterbalance the loss in revenue that derived from payments in silver. Therefore, the measure seems to have been an element of a well-considered financial policy, the aim of which was to preserve the solvency of the kingdom.

Nevertheless, signs of difficulties, though not perhaps as yet really serious, become evident in the last years of Louis's reign. In 1381, after many decades of stability, the value of the penny began to fall. This was not the consequence of a further raising of the gold price, but the result of a debasement. It was in terms of the silver currencies of Vienna and Prague that the Hungarian penny began to sink, which indicates that its silver content was somewhat reduced. In 1382, the year of Louis's death, one florin was worth 180d while, in terms of silver, this figure ought to have been only 160d. There are indications that this light debasement of 11 per cent may have been due to financial troubles. In 1380, King Louis mortgaged the castle of Steničnjak in Slavonia for 10,000 florins, a new method of making use of royal estates that was later to be frequently employed. His only reason for doing so can have been to raise funds. It is clear that the treasury was experiencing difficulties by this time, but we can but speculate as to their cause. War expenses cannot have played a part, for the last years of Louis's reign were practically free from armed conflicts. We may suppose that a sudden fall in the yield of the goldmines had occurred. This would provide an explanation for the financial troubles that were soon to come and which the kingdom would never be able to master.

THE REFORM ERA

A decisive change in politics occurred only in the last years of Louis's reign. Weakened by illness, the king had become progressively less active and spent an increasing amount of time at prayer. His mother, who had returned from Poland in 1376 and was well into her seventies, did the same. Her place at court was taken by her daughter-in-law, the younger Elizabeth, whose influence had grown steadily since she had given Louis a series of heiresses. It was probable, and by 1374 it had become a certainty, that the crown would pass sooner or later to one of her under-age daughters. Measures had to be taken to make the eventual succession as smooth as possible, and to prevent those who might oppose it from making trouble.

The real threat to royal authority came not from the county nobility but from within the court. By this time it had become clear that the descendants of the Angevin barons were well on the way to forming a new aristocracy that might in due course endanger the authority of the Crown. For the moment, no family was able to defy the king or to restrict his power in any way. The combined possessions of the Lackfi hardly amounted to what any major royal dignitary had at his disposal. Moreover, none of the private fortunes was territorially concentrated. The lands of the Lackfi were dispersed in fifteen counties from Transylvania to the border of Styria; those of the descendants of Mikcs were scattered in eleven counties from the frontier of Poland to Slavonia. As was later made clear, the threat lay in the magnates' hunger for land and their growing self-consciousness. Whilst the fidelity of these men was beyond question, there can have been no doubt that an individual's main objective was to increase his family's wealth. They had also become accustomed to having permanent seats on the royal council and to sharing the offices among themselves. That these developments would have disastrous consequences after the king's death, especially given the accession of a young daughter rather than an adult male, would have been easily foreseeable at the time. Indeed, we may suppose that such predictions prompted the reform measures taken in the last years of Louis's reign.

Beginning in 1373, a slow but decisive change in the personnel of the government took place. One after another, the warrior barons, like the Lackfi, disappeared, to be replaced in the positions of power by men of a wholly different stamp. The long series of high-born, warlike and illiterate barons was followed by a small group of new leaders, men who though not distinguished by birth or military talent, excelled in their professional skills.

Two men of equal weight stood at the head of the movement. Both enjoyed the full support of the young Elizabeth, who seems to have directed events from behind the scenes. One of them was Nicholas Garai, a high-born magnate who took the office of palatine in 1375 and held it for ten years. His uncle, Paul, had been a baron in the service of both Charles and Louis, while Nicholas himself had governed the banate of Mačva since 1359. Having becoming palatine, he gradually secured most of the other offices for his kinsmen and allies and pushed aside everyone with whom he could not or would not come to terms. Stephen Lackfi junior, the voivode of Transylvania, went on a pilgrimage to the Holy Land in 1376, only to find on his return that in the meantime he had lost all his influence. At the time of Louis's death most of the honours, among them almost all the key positions, were in the hands of Garai and his allies. Peter Cudar, then governor of Galicia, was the only serious opponent whom they were unable to remove. However, the moment came in December 1382, shortly after Louis's death. Peter was arrested upon the accusation that he had handed over several castles to the Poles. The power of Garai and Elizabeth had thus became virtually unrestricted.

While Garai seems only to have prepared the ground for reform, it was put into practice by his ally, Demetrius, a clergyman of very modest – probably peasant – origins, who rose from being a simple court cleric to the highest church offices. From 1359, he administered the kingdom's finances, with the new title of treasurer, and then became, successively, bishop of Srem, Transylvania and Zagreb. He was appointed archchancellor in 1377, and became archbishop of Esztergom, and also cardinal, in 1378. Another of the reformers, 'Master' James, was a nobleman, but from a local family of Spis and was called simply 'James of Spis', even after he had become a baron. He was a lawyer by profession, and rose from the status of notary to being protonotary, first of the judge royal and then of the palatine. While the lords whom he served changed continually, he remained in office as a greatly respected expert, and then became a baron himself. He held the office of judge royal from 1373 until his death in 1380.

Also a member of the reforming group, Nicholas Zámbó seems to have been valued for his financial expertise. He came from a petty Transdanubian noble family and began his career as one of the queen-mother's squires. As such he became a chamber count and castellan of Óbuda. He administered the royal finances with the title of archtreasurer from 1377, and was appointed *magister tavarnicorum* in 1382. It is remarkable that in this capacity he went on to engage in financial affairs with the Italians who were at that time renting the chambers – something that not many of his fellow barons can be said to have imitated.

A most conspicuous feature of the new government was that all of its members refrained from amassing fortunes for themselves. Not a single land-grant is known to have been given to them, despite the fact that they were well placed to obtain such favour. What is especially surprising is that estates were not even acquired by those among them, like James or Zámbó, who would have needed significant amounts of land to consolidate their social standing. Somewhat unusually for a prelate, Demetrius did not even favour his own brother, except for admitting him to the royal household. The apparent unselfishness of the 'reform men' can best be explained by their determination to keep the royal domain as intact as possible.

THE REFORMS

Until 1374 the only royal seal that had the legal force of authenticity was the great seal. The king took it on his travels and used it to handle everyday affairs. In the form of a double-sided majesty seal, it was attached pendent to every royal grant. The obverse showed the ruler, whilst the double cross on the reverse, taken from the Holy Crown, represented the 'realm', as opposed to the changing person of the monarch. The two sides of the great seal thus reflected the legal maxim that supreme power was divided between the king and his 'realm'. During at least Louis's reign, it was held that the list of dignitaries included in royal grants was a written expression of the same division of power.

Under the Angevins other royal seals were employed for government purposes, especially for issuing writs. The signet (*sigillum anulare*) of the king, 'the one which he wears on his hand', had a major part to play for a long time. A 'minor' or 'secret' seal (*sigillum secretum*) also appeared in 1331, but its role only began to increase from 1347, when Louis took it with him during his first Neapolitan campaign and used it there as an instrument of power. Although the secret seal quite often accompanied his travels thereafter, Louis was unable to make effective use of it, since the great seal was needed in order to make grants or indeed any other important decisions.

A permanent office that used the royal 'middle seal' (*sigillum mediocre*) was opened at Visegrád under Charles and functioned as a place of authentication. Its head was the 'count of the chapel' (*comes capellae*), an influential court cleric who, for some unknown reason, bore the title of secret chancellor (*secretus cancellarius*) until 1374. He had in fact nothing to do with the secret seal, and had little involvement in politics.

In 1374 the secret seal was declared to have the force of authentication and thereby made the main instrument of royal decision-making, a role that it was to keep until the end of the Middle Ages. The secret chancellor, who now became the keeper of the secret seal, was henceforth to be a dignitary of particular importance. He was to accompany the ruler on all of his journeys, even those abroad, and as a consequence the signet completely lost its former role.

In 1376 or 1377 new measures were taken concerning the great seal, and a new office with the name of Lord Chancellor (*summus cancellarius*) was created. Hitherto, except for the years 1356–66, the great seal had been in the custody of the vice-chancellor, who was the provost of Székesfehérvár until 1351 and one of the bishops thereafter. There was also a chancellor, of course, but his office was hardly more than a title and was left vacant for long periods. As a matter of course the first Lord Chancellor was Demetrius, who was to keep the obverse of the great seal, while its reverse was to be in the queen's custody. The Lord Chancellor was empowered to use the great seal for settling routine affairs in the king's absence and to issue documents in his name.

The Lord Chancellor also became the head of a third central law court of general competence. Established in 1377 at Visegrád, it was called 'the king's special presence' (*specialis praesencia regia*). The other two central courts were those of the palatine and the judge royal. There had been two palatinal courts, held at Buda and Vizsoly (south of Košice), but they were united by Charles in 1342 and transferred to Visegrád. The personal court of the king, led by the judge royal, also resided at Visegrád from 1324.

According to ancient custom the high judges did their work in the company of assessors drawn from among 'the prelates, barons and nobles'. The hearing of cases began on the eighth day (*octava*) following a notable feast – Epiphany, St George, St James, Michaelmas, among others – and lasted for several weeks. Since as many as eight or even ten such terms were appointed each year, the 'octaval courts' were working almost continuously. They were only suspended when the ruler proclaimed a general levy, the next term being set for the fifteenth day after the army's demobilisation. We have no information concerning the number of lawsuits, but there must have many hundreds of them each year, thereby attracting a good many people to the capital.

Demetrius also made an attempt to improve financial administration. He had occasionally been called royal treasurer (*thesaurarius*) between 1359 and 1370, and though we do not know exactly what his functions were, it is certain that he had, or acquired, some skill in financial matters. It is only from 1377 that we regularly meet a treasurer (or arch-treasurer, as he was often called until 1439), and so we may perhaps conclude that the office was created at about this time, most probably on the initiative of Demetrius himself. Initially, the functions of the treasurer were rather limited. He was, of course, the keeper of the treasury, which was called *domus tavernicalis* and located at Buda; he collected the tax from the towns; and he also received the accounts of the chamber counts. But as yet he did not have control over the royal revenues in general, as he was to have later. More important was that the office was generally held by a lay lord who had some accounting skill, and so for the first time there was a man in the royal council who was able to understand and handle financial matters.

Both the Angevin kings made efforts to increase the number of royal towns and to strengthen their position. When the county of Vas was recovered from the Héder in 1327, the first thing Charles did was to confirm the old privileges of Körmend and Vasvár and to grant new ones to Kőszeg and Sárvár. Around 1370 there were, throughout the kingdom, at least 70 royal towns (*civitas*) and 'free villages' (*libera villa*) that had been privileged in this way, not including the Saxon and mining towns and those belonging to the queen. In order to allow them to be autonomous, they were all exempted from the judicial authority of the count or the castellan, and paid their tax to the treasury rather than to the lord of the honour. During the reform years the number of towns was increased by further exemptions. In the county of Trenčín, four great villages were removed from the authority of the count in 1375 and 1376 and were declared to be 'cities'.

The court of appeal for the towns, and their supreme judge, was the *magister tavarnicorum*. His law court had for a long time been assisted only by noblemen and brought judgement in the cases of townspeople according to the common law. In 1376 the court was suppressed temporarily and the judge royal, James of Spis, was appointed judge of 'all the royal towns'. In 1378 the court of the *magister tavarnicorum* was restored, but also reformed. Henceforth it was to be assisted by burghers who were delegated by the towns themselves, and was to use the towns' own customary law in its procedure.

PROFESSIONALS

Behind this series of reforms was an increase in the number of lay professionals – a characteristic of the Angevin century. Hungary was one of those lands that made use of a local law, rather than Roman law. Hence justice was administered by laymen who had to possess a thorough knowledge of common law, even though they did not need much skill in Roman or canon law. In the thirteenth century it became normal for the verdicts to be put down in writing, and henceforth the judges were also expected to have a good command of Latin. The appearance, in about 1326, of paper, which was much cheaper than parchment, brought about the large-scale production of legal documents.

The palatine and other high justices, being both illiterate and actively engaged in politics and warfare, were neither suitable nor probably willing to sit in judgement. Consequently, as a rule they exercised their judicial authority through professional deputies: the vice-palatine (*vicepalatinus*), the vice judge royal (*viceiudex curiae*) as well as the protonotaries (*protonotarius*) of the high justices, all of whom were professional lawyers. The personnel of the law courts, consisting mainly of notaries, had also to have a fair skill in drafting every kind of legal document, and so had those who did similar work elsewhere.

Working in the chancellery, the law-courts, the places of authentication or in the administration of the counties required, therefore, a good command of Latin and a fair knowledge of common law. Both could be acquired in the grammar schools, and those who acquired them were called 'literate' (*litteratus*) in Latin and *deák* in Hungarian, a word which was also to be the term given to Latin, as a language, in the early modern age. All the notaries who made up the personnel of both the chancellery and the law courts had this kind of education, and in the fifteenth century even the places of authentication, although themselves ecclesiastical institutions, began to employ lay notaries. Since all legal documents were drafted in Latin, neither Hungarian nor other vernaculars (except for German in the towns) were ever used by laymen as a written language before the fifteenth century.

Given that literacy was regarded as something quite alien to noble status, laymen who earned a living in this way occupied a position of low prestige. Those who did so were of modest origin, sons of petty noblemen, burghers or even peasants. Barons and other magnates who needed to handle written documents could afford to employ notaries of their own, and all of them did so. That written communication became fairly common at all levels of society is shown by the surviving correspondence of Benedict Himfi, one of Louis's barons. In the letters that Himfi received we find that his cook, Andrew, was not content with his position and asked for another one; that the bishop of Győr sought repayment of a sum of money, which had been borrowed during a campaign; and that the people of the royal village of Hodoş informed him, as their lord, of their firm intention to keep the schoolmaster whom they had elected.[11] It is probable that Himfi was as illiterate as any other lord of his time and that he had a notary who read out the incoming letters and drafted his replies.

Education of a higher level than this was important only for members of the Church. Clerics who had studied at universities, mainly in Italy, played a crucial role in the maintenance of diplomatic relations with the Holy See and other princes. Their special skill was not, however, needed in the royal administration. This may be the reason why all attempts to found a university in Hungary during the

Middle Ages failed. After universities had been founded in Prague in 1348, in Cracow in 1364 and finally in Vienna in 1365, Pope Urban V sanctioned one at Pécs in 1367, though without a faculty of theology. The petition for its founding was issued in Louis's name, but he offered it no financial support, nor did he insist that it be located at his own residence, as would have been normal. We must conclude, therefore, that the initiative came from William of Bergzabern, bishop of Pécs and a German by origin. It was he who provided, from his own wealth, the material resources of the new establishment, which naturally found a place in his own city. The university did function for a period, for an Italian professor of canon law is known to have taught there, but it is unlikely to have long survived William's death in 1374.

Chapter 12

The Years of Crises (1382–1403)

Louis's death cut the ties that had hitherto bound the barons to the dynasty. It was soon clear that in this respect the king was not to be replaced. The ensuing events fully justified the fears of the reformers, for the real centre of authority soon came to be the royal council, within which those who strove to increase the power of their own family, rather than that of the king, prevailed. Five years after his passing, Louis's absolute monarchy was no more than a distant memory. In fact, the extinction of the Angevins' male line had brought with it the beginning of a long series of crises. Calm did not return until 1403, when royal authority was restored.

QUEEN MARY (1382–1395)

Louis's throne passed to the eleven-year-old Mary, who was crowned on 17 September 1382, the day following her father's burial. The succession was effected without difficulty; the regency was bestowed upon the queen-mother, while the reins of government were picked up by Garai and Cardinal Demetrius. Nevertheless, it was clear from the outset that this could only be a temporary solution. Being ruled by a woman must have appeared wholly absurd in a land of patriarchal customs, and where the nobility, regardless of their political sympathies, expected to be led to war by the king in person.

The political elite was, however, dangerously divided over how to find a definitive solution. While the court acquiesced in Louis's will, and accepted Sigismund of Luxembourg, Mary's bridegroom, as king, the bulk of the nobility objected to the very idea of succession in the female line. In their eyes the only lawful heir was Charles of Durazzo, the last Angevin in the male line. Having been brought up in Hungary, Charles was after all not a foreigner, and it was hoped that his accession would bring about the fall of Garai and other unpopular barons. In these circumstances the outbreak of a political crisis was only a matter of time.

There were no immediate problems, however. For the time being Charles was unable to make a bid for the Hungarian crown, since his own throne was seriously threatened by Louis of Anjou, the uncle of Charles VI of France. Louis regarded himself as Joan's heir and, at the head of a French army, embarked upon the conquest of the kingdom of Naples in June 1382. Consequently, in Hungary, it was only John Palisnai, prior of Vrana, who dared openly to take sides with Charles, and the court was able to act against him in concert. The banate of Croatia, where the revolt had broken out, was put under the control of Stephen Lackfi. By the autumn of 1383 he had succeeded in suppressing the revolt. Nevertheless, it was feared that Charles's eventual arrival in Hungary would have unpredictable consequences. In order to thwart his plans, Garai and his partisans resorted to diplomacy. The most obvious solution was to enter into an alliance with Charles's enemies, the Valois, and ask them for a king. The French court was contacted as quickly and secretly as possible, and by the beginning of 1384 the betrothal of Mary and Louis of Orléans, Charles VI's brother, had been agreed. Moreover, to check expressions of opposition at home, a diet was convened, which is something that had not happened since 1352. On 22 June 1384 Mary solemnly confirmed the statute of 1351.

By that time, the crown of Poland had already been lost. Since the Polish barons insisted that their ruler should reside permanently in their kingdom, they were from the outset reluctant to acknowledge Mary as queen. At first, Elizabeth considered taking up arms; but, in March 1383, she contented herself with the accession of Mary's sister, Hedwig, to the Polish throne. She was to rule with her husband, William of Austria, but the Poles found a more convenient solution. After annulling Hedwig's marriage, they crowned her queen in October 1384, and two years later made her marry Jagiełło, prince of Lithuania, who became king of Poland under the name of Wladislas II. Thus the Polish union with Hungary was replaced by another with Lithuania which, besides proving more advantageous in the long run, also presented some immediate benefits. Wladislas annexed Galicia to Poland as early as 1387, and the short-lived 'voivodate of Russia' came to an end.

So troubled was the internal situation in Hungary that the Polish problem attracted little attention. The loss had simply to be accepted. News of the planned French marriage divided the court. The judge royal, Nicholas Szécsi, the Lackfi and the *magister tavarnicorum*, Nicholas Zámbó, openly opposed the queen-mother and renounced their allegiance to her in August 1384. They continued to support the young Sigismund, partly because to set him aside would have been to violate Louis's will, partly because Prague was much nearer to Hungary than Paris and they were naturally anxious to avoid rousing the anger of the Luxembourgs. They had also had enough of the overweening power of Garai and his party. In response to their open resistance, Elizabeth deprived them all of their offices and put Garai's partisans in their place. The kingdom was on the verge of civil war.

However, the most serious threat came from Naples, where events in the meantime had taken an unexpected turn. In 1384 Louis of Anjou died and Charles was quickly able to reconsolidate his rule. His partisans in Hungary immediately invited him to take possession of the throne that was rightfully his. The movement was directed by Paul of Horváti, bishop of Zagreb, and his brothers, all former partisans of Garai. They proceeded with the utmost secrecy, so that in September 1385 the news of Charles's landing in Dalmatia and his march on Buda provoked a panic. By that time war had already broken out with both the Luxembourgs and Bosnia. The armies of Wenceslas, led by his cousins, the Margraves Jodocus and Procop of Moravia, invaded the county of Pressburg and captured one castle after another. In addition, King Tvrtko of Bosnia reoccupied those territories that he had been forced to cede to Louis in 1357, while his lieutenant, the 'great-voivode', Hrvoje, pushed forward to the River Sava, invading the counties of Dubica and Vrbas, which had belonged to Hungary since the Árpádian period. A general feeling of crisis swept the country, and those noblemen who were wealthy enough to have a castle took refuge 'in order to protect their bodies'.[1]

THE CRISIS OF 1386

The news of Charles's arrival forced Elizabeth to yield and the planned French marriage was abandoned. While her envoys in Paris prepared for Louis of Orléans's journey, she made peace with her enemies and bestowed the office of palatine upon Szécsi. The marriage of Mary and Sigismund was celebrated in October, but it turned out to be too late. Charles's arrival was prepared with much foresight. He came not as an enemy at the head of an army, but as a friend in the company of his own Hungarian supporters, claiming that his only aim was 'to unite the realm's divided nobility'.[2] It was impossible either to meet him with an army or to prevent him from convoking a diet. This was attended by a huge number of nobles and, as could have been predicted, Charles was able to secure their overwhelming support. The general feeling was unmistakable. Sigismund fled to his brother in Prague, and, following Mary's abdication, Charles was crowned king on 31 December 1385.

The reign of Charles II (1385–1386) was not, however, to be of long duration. Elizabeth feigned kind feelings towards him as her kinsman, but it seems that she quickly took the decision to dispose of him. After the nobles had departed for home, the new king, without a retinue of his own, was left defenceless. He was wholly at the mercy of his enemies and on 7 February 1386, 39 days after his coronation, they fell upon him in the castle of Buda and took him, severely wounded, to Visegrád, where he died on 24 February. Elizabeth seized the reins of power in the name of Mary and immediately rewarded those who had perpetrated the king's downfall. Blaise Forgách, the Master of the Cup-bearers, whose blow mortally wounded the king, was given the castle of Jelenec, near Nitra. In April, King Wenceslas brought Sigismund to Hungary, and by the Treaty of Győr the queens were forced to accept him as prince consort. Until his coronation Sigismund was allotted the provinces once held by Duke Stephen, while to meet their expenses the margraves of Moravia were allowed to retain, as a mortgage, Pressburg and the castles between the Rivers Morava and Váh, land which they had occupied in 1385.

In Slavonia and the southern counties the war had already broken out. The Neapolitan party, led by the Horváti, declared Charles's little son, Ladislaus, heir to the throne, and took up arms in his name. Elizabeth thought that the mere presence of her daughter would be enough to calm the rebels, and marched southwards with a modest following. It turned out that she had seriously misjudged the situation. On 25 July 1386 her enemies fell upon her small army at Gorjani and slaughtered Garai together with all who were held responsible for Charles's death. Their heads were sent to Charles's widow in Naples. The queens were imprisoned at the bishop of Zagreb's castle of Gomnec.

With the fall of Elizabeth and Garai the fate of the Angevin monarchy was decisively sealed. For the first time since the beginning of the century the kingdom was left without a lawful ruler, and government was taken over by the barons. They formed a formal alliance, which they called a 'league', and a new seal was carved with 'the seal of the regnicoles' (*sigillum regnicolarum*) as the inscription. Parliamentary ideas were apparently not alien to them, but, according to their own interpretation, it was the league as a body that was to represent the realm and to act in its name; and the barons did not intend to share their power with the provincial nobility. In the political sphere they tried first to find a peaceful settlement. In August 1386 they summoned a diet to Székesfehérvár. Here, while reserving the rights of the captured queens, they offered terms to their adversaries. In the name of Mary they promised them a general pardon in return for their submission, and offered the ringleaders offices 'suitable to their status and rank'.[3] The Horváti did not yield, however; indeed, in January

1387 they had Elizabeth strangled in her prison. According to later report, the deed was done before her daughter's very eyes.

An armed conflict was now inevitable. The barons – or possibly the diet – made Stephen Lackfi palatine and conferred the regency upon Sigismund, who took the title 'leader and captain (*antecessor et capitaneus*) of Hungary'. War broke out on all fronts. By December an army of the league had recovered Timişoara and its region, and in January 1387 Sigismund himself marched into Slavonia to rescue the queens. Although he failed, the throne could no longer be left vacant, and he was crowned king on 31 March 1387 at Székesfehérvár. Since Cardinal Demetrius had died in February and the archbishop of Kalocsa seems to have been staying abroad, the ceremony was performed by the bishop of Veszprém as the senior prelate.

KING SIGISMUND AND THE LEAGUE

The fact that Sigismund acceded to the throne through election rather than by hereditary right was of the utmost importance. In order to become king he had to accept the conditions that the league presented to him before his coronation. Moreover, he had to join the league himself, which was in itself an almost irreparable degradation of royal dignity. It was also clearly explained to him that he was expected thereafter to share royal authority with the members of the league. He had to promise that he would respect the kingdom's 'ancient good customs', that his counsellors would be chosen from among the prelates, the barons and their 'heirs and successors', and that he would bestow neither offices nor estates upon foreigners. The barons also authorised themselves, if necessary, to force the king 'by every possible means' to respect the promises that he had undertaken.[4]

Although a list of the league's members has not survived, we can reconstruct it with a high degree of certainty. Besides a few prelates some 20 lay barons belonged to it, representing altogether 12 magnate families. Their intellectual leader seems to have been John Kanizsai, bishop of Eger, who was immediately promoted to arch-chancellor and archbishop of Esztergom. Other leading personalities of the league were Palatine Lackfi, as well as some of Garai's former allies, such as the judge royal, Emeric Bebek, and the two Ladislaus Losonci, the elder being voivode of Transylvania and his younger cousin, ban of Slavonia.

After the coronation the fears that had once so exercised Cardinal Demetrius and Garai were indeed realised. It soon became clear that the main purpose of the league's members was to increase the wealth of their families, and for the time being there was no one to check their ambition. Immediately after Sigismund's accession to the throne there began a rush for parcels of the royal domain. It may well be that, for a while, the young ruler enjoyed being generous; but it hardly mattered since he really had no alternative. The result was disastrous: within a few years, the wealth of the Angevins, which had seemed inexhaustible at the beginning of Sigismund's reign, had vanished. By 1396 as many as 80 of the 150 castles that had been royal seigneuries had passed into private hands, some by purchase or mortgage, but most by hereditary grant, and those who acquired them were mainly officeholders.

Some examples will serve to demonstrate the extent of the change that took place. In the counties of Vas and Sopron all of the seven royal castles that had been under the count's command in 1386 had been granted away by 1392. Kanizsai and his brothers acquired, as hereditary grants, Kapuvár in 1387 and Bernstein in 1392, while Lockenhaus and Sárvár were mortgaged to them in 1390. Neuhaus was given 'perpetually' to Nicholas Szécsi and his sons in 1387, Güssing went to Ladislaus Sárói, count of Timiş, in 1391, while Kőszeg was acquired by the sons of Palatine Garai in 1392 in exchange for their domains lying in Mačva. In Abaúj only one of the six royal castles had been spared by 1392. In Nitra, Bars and Hont 17 castles had been granted away by 1395. Not only castles but also more than one third of the royal towns fell victim to the barons' hunger for land. Confining ourselves to important towns, it was during these years that Csepreg, Körmend, Kőszeg, Pápa, Zalaegerszeg and Güssing in Transdanubia, Nagykőrös, Gyula and Ineu east of the Danube, Sárospatak, Sátoraljaújhely, Gönc, Vinohradiv, Mukačeve, Beregove, Ľubovňa and Podolinec in the northeast and Skalica, Nové Mesto nad Váhom, Beckov, Bánovce, Topoľčany and Prievidza in the north-west became parts of private lordships permanently or at least for a very long time. The vast honours of the Angevin period were now replaced by magnate family estates of a size that had hitherto been unheard of. Around 1396 about half of all castles were in the hands of some 30 noble families, dominated by those who were members of the league. The Lackfi had ten castles, the Garai and the Kanizsai nine each, the Bebek, the Jolsvai and the Losonci each had seven, along with dozens of villages and thousands of tenants.

Sigismund soon tried to loosen his dependence on the league. In 1392 he removed Lackfi from the office of palatine, which was an unusual step, for this office was normally held for life. At the same time he put an end to his ill-considered grants. Thereafter, he rewarded only his most faithful supporters. Moreover, despite his solemn promise, from the outset he had counsellors who were not members of the league. Some of them were chosen from respectable families, like Nicholas Garai junior, who was the son of the late palatine; others were knights of his household whom he raised to high office and invested with enormous fortunes. Nicholas Perényi, the son of one of King Louis's knights, was made Master of the Cup-bearers in 1387 and ban of Severin in 1390, and was given the seigneuries of Sárospatak, Füzér and Trebišov. After his death at Nicopolis, Perényi's influence, with most of his wealth, was inherited by his younger brother, Emeric, who was later chancellor of the privy seal. The king's most influential adviser, apart from Kanizsai, was Stibor of Ściborz, a knight of Polish birth, who was made count of Pressburg in 1389 and voivode of Transylvania in 1395. He received from Sigismund no fewer than nine castles with some 140 villages along the north-western frontier and from one day to the next became one of the greatest landowners of the kingdom.

THE CRUSHING OF THE ANGEVIN PARTY

After his accession Sigismund had to face two great challenges, one of them being the suppression of the Neapolitan party and the other to recover the territories that had passed under Moravian rule. It took several years to accomplish them both, and in the meantime other problems arose, of which the most important was to be the expansion of the Ottoman empire.

The southern counties and Slavonia were pacified as early as 1387. Queen Mary, who in February had been moved from Gomnec to Novigrad in Dalmatia, was liberated from her prison in June with the help of a Venetian fleet. Her status remained somewhat uncertain. In theory she was to be co-ruler with her husband, and in fact she did exercise royal prerogatives in a formal way. She had a great seal of her own, and she granted estates in her own name until 1393, but these were not her own acts, being merely confirmations of Sigismund's grants. Nor did she actively interfere in government affairs. On 17 May 1395 she died while pregnant following a riding accident. Her sister, Hedwig, laid claim to the crown and Wladislas of Poland, acting in his wife's name, invaded the north-eastern counties of Hungary. He was driven back, apparently without much difficulty, by Kanizsai and the palatine, Eustache Jolsvai, Sigismund being engaged in a war against the Ottomans at this time.

The suppression of the Angevin party was only completed in 1394, for the rebels found a powerful supporter in Tvrtko of Bosnia, who gave them refuge and actively supported their counter-attacks. He also occupied most of Croatia and Dalmatia between 1387 and 1390, and all the efforts of Sigismund to take these back ended in failure. Tvrtko died in March 1391, but the situation only changed in 1393, when his successor, Stephen Dabiša, made peace with Sigismund. He returned

Tvrtko's recent acquisitions, but was allowed to keep the territories in the west of Bosnia that had been conquered in 1385. Hrvoje also submitted in 1393, but retained his acquisitions south of the River Sava. In return for these concessions Sigismund received support from Dabiša against his Neapolitan enemies. In July 1394 he took Dobor in Bosnia. John Horváti was taken captive there and, on Queen Mary's orders, was tortured to death at Pécs. At the same time, Nicholas Garai junior, with Bosnian support, finally succeeded in reducing Croatia.

It seems that the opposition led by the Horváti had been very popular among the nobility. John Thuróczy's chronicle preserves traces of a contemporary ballad, clearly pro-Angevin in tone, which tells the story of 32 valiant knights, one of whom was Stephen Héder-vári, called 'Kont'. They fought on the Angevin side and were put to death on Sigismund's orders after a battle fought somewhere between the Rivers Sava and Bosut in the spring of 1388. One of Hédervári's squires was also ruthlessly executed, although still a child, for he was not willing to serve the king whom he called a 'Czech swine'.[5]

Winning back the lands held by the margraves of Moravia proved to be less difficult, but Sigismund found that it could only be achieved by giving up Brandenburg, his family inheritance. In 1388 the greater part of the province was mortgaged to Margrave Jodocus for the enormous sum of 565,000 florins and from him Sigismund redeemed Pressburg and its county on 1 January 1389. Jodocus's brother, Procop, was unwilling to abandon his claims peacefully, and so in 1390 it was necessary to take his strongholds in Hungary by force of arms. This, however, was to lead to a constant state of hostility and further wars between him and Sigismund.

THE ROAD TO NICOPOLIS

During the period of internal wars in Hungary, relations between the kingdom and its neighbours changed profoundly and irreversibly. Ottoman expansion reached Hungary in 1389 and the kingdom was soon compelled to adopt a defensive policy to counter this threat. From this time until the catastrophe of Mohács, Hungary lived, almost without interruption, under the constant menace of Ottoman raids and invasions, which, besides straining her economic and military forces to the limit, also led to internal conflicts. Proud of their ancestors' warlike traditions, the nobility found the necessity of a defensive policy unacceptable. They demanded the same offensive attitude towards the Ottoman empire as had for so long prevailed towards others. The failures that were bound to follow were invariably blamed on those who happened to be in power.

In early 1389, Lazarus, prince of Serbia, confirmed his allegiance to Sigismund, but he was killed in June at the battle of Kosovo, and his son Stephen Lazarević soon became an Ottoman vassal. In early 1390 Turkish troops devastated the region of Timişoara, in 1391 they did the same in Srem, and thereafter their incursions became regular occurrences. Sigismund took the threat seriously from the very first moment. As early as the autumn of 1389 he led an expedition to Serbia, taking Čestin and Borač by siege, and he repeated the action in 1390 and 1391. In 1392 he pushed forward as far as Ždrelo, but Sultan Bayezid, who arrived there in person, refused to give battle. In 1393 the barons led a campaign along the southern frontiers, and Sigismund was also there in August 1394. In early 1395 he mounted an expedition against Moldavia and forced its prince to submit, but this success proved only temporary and Moldavia soon shifted back under the influence of Poland. By this time Wallachia had passed temporarily under the suzerainty of the Ottomans, who raided Transylvania for the first time in 1394. Mircea cel Bătrîn, prince of Wallachia, who had hitherto opposed Hungary with Polish support, asked Sigismund for help in order to regain his land. On 7 March 1395, in Braşov, he agreed to be a vassal of Hungary. However, on 17 May the Hungarian army sent to Wallachia was defeated and its commander, Stephen Losonci, killed. In July Sigismund himself invaded the province, restored Mircea to his throne and recovered from the Ottomans the castle of Minor Nicopolis on the Danube.

These wars were exhausting and yielded only meagre results. Consequently, Sigismund decided to settle the Turkish problem once and for all. He set about organising a major enterprise with the ambitious aim of driving the Ottomans out of Europe. In 1395 his envoys made a tour of the courts of Europe and an embassy may also have been sent to the Mamluk sultan of Egypt. As a result of these efforts the Pope declared the planned expedition a crusade, and by the summer of 1396 an army of considerable size had assembled. Alongside the Hungarians and their Wallachian auxiliaries, the core of the army was made up of Frenchmen, with John of Nevers, heir to Burgundy, at their head, though knights also came from Germany, Bohemia, Italy and even England. In August the army, led by Sigismund, invaded Bulgaria along the Danube and laid siege to Nicopolis. Bayezid, leading the counter-attack in person, marched to relieve the beleaguered castle, and it was there that a European army faced the Ottomans for the first time. The battle, which for a long time was to determine the nature of Hungaro-Ottoman relations, took place on 25 September 1396. The crusader army was virtually destroyed, allegedly as a consequence of the ill-considered actions of the French knights. As for Hungarian casualties, several barons were killed, Palatine Jolsvai captured, and

Sigismund himself barely escaped with his life, fleeing on a ship to Constantinople and returning by sea to Dalmatia in January 1397.

The catastrophe of Nicopolis demonstrated that the Ottoman empire represented a power against which Hungary was unable to wage an offensive war, even with support from abroad. The hope that Ottoman attacks might be stopped through a single determined effort vanished. From this point on priority was given to defence rather than to offensive campaigns. The kingdom had to learn how to live with the constant menace of Turkish incursions.

The Ottomans did not try to conquer Hungary for a long time. In contrast to the Balkan states, which were easily crushed, the kingdom was to remain a rival of the empire right up to the end of the fifteenth century. For the time being it was not Hungary's existence that was threatened but the supremacy that it had been able to impose upon its southern neighbours. However meagre the palpable results of Louis the Great's wars had been, they had demonstrated that Bosnia, Serbia and Wallachia belonged to Hungary's sphere of influence. The Ottoman conquest caused Hungary to lose this position: instead of launching offensive campaigns, the kingdom was forced now to defend itself. Nor should the humiliating effect of the Turkish incursions be underestimated. Hungary, which had not suffered a major external attack since the Mongol invasion, now found herself exposed to plundering raids by the Ottomans year after year.

THE DIET OF TIMIŞOARA

The immediate consequence of the defeat of Nicopolis was a revolt by the Lackfi. The former palatine, who had been deprived of office since 1392, contacted Ladislaus of Naples and was joined in his conspiracy by his nephew, Stephen Lackfi junior, and by a grandson of Ban Mikcs. But that was all the support he could muster. The rest of the league remained faithful to the king, who was therefore able quickly to put down the revolt after his return. The two Lackfi were enticed to the royal court and killed there in February 1397, and the enormous wealth of their family and of their supporters was confiscated.

From this time on Sigismund became increasingly determined to rule alone. The barons of the league were slowly but steadily pushed aside. Only Kanizsai and Detricus Bebek, the new palatine, remained in office after 1398. Their place was taken by hitherto unknown persons, partly from the household, partly from abroad. Immediately after the suppression of the revolt the king took into his service Count Hermann of Cilli (Celje) from Styria, who was to remain his closest confidant (before even Stibor) until his death in 1435. Cilli was given, as hereditary grants, first the town of Varaždin in 1397, then the district of Zagorje in 1399. From this time on, he and his successors gave themselves the title 'count of Cilli and Zagorje' and were the greatest landowners in Slavonia. Cilli's staunch ally was Eberhard, a cleric who probably came from the Rhine region and who in 1397 was appointed bishop of Zagreb. He summoned to Hungary his nephews, lords of Alben in Germany, and persuaded the king to invest them with large estates. It was in 1398 that Filippo Scolari, who was the Buda representative of the trading house Bardi of Florence, was engaged by Sigismund. He was a count of the chamber for the time being, but was later to make an astonishing career under the name of Pipo of Ozora.

Sigismund's endeavour to enlarge his independence manifested itself no less in his reforming activities. In October 1397, in response to the disaster of Nicopolis, he convoked a diet to meet at Timişoara with the intention of organising effective defence against the Ottomans. Forty-five of the 70 articles that were accepted simply reiterated the Golden Bull and Louis's decree of 1351, but the remaining 25 contained important innovations. Whilst being willing to confirm in principle the nobility's freedom from compulsory mobilisation for an offensive war, he suspended this privilege in view of 'the great necessity of this kingdom'. He promised that 'once the present wars are over', that is, after the Ottoman threat had passed, the nobles would regain their ancient liberties. But for the time being he required them to take up arms 'in person', whenever he called them, and to make war on the frontiers, or even beyond, under his leadership or (in his absence) that of the palatine. Those not complying with royal orders would be liable to a fine of one florin per tenant if they had any, and of three marks, equalling twelve florins, per head if they did not. He also ordered that all the landowners 'must equip, as a soldier should be, one archer from every 20 peasant tenants and lead him to war.'[6] With a view to enforcing the edict as smoothly as possible Sigismund ordered a general census of landowners and their tenants in every county. This is the first such attempt that we know of in medieval Hungary, though unfortunately only the roll from the county of Ung has survived. Troops were being raised from landowners according to the number of their tenants as early as 1398. Known as *militia portalis*, these troops would constitute an important part of the army in the fifteenth and sixteenth centuries.

The nobility received little in return for these encroachments upon their liberties. Sigismund agreed not to grant 'promotions' of daughters in cases where there was a male heir within the fifth degree of kinship. In another article, he promised that he would remove all 'foreigners' from their offices, but stipulated that exception should be made for Stibor, Eberhard and Maternus, bishop of Transylvania.

These were, of course, the very persons against whom the protests underlying this article had been aimed in the first place.

The burden of war had also to be borne by the Church. Albeit 'only for the time of the war against the heathens', the king seized half of all ecclesiastical revenues, the tithe included, promising that the money would be spent solely on the defence of the kingdom.[7] Finally, referring to the fact that he had often been forced to yield to extortion in the past, Sigismund had himself invested with the authority to recover all estates that had been given – whether as a hereditary grant or as a mortgage – to persons who had done nothing to merit them; but he would issue special letters patent to his adherents to exempt them from this provision.

Although the decree of Timişoara had been prompted by the Ottoman threat, the ultimate insolubility of that problem soon discouraged Sigismund. With growing intensity, his attention was drawn to the affairs of the Luxembourg dynasty. His brother, Wenceslas, had no children and Sigismund could expect one day to succeed him in Bohemia and Germany. In his struggle with baronial leagues Wenceslas frequently turned to his brother for help, and Sigismund did in fact devote much of his time to Bohemian affairs. He went there in person in 1393 and 1396, while in 1397 he took the field against Procop, his old enemy. He left for Moravia at the end of 1399 and having spent nearly a year abroad, only returned in December 1400. In the meantime, the crisis in Hungary had come to maturity.

SIGISMUND'S VICTORY

On 28 April 1401 the barons, led by Archbishop Kanizsai and Palatine Bebek, arrested the king in the castle of Buda. They demanded that he should get rid of his foreign counsellors once and for all. Sigismund refused to yield, preferring captivity, and the government was assumed by the prelates and barons in the name of the Holy Crown, which was now regarded as vacant. Kanizsai took the title of its 'chancellor', while the council issued orders under the 'seal of the Holy Crown'. Various plans were put in motion with a view to filling the throne: Ladislaus of Naples, Wladislas II of Poland and William of Austria emerged successively as possible candidates. However, the barons were unable to come to an agreement, and Sigismund's captivity did not last for long. It was Nicholas Garai, the king's faithful supporter, who secured his release on 31 August 1401. Garai brought the king to his castle of Siklós and handed over his own son and brother as hostages. Through Garai's mediation a compromise was finally agreed upon at Pápa on 29 October, as a result of which Sigismund was restored to his throne. In return he granted immunity to the rebels, and promised to remove his foreign followers with the exception of Stibor, a promise that he was determined to break as soon as possible.

Thus it was Sigismund who won the first battle, and Wenceslas, observing events from a distance, was of the opinion that his brother was 'more powerful than ever before'.[8] Acting as if his captivity had never occurred, Sigismund began immediately to reinforce his authority. Not only did he refuse to remove his foreign supporters, but, adding insult to injury, he also became betrothed to the daughter of Hermann of Cilli, Barbara, whom he married in 1405. Since Cilli's other daughter, Anne, was Garai's wife, the three families became linked to one another by affinity. Before returning to Bohemia in January 1402, Sigismund took some important security measures, bestowing the most important royal castles upon his adherents. In September he paid a short visit to Pressburg in order to sign a treaty with Albert IV of Austria, who was an old friend. Sigismund designated him as governor of Hungary during the period of his own absence, and made the assembled barons and nobles promise that in the event of his dying without a male heir they would accept Albert as king. He removed Detricus Bebek from the office of palatine, putting Garai in his place, thus disposing of his last enemy, with the exception of Kanizsai, who still held the dignity of arch-chancellor.

These measures prompted the leaders of the opposition to take a decisive step. They offered the crown to Ladislaus of Naples, who had already sent troops to Dalmatia in 1402. At about Christmas 1402 they made a solemn oath of allegiance to him at the tomb of Saint Ladislaus in Oradea, and at the beginning of 1403 the revolt broke out. This time the rebels had a real chance of victory. They were led, as in 1401, by Kanizsai and Bebek, but their movement was much stronger than before, for they were joined by the archbishop of Kalocsa, the bishops of Eger, Oradea, Transylvania and Győr, Emeric Bebek, prior of Vrana, son of Detricus, and by nearly all the magnates, with the exception of Garai and some of his kinsmen. The provincial nobility rallied to the revolt in great numbers, and the general feeling of discontent even drove some of the king's former supporters into opposition. The rebels of the eastern counties were led by the two voivodes of Transylvania, Nicholas Csáki and Nicholas Marcali, both of them the king's own creations.

Against the rebels Sigismund could rely on his barons, his household and the towns, which all remained faithful to him. The most important castles, such as Buda, Visegrád, Pressburg and others were securely held by his foreign captains. Yet his throne was saved by the swift and determined action of Stibor, Garai, John Maróti, Peter Perényi and several other barons who promptly mobilised their contingents and within weeks dispersed the enemy, who had been gathering in rather too leisurely a fashion. At the end of July Sigismund himself arrived from Bohemia, and by the time the army of the eastern provinces crossed the Tisza he had reached Pest. He surrounded Esztergom, Kanizsai's residence, then had the Holy Crown brought from Visegrád and set upon his head in a public ceremony, making palpable that he was the real lord of the kingdom. King Ladislaus had arrived at Zadar in the company of Angelo Acciajuoli, legate of Boniface IX, on 19 July and was crowned there by Kanizsai on 5 August, but this was too late. He left for Italy as early as November, after appointing one of his supporters, Hrvoje, as duke of Split and bestowing upon him the government of Dalmatia. Sigismund's authority was never fully restored in this province, a fact that was to bring about its permanent loss by Hungary.

The barons could do nothing but surrender. The first to lay down their arms were Csáki and Marcali, who on 8 October mediated an agreement with the other rebels at Buda. The king granted a pardon to all those who would submit before a fixed date, and promised to restore their possessions and to annul the grants that he had made to their detriment during the revolt. Bebek and Kanizsai and their kinsmen, who did not lay down their arms before the term expired, were accorded a special pardon, but some of their castles were confiscated and Esztergom itself taken into royal hands for some years. By the spring of 1404 virtually the whole kingdom had been pacified, only a couple of fortresses continuing to resist the king's troops.

Sigismund's struggle with his barons ended with his complete victory. He was to have no difficulty in maintaining his control over Hungary during the 34 years that remained of his life. Many years would be spent far away from the kingdom, yet he would never again face opposition. His enemies at home, weakened and demoralised, could only accept defeat and wait for better times.

Chapter 13

Sigismund's Consolidation

That internal order in Hungary remained undisturbed during the next few decades was probably due to the restraint that the king had shown after his victory. In important political affairs he had no intention of respecting the sensitivity of his subjects, and there had certainly never been as many 'foreign' office-holders in the kingdom as during these years. But Sigismund resisted the temptation to wreak vengeance and was even willing to make some minor concessions. Instead of destroying his enemies he simply pushed them aside. The defeated nobility were allowed to enjoy the fruits of their recent acquisitions, but were no longer to have a say in political matters. In this way Sigismund was able to obtain a certain degree of security, though not popularity. The dislike that he had aroused from the beginning remained alive, but it was not transformed into an implacable hatred that could have incited his enemies to take desperate actions against their ruler.

THE PILLARS OF THE REGIME

Those who had submitted to the king in good time were not seriously threatened. We do know that Sigismund imposed heavy fines upon several barons, and even confiscated some of their estates, but full-scale retaliation was reserved for those who had resisted him till the last moment. After the last date for pardonable submission had passed, these men faced a complete loss of property. In November 1403 Sigismund began to distribute among his supporters the lands that had been confiscated from the rebels. The greatest estates were naturally given to his victorious commanders, the minor ones being divided among their retainers. Strangely enough we no more hear of executions than in the time of Charles I. Indeed, some of the 'notorious rebels', who were forced to seek refuge abroad, later managed to enter the service of a new baron, thereby once again accumulating some wealth.

Sigismund's attitude towards the Church and the disloyal prelates was more severe. He seized the estates of both the archbishopric of Esztergom and the bishopric of Győr. The archbishop of Kalocsa died in exile at Naples, while Thomas Ludányi, bishop of Eger, who had been driven out of his castle only after a siege, took refuge in Poland. For some time, even relations with the Papacy became frosty, for Boniface IX had thrown the whole of his political weight behind Ladislaus. In 1404 Sigismund ordered that no one should be allowed to obtain an ecclesiastical benefice in Hungary by virtue of a papal bull without asking for royal permission. He reserved to himself the right to fill benefices, and even prohibited clerics from accepting and proclaiming papal charters and other documents arriving from Rome without his consent (*placetum regium*). The break in relations with the Holy See furnished Sigismund with a pretext for leaving the vacant sees of Veszprém and Vác unfilled for some years, allowing them to be governed through his own men. He may also have suspended the payment of taxes due to the papal chamber, though the only piece of evidence we have in this respect is his edict for Bohemia of 1403, which he issued as regent in the name of Wenceslas.

Of the three Popes it was John XXIII whom Sigismund finally recognised in 1410. He normalised his relations with him, but did not abandon his claim to govern the Hungarian Church himself. In 1417, when the papal throne was vacant, he managed to persuade the cardinals, assembled at the council of Constance, to confirm the overlordship of the kings of Hungary over their Church. By virtue of this supreme right the highest ecclesiastical benefices were to be filled through royal nomination, the Pope having only the right of formally confirming the ruler's candidate. Though Pope Martin V later refused to acknowledge the council's bull, neither he nor his successors were able to modify the established custom.

It was only natural in the early years after the revolt that influence and offices were reserved for those who had actively helped Sigismund to defeat his enemies. In 1408, on the occasion of the victory against Bosnia, the king bound them together in a formal league, founding the Order of the Dragon (*Societas draconica*), the members of which made an oath of fidelity to one another to perpetuate their alliance. The order, which was named after its symbol, was in the beginning composed of the king himself, Queen Barbara and 22 barons – mainly those who had played an outstanding role in the suppression of the revolt. (Naturally, new members were adopted later on.) It was only after this, from 1409 onwards, that Sigismund began to show mercy to earlier rebels, readmitting some of them to offices. It was at that time that Simon Rozgonyi, who had joined the rebels despite being a household knight, was appointed to the office of judge royal. In 1410 John

Bebek became *magister tavarnicorum*, and Ladislaus Újlaki, one of the ringleaders in 1403, was appointed ban of Mačva. Archbishop Kanizsai was appeased by his appointment to the head of the imperial chancellery. From this time on the former rebels or their sons were once again given access to the *aula*. In 1422 even the exiled Bishop Ludányi was restored to Eger. All this, however, was no more than a compromise made for the sake of internal stability, for political power remained firmly in the hands of the king's former supporters.

The two buttresses of the regime were Nicholas Garai and Hermann of Cilli, both of whom were Sigismund's relatives and his intimate advisers until their deaths. Garai held the office of palatine for 31 years (1402–33), his unwavering fidelity receiving its due reward in the form of lavish grants. At the time of his death he possessed 13 castles and several other estates, stretching from the Austrian border to the county of Timiş, among them Kőszeg, Pápa, Csesznek and Siklós. Count Hermann, his father-in-law, rarely held any office – he was ban of Slavonia from 1406 to 1408 and then again from 1423 to 1435; but his informal influence on matters of politics was nevertheless considerable. Just like his father, Garai was a convinced champion of resolute royal power, and Hermann seems to have been his staunch ally in all his efforts to strengthen central authority. This is why in Hungarian historiography, based as it has been upon the traditions of the nobility, these men have until recently had an evil reputation. The 'Garai-Cillei league', so the old story ran, manipulated the helpless king like a mere puppet, using him as an instrument in the service of their own selfish aims. This interpretation, whilst being naive in the light of the facts, went back to a legend that was widely known in the fifteenth century. The fullest version of it has been preserved in John Thuróczy's chronicle. According to him, the captive Sigismund was entrusted to the Garai brothers by the king's enemies, who knew 'the implacable hatred that these nurtured towards the king because of the murder of their father'. However, taking pity on the young ruler, who wept miserably in his prison, the mother of the Garai dissuaded her sons from taking vengeance. On hearing this, Sigismund 'immediately threw himself at her feet', adopted her as his mother and promised to love her sons as his own brothers.[1] Now it is evident that these events never took place. What the chronicle has preserved would appear to be one of those stories with which nobles in out of the way manor houses passed the time while waiting for Sigismund's demise.

FOREIGNERS AND PARVENUS

The king's other chief advisers were all foreigners. Stibor, a Pole, administered the estates of the archbishopric of Esztergom and the bishopric of Eger after the revolt, and died as voivode of Transylvania in 1414. Pipo of Ozora, an Italian, became count of Timiş in 1404 and governed seven south-eastern counties until his death in 1426, while his kinsmen occupied the sees of Kalocsa and Oradea. At the same time Pipo retained his office as count of the chamber of salt, and from 1415 even extended his influence over the entire financial administration. Eberhard, a German, became Kanizsai's successor as arch-chancellor in 1404, and when he died in 1419 his office passed, together with the bishopric of Zagreb, to his nephew, John of Alben, who had been the queen's chancellor since 1406. In 1423 Alben was appointed imperial chancellor and head of the Hungarian secret chancellery, which meant that he had exclusive control of all of Sigismund's seals until his death in 1433. In the last years of the reign it was Matko of Talovac, the descendant of a merchant family from Dubrovnik, who gathered extensive powers in his hands. He began his career in 1429 as castellan of Belgrade, became ban of Slavonia in 1435 and then ban of Croatia one year later, while his brother Franko functioned as ban of Severin. At the time of Sigismund's death, they and their two younger brothers were governing the possessions of the archbishopric of Kalocsa, and those of the bishoprics of Cenad and Zagreb and the priory of Vrana. They were also organising the defence of the frontier from Turnu Severin to the Adriatic Sea. According to a contemporary list they were in command of no fewer than 52 castles.

Besides these foreigners, several others were given offices in the kingdom of more or less importance. Among them were Sigismund's sister, Marguerite, and her brother-in-law, Frederick of Hohenzollern, who governed several counties for years by means of their German followers; lords from Bohemia and Moravia who had joined Sigismund as a result of his lieutenancy in Bohemia; Stibor's kinsmen and retainers from Poland who guarded his castles; Florentines from Pipo's family; Styrians in the households of Hermann of Cilli and the queen; and also Dalmatians who had fled to Hungary after the arrival of Ladislaus of Naples. After Sigismund ascended the imperial throne in 1411 the number of foreigners further increased. From 1419 to 1423 the archbishopric of Esztergom was governed by Georg von Hohenlohe, bishop of Passau and imperial chancellor. The county of Trenčín was mortgaged to Louis, duke of Brzeg in Silesia, until 1421. The dukes of Masovia, Garai's brothers-in-law, administered the bishopric of Veszprém in 1412. In this year eight out of the 14 bishoprics were in the hands of foreigners, and 23 counties were governed by counts who had not been born in Hungary. Although the role of foreigners had been something of a raw nerve since the time of Saint Stephen, there had never been a period in Hungarian history when their influence was as great as it was during the last 30 years of Sigismund's reign. The completeness of the king's victory in 1403 is perfectly shown by the extent to which he was able thereafter to disregard public opinion.

It must be added, however, that few of the foreigners settled permanently in Hungary. Most did not acquire hereditary possessions and so did not become, to use a later term, *indigenae*. There were, of course, some exceptions: the sons of Onofrio Bardi, Pipo's financial deputy, became lords of Bojnice, and some of the captains of Stibor and Cilli found a place among the provincial nobility. But it seems that Cilli generally rewarded his men by means other than land grants. The Czechs and Moravians returned home with Sigismund when he was crowned king of Bohemia in 1420, while the Italians, coming from a civic milieu, were not really attracted by the noble way of life. On the other hand, it was purely accidental that the composition of the aristocracy was to be hardly affected by a period of foreign influence that lasted several decades. For Pipo died without heirs, the Stibor died out in 1434, the Wolfurt from Swabia disappeared in 1438 and the Cilli in 1456. The descendants of the Talovac were impoverished, while the last of the Alben, who no longer enjoyed the king's favour, moved back to Germany in 1436.

However great the number of foreigners might have been, most of Sigismund's supporters were Hungarians. The leading elite was largely transformed during the course of his reign. At the time of his death half of the 40 or so greatest landowners could be regarded as *homines novi*, and only five of them were foreigners. Nine of the founding members of the Order of the Dragon should be seen as belonging to this group of new barons, among them the secret chancellor, Emeric Perényi; the later judge royal, Peter Perényi; the ban of Mačva, John Maróti; the voivode, James Lack; Peter Lévai, called 'the Czech', the son of Ladislaus Sárói; and Nicholas Csáki. They, together with the Marcali, Jakcs, Rozgonyi, Pálóci, Bátori and Ország constituted the new political elite. They were all descendants of ancient noble families, they had belonged to the household, and were chosen by Sigismund to hold important offices and given suitable possessions. Each of them could trace his origins back through at least four or five generations, and some of their ancestors had already been in royal service under the Angevins. Now, when new men were needed to fill the governing elite, their advantageous position served as a launching pad for a series of brilliant careers. Matthew Pálóci, for example, who had been a simple squire of the household at the time of the revolt, became castellan of Diósgyőr in 1410 and then royal counsellor. He functioned as secret chancellor from 1419, as judge royal from 1425, and finally as palatine from 1435 until his death in December 1436. The important ecclesiastical benefices were also destined for the new barons' brothers or sons. George Pálóci, a brother of Matthew, became bishop of Transylvania in 1419 and archbishop of Esztergom in 1423, while two of the Rozgonyi were bishops simultaneously from 1428.

THE GOVERNMENT

After 1410 the royal council developed towards a higher degree of proficiency. It began to include members who were not drawn from among the barons and who were consequently entitled 'special counsellors' (*consiliarius specialis*). Besides one or two royal captains, we mainly find among them men with special expertise: lawyers like Benedict Makrai and Stephen Aranyi; financial experts like Leonhard Noffri, an Italian, and Marcus of Nuremberg, a German; and administrators like the vice-chancellor, Ladislaus Csapi. Mark of Nuremberg was the initiator of the urban reforms of 1405, while Aranyi worked out the conception underlying the military reforms of 1432. In several respects their role recalls the activities of those who had elaborated the reform plan of the 1370s. But, whereas the latter had all been barons, Sigismund's experts may be called civil servants. They did not benefit from the income of an honour, nor were their services normally rewarded by grants of land, so they probably received a regular salary.

After 1403 Sigismund relied upon his barons and the household, and governed with the same unrestricted power as Charles or Louis had before him. No diets were summoned until 1435, and decisions continued to be made at court. The royal council and the household retained their exclusive grip on leadership. Nor was the ideology modified. Sigismund continued to refer to his 'plenitude of power' as his Angevin predecessors had done, and he used it in the same way. He was prepared to strike down even the greatest barons if he judged it necessary. In 1424 Nicholas 'of Salgó', who was a great-grandson of Thomas Szécsényi and whose father was a member of the Order of the Dragon, was condemned for counterfeiting coins. In spectacular fashion, the king razed his castle to the ground and confiscated the whole of his patrimony. In 1435 the son of James Lack, the voivode, met a similar disaster. The extent of royal authority is perfectly shown by the fact that in 1427, when the only son of Palatine Jolsvai died without heirs, it was sufficient for the court to send a squire to take over his immense heritage.

Nor did the king's frequent absences endanger internal stability. After Sigismund had become 'king of the Romans' in 1410 he spent nearly half of his time abroad. Not counting stays that lasted less than half a year, he spent altogether fourteen years away from Hungary. His longest absence was caused by the war against Venice and the council of Constance (December 1412 – February 1419), while the others were made necessary by the Hussite wars (December 1419 – April 1421,

October 1421 – April 1422), the council of Basle and the imperial coronation (June 1430 – October 1434) and the taking over of the reins of power in Bohemia (May 1436 – December 1437). Thus, for the first time in Hungarian history, the kingdom was left for years without its ruler. Nevertheless, internal order remained stable and government was never impaired. On 6 January 1414, after the proclamation of the council of Constance, Sigismund, then at Cremona, appointed Garai and Kanizsai, the imperial arch-chancellor, as his lieutenants (*vicarius*) for the time of his absence, conferring upon them the right of coinage and of granting pardons in his name. However, Garai remained in his entourage until 1418, and effective government in Hungary was led by Kanizsai, under the control of the arch-chancellor Eberhard and other barons who had stayed at home. The situation was similar between 1430 and 1434, during the king's second long absence from the kingdom. This time he was replaced by a council, the members of which bore the title of 'lieutenant general' (*vicarius generalis*). The council was led by the arch-chancellor, Archbishop George Pálóci who was assisted by the bishop of Eger, Peter Rozgonyi, Palatine Garai, the judge royal, Pálóci, the chief treasurer, John Rozgonyi, and by the *magister tavarnicorum* Peter Berzevici (until his death in 1433).

Since Sigismund took his secret seal on all of his journeys, his presence was felt even during his absences. He was always accompanied by part of the household and by several barons and their retinues, and they were often rewarded by grants and privileges. He also regularly received visitors from Hungary, who kept him informed of events at home. He would then take action if it seemed to him necessary. When Stibor died Sigismund sent a letter of condolence to his widow from Cremona. In 1431 he dispatched a message from Nuremberg to the ban of Mačva prohibiting him from contracting a marriage for his daughter that was not to the king's liking. In 1433 it was from Mantua that he forbade Ladislaus Szécsényi to mortgage one of his castles to his proscribed cousin, Nicholas 'of Salgó'.

Sigismund's exceptional authority was based not upon the royal honours, as had been the case under the Angevins, but upon his own prestige and the support of his barons. By the 1390s, the granting away of royal castles had undermined the foundations of the old regime. There was almost nothing left with which to endow the office-holding barons. The honour that had formerly been held by the judge royal had ceased to exist by 1392, after its centre, the castle of Bystrica (Považský hrad), had passed into private hands. In 1409 the few remaining castles in Slavonia were allotted for the maintenance of Queen Barbara and granted away permanently after 1419. What had been left of the honour of the ban of Mačva was given by hereditary grant to the prince of Serbia in 1411. The most important of the transformations came after the king's captivity, with the suppression of the palatine's honour in 1402. Detricus Bebek, who was removed from office at that time, was the last palatine to hold royal castles as part of his office. His successor, Garai, received none. The royal castles were henceforth usually governed not by barons but by castellans appointed from the household. From the 1410s onwards they were often given the title of 'captain' (*capitaneus*), which seems to show that the nature of their commission had changed. Initially most of them were foreigners, but later Hungarian nobles came to form the majority within the group. Considerable power was enjoyed by some of them, like the two Stephen Rozgonyi, who governed 13 castles in the 1430s, including ones as important as Pressburg, Komárno, Tata or Timişoara. These castellans and captains, however extensive their commissions might be, were no longer powerful barons but simple agents of the royal will. Even if they happened to hold their office as an honour, their duty involved no more than the execution of royal orders. They played no part in the direction of affairs of state. The system of royal honours, which had been the very basis of government since the time of the Árpádians, ceased to exist and what had hitherto been the rule now became an exception. Only the voivode of Transylvania, the ban of Croatia and the counts of the Székely, of Timiş and of Pressburg were allowed the exceptional privilege of holding castles and estates by office. Indeed, the very fact that royal honours had once existed fell into oblivion, to such an extent that, until recently, nothing of their existence had been known.

THE ROYAL DOMAIN

Sigismund tried to conserve – and even build upon – what remained of the royal domain with all possible means. He took possession of escheated properties with the same determination as his predecessors. His methods are well illustrated by the example of the castle of Turna, which he twice confiscated on the pretext of it having no legal heirs. In 1406 he extorted it from the collateral heirs by means of threats, then in 1436 he took it from the new owners by an unlawful verdict that, even today, seems astonishing. Between 1397 and 1437 a total of 62 castles and many other seigneuries (as in 1404 that of Debrecen and in 1420 the possessions of the last branch of the Lackfi) devolved upon the king through escheat or confiscation. Twenty-three cases out of the 62 directly followed the revolts of 1397 and 1403. The heritage of Stibor junior, who died in 1434, was undoubtedly the best catch, for it comprised 11 great seigneuries in Hungary and several others in Moravia. When cousins from Poland appeared and laid claim to it, Palatine Pálóci obediently adjudged the whole of it to the Crown.

While the royal domain was gradually swelling through escheats and confiscations, from 1392 grants became smaller in size. With the exception of Garai, Cilli and Stibor, the king's supporters, both old and new, were much more moderately rewarded than the members of the league had once been. Sigismund can even be said to have become stingy as he grew old. The Talovac had been serving him for eight years before he finally deigned to bestow upon them the greater part of the Alsáni heritage. The Pálóci were given the escheated estate of Sárospatak as late as in 1429, while the Rozgonyi had to content themselves with a couple of villages. But even this level of economy was not sufficient to allow the royal domain to regain, or even to come close to regaining, the material importance that had been its chief characteristic in Louis's reign. Its further dissolution had nevertheless been arrested. According to a list of 1437, 52 castles were still in royal hands, not counting the border castles held by the Talovac on the Danube, in Bosnia and Croatia, to which the five castles of the voivode of Transylvania and the four of the count of the Székely should be added. This was somewhat more than had been at the ruler's disposal in about 1396.

The wealth of the queen had been greatly increased since Louis's reign. Although the two Elizabeths were far from poor, the extent of their possessions was not comparable to that of the royal domain. At the time of Sigismund's death, Barbara of Cilli was richer than her predecessors had ever been. As a result of the continuous growth of her property, in 1437 half of the 52 royal castles were owned by her, the core of her possessions being Óbuda and its appurtenances on the Great Plain, among them the town of Kecskemét with the authority over one part of the Cumans, called the 'Cumans of the Queen'. In 1409 she was given the former estates of the ban of Slavonia. When in 1419 a rumour arose that she had had a love affair with a German knight during her husband's stay at Constance, Sigismund deprived her of her possessions, dissolved her court and exiled her to Oradea. However, a couple of years later, he pardoned her, perhaps out of regard for Count Cilli, and in 1424 lavishly recompensed her for the loss of her former estates. She was now given, besides other estates, the counties of Trenčín and Zvolen and the revenues of the chamber of Kremnica. Later on several important estates of the northern region were mortgaged to her: Diósgyőr in 1427, the county of Liptov in 1430 and one part of the Stibor heritage in 1434. In 1427 she was permitted, once more, to have a household of her own, although its composition was somewhat more modest than that of her previous entourage. Whereas formerly its highest offices had been held by illustrious barons, as in the time of the Angevins and Mary, now they were filled by simple knights who were in no sense regarded as barons.

The number of royal castles having diminished to a dangerous level, their role was partly assumed by fortified towns. During the Angevin period there had been no recognition that such towns might one day play a role in the consolidation of royal authority. They had been considered merely as a source of revenue. However, during the course of successive revolts, it suddenly became apparent that they could also be a force to be reckoned with in the field of politics, as natural allies of the ruler in his struggle against the nobility. On the one hand, the leading elite in the towns was mostly of German and (to a lesser extent) Italian ethnic origin, which meant that they existed outside the world of noble solidarity. On the other hand, in the event of the weakening of central authority, they had every reason to fear the loss of their privileged position and that they would fall under lay or ecclesiastical lordship.

As early as 1402 Sigismund conferred staple right upon some of the towns for the very reason that they had remained faithful to him in the time of his 'necessity', that is, his captivity.[2] After 1403, Pressburg, Košice and Sopron – the most important towns – were entrusted to foreign captains, Buda together with its newly built castle being in the hands of the Nassis brothers from Dalmatia. Later on the king tried to increase the political weight of the towns. He urged, for instance, Prešov, Bardejov, Kežmarok, Spišská Nová Ves and Cluj to enclose themselves with a circuit of walls and even provided financial support for this costly undertaking. In 1405, for the first time in Hungarian history, Sigismund held an assembly for the envoys of the towns, in the course of which he enacted laws with obvious political implications, such as the one by which he conferred upon each of the fortified towns the right to execute criminals. Several of the other royal towns were now promised that they would obtain the privileges enjoyed by the free royal cities if they too built circuits of walls. It was not Sigismund's fault that most of these efforts ultimately came to nothing, partly through lack of resources, partly because of the indifference of those concerned. The walls of Debrecen, for example, were never erected, and the town itself was granted away to Prince Stephen of Serbia in 1411. The political importance of the towns had nevertheless been considerably increased, and they were to play a significant role in the internal struggles of the 1440s.

THE COUNTIES

Sigismund also tried to win the support of the provincial nobility. His chances were less than promising, however, since the old hostility between court and province had if anything been intensified rather than appeased. Nevertheless, since the 1390s Sigismund's chief enemies had been the baronial league and the old aristocracy, who were ever willing to revolt. Confronted as he was by such animosity, the counties could even be considered as potential allies. That is why he took several measures during his long reign that considerably enlarged the authority of the counties in the fields of policing and of civil and military administration. Hitherto the counties had not possessed such extensive powers. They had had the right to execute criminals, to proclaim royal ordinances and, at least since the time of Charles I, to carry out inquiries upon royal orders. Since the 1350s they had also been able to convoke 'proclaimed assemblies' (*proclamata congregatio*) with a view to making official inquiries into local affairs. Apart from these functions, however, they had remained essentially an organ of the local nobility. It was only under Sigismund that the long process began, in the course of which the counties, assuming ever more responsibilities, were slowly transformed into the local organs of central administration.

As early as 1397 the decree of Timişoara authorised the deputy counts and the noble magistrates to proceed in cases involving 'violent trespasses' (*actus potentiarii*), that is, acts of aggression committed by one landowner against another. In essence, this particular group of crimes involved the seizure of someone else's property, the shedding of blood and the unlawful occupation of another's possessions. The county, whose responsibility had hitherto been restricted to the process of inquiry, was henceforth obliged to provide an 'immediate' remedy for the complaint. Only in the event of an appeal was the case handed over to the great judges of the kingdom. With regard to such cases, it was of crucial importance that the law annulled all those former exemptions that were liable to infringe upon the county's competence. From 1409, the procedural mechanism was the 'proclaimed assembly', which was to be attended by the entire political community of the county in order to act as witnesses in some of the most serious cases.

The county's role in the field of military administration had also been increasing since it had been given the responsibility of preparing the registers that were necessary for the mobilisation of the *militia portalis*. But in this respect the decisive moment was to come only in the 1430s, when in the face of the threats presented by the Ottomans and the Hussites, Sigismund attempted to reorganise the army. During his stay at Siena in 1432 he commissioned a comprehensive military reform project, the aim of which was to establish a relatively well-equipped army instead of the hitherto regularly summoned but almost useless general levy of the nobility. 'What benefit would arise from a general levy of the gentlemen of the realm for the defence and preservation of the kingdom,' he asked, 'if many of them, hindered by poverty, age, or other weaknesses, appear on crutches rather than with arms?'[3] The king, therefore, suggested that, instead of summoning everyone in person, the poorest nobles should be given an exemption, with the ensuing loss in effectives being retrieved by means of the *militia portalis*. He demanded the equipment of three archers from each group of one hundred tenants, promising in return that neither his own nor his barons' possessions would be exempted from this obligation. He also suggested that campaigns, which had traditionally lasted for only fifteen days, should be prolonged for 'as long as it may seem necessary to the lord king.'[4] Finally, he wanted to know whether Serbia, Bulgaria and the other 'realms' of the Hungarian crown were to be regarded as parts of Hungary, within which the levy could be summoned.

Sigismund was evidently appealing to the vanity of the whole nobility and to their respect for tradition when, turning to the chronicles to buttress his arguments, he proposed that the warriors of each county 'should take the field under the leadership of the count of their own county, as was the ancient custom';[5] but he seems also to have wanted to carry through his reforms with the support of the lesser nobility. Not only did he insist that his proposals should be sent to all counties in a written form and be discussed by them in their assemblies, he also wanted that every nobleman, 'one by one, should give his opinion freely according to his feelings without fear.'[6] He did not fail to emphasise that his reforms were conceived 'in order to alleviate the burdens of the poor nobles'.

The future of the proposed reform was to be decided by the diet that, after 38 years of non-parliamentary government, was summoned by the king to meet in Pressburg in March 1435. Of all the king's proposals, however, only the one concerning the *militia portalis* was agreed to. In all other respects, the burden of the kingdom's defence was shifted onto the king and the barons. Demagoguery, which had entered Hungarian history for the first time as a political weapon, had not yet produced the desired effect. The consequences of the decision – the fatal weakening of the kingdom's armed forces after Sigismund's death – were, however, not difficult to foresee.

THE REFORM OF JUSTICE

Considerably more success was achieved by the king in his reform of the administration of justice, a project discussed by the same diet and equally intended to strengthen the position of the counties within the regime. The two most important issues were the modernisation of the court of the 'special presence' and the abolition of the universally hated institution that was referred to as the king's 'personal presence'.

Since Louis's reign the central courts of justice had been holding their sessions at the royal court, first at Visegrád, then from 1406–8 at Buda, Sigismund's new residence. We may remember that, since the reforms of the 1370s, there had existed four such courts, including those of the palatine, the judge royal, the *magister tavarnicorum* and the 'special presence of the lord king' under the nominal direction of the arch-chancellor. These were regarded as the 'ordinary judges' of the kingdom. The court of the 'special presence' grew in importance during Sigismund's reign, when it was led, in the name of the arch-chancellor, by a certain 'Master' James, who bore the title of *protono-tarius* or *diffinitor causarum*. Having perhaps been inspired by the reforms of the 1370s, he handled the court's cases with an almost abso-lute independence from 1395 to 1428, frequently going as far as to annul the decisions of other high courts. Although he was one of the kingdom's most powerful office-holders, not even his full name has come down to us, since he seems to have been a burgher and never acquired an estate. Yet the court of the 'special presence' became attached to his person to such an extent that it ceased to exist upon his death in 1428.

All these courts administered justice on the basis of noble customary law, and no serious objections were ever expressed concerning their activity. What seemed really injurious to the nobility was the king's personal judgement, and more exactly the way it was administered, which had been introduced by Sigismund himself and which, since the establishment of the 'special presence', had been referred to as his 'personal presence' (*personalis praesentia*). In fact, this was not a law court in the real sense of the word, but rather the ruler's personal decision, made in his capacity as supreme judge and with the participation of his barons and prelates. Nor was it located in one single place, but could be assembled anywhere within the realm's boundaries, which meant that the parties concerned were normally summoned to the place where the king, 'guided by God, happened to stay at the moment.' While this practice in itself was sufficient to make this institution seem odious, it was impossible to overlook that it was above all used as a means of power. Sigismund adopted the practice of deciding in person all those cases that in some way concerned his own interests. In such cases he might without hesitation annul the verdicts pronounced by the ordinary courts of law, and by his 'special grace' make decisions, not surprisingly on behalf of his supporters, that were not compatible with approved custom. This manner of judgement was much criticised and finally suppressed when Sigismund embarked on one of his lengthy absences from Hungary in 1430. 'Personal presence' was henceforth the name of the royal court headed by the arch-chancellor, and it was ranged defini-tively among the ordinary courts by the diet of 1435.

Several articles of the 'greater law book' (*decretum maius*) of 1435 were intended to protect 'those below' from the powerful, that is, the lesser nobility from baronial aggression. One of their primary objectives was to check the acts of tyranny that had become all too frequent. The county had been accorded powers to proceed in such cases in 1397 and these were now confirmed. Although its competence was in several respects limited, the comital court henceforth functioned with royal authorisation. The deputy count and the noble magistrates were counted among the 'ordinary judges' of the kingdom, and as such had to swear an oath when they entered office. In order to restore the declining prestige of the noble magistrates it was ordained that they should be chosen from among the wealthier nobles of the county. Those who refused to accept the office would be liable to pay a fine. However, this measure failed to bring about the desired result, for the magistrates continued to be chosen from among the poorest nobles, those who had no tenants.

The growing political weight of the county modified its very identity. Hitherto the 'county' had been that ancient territorial unit, partly dating back to the eleventh century, within which the count exercised the *ius gladii*. Where possible, it was bounded by natural frontiers, such as rivers or streams, which might divide a village in two. (As late as the nineteenth century there were villages whose two halves belonged to different counties.) However, the competence of the county court was profoundly altered in 1405, when it was declared to be a court of appeal for every noble, 'whatever status and dignity he may belong to.'[7] Thereafter, the 'county' was to mean a certain number of estates rather than a territory in the former sense. The old, natural frontiers of a county were now replaced by those of the estates that were subjected to the county court. The question of which county a particular estate belonged to – in other words, to which court it was submitted – thus became of great importance for landowners. With increasing frequency from 1411 landowners sought from the king the official attachment of individual estates to another county, generally a neighbouring one, where conditions seemed to them more favourable, and where in most cases the bulk of their other possessions lay. As a result, by the start of the modern period, the ancient county boundaries had been considerably modified.

FINANCES

Taking into account all the difficulties confronting Sigismund during the course of the consolidation of his authority, there was but one that he was definitely unable to cope with. This was the constant shortage of money. As far as we know, he was the first Hungarian ruler to face a serious and constant problem in this regard. Although not uncommon elsewhere, in Hungary it was unprecedented that the entire reign of a king should be overshadowed by the anxiety caused by his never ending financial difficulties. And it seems all the more surprising, given the circumstances of the rule of Louis the Great, who appears to have avoided such problems till the very end of his reign. It has not been by chance, therefore, that in Hungarian historiography Sigismund has long been presented as the incarnation of prodigality, hastiness and financial irresponsibility.

Royal finances continued to be administered by Italian (mainly Florentine) merchants, but after 1390 financiers from Nuremberg also had a growing influence. The increasing political role of money is well illustrated by the exceptional influence that some of these experts acquired. It was now, for the first time, that someone primarily engaged in financial matters, like Pipo of Ozora, managed to join the ranks of the barons. When, in the 1410s, Sigismund attempted to centralise royal finance, he put Pipo at the head of all of the chambers and designated Buda as the centre of financial administration. After Pipo's death in 1426 financial administration was decentralised for some time, but in the 1430s it was once again concentrated, this time in the hands of the Talovac and the sons of Onofrio Bardi of Florence.

The process of devaluation that had begun in the last years of Louis's reign continued at an accelerating rate. One florin was equivalent to 192d in 1385, to 240d in 1386 and to 300d in 1389. Evidently the 'collapse' of the Hungarian penny was not unrelated to the internal troubles. In 1390 Sigismund succeeded temporarily in restoring stability. While leaving in circulation the 'small' pennies of 1387, he ordered the issue of a 'new money' (*nova moneta*), which was greater in size than any of Louis's pennies and worth three 'small' pennies. For 13 years one hundred pieces of the 'new money' were taken as equivalent to one florin, and the process of stabilisation seemed to be successful. But the troubles of the year 1403 decisively undermined the financial balance, and the treasury had again to proceed to a debasement. The price of the florin in terms of the 'new' pennies rose from 100 to 132 in 1403, and reached 160 in 1407, 200 in 1421, 225 in 1423, and 320 in 1426, while the minting of 'small' pennies ceased in 1410. The fall in value of the silver currency seriously affected both royal and seigniorial revenues, and prompted the king to attempt another monetary reform in 1427. From that time to 1437 two types of pennies were in circulation: the 'new greater money', made of silver, one hundred of which equalled one florin, and a small coin, called a ducat and, from 1430 onwards, a *quarting* (or *fyrling*), which was originally worth a quarter of a new penny. Whereas the greater penny maintained its value until Sigismund's death, the smaller one soon fell victim to the manipulations of the treasury. Its fineness decreased at such a rate that soon it contained almost nothing but copper. The result was economic anarchy. Trust in these silver coins was irreparably damaged, and, although the government officially devalued the *quarting* several times, its market value fell even more drastically. In the last years of Sigismund's reign, 6,000 to 8,000 *quartings* were equivalent to one florin instead of the original 400. In 1437 another attempt at stabilisation followed, this time with tragic consequences. The bishop of Transylvania, who had long been reluctant to collect the tithe because of the poor quality of the coins, now demanded that the arrears be paid in the new, good money. The response to this ill-considered step was a peasant revolt about which more will be said in a later chapter.

ORDINARY REVENUES

It is from the last period of Sigismund's reign that the first scraps of evidence concerning the royal budget are available. One third of the income, that is, some 100,000 florins, came from the salt monopoly. Its importance can be measured by the simple fact that Pipo handled it himself until his death in 1426. In 1427 the king took the administration of the salt chambers into his own hands and, somewhat unusually, entrusted them to persons sent out from his household. It was at that time that the centre of salt mining shifted from Transylvania to Maramureş. From 1435 until the end of the Middle Ages the count of the salt chamber of Maramureş was responsible for everything that concerned the commerce of salt. Its production and use were characterised, both then and later, by a good deal of waste. Salt was put into circulation in cubes of different size but of equal price, while salt rubble, a necessary by-product of the mining, was simply thrown away. In 1454 it was estimated that a rationalisation would bring a 20 to 25 per cent increase of the annual income. Sigismund explained to the Estates in his reform project that 'salt is sold by weight in the whole world',[8] but neither he nor his successors were able to break the ancient 'custom' in this matter.

The second most important of the ordinary revenues seems to have been the 'chamber's profit' (*lucrum camerae*). It will be recalled that this was an annual tax of the peasantry, introduced in 1336 by Charles I with the aim of replacing the regular renewal of money. It was paid by the entire free peasant population of the kingdom and also by the king's people, with the exception of the ancient villages of *udvornici*. Although there were some lords whose tenants had been exempted from it by means of a special royal privilege, the overall number of these exemptions was not significant. The basis of the imposition had always been the *porta*, that is, the gate of a peasant yard, 'through which a cart loaded with hay or crops can enter'.[9] The *porta* was, therefore, originally identical to the peasant household. By the fifteenth century one *porta* was generally inhabited by more than one family, so the word took on the meaning of a tax unit. The tax itself was not heavy. During Sigismund's reign it amounted to only one fifth of a florin per year, and could be discharged in pennies. The 'chamber's profit' was nevertheless one of the most important items among the royal revenues, since at the end of Sigismund's reign there were some 400,000 taxable *portae* in the kingdom, representing an annual income of about 80,000 florins.

Originally it was the counts farming the chambers who collected this tax, proceeding village by village within each county. Their chief instrument was a small wooden rod, or tally, called a *dica,* with notches showing the number of *portae*. When the tax was paid one half of the tally was left with the landowner as a sort of receipt. This type of taxing was itself called *dica* and for many centuries its collectors were referred to as *dicators*. In 1427 the king entrusted this source of revenue, just as he had the salt income, to his own tax-collectors. It was probably they who, for the first time, drew up written lists of taxpayers and part of this work, listing the tax receipts of five counties, has survived until the present day. It seems that, from this point on, such registers were regularly made, but with few exceptions those of the medieval period have been lost. Since the collection of the tax was carried out under the supervision of the noble magistrates, each county was divided into two or four districts according to the number of its magistrates. In 1427 when we first meet these districts they were called *reambulatio*. Their later name was *processus*, and from the sixteenth century until recent times they served as the basic framework of administration within a county.

In view of the almost complete lack of evidence, the income derived from the mining of precious metals can only be estimated tentatively. Nevertheless, it seems to have slipped back to third place among the various categories of income received by the treasury. We may infer a sharp decline in the production of gold from the fact that it tended to be replaced by salt as a means of paying the army. In 1454 the total income from the precious metals was put at no more than 24,000 florins, half of which came from the chamber of Kremnica, a quarter from that of Baia Mare, the rest being shared by the chamber of Sibiu and the mints of Buda and Košice. It is beyond doubt that in Sigismund's time they all had yielded much more. In 1427 (the year when it was granted by the king to his wife) the chamber of Kremnica alone was expected to produce some 28,000 florins per year. If the output of the other chambers had been proportionally greater in 1427 than in 1454, then we may put Sigismund's total annual revenue from the monopoly of gold and silver at about 55,000 to 60,000 florins. In 1429, in an effort to win the support of the Teutonic knights for the defence of the southern frontiers, Sigismund promised them 150,000 florins from the yield of the mints of Sibiu and Braşov alone, but this sum is so high that it cannot be taken seriously.

The revenues stemming from the so-called 'thirtieth' (*tricesima*) were also far from negligible. This was a tax imposed on both domestic and foreign trade, consisting, from the time of Mary and Sigismund onwards, of one thirtieth of the value of the merchandise to be sold. It was collected by special 'counts' and their *tricesimatores*. Whereas in 1427 its yield amounted to some 20,000 florins, in 1454 the corresponding figure was hardly half this amount.

The tenants of Slavonia and Požega did not pay the 'chamber's profit' but rather a special tax called 'marten's fur' (*marturina*). Although the number of exemptions was far greater here than elsewhere in the kingdom, the government derived some 8,000 florins from this tax in 1427. The Romanians of Transylvania paid the 'fiftieth' (*quinquagesima*), a tax of their own that in 1454 was expected to yield '2,000 florins at the least'.[10] As for the Jász and the Cumans, they were not yet regarded as tenants and paid a special tax in both kind and money, the latter amounting to 10,000 florins in the middle of the century. The royal towns were exempted from the 'chamber's profit' along with the Saxons who enjoyed similar privileges. The Saxons of Transylvania collectively paid the value of 13,000 florins in silver, while the 11 Saxon 'towns' (they were in fact large villages) of Spis together paid 700 florins. As their ordinary tax (*census*), the royal towns paid a fixed sum: Buda and Pest together paid 4,600, Košice 2,000, Szeged 1,000, Székesfehérvár 600, Esztergom and Timişoara 400 each. The annual revenue obtained from the tax of the Saxons and the royal towns can be estimated at some 30,000 florins, to which should be added the tax paid by the Jewish communities, which amounted to 4,000 florins in 1454.

In 1454, when the kingdom had long been in a state of complete disorganisation, the ordinary revenues of the chamber were still expected to yield 218,000 florins. The fragmentary evidence that we have seems to attest that Sigismund was able to squeeze twice as much as his successors from at least some of the resources. This, of course, was the consequence of the strength of royal authority and the relative stability of internal order in Hungary. On the whole, Sigismund's annual ordinary revenues can be put at some 300,000 gold florins, a sum that was probably surpassed in unexpectedly good years.

EXTRAORDINARY REVENUES

Sigismund could dispose of another source of money which, though intended to be extraordinary, had in fact become ordinary. This was the heavy tax that he imposed upon the Church in 1397 in order to meet the expenses of the Ottoman war. Henceforth half of the annual income of all ecclesiastical benefices had to be delivered to the treasury, and Sigismund did his utmost to exploit this new source of revenue to the full. The exact amount raised is not known, but an estimate of some 100,000 florins a year would surely not be far from the truth. The Premonstratensian provost of Leles is known to have paid 215 florins, while the income of the archbishop of Esztergom, Hungary's richest prelate, amounted to 23,500 gold florins in 1419. Moreover, the king had the habit of leaving bishoprics unfilled for a while, collecting their revenues during the vacancy. At the time of his death four important benefices were vacant and governed by lay 'governors' (*gubernator*) who had, of course, been appointed by Sigismund.

Some 400,000 gold florins were delivered to the treasury every year, but they were not sufficient to prevent Sigismund from experiencing recurrent financial shortages, which obliged him to resort to occasional resources. From the very beginning he had recourse to the imposition of extraordinary taxes (*collecta*). As early as 1387 he demanded a property tax called the 'seventh' from peasants and townsmen alike in order to meet the costs of his war against the Horváti. The imposition of 1397, assessed (for some unknown reason) at 1 florin and 21 pennies per peasant holding, must have yielded some 500,000 florins in all. In 1435 the king collected the tax called the 'fiftieth', which had been ordered by the council of Basle to finance the war against the Ottomans. For his Turkish and Hussite wars he frequently required 'occasional' sums from the royal towns, in addition to their ordinary payments, and they were obviously not in a position to evade his demands.

A good many of the king's financial manoeuvres involved mortgaging operations. The sum that he was able to collect in return for mortgaged estates during the five decades of his reign in Hungary could be put at some 500,000 florins. From the 1420s he devised various new methods of raising more money from a single estate. Before giving the castle of Šintava to the Pálóci by hereditary right, he mortgaged it to them in 1426 for 10,060 florins. He also adopted the practice of forcing the mortgagees to lend him further sums by threatening to confer the mortgage upon someone offering more. When he recovered Šintava from the Pálóci by exchange he gave it to the Rozgonyi in return for a loan of 7,403 florins. He later charged it with a further sum of 3,482 florins. If he showed so little consideration for his most faithful men, others are unlikely to have been treated less harshly.

There was no financial resource that Sigismund did not try to exploit. As has already been mentioned, in 1388 he mortgaged Brandenburg for 565,000 florins. In 1402 Neumark was sold to the Teutonic Order for 63,200 florins. On one occasion he went as far as to detach a portion of his own kingdom. In 1412 Sigismund borrowed 37,000 *schocks* of silver groats of Prague, equalling 100,000 florins, from Wladislas II of Poland for the war against Venice, in return for which he mortgaged to him one part of Spis, including the seigneury of Ľubovňa, the towns Podolinec and Hniezdne, and 13 Saxon towns, among them Spišská Nová Ves. The area thus conceded was only restored to Hungary by Queen Maria Theresa in 1772.

As for Sigismund's expenditures, they must have greatly increased in the later part of his reign. The defence against the Ottomans consumed more and more money, but costlier still was the king's western policy, especially his long sojourns abroad and his wars against the Hussites. All these expenses had to be met from his Hungarian revenues, for the Empire played hardly any role as a source of money. Only the imperial cities and the Jews paid a regular tax; but, combined, this is unlikely to have amounted to more than 20,000 gold florins a year and was consequently insignificant in comparison with Sigismund's revenues from Hungary.

Chapter 14

Sigismund's Foreign Policy
(1403–1437)

In the latter part of his reign Sigismund's activities assumed European dimensions. Many of his actions following his accession to the imperial throne in 1410 and his consecration as king of Bohemia should properly be viewed as part of the history of Germany and Bohemia and cannot be analysed from a strictly Hungarian point of view. It is, of course, not always easy to distinguish the 'Hungarian' aspects of his activities from those that are more 'supranational' in character, for his court, his treasury and his army remained undivided. Nonetheless, in the following pages those events that cannot be regarded as belonging to the main course of Hungarian history will be treated only briefly, for they have been conveniently described in easily available textbooks. Only the events that had an immediate impact upon the history of Hungary, which are less widely known, will be discussed in detail.

SIGISMUND AND THE WEST

Sigismund's European career began with his election as king of the Romans. On 20 September 1410, after Rupert of the Palatinate had been deprived of his throne, half of the electors chose Sigismund to be his successor, the other half electing his cousin, Jodocus, margrave of Moravia, on 1 October. But Jodocus died as early as January 1411 and a second election on 21 June confirmed Sigismund on the imperial throne. He was crowned on 8 November 1414 at Aachen, during the course of his first visit to the West, and was to remain ruler of the Holy Roman Empire until his death in 1437.

Between 1414 and 1418 his attention was turned almost exclusively to the general council of Constance. In fact, it was the emperor himself who prepared its convocation when, during his journey to Lombardy, he negotiated with Pope John XXIII at Lodi in November 1413. The council was opened in November 1414, and Sigismund himself entered the city of Constance on Christmas Day. As is generally known, he was present when John Hus was put to death as a heretic on 6 July 1415. Two weeks later he set off on a long journey in western Europe. In the autumn he discussed the problems facing the council and the schism with King Ferdinand I of Aragon at Narbonne and Perpignan, then, having met Charles VI of France at Paris in April 1416, he stayed from May until August with Henry V in England, trying to mediate in the Anglo-French conflict. The result of his visit to England was a treaty of alliance, signed by the two rulers on 17 August at Canterbury. Sigismund returned to the council on 27 January 1417, having *en route* made a short stay at Luxembourg, from where his family originated. In the course of his journey he succeeded in removing the main obstacles that had so far hindered the work of the council, and the election of Pope Martin V on 11 November put an end to the Great Schism that had divided the Church for almost 40 years. On 21 May, one month after the council's dissolution, Sigismund left for home, but he was apparently in no hurry, for he spent some time at Passau with Bishop Hohenlohe, whom he had appointed as imperial chancellor, and arrived in Pressburg no earlier than January 1419.

The next problem he had to face was the Bohemian succession. King Wenceslas died on 16 August 1419 and his crown was to devolve upon Sigismund. In fact, power was seized by the pro-Hussite Estates who refused to elect him unless he consented to their most important demands. Despite the fact that he had not approved of the execution of Hus, Sigismund was unwilling to negotiate. He summoned an imperial diet to Wrocław in Silesia, where on 17 March 1420 he proclaimed Martin V's bull declaring a crusade against the Hussites. The result was a desperate struggle lasting ten years, fought primarily by the Czechs against the Empire, but also involving the activity of Hungarian armies, and, more importantly, spreading over Hungarian territory during the last phase of the conflict.

Sigismund suffered serious defeats throughout the war. Right at the start he managed to break through and reach Prague, where he was crowned king on 28 July 1420. But he was forced to withdraw soon afterwards and was heavily defeated at Vyšehrad, near Prague, on 1 November. As a result, for a long time his rule was confined to the Catholic provinces of Moravia and Silesia, and 16 years were to elapse before he was able to make a second visit to his capital. In the first years of the conflict he relied on his Hungarian and Moravian troops to suppress the rebels, and turned to the German Estates only after he had suffered serious setbacks. In the autumn of 1422 the diet at Nuremberg decided to launch a general attack, but the new campaign, which finally took place in 1426, ended with another defeat at Ústí nad

Labem. The last effort, a large-scale crusade, intended to annihilate the rebels through a decisive blow, was led by Giuliano Cesarini, the legate of Pope Martin. Sigismund had travelled to Germany as early as the summer of 1430 to direct the preparations in person, and followed the events of the next year from Nuremberg. But, in spite of its careful organisation, the crusade ended in catastrophe in August 1431 at Domažlice, to the south-west of Plzeň.

After the defeat, Sigismund went to Italy in November 1431 with the aim of realising his long cherished dream and acquiring the imperial crown. Having been crowned king of Italy on 28 November at Milan, where he was entertained by Duke Filippo Maria Visconti, he endeavoured to reach Rome. It took a long time to accomplish this apparently simple task, for his war with Venice necessarily brought Sigismund into conflict with Florence and Pope Eugene IV, who were allies of the Republic, and forced him to waste nine long months, from July 1432 to April 1433, in Siena. It was only on 21 May 1433 that he was able to enter Rome, where the imperial crown was finally placed upon his head by the Pope himself. However, the price of his newly acquired title was a peace treaty with Venice, signed on 4 June, which left Dalmatia in the hands of the Republic, this time (as was to become clear later) definitively.

THE OTTOMAN PROBLEM AND THE BUFFER STATES

In the meantime the Ottoman expansion had remained the most pressing problem facing his Hungarian kingdom. After the defeat of Nicopolis hopes of breaking Ottoman rule in Europe through offensive warfare dispersed, and the establishment of an effective defence – the concept and how to achieve it – came to the forefront of Hungarian foreign policy. Henceforth Sigismund adhered consistently to this defensive outlook. Although later, when he became the head of the Holy Roman Empire, he frequently referred to the importance of uniting all the forces of Christendom, using this as a political weapon against his enemies whenever it seemed advantageous to him, his words were not meant to be taken at face value. In fact, the idea of an 'eternal peace' with the Sultan was by no means alien to him,[1] and he planned no further large-scale attacks towards the south, not even when circumstances were seemingly favourable for such an expedition. He turned all of his attention to the question of defence, and with considerable success multiplied the means of maintaining it effectively.

The occasion for a counter-attack presented itself after Tamerlane had defeated and captured Sultan Bayezid in the battle of Ankara in 1402. As a result, the Ottoman empire not only lost its possessions in

Asia Minor, but its position in Europe was also shaken, at least temporarily. It remained politically paralysed even after Tamerlane died in 1405, for the struggle for the throne between Bayezid's sons made it impossible for the Ottomans to tighten their grip on their vassals, let alone launch offensive campaigns. It was only in the reign of Mehmed I (1413–21) that the empire began to recover from the blow, but it still took some years for it to become as powerful and expansionist as it had been before Tamerlane's attack. Indeed, the policy of conquest was only resumed by Mehmed's son, Murad II (1421–51).

It was only after he had put down the baronial revolt that Sigismund could consider turning the political instability of the Ottoman empire to his own advantage, and this time he was not slow to take action. Although not risking another attack, in the next few years he did put a new system of active defence into effect. Profiting from the slackening of the ties that had linked the Balkan princes to the Ottomans, he tried to draw them under his own suzerainty. Although this may seem no more than the simple renewal of Angevin ambitions, his objective was in fact different in two respects.

Firstly, while Louis had wanted to impose his suzerainty upon his southern neighbours without offering them anything in return, the essence of Sigismund's policy was to give them an interest in acknowledging Hungarian overlordship. His principal means was the granting of estates in Hungary to the 'vassal' rulers, something that Louis had been unwilling to do except in the case of the voivode of Wallachia, who had received the district of Făgăraş from the king. The second difference in Sigismund's policy concerned what he expected from the buffer states in exchange for these grants. What he wanted was neither taxation nor unwavering fidelity but sacrifice. He tried to use his southern neighbours as a kind of a *cordon sanitaire*, intended to ward off Ottoman attacks. As an important novelty, the vassal princes were left to decide for themselves how they were to achieve what they were expected to do, and what kinds of compromises would be needed. If necessary they might look for a *modus vivendi* with the Ottomans and Sigismund had no objection to this. It was these principles that from 1403 governed his policy, with varying success, towards Wallachia, Serbia and Bosnia.

The Serbia of Stephen Lazarević, who took the Byzantine title of despot in 1402, became the model buffer state. Stephen had been Bayezid's faithful subject since the battle of Kosovo and fought in his army at Ankara, but after that defeat he changed sides and in 1403 placed himself under Sigismund's suzerainty. In 1408 he was among the first members of the Order of the Dragon, and from 1411, as a consequence of constant royal grace, became one of the greatest landowners in Hungary. Together with Belgrade, he was given all the estates that remained in Hungarian hands beyond the River Sava, and also enormous properties in Hungary, such as Sremska Mitrovica, Slankamen, Bečej, Bečkerek and Vršac in the south and Mezőtúr, Debrecen, Hajdúböszörmény, Satu Mare, Baia Mare, Baia Sprie, Mukačeve, Beregove, Tállya, Tokaj, Boldogkő and Regéc in the north, all of them having many appurtenances. In return for these grants the despot remained Sigismund's faithful ally. He spent a good deal of time at court, and even accompanied Sigismund to Cracow in 1423. Until the despot's death in 1427 the southern counties of Hungary were spared from Ottoman raids. He also succeeded in retaining his own land by recognising Ottoman suzerainty in 1413 and, thereafter, paying a regular tax to the Sultan.

Along the southern border of Transylvania a similar defensive role was intended for Wallachia. Mircea, its ruler, who had been Sigismund's ally since 1395, was rewarded with estates in southern Transylvania, receiving first the 'duchy' of Făgăraş and in 1399 the castle of Bologa, which was later exchanged for Bran. Mircea was so resolute an enemy of the Ottomans that not only did he refuse to make peace with them but he also overtly supported the opponents of Mehmed I. At the same time he also tried to maintain his independence from Hungary, and in 1411 he secretly asked Wladislas of Poland for help in the event of a Hungarian attack against his principality.

The role of buffer state was most difficult to impose upon Bosnia. Sigismund certainly did his utmost, as is shown by the fact that by 1410 he had already led four campaigns into this region. Since the death of Tvrtko, central authority had much weakened and large regions had passed under the rule of magnates, Hrvoje being the most powerful among them. This disintegration could well have served Sigismund's purposes, but the general dislike for Catholicism and for the king of Hungary as its champion was an obstacle that proved to be insurmountable. Whether the Bosnians followed a kind of Orthodoxy or were Patarenes is disputed; but it is certain that they preferred Ottoman rule to Hungarian suzerainty. Sigismund was, therefore, obliged to embark upon the systematic conquest of the country, a very expensive enterprise that yielded only short-lived results.

From 1404 Sigismund's protégé in Bosnia was King Stephen Ostoja, his rival being Tvrtko II. It was in that year that the ban of Mačva, John Maróti, took Srebrenik in northern Bosnia and put a Hungarian garrison in Bobovac, the royal residence. In the autumn of 1407 Sigismund himself appeared in Bosnia, but was soon forced, allegedly by illness, to turn back. He returned there twice during 1408. In May he occupied Dobor and ordered the slaughter of some 120 captured Bosnian nobles, while in September he pushed forward to Maglaj.

Although little is known about these campaigns, they seem to have been successful, leading to the temporary submission of Bosnia. In early 1409 even Hrvoje, Sigismund's most resolute opponent, surrendered. As a reward he was allowed to retain his former acquisitions, along with his title of duke of Split, and he was appointed by Sigismund as his lieutenant in Bosnia. He also received possessions in Hungary, namely Požega together with its county, and the seigneury of Segesd in Somogy. Surely a sign of Sigismund's victory in Bosnia was his founding of the Order of the Dragon at Pécs in December 1408, followed soon after by his adoption of Hrvoje as one of its members. Nevertheless, the situation in Bosnia remained unstable, so much so that in 1410 Sigismund found it necessary to embark on what was to be his last expedition there. He advanced as far as Srebrenica, which was famous for its silver mines. It was rumoured that he wanted to assume the crown of Bosnia himself. It seems, however, that he changed his mind and confirmed Ostoja as king, though he took Srebrenica from him and gave it to the prince of Serbia in 1411. Moreover, he left Hungarian troops in Srebrenik, Dubočac, Vranduk, Toričan, Vesela Straža and probably also in some other castles.

The submission of Hrvoje involved the return of Split, Trogir and Šibenik to Hungarian suzerainty. Hrvoje's brother-in-law, John Nelipčić, count of Cetina, also recognised Sigismund's overlordship, which represented, in effect, the submission of southern Croatia. All the rest of Dalmatia, however, was lost to Hungary. Ladislaus of Naples realised that after the desertion of Hrvoje he would be unable to maintain his rule in Dalmatia. Consequently, in July 1409 he sold the remainder of his territories, together with his rights concerning the whole, to the Republic of Venice for 100,000 ducats. Venice immediately took possession of Zadar, Nin, Vrana and Novigrad, together with the islands of Pag, Cres and Rab, and in February 1410 began the siege of Trogir and Šibenik.

The tension between the Republic and Hungary had long been growing. At first Venice had supported Sigismund and Mary against the Horváti and their other enemies and, finding the union of Hungary with Naples a dangerous possibility, had refrained from assisting Ladislaus of Naples. However, from 1400 Venice refused to pay Sigismund the annual sum of 7,000 florins that was due to him according to the terms of the Peace of Torino. At the same time the Republic began a large-scale expansion on the Italian mainland and along the Balkan coast of the Adriatic. The occupation of Dalmatia was part of this new expansionist policy, and the attack against the cities that continued to adhere to Hungary was an overt act of war.

In response, Sigismund mobilised his army and attacked the Republic in 1411. The main theatres of war were to be Istria and Friuli where the Hungarian commanders, Stibor and Pipo, operated with considerable success during the first phase of the conflict. The tables were turned in 1412, however, when Voivode Nicholas Marcali was defeated near Motta, and Šibenik surrendered to the Venetians after a siege lasting two years. In January 1413 Sigismund himself invaded Friuli, but was unable to stem the flow of events that were now running against him. In April at Castelleto he agreed to a five-year armistice on the basis of the *status quo*. As a matter of fact his attention was being drawn to other problems, and by the time war broke out again in 1418 he seems to have accepted the loss of Dalmatia. In June 1420 Split and Trogir, the last footholds of Hungarian rule, submitted to the Republic. Fighting flared up once again in 1431, and the long series of wars with Venice was ended by another armistice, signed at Rome in 1433. It was designed to last for only five years, but in fact became a permanent settlement, and Dalmatia was definitively lost to the crown of Hungary.

During Sigismund's prolonged stay in the West the southern line of defence began to crack at several points. The first opening appeared, as was to be expected, in Bosnia. In 1413 Hrvoje attacked his neighbour, Sandalj Hranić, prince of Hum (Hercegovina), another Hungarian protectorate. Sigismund's response was to declare Hrvoje to be a rebel, ordering the confiscation of all the lands that had been given to him. Although Split, the islands of Korčula, Hvar and Brač and the counties of Dubica, Vrbas and Sana immediately accepted Hungarian suzerainty, the consequences of Sigismund's decision were irreparable. Hrvoje, having vainly protested against the verdict before the Hungarian barons, turned to the Ottomans, who during the winter of 1413–14 helped him to recover a number of castles from the Hungarians, with the exception of Srebrenik and other fortresses that were able to offer resistance. The sudden collapse of the Hungarian defensive line in Bosnia opened the way into Slavonia, and Ottoman raiders appeared there for the first time in the summer of 1414.

The Hungarian barons reacted at once and attempted to regain the lost ground. The general levy was proclaimed, and in the summer of 1415 a great army, led by John Garai, the palatine's brother, John Maróti and other barons, marched deep into the heart of Bosnia. Near Doboj, in the valley of the River Bosna, they suffered a heavy defeat at the hands of Hrvoje and his Turkish allies. Most of the Hungarian invaders were killed, some of them taken prisoner. Paul Csupor, ban of Slavonia, against whom Hrvoje bore a grudge, was executed, while the others were ransomed for 65,000 florins, a sum that had to be raised by imposing an extraordinary tax in September 1416. Yet by far the most important consequence of the defeat was the end of Hungarian influence in Bosnia. King Ostoja and Sandalj went over to the Ottomans, who appeared in 1415 on the marches of Carniola, in the region of

235

Celje. Only Srebrenik and its province remained in Hungarian hands, mortgaged to John Garai in 1422 and then to Matko of Talovac in 1430.

It was not until ten years later that Bosnia became part of the Hungarian defensive belt again. The new king of Bosnia, Tvrtko II (1421–1443), was soon forced to seek Sigismund's assistance against enemies at home. Having contacted the king of Hungary in 1425 or 1426, he accepted Hermann II, son of Hermann of Cilli, as his heir in 1427, and married one of the daughters of John Garai a year later. However, his Hungarian orientation only served further to weaken his authority within his own kingdom, while the Ottoman incursions were becoming increasingly intense. Finally, in 1434, Sigismund decided to send Matko of Talovac to Bosnia. To some extent, this did succeed in consolidating Tvrtko's position, since Hungarian garrisons were installed in the castles of Jajce, Vranduk, Bočac and Komotin. Thus, at the time of Sigismund's death, Hungary's control over Bosnia could be said to have been firm.

The situation in Wallachia after the death of Mircea in 1418 was in many respects similar to that in Bosnia. In the next few years the principality was kept under constant pressure by the Ottomans, who tried to put their own candidates on the throne, while their opponents were unable to hold out without help from Hungary. Problems had begun to arise during Mircea's lifetime. In 1417 Sultan Mehmed I led a retaliatory campaign against him, forced him to pay a tax, captured three of his sons and occupied Turnu Severin and other castles along the Danube. The situation seemed so dangerous that, on arriving from Constance, Sigismund decided to intervene immediately. In November 1419 he recovered Turnu Severin with the help of Michael, Mircea's successor, and put it under Hungarian control. At the same time he ordered the strengthening of the frontier between Turnu Severin and Golubac, the section that was most exposed to Ottoman attacks. In the summer of 1420 Michael died whilst fighting the Ottomans. The latter then placed one of their hostages, Radu II, on the throne of Wallachia, and after 26 years of relative calm resumed their incursions into Transylvania. In September 1420 they defeated the voivode, Nicholas Csáki, near Haţeg, and in 1421 devastated the area surrounding Braşov. The following year Mircea's nephew, Dan II, seized power, but he was unable to proceed without help from Hungary and needed several years to consolidate his authority. Every year from 1423 to 1426 Pipo and Csáki marched to Wallachia to support Dan against Radu and his Turkish allies. In the end Sigismund himself intervened. He went to Braşov in December 1426, and for several months directed the military operations in person. His army – of which, curiously enough, one of the commanders was Prince Peter of Portugal – won a decisive winter victory over Radu's troops. Dan's position was thereby stabilised, so that in April 1427 he was able to receive Sigismund in his own residence at Câmpulung. The relative calm lasted for five years. In June 1432 Ottoman troops invaded Wallachia, forced the new prince, Alexander Aldea, to become the Sultan's vassal, and, proceeding into Transylvania, devastated the environs of Braşov and Sibiu. The situation remained critical until 1436, when another Hungarian army managed to put Vlad, called 'Dracul', in charge of the principality. He had been brought up in the Hungarian court, where he became a member of the Order of the Dragon – hence his sobriquet.

At the time of Sigismund's death there was no immediate threat from either Wallachia or Bosnia, but in Serbia the defensive line had already been irreparably damaged. The events that led to this development began in May 1426 when at Tata a treaty settling the future of Serbia was concluded by Sigismund and Despot Stephen. It was agreed that Stephen's principality, together with his estates in Hungary, would devolve after his death to George Branković, his sister's son. However, Belgrade and Golubac, both strongholds of strategic importance, would pass under Hungarian rule. The treaty could only be partly enforced. Stephen died on 16 June 1427, and Sigismund took possession of Belgrade in October, but in the meantime Golubac had been sold by its captain to the Ottomans. Sigismund tried at once to fill the gap which had opened up on his frontier: he laid siege to the castle in the last days of April 1428, but when Sultan Murad arrived in person to relieve it he was forced to withdraw. On 12 June Sigismund was attacked whilst crossing the Danube and suffered serious losses, barely escaping with his life.

For the first time in its history Hungary became the immediate neighbour of the Ottoman empire, and the consequences were not slow to appear. The southern marches, including the counties of Caraşova, Kovin, Timiş and Torontal, were henceforth constantly exposed to Turkish incursions. Judging from the list of its parishes drawn up between 1332 and 1337, the region had been densely inhabited, the place names suggesting a predominantly Magyar population. They now fell victim to the raids or moved to better protected areas, and their place was taken by groups of Serbs coming from the Balkans. As a consequence, by the end of the Middle Ages the ethnic composition of the region had been completely modified.

The burden of warding off, or at least slowing down, the Ottoman incursions was borne by a chain of border castles on the Danube between Turnu Severin and Belgrade. Whereas before 1390 only Orşova, Hram and Kovin had been standing, by 1429 14 new fortresses had been built. While most of these fortifications seem to have been erected after 1419 by the governor of the region, Pipo of Ozora, the last – Pescari (Szentlászló), located opposite Golubac – was constructed by Sigismund himself in 1428. In 1429 Sigismund turned to a solution that had never been contemplated before and entrusted the defence of this section of the frontier to the Teutonic Knights. Besides undertaking to meet all of their expenses, he handed over to them the lordship of the scattered royal estates in the territory that had been conceded to them. The Knights did take possession of the banate of Severin late in 1429, and their captain, Nicholas von Redwitz, was admitted to the ranks of Hungarian barons with the title of ban. However, in 1432 he suffered so serious a defeat at the hands of the Ottomans that Sigismund was soon obliged to retrieve the castles from the Order.

The defence of the southern marches laid an unprecedented burden on the treasury. The total expenses of the Teutonic Knights, estimated at the almost astronomical sum of 315,000 florins annually, were to be met from various sources of revenue: the mints of Braşov and Sibiu, the salt of the chamber of Szeged (among others), and the 'silver of Transylvania'.[2] Moreover, the king also conceded to the Knights the Romanian tax, paid in sheep, for three years; the tax of the Cumans and the Jász for two years; the tithe levied on wine of the diocese of Kalocsa; and the fishing rights in that section of the Danube that belonged to the Order. Although these promises, especially those involving money, were evidently impossible to keep, the 13 castles handed over to the Knights were guarded, according to an official register from around 1430, by 1806 men. Among them were 178 crossbowmen and 260 'servants having to do everything they are ordered to, but also doing military service'. The remaining 1368 probably represented 342 lances, reckoning one lance for each four men.[3] Since the monthly pay of a lance was 25 florins, that of a crossbowman six, and a boatman three, a total of 124,776 florins was needed every year to pay the 1806 men. To this sum should be added, of course, the money necessary for the maintenance of Belgrade and the border castles in Transylvania and Croatia. All in all, the most serious consequence of the Ottoman threat was that the kingdom of Hungary was obliged, earlier than most other monarchies of Europe, to keep a large number of soldiers continually at arms, a measure requiring resources far beyond its economic potential.

In the last decade of Sigismund's reign the Ottoman menace was joined by the threat posed by the Hussites. It was in the beginning of 1428 that their plundering armies first reached Hungary and firmly established themselves in Skalica on the border of Moravia. Having defeated the Hungarian barons who had been dispatched to stop them in April 1430, they ravaged the valley of the River Váh in 1431 and then occupied Trnava in the following year. In 1433 they ventured as far as Spis and sacked Kremnica. Against this military machine, the Hungarian government proved as impotent as had the princes of Germany, for the clumsy, slowly mobilised general levy was unable to halt the swiftly moving Hussite troops. By the beginning of the 1430s the Hussites represented a problem quite as pressing as the Ottoman expansion, and they played an equally decisive role in the birth of the military reforms of 1432.

The devastation continued until the Hussite movement itself was suppressed. Disheartened by the successive defeats suffered by imperial armies, both Sigismund and the Roman Church accepted the need for a peaceful solution. In 1433 the Treaty of Prague (*Compactata Pragensia*) was signed, which permitted Hussite religious practice with certain limitations. On 30 May 1434 the radicals who had set themselves against the compromise were beaten at Lipany. The Hungarian government soon recovered Trnava and Skalica from the Hussites, whose captains were taken into the service of Sigismund and Queen Barbara.

In the meantime a new general council had been assembled in 1431 at Basle. This was intended to settle not only the Hussite problem but also that concerning the reform of the Church. The latter had already figured on the agenda of the council of Constance, but the real discussion only began in Basle. Relations between the Pope and the extreme wing of the reformers were becoming increasingly strained; and, on his return from Rome, Sigismund spent half a year at the council, from October 1433 to May 1434, in an effort to mediate between the parties. Having arrived home, he engaged in negotiations with the Estates of Bohemia with a view to restoring his rule there. In the beginning of 1436 they came to terms at Székesfehérvár, and in May Sigismund set off on what was to be his last journey. He died on 9 December 1437 at Znojmo, on his way back from Prague.

Sigismund's rule has not had a good reputation in Hungary. He has never figured among her greatest rulers; indeed, modern historiography has regarded him as one of the worst. This verdict very much reflects the sentiments of the contemporary nobility, who found Sigismund's personality and political attitudes wholly unattractive, since they were out of keeping with their ideal of a king. Sigismund is depicted as a kind and majestic personality by his contemporaries. He had an excellent command of Latin and several languages, he willingly indulged in refined conversation, and was able to follow, and sometimes even to influence, theological discussions. He was also known for being a diplomat of the first rank, and enjoyed negotiations more than war. What he was really skilful at was finding agreement between opponents in the most hopeless of situations. On the other hand, he was only willing to take the field once all possibility of a peaceful solution had disappeared. These qualities were hardly likely to increase his popularity among a warlike and illiterate nobility. In the eyes of his Hungarian subjects, Sigismund was above all a poor soldier and a coward who had fled at Nicopolis and Golubac, and who gave up Dalmatia.

There were, of course, other, more reasonable causes underlying this instinctive antipathy for Sigismund. He is known to have ruled with a rod of iron, showing no respect for the 'liberties' of the nobility and sometimes even encroaching upon them through his reforms, which were later referred to as 'harmful novelties'. Moreover, he foisted many 'foreigners' upon the Hungarian nobility. His foreign policy and the fact that he spent ever more time abroad, especially after 1410, also contributed to the aversion felt for him. It would seem that the problems at the centre of his interests during these years were far beyond the political horizon of his subjects, who were unable to appreciate the scale of the issues raised by either the council movement or Hussitism. In the eyes of his subjects (excluding his small circle of advisers), Sigismund was a ruler who, instead of checking the Ottoman expansion, had wasted the financial and human resources of the kingdom on goals that were not in keeping with the interests of the 'nation'.

In fact, when viewed in a European context, Sigismund can be seen as an outstanding figure in history. He was appreciated by his Western contemporaries as the leading politician of Europe, and he is still appreciated as such by modern historiography. His policy was determined partly by personal ambitions, partly by dynastic perspectives. In the long struggle for the attainment of his aims, Hungary merely played the role of a safe hinterland, a permanent base where money and soldiers could always be raised. But, for the very reason that it was from here that he drew the resources necessary for the realisation of his ambitious plans, Sigismund always regarded himself above all as king of Hungary. It was here that he maintained his permanent residence and he did everything he could to make it worthy of his exalted position.

The cultural life of this period was on the whole a continuation of what had been established under Louis. It was still dominated by the ideal of the Christian knight, its norms, life-style and artistic taste being formed by the royal court and mediated for the wider public by the barons and knights living there. Yet a new phenomenon, the birth of magnate dynasties, was also bound to have an effect on cultural development. The Angevin barons spent most of their time at court, and this determined their way of life and their of view of themselves and the world. Their successors under Sigismund created new centres in the provinces, which were later to have a decisive influence upon the culture of the noble class as a whole. A new and particular complexion was also given to cultural life by the royal towns in accordance with the growing role that their burghers were playing in politics.

It was under Sigismund that Buda became the unquestioned capital of the kingdom. Louis had already begun the construction of a royal palace at the southern end of the castle hill, and between 1346 and 1355 the court and tribunals resided at Buda while reconstruction work was carried out at Visegrád. In the early years of his reign, Sigismund had Louis's palace transformed into a castle. It is first documented in 1402 and between 1406 and 1408 he moved there permanently, together with the chancellery and the central law courts. Large-scale building work appears to have been undertaken in the 1410s, when the king recruited foreign craftsmen during his travels in the West and sent them home to work at Buda. Judging from contemporary reports, the most outstanding construction was the 'Fritz' palace (later popularly called 'fresh palace'), which made a lasting impression on foreign visitors. (It was so completely destroyed in Ottoman times that even its exact location is disputed.) In the vicinity of this palace a collegiate church consecrated to Saint Sigismund was built in 1424. The many pieces of sculpture, of a high artistic level, which were discovered during the excavations of the palace in 1974, must in some way have been connected with these buildings. Another of Sigismund's residences, much favoured from 1409, was Tata, an estate acquired from the Lackfi, where he built a splendid castle for hunting. Around 1430 he considered shifting his permanent residence to Pressburg and ordered the complete reconstruction of its castle. The amount of work undertaken there is shown by the several thousand florins that were spent on it every year and (according to the accounts of 1434) the fact that a team of about 220 to 240 persons was working there continuously.

The barons tried to follow the example of the king, albeit on a more modest scale. Most of them constructed new and more comfortable houses to replace their inaccessible, mountain-top eyries. There are examples of this from as early as Louis's reign, but a general trend of building activity is only discernible from around 1400. It was at that time that new castles were erected by the Kanizsai at Eisenstadt, by Nicholas Garai at Pápa, by Hermann of Cilli in Varaždin and by John Maróti at Gyula. They were all meant to be comfortable residences and generally imitated the castles of King Louis, especially Diósgyőr, in their rectangular plan and four corner towers. When earlier castles were rebuilt – as were Beckov by Stibor or Siklós, Kőszeg and Csesznek by the Garai – a choice seems to have been made to improve comfort and accessibility. Besides the barons the wealthier nobles also wanted a fortified residence of their own. It was in the early fifteenth century that smaller castle-like timber buildings, called *castella* in Latin and *kastély* in Hungarian, were being erected all over the land.

Nor did the ancient habit of founding churches disappear. Stibor founded a house for the Augustinian Canons at Nové Miesto nad Váhom, Nicholas Garai a chapel in the church of Our Lady at Buda, and Pipo of Ozora another in the basilica of Székesfehérvár. John Maróti (of Morović) had the parish church of Morović transformed by the Pope into a collegiate chapter. All this did not imply that the ties that had so far linked the magnates to the royal court were to slacken. The barons continued to spend the greater part of their life in the king's entourage, so most of them maintained a permanent residence in the city of Buda. That of the Garai, for instance, contained no fewer than 20 rooms.

By comparison with the Angevin era, the intellectual and political horizon of the nobles who lived at court broadened to a considerable extent. On more than one occasion, Buda, Tata and Pressburg hosted meetings of princes and splendid festivities that were attended by a large number of foreigners. The most outstanding event in this respect was the series of feasts, lasting for several weeks, which pledged the reconciliation of Sigismund and Wladislas of Poland in 1412. In 1424 Sigismund received Eric of Denmark and co-Emperor John VIII of Byzantium, and in 1429 the imperial diet was held in Pressburg. Even more important from a cultural point of view were Sigismund's journeys in the West, since he was accompanied by a great number of Hungarian prelates, barons and knights. Constance seems to have been especially popular as a destination. Given that some of the lords, like Archbishop Kanizsai, arrived at the council with large retinues, the Hungarians who turned up at Constance should probably be numbered in the hundreds. Sigismund was escorted to Paris, London, and later to Italy by a substantial entourage. In 1433 many of them attended the imperial coronation at Rome: about 140 Hungarians – barons and their retainers, knights, guards, cooks and others – are known to have asked the Holy See for favours of various kinds on this occasion.

That part of the nobility which took part in the king's journeys began to imitate some of the trappings of chivalry. After 1414 the use of coats-of-arms, which had hitherto been limited to the most illustrious kindreds, quickly spread among the lesser nobility. However, closer contacts with the West showed clearly just how moderate was the Hungarian nobility's wealth as compared with what they found in western Europe. Stephen Rozgonyi senior, royal castellan and knight, complained to his brother about the high prices in Paris: he found the shops wonderful, but 'since I do not have money', he wrote, 'I prefer not to look at them.'[4] However, there is no evidence that these new experiences had any significant effect on Hungarian noble mentality. There are no signs of chivalric poetry flourishing at court or elsewhere during this period; indeed, there is not even a single surviving work that would pass as lay literature. Noblemen who were more curious than normal were obviously regarded as eccentrics. Such a person was Lawrence Tari, Master of the Cup-bearers, who could write his letters in Latin, and also enjoyed adventurous travels. Between 1409 and 1411 he made a pilgrimage to Santiago de Compostela and from there to the Purgatory of Saint Patrick in Ireland.[5] His memorable 'journey in Hell' soon gave birth to a legend that was elaborated by several poets in the sixteenth century. Nicholas Szécsényi 'of Salgó', who died in exile at Venice in 1438, was another nobleman of unusual tastes. In his will he ordered that if 'love-letters' or 'books and documents which hurt the right and the spirit' were found among his things they should be burnt.[6]

There were a few foreigners whose different cultural world had been brought with them from their homeland. When he was still a simple retainer of Kanizsai, Pipo of Ozora stupefied the king and his barons by his ability to calculate what 12,000 soldiers would cost for three months. Later, when he became a baron, he made a point of taking Hungarian habits, growing a beard among other things, but his attraction to Italian culture persisted. His castle at Ozora, which seems to have imitated Florentine patterns, was constructed by Manetto Ammannatini, a disciple of Brunellesco, who remained in Hungary for many years after his master had died. Masolino is also said to have worked for Pipo for some time around 1426.

It may be attributed to a general lack of interest that Sigismund's efforts to found a university in Hungary failed. He first tried to establish one at Óbuda in 1395 under the direction of his secret chancellor, the provost, Luke Szántói. It may have ceased to exist when Luke, then bishop of Oradea, became involved in the revolt of 1403. In 1410 Sigismund restored the university with the permission of Pope John XXIII, and invited some renowned foreign scholars to be teachers. They later attended the council of Constance on behalf of the university. Around 1419 this new attempt also failed: the reasons are not clear, but Sigismund seems now to have given up the fight. Nevertheless, from the beginning of the fifteenth century many people went abroad to study. Being the nearest, the university of Vienna was the most favoured destination, while Cracow was chosen only from the second half of the century. A number of Hungarians had also gone to Prague prior to the Hussite revolution of 1419, but that event effectively closed it to Catholics as a source of learning.

Chapter 15

Trade and Towns

The age of the Angevins and Sigismund was a decisive period in the economic development of Hungary. Between 1323 and 1437 the kingdom experienced a transformation the extent of which was to remain unparalleled until the eighteenth century. The most tangible sign of change was the proliferation of towns and their rapid consolidation. Whereas around 1240 there existed but a handful of settlements that could be called towns in the Western sense of the word, two hundred years later we find several dozen such settlements scattered throughout the kingdom. Buda, from which the capital of Hungary was to be born, serves as a symbol of what had happened during this period. While at the time of the Mongol invasion sheep still grazed on the site of what was to become Buda, by the death of Sigismund it had become an important central European city.

GENERAL FEATURES

The spectacular process of urbanisation indirectly influenced the rural world as well. The weekly markets of the villages, which had existed since the Árpádian era, gained a new lease of life in the course of the fourteenth century, and hundreds of new ones were also created. These markets were frequented by the surrounding population, nobles and peasants alike, and the most important among them soon began to show signs of a form of urbanisation. It was by the end of our period, from these origins, that a new type of regional centre, called a 'market town' (*oppidum*), had grown up. The 'market town' was a settlement of a form halfway between a village and a town. It was typical of central Europe, being also found in southern Germany and Austria where it was referred to as a *Markt*. Thanks to its function as a market, each *oppidum* became the economic centre of the surrounding region, and some of them assumed an increasingly urban outlook. It was also in the fourteenth century that the use of money became general, showing that the majority of the rural population had by that time joined in the production of goods. By the reign of Sigismund all other currencies had been squeezed out by the king's penny, a fact which demonstrates that through the expansion of internal commerce the whole of the Carpathian basin had been moulded into a single market economy.

Political stability obviously contributed to these developments. With the exception of certain critical years, this was a peaceful period, creating favourable conditions for commerce; and the king's authority was strong enough to enable him to enforce his decisions. It would, of course, be anachronistic to speak of an 'economic policy' at this time, but the government did have ideas that amounted to something similar. More than one institution ensured that the kingdom would be regarded as a unit, not only from a political point of view but also in terms of its economy. There was, firstly, the monopoly of coinage by which the government was able, at least to a certain extent, to regulate the circulation of money; secondly, the monopolies regulating the trade of precious metals and livestock; and, finally, the thirtieth, that is the customs duty on external commerce that was paid on the frontiers. King Charles I had probably himself played a decisive role in the development of the mining industry. He and his successors supported the towns by granting them privileges. They also founded new ones, and protected their burghers against foreign competition as well as against the nobility. In 1405, after consultation with the envoys of the towns, Sigismund issued a decree that dealt with almost every aspect of what we could call a 'national economy'.

Although it is undeniable that Hungary went through a period of economic development, the limits of her prosperity are no less evident. The view, often expressed in the past, that Hungary had attained more or less the same level as western Europe by the end of the Middle Ages and that her falling behind, which would become so obvious later, was a consequence of the Ottoman conquest is no longer accepted by modern historians. Figures concerning urbanisation in Hungary suffice to prove the contrary. The combined population of the most important towns of the kingdom was less than that of a middle-sized town in Lombardy. Buda was a huge city by local standards, but was smaller than Cracow, not to mention Prague or Vienna. The modest proportions are an indication of the strictly limited nature of urban development, which was obviously due to the primitive beginnings from which it had grown. We know that, in the West, urbanisation had been a consequence of the rapid expansion of industry, which had become the main source for the accumulation of capital by the late Middle Ages. In Hungary not a single branch of handicraft was able to gather sufficient force to provide an impetus to economic development. No industrial products are to be found among exported goods. To sum up, the Hungarian economy was unable to progress to that phase from where a development generated by its own force would have been possible. It remained instead at the level characteristic of western Europe before the great take-off of the twelfth and thirteenth centuries. Hungarian towns were strong enough to draw their surroundings into the monetary economy, but too weak to transform them according to their own image; the force they had came almost exclusively from long-distance trade. The predominance of trade, besides hindering the accumulation of capital and urban growth, had a major effect on the towns of Hungary. It determined their geographical location, had a decisive influence upon their social life and government, and limited the political role that they were able to play.

Beyond these facts not much is known about the structure of the economy. Few data exist by which the problem could be analysed. In 1427 the revenue of the treasury from the thirtieth, levied upon the value of goods, amounted to 20,000 florins. Allowing for exemptions, of which there were many, this sum seems to imply that the volume of foreign trade exceeded 500,000 florins. The only source that gives us a glimpse of what this trade consisted of is the register of the customs house of Pressburg for the financial year 1457–8. According to this record, the overall value of the goods upon which a duty was levied amounted to 186,000 florins. Only 11 per cent of the duty was imposed on exported goods, the rest being levied on imported articles. The balance seems, at least for this particular year, extremely unfavourable. Among the imports, textiles played a predominant role with 79 per cent. Next came ironwares with 12 per cent, due to the enormous quantity of knives coming from Austria. Most of the textiles were luxury fabrics of the finest quality, but also arriving in the kingdom was a great quantity of cheap 'grey' cloth, destined for ordinary people.

It is evident, however, that the information furnished by the Pressburg duty register cannot be used to reconstruct the overall pattern of the kingdom's foreign commerce. Spices, for instance, represented only four per cent of the taxed value at Pressburg, but it is beyond doubt that much greater quantities were imported, presumably through another customs office. Other factors are also likely to have distorted the picture. Judging from sixteenth-century information it seems that the customs offices specialised in different types of goods, and while at Pressburg imports happened to dominate elsewhere there could have been a predominance of exports. In the early modern period the value of exports, at a national level, surely exceeded that of imports, and this may already have been the case in the middle of the fifteenth century. In the Angevin era, however, the situation seems to have been different. At that time it is clear that the commercial balance of the kingdom was highly unfavourable, imports being paid for by a massive outflow of precious metals, mainly in the form of gold florins.

THE PRODUCTS

In Hungary the main and almost only motive power of the fourteenth-century economy seems to have been the enormous deposits of gold. However rich this kingdom may have been in other metals, it was above all as a producer of gold that Hungary was present on the international market. In Europe gold was never found in large quantities outside the Carpathian basin, and the volume of production in that region began to grow rapidly in the 1320s. The most important new mine was found at Kremnica, but others were also opened at Baia Mare, in Transylvania and elsewhere. It is impossible to say exactly how much gold was extracted, but scholars are unanimous in considering Hungary to be one of the leading producers in the world. The only piece of information that makes conjecture possible comes from the financial year of 1434–35, by which time production had already been in decline for several decades. In that year 1,600 marks, that is 393 kg, of pure gold were extracted in the chamber of Kremnica alone. Judging from this amount the estimates that put the annual production in the fourteenth-century at 1,500 kg, equalling some 420,000 florins, cannot simply be rejected as exaggeration.

However we interpret this evidence, the impact that Hungarian gold is known to have had upon the fourteenth-century European economy can only be explained if the volume of production was indeed significant. Gold coins had been minted since 1252 in Florence and since 1284 in Venice, but the Hungarian florin, which was struck from 1326 onwards, was the first to appear north of the Alps. It seems to have circulated in such quantities that its influence was felt throughout the continent. In Italy, the price of gold in relation to that of silver had been growing continuously since the middle of the thirteenth century; but as early as 1328, it began to fall. In Florence the amount of gold available grew so rapidly that in the middle of the century 350,000 to 400,000 florins were minted annually. The gold ducat of Venice was also issued in ever-increasing quantities, and in 1338 it was made the basis of the Republic's financial system in place of the hitherto used silver groat. As a consequence of the activities of the Italian banking houses Hungarian gold also reached more distant countries. One after another, the lands of western Europe, which now had abundant supplies of gold at their disposal, began to use gold coins. Flanders did so in 1336, France in 1337, Emperor Louis of Bavaria in 1339, Lübeck in 1342 and England in 1344. With the exception of the Baltic region, it soon became the norm everywhere to account in gold coins, and payments were generally effected in gold. Since gold from Africa continued to reach the continent through Arab, Italian and Spanish merchants, it is likely that this also had some part to play in these events; yet, given the chronological coincidences outlined above, it seems clear that they were essentially the result of the unparalleled boom of gold production in Hungary.

Compared with gold, all the other exported goods, metals and agricultural products, were bound to play a secondary role. Not even silver could equal gold in importance, although large-scale mining of this precious metal did continue in the later Middle Ages. The volume of silver production may have been as great as in Bohemia, and we have some information concerning its export; but the greater part of it seems to have been used to meet the demands of the domestic market.

Copper was a relatively important item, since the greatest mines of central Europe lay in Hungary. Copper of Hungarian origin had been continuously present on the international market since the middle of the thirteenth century. It reached the West via Poland's Baltic Sea ports, while its commerce in the Levant was usually controlled by Venice. The exploitation of copper was profitable enough to arouse the interest of the Medici in the 1380s. However, around 1390 the Italians were driven out by entrepreneurs from Nuremberg, and the production of copper was to remain a business dominated by Germans until the end of the Middle Ages. The value of Hungarian copper was enhanced by the great amount of silver it contained, which could be extracted by adding lead to it. The instrument necessary for this process, called *Saigerhütte* in German, seems to have been invented by craftsmen from Nuremberg around 1400, and was first put to use in the mines of northern Hungary. L'ubietová and Gelnica continued to be the two main centres of copper mining until the middle of the fifteenth century, when they were gradually outstripped by Banská Bystrica.

Alongside copper, the mining of iron should also be mentioned, though the volume of output cannot have been very significant, for the treasury never laid claim to it and the greater mines always remained in private hands. Most of them were to be found in present-day Slovakia, to the south of Spis and north of Gemer, but there were also some in Transylvania. The iron from Slovakia, just like some of the copper, was exported through Cracow. It was in the fourteenth century that the production of iron was given an enormous stimulus throughout Europe by the appearance of the smelting furnace (*Floßofen*) and the foundry. Both of these inventions soon reached

Hungary via Germany: we know that a foundry existed in Štítnik as early as 1344, while furnaces are mentioned from 1376 onwards. Among the minerals, salt should also be mentioned, for, as we have already seen, it was one of the main resources of the treasury. Salt was sold within the kingdom at a fixed, that is very high, price, and the treasury tried to prevent the import of cheap salt from the Empire and Dalmatia.

The remaining Hungarian exports were all agricultural products. Wine was exported to as far away as Bohemia, Poland and northern Germany, but by some margin the most important role was played by livestock. It was at this time that cattle, which in the early modern period would be exported in their tens of thousands, first appeared on the market. These were not the small draught oxen so commonly used in the Middle Ages, but heavy-bodied beef cattle, which began to be bred on the immense pastures of the Great Plain during these decades. They were driven along the Danube to Nuremberg and the towns of southern Germany where they played a decisive role in alimentation. What was not sold locally seems to have been taken by German merchants through the Alps to Lombardy and Venice. The first signs of the export of cattle date from around 1360, and from the 1380s it becomes fairly common. The golden age of this trade was, however, to come later.

During the last centuries of the Middle Ages, as under the Árpádians, the role of cattle was still eclipsed by that of the horse. Bertrandon de la Broquière, a knight from Burgundy who crossed the Great Plain in 1433, said nothing about cattle but was amazed by the abundance of horses. On his way he saw 'an enormous amount of wild horses bred for sale', which 'live freely like wild beasts', and was told that in the markets of both Szeged and Pest he could buy them by thousands.[1] So it is not surprising that the treasury tried to monopolise the export of horses and as late as 1400 prohibited the activities of individual entrepreneurs by a series of measures.

With sheep the situation was different. From the earliest times they had been bred in great herds, and with the immigration of the Romanians, who were sheep-rearers *par excellence*, their number even increased. Many centuries later, after the introduction of western breeds of sheep, there would be a short time before the appearance of Australian wool when the fleece from Hungarian sheep would take first place on the world market. In the Middle Ages, however, sheep were important only as a source of nourishment. Their wool, as elsewhere in eastern Europe, was unfit for the manufacture of fine cloth, while the proper treatment of their skin would have necessitated skill and capital. The economic importance of sheep-rearing was, therefore, insignificant by comparison with its volume. In contrast to the situation in England, the abundance of sheep in later medieval Hungary could not provide a basis for the development of cloth manufacture.

The structure of imports shows that the domestic market had preserved its traditional features. Although commerce relied to a growing extent upon the purchasing power of the lower classes, the bulk of imports were still destined to satisfy the prestige needs of a small elite. Some light is shed on this by a list drawn up in Venice in 1264 that enumerates goods, worth a total of 1485½ marks, which were delivered to the future King Stephen V and his court in Transylvania. Among the 122 items we find above all textiles (cloth of Ghent, purple and silk from Milan, from the 'Tartars' and from 'overseas') and jewellery, for which the king paid with silver and, to a lesser degree, with salt.[2] Essentially similar in structure, though more abundantly supplied, was the market in the fifteenth century, which is known from the Law Book of Buda and also, with fewer details, from a general regulation concerning the thirtieth issued in 1436. The latter contained some 80 import items, among them 25 kinds of cloth (as against 49 in the Law Book) along with other textiles from East and West, threads, spices, oil, raisins, parchment, paper, combs, mirrors, shoes, ostrich plumes and many other goods. Among the types of cloth were a great many expensive Florentine textiles, many kinds of Flemish and German fabric, 'English' and 'Londisch' stuff of middling quality, but also cheap cloth from Bohemia and Moravia, which had been imported in growing quantities since the thirteenth century.[3]

A great difference can be observed in the price of domestic and imported goods. At the beginning of the fifteenth century the average price of an ox in Hungary, counted in silver, corresponded to the value of three or four florins, and an ordinary horse could not have been much more expensive. According to de la Broquière, a mount of the finest quality could be bought for ten florins, whereas its price could be five times as much elsewhere. On the other hand, one bolt of cheap Bohemian cloth cost seven florins, while the same amount of the finest Italian textile was sold for 45 florins, equalling the price of ten to fifteen oxen. Hungary was, therefore, a relatively cheap country for foreigners, and it is not surprising that in a Florentine short story of 1389 it was referred to as the paradise of businessmen.[4]

THE TOWNS

The nature of urbanisation in Hungary was determined by two factors outlined above, one of them being the production and export of gold and the other the import of luxury goods. The network of towns that came to life in the thirteenth and fourteenth centuries was essentially created by these economic circumstances. The most important towns were born at places where consumption was concentrated: in the middle of the kingdom where the court resided; along the frontier where merchants from abroad entered the kingdom; and in the mining regions where precious metals were produced. The wealth and size of the towns depended on how favourable their situation was within the system of consumption, and were proportional to the extent of their foreign relations.

Seen from a political point of view, the process of Hungarian urbanisation followed more or less closely the Western pattern. A Frenchman travelling in Serbia realised with astonishment that 'the towns are not surrounded by ramparts and walls',[5] that their buildings were made of wood, and their privileges, if they had any, were of a very restricted nature. A traveller in Hungary was not to meet such a surprise. All the towns that had been founded in the thirteenth and fourteenth centuries enjoyed wide-ranging autonomy, and at least some of them were protected from the outside world by stone walls. It was these settlements that contemporaries regarded above all as 'cities' (*civitates*), and their inhabitants as 'burghers' (*cives*). It should be noted that some important settlements whose lord was not the king did not enjoy the right of self-government, yet they can nevertheless be considered towns from an economic point of view. Outstanding examples of this type of town were Pécs and Oradea, both of which were centres of episcopal sees and owned by the bishop and his chapter.

Privileged towns were founded by the king alone, since no one else had the authority necessary for such an act. The decisive moment in the act of foundation was the exemption of the settlement and its appurtenances (forests, waterways, arable lands, pastures) from the authority of all secular judges. In practice this meant that the territory of the town in question was to be subjected neither to the local count, nor to the king's castellan, nor to any other royal officer, but solely to the king himself. Its free inhabitants, the burghers, constituted a *universitas*, a community, which effectively became the owner of the town's territory, that is, the lord and exclusive user of its land.

The nominal landlord of the town continued to be the king, however, and he derived important rights from his elevated position. First, he demanded an annual tax of fixed amount (*census/taxa*) which, in contrast to what was normal for villages, could be paid as a lump sum by the community and then divided among its members in proportion to their wealth. During the Angevin period the towns managed to enforce the fundamental principle according to which the obligation of tax-paying concerned not only the citizens themselves but also those noblemen and clerics or ecclesiastical institutions who had property within the town's territory. In the fourteenth century the towns' right to pay the 'chamber's profit' in one sum, just as they did their tax, was also regarded as an old privilege. Besides requiring a tax the king's lordship had other tangible consequences. Once a year he could stay within the town walls at the citizens' expense and he could also demand several kinds of New Year gift. Yet this dominance, burdensome as it may have seemed, was very far from what we normally call 'seigneurial power' and was already becoming transformed into a simple suzerainty.

This was partly a consequence of the community's self-government, that is, of what we can regard, together with the free possession of the town's territory, as the basic condition of urban life. At the time of its foundation the members of the community were accorded the right to elect a mayor of their own, who was generally called a judge (*judex*) in Hungary, and a council, which consisted of 12 jurors (*iurati*) in the royal towns. The town's territory was thereby transformed into a liberty. Its judge was given an exclusive judicial authority over the entire population of the urban community. This involved both major and minor cases. The secular liberty was generally complemented by some form of ecclesiastical autonomy. The church in most towns was an 'exempt parish' (*exempta plebania*), that is, it was freed from the authority of the archdeacon and owed submission directly to the bishop (or the archbishop of Esztergom himself). This normally involved the right of the citizens themselves to elect their priest, and that of the parish priest to retain the whole tithe as a 'free tithe' (*libera decima*).

One aspect of the towns' liberty was the use of their own law-codes, rather than the kingdom's customary law. Most of these law-codes were adopted from Germany, and that of Buda had come to enjoy the greatest authority by the fifteenth century. Their comprehensiveness is well attested by the fact that the law-code of Buda, which was compiled around 1420, contained no fewer than 403 articles. At first the only court of appeal for the towns was the tribunal of the *magister tavarnicorum* of the king who, unlike the other great judges of the kingdom, had administered justice according to the laws of the towns and in the company of burghers since the reforms of the 1370s. By the second half of the fifteenth century this practice had led to the emergence of a law-code common to all royal towns, called *ius tavernicale*, which was in fact a somewhat modified version of the law of Buda. Moreover, in 1405 Sigismund authorised the towns to appeal to the court of that town whose laws they used, rather than to the *magister tavarnicorum*, thus introducing in Hungary the institution (of German origin) of 'mother towns'.

These legal rights, which were frequently more extensive than the Western models they followed, were complemented by important economic privileges, such as exemption from internal tolls, whoever owned them. This exemption, which was accorded to practically all towns, sometimes extended throughout the whole kingdom, but was normally limited to a certain region, in some cases covering no more than one or two counties. These rights were completed in 1405 by Sigismund's decree, which exempted all merchants from paying tolls at the royal tollhouses. As there were, for instance, no fewer than 37 such places along the road from Vienna to Buda, the economic importance of these privileges should by no means be underestimated.

When a town was founded, the toll of the local weekly market, which would otherwise be paid to the landlord, was generally made over to the community. Besides this ancient type of market, the fair (*forum annuale* or *nundine*) also became common from the middle of the fourteenth century. It took place once a year, generally on the two weeks preceding and following the day of the local patron saint, and was intended for long-distance merchants. At first, to have a fair was regarded as an exceptional privilege, extended only to Székesfehérvár, Esztergom and Buda, the three royal residences; but from Louis the Great's time it was granted to other towns, first to Pressburg and Sopron in 1344 and Košice in 1347. Around 1400 some of the greater towns held more than one fair a year, and dozens of landlords secured one for their villages. During the period 1387–1410 Sigismund granted privileges to found no fewer than 27 weekly markets and 28 annual fairs.

THE ROYAL TOWNS

Since the foundation of Trnava in 1238, Béla IV and all his successors had been generous in granting privileges of varying extent, the most generous being Louis at the time of the reforms of the 1370s. It is impossible to determine the exact number of these grants, for many of them have disappeared. At any rate, before 1389 there were at least one hundred settlements owned by the king that were always or occasionally referred to as 'cities' (*civitas*).

It is unlikely that the legal definition of a town was fixed right from the outset. At first the extent of the privileges seems to have counted most. An equally important distinction was made during the Angevin era between those settlements that paid their annual tax and the 'chamber's profit' in a lump sum and those paying them by holdings. Not all the towns were of the same rank, therefore, and many of them had to content themselves with a limited amount of autonomy, especially those owned by the queen. The council of such places, sometimes referred to as 'free villages' (*liberae villae*) in order to distinguish them from towns enjoying fuller privileges, consisted of six (or four) jurors instead of twelve.

In the course of the fourteenth century a new concept emerged, according to which only those towns surrounded by walls deserved the name 'city'. When Charles I granted full autonomy to the royal 'guests' of Tekov in 1331, he promised that he would give them the privileges of the 'other royal towns' if he saw 'their number increasing', and he ordered them to surround their settlement with a wall as soon as possible.[6] In Louis's decree of 1351 the 'walled town' (*civitas murata*) emerges as an important legal category, and from the 1370s the other *civitates* were increasingly referred to as 'market towns' (*oppidum*). Their Hungarian name was *mezőváros*, but although the Hungarian word *mező* was a synonym of pasture, the term had nothing to do with agriculture. It simply referred to the fact that these settlements lay on the open fields, that is, that they were not surrounded by walls. The terminology had become more or less fixed by the fifteenth century: henceforth the word *civitas* normally denoted a town fortified by stone walls, while *oppidum* stood for one having no walls at all. The only exceptions were the episcopal cities, which were traditionally called *civitas* even if they had neither walls nor privileges, as was the case with Veszprém, for example. When Sigismund tried to increase the number of royal towns in 1405, he granted urban rights to Debrecen and other 'free villages' upon the explicit condition that they would build a circuit of walls.

It was from these beginnings that the different categories of town had grown by the end of the fifteenth century. Henceforth the most illustrious group of the 'free royal towns' (*liberae civitates regiae*) was represented by eight walled towns that came under the jurisdiction of the court of the *magister tavarnicorum*: Buda, Pressburg, Trnava, Sopron, Košice, Bardejov, Prešov and, from the time of King Matthias, Pest. The three 'capitals' of the Saxon community of Transylvania, Sibiu, Braşov and Bistriţa, though not attached to the same court, were nevertheless regarded as forming part of the first group. The rest of the royal towns formed a group of a somewhat lower rank, comprising the walled towns of Zagreb, Székesfehérvár, Esztergom, Levoča, Visegrád, Skalica, Krupina, Cluj and Sabinov, and also unfortified towns such as Szeged, Zvolen, Timişoara and the centres of the Saxon districts of Transylvania. A separate category was formed by the 'free' mining towns, governed by the royal chamber, among which Baia Mare and Baia Sprie in the east and Kremnica, Banská Štiavnica, Banská Bystrica, Pukanec, Ľubietová, Nová Baňa and Banská Belá in the north enjoyed a relatively high degree of autonomy.

Around 1500 the inhabitants of the 40 or so towns belonging to these three categories formed the estate of free burghers. There were many other towns, of course, but these had already passed under private lordship and their inhabitants were not considered free burghers. Some of these towns were fortified, as were Kőszeg, Eisenstadt, Stadtschlaining,

Trenčín and Beckov along the western frontier, and Pécs, Siklós and Kežmarok in other regions, but the overwhelming majority belonged to the category of *oppida*. The most illustrious among them were those under the seigneury of the king (such as Komárno, Tata and Nagymaros) or queen (as were Óbuda, Ráckeve, Miskolc, Beregove and the 'five towns' of Maramureş). Although they regarded themselves as 'towns', they were not 'free' towns, for they continued to be subjected to the authority of a castellan. The same was true of the five towns of the Transylvanian salt mines, namely Turda, Dej, Sic, Cojocna and Ocna Sibiului, whose lord was the royal treasury.

In order to present an outline of urban development in Hungary it has been essential to define what constitutes a town from a legal point of view. Yet the town in the legal sense of the word should not be confused with the more general idea of the town as a commercial centre. The privileges granted by the king could, of course, create a highly favourable starting point for the development of a particular settlement, but they could not compensate for the lack of natural conditions, which were at least as important as the legal background. Although most of the important commercial centres were indeed free royal towns, many royal foundations turned out later to be poorly situated economically and were consequently unable to develop despite their extended privileges. On the other hand, an economic upswing did not necessarily depend upon the granting of a privilege. Oradea, which was inhabited by the tenants of its bishop and chapter and had neither walls nor self-government, became one of the most important trade centres of the kingdom thanks to its favourable location. Since our aim is to provide an outline of urban development in general, we will focus now on the economic aspect of the process. All economically important places will be treated as part of the urban network, regardless of their place within the legal hierarchy of settlements.

THE ROLE OF BUDA

The middle of the country, where the royal residences were grouped, became as a matter of course the focus of the main commercial routes and, consequently, of the urban network as well. The most important consumer was necessarily the royal court where the greatest wealth was concentrated. The production and commerce of precious metals remained a royal monopoly throughout the Middle Ages, and the income of the treasury was shared by those who stood close to the king. Originally every foreigner was obliged to go to the king with his merchandise, and the court remained the natural destination of all the principal trading routes even after this tradition had fallen into oblivion. It is, therefore, no surprise that the two settlements that first obtained urban privileges were Székesfehérvár and Esztergom, the two early residences of the Árpádians. Both of them grew out of a community of 'Latin', that is Walloonian, merchants who may have received their privileges as early as the twelfth century. The 'law' of Székesfehérvár served as a model for the foundations of Béla IV and his successors: that is, the inhabitants of the towns that were then founded were accorded the privileges enjoyed by the burghers of Székesfehérvár. In the fourteenth century, when Buda finally outshone Székesfehérvár, the law of Buda became the new model for the foundation of towns, even though the two sets of privileges were roughly identical.

By the beginning of the fourteenth century Buda had grown to be the capital of the kingdom. Its location at the most convenient crossing of the Danube marked it as a natural centre of the Carpathian basin. The town, founded in 1247 by Béla IV on the castle hill, soon became the cornerstone of the kingdom's economic life. Indeed, its dynamic development was not even interrupted by the fact that between 1323 and 1406 the court resided at Visegrád, which was one or two days' journey from Buda. From the point of view of commerce, Visegrád was so unfavourably sited that not even its importance as the centre of government enabled it to rival Buda. By the time the latter definitively became the kingdom's capital in the early fifteenth century it had surpassed all the other towns in both size and importance.

Buda, in the narrowest sense, meant the town that was built on the castle hill (see Map 7). Its extent at that time is still shown by its modern walls, built in the eighteenth century, which follow the line of the medieval fortifications. In the Angevin era, the territory within the walls was densely packed with two-storied stone buildings, some of which have been preserved. The quarter of the 'Hungarian' burghers was situated around the market place called *Szombatpiac* ('Saturday market'), next to the Vienna gate. Their ancient church was destroyed during the Second World War, and only its tower has survived. During Louis's reign, the Jews, whose memory has been maintained by two small synagogues, were transferred here from the southern end of the castle hill. Alongside the Hungarians, in the 'Latin' (present-day Országház) street, were the houses of the rich Italian merchants. The German burghers, who monopolised the town's government, lived on the southern part of the hill. The church of Our Lady (now Matthias church) was their parish church, and next to it, on the site of the Hotel Hilton, was the friary of the Dominicans, while that of the Franciscans stood in the vicinity of the royal palace. The Saint Peter suburb, the modern Víziváros, which lay along the Danube under the castle hill, also belonged to the town. By the end of the Middle Ages most of the burghers had moved down there, while many houses in the castle had been bought by lay and ecclesiastical lords.

North of the Saint Peter suburb, but closely connected to it, lay the market towns of Felhévíz, famous for its thermal baths, and Óbuda, which boasted an eleventh-century collegiate church and a rich monastery of the Clares, founded by Louis's mother, Elizabeth. Pest, on the other side of the river, had long been a market town as well, with a hospital and two mendicant friaries. Although it functioned as the chief market for the livestock trade of the Great Plain, it had long been regarded as a mere suburb of Buda. Its judge, assisted by only four jurors, was appointed by the council of Buda. It became an independent royal town only in the time of Matthias Corvinus, when the wall, fragments of which can still be seen here and there among the huge buildings of the modern city, was erected. Although at that time the two banks of the river were not linked by a bridge, Sigismund 'planned to draw a huge chain over the Danube to block it'. In order to realise his plan he hired master masons from France who began to construct an enormous tower on the left bank of the river. De la Broquière noted that it was as high as 'three lances' in 1433, but he was proved right in his judgement that the chain, like many of the emperor's over-ambitious plans, would finally come to naught.[7]

THE URBAN ECONOMY

The main trading routes of the kingdom converged at Buda and Pest. The most frequented among them were those which, running to the north, north-west, north-east and east, connected the capital with Vienna, Prague, Cracow and the ports of the Black Sea. Not surprisingly, the most important towns emerged at the points where these routes entered the kingdom. Pressburg, which received its first privileges in 1291 from Andrew III, became the second largest town of the land thanks to its location on the Danube along the old road that led through Vienna to Regensburg. Another route, which branched off it at Győr towards Wiener Neustadt, crossed the frontier at Sopron. The chief town along the road to Bohemia and Moravia, which came from Prague through Brno, was Trnava, founded by Béla IV in 1238. From the beginning of the fourteenth century the growing importance of the commerce with Poland led to the boom of Levoča, Prešov and Bardejov (the latter founded by King Louis), and especially of Košice which lay at the junction of the roads leading from Levoča and Prešov to Buda and became the third largest town of the kingdom. Yet nowhere else is the urbanising effect of long-distance trade as perfectly illustrated as in Transylvania, through which pepper, a commodity of great importance, arrived in Hungary from the Genoese ports of the Black Sea. Two great commercial centres, Sibiu and Braşov, were born along this route, at the entrance of the passes of Bran and Turnu Roşu, the two points where the otherwise impassable range of the Southern Carpathians could be crossed. The two roads from there converged at Cluj and led towards Buda along the valley of the Criş, branching off towards Košice and Cracow at Oradea, which consequently developed into the economic centre of eastern Hungary.

Little is known about the kingdom's southern trading relations. The Balkan market was controlled by Dubrovnik whose commercial activity seems to have been directed principally towards the Adriatic sea. Nor was the Republic of Venice a prime commercial partner of Hungary, for it was much more attracted by the western European market than by what it could hope to buy and sell in Hungary. The Republic vigilantly protected its dominance over the Adriatic sea, but its merchants did not enter Hungary beyond Zagreb. The urban development of the region was entirely in keeping with this situation. Apart from Zagreb, which was the centre of Slavonia, the southern part of the kingdom at the end of the Middle Ages had only three commercial centres of relative importance. These were Pécs, Szeged and Timişoara, none of which lay near the frontier. In all likelihood their burghers made their living less from commerce with the Balkans than from the livestock trade and the distribution of such imported goods as arrived from the West through Buda. However, the situation in the south may have been different in the Angevin period. At that time, Srem, a small region of southern Hungary, was still ahead in the process of urbanisation. In 1342 its largest town, Slankamen, paid a tax six times higher than that levied in Pécs and two and a half times more than that paid by Trnava. Among the many towns that were clustered in this region, in a relatively small area, Eng and Sremska Mitrovica appear to have been wealthier than Pécs. The prosperity of Srem probably came from the production and commerce of its famous wine, which was exported to distant lands. Its economic boom was checked by the Ottoman incursions that began in 1390. The towns were impoverished or completely destroyed. Eng, which had as many as three parishes and a Franciscan friary, was so completely devastated that it disappeared after 1408. Today its site is not easy to locate.

What we know about them makes it clear that the towns of Hungary were given life by long-distance trade. It was most profitable for those few that had obtained staple rights. This had the same meaning as elsewhere in Europe. Both foreign and native merchants were obliged to stop in the privileged town, open their carts and offer their merchandise for wholesale. In this case the profit deriving from both resale and retail (as, for example, from the sale of cloth by the ell) went to the local burghers. Originally, staple right, like that of holding fairs, had been restricted to the royal residences, and even though Győr and some other towns were granted it after 1271, it was effectively exercised by only Buda and Košice. In 1402 Sigismund temporarily accorded staple rights to Pressburg, Sopron, Bardejov and Levoča, but withdrew his ordinance a couple of months later. In 1405 he abolished the staple right of Buda with regard to native merchants, 'lest because of the profit and growth of one city the whole community of our realm suffers loss, damage, and injury.'[8]

The provision of food played a basic role in the economy of towns. While butchers were, as a rule, members of the governing elite, only a small fraction of the townspeople engaged directly in arable farming. It was the urban community itself that tried to acquire landed property in order to raise funds from its own peasants through taxation. By the middle of the fifteenth century most of the royal towns had become landlords: Trnava owned four villages, Sopron seven, and Košice no fewer than seventeen. Buda, which possessed no villages at all, was supplied by the merchants of Pressburg, who purchased their crop on the Little Plain, a fertile region south of their town. Vine-growing and the wine trade played an outstanding role in several of the towns. Sixty per cent (and as high as 80 per cent at the end of the Middle Ages) of the burghers of Sopron owned vineyards on the sunny hillsides around their town. The inhabitants of Pressburg and Trnava, while having vineyards of their own, preferred to lease them from the greatest land-owners of the county. The hillsides around Buda, a residential area today, were covered by the vineyards of the local burghers until the Ottoman conquest.

Manufacture played a much more limited role in the life of the towns than either commerce or food provision or even the wine trade. Nowhere did export-orientated handicrafts emerge, with the exception of Bardejov, where the production of linen was developing rapidly from the early fifteenth century. In 1411 Sigismund tried to introduce *barchent* weaving at Košice, and ordered the settlement of skilled craftsmen there, but his attempt failed, being based on nothing more than royal will. Of course, a number of artisans lived in every impor-tant town. At Buda, for instance, 61 crafts were represented in the first half of the fifteenth century, whereas at Sopron their number grew from 32 to 52 between 1379 and 1441. But in the main these tradesmen produced cheap articles for everyday use. Wealth and pres-tige were attached only to those crafts that supplied the elite, as was the case with those of the goldsmiths and leather-workers, both of which had a long-standing tradition in Hungary. Consequently, as a rule craftsmen were poorly organised, and their influence was negligible. Although from the reign of Louis onwards guilds do appear here and there, their number and political weight were insignificant. No more than ten guilds are thought to have existed at Buda in the time of Sigismund, and their number was even smaller elsewhere. At Sopron, for instance, they are first mentioned as late as 1425.

All the towns in Hungary, including even Buda, the largest among them, were rather modest in size. In 1436, when considering transferring the general council of Basle to Buda, Sigismund ordered a survey of the town's accommodation. At that time there were 322 houses in the 'castle', containing 679 rooms, 1416 pantries, 710 shops, 360 caves and 2,607 stables, whereas in the suburb there were only 673 rooms, 1,860 pantries, 32 shops, 267 caves and 2098 stables in as many as 645 houses.[9] Obviously the castle had a more urban character than the suburb, but their combined population must have remained under 10,000. By the end of the Middle Ages the agglomeration of Buda, including Pest and the suburbs, may have numbered nearly 20,000 inhabitants, but all the other towns lagged far behind. Pressburg had fewer than 1000 households in 1434, and the same seems to have been the case at Košice. At Sopron, one of the chief towns in Transdanubia, only 750 to 800 tax-payers were registered between 1424 and 1438, and Bardejov appears to have had even fewer.

URBAN SOCIETY

One result of the kingdom's western orientation was that the cities of the Empire had a decisive influence upon commerce. Lacking sufficient capital, the burghers of Hungary were condemned to a passive role and rarely got beyond Vienna which, because of its staple right, was always able to control Hungary's commerce in that direction. At the time of his conflict with the dukes of Austria, Charles I tried to counterbalance Vienna's overbearing presence by increasing the economic importance of the route to Prague. In 1336 he launched a commercial war against the Habsburgs in alliance with King John of Bohemia, granted royal letters of protection to the merchants of Bohemia and Moravia, and even reduced toll tariffs in their favour. Charles's successors generally maintained good relations with Austria, and so Louis extended these privileges to the merchants of Vienna in 1366, who also obtained from Sigismund the right of free trade all over Hungary in 1402. By that time similar privileges had been granted to a number of towns in Germany: Cologne in 1344, Nuremberg in 1357, Regensburg in 1359 and Aachen in 1369.

It is, therefore, not surprising that, right from the beginning, ethnic Germans played a no less crucial role in the process of urbanisation in Hungary than they did in Bohemia and Poland. Not only had the towns of Transylvania and Spis been inhabited by Germans since the very birth of these settlements, but also the most important towns throughout the kingdom. Since the middle of the thirteenth century the first settlers had come from the Empire, above all from Vienna and Regensburg. Most settlements of some importance were dominated and governed, at least in the beginning, by an elite of German origin. Official documents at Sopron and Pressburg were drawn up in German from the time of Louis the Great, and even the law-code of Buda was written in German. According to this code, only two Hungarians could be elected as members of the council, while the judge was to be a person whose four grandparents were of German birth.

The activity of the Italians was more limited and less enduring than that of the Germans. They were only interested in large-scale business. Above all, they were keen to establish good relations with the royal court. Only a few Italians settled down permanently, mostly at Buda, where they constituted a kind of elite within the local merchant community, and controlled the wholesale of spices, silk and cloth. They had been quite influential for a long time. In Louis's reign, Italian financiers – Jacopo Saraceno from Padua, Francesco Bernardi from Florence, Bartolommeo Guidoti from Bologna and others – administered the kingdom's revenues and also engaged in credit operations. They temporarily lost their position after the accession of Sigismund, for in 1394 he entrusted the administration of the mines, the coinage and the thirtieth to Ulrich Kamerer and a certain Marcus, his companion from Nuremberg. Somewhat later the influence of Pipo of Ozora helped the Florentines to regain the positions that they had lost, mainly within financial administration, which they continued to control until the middle of the century.

Due to the importance of long-distance trade, the governance of the towns was in the hands of rich merchants and entrepreneurs throughout the Middle Ages. A handful of influential families held all the leading posts within the municipal administration. The original elite consisted of the descendants of the founders, who had still been land owners rather than merchants and had frequently contracted marriages with distinguished noble families. It was only after 1370 that the towns – especially Buda – became dominated by a new merchant elite, which was strongly linked, both economically and by ties of kinship, to the towns of southern Germany. In order to protect domestic capital, association with foreign merchants was prohibited by the king as well as by the law-code of Buda; but the trading companies of Germany were nevertheless able to control the Hungarian market through their local representatives and relatives. In the meantime the originally tiny group of Hungarian burghers was also being swelled by a continuous influx of rural immigrants. As a result of this, in some towns, like Buda and Cluj, Hungarians had come to form the majority of the population by about 1500.

The uncontested dominance of the merchant class prevented the outbreak of serious social conflict between the 'rich' and the 'poor' or between merchants and craftsmen. Only in Pressburg and Sopron did the 'commotion' of the poor lead to the establishment, in 1414 and 1427 respectively, of an 'outer council', which was to control finances and in which craftsmen were also given some seats. Buda was an exception, however, for two serious revolts took place there in the first half of the century. The first, led by a group of wealthy burghers, broke out in 1402, when the assembled townspeople dismissed their leaders and elected a council of 36 members, in which the poor were represented. On the whole the movement was socially motivated, but it enjoyed the support of the rich Italians and was directed mainly against the German elite. Its outbreak must have been linked in some way to the revolt of the barons against Sigismund, and it collapsed together with that revolt in the autumn of 1403. The king ordered the confiscation of the Italians' property, sent the members of the new council into exile and restored the town's previous regime. The second revolt, which broke out in 1439, was more acute and also more important in its consequences. By that time 'Hungarian' and 'German' parties had come to exist in the town, and the revolt was brought about by the murder of the leader of the 'Hungarians'. The mob attacked and robbed the houses of the rich, making no distinction between Germans and Hungarians, and by the time the rebellion was finally put down both parties were willing to find a compromise. Henceforth 'German' and 'Hungarian' burghers were to enjoy equal rights within the town's government. The Hungarians were to provide half of the council: that is, to have equal representation in a great council of one hundred members, which was to elect the judge, who every second year was himself to be Hungarian.

THE MARKET TOWNS

Mapping the urban network of medieval Hungary reveals conspicuous gaps. Most of the important towns lay north of a line drawn through Sopron, Buda, Oradea and Baia Mare, with only a handful being south of it. Not only the Great Plain but also Transdanubia, though relatively densely populated, preserved their predominantly rural character until the modern period. The urbanisation of towns like Zalaegerszeg, Veszprém, Kaposvár and Szekszárd, not to mention smaller settlements, has only taken place during the last two hundred years.

Yet the beneficial effect of long-distance trade was also felt in these regions, and not only in the 30 or 40 settlements that were directly interested in it. Their growth gradually gave new life to the kingdom's whole economy and led to the formation of a dense network of markets. Where there were no real towns their functions were taken over by rural markets and by a multitude of market towns. Commercial relations became ever closer both between the towns and their surroundings, and between the regions themselves, which as a consequence by 1400 had been united in a single market area, represented by the common use of the same money.

One of the signs that shows the development of the domestic market is the proliferation of market towns. About 300 settlements termed *oppidum* occur in the sources before 1440, and another 470 during the period between 1440 and 1526. About 200 of them displayed some urban characteristics, but the rest were simple villages both in their appearance and by the nature of their economy. Their inhabitants lived off agriculture and were treated and taxed as simple tenants. They held markets and some of them even had fairs. They were more populous than average villages, but resembled them in every other respect.

What is meant by these two types of settlement can best be illuminated by the example of the estate of the Bánfi around Lendava. In 1389 this seigneury, as is shown by the document describing its partition, spread over 725 square kilometres, comprised 90 villages, eleven inhabited *praedia* and four 'towns', called *civitas* by our source and *oppidum* by later ones. In an average town we find one hundred households as opposed to eighteen per village. Each 'town' had a market, and there was even a Franciscan friary in Szemenye, but the inhabitants of these towns were mostly peasants. Among the 50 inhabitants of Dobrovnik there were only five craftsmen: two smiths, a quiver-maker, a weaver and a shoemaker. Only Lendava, the centre of the estate, can be seen as a market town in the true sense of the word. The Bánfi who resided in the castle above the town regarded it as their most important settlement. Indeed, in 1366 they obtained for it the privilege of holding a fair, being among the first in the kingdom to do so. In that half of the town which was included in the land division of 1389 there were no more than 43 tenants, but 19 of them lived off something other than agriculture. Besides the typically rural crafts (four tailors and a shoemaker) there were other specialised tradesmen, like a weaver, a carpenter, a sword-maker, a bow-maker, a butcher, a cook, a dog-keeper (*canifer*), even a goldsmith, a merchant and a surgeon (*cyrologus*), which surely suggests a modest level of urbanisation as a whole.[10]

The market towns were intended to meet the demands of the landlord and the local elite as well as those of the peasantry. Their most important function seems to have been the distribution of imported goods, which generally reached them through the intermediary activities of the merchants in the greater towns. Telling evidence of the growing purchasing capacity of the peasantry is to be found in the increasing importation of cheap commodities such as knives from Austria and cloths from Bohemia, Moravia, Silesia and Poland. Most of the market towns on the Great Plain lived off the livestock trade, while other regions profited from the trade in crops and wine.

However, not even the greatest of the market towns of this period as yet showed the outward signs of urbanisation. Their houses were built of wood or adobe, the construction of stone buildings not beginning before 1450 and even then only sporadically. Nevertheless, there emerged a relatively small group of rich peasants who, not contenting themselves with the sale of their own produce, invested their capital in business activities. Many of them later moved to greater towns and became respected members of their citizenry, while others sent their sons abroad for study at a university. Those who came back had a good chance of obtaining the parish of their borough, a canonry or another suitable church benefice. There were chapters where half of the canons were sons of townspeople, many of them coming from market towns.

The inhabitants of a greater market town regarded themselves as 'burghers' (cives) and their town as a 'town' (civitas). In fact they were tenants living under seigneurial power, and their lords not only called them peasants but treated them as such. It is possible that this contrast explains why the radical ideas of the age were received more intensely in the market towns than elsewhere. Heretics called valdenses appeared in Sopron in the 1380s, but the main breeding-ground of Hussitism in Hungary were the market towns of Srem where the seeds of 'heresy' were sown by young burghers who had studied at the university of Prague. Two of them, Thomas and Valentine, prepared the first Hungarian version of the Bible, parts of which have come down to us in three codices. The spread of the Hussite doctrines was so conspicuous that Pope Eugene IV entrusted their extermination to Giacomo della Marca, vicar of the Franciscans in Bosnia, in 1436. Giacomo, who had been working as an inquisitor in the dioceses of Cenad and Pécs since 1434, set up his residence at Sremska Kamenica, near modern Novi Sad, in the very centre of the movement. His work proved highly successful, and the leaders who were not burnt alive or imprisoned went into exile. The two translators of the Bible, followed by many of their supporters, went to Moldavia in 1439, and with them the short history of Hussitism in Hungary came to an end.

THE TRIUMPH OF MONEY

The increasing volume of commerce and the multiplication of markets implies the general use of money. In the first half of the fourteenth century people still preferred counting in marks, *fertones* and *pensae* instead of pennies, and in the eastern provinces bars of silver continued to be used as a means of payment. Many payments were effected by means of a combination of money and 'estimated goods' (*partim in denariis, partim in aestimatione*), and in the 1330s some of the parish priests on the Great Plain paid the collectors of the papal tenth with objects made of silver. The situation changed rapidly during Louis's reign when the penny and the florin came into general use all over the kingdom. Payments in bars of silver are last recorded from Transylvania around 1380. The mark continued only in the vocabulary of the law courts, where the sums of the fines imposed by them were given in marks even if the fines were commonly discharged in pennies or movables.

The use of money, by now fairly general, was accompanied by the disappearance of local money. Until the mid-fourteenth century each chamber minted coins according to its own 'account' (*computus*), a fact which resulted in there being in use eight to ten pennies of varying weight and fineness, the exchange rates of which had caused much difficulty to the papal tax-collectors. The value of the local pennies was generally established by reference to the groat of Bohemia, which weighed 3.5 grams. Four of the best pennies and 20 of the smallest ones had the value of a groat. In the 1350s local mints were closed down, and one single penny, that of the chamber of Buda, took their place. The only other currency that remained in use – and then only in western Hungary, from Pressburg to Zala – was the penny of Vienna.

It was more difficult to suppress the local moneys of account, all of which were rooted in ancient custom. East of the River Tisza and in Transylvania the weight of silver was computed in marks of 'fine silver', that is of a fineness of 900/1000, whereas elsewhere the 'commercial' mark (*mercimonialis*), of a fineness of 750/1000, was in use. The situation was complicated by the fact that the weight of the mark itself varied extensively, from the mark of Buda (245.5 grams) through the 'Hungarian' mark (233.8 grams) to the mark of Transylvania (206.7 grams). Each region adhered to its accustomed mark and its special way of reckoning: they remained in use for some time, even after the king's penny had established its dominance all over the realm, and became the bases of eight to ten local moneys of account. In the south-west, for instance, the penny was counted in marks, in Slavonia five *pensae* (i.e. 200d) and in Baranya six *pensae* (i.e. 240d) giving one mark. In the eastern regions several types of 'florin' were in use, among them one of '38 groats' (one groat being equal to four pennies) in the region of Košice or another of '32 groats' in Transylvania. This chaotic state of affairs was finally ended by the decree of 1405, which ordered the general use of the computation of Buda. This meant that thereafter

100d were counted everywhere as equivalent to a florin and 400d were worth one mark. The strength of the 'national' market is well shown by the fact that both the groat (as a money of account) and the *pensa* went out of use within years. It was also in 1405 that the king tried to generalise the use of the measures of Buda, but his efforts were to no avail and local measures continued to be used until as late as the nineteenth century.

Chapter 16

The Rural Landscape

The reigns of the two Angevins and of Sigismund of Luxembourg mark the apogee of medieval Hungary. The process of modernisation that had begun in the thirteenth century, culminating between 1323 and 1437, broke down with the death of Sigismund. No social and economic transformation of comparable depth and comprehensiveness was to take place before the eighteenth century.

POPULATION GROWTH AND NEW SETTLEMENTS

The stable political system favoured not only commerce but also the life of peasants. The troubles that shook the country between 1382 and 1402 left few lasting traces. More damage was caused by external attacks, though the Ottomans were as yet unable to penetrate beyond the southernmost counties, and the devastation caused by the Hussites was limited to a period of only a few years. The destruction was considerable but only affected a small fraction of the population, while the great majority of people enjoyed the benefits of strong royal authority and were able to rely on the support of the court as well, for the initiative to modernise the country came from the immediate entourage of the king. Nothing in this respect had changed since the time of St Stephen.

The pace of development seems to have been fairly rapid even when compared with western Europe. Whether or not we accept that an age of enormous achievements may be termed an 'age of crisis', the West had certainly to cope with the trauma caused by the Black Death and its consequences. The situation in Hungary and in central Europe in general was much more favourable. The symptoms of the crisis were few, if not entirely absent, while the positive impulses of the period were as strong as in the West. Consequently, it was during this period that the economic and cultural gap between the two regions of Europe was significantly reduced, though it should be emphasised that it never disappeared completely.

The clearest indications of undisturbed development were population growth and the settlement of the hitherto uninhabited mountain regions. The thirteenth and fourteenth centuries saw the greatest period of *défrichement* in the Carpathian basin. By the middle of the fifteenth century there was no room left for new settlers, with the exception of the northern and north-eastern fringes of the counties of Trenčín, Orava, Šaríš, Zemplín, Ung, Bereg and Maramureş, which remained almost uninhabited until 1500 and beyond.

The process began in the thirteenth century with the settlement of the huge royal forests in Zvolen, Turc, Liptov and Spis. During the Angevin period the hitherto deserted woodlands of Trenčín, Orava, Gemer, Šaríš, Zemplín and Ung were gradually spotted with human settlements. When, in 1243, Béla IV granted the region of Plešivec (in Gemer county) to the ancestors of the Bebek family, ten localities were enumerated there; by 1320 the number of villages had grown to 29. In 1427 51 villages with 1,181 peasant holdings were registered in the same area. The scale of settlement is demonstrated by the fact that this figure represented nearly a quarter of the total number of holdings in the county. The northern part of Šaríš county, along the border of Poland where later was to be formed the seigneury of Makovica belonging to the Cudar, seems to have been covered by wholly uninhabited woodland around 1300. In 1427 about 50 villages were dispersed here, with a total of 1,471 holdings. It was also during the same period that the greatest estate of the whole country, that of the Druget family in present-day Slovakia and Ukraine, was populated. In 1437 106 villages were listed here with some 3,200 households (*mansio*). The same process was going on throughout the eastern peripheries of the kingdom, in the counties of Bereg, Ugoča, Maramureş, Satu Mare, Szolnok, Crasna, Bihor, Zărand, Arad and Timiş, in Transylvania itself and on the marches of Severin. In all these regions thousands of new villages were established on estates where no man had ever lived since the dawn of human history. For example, in 1292 Andrew III authorised Count Alexander Ákos to settle Romanians on the domain of Ilia, north of the River Mureş, and by the middle of the fifteenth century some 50 tiny villages shared this territory. Many similar examples could be cited from any of the above-mentioned regions.

Before the great period of settlement the population density must have been quite low, perhaps as low as five to seven inhabitants per square kilometre at the beginning of the fourteenth century. 'The kingdom appears to be empty because of its sheer size': this was the impression gained in 1308 by the French Dominican friar whose testimony has already been noted.[1] The papal tax lists from the 1330s also show the peripheries of the country to have been almost completely devoid of parishes. By the 1430s, when it first becomes possible to assess the overall population of the country, the situation had completely changed. At that time, 400,000 tax-paying peasant holdings were registered on the 295,000 square kilometres of the kingdom (excluding Slavonia), from which a population of some 3 to 3½ million people may be surmised. This would mean a density of ten to twelve inhabitants per square kilometre.

ETHNIC CHANGES

The process of settlement brought about important modifications to the ethnic structure of the region. It was at this time that the extensive peripheries of the Carpathian basin became inhabited predominantly by Slovaks, Ruthenes or Romanians. We rarely have direct information about the provenance of the settlers, yet it is evident that the territories that were populated at that time were later inhabited by non-Hungarians. It seems reasonable, therefore, to conclude that the settlers were foreigners, even if the names of their settlements were often registered in Hungarian, which was the language of their lords.

The northern mountain ranges, from Trenčín to modern Ukraine, became a Slovak-speaking region. Slav groups had, of course, been living there before the Hungarian conquest, but not it seems in significant numbers. It is in the fourteenth century that their villages begin to appear in great numbers in the sources. Many of them can be proved to have been recently settled. Immigration was organised by German entrepreneurs, mostly burghers, who were called *scultetus* (from the German *Schultheiß*) in the east and *advocatus* (German *Vogt*) in the west. They concluded a mostly written agreement with a lord for the settlement of a piece of woodland. The settlers themselves were undoubtedly Slavs, who seem to have been recruited in Poland and Moravia. For the northern part of Trenčín county after 1324, we have relatively plentiful information about the activity of the *advocati* commissioned by the judges royal who held the region as part of their honour. By 1439, when the appurtenances of the seigneuries there are first enumerated, most of the modern localities had already come into existence. The same can be said of the three counties of Orava, Liptov and Zvolen by the middle of the fifteenth century. Many of the villages that had been founded bear a name which clearly indicates the circumstances of their birth: there are names in -*vágás* ('clearing') and -*poruba*, its Slovak equivalent, which hint at assarts within woodlands, while the many Slovak toponyms *lehota* ('lightening') refer to newly founded and privileged settlements.

The settlers in present-day Slovakia were freeholders who were attracted by favourable conditions. At the time of their settlement they were granted an exemption from the payment of taxation, generally of 16 years' duration, during which they could clear the forest, found their village, build up their farmsteads and put the newly reclaimed land under cultivation. Their future services were precisely fixed: they consisted of payments in money and sometimes in kind, but no labour service was required. They enjoyed relatively extensive privileges, in accordance with the liberal norms of the settlements under 'German law' that had already become common in Bohemia and Poland. As for the *scultetus* or *advocatus*, he received a double-size holding that was exempted from all sorts of taxes and services. Moreover, he and his descendants became the perpetual reeves of the new settlement with the right to proceed in minor cases and to collect the fines imposed. It was his privilege to have a mill, to run a brewery and a tavern, and to pursue the basic crafts. He also frequently had a share in the seigneurial tax of the village.

It was also during the rule of Charles I that the immigration of Romanians and Ruthenes into the north-eastern regions began. In Maramureş, which had been almost completely deserted under the Árpádians, Romanians are first mentioned in 1326. In the neighbouring counties of Ung, Bereg and Satu Mare they appear in 1337, 1338 and 1357 respectively. The earliest sources clearly refer to newcomers. The scale of the process is clearly demonstrated by the fact that whereas in 1398 393 tenants were registered on the highland part of the estates of the Druget family in the county of Ung, in 1437 622 of them lived in the same area, and the number of villages had grown from 20 to 29. Yet this did not mean that there was no further room for settlement: in 1437 the population density was still under 1 per square kilometre, and dozens of new villages were later to be founded here (see Map 5).

The appearance and spread of the Romanians in Transylvania and neighbouring counties can be followed with relative certainty. We have already seen them appear on the slopes of the southern Carpathians in the twelfth century at the latest. In 1288 they are first mentioned on the land of the Saxons; they then turn up in the counties of Hunedoara and Alba in 1292 and 1293 respectively. From here they spread westwards and eastwards, through the counties of Zărand (1318), Caraşova (1319), Bihor (1326), Arad (1337), Crasna (1341) and Timiş (1343), and within Transylvania itself, in the counties of Turda (1342), Cluj (1344) Bistriţa and Dăbâca (1366). They had already reached Szolnok Interior before 1353, presumably from neighbouring Maramureş.

Having first appeared, they are frequently referred to in each of these counties. Moreover, we have ample evidence to prove that their arrival in great numbers was the outcome of a conscious settlement policy on the part of the local lords. In 1335 a certain Voivode Bogdan, perhaps the future ruler of Moldavia, moved 'from his land to Hungary', and the archbishop of Kalocsa spent almost a year in the county of Caraşova to handle the affair on the king's behalf.[2] In 1337 William Druget settled Romanians on one of his estates in Ung county, while in 1341 a noble family of Bihor planned to 'gather Wallachians' on their lands. It is, of course, evident that Romanians may have arrived several decades before their first appearance in the written sources. Yet if the available data are plotted on a map, it is impossible to avoid the conclusion that the immigrants came from the north-east and the south, that is, from Moldavia and Wallachia. The process seems to have reached a peak in the first half of the fourteenth century, during the reign of Charles I.

AGRICULTURE AND THE VILLAGE

Agriculture went through a profound transformation in the thirteenth and fourteenth centuries as a consequence of what is called the first agrarian 'revolution'. By the second half of the thirteenth century the most primitive form of settled agriculture, dominant under the early Árpádians, gave way to more developed forms. The land of the village community was divided into fixed parcels, which were put to use on a rotational basis: while one part was cultivated, the other was left fallow for some years. This kind of open-field system was a fairly extensive, but at the same time relatively modern, form of land cultivation, made possible by the abundance of arable land and made necessary by the large number of animals. On the basis of our evidence relating to the thirteenth and fourteenth centuries the number of major animals in an average household can be put at about 30, which would mean that there were hundreds in each village. One fifth seems to have been cattle, the rest being sheep, goats and pigs. The animals wintered on the land under cultivation, manuring and treading it intensely, while in the summer they grazed on the fallow land. Horse-breeding, on the other hand, had become quite rare among the peasantry.

An essential element in this sort of open-field system was the prescribed order of cultivation. The land under cultivation remained the undivided property of the village community. That part of it which had been manured and trodden by the animals was distributed among the villagers, each of whom received a parcel in proportion to the number of his animals. Since the parcels were traditionally allotted by bow-shots, the parcels themselves were called 'arrows'. The 'arrows' were separated by long strips of grass, whence the name of the distribution itself (Hung. *füvönosztás*, literally 'distribution by grass'). The open-field system naturally involved strict rules governing the nature of the crops to be grown and all other aspects of communal land cultivation.

The new system of cultivation was directly connected to new agrarian techniques. The thirteenth century saw the appearance of the great asymmetric plough, pulled by eight to ten oxen. The land that could be turned over by it in one day was called a *jugerum*, which took the form of a long strip, one of the chief characteristics of the open-field systems. The Hungarian *jugerum* of that time was a little larger than an acre (4,300 square metres). An average peasant holding had about 20 acres in the western counties, and 55 to 60 in the new settlements in the north-east. The new technique naturally resulted in higher yields. Whereas in the early thirteenth century the crop yield was only twice as great as the amount of seed used, a century later the yield was already 3 or 4 to 1 throughout the country.

Although the dominant form of open-field agriculture was still the two-field system, its three-field variant was also employed in some places. It was based on the annual rotation of the fields, one being sown in the spring, the other in the autumn, the third being fallow. The land was no longer redistributed periodically, the individual parcels remaining permanently attached to particular peasant holdings.

The settlement of the peripheries, the emergence of the standard peasant holding and the new agrarian techniques profoundly modified the traditional form of the village. The irregular, widely dispersed settlements of the early Árpádian period gradually gave way to a new, German type of village, which generally consisted of a single street, with the inner holdings lying on the two sides and their appurtenances dispersed throughout the village territory. The inner holding as a rule took the form of a long rectangle, with its shorter side facing the street, whence a wide gate led into the court. The house was always constructed on one side of the court. By the thirteenth century the small hovel of the earlier period had been replaced by an oblong house with three rooms. It was generally a wooden construction, adobe and stone not being used for rural buildings before the early modern period. The entrance was in the middle of the house and led into the kitchen, which was equipped with an oven. From the kitchen two other doors led to the living room on one side and to the pantry on the other. The farmyard was beside and behind the house and was joined by a garden, and sometimes also by a small piece of arable land, at the other end.

This type of village and house remained common in Hungary until the nineteenth, indeed even the twentieth, century. One of its variants in the woodland areas of present-day Slovakia was also adopted from Germany and appeared together with the settlers. Its distinguishing feature was that the parcels of arable land were not dispersed throughout the village territory but lay at the two sides of the village in long strips, which were contiguous to the inner holding and ran up to the very edge of the forest. On the Great Plain a third type of settlement was dominant in the early modern period, but it is open to discussion whether its specific form dated back to the Árpádian period or was the result of a later transformation. These villages had no regular streets, the houses lying in more or less disordered clusters or forming concentric circles instead. Although rare in Hungary, other forms of rural settlement were to be found in areas where a relatively numerous lesser nobility existed. Such a region was the Göcsej in the county of Zala, where the houses of the nobility were widely dispersed, the parcels of arable land lying among the houses.

The size of an average village depended upon local circumstances. In 1427, 21,257 *portae* (tax-units) were registered in 1,059 localities within five north-eastern counties, which gives 20 *portae* (perhaps corresponding to 25–30 households) for an average village. In fact, while there were micro-villages with only one or two *portae*, which became deserted during the following decades, most of these villages were considerably larger and still exist with their names unaltered. In the counties of Abaúj and Tolna the average village territory was around 2,800 acres at the end of the Middle Ages. Yet there existed great regional differences. The Great Plain was characterised by populous villages with extensive territories, whereas in the southern part of Transdanubia and south of the Drava small villages were more usual. For example, around 1500, in the county of Vas the extent of a village's territory was 2,100 acres on average, while the corresponding figure in Zala was 1,700 acres.

THE PEASANTRY

The material foundation of peasant life was the holding, called *sessio* or *curia iobagionalis* in Hungary. In the narrow sense it was the peasant's dwelling within the village together with the adjoining farmyard. Later it was called the 'inner holding' and its size was, at least theoretically, invariable within a village. Yet the *sessio* as an economic unit was not restricted to the farmyard. Each peasant who had an inner holding also had a share in the arable land, meadows, pasture and woodland pertaining to the village – that is, in everything that was not reserved for the lord. This complex was later called the 'outer holding'. The arable land and the meadows were allotted in the form of strips in that part of the village territory that was under cultivation, the pasture and the woodland remaining undivided and used in common by the village community.

The *jobagio* and his holding (*sessio*) were inseparable from each other. The holding was the basic unit of agrarian production, and only those who possessed such a holding were counted among the *jobagiones*. Yet the division of the holding began as early as the end of the fourteenth century, gradually leading to the appearance of half-holdings, quarter-holdings and so on, which meant that several, economically independent, families lived on one and the same holding, their shares in the village territory being proportionate to the size of their holding within the village. From the end of the fourteenth century we also find a growing number of *inquilini*, that is, peasants who possessed little or no arable land in the village territory and whose inner holding, if they had one, consisted merely of the site of their dwelling. Although the great majority of the fifteenth-century peasantry consisted of *jobagiones* with half- and quarter-holdings, it comprised several different strata, ranging from the well-off peasants with entire holdings to the *inquilini*.

After the great transformation of the agrarian system the holding became the basis upon which tax and other services were assessed. Indeed, peasant services continued to be determined with reference to the holding even after it had been divided between several households. Although the extent of the services was sometimes fixed by a formal contract, most frequently it was regulated by custom. Relatively the most burdensome of all was the money tax, called *census*, whose amount varied throughout the country between half a florin and one florin. The peasants were also required to offer 'gifts' (*munera*) to their lord on two or three important feast days of the year. These mostly involved a fixed amount of food (cake, hens, eggs, etc.). Labour service, the third main component of peasant obligations, was not significant before the end of the Middle Ages. Most of the lords in the fourteenth and fifteenth centuries did not themselves engage in agrarian production, which meant that their 'demesne' (*allodium*) amounted to no more than a few holdings and accordingly needed little peasant labour. Consequently, the labour service required from a single holding was limited to a few days' work per year and mostly took the form of transport. The last group of seigneurial dues was paid in common by the village community and divided by the local leaders among its members. The *jobagiones* also paid a yearly tax, the *lucrum camerae,* to the royal treasury, and the tenth of their crop was, of course, due to the Church.

In reality, the holding was a hereditary piece of land: the *jobagio* could not be deprived of it by his lord and his offspring inherited it without restriction. Yet it would not be transformed into real property until the nineteenth century, and in the later Middle Ages it continued to be subjected to noble property law, in terms of which the whole territory of the village, including both inner and outer holdings, was considered to be the lord's property. This legal fact was expressed by the common Latin name of the village, which from the thirteenth century was not *villa* but 'possession' (*possessio*). Within its boundaries the peasant was not a proprietor but merely a perpetual tenant. True, in the case of individual assarts and vineyards, his tenancy came fairly close to what we would call a freehold. However, neither the assarts nor the vineyards were regarded as belonging to the peasant holding proper.

The most important vine producing regions were almost the same as today: the hills around Pressburg and Sopron; those north of the Balaton; the region of Tokaj, called Hegyalja ('below the mountains') in the north-east; the Macra hills east of Arad; and the southern slopes of the Fruška Gora in Srem, whose wine enjoyed an international reputation. But wine was also produced in many regions that offered unfavourable conditions for viticulture. Wine was much in demand in the local markets and played an important role in exports, and this is sufficient to explain why not only peasants but also burghers, nobles and even churchmen engaged in its production. Like all other land, vineyards were subjected to seigneurial authority, but they had enjoyed a special status since the thirteenth century, their owner having the right to sell or bequeath them to whoever he wanted as long as he cultivated them regularly. The same was true of cleared land (*terra exstirpata*), on which grain, especially wheat, was produced. This name was given to those parcels of arable land that did not belong to the common land of the village community but remained the individual possession of a *jobagio*. These parcels were regarded as the hereditary possession of the man who had laboriously cleared them for cultivation.

The specific tax of vineyards and assarts seems to have been what was referred to as the 'ninth' (*nona*) by contemporary sources. It meant in fact the 'second' tenth part of the crop, which was due to the lord after the tithe had already been paid, and it accordingly amounted to one ninth of the remaining crop. As a sort of tax it is first mentioned by Louis the Great in his law of 1351. The ruler engaged himself to collect, in his own villages and in those of the queen, 'from all our peasant tenants holding ploughlands and vineyards the ninth part of all their crops and vines', and ordered the barons, the nobles and the ecclesiastical landowners to do the same on their own estates.[3] Those not complying with the law were to be treated as rebels and the ninth was to be collected by the king from their lands. It would be logical to infer from this that the ninth was one of the regular services and was paid by all *jobagiones*. Yet it was never enumerated among the regular payments of the peasant holdings before the middle of the fifteenth century. It is therefore more probable that the law concerned only the *jobagiones* possessing assarts and vineyards and was meant to regulate their way of tax-paying. In the case of vineyards the ninth replaced a former tax in kind of fixed amount called 'hill tax' (*tributum montis*), also referred to as *bergrecht* (*ius montium*) in the western counties, which had been paid since the thirteenth century. At first it amounted to one 'bucket' of wine from 'each vineyard', then later to one tenth of the yield and was called *nona vinorum* after 1351. It is highly probable, though still needs to be proved, that the individual assarts were taxed in a similar way, and the tax that is mentioned in our sources as the 'ninth of corn' (*nona frugum*), mostly together with the *nona vinorum*, was in fact the seigneurial due imposed on them.

The holding was, therefore, not the only basis of peasant subsistence: many of the *jobagiones* had vineyards, assarts, animals, or were engaged in some kind of handicraft, which meant that they were much stronger economically than the small size of their holdings would indicate. It was this fact that led to the emergence of arbitrary seigneurial taxation at the end of the Angevin period. The model for this was the 'extraordinary' taxation levied by the king. The royal example was followed in the second half of the fourteenth century by other lords, who with growing frequency demanded irregular taxes whose amount generally exceeded that of the traditional ones. Yet this new type of taxation was, in a way, more equitable than the system of customary dues, for the collection of which the economic strength of individual households was not taken into account. The extraordinary tax was imposed on, and proportional to, the totality of a peasant's economic resources.

There was a reluctance among poorer lords to let their peasants move away. Most of these *jobagiones* wanted to settle in towns, market towns or on greater estates, whose lords could offer more favourable conditions. That the lesser nobility should try to prevent the departure of their peasants, retaining them on various pretexts, is hardly surprising. This is the explanation for Sigismund's repeated confirmation of the right of free movement. His first mandate, of 1391, concerned only Transylvania, but was extended over the whole country in 1397. The latter disposition was repeated at the diet of Timişoara, in two decrees in 1405 and again in 1407 and 1409. The frequent confirmation of the law clearly indicates that this right was universally acknowledged but also that its enforcement was far from smooth. A normal aspect of everyday rural life in the fourteenth and fifteenth centuries was so-called 'abduction'. This was the arbitrary transfer of a *jobagio* to a greater lord's estate by his retainers and peasants, the initiative frequently coming from the *jobagio* himself.

In the year of Sigismund's death a peasant revolt broke out in Transylvania. It was the only significant uprising of the subjected masses before the great peasant war of 1514. Paradoxically, the revolt was caused not by the increase of service dues but, at least indirectly, by the emperor's monetary policy. In 1434 the bishop of Transylvania refused to collect the tithe while low-quality money was in circulation, but then in 1437 demanded the arrears in one sum after the appearance of good money. The peasants' unwillingness to pay their accumulated tithe prompted the bishop to turn to the weapon of excommunication. The other chief grievance of the peasants was their lords' reluctance to respect their right of free movement. Although the revolt broke out in northern Transylvania, it soon spread to the counties of Satu Mare and Szabolcs. In June 1437 an army of peasants entrenched itself on a hill at Bobîlna and sent envoys to the voivode, Ladislaus Csáki. The rebels called themselves the 'university' of the Hungarian and Romanian 'inhabitants' (regnicolae) of Transylvania.[4] They were led by six captains: a petty noblemen called Anthony Budai Nagy, one Romanian and three Hungarian peasants, and a burgher from Cluj. Although the voivode executed the envoys, he pretended to be willing to negotiate in order to gain time. On 6 July a formal contract was signed at the monastery of Cluj-Mănăştur, which considerably reduced the tithe, abolished altogether the ninth of wine and grain, and confirmed the peasants' right to move freely and to make a will. The general observance of these points was to be controlled by an annual assembly on the Bobîlna hill of the representatives of the boroughs and villages. Nobles failing to respect the treaty were threatened with serious penalties. Finally, the parties sent envoys to Sigismund and asked for his arbitration, the peasants promising to acquiesce in the emperor's decision without further hesitation.

In the meantime the voivode and the nobility prepared themselves to take revenge. On 16 September the nobility of Transylvania, the Saxons and the Székely allied themselves at Capîlna and promised mutual aid against 'everyone', that is, against the rebellious peasants.[5] On 6 October a new treaty was signed with the rebels at Apatiu (Dăbâca county), which somewhat increased the money tax of the peasants and made no reference to the annual assembly. Upon receiving the news of Sigismund's death in December the nobility launched a counter-attack. They defeated the rebels in a pitched battle and laid siege to Cluj, which had joined the peasants. The town fell at the end of January 1438; it was immediately deprived of its urban privileges and its inhabitants were declared simple jobagiones. (They recovered their liberties from King Wladislas six years later.) The leaders of the revolt were executed at Turda, some of the participants being punished with mutilation. Order was soon restored, and on 2 February the victors renewed their former alliance, which was later transformed into the perpetual alliance of the 'three nations', that is, of the Transylvanian Estates.

Chapter 17

The Age of John Hunyadi (1437–1457)

In both the short and the long run, Sigismund's death caused decisive changes within the kingdom's political order. Its short-term consequence was that the power which had hitherto linked the magnates to royal authority, and thus effectively checked the political ambitions of the noble Estates, disappeared along with the emperor. These ambitions were now unleashed, which led first to the weakening, and later to the collapse, of central authority. Only two years after the emperor's death, in 1439, the nobility was already able to impose its conditions upon the new ruler. More than two decades were to elapse before Matthias Corvinus, a sovereign of Sigismund's stature, attempted to restore, and at the same time to reshape, the foundations of royal power.

The changes were even more important in the long term, in so far as they brought about a complete transformation of both the structure of the state and of political ideology. For laid at that time were the foundations of the system of institutions and ideas, which is generally referred to as *Ständestaat* or *Ständewesen* in historiography influenced by German terminology, and which was to constitute the political framework of the Hungarian state until the revolution of 1848. The essence of the new system was the radical extension of the right of decision making, in theory to all the landowners of the kingdom, but in practice to that part of them which was involved in politics – the nobility. Whereas decisions had hitherto been made by the king and the royal council, henceforth all important decisions had to be discussed and accepted by the diet (then commonly referred to as *congregatio generalis regni*), which was the general assembly of the 'kingdom's inhabitants', where the nobles either appeared in person or were represented by envoys. This assembly was, therefore, the institutionalised decision-making body of the 'society of possessors' – the Estates. As such, it was by far the most conspicuous institution of the new era.

278

KING ALBERT

Sigismund's only child was a daughter, Elizabeth, who was born in 1409 to his second wife, Barbara of Cilli. In 1421 her father made her marry Albert V of Habsburg, duke of Lower Austria, to whose family he was attached by a long-standing friendship. Sigismund intended to bequeath his kingdoms to the young couple, but after his death the initiative was taken by his barons who, while partly approving of the emperor's plan, set about a radical transformation of the regime. On 18 December 1437 Albert was elected as king of Hungary; but Elizabeth's right to the throne was rejected and only her husband was crowned at Székesfehérvár on New Year's day 1438. Albert's election was conditional upon wide-ranging concessions. He had to promise to annul all the 'innovations and harmful customs' that had been introduced by his predecessors,[1] which amounted to the abolition of the whole edifice of Sigismund's reforms; and he had to agree to put an end to the influence of foreigners and to the taxation of the Church. Moreover, he had to engage himself to make practically every political decision – from the use of royal revenues to the making of official appointments – with the consent of the prelates and the barons. This meant, in effect, that the totality of power had shifted under the control of the royal council.

Albert, who followed his father-in-law on the thrones of Germany and Bohemia as well, was not inclined to keep his promises. Having appointed new office-holders in April 1438, he left for Bohemia and entrusted the government of Hungary to his wife. Elizabeth seems to have inherited her father's authoritarian attitudes and tried to govern as if nothing had changed. The nobility was already on the verge of revolt when Albert arrived back in Hungary. He immediately convoked a diet to meet at Buda in May 1439, where he was forced by the crowd to capitulate. The law that he was forced to sign at that time was similar to his pre-election promises, except for the fact that the power was now made over to the diet instead of to the royal council. The Estates movement started out with the slogan of 'restoring the ancient laws and customs of the realm' and acted accordingly against the 'new customs' introduced by Sigismund.[2] The royal couple were forbidden to confer offices upon foreigners or to grant them estates. Also prohibited was the taxing of ecclesiastical benefices and administering them through laymen. The defence of the realm was once again declared to be the ruler's duty, while the general levy of the nobility could only be proclaimed in a case of emergency and for service within the frontiers. The right to control the quality of coinage and to choose husbands for the royal daughters was also conferred upon the Estates. In contrast to his promises of 1437 the king was allowed to elect his advisers freely (with the exception of foreigners, of course), but the filling of the office of palatine was for the first time to be subject to the consent of the Estates.

The movement of 1439 not only swept away Sigismund's reforms, but sealed the fate of that part of the royal demesne that had, up to now, been preserved. At the time of the emperor's death, there were still as many as 60 castellanies at the ruler's disposal. Nearly half of these were lost during the weeks following the diet. It is clear that Albert was not acting of his own free will when he made a whole series of lavish grants, especially to the leaders of the opposition. The disintegration of the royal demesne, which had been so extensive in the time of the Angevins, was practically complete. From now on the king himself was but one of the kingdom's major landowners.

The political upheaval fatally weakened royal authority, the grave consequences of which soon became evident. Although Hungary had long suffered from the incursions of the Turkish marauders, the territorial integrity of the kingdom had so far never been threatened. Even Hungary's dominance over the neighbouring principalities of the Balkans had to some extent been maintained. After Sigismund's death the kingdom had to face a new challenge: the overtly expansionist policy of the Ottoman empire. As early as 1438 Sultan Murad devastated Transylvania. There was no resistance. In the spring of 1439 he invaded Serbia, which had been a vassal of Hungary for years, and in August he took Smederevo, the residence of Despot Branković, after a two-month siege. Hungary, as reformed by the diet, proved unable to thwart the attack. Although the general levy of the nobility was proclaimed, the Hungarian army was mustered only with great difficulty and remained immobile in the region of Titel during the last days of the siege. It soon dispersed without having risked a counter-attack. By then it had been decimated by dysentery, to which the king himself fell victim on 27 October 1439.

The next Ottoman offensive was directed against Hungary. In the spring of 1440 Murad laid siege to Belgrade, the southern gate of the kingdom. That his attack failed was due to the resistance of Jovan of Talovac, prior of Vrana, who, supported only by his own brothers, successfully opposed the sultan's army for several months. No help from elsewhere was to be expected, for in the meantime the kingdom had been drifting onto the threshold of civil war.

DOUBLE CORONATION AND CIVIL WAR

The occasion for an open conflict between court and nobility was furnished by the unsolved problem of the succession. The widowed queen, Elizabeth, was pregnant, and wanted to secure the throne for the baby to whom she would hopefully give birth. This would naturally have meant her hands on the reins of government, which was something the Estates were by no means willing to accept. They offered the crown to the 16 year old king of Poland, Wladislas III (born from the fourth marriage of Wladislas II Jagiełło) who, having accepted their conditions, entered Buda in May 1440. However, at the time of his arrival the throne was no longer vacant: in February Elizabeth had given birth to a son, who was crowned king of Hungary as Ladislaus V on 15 May.

The ceremony could be regarded as regular, apart from the fact that the Estates had not consented to it. It was carried out by Archbishop Denis Szécsi at Székesfehérvár, the traditional place, and with the Holy Crown, which had previously been stolen from the castle of Visegrád by one of Elizabeth's ladies-in-waiting, Helena Kottaner (the episode is known from the memoirs of Kottaner herself). The queen, who obviously hoped to disarm her opponents by this *fait accompli*, miscalculated the political situation. The Estates' desire to rule was much stronger than their respect for the Holy Crown, a fact that was expressed by a decision of far-reaching ideological implications. On 29 June 1440 they solemnly invalidated Ladislaus's coronation, justifying this by reference to the new idea that 'the crowning of kings is always dependent on the will of the kingdom's inhabitants, in whose consent both the effectiveness and the force of the crown reside.'[3] Royal authority was therefore 'with a common will' conferred upon Wladislaus, a person who, in contrast to the infant king, was able to defend the kingdom 'in a state of need'. Wladislaus was crowned at Székesfehérvár on 17 July. Since the Holy Crown was in Elizabeth's possession, another crown was taken from Saint Stephen's reliquary, upon which the Estates transferred for the occasion 'all the force and all the efficacy of the previous crown' until this was regained.[4]

Wladislaus's coronation was a very important step, both politically and ideologically. From an ideological point of view it declared for the first time the Estates' supremacy over royal authority, and the priority of the principle of election over that of legitimacy, which had never before been contested. Ladislaus V was Albert's lawful heir, while in favour of Wladislaus, who was not attached to any of the previous Hungarian kings by ties of kinship, it was only possible to refer to the notion of *idoneitas*. From the political point of view, the double coronation led to a civil war, which split the political community into two parties, and to a division that was to last for some twenty years. The kingdom's unity was not to be restored until the accession of Matthias, and even then not immediately.

The struggle between the partisans of the 'Bohemian Ladislaus' (Ladislaus V, 1440–1457) and those of the 'Polish Ladislaus' (Wladislas

I, 1440–1444) lasted with a brief pause from the summer of 1440 until 1445. The forces were more or less evenly balanced. Wladislas had the support of most of the barons and of the nobility, but Ladislaus could rely on the wealthiest magnates, such as Ladislaus Garai, the counts of Cilli, the despot George Branković, Archbishop Denis Szécsi and his brothers, John Perényi, then *magister tavarnicorum*, and others. Characteristically, the towns also threw in their lot with Ladislaus V wherever they could. As for help from abroad, Wladislas received little assistance from the Polish Estates, while the queen's party was well supplied from Austria and the Bohemian provinces. Right from the outset, the cause of the infant Ladislaus was espoused by Frederick III, who had become the head of the Habsburg dynasty after the death of Albert. In 1440 Elizabeth, in return for financial support, appointed Frederick as the guardian of her son, entrusted the Holy Crown to his care, and mortgaged to him the town of Sopron.

The civil war, which raged with full force in the first two years (1440–1442), consisted mainly of assaults against castles and the regular devastation of the enemy's lands. In this respect the greatest success was undoubtedly achieved by Elizabeth's Bohemian condottiere, John Jiškra z Brandýsa. In 1440 the queen entrusted to him the defence of Košice, whence he gradually extended the influence of Ladislaus's party as far as Spiš and Zvolen. The bulk of his army consisted of Bohemian mercenaries, hardened in the Hussite wars. They took to Hungary the art of war that had proved so effective in the past. In the hands of Jiškra they soon became a well disciplined and virtually invincible army. The necessary material basis was secured by Jiškra himself, partly from the confiscated royal revenues of the occupied territory (mines, *lucrum camerae*, thirtieth, *census* of the towns), partly from loans offered by the burghers living under his authority. For the towns regarded Jiškra as their protector against the nobility, and were accordingly willing to make considerable financial sacrifices in his favour.

While Jiškra defeated the armies that were sent against him one after another, in the remaining part of the kingdom Wladislas's partisans slowly got the upper hand. At the very beginning of 1441 two of his leading followers, Nicholas Újlaki, ban of Mačva, and John Hunyadi, ban of Severin, routed the queen's followers near Bátaszék, annihilating the last army that Elizabeth was able to muster from the central and southern parts of the kingdom. Wladislas entrusted the pacification of the eastern regions to his victorious commanders, while he himself took several Transdanubian castles during the spring. By the beginning of 1442 the scales seemed to be tipped in Wladislas's favour, but he failed at the siege of Nitra and thereafter the opposing forces remained balanced. The greater part of the country acknowledged Wladislas as its king, but most of the northern counties, from Trenčín to Šaríš, obeyed Jiškra, while the key places in the west were controlled by Elizabeth's partisans. Not only were the castles of Komárno, Győr and Nitra, and the cities of Sopron and Pressburg in their hands, but also the fortress of Esztergom in the very heart of the country, which had been successfully defended by Cardinal Szécsi, leader of the legitimists, against Wladislas's assault in 1441. The peace talks, which began in 1442, were interrupted by Elizabeth's sudden death on 16 December, but the renewed fighting did not really modify the existing state of affairs. The direction of Ladislaus V's party was taken over by his guardian, Frederick III.

THE RISE OF HUNYADI

It was thanks to the civil war or, more precisely, to the battle of Bátaszék that a hitherto relatively unknown captain, John Hunyadi, suddenly moved to the forefront of politics. His father, Voyk, was a Romanian noble from Wallachia, who had served Sigismund as a household knight and in 1409 received from him the borough of Hunedoara (Hunyad), together with the domain belonging to it. Hunyadi seems to have been born a few years earlier, in around 1405. Like other young noblemen he spent his youthful years at the courts of various barons. One of them was Stephen Újlaki, ban of Mačva, to whose younger brother, Nicholas, Hunyadi was later bound by a firm friendship. In 1430 Hunyadi accompanied Sigismund on his journey to the West and is supposed to have learned some of the basic elements of modern warfare in the court of Filippo Maria Visconti, duke of Milan, whom he served for two years. He became a household knight himself in 1434 and for some years took part in the defence of the southern frontiers under Franko of Talovac, ban of Severin. It must have been upon the latter's recommendation that in 1439 Albert entrusted to Hunyadi (before long with the title of ban) the defence of the border castles belonging to the banate of Severin. Hunyadi was still not a baron, however. When he joined Wladislas's camp in 1440, he was not counted among the leaders but was regarded merely as one of the less important captains.

After the victory of Bátaszék, in February 1441, Wladislas conferred extraordinary powers upon Nicholas Újlaki and Hunyadi. He appointed them jointly and with equal authority to be voivodes of Transylvania, counts of the Székely and of several counties, and also commanders of Timişoara, Belgrade and all the border castles on the Danube. In order to enable them to perform their duties he made over to them the administration of the revenues deriving from the royal monopoly of salt. At the same time Újlaki remained captain of Székesfehérvár and ban of

Mačva, while Hunyadi retained the banate of Severin. Their accumulation of offices and territorial power thus reached a level that had not even been attained by the Talovac brothers before 1437. In half of the kingdom, from Székesfehérvár and Pécs to the eastern Carpathians, all power was concentrated in the hands of the two barons. Their enormous authority is partly explained by the fact that at the time of their appointment the partisans of Elizabeth still held strong positions in both Transylvania and the south-eastern counties. The original task of the two commanders was to be the elimination of these positions.

Újlaki, who was fighting with the enemy in the region of Pécs and beyond the River Drava, left the military work in eastern Hungary to his friend. Hunyadi completed his mission successfully within a surprisingly short time. It required little more than his appearance to prompt Wladislas's enemies, among them Branković, to submit. By the time he entered Cluj in April 1441, the eastern part of the kingdom had been entirely pacified. In the years to come, the work was to be divided between the two barons in the same way. Újlaki remained active in the central and Transdanubian counties and conceded the government of the territories east of the Tisza to Hunyadi. In Transylvania Újlaki's role in judicial authority was exercised through his vice-voivodes, and he had a share in the monopoly of salt; but he left the military command and the castles in the hands of his fellow baron. Hunyadi never loosened his grip on them and Transylvania remained the basis of his political influence from 1441 until his death. His power was always founded upon those castles in Transylvania and in the southern marches that had come into his possession in 1441, together with the estates that he had taken from Elizabeth's partisans or which had become vacant for other reasons. Although somewhat later he made Wladislas grant some of these castellanies to him, this step was of limited significance, for he actually regarded them all as his own possessions. Nevertheless, it was in the centre of the family's patrimony, at Hunedoara, that he set up his residence in the form of a splendid castle, which in a rebuilt form can still be seen today.

In the midst of instability and confusion, Hunyadi's province was an island of stability and order. After he had broken the resistance of Ladislaus's followers, the territory under his authority was no longer disturbed by civil war. While fighting continued in other parts of the kingdom, Hunyadi was able to devote his attention to the problem that had been his principal concern right from the outset: thwarting the increasing Ottoman threat. It was in this field that he soon acquired a worldwide reputation.

Hunyadi's entry as a major player in the game led immediately to a turnaround in the course of Hungaro-Ottoman warfare. Having, with Újlaki, taken over the defence of Belgrade from the Talovac brothers in

1441, he marched into Serbia and defeated Ishak, bey of Smederevo. In 1442 he achieved two successive victories, each of them quite important. On 22 March he routed the Turkish army of Bey Mezid that had been devastating Transylvania; then, in September, in the Carpathians, along the upper valley of the Ialomiţa, he annihilated the troops led by Shehabeddin, beylerbey of Rumelia, commander of the Ottoman troops in Europe. Needless to say, these triumphs made little impression on the inexhaustible resources of the Ottoman empire, yet this series of victories, of a kind hitherto unheard-of, was resounding enough to make Hunyadi an idol of the 'nation'. He acquired the reputation of being an invincible commander, who had no difficulty in defeating any kind of enemy. Indeed, it seemed to everyone that, as John Thuróczy put it later, he was the long-awaited hero who would once again lead the Hungarians to victory and raise the kingdom from its miserable state. Henceforth, noble public opinion regarded Hunyadi with such a degree of admiration that it could not be shaken by future developments. Each of his victories reinforced the common belief in his invincibility, while his failures were generally explained away by reference to treachery or unforeseen circumstances. For Hunyadi, the way was paved to the office of governor and even to the throne, although his death was to prevent him (but not his son) from gaining the latter.

THE CRUSADE OF VARNA

The course of events was such as to push Hunyadi into the spotlight of international attention immediately after his first victories. At the council of Florence in 1439 the union of the Catholic and Orthodox churches was virtually achieved, and from Rome it seemed as if it was only the Ottomans' presence in the Balkans that stood in the way of a definitive settlement. The cause of the union was thus linked to the plan of liberating the Balkans, which had been off the agenda since the defeat of Nicopolis. Displaying great energy, Pope Eugene IV set about the joint organisation of the two enterprises. In the spring of 1442 Cardinal Giuliano Cesarini, then the leading statesman of the Holy See, came to Hungary in order to mediate peace between the parties and to mobilise the kingdom's forces for an offensive war against the Ottomans. By the time he completed his mission, it had become evident that the leading role in the projected expedition would be played by Hunyadi.

Cesarini was, of course, unable to restore the kingdom's unity, but he did succeed in negotiating an armistice for one year, during which the campaign against the Ottomans could be launched. In October

1443 a huge Hungarian army, led by Wladislas and Hunyadi, invaded the empire, and, although it was forced by severe weather conditions to turn back from Sofia, it finally arrived home victoriously in January 1444. The so-called 'long campaign' was not so much a military as a moral success. The Hungarians did not annihilate the enemy, nor did they recover a single piece of land, but they managed to control the course of events throughout the expedition and won three major battles. The psychological effect of the campaign thus became enormous. Whereas the series of defeats filled the sultan with anxiety, it spurred his enemies to further efforts, and at the same time made the belief in Hunyadi's pre-eminent abilities virtually unshakeable.

The triumph was so resounding that it broke the standstill and promoted the formation of a Christian coalition for the purpose of liberating the entire Balkan peninsula. Besides the Pope and Wladislas, the coalition was joined by Philip the Good, duke of Burgundy, and by the two republics of Venice and Genoa. The plan was astonishingly simple. The naval forces of the sea powers were to cut all lines of communication between the Asian and European provinces of the Ottoman empire by closing off the Straits, while the Hungarian army, led by Hunyadi, would drive the sultan's European forces into the sea. The chief promoter of the enterprise was Cesarini, then staying at Buda. During the diet of April 1444 he made the king swear to launch the projected campaign. Preparations were immediately started, and in June the allied navy set sail. On 25 July Wladislas left Buda aiming 'to destroy those accursed Turks', as he observed in a letter to the king of Bosnia.[5] The invasion seemed full of promise, for the Hungarian troops were accompanied by Polish contingents and foreign mercenaries hired by the Pope. The expedition was joined by the army of the prince of Wallachia, while the king of Bosnia and Scanderbeg's Albanian rebels also promised their support.

That this promising enterprise ended in catastrophe was due to an unexpected turn of events. Murad was so frightened by the threat posed by the Christian coalition that he was willing to make peace at any cost. As early as the winter of 1443–4 he asked his father-in-law, Branković, to mediate, with the promise of restoring Serbia to him if he could break up the coalition. The despot picked out Hunyadi as the weakest link of the chain and persuaded him to support the sultan's peace offer. In return, Hunyadi was promised Branković's immense estates in Hungary. It was after such preliminaries that the famous Hungaro-Ottoman 'false' peace was signed – a peace that undermined the cause of the crusade, and which for centuries has given rise to conjecture and accusations. Did Wladislas really make peace, and, if so, why? If he did sign the peace, why did he breach it immediately, and who is to blame for the disastrous consequences that followed? What in fact happened?

On 12 June 1444, while Wladislas was preparing for war, Murad signed a preliminary peace treaty at Adrianople, in which he engaged to evacuate Serbia, to pay a tribute of 100,000 gold florins to the king of Hungary and to assist him with 30,000 soldiers in case of war. The treaty, which was clandestinely obtained by Branković's envoys in the name of Wladislas, was to be valid for ten years, counted from the day upon which it was ratified by the other party. On 1 August Murad's envoys met Wladislas and his barons at Szeged. The Hungarians were surprised by their appearance and astonished by the exceptionally advantageous peace offer. Hunyadi, the commander-in-chief, immediately insisted that the offer should be accepted, and negotiations proceeded behind locked doors.

Secrecy was indeed advisable. Cesarini wanted to make war at any cost, but this was inconceivable without Hunyadi's participation. In order to achieve his ends, the cardinal engaged in a complicated intrigue. He fell in with the peace, but in such a way that made it certain that the war he had been planning would not be endangered. On 4 August he made Wladislas and his barons swear in public that the treaty to be signed with the Ottomans would automatically become void, 'even if it happened to be ratified on oath',[6] and that the campaign would be launched immediately. When the way was thus paved, the 'peace' could finally be concluded on 15 August, not at Szeged, where the suspicion of the Turkish envoys might have been aroused by the gathering troops, but at Oradea. According to Thuróczy, the treaty was confirmed, on the Hungarian side, by Hunyadi rather than by the king himself. Wladislas had probably become tired of repeated oath taking. The sultan, suspecting no fraud, carried out his part of the agreement. On 22 August, Branković took possession of Smederevo and the other castles in Serbia. He handed over to Hunyadi the stipulated reward, consisting of Debrecen, Hajdúböszörmény, Satu Mare, Baia Mare, Mukačeve, Beregove, Vršac, and the immense estates belonging to them. Hunyadi's participation in the war was secured when Wladislas promised him the kingdom of Bulgaria in the event of victory. On 22 September the army crossed the border and marched into Ottoman territory along the Danube.

The peace of Oradea had disastrous consequences. During the preceding two weeks, news from the negotiations had reached the allies and drove them into uncertainty. As a result, the sultan had no difficulty transporting his troops from Asia, where he happened to be staying, to Europe, and to march against the invaders. On 10 November 1444 at Varna the Ottoman army, numbering perhaps 40,000 men, annihilated the allied forces. Hunyadi's army had probably been outnumbered two to one. Wladislas and Cesarini were killed in the battle, along with two bishops and many barons, while Hunyadi barely escaped with his life.

HUNYADI'S REGENCY

The king's death unleashed an anarchy that can only be compared to the age of Matthew Csák. The work of the law courts had been suspended since 1439, while all kinds of unauthorised castles and forti-fied places had been proliferating throughout the kingdom. During the civil war, supporters of both sides had obtained from their respec-tive rulers grants of land that belonged to members of the opposing party, with the land being retained by the one who finally emerged as the more powerful. After the defeat of Varna matters went from bad to worse. In the summer of 1445 Frederick III occupied the castles of the western borderland, including Kőszeg and Eisenstadt. In Slavonia the counts of Cilli struck a decisive blow against the Talovac brothers, who were supporters of Wladislas: the castles of the bishopric of Zagreb and of the priory of Vrana were taken, and the city of Zagreb itself was occu-pied. In the north, Jiškra extended his authority over the region of Spiš. Moreover, the kingdom faced the possibility of Ottoman revenge.

The only way out of this dangerous situation was a compromise between the parties. The diet of April 1445, in which the towns were represented for the first time, worked out an agreement and set up a regency council, on which the leaders of both parties were given places. The partisans of Wladislas acknowledged Ladislaus V as their king, provided that Frederick set him free, along with the Holy Crown. In order to restore order, seven captains were elected and invested with extraordinary authority. Six of them were supporters of Wladislaus (Hunyadi, Újlaki, George Rozgonyi, Emeric Bebek, Michael Ország, Pancrace of Liptov), the seventh being Jiškra. The castles that had been erected without permission were to be destroyed, and all royal grants that had been made since the death of Albert, regardless of their beneficiaries, were annulled for the time being.

Since Frederick was unwilling to release Ladislaus, a new diet assem-bled on the field of Rákos, near Pest, with the massive participation of the nobility. On 6 June 1446 it elected a regent, with the title of 'governor' (*gubernator*), for the period of the king's minority. The vote went, as a matter of course, in Hunyadi's favour. Not only did he enjoy the support of his party and of the nobility in general, but he had been the most powerful person in the kingdom since his unscrupulous and successful bargain with Branković. As the new head of the kingdom, he was now given a limited form of royal authority. He could not grant away estates consisting of more than 32 peasant holdings (somewhat more than an average village), nor did he enjoy the supreme judicial authority of the king. Nor, indeed, could he administer royal finances at will. The regency council, within which the 'national party' prevailed, continued to function, and its authority was even quite considerably augmented. It exercised royal power along with the governor, this being expressed (among other ways) by the fact that the laws were issued not in the name of Hunyadi, but in that of the 'kingdom's prelates, barons, nobles and notabilities' – that is, in the name of the Estates.

Perhaps even more important than the election of a regent was the fact that the anarchy was suppressed. The desire for order was so strong that, surprisingly enough, most of the barons submitted themselves to the decisions of the diet and restored those castles and possessions that had been unlawfully occupied in the 'time of troubles', that is, during the civil war. Courts of law also returned to their regular work. The functioning of the newly organised state was regulated by the diet that met in March 1447. In accordance with the decrees of the previous year, it was ordained that a diet should be convoked to meet every year on Whitsun Day, where all the nobles with more than 20 tenants should appear in person. The commission of the captains elected in 1445 was suspended, whilst the governor and barons were ordered to resign their offices until the assembly was dissolved. Moreover, it was decreed that in the event of the king's death, the right to elect a new ruler should reside in a joint body consisting of the barons and the envoys of the counties. The election should be unanimous. In September 1447 a new diet elected Ladislaus Garai, head of the legitimists, as palatine, thereby turning the peace that had been established in 1445 into a practical alliance between the parties.

The authority of the governor and of the Estates did not, however, extend over the whole kingdom. Jiškra and the counts of Cilli were practically independent of the government, while Frederick still occupied considerable territories in the west. Although the six years of Hunyadi's regency witnessed constant efforts to restore unity, this had no more been achieved in 1452 than it had been in 1446.

The government had first to acquiesce in Frederick's conquests. In the autumn of 1446 Hunyadi himself marched against Austria, but he could do little more than devastate the territory around Vienna. On 1 June 1447 the barons had to sign a truce, which left Sopron, Kőszeg, Eisenstadt and some other border castles and estates in Frederick's hands. The German king for his part restored the town of Győr, which had been occupied by his mercenaries since the outbreak of the civil war; but it was restored on condition that its bishop would be a staunch partisan of Ladislaus V. Both the infant king and the Holy Crown remained in Frederick's custody. Although the truce was not followed by a peace treaty, the war with Frederick did not flare up again until 1459.

Hunyadi had also to resign himself to the domination of Slavonia by the counts of Cilli. The province of Ulrich, grandson of Herman, who had married the daughter of Branković and had been elevated to the dignity of an imperial prince by Sigismund in 1436, comprised several loosely connected pieces of land located between the Habsburg lands of Styria, Carniola and Carinthia. Having expelled the Talovac brothers from Slavonia in 1445, Cilli took the title of ban of Slavonia and as such ruled the province with practical independence. His power was based upon the possession of more than 20 castles, partly inherited from his grandfather, partly conquered in the years of civil war. At first Hunyadi tried to break Cilli's power, and in the spring of 1446 he invaded his lands as far as Styria. In June he compelled the diet to elect new bans in place of Cilli and attempted once again to regain Slavonia. But Cilli's position in the province remained impregnable, and in June 1448, after another unsuccessful campaign by Hunyadi, he even managed to consolidate it by means of a peace treaty. Cilli formally submitted himself to the authority of the Estates, in return for which he was officially confirmed in the banate, along with his father, Frederick, and was allowed to retain his territorial gains not only in Slavonia, but also in upper Hungary, where Trenčín and the castles belonging to it had been mortgaged to him in 1439. In order to seal the peace, Hunyadi's elder son, Ladislaus, was betrothed to Count Ulrich's daughter.

Yet it was at the hands of Jiškra that Hunyadi and the Estates suffered their most serious setbacks. Jiškra showed unwavering loyalty towards Ladislaus V and adopted the title of king's 'captain general'. His immense province spread from the mining towns around Kremnica to as far as Košice and Šaríš and he was unwilling to hand it over to anyone except the future king. His conflict with the Estates originally arose from the fact that he had the most important royal resources at his disposal, among them the richest gold and silver mines. Moreover, contrary to the decrees of the diet of 1446, he refused to give up the baronial and noble estates that he had occupied during the war. Further trouble was caused by the depredations of his mercenaries, whom Jiškra was unable to keep under firm control. Lacking regular payment, they continued to live off looting even after the end of the civil war in 1445.

At first the Estates tried to come to terms with Jiškra, and even legitimised his rule by appointing him as one of the seven captains-in-chief. In 1446 he was permitted to retain the usurped royal revenues for three years, provided that he paid his troops regularly and restored the castles that he had occupied. But, since Jiškra was partly unwilling and partly unable to keep his promises, war broke out again in 1447 and went on, with brief pauses, until 1452. In the course of these five years Hunyadi led no fewer than four campaigns to upper Hungary, but without achieving any positive result. Instead of systematically reducing Jiškra's strongholds, an enterprise for which neither his equipment nor his patience sufficed, he contented himself with devastating the enemy's lands and trying to take some hastily constructed wooden fortresses. On one such occasion, at the siege of a fortified monastery near Lučenec in 1451, he suffered such a serious defeat at the hands of Jiškra, who had hurried to relieve the place, that several Hungarian barons were killed in the battle. However, this was to be the last act of this unhappy and dispiriting war. Upon receiving the news that Ladislaus had been set free, the peace was signed on 24 August 1452, according to the terms of which Jiškra was able to retain all the possessions and revenues then in his hands. He was also given 10,000 gold florins in return for the demolition of his castles and 12,000 for his prisoners.

As for the Ottoman problem, the threat of an invasion had for the time being passed. However, Hunyadi wished to repair the damage caused by the defeat at Varna by achieving a resounding victory. The new Pope, Nicholas V (1447–1455), was of the same opinion, and sent Cardinal Carvajal as a legate to Hungary to make the necessary preparations. Having put a pro-Hungarian voivode on the Wallachian throne by means of a rapid strike in December 1447, Hunyadi launched the campaign against the Ottomans in the autumn of 1448. The Hungarian army, reinforced with Romanian troops, headed for Albania with the aim of joining up with Scanderbeg's rebels. It was on the plain of Kosovo Polje, of ominous memory, that they met the army of Murad II. Although very large by western-European standards, Hunyadi's army was heavily outnumbered. The battle lasted for three days (17–19 October) and ended in the heavy defeat of the Christians. The greater part of their army perished, and Hunyadi was practically the only baron to escape with his life.

The defeat of Kosovo Polje turned the conflict between Hunyadi and Branković, which had been caused by the breach of the peace of Oradea, into an open war. The prince of Serbia had kept his bargain with Hunyadi, but had also carefully respected the peace concluded with the sultan. He consequently refused to take part in the war, which led to accusations of treason from the Hungarians. Branković blamed Hunyadi for the embarrassing situation that he found himself in as a result of the broken peace, and reclaimed the estates that he had handed over to Hunyadi. On the way home from the battlefield of Kosovo Polje, Hunyadi fell into the hands of the Serbian prince, who was able in these circumstances to extort some of these estates from his captive. When the governor finally reached home, his revenge was swift: in 1450 he forced the diet to sentence Branković to forfeiture of property and he also began to wage a regular war against him. It was only in 1451 that the barons finally mediated a peace between the two magnates. Hunyadi restored to his rival the possessions that he had occupied during the campaign, but retained all that had been made over to him in 1444 in return for 155,000 florins. The settlement was made complete by the betrothal of Hunyadi's younger son, Matthias, to Branković's granddaughter, the daughter of Ulrich of Cilli.

Against all expectations Hunyadi's position was not affected by his failures; indeed, he was even able to strengthen it. It is true that he faced strong opposition from among the barons, but the nobility continued to regard him as their leader and he could still rely on Újlaki's support. In 1450 he and Újlaki formed a league with Palatine Garai. To their own advantage, and behind the backs of the regency council, they made peace with Frederick III. Garai regained the castle of Devín (near Pressburg), which had fallen into Austrian hands during the civil war, and the allies consented to Frederick's continued guardianship of Ladislaus V until 1458 when the king would reach the age of 18. Frederick thereby prolonged his authority over Ladislaus's Austrian provinces, while Hunyadi extended his term of office as governor. More than that, the emperor promised in due course to hand over the young king to Hunyadi himself. It must have been as a consequence of this peace that Hunyadi was finally able to force George Rozgonyi to deliver the castle of Pressburg and the cities of Trnava and Skalica. When in 1454 he also recovered Trenčín and Považská Bystrica from Cilli, his position in the north-western counties of the kingdom was considerably reinforced.

KING LADISLAUS V

The end of Hunyadi's regency was brought about by the armed revolt of the Austrian and Bohemian Estates, which broke out unexpectedly during Frederick's coronation in Rome. The rebels, supported by the Hungarian Estates and by the counts of Cilli, laid siege to the city of Wiener Neustadt, and the emperor, who had just returned from Italy, was forced to yield. On 1 September 1452 he handed over Ladislaus V to Count Ulrich, who was a second cousin of the young king and now became his guardian. The Hungarian Estates welcomed the return of a lawful ruler to the kingdom, even though the restitution was far from complete, for the Holy Crown, the town of Sopron and the castles taken in 1445 were left in Frederick's hands.

Ladislaus's liberation provided a legal basis for the long-awaited internal consolidation. For the first time since 1439 the realm had a king whose legitimacy was undisputed. So was the act of his coronation, despite the declaration of the Estates in 1440, and no one now suggested that the ceremony should be repeated. The guidelines for the kingdom's future government, and for the regulation of the state of affairs that had emerged during the years of upheaval, were discussed by the barons during their negotiations in Vienna. Their decisions were enacted as laws by the diet in Pressburg in January 1453. A veil was to be drawn over the events of the past: the king pardoned all those who had taken arms against him on Wladislas's behalf. The distribution of landed property was regulated on the basis of the *status quo*; the grants of both Elisabeth and Wladislas were annulled, and the barons were confirmed in their recent acquisitions by means of new and valid royal charters. Everyone received his reward, regardless of the party he had belonged to. A large proportion of the estates that legally belonged to the Crown, but which in 1439 or later had passed into private hands through mortgage or usurpation, fell victim to the general reconciliation. The strongholds that had been constructed without permission were once again ordered to be destroyed, and every unlawfully occupied property had to be returned to its owner. The offices of government that had ceased to exist after 1439 were restored: the greater chancellery, led by the new arch-chancellor, Cardinal Denis Szécsi; the secret chancellery, under the direction of John Vitéz, bishop of Oradea, a famous humanist and partisan of Hunyadi; and the courts of the king's personal and special presence. The royal council was also re-established by the filling of the household offices that had been left vacant for years; but, at the same time, the diet, a new institution that had emerged from the civil war with its authority strengthened, was also left intact, at least formally.

The changes did not modify the actual distribution of power, however. Hunyadi remained the effective lord of the kingdom. Admittedly, he had to resign the regency at the end of 1452, but he was compensated in every possible way. He received the title of 'captain general of the kingdom', and was allowed to retain the royal castles and revenues that were at that time in his hands, with the exception of 24,000 gold florins, which were to be handed over to the king annually, for the expenses of his household. He also achieved a privileged position among the most illustrious families of the kingdom. Ladislaus granted him the district of Bistriţa, belonging to the Saxons of Transylvania, together with the hereditary title of 'perpetual count' (*perpetuus comes Bistriciensis*). Hereditary titles had hitherto been unknown in Hungary. The lords of the western regions had sometimes titled themselves 'counts' (*Graf*) in the German way, but it had never been officially acknowledged. Only the province of Zagorje, given to the counts of Cilli by Sigismund in 1399, and the comital title that went with it, could be seen as resembling a county belonging to the Empire. What appears to have prompted Hunyadi to obtain this privilege was, quite simply, his desire to secure for his family a rank as exceptional as that enjoyed by the counts of Cilli.

In the next few years Hunyadi gradually became isolated. His unconcealed efforts to increase his own power set him on a path that even his friends were unwilling to follow. He still had many partisans among the nobility of the eastern part of the kingdom, but only some of the barons, like Michael Ország, the future palatine, and the young Sebastian Rozgonyi, remained loyal to him. Even Újlaki became alienated from him. While not overtly breaking their friendship, Újlaki joined the baronial league – led by Cilli, Garai and the judge royal, Ladislaus Pálóci – which wanted to restore royal authority. The league, which was in fact quite obviously directed against Hunyadi, was formed in September 1453 and confirmed two years later.

A sign even more alarming than the alienation of Újlaki was that the bishop of Oradea turned against Hunyadi. John Vitéz was an educated and talented member of the chancellery, who seems to have played a decisive role in working out the ideology of the Estates movement that unrolled its banner in 1439. He was a whole-hearted supporter first of the 'national' party, then of Hunyadi himself, who made him bishop of Oradea in 1445 and entrusted to him the education of his younger son, Matthias. Vitéz was in charge of the governor's diplomatic relations, and it must have been due to Hunyadi's influence that in 1453 he was appointed secret chancellor. At the head of his new office, however, he began to work for the restoration of central authority, which necessarily led to a clash with his former patron. Vitéz's attitude clearly shows how profoundly the political climate had been transformed since the 1440s. Now that the new principles of parliamentary government were acknowledged by everyone, the old opposition between 'royal' and 'national' parties no longer made sense. The latter lost its former character, and was gradually transformed into a political faction consisting of Hunyadi's partisans. What gave this group its coherence were not the interests of the Estates or those of the kingdom, but simply the political ambitions of a party led by the Hunyadi family and their followers.

The interests of Hunyadi and those of the court clashed over the control of the royal castles and revenues, for as long as Hunyadi freely disposed of them all no effective central power was possible. As early as January 1454 the king, on the advice of Vitéz, tried to persuade the diet to deprive Hunyadi of at least the administration of the royal revenues. He had no chance of succeeding, for as long as the court remained in Vienna or Prague, the influence of the ex-governor would continue unchecked. The situation began to change in February 1456, when the king came to Buda for the first time. Hunyadi was forced to make concessions: while retaining most of his authority as captain general, he resigned part of the royal revenues and some of the royal fortresses, among them Buda, Trnava and Diósgyőr.

THE SIEGE OF BELGRADE

That Hunyadi was able to maintain his pre-eminent position for several years was to a considerable degree due to the ever-present Ottoman menace. The defeat of Kosovo Polje was followed by a pause in hostilities. Sultan Murad, who had business to look after elsewhere, signed a treaty with the Hungarians in 1450 and this was confirmed by his successor, Mehmed II (1451–1481). However, it was soon apparent that the accession of Mehmed meant the beginning of a new phase of Ottoman expansion, which was to be much more successful than the previous ones. The first waves of this resurgent military threat soon reached Hungary. Constantinople fell in 1453, and Mehmed immediately transferred his residence from Adrianople to the newly conquered city. In 1454, when the peace of Oradea expired, he attacked Serbia and laid siege to Smederevo, Branković's capital. In the following year he renewed his attack, this time occupying the whole of Serbia with the exception of Smederevo. As the expedition of 1456 was to be directed against Belgrade, it was not surprising that Hunyadi would once again be pushed to the forefront of events as the potential saviour of the kingdom. His reputation may have been shaken by his defeats since 1444, but he was indisputably the only man capable of successfully opposing the Ottomans.

The preparations for a counter-attack began as early as 1453. Immediately after the fall of Constantinople, Pope Nicholas V proclaimed a crusade. The war against the Ottomans frequently emerged as a subject for discussion at the imperial diets in Germany in 1454–1455, although no definitive decision was made. Not surprisingly, Hungary was swept by a wave of panic, and the diet that assembled in January 1454 at Buda consented to large-scale measures in order to mobilise a national army. It proclaimed the general levy of the nobility, and renewed the institution of the *militia portalis*. Four cavalrymen and two archers were to be equipped by every 100 peasant holdings, a demand that surpassed all previous recruiting measures. But the projected offensive never took place; all that happened was that in the autumn of 1454 Hunyadi marched into Serbia at the head of a small army and defeated the forces left behind by the sultan at Kruševac. Planning continued in 1455 and the diet levied an extraordinary tax, but that was all that took place. The cause of the anti-Ottoman war was given renewed impetus by the new Pope, Calixtus III (1455–1458), who tried to mobilize the whole power of the Church in order to launch a new crusade. Although the princes of Europe turned a deaf ear to the Pope's request, he nevertheless aroused enthusiasm among the common people in several places. He received much help from the Franciscans, who deployed the skills of their popular preachers in the service of the 'holy war'. As a result of their unremitting zeal, by the summer of 1456 a huge crusading army, consisting mainly of Germans and Bohemians, had assembled in the area around Vienna, ready to march against the 'infidels'.

However, this host never confronted the sultan, who began the siege of Belgrade on 4 July with an army which modern scholars have put at 60,000 to 70,000 men. Hunyadi, assisted by the Franciscan Giovanni da Capestrano, had successfully organised the castle's defence and had assembled a significant army in the vicinity. In the region of 25–30,000 crusaders, 'peasants, craftsmen and poor people', rallied to Hunyadi's camp under the influence of Capestrano's impressive sermons. On 21 July the Ottomans' general offensive on Belgrade collapsed, and on the following day they were also defeated in a pitched battle. The sultan withdrew with the remnants of his army and with memories that prevented him and his successors from launching an attack of the same dimensions for 65 years. News of this resounding victory soon reached the West. The day on which the Pope received the news, 6 August, the day of the Lord's Transfiguration, was declared a general feast throughout the Christian world. He had previously ordered that all the bells should be rung at noon to encourage the soldiers, but his bull was not published until after the battle, and thus the tradition, which continues in Hungary to this day, is generally thought to be commemorative of the victory itself.

The victory presented an excellent opportunity for a counter-attack, especially in view of the fact that considerable forces were gathering in the heart of Hungary. But no offensive took place, because the crusaders were already on the edge of open revolt. Anger against the 'powerful', who had kept themselves far from the battle, had already been growing during the fighting. Agitation became so intense after the victory that Hunyadi and Capestrano decided to disband the army. Both of them soon died, however. On 11 August, Hunyadi fell victim to the plague that had broken out in the crusaders' camp, and Capestrano followed him to the grave on 23 October.

Hunyadi was succeeded by his elder son, the 23 year-old Ladislaus. He seems to have inherited his father's ambition and slyness, but apparently not his talent. Within a couple of days he found himself in conflict with the king and Cilli, who demanded that the castles and revenues that had been held by Hunyadi should be handed over. Cilli had himself appointed captain general of the realm. Together with the king, and at the head of the foreign crusaders who had recently arrived, he marched southwards with the aim of taking possession of Belgrade and the other stipulated fortresses. To preserve his position, the young Hunyadi decided upon an extremely hazardous course of action. At the assembly of Futog he feigned submission and then enticed his opponents into the castle of Belgrade. There, on 9 November 1456, he had Ulrich murdered by his henchmen, and made himself master of the king's person. Hunyadi had himself appointed captain general, then took the king to Timişoara. Before being set free, the king was made to swear that the death of Count Cilli would never be avenged.

Ladislaus Hunyadi seems to have seriously miscalculated the possible consequences of his actions. The unprecedented murder turned everyone but his most determined followers against him: not only John Hunyadi's enemies, like Garai, but also his friends and supporters, like Újlaki and Ország, agreed that Ladislaus should be bridled. Paying for perfidy with perfidy, they soon made their opponent believe that he had nothing to fear; and the king too showed himself a master of deception. On 14 March 1457, when Ladislaus was staying at Buda with his brother Matthias, both were arrested, together with their supporters. The royal council, functioning now in its capacity as supreme court, convicted the Hunyadi brothers of high treason, and on 16 March Ladislaus was beheaded in St George's square in Buda. His supporters were pardoned, but Matthias was held by the king, who immediately left Hungary for Bohemia.

The retaliation failed to bring about the desired consolidation, however. Hunyadi's partisans, in possession of his family's immense and still intact resources, reacted with open revolt. It was led by Matthias's mother, Elisabeth Szilágyi, together with her brother, Michael, while the royal troops were commanded by Újlaki and Jiškra. Fierce but indecisive fighting continued for months, and was ended only by the news of Ladislaus V's premature death in Prague on 23 November 1457. Since the king had no lawful heir, the kingdom was once again left without a ruler.

Chapter 18

King Matthias Corvinus (1458–1490)

The death of Ladislaus V left the thrones of Bohemia and Hungary vacant. There were two legitimate heirs: Casimir IV, king of Poland, and William, duke of Saxony, both of whom were brothers-in-law of the late ruler. But the duke laid no claim to the inheritance, while the king of Poland was prevented from entering the lists by his war with the Teutonic Order. Ladislaus's closest relative in the male line was the emperor, Frederick III, who immediately took possession of Austria, but had no acceptable title to any of the deceased king's other domains, even though he still retained the Holy Crown.

ACCESSION AND CONSOLIDATION

Finding a new king was the responsibility of the diet. Practically the only candidate was Matthias Hunyadi, who was at that time staying in Prague. Designating anyone else would have caused an immediate relapse into a state of civil war. Matthias was supported not only by the legate of Pope Calixtus III, Cardinal Carvajal, who was then sojourning in Hungary, but also by Archbishop Szécsi himself. Even Palatine Garai promised to accept young Matthias as king, though on the condition that he would marry Garai's daughter.

At the diet that assembled at Pest in January 1458, at which the nobility were required to appear in person, the influence of the 'Hunyadi party' was bound to prevail. Szilágyi presented himself at the head of his 15,000 followers, which could not fail to impress the barons in council in the castle of Buda. By promising them that the future king would not take revenge for the execution of his brother, Szilágyi managed to come to terms with them; and on the following day, 24 January, he stirred an enthusiastic crowd on the frozen Danube into acclaiming Matthias as king. At the same time he had himself appointed governor for five years and immediately issued a couple of laws to prove his willingness to guarantee the liberties of the nobility.

George Poděbrad, governor of Bohemia, had reason to be content with what had happened in Hungary, for it indirectly paved the way for his own election as king. Having betrothed his daughter to Matthias, George released the young king without further hesitation. Matthias was obliged to pay a ransom of 60,000 gold florins, but George immediately remitted it as part of his daughter's dowry. On 14 February Matthias entered Buda, where he was solemnly enthroned in the church of Our Lady. No coronation was possible, since the Holy Crown was still in the possession of Frederick III in Austria.

If the testimony of a later horoscope is to be trusted, Matthias was 15 years old at this time. No one, least of all Szilágyi, seems to have rated him as an active player in the field of politics, at least for the time being. In view of this it must have caused real surprise when the young king took the initiative within weeks. As early as the end of June he removed Garai from the office of palatine and appointed his father's old friend, Michael Ország, as his successor. At the same time he suppressed the regency, seeking to appease his uncle by granting him the county of Bistriţa; but this apparently failed and Szilágyi was arrested on 8 October. He was kept in custody for almost a year. Henceforth, until the very day of his death, Matthias kept a firm grip on the reins of government. He always acted with the same resolution, swiftness and determination, both at home and in the field of foreign policy. As a result, within a couple of years he was able to make his kingdom, which had been drifting from one crisis to another since the death of Sigismund, the leading power of central Europe.

His most urgent task was to regain the Holy Crown and legitimise his rule. Immediately after acceding to the throne he initiated negotiations with Frederick III, but because of the harsh conditions set by the emperor his efforts bore no fruit. The situation was complicated by the fact that at the beginning of 1459 Garai, along with other magnates from the western parts of the kingdom who were disappointed in Matthias, sought to designate Frederick as king of Hungary. On 17 February they made an oath of fidelity to him in the castle of Güssing. However, relying on the support of most of the barons, Matthias was able swiftly to defeat the rebels in April. Garai had died in the meantime and Matthias made peace with his widow. Driven by the desire to mount a crusade against the Ottomans, Pope Pius II employed all possible means to bring about a reconciliation between Matthias and Frederick; but a settlement was only reached in April 1462, upon which was based the peace treaty, ratified by Matthias's envoys on 19 July 1463 at the emperor's residence, Wiener Neustadt. Matthias finally recovered the Holy Crown, but it cost him 80,000 florins, as well as several important concessions. Frederick, who adopted Matthias as his son and expected the young king to address him as his father, retained his Hungarian royal title, which he had been using since 1459. Of the Hungarian domains that Frederick controlled, only Sopron was returned. Moreover, if Matthias failed to father a legitimate male heir, Frederick or his successors would inherit the Hungarian throne. If all these stipulations fell short of bringing about a definitive settlement to the conflict between the two rulers, they nevertheless normalised their relationship for some years.

The peace with Frederick also facilitated the internal consolidation of the kingdom. From the outset, this process was hindered by the rule of Jiškra and his Czech mercenaries in upper Hungary. Jiškra was reluctant to acknowledge Matthias as his lord and initially worked for the election of Casimir IV. After this failed, he went over to Frederick III. Matthias launched military operations against him as early as April 1458, but the multitude of Jiškra's strongholds made the king's task difficult. Having secured the support of Košice and the other royal towns, Matthias cleared several counties of mercenaries by the end of 1461. Spiš and Zvolen had yet to be recovered, but further fighting was rendered unnecessary by the treaty signed with Frederick, which entailed the disarmament of Jiškra. Once isolated, the condottiere submitted to Matthias at Vác in May 1462 and handed over his castles, in return for which he was given 25,000 florins with the castles of Lipova and Şoimoş on the River Mureş. Henceforth Jiškra put his military skills at the disposal of his new lord and died an esteemed Hungarian baron shortly before 1471. Yet Jiškra's submission by no means brought about the immediate pacification of the whole of northern Hungary. Although most of his soldiers were engaged by the king, plundering mercenary bands continued to cause trouble for some years. The last of these was annihilated by Matthias himself at Kostoľany on the River Váh in 1467, when the king had 150 men hanged, including their commander, Jan Švehla.

Another region in need of consolidation was Slavonia, where the disappearance of the counts of Cilli at the end of 1456 had left a power vacuum. The man of the hour there was Jan Vitovec, condottiere of the late Count Ulrich. He had been appointed to the office of ban by Ladislaus V, and with Frederick's consent had taken control of most of the Slavonian estates of the counts of Cilli. Matthias acquiesced in this *fait accompli* and in 1463 not only confirmed Vitovec in the office of ban, but also made him perpetual count of Zagorje. He thereby obtained a faithful supporter, who assisted him in acquiring the rest of the Cilli inheritance, which meant that Matthias's position in Slavonia could be said to be firm from the end of 1465.

In the meantime the Ottoman threat had apparently intensified. Although Mehmed II did not engage in an offensive war against

Hungary, he systematically suppressed the Hungarian king's vassals in the Balkans. The first to fall victim was Serbia, which had become considerably smaller since the Ottoman attacks in 1454–55 and had lost its internal coherence after Branković's death in 1456. Profiting from this situation and from the crisis in Hungary, the sultan took the castle of Golubac in the summer of 1458, and then Smederevo, the princely residence, on 29 June 1459. Serbia ceased to exist as a political entity for several centuries; the members of the Branković family, together with many of their subjects, fled to Hungary, where the former were given large estates by Matthias, while the latter were used by him to strengthen his army and frontier defence. In 1462 Ottoman troops invaded Wallachia and drove out Vlad Ţepeş, a protégé of the Hungarians. The prince, who was widely known for his cruelty (and was later to be the model for Bram Stoker's *Dracula*), first sought refuge in Transylvania, then lived in the castle of Visegrád as Matthias's prisoner. Wallachia was henceforth one of the sultan's faithful vassal states. In the summer of 1463 it was the turn of Bosnia, where Mehmed, in the course of a lightning campaign, captured and beheaded King Stephen Tomašević, and transformed his kingdom into an Ottoman province. The last country to pass under Ottoman rule was Hercegovina, the principality of the late Sandalj Hranić, which was occupied in 1466.

The Ottoman advance thus destroyed the system of buffer states that had been created by Sigismund. From the 1460s onwards Ottoman and Hungarian garrisons faced one another along the entire southern frontier, from Omiš on the Adriatic coast to Turnu Severin on the lower Danube. Matthias was unable to check these unfavourable developments. In the early years of his reign, the internal situation of the kingdom made it impossible for him to mobilise substantial forces, while the failures of his father had taught him to avoid a direct confrontation with the sultan's army. The whole of his Ottoman policy was based upon this perception. This is why he had not intervened before the fall of Bosnia, and only did so after the Ottoman troops had left. In the autumn of 1463 he tried to recover Bosnia, but it took him nearly three months to take Jajce, the former royal residence. Together with a handful of smaller local fortresses, the castle of Jajce was to remain one of the bastions of the Hungarian defensive line until 1527. In the summer of 1464 Mehmed II tried to retake it, subjecting it to 43 days of bombardment, but he withdrew when Matthias appeared at the head of his army. It was then that the king occupied Srebrenik and a number of other castles; but he besieged Zvornik without success, and suffered serious losses during his withdrawal.

The first and most critical phase of Matthias's rule ended with his coronation, which took place on 29 March 1464. At the diet, which was held at the same time at Székesfehérvár, he solemnly confirmed King Louis I's law of 1351, which contained the Golden Bull, and Sigismund's 'major' decree of 1435. He had a great seal made and obliged those who had received letters of grant from himself or Ladislaus V to present them within a year for confirmation with the new seal. The latter, along with the secret seal, was entrusted to Stephen Várdai, archbishop of Kalocsa, and John Vitéz. Both bore the title of 'arch- and secret chancellor', but the chancellery was effectively directed by Várdai. An important reform was also carried out in the field of judicial administration. Instead of the courts of the royal presence, which had been transformed several times, one central court of justice was established, whose competence extended throughout the kingdom and whose judge, from the 1470s onwards, was referred to as the 'lieutenant of the royal personal presence' (*personalis praesentiae regiae locumtenens*), or simply 'the Personal'.

Although the coronation ceremony symbolically closed the period of stabilisation, it by no means brought all opposition to an end. A new system of taxation, which was put into effect three years later, led to considerable unrest, above all in Transylvania, where the method of assessment seemed especially injurious. On 18 August 1467 at Cluj-Mănăştur the 'three nations' entered into a formal alliance against the king, and elected as their leaders the three barons then holding the office of voivode: John Szentgyörgyi, his brother, Sigismund, and Berthold Ellerbach. Matthias marched swiftly to Transylvania, and the revolt was put down without a fight within a couple of weeks. On 3 October he sat in judgement on the rebels at the assembly of Turda. The voivodes, whose active involvement in the conspiracy could not be proved beyond doubt, were spared, but the noble leaders of the revolt were punished with exemplary harshness. Executions continued for weeks, and the king rewarded his followers lavishly with the estates confiscated from the rebels. Having mopped up the revolt, Matthias marched into Moldavia with a view to forcing Prince Stephen 'the Great' to obedience. He was defeated near Baia on 15 December 1467 and compelled to withdraw, but the completeness of Matthias's triumph in Transylvania is shown unequivocally by the fact that his standing was not in the least shaken by his failure in Moldavia.

WARS IN BOHEMIA AND AUSTRIA

As soon as the southern frontier had been consolidated and Transylvania pacified, the king's ambitions turned decisively towards the west and the north-west. Admittedly, at the level of words Matthias always remained an enthusiastic champion of the war against the Ottomans, and referred to himself as the only defender of Christendom, but it was simply a matter of political propaganda, intended to secure the financial support of Venice and the Holy See and to arouse the sympathy of European princes. In fact, he contented himself with thwarting and, when possible, avenging Ottoman incursions. Further modification of the southern defensive line was not among his plans: he rightly considered it to be beyond his power. In his letters he was at pains to point out that he could do nothing against the sultan without help. But, as the maintenance of his rule depended upon political achievements, and his army had to be employed as well, he looked elsewhere for aggrandisement. As his biographer, Bonfini, put it later: 'In order to rule in peace at home, he made war abroad.'[1] The first target to present itself was Bohemia.

Matthias had been contemplating a war against Bohemia for some years, perhaps since the death of his first wife, which had severed the ties with King George. The young queen, Catherine Podebrad, whom he had married in 1461, died in childbirth shortly before the coronation. Relations between Matthias and his father-in-law had been full of tension during Catherine's lifetime, for George continually allied himself with Emperor Frederick III against his son-in-law, despite the fact that Matthias would have been his natural ally. The attitude of King George is explained by the fact that, as leader of the utraquists, he badly needed the emperor's benevolence, as security against his own catholic subjects and neighbours, as well as against the Pope. Although the use of the secular chalice had been sanctioned by the *compactata* of Prague, and accepted by the council of Basle, there were signs that the Holy See wished to revise its former point of view. Another source of tension between Matthias and Poděbrad was the presence in upper Hungary of Czech mercenaries, who, while acting independently of the king of Bohemia, could in fact count on his sympathy.

The pretext for an armed intervention in Bohemia was furnished by Pope Paul II, who decided finally to settle the Hussite problem. At the end of 1466 the papal consistory declared Poděbrad a heretic, deprived him of his throne, and proclaimed a crusade against him. The Catholic magnates of Bohemia and Moravia, encouraged by the Pope's attitude and displeased by their ruler's centralising tendencies, unfurled the banner of revolt and looked for another king. Their first candidate, Casimir IV of Poland, was easily bought off by George, who designated Casimir's son, Wladislas, as his own heir in Bohemia. After the margrave of Brandenburg had also declined their invitation, they turned to the king of Hungary, whom the Pope had recommended right from the beginning. For Matthias, who as early as 1465 had informed the Pope that for the sake of Christianity he was willing to fight 'both against the Czechs and against the Ottomans',[2] the offer came at exactly the right moment. Being urged by the Pope and the Bohemian magnates, Matthias's offensive attitude was given further impetus by Frederick III. When, in early 1468, Victorin Poděbrad, son of King George and governor of Moravia, attacked Austria, the emperor turned to his 'son' for help. Matthias was naturally more than ready to intervene. On 31 March 1468 he declared war on Victorin, and the long and tiring struggle for the Bohemian crown began.

The first phase of the war ended with rapid success for Matthias, who for three years led his troops in person. Having cleaned up Austria, he invaded Moravia, which he conquered in the course of 1468 together with the greater part of Silesia. In June he marched into Brno, and after a prolonged siege even managed to starve the castle of Špilberg, situated upon a hill above the city, into surrender. In February 1469 Poděbrad almost succeeded in changing the course of events by forcing his opponent into a militarily unfavourable situation from which he could not avoid starting negotiations. While these were proceeding, however, Matthias's partisans prepared the way for his election as king of Bohemia. This effectively took place on 3 May 1469 at Olomouc. The war flared up immediately, but this time it was Matthias who achieved the upper hand. In June he captured Prince Victorin, and during the following spring he finally stabilised his rule over Moravia.

The greater part of the domains belonging to the Bohemian crown was from now on to be ruled by Matthias, but the struggle was far from over. Not surprisingly, his achievements filled all of his neighbours with anxiety and a triple alliance, consisting of the rulers of Austria, Bohemia and Poland, gradually formed. The relationship between Matthias and Frederick had been deteriorating since 1469, when Ottoman troops invaded the Austrian provinces for the first time. The emperor accused Matthias of letting the Turkish marauders through his kingdom and of clandestinely aiding the rebellious Estates of Styria, while the Hungarian king demanded the financial support for the Bohemian war that Frederick had promised him. In February 1470 the two rulers met in Vienna with the aim of settling their differences, but by the end of the negotiations their disagreements had become sharper than ever.

In March 1471 Poděbrad died, and, in accordance with his last will, Wladislas, the 15 year old son of Casimir IV, was elected as his successor, which meant that Poland had become directly interested in the struggle for the Bohemian crown. The principal focus of the war soon shifted to Hungary, where another conspiracy was organised with the aim of overthrowing Matthias. This time the movement was led by Archbishop Vitéz, who was supported by his nephew, the famous humanist, Janus Pannonius, bishop of Pécs, and by some other barons. The conspirators contacted Casimir IV, and offered the Hungarian crown to one of his sons, also called Casimir. The Polish prince organised a military intervention immediately, but by the time he marched into Hungary in October, Matthias had already regained control of the situation. At the diet that had assembled in September not only was he assured of the support of the Estates, but also of that of the great majority of prelates and barons. Prince Casimir had to leave the kingdom in December; Janus fled and Vitéz submitted to the king. Matthias's authority was as solid as ever.

The failure of the Polish attack was followed by a series of truces and peace talks, during which Matthias could count on the consistent and wholehearted support of the Holy See. The negotiations began to bear fruit in 1474. The peace treaty with Poland, signed in February, was ratified by the Hungarian Estates two months later. However, in the meantime Wladislas, who had been staying with Frederick at Nuremberg, had persuaded the emperor to form an anti-Hungarian alliance, which once again offered the prospect of breaking Hungarian hegemony. Casimir immediately joined the coalition, and in October he marched into Silesia at the head of an enormous army, uniting his forces with those of Wladislas. Having previously devastated the whole region, Matthias waited for the attack behind the walls of Wrocław. The allied forces laid siege to the city in October, but were soon desperately short of supplies. Within three weeks they were compelled, despite their overwhelming numerical superiority, to seek a truce. The ensuing treaty, signed on 8 December 1474 and due to expire on 25 May 1477, was the last act of the war for the kingdom of Bohemia. The division of the lands belonging to the Bohemian crown, which was made by the envoys of Matthias and Wladislas at Brno in March 1478, was accepted by the king of Hungary, with minor modifications, on 20 September. It was ratified by the two rulers on 21 July 1479 during the course of splendid festivities at Olomouc. According to the terms of the treaty, Wladislas was to retain the kingdom of Bohemia proper, while the greater part of the territory once ruled by the king of Bohemia, that is, Moravia, Silesia and Lausitz, remained in Matthias's possession. Wladislas was entitled to redeem these domains for 400,000 florins after Matthias's death. Both rulers could use the title of king of Bohemia, but whereas Matthias was obliged to address his opponent as such, it was not to be the case the other way round. The peace treaty between Hungary and Poland had been signed somewhat earlier, on 2 April 1479, and thereafter until Matthias's death the three countries coexisted peacefully.

The relationship between Austria and Hungary, on the other hand, had been gradually deteriorating, especially after one of Matthias's most trusted advisers, John Beckensloer, archbishop of Esztergom, fled to

Austria and joined the emperor's service. As long as the prospect of an alliance with the kings of Bohemia and Poland existed, Frederick took sides with them, and in June 1477 it was Wladislas whom he declared to be the lawful ruler of Bohemia and Elector of the Empire. Matthias immediately attacked Austria, laid siege to Vienna, and in December 1477 forced the emperor to accept his terms. Frederick acknowledged him as king of Bohemia, and engaged himself to pay an indemnity of 100,000 florins. The peace did not, however, last for long. Frederick worked hard to secure the see of Salzburg for Beckensloer. Determined to thwart the emperor's plan, Matthias occupied the Styrian castles belonging to the archbishopric in 1480. When, despite the king of Hungary's efforts, Beckensloer did become archbishop of Salzburg, the outbreak of war became only a question of time. In January 1482 Matthias laid siege to Hainburg, the most important Austrian border castle, then formally declared war on Frederick in April.

Although Matthias was careful to emphasise that he wished to fight Frederick as archduke of Austria and not as emperor, the war in fact became one between Hungary and the Empire. But despite the support that Frederick received from imperial troops, the war was marked from the very beginning by Matthias's military superiority. No pitched battle was fought, but the most important of Frederick's strongholds fell successively, most of them after several months' siege. Hainburg was taken in September 1482, Kőszeg in December, Bruck and Korneuburg two years later. On 29 January 1485 the king of Hungary surrounded the city of Vienna, which was compelled to open its gates on 1 June. Wiener Neustadt, the emperor's residence, fell on 17 August 1487. The peace treaty, signed at Sankt Pölten on 16 December, left Lower Austria and Styria in Matthias's possession with the exception of a few castles.

Frederick seems to have acquiesced in his defeat, and at the time of Matthias's death, the Hungarian king's empire spread from Bautzen to Belgrade and from Enns to Braşov. But not even these spectacular military achievements could conceal the fact that by far the most important aspect of Hungarian foreign policy, namely the defence against the Ottomans, had been permanently relegated to the background.

HUNGARY AND THE OTTOMAN EMPIRE

The relationship between Matthias and the sultan followed a course that was frequently changing direction and it cannot be argued that they lived in a permanent state of hostility. Although the king of Hungary's diplomatic correspondence with the Pope and other Christian princes seems to show that the war against the Ottomans had never ceased to be his primary concern, his letters were precisely calculated to create such an impression. They are full of phrases like 'the Ottomans are our eternal enemies', and he took some delight in reiterating that his kingdom was the 'bastion and bulwark of the whole of Christendom'. His slogans were entirely in keeping with the political rhetoric of his age, for highly ambitious plans were always at hand in the West. For several decades, experts in Rome, Venice and elsewhere seriously considered the possibility of a great crusade; and in the plans they made the king of Hungary was always given a leading role. None of these plans was ever put into effect, however, for reality was more complex than people thought, and some important aspects of that reality seem to have remained hidden from even the best informed of contemporaries.

No serious Hungaro-Ottoman clash took place during the ten years following the Bosnian war of 1464, despite the fact that it was during this same period, between 1463 and 1479, that Venice fought her bloodiest war against the Ottoman empire – a war in which the republic counted Matthias among its allies. Yet the southern frontier of Hungary was so calm during these years that even the usual Turkish incursions disappear from the sources for a while; and when they reappear they are directed not against the kingdom of Hungary, but against the Empire and Venice. In 1469 Ottoman troops, coming from Bosnia, devastated Carniola and Carinthia for the first time, and the domains of the Habsburgs suffered ten further attacks before 1490. The Ottoman marauders also appeared frequently in the Venetian provinces of Istria and Friuli. In order to reach their goal, the Turkish contingents had to cross Croatia and Slavonia, both belonging to the Hungarian crown. It was conspicuous that these territories were, as a rule, spared, and it was therefore not entirely without reason that Matthias was accused of colluding with the Ottomans under the veil of his bellicose rhetoric. In 1465 and 1468 Ottoman envoys arrived in Hungary. Although their offers were officially rejected, it seems probable that a secret peace treaty was signed on the first occasion, which was then regularly prolonged until 1473. The emperor seems to have been correct in his suspicion that in return for the peace Matthias allowed Ottoman troops to pass through his lands on their way to the Austrian provinces.

After a long period of peace Hungaro-Ottoman relations apparently began to deteriorate. Having won a decisive victory over the Akkoyunlu sultan, Uzun Hasan, Sultan Mehmed unexpectedly refused to prolong the peace at the end of 1473. It must have been as a consequence of this refusal that in the beginning of 1474 Ali, bey of Smederevo, carried out an incursion into Hungary that was much more audacious than any that had previously been mounted. Having marched deep into the heart of the kingdom, he set fire to the town of Oradea on 8 February and withdrew unscathed from the country, carrying away 16,000 prisoners. Matthias's reaction was to ally himself with his former enemy, Stephen, prince of Moldavia, to whom he sent auxiliary troops under the command of Blaise Magyar, voivode of Transylvania. In January 1475 the Christian army annihilated that of the beylerbey of Rumelia at the battle of Vaslui in Moldavia. Not content with this victory, Matthias led his troops against the castle of Šabac, on the southern bank of the River Sava, and captured it on 15 February 1476 after a six-week siege. Šabac was a simple wooden fortress, constructed by the Ottomans a few years before. Its occupation was by no means an outstanding victory, but Hungarian propaganda proved very skilful in making it appear as such. The siege of Šabac even gave birth to a Hungarian heroic epic, which is in fact the first of this genre to have survived. Matthias also considered attacking the much more impressive castle of Smederevo, and constructed wooden fortresses in the vicinity, but the sultan appeared swiftly and destroyed them before the king could make up his mind. Mehmed also tried to force Moldavia to obedience in the summer of 1476, but Prince Stephen avoided battle and the sultan left empty-handed. Peace was then temporarily restored, and in his letter to Mehmed in 1478, Matthias could once again refer to their 'mutual peace and friendship'.[3]

The last series of Hungaro-Ottoman clashes in Matthias's lifetime took place between 1479 and 1481. In 1479 Transylvania and the southern part of Transdanubia, which had hitherto been spared by the marauders, were attacked simultaneously; but on 13 October near Orăştie the army that was devastating Transylvania was destroyed by Voivode Stephen Bátori and Paul Kinizsi, count of Timiş. In 1480 Croatia was pillaged by the Turks whilst returning from Styria. Matthias retaliated by sending Kinizsi to ravage Serbia, while he himself invaded Bosnia in November and marched as far as Sarajevo. The sultan's counter-attack was prevented by his death in 1481. His successor, Bayezid II, was much less bellicose. In October 1483, after a series of minor conflicts, he made peace with the Hungarian king for five years, which was prolonged in 1488 for a further two years. This did not prevent him from bringing the Moldavians to heel, however. In 1484 he took the two southern strongholds of the principality, Kilija and Belgorod (Akkerman), and thereafter Prince Stephen was forced to pay a symbolic annual tax to the sultan.

Though seldom attacking, Matthias paid a good deal of attention to defence against the Ottomans. It was he who, following in the footsteps of Sigismund, established the southern system of border castles that was to be held firmly until as late as the 1510s. He suppressed those governmental offices that could no longer be justified from a military point of view. The office of the count of the Székely was united with that of the voivode of Transylvania in 1462 (permanently in 1468) and the banates of Slavonia and Croatia were combined in 1476. In 1478 Matthias abolished the banate of Mačva, to which neither border castles nor estates any longer belonged. On the other hand, in 1479 he restored the unified military government of the south-eastern counties by giving the count of Timiş the title of 'captain general of the inferior parts' and putting him in charge of all the border castles from Belgrade to Turnu Severin. The new captain general was officially authorised to collect the annual tax of the southern counties for his own use. From this source he had to pay not only the garrisons of his castles but also the light cavalry, which was mainly recruited from among Serbian refugees. Their primary task being pillaging, they had been called 'hussars' since Sigismund's time (the Serbian word originally meant 'marauder'). Thousands of mostly Serbian peasants were exempted from tax-paying in return for military service. The status of these soldiers, the so-called *vojniks* ('warriors'), was therefore similar to that enjoyed by the Serbian soldiers of the military frontier in the eighteenth and nineteenth centuries. The garrisons of the border castles were completed by companies of lightly armed boatmen called *nazadistae*. The castles most exposed to Ottoman attacks were organised into districts, their centres being at Turnu Severin, Belgrade, Šabac, Srebrenik and Jajce. Although their commanders were generally referred to as 'ban' from the 1480s onwards, they were not counted among the barons, for the first four were subordinated to the captain general of Timiş, and the captain of Jajce to the ban of Croatia.

THE ARMY AND FINANCES

The traditional forms of military organisation also lived on, especially the *banderia* of the prelates and the barons, which played an important role throughout Matthias's wars. From 1459 a few efforts were made to revive the institution of the *militia portalis*, but the core of the royal army was composed of mercenaries. Matthias was one of the first European princes to set up and maintain a considerable mercenary army on a permanent footing. He seems to have hired the first units from among Jiškra's troops in 1462, and probably employed such mercenaries continuously thereafter. Their number increased rapidly during the Bohemian and Austrian wars. According to Bonfini, during the muster at Wiener Neustadt in 1487 the king inspected 20,000 heavily armoured cavalry and 8,000 infantry, at least half of which must have consisted of his own mercenary troops. This army, or part of it, later became known as the 'Black Army'. It was made up of Czechs, Germans and some Hungarians, while it is clear that most of its captains were foreigners, such as Černahora, Haugwitz, František Hag, Jan Zelený and others. The army was, of course, complemented by a considerable artillery train.

Under Matthias's masterful control, the mercenary army proved its effectiveness several times during the wars against Bohemia and Austria, but maintaining such a force imposed a heavy burden upon the treasury. Allowing three florins as the monthly pay of a heavily armoured cavalryman, and two florins for that of an infantryman, the maintenance of 10,000 soldiers must have cost at least 200,000–300,000 florins a year. To this must be added the money needed for the upkeep of the southern border castles, which already under Sigismund had amounted to a considerable sum. We may reasonably assume, therefore, that the soldiers were not always regularly paid, and that they had to live off looting in wartime. As long as there were wars this stopgap solution seems to have worked perfectly, for there is no evidence of a revolt by unpaid soldiers during Matthias's lifetime.

In view of the fact that in 1454 the prospective revenues of King Ladislaus V were estimated at little more that 250,000 florins *per annum*, it is clear that the kingdom's traditional resources would not have sufficed for even the partial payment of the mercenaries. Consequently, Matthias had to carry out a comprehensive reform of royal finances. In 1467 he entrusted their administration to a converted Jewish merchant from Vienna, John Ernuszt (alias Hampó), who, as treasurer, managed all the revenues, ordinary and extraordinary alike. It seems to have been at this time that it first became possible for the treasury to account systematically for its revenues and expenditure, and to set up a primitive budget. The king consented to Ernuszt's introduction of a new, stable penny, 100 of which were to be worth a gold florin. From this time onwards the thirtieth was to be collected as 'the crown's customs' (*vectigal coronae*), the change of name meaning that all previous exemptions became void.

However, the most effective means of increasing the treasury's revenues proved to be the extraordinary taxation of the peasantry, which took place every year from 1458 onwards. The extraordinary tax was much heavier than the 20 pence hitherto paid as the *lucrum camerae*. The basis of the assessment was likewise the *porta*, but the tax generally amounted to as much as a florin a year. Moreover, it was levied 43 times in the course of 32 years, which means that it was sometimes collected twice within the same year. The annual tax of a *porta* amounted, therefore, to some 1.32 gold florins on average, despite the fact that in 1467 the *lucrum camerae* was suppressed, or, more precisely, became part of the generally collected portal tax. Since most of the *portae* were actually inhabited by more than one peasant household, Matthias also tried to collect the new tax by households rather than by *portae*. This measure aroused vigorous resistance, however, especially in Transylvania, where it led to the revolt of the Estates, and the king consequently judged it wiser not to enforce it.

As for the king's overall revenues, we have several contemporary estimates, the most reliable of which seems to be the report of the Neapolitan envoy Fontana from the year 1476. Besides the portal tax, 250,000 florins seem to have come in an average year, above all from the monopoly of salt (80,000), from coinage (60,000), from the thirtieth (50,000) and from the towns (47,000, including the tax of the Saxons of Transylvania). The overall number of *portae* at the end of Sigismund's reign can be put at 400,000, which fell to some 265,000 by 1494–95. For Matthias's reign, the existence of at least 300,000 *portae* can be postulated, therefore, which, assuming an annual tax of 1.32 gold florins for each of them, would give an additional 400,000 florins a year. Consequently, the king's entire annual revenues must have fluctuated at around 650,000 florins, depending on how many *portae* were registered, and on whether the tax was levied once or twice. It is worth noting that by comparison in 1475 the annual income of the Ottoman Empire amounted to 1,800,000 florins.

THE KING'S SUPPORTERS

The stability of Matthias's rule during the period after 1471 can be explained by reference to his revenues (which were more than twice those that Sigismund had at his disposal), by his standing army and by his successes in the field of foreign policy. The way in which he was able to establish a surprisingly stable regime is much more difficult to account for, however.

It goes without saying that Matthias could rely from the very beginning on his own kinsmen and retainers, among whom the Szapolyai brothers played the most outstanding role. Emeric was Matthias's archtreasurer between 1460 and 1464, became governor of Slavonia, Croatia and Bosnia in 1464, and died in 1487 whilst holding the office of palatine. His younger brother, Stephen, distinguished himself as captain general during the war against Jiškra. In 1464 the king granted them the newly recovered region of Spiš, together with all its castles and towns, with the sole exception of Levoča, which remained a royal city. At the same time he authorised them to use the title of 'perpetual count', a favour previously accorded to no more than three persons – Michael Szilágyi, Jan Vitovec and Nicholas Újlaki. Despite the fact that Emeric's loyalty wavered more than once, the king's generosity knew no bounds. By the end of Matthias's reign, Stephen, then governor of Austria, had become the second greatest landowner of the kingdom.

Since none of Matthias's other favourites had a career comparable to those of the Szapolyai brothers, it is highly probable that a special relationship – perhaps one deriving from illegitimate birth – attached them to the Hunyadi family. Nevertheless, following in Sigismund's footsteps, the king willingly conferred the most important governmental positions on his own personal followers and systematically helped them to rise into the highest strata of society. Many people made enormous fortunes from royal grants during these decades: above all the king's cousins, the brothers Pongrác of Dengeleg and the Geréb of Vingard, and some of the former retainers of John Hunyadi or their sons, such as Ban John Túz, the voivodes of Transylvania, Blaise Magyar and Nicholas Csupor, and Peter Szokoli, count of Timiş. Some of them rose into the ranks of the barons through service as military commanders or condottieri: these included Vuk Branković, who had fled from Serbia and was given the title of despot; the Serbian Jakšić brothers; Ban Ladislaus Egervári; or the first captain general of Timiş, Paul Kinizsi, a man of obscure origin. John Ernuszt, ban of Slavonia, the initiator of the financial reforms, was also able to bequeath a number of domains to his heirs. Among the barons an important role was played in the process of stabilisation by the traditional allies of the Hunyadi party, such as Voivode Sebastian Rozgonyi (a relative of the king through his wife), who died young, and Stephen Bátori. The latter, while serving as judge royal from 1471, and then also as voivode of Transylvania from 1479, rose to be the third richest landowner in the kingdom.

Nevertheless, the king was far too circumspect to allow his rule to be founded solely on the support of kinsmen and followers. From the outset it was clear that he did not intend to rule merely as head of the Hunyadi party, but wished to rely on each of the baronial groups. Among those who had once been his father's allies, Nicholas Újlaki retained his authority and the banate of Mačva until his death. Moreover, Matthias made him perpetual count of Teočak in Bosnia in 1464, and conferred upon him the title of 'king of Bosnia' in 1471. Michael Ország functioned as palatine for 26 years until his death, while Ladislaus Pálóci, appointed judge royal in 1446, also retained his office until the very end of his life. The king showed conspicuous respect towards those who had been the most determined enemies of his own family, perhaps because their efforts to strengthen central authority converged with his own aims. Cardinal Szécsi remained arch-chancellor until 1464, while John Rozgonyi, also a resolute follower of Ladislaus V, served as *magister tavarnicorum* for 11 years and died as judge royal in

1471. It is highly characteristic that Matthias chose as his foremost adviser and as leader of the arch- and secret chancellery (alongside John Vitéz and later instead of him) Stephen Várdai, archbishop of Kalocsa, who had previously been a faithful supporter of Ladislaus V. It was for him, and not for Vitéz, that Matthias obtained the cardinal's hat. The powerful Szentgyörgyi brothers, former partisans of Frederick III, were bought off by the voivodate of Transylvania. It was surely thanks to the king's prudent policy that whenever his rule was in danger – in 1459, 1467, and, finally, during the conspiracy of 1471 – he was always able to rally the support of the great majority of barons.

An important element contributing to the strength of the political regime was the king's right to fill vacant episcopal sees, a right that Matthias exploited to the full. Episcopal elections, which before Matthias's accession had already become purely formal, were finally suppressed in 1458. Henceforth, the person of the future bishop was to be decided by the king alone, who always enforced his will even against the Pope. The only occasion when Matthias faced serious resistance was in 1486, when he designated Ippolito d'Este, the six-year-old nephew of his wife Beatrice, as archbishop of Esztergom. Innocent VIII was stupefied: 'It is a foolish thing,' he wrote, to confer the government of the Hungarian Church 'upon a child who is still almost an infant.'[4] The king remained inflexible, however, and it was the Holy Father who in the end had to yield. Ippolito later became a cardinal and until his death in 1520 lived at Ferrara, partly from the revenues which, administered by his Italian stewards, arrived regularly from Hungary.

Further conflicts rarely emerged, for throughout his reign Matthias enjoyed the special goodwill of the Holy See, and his appointments always obtained at least tacit consent. His candidates were either brothers or sons of his favourite barons, or simple clerics, who had made a name as diplomats, financial experts or as members of the chancellery. In addition to some foreigners, such as the Silesian John Beckensloer, the Moravian John Filipec, or the Italian Gabriele Rangoni, there were among them talented sons of peasants and burghers, such as George Handó, archbishop of Kalocsa and his successor, Peter Váradi; and Urban Nagylucsei, bishop of Győr and later of Eger, and his successor Thomas Bakócz, who in 1497 exchanged his bishopric with Ippolito for the archbishopric of Esztergom. That throughout his reign Matthias should have enjoyed the unconditional support not only of his barons but also of his prelates is, therefore, wholly understandable.

It was with the same determination that Matthias enforced the Crown's right of escheat. The principle according to which the possessions of families that died out in the male line devolved to the king, who was entitled to dispose of them at will, was still flourishing during

Matthias's reign. It was certainly to the king's advantage that a whole series of great fortunes happened to become available through the lack of a male heir – namely those of the Szécsényi (1460), Bebek (1469), Cudar (1470), Kórógyi (1472), Maróti (1476) and Marcali (1487) families and that of Count Martin Frankopan in 1479. 1481 saw the death of the childless Job Garai, who was son of Palatine Ladislaus and one of the greatest landowners of the kingdom. Neither Michael Szilágyi, who was executed by the Ottomans in 1461, nor Voivode Nicholas Csupor, who died in the Polish war of 1474 and possessed, in addition to his own domains, the estates of the Kórógyi family, had a legitimate heir. As with several other aspects of his policy, in enforcing the right of escheat Matthias seems to have been following Sigismund's example. But it is highly characteristic of the changing circumstances that he was sometimes obliged to take firm measures in order to enforce his will. In 1459, when John Rozgonyi junior died, and again in 1469, following the death of Paul Bebek, Matthias had to threaten to besiege the widows before he was able to take possession of their castles.

In addition to the royal estates there were other sources at the king's disposal, above all the enormous wealth of the Hunyadi family itself. This was incorporated into the royal domain in 1458 and was frequently used by Matthias to reward his followers, especially in the first years of his reign. It was at that time that he established the new office of the *provisor* of Buda castle, to whom he subjected a growing number of domains pertaining to the Crown. In 1459 he confiscated the still considerable possessions of the despots of Serbia on the pretext that they had been disloyal by surrendering Smederevo to the Ottomans. Most of the estates that he recovered from the Czechs in upper Hungary between 1458 and 1462 were not returned to their previous owners but turned instead to his own uses. After the suppression of the revolt of 1467 he confiscated the possessions of one branch of the Losonci family and many of the Transylvanian nobility suffered the same punishment. In 1474 he regained, partly through purchase, a whole series of estates (including the counties of Orava and Liptov) from their Polish lords.

THE KING AND THE DIET

Besides his own determination and uncompromising attitude, it was the support of his prelates and barons that helped Matthias through the first, most difficult years of his reign. It was their fidelity that counted most; to the towns, which were his natural allies, he paid relatively little attention, but he did try to check the political ambitions of the nobility. The events that had taken place since the death of

Sigismund had made it clear that the main obstacle to the consolidation of royal authority was the diet. It was, of course, impossible wholly to ignore its existence, but the king did have the power to lengthen the intervals between its sessions and to limit its field of activity. Between 1458 and 1476 Matthias held 15 diets, which means that hardly a year passed without an assembly being summoned. On the other hand, during the 13 years extending from 1476 until his death only five diets are known to have been held, which shows in itself that the influence of the Estates had decreased radically. This impression is further reinforced by an examination of the composition and procedure of the assemblies and of the laws accepted by them.

In accordance with the intentions of the king, the diet was dominated not by the masses of the nobility but by the barons. Although, on the very first occasion, in June 1458, Matthias had been forced to agree to hold a diet on Whitsun Day every year, with the personal participation of the kingdom's inhabitants, he had no intention of keeping his promise. On the contrary, he almost always negotiated with the envoys of the counties, and it was only exceptionally – after 1464 only twice – that he consented to the appearance of the nobility in person. For the towns, which were invited to a diet only once between 1464 and 1490, the king held separate assemblies. The burghers seem to have acquiesced in this situation without complaint, especially since their participation at the diet, whose work they influenced very little, was felt to be more a burden than a privilege. In their absence, however, the Estates were represented by the barons and by deputies of the county nobility, and almost all decisions were the result of bargaining between these groups and the king.

Besides tradition, the regular convocation of the diet was explained by the necessity of obtaining the Estates' consent to extraordinary taxation. In return for their consent, the diet would make their usual declarations: that the king should respect the privileges of the nobility; that the general levy should not be summoned except in cases of extreme danger; and that neither offices nor estates should be conferred upon foreigners. Matthias was willing to accept these conditions, but most of his laws remained a dead letter. He seems to have consented to everything that was presented to him, but had not the slightest intention of respecting those contrary to his own interests. By far the best example of this concerns taxation. In 1458 he promised under oath to limit himself to the *lucrum camerae* and never to collect unlawful taxes from the inhabitants of the kingdom and their tenants. He frequently reiterated his promise thereafter, yet regularly levied extraordinary taxes, sometimes without a diet's consent, merely contenting himself with a decision of the royal council. Having achieved the consolidation of royal authority, Matthias felt even less

315

inclined to bother with the demands of the Estates. By 1475 they had become so subservient as to request 'His Majesty' not to oppress them with new taxes, in return for which they engaged themselves to take the field 'whenever the kingdom's necessity demands'.[5] Yet what Matthias needed was money, not the militarily worthless general levy, and in 1478 he obtained the Estates' vote for the tax (one florin per *porta*) to be levied for six successive years.

As the years passed, the king's authority became increasingly unrestricted, and his government more and more authoritarian. The most important decisions were made by himself and his intimate advisers, while the Estates, including the barons, had to content themselves with the pleasure of acknowledging them. Like Sigismund before him, he delighted in referring to the 'plenitude' of his power, encroached upon the laws that he had once sanctioned, and did not hold back from other high-handed measures. Already in the first part of his reign he had once gone as far as to slap Archbishop Vitéz in the face, and in his later years he became increasingly unwilling to restrain himself. In 1484 he imprisoned his arch-chancellor, Archbishop Péter Váradi and refused to free him, despite the repeated protests of the Pope. In 1487 the same fate awaited his other favourite, Nicholas Bánfi, count of Pressburg, who also lost several of his estates. Matthias tried to dispense with the barons by relying upon the royal household, that is, the group of personal followers who carried out his orders and governed the counties and royal castles. From about 1460 the most distinguished members of the household bore the title of *cubicularius,* and from the 1470s two royal secretaries (*secretarius*) were charged to report on the affairs of the chancellery. In the meantime important institutional reforms were carried out. During the diet of 1486 the king had a voluminous law-code sanctioned, which modernised the administration of justice and considerably increased the authority of the comital courts. It abolished the institutions of the palatinal eyre and the 'proclaimed' congregations, and the deciding of lawsuits by duel; and it annulled all the exemptions that had limited the competence of the courts. It was also decided at that time that the count's deputy (*vicecomes*) had to be chosen from among the well-to-do nobles of the county. Another law of 1486 regulated the authority of the palatine, sanctioning the established custom that he was the second most important person in the kingdom, whereby he was entitled to function as regent in the event of king's absence or minority.

In his last years the king became primarily concerned with the problem of the succession. He had no children from his first wife, after whose death he had some difficulty in finding another suitable bride. Both Frederick III and Casimir of Poland turned down his proposals, presumably because his family was regarded as insufficiently distinguished. Consequently, it took him a long time to remarry. Finally, on

22 December 1476 he married Beatrice, the daughter of Ferrante of Aragon, king of Naples (she had been crowned as queen before the wedding, on 12 December). However, his second wife also remained childless, which forced Matthias to look for another solution. His only child was a bastard son, born in 1473 to the daughter of an Austrian burgher. Matthias originally intended for him to become a bishop; but as time passed by it became increasingly probable that, despite the stigma of his illegitimate birth, little John Corvinus would be the only means of prolonging the dynasty.

It was in 1482 that the king finally decided to introduce the child into the political arena. He officially acknowledged him as his son, gave him the title of 'duke of Liptov' (*dux Liptoviensis*), and granted him many estates, among them the most valuable pieces of the Garai heritage. Henceforth he employed every possible means to increase the young duke's wealth, including arbitrary measures if necessary. In 1483 he granted his son the castle of Šariš, previously confiscated from the Perényi family, then, in 1484, the immense fortune of his own mother, Elisabeth Szilágyi, with the towns and castles of Mukačeve and Debrecen. In 1487 he gave Corvinus the estates of Nicholas Bánfi, then the Slavonian castles of the sons of John Vitovec and Victorin Poděbrad, whom he had forced into exile by accusing them of disloyalty. It was at that time that Matthias tried to win the hand of Bianca Sforza of Milan for the duke, which leaves us in no doubt as to his intentions concerning the succession. In 1489 he made the barons and the captains of the royal and ducal castles, together with the towns, promise on oath that in the event of his death they would obey Corvinus. His precautions were justified, for he did not have long to live. At the beginning of April 1490 he suddenly fell ill after a banquet in Vienna, where he spent much of his time during the last years of his reign. He died a few days later on 6 April.

The death of the 47 year old king meant that the last ruler of indisputably high stature disappeared from the political scene of medieval Hungary. A general review of his career makes it clear that the ideal that he tried to follow was not his father but rather Sigismund of Luxembourg. Although he did not know his imperial predecessor personally, he would have been able to form a graphic image of him through the memories of his tutor, John Vitéz, or those of his palatine, Michael Ország. Sigismund's empire, comprising several kingdoms, his international prestige, his unshakeable authority and dominant personality seem to have been the standards that Matthias tried to follow throughout his life. His Bohemian, Austrian and Ottoman policy, as well as his government in Hungary, his Sigismund-like, authoritarian interpretation of royal power, can be explained by reference to this attitude of mind. In order to follow as closely as possible in the footsteps of his model, he even reached out for the imperial crown, although in this respect he must have been fully aware of the insurmountable obstacles that stood in the way of his ambitions.

It must be admitted that, apart from some of his laws, his work did not prove to be enduring. His conquests were lost within a couple of weeks, and the royal authority that he had built up vanished with him. Nevertheless, his extraordinary political and military talent cannot be disputed. As a child, he had found himself at the head of a disorganised, crisis-stricken kingdom. At his death, he was the highly respected ruler of a considerable empire. Yet it is not his political achievement but his role as an open-handed patron of Renaissance art that best shows the inborn sovereignty of his personality. The roots of the Renaissance in Hungary, which is indeed an enigma in the history of culture, are to be found in the king's extraordinary personality.

PATRONAGE OF THE ARTS AND HUMANITIES

It seems to have been John Vitéz who instilled into Matthias, his pupil, the taste for modern culture. Although he never visited Italy, the bishop was a devoted humanist. He wrote carefully composed Latin letters, collected books, and soon after his appointment as archbishop of Esztergom founded a university at Pressburg in 1467. As early as 1447 he sent his nephew, John, to Ferrara to be educated in the famous school of Guarino Veronese. The boy, known later as Janus Pannonius, spent 11 years in Italy, by the end of which he had mastered contemporary Latin and Greek culture at the highest possible level. After his return to Hungary, Matthias appointed him bishop of Pécs and then ban of Slavonia, and entrusted important political missions to him. Their relationship seems to have remained free of conflict until around 1470. We do not know what it was exactly that finally turned Janus and Vitéz against the king; all that is certain is that after the failure of their conspiracy Janus found it advisable to emigrate. He died in the spring of 1472, en route to Italy, in the castle of Medvedgrad near Zagreb. Vespasiano da Bisticci found him worthy of commemoration in one of his biographies.

It was not only Janus whom Matthias held in the highest esteem but also manuscripts. The beginnings of his famous library date back to the 1460s, and its development remained one of his deepest concerns until the end of his life. He strove for a collection where the whole body of knowledge of the ancient and modern world would be available, which led him to search systematically for curios. He exchanged books with the great Lorenzo Medici, was a regular customer of Bisticci's bookshop in Florence, and maintained relations with other collectors as well. For a time a workshop, allegedly consisting of 30 artisans, produced books for him at Buda. According to a later visitor, the humanist archbishop of Esztergom, Nicholas Oláh, the *Bibliotheca Corvina* filled two halls of the palace at Buda, one containing the works of the Greek authors, the other those of the Latin writers. Scholars think that at the time of the king's death his library may have comprised as many as 2,000 volumes, which would mean that it was the second greatest collection of books in Europe, after that of the Vatican. Most of these splendidly ornamented volumes were later lost. A small fraction of them were taken to Istanbul after the Ottoman conquest, whence 18 pieces returned in 1869 and 1877 as a gift of the sultan. Today, 216 Corvinas are known to exist all over the world. Only a third are kept in Hungary, the others contributing to the magnificence of various European and American collections.

Matthias's large-scale building activity served to display his princely authority in the same way as his beloved library, and it was characterised by the same taste for delicacy. It seems to have been due to the influence of his Neapolitan wife that the king, who never visited the Italian Peninsula, became an adherent of the most recent trends of contemporary art. The complete reconstruction of the castle of Buda began in 1479 with the addition of two Renaissance wings to the palace, together with a hanging garden; and it was at the same time that the royal residence at Visegrád was reshaped in Renaissance style. The reconstruction was directed by Chiementi Camicia of Florence and then by Giovanni Dalmata, from Trogir. Even artists as renowned as Benedetto da Maiano and Filippo Lippi are said to have worked for the king. The ornamental well of his palace at Buda was designed by Verrocchio, and his portrait was painted by Mantegna. As far as we know these were the earliest manifestations of the new Italian style north of the Alps.

The works of art were almost completely destroyed during the sixteenth and seventeenth centuries, and very few of them can be seen today. The excavations at Visegrád have uncovered some parts of the palace built by Matthias, while in the castle of Buda fragments of red marble were found during the reconstruction following the Second World War. Such evidence alone would have been hardly sufficient for us to imagine what had vanished. Fortunately we also have Bonfini's detailed description of the palace of Buda, while in the middle of the sixteenth century Nicholas Oláh was still able to see and record for posterity the declining but astonishing splendour of Visegrád.

Matthias endeavoured to fill his Renaissance palaces with men of letters worthy of the splendid environment, but his efforts did not bear abundant fruit. His dream was to gather around himself the best scholars of his age, but very few of them were willing to settle permanently in his distant kingdom. One of the exceptions was

Regiomontanus, the leading astronomer of his time, who had previously dedicated one of his works to the Hungarian king. He was in charge of the Greek codices at Buda from 1468 to 1471. The most illustrious Italian humanists remained Matthias's distant admirers. Ficino and Pomponio Leto, for instance, dedicated their works to him, while Poliziano helped him to acquire new books for his library. Otherwise the king had to content himself with the company of humanists of the second rank, like Taddeo Ugoleto, Galeotto Marzio or Antonio Bonfini. Ugoleto was in charge of the library and, at the same time, tutor of the young John Corvinus. Galeotto also spent several years at court and considered his main task to be the conferring of praise on his princely host, a task that he carried out with taste and moderation. Bonfini, who was the last to arrive in 1486, became the posthumous historian of the king. In his voluminous work, completed in the 1490s, he narrated not only his master's reign but also the entire history of Hungary from the beginning, rewriting in a humanistic style the local chronicles upon which he was able to draw. He is the source of the king's epithet 'Corvinus', which has become definitively attached to Matthias's name. In accordance with the traditions of his age Bonfini claimed that the Hunyadi family, whose arms depicted a raven (*corvus*), descended from the ancient Roman *gens* of the *Corvini*.

The group of foreign scholars living at court, Italians and others, was completed by a small circle of Hungarian humanists. It comprised but a handful of persons within the palace, most of them prelates, like Nicholas Bátori, a member of the aristocracy, who had been educated at Ferrara, or Peter Váradi, son of a simple burgher. The centre of the circle was the king himself. Matthias, who spoke German, Czech and Italian, seems to have had a good command of Latin as well, for Galeotto noted that he once made an error of grammar. He read a lot, and willingly engaged in sophisticated discussions at the dinner table, the direction of which he always controlled. With the arrival of Beatrice the outward features of Italian fashion appeared as well. Outsiders could but respect the eccentric habits of their ruler and his wife, but they did not conceal their contempt for the other humanists at court. Galeotto tells us that Bishop Bátori was laughed at because he was always seen reading.

It must have become evident by now that Matthias's Renaissance court remained no more than a small island within what was an ocean of a profoundly alien culture. It was the strange initiative of a strange personality, which had nothing to do with the culture of the elite, let alone with that of the country in general, nor did it exert any influence upon it, at least for the time being.

A glimpse of the general attitude of the contemporary nobility can be gained through the official document of the Peace of Pressburg of

1491. In accordance with the new practice that was at that time becoming general all over Europe, the document should have been signed by the four barons who represented the kingdom at the conclusion of the treaty. Yet three of them – the judge royal, Stephen Bátori; the Master of the Horse, Ladislaus Ország, the only son of Palatine Michael; and the arch-chamberlain, Ladislaus Rozgonyi – were unable to sign their names. Though all of them were contemporaries of the Renaissance ruler, none of them had learned to write, even at the most primitive level. This can only be explained by the fact that the contemporary Hungarian nobility were 'active' illiterates – that is, that they were not only without the basic elements of written culture, but did not feel the need to learn them, probably regarding literacy as incompatible with their status. If this was the case in the most illustrious families, there can be no doubt that it also applied to the lower strata of society. In fact, while the attitude of the aristocracy was to go through a profound change during the next few decades, the acquisition of literacy by the nobility was to be a much later development.

Writing remained the privilege of those men whose profession demanded the use of the written word. Besides the clerics, these included the laymen working in the chancelleries, the courts, the counties and the places of authentication. Their culture was essentially Latin-based, of a secular nature, and was mainly limited to the sphere of law. Their work consisted of the drafting of charters and other legal documents, an activity for which they were prepared by their schooling. If an 'intelligentsia' can be spoken of in this period, it was composed of this small group of no more than several hundred people, most of them notaries. Their intellectual horizons, needs and mentality seem to be perfectly represented in the historical work of one of their leaders, John Thuróczy.

Thuróczy, who came from the lesser nobility of the county of Turc (Turóc), worked as a notary at the court of the judge royal and then at a place of authentication, before becoming, at the end of his life, Personal, one of the chief judges of the kingdom. It was at that time, and encouraged by his colleagues, that he wrote his work entitled *Chronica Hungarorum*, which was printed simultaneously in Brno and Augsburg in 1488. In accordance with its title, this rather slight work was written in the manner of the chronicles. Its author, following the ancient tradition, merely brought together those previous works that were available to him, limiting his own contribution to sporadic corrections. It was he who preserved for posterity the *Gesta* of John Küküllő, by inserting it verbatim into his own compilation. His knowledge of classical authors did not go beyond the level that could have been attained in one of the common chapter schools. The independent part of his book is the description of the events following 1387, during the writing of which he sometimes drew on charters preserved in the chancellery, but mostly relied on the memory of his older contemporaries, among them Michael Ország. He did make some apt remarks, but his intellect was far from outstanding and his sense of chronology very poor, and as a consequence the quality of his work was not comparable to those of his contemporaries, such as Thomas Ebendorfer of Austria or Jan Długosz of Poland. Also highly conspicuous is his national bias, combined with a good deal of naiveté. His colleagues must have found much delight in statements such as 'the Hungarians surpass by far all the other nations in valour and martial virtues'.[6]

It is not surprising, therefore, that Janus Pannonius did not have a high opinion of the cultural level of his homeland:

> In Latin soil I wrote, perhaps, in a style more Latin,
> but now, in a barbaric land, I babble out barbaric lines.
> Put Vergil here, and Vergil's lyre will grate!
> Let Cicero come here, and Cicero will be mute.[7]

Chapter 19

Hungary at the End of the Middle Ages

The reigns of Matthias and of his two successors from the Jagiellonian dynasty, Wladislas II, (1490–1516) and Louis II (1516–1526), can be characterised by two divergent lines of development. On the one hand, we see, at least from the 1470s onwards, unmistakable signs of a general economic upswing that went hand in hand with a marked improvement in the living standards of the population. One could almost say that, in terms of the level of its civilisation, Hungary would not again come so close to the Western world before the nineteenth century. On the other hand, it was also at this time that the boundaries that divided society into two sharply separated castes, those of land-owners and tenants, definitively hardened. The two lines of development were not, of course, wholly independent of each other. As it became more evident that the general course of economic development would lead to a progressive decrease of social inequality, so the nobility became more determined to block the path to upward social mobility, through the strengthening of their own privileges, in the face of pressure from the rest of society and particularly from the wealthier groups of the peasantry. The sharpening conflict culminated dramatically in the great peasant war of 1514.

ECONOMIC DEVELOPMENT

The decades around 1500 show clear signs of economic prosperity. Although the growth of the western towns, such as Sopron and Press-burg, came to a halt, this was counterbalanced by the spectacular development of Buda and Pest and of the economy of the eastern regions, especially the market towns. This should above all be seen as a consequence of the profound changes that had occurred within the structure of commerce. Imports continued to consist mainly of luxury goods – Italian and Western cloths, spices and so on – but the proportion of cheap mass products was continuously growing and was a sure sign of ever-increasing demand. An even more important phenomenon was that the major part of exports now consisted of domestic raw materials, the value of which surpassed that of imports by the end of the fifteenth century at the latest. The production of precious metals continued on a considerable scale, and the Hungarian gold florin retained much of its prestige on the international market, but its place within the export trade was taken by other items, such as copper and cattle. The enormous increase in the volume of international commerce is demonstrated by the fact that royal revenues derived from the thirtieth, which had amounted to some 20,000 florins under Sigismund, had grown to 50,000 florins by the reign of Matthias and further increased under his successors. The principal commercial routes remained those leading towards the Empire, Venice, the Black Sea and Cracow, but the Balkan route had also grown in importance by the end of the fifteenth century. Even Turkish merchants were to be seen in Buda in the inter-war periods.

Although copper mining had previously not been entirely unknown in the region, its spectacular rise began only in the 1470s, with its centre at Banská Bystrica. The initiative came from John Thurzó, an entrepreneur of Hungarian origin from Cracow, who employed the most up-to-date techniques of drainage and also the process of roasting, by means of which silver could be extracted from copper. He gradually acquired the copper mines, which were among the richest in Europe, and in order to exploit them associated himself with the Fugger of Augsburg in 1495. The new enterprise operated on a scale hitherto unheard of in Hungary. Within four years (up to 1499) the associates invested 277,500 florins in the 'common Hungarian business'. In the course of 32 years (before 1526) they produced 42,000 tons of copper and 84,000 kg of silver, and made a profit of 869,000 florins in all. During the best years (1504–13) the annual profit was around 60,000 florins, which was completed by the income from the coinage of Kremnica, rented by Thurzó from the Chamber for 14,000 florins a year.

Simultaneous with the upswing of copper working was the unprecedented increase in the export of cattle to the Empire and Italy. At the beginning of the sixteenth century, 8,000 to 20,000 cattle were driven to Austria every year, and hardly fewer to Venice. Although the export of wine and animal skins was far from negligible, oxen remained the most important item of Hungarian exports for a very long time. Those to profit from an expanding economy were Buda and its surroundings and the regions directly involved in cattle breeding. By far the most favourable conditions were to be found on the Great Plain, where hundreds of villages had been left deserted since the Mongol invasion, and enormous pastures awaited the entrepreneurs. For example, the inhabitants of Debrecen had access to some 120,000 acres of land, those of Nagykőrös using almost 75,000 acres. Merchants engaging in the cattle trade could amass enormous fortunes. Some of them drove as many as ten thousand cattle to market at one time, and employed hundreds of highly specialised armed retainers, called *hajdúk*. It was at this time that Pest, the chief cattle market, became a commercial centre of national importance, and Szeged grew to become one of the most populous towns of the kingdom.

Where the land was not suited to stock raising, wine production played a similar role, especially in the western parts of the country. Hungarian wine was highly appreciated in both Bohemia and Poland and even reached Brandenburg. The market towns of Transdanubia, the Little Plain (the region between Pressburg and Győr) and the Hegyalja (around Tokaj) all prospered thanks to wine production.

The growing buying capacity of the peasantry and the increasing internal traffic are well attested by the proliferation of markets and fairs. The second half of the fifteenth century was a period of boom for the market towns and saw a special kind of 'rural urbanisation'. The rural population tended to settle in the towns and boroughs, and in some areas half, or even three-quarters, of the entire population was concentrated in a handful of major localities. In 1469, for instance, 77 per cent of the peasants belonging to the castle of Korog (Vukovar county) lived at Osijek and five other boroughs, the remaining 23 per cent being dispersed in the 21 villages of the estate. Though most of the boroughs remained agricultural settlements of a clearly rustic outlook, some of them show unmistakable signs of a slow urbanisation, such as the establishment of guilds and the appearance of stone-built houses. Remnants of gothic dwellings that were erected during this period of prosperity are still sometimes discovered in the centre of little towns like Ráckeve, Gyöngyös or Pásztó.

LANDLORDS AND PEASANTS

The spectacular expansion of the economy was not, however, followed by a profound transformation of society. The increasingly caste-like social structure set a limit on the upward mobility of the peasantry. The main obstacle that made the restructuring of society impossible was the special nature of seigneurial power in Hungary: this involved *sensu stricto* property rights and amounted to much more than a lord's more or less exclusive judicial authority over his subjects. To be a landlord meant the enjoyment of a perpetual and practically inalienable property right to a well-defined parcel of the kingdom's land. Such a parcel of land was called a 'possession' (*possessio*) if inhabited by peasants and 'puszta' (Wüstung, *praedium*) if uninhabited. From the fifteenth century onwards, 'possession' was practically synonymous with 'village'. Each village was surrounded by 'true and ancient' boundaries, and whatever lay within them was regarded as belonging to the village's 'appurtenances' (*pertinentiae*). Consequently, both the land and its 'utilities', that is, all sorts of profits associated with the land and its users, belonged exclusively to the landowner.

The owner's lordship consisted, in fact, of judicial authority over those living within the boundaries of his domain, for whom he could act as their natural judge. From our point of view, however, it is even more important that landowning amounted to a property right with which no other right of that kind was compatible. The lord's right extended not only to woodlands, lakes, rivers and pastures, but also to every single parcel of land within the village boundaries, the peasant holdings included. These holdings were not 'properties' in the legal sense (though they resembled them in many respects) and they existed only in a state of subordination to the estate. The peasant enjoyed personal freedom and was not restricted in the use of his holding, which could even be the object of a legal testament. Sometimes he obtained exemption from all kinds of service dues. Yet he had no right to detach his holding from either the village community or from the common shackles of seigneurial authority. He could never become a lord himself. He remained a peasant (*rusticus*) until his death, no matter how complete his personal freedom otherwise was. 'The rustic, apart from the pay for his labour, has no perpetual right in the lands of his lord, but the proprietorship of the entire land belongs to the lord.'[1]

It was by means of such a distinction that the population of Hungary was split into two sharply separated groups, composed of lords and subjects. It was privileges based upon property rights, and not material wealth or a distinctive way of life, that put up a barrier between them. There existed rich peasants and poor noblemen; yet their social difference remained insuperable. In the Hungary of the late fifteenth century every single piece of land had a lord of its own. The landlord belonged to the order of the privileged, and as such could regard himself as an 'inhabitant of the kingdom' (*regnicola*), enjoying the rights pertaining to his status. Those living 'under alien roof', on the other hand, were as a rule deprived of all kinds of political rights, legal competence included.

THE PEASANTRY

With the sole exception of the land of the Székely, all villages were subjected to seigneuries. Their inhabitants – the peasantry – made up some 86 per cent of the entire population. Most of the peasants were called *iobagiones* (from Hung. *jobbágy*), a legal category that comprised those who possessed at least the eighth part of an original holding (*sessio*). Those possessing less or no land at all were called *inquilini* (Hung. *zsellér*): they were 'householders' if they lived in their own house and 'houseless' if they lived under the roof of another peasant. As the inhabitants of a given estate were rarely registered in their entirety, we can only estimate the relative proportions of the different groups. It seems that around 1500 one peasant in four was counted among the *inquilini*. On most of the estates there also lived *libertini*, peasants who by virtue of some kind of privilege were exempted from seigneurial dues and, in most cases, from royal taxes as well. This privilege was enjoyed, above all, by village reeves, but sometimes also by others, such as millers. Overall, however, the number of *libertini* cannot have amounted to more than 4 to 5 per cent of the peasantry.

At the end of the Middle Ages, the average peasant holding was the half-*sessio* which amounted to 20 to 30 acres. This was sufficient, at best, to provide the tenant with a subsistence income, for the dominant form of cultivation was the two- or the three-field system (that is, only half or two thirds of the arable land was tilled), and the average return was hardly higher than four or five times the seed. Nevertheless, our sources often reveal the presence of rich peasants possessing several entire holdings, dozens of cattle and pigs, important items of movable property, jewellery and even a considerable amount of cash. Most of them had made a fortune from the trade in cattle or wine, and they sometimes accumulated enough capital to rent the ecclesiastical tithe, just as landlords used to do. The extent to which rural society was divided is shown by the scale of the extraordinary taxes paid by the tenants of Korog castle in 1469. While the great majority paid a sum varying from half a florin to three and a half, there were three who paid eight florins and 30 people paid less than 25 pence (a quarter florin). A handful of peasants had to pay no more than ten or 12 pence, and 14 per cent of the tenants were exempt from tax-paying, most of them presumably on account of their poverty.

Differences in wealth were greatest in the market towns, where the bulk of the *inquilini* lived. These people were only modestly burdened with royal taxes, and paid to the Church not the customary tithe but the so-called 'Christian money'. Not all the landless villagers were necessarily poor, however. Some of them made a comfortable income by engaging in handicrafts, while others rented uninhabited land from the landlord for stock-raising or cultivation. Wine production in particular provided a living for many of them. In the year 1502, 70 per cent of the population of the village of Szabadbattyán, near Székesfehérvár, paid no tax except that assessed on their vineyards, which means that they were in fact well-to-do *inquilini*. Nevertheless, the vast majority of the landless peasants should be imagined as a predominantly poor and ever-growing mass of people, who possessed neither livestock nor vineyards, paid no taxes and struggled to maintain themselves as day-labourers hired by rich peasants.

On the whole, by 1500 the living conditions of the peasantry had improved rather than deteriorated. They could freely change their place of residence, they were allowed to bear arms and to hunt and they sometimes even took the field alongside the nobles. They were not afflicted by humiliating costume restrictions: they could clothe themselves with precious furs if they had the means to do so. Famine was a rare visitor among them. Although sometimes there was less bread than necessary – the common crops were wheat and barley – they had no difficulty in supplementing their diet with pulse, meat, fish and even game. As the density of the population remained rather low, there were abundant expanses of woodland and pasture throughout the country. At the beginning of the sixteenth century an average household raised two or three cattle and – at least in the eastern part of the kingdom – no fewer than eight pigs, not to mention poultry. In the 1510s it was quite natural for the servants of the domain of Ónod to eat meat every day, sometimes even twice, and we have no reason to believe that the diet of the peasantry in general was significantly worse.

DEMOGRAPHY

The *iobagiones* are the only group to appear in the royal tax registers and the other sources also generally exclude the rest of the peasantry from their enumeration of villagers. It was they who bore the lion's share of the service dues, seigneurial, royal and ecclesiastical, and all that we know about the overall size of the population is based upon data concerning them.

As regards the distribution of *iobagiones* throughout the kingdom, a more or less reliable picture can be obtained from the accounts of the royal treasurer, Sigismund Ernuszt, bishop of Pécs, arising from his activities in the years 1494 and 1495. They give for both years, among other things, a detailed record of the one-florin tax assessed on each *porta*. In 1494 161,500 florins were assessed upon the same number of *portae* in 43 counties of Hungary proper and 31,500 in the seven Transylvanian counties. The accounts do not contain the figures for 14 southern counties, whose tax was allocated, as was usual, to the captain general of Timiş to cover his expenses. Drawing on Ottoman records of the mid-sixteenth century, the overall number of *portae* in that region can be put at 73,000 at least. The number of tax units in Hungary and

Transylvania around 1500 can therefore be estimated to have been in the region of 266,000. The southern part of Slavonia was exempt from tax-paying on account of the Turkish raids, while the northern part, being smaller, paid a tax of 15,500 florins in all. In that region, the basis of the assessment was the 'hearth' (*fumus*). Since traditionally every 'hearth' paid half a florin, we should count 31,000 'hearths' for that part of Slavonia, though what this meant in terms of *portae* is impossible to determine.

With the exception of Slavonia, there was, on average, one florin, or rather one *porta*, per square kilometre of territory. The most densely populated regions seem to have been the area around Buda and the south-eastern part of Transdanubia. There was an assessment of 2.63 florins per square kilometre in the county of Baranya, and 2.28 in that of Tolna. At the other extreme were some almost uninhabited border counties, such as Orava (0.15 florin per sq. km) and Maramureş (0.18).

Although the number of *portae* is approximately known, it is impossible to formulate an estimate of the overall population of the country that is anything more than a wild guess. Above all, this is because the concepts of '*porta*' and 'household', which had originally been more or less identical, had become increasingly separated in the course of time. Since the royal tax of the peasants was assessed on *portae*, peasant families found it advantageous to live together. Consequently it became commonplace for one *porta* to house more than one family, which in turn led to a drastic reduction of the number of *portae*. At the time of Sigismund's death (1437) some 400,000 were taxed in Hungary and Transylvania, which must have corresponded, even then, to a significantly larger number of households (500,000 to 600,000, according to one estimate). By 1494 the number of *portae* had decreased by a further third. As a consequence, the number of deserted holdings reached an unprecedented level throughout the country. In 1478 only 38 per cent of holdings on the immense estates of the Garai were inhabited, all the others having either an empty house or no dwelling at all.

It is evident, therefore, that the 266,000 *portae* of the late fifteenth century corresponded to a considerably larger number of peasant families, but we do not know exactly how many. Nor do we know what proportion of the entire population paid the *taxa portalis*: that is, what percentage of the population were *iobagiones*. The size of the average peasant household also remains unknown. The only source that sheds some light on the structure of contemporary peasant families is a register made in 1525 concerning the village of Nyék (present-day Vinica) in the county of Hont. This is the only document of its kind listing both the heads of family and the women and children. In this village 348 persons lived in 44 households, which gives an average household of 7.9 persons. Three-quarters of the households were composed of 6 to 10 souls, but there were also among them smaller (3) and much larger (16) ones. There were equal numbers of men and women (174), while there were 112 children, which gives an average of 2.5 children per family. More than half of the households consisted of a couple with 4 or 5 children, but nearly one third of the inhabitants lived in households containing more than one family. It is difficult to judge to what extent this isolated piece of evidence may be used as a basis for generalisations. Two, slightly later sources (both from the mid-sixteenth century) show households with an average of 6.3 and (in the market town of Szigetvár) 13 persons, which seems to suggest that a household in Hungary had more than the usual 4 or 5 members.

All in all it is almost impossible to determine how large the population of Hungary was at the end of the Middle Ages. Indeed, current estimates vary between 2.5 million and 5.5 million, which only serves to underline the prevailing uncertainty surrounding this issue. A recent and extremely careful calculation proposed a minimum of three million, a figure that is almost certainly too low to be accepted without hesitation, especially in view of the fact that in the eighteenth century, after the destruction wreaked by two centuries of almost incessant warfare, nine million people lived on the same territory. It seems, therefore, that the population of Hungary at the end of the Middle Ages (including Slavonia) should not be put at less than 4.5 million. This figure would give an average population density of 14–14.5 people per square kilometre, with a maximum of 37.5 in the county of Baranya and a minimum of two in that of Orava.

The number of settlements in Hungary and Transylvania during the first half of the sixteenth century can be estimated at 16,500, to which should be added some 3,000, most of them small hamlets, in Slavonia. With the latter region excluded, an overall average per settlement of 17.5 *portae* – or 250 people – can be arrived at. However, the size of the settlements varied greatly throughout the country. In the southern and south-western part of Transdanubia, as in the mountainous area along the eastern edge of Transylvania, there were hundreds of tiny hamlets whose population remained under 100 people (7 *portae*). On the Great Plain, on the other hand, much larger villages with 500 to 600 souls (35 to 40 *portae*) were the rule.

ETHNIC GROUPS

Differences in the form and size of settlements were at least partly determined by the ethnic origin of the population. The villages of the Croats, Slovenes and Romanians were mostly small settlements, those of the Hungarians being considerably larger, though the many

Hungarian hamlets of southern Transdanubia were an exception to this rule. As regards the ethnic and linguistic structure of the country at the end of the Middle Ages, we can do no more than offer conjectures, mostly on the basis of toponymical evidence and lists of tenants that have survived in considerable numbers. It is important to note, however, that toponyms should be treated with considerable caution, since foreign place names were sometimes translated by the Hungarian authorities into their own language.

What seems certain is that the ethnic map of the Carpathian basin was nearly as heterogeneous as it is now. The linguistic boundary between the Hungarians on the one hand and the Croats, Slovenes, Germans and Slovakians on the other seems to have changed very little since the end of the Middle Ages. In Slavonia there lived very few Hungarians, present-day Burgenland was mostly inhabited by German-speaking people, while the northern counties of upper Hungary (modern Slovakia) were almost exclusively populated by Slavs. (In the case of Slovakia it must be emphasised, however, that the linguistic boundary is far from identical to the modern state boundary, the Treaty of Trianon having ceded large areas inhabited by Hungarians to the republic of Czechoslovakia.) It is likewise beyond doubt that most of the greater towns were dominated by Germans.

The eastern part of the country seems to have gone through a deeper transformation since the Middle Ages, though its stages cannot be followed exactly. All the evidence that we have seems to suggest that the number of Romanians in Transylvania and in the neighbouring counties of Hungary increased continuously since the fourteenth century and that they outnumbered the Hungarians by the eighteenth century at the latest. In the modern era we find in this region many Romanian-speaking villages with Hungarian names. These were probably Hungarian settlements originally, only becoming 'Romanian' in later centuries. However, details of this transformation can rarely be established with precision.

The ethnic structure and settlement patterns of the Great Plain and eastern Transdanubia have changed even more profoundly since the end of the Middle Ages, mostly as a consequence of the Ottoman expansion. Before the first Turkish incursions around 1390, both the area south of the River Maros and the southern bank of the Drava between Osijek and Belgrade were, judging from toponyms, still inhabited by a mainly Hungarian population. On the territory belonging to the bishopric of Cenad beyond the River Maros there were 168 parishes, while in the three archdeaconries of the bishopric of Pécs that lay beyond the Drava there were 145. All these villages, as well as the smaller settlements of the same areas, bore Hungarian names, which seems to prove that, at least in the beginning, they were inhabited by

Hungarians. By the middle of the sixteenth century nearly one-third of these 313 parishes had become deserted, and those that still existed were already populated by Serbs. The newcomers, of course, converted the old toponyms into their own language, making Vizić from Füzegy, Jebel from Széphely, Ilok from Újlak, and so on. The Ottoman wars further decimated the surviving population, and by 1700 both the Great Plain and the eastern part of Transdanubia had become practically uninhabited. The later, highly mixed ethnic structure of the region dates back to the eighteenth century, when the deserted area was repopulated with German, Hungarian, Serbian, Croatian and Slovakian villages. By that time most of the medieval settlements had vanished and in most cases no traces survive to preserve their memory.

All this hints at destruction on an incredible scale, which led in the long term to an almost complete change in the region's ethnic structure. Details of the process can be guessed from a handful of isolated examples. The town of Eng, one of the largest settlements of Srem, which boasted three parish churches and a Franciscan monastery, is last mentioned on the occasion of an Ottoman incursion in 1391. It appears again in the 1570s as a middle-sized village called Vengince, inhabited by Serbs. In the market town of Horváti, in the county of Vukovar, the former manor house of the notorious ban, John Horváti, was still standing in 1478, but the church was already in ruins and only 12 out of the 47 houses in the settlement were inhabited. By 1565 it had been completely deserted and its land was cultivated by the peasants of the neighbouring village of Mikanovci. Peciu Nou, south of Timişoara, was counted among the market towns in the fifteenth century, but was registered as a deserted village in 1554 and later. In the domain of Cseri, in the same county of Timiş, 70 to 80 small Hungarian and Romanian villages are known to have existed in the time of Sigismund, but their new lord in 1508 found three-quarters of them to be deserted 'on account of the almost incessant incursions of the Turks'.[2] By the 1520s the first wave of Serbian immigration had reached the villages around Timişoara. On the other hand, the Hungarian population of Transdanubia and the region between present-day Novi Sad and Subotica had remained intact for the time being. In 1525 the overwhelming majority of the 1,420 peasants living in the 26 villages of the domain of Futog bore Hungarian names.

On the basis of the evidence that we have, it would be foolhardy to attempt to determine the respective proportions of the different ethnic groups within the overall population of the Carpathian basin. It can nevertheless be said with relative certainty, that – with the sole exception of Slavonia – the Hungarians were still largely dominant, for the most densely populated regions, such as Transdanubia and the Great Plain, were inhabited exclusively by this ethnic group.

THE KINGDOM AND ITS OWNERS

The kingdom of Hungary was one of Europe's largest countries at the end of the Middle Ages. Its territory amounted to 318,000 square kilo-metres, divided between Transylvania (56,000 sq km), Slavonia (23,000) and Hungary proper (239,000). To this should be added Croatia and the four provinces over the River Sava in the south, namely the banates of Jajce, Srebrenik, Šabac and Belgrade. Alto-gether, the countries subjected to the Holy Crown of Saint Stephen covered some 330,000 sq km. In reality, this territory was somewhat smaller, for a part of Spis (762 sq km) had been mortgaged to Poland since 1412, while the Habsburgs had been in possession of six castles and their domains since 1445: Eisenstadt, Hornstein, Forchtenstein and Kobersdorf in the county of Sopron, Kőszeg and Bernstein in that of Vas (1,592 sq km in all).

There were 57 counties in Hungary proper, seven in Transylvania and four in Slavonia. The territory of an average county was 4,000 sq km, but this average conceals enormous differences in size, for the greatest county, Bihor (11,727 sq km) was almost 18 times greater than the smallest one, Turna (657 sq km). The three districts of the *Jász* and the Major and Minor Cumans (5,614 sq km altogether), the banate of Severin (5,500 sq km) and, in Transylvania, the seven Székely seats (12,700 sq km) and the territory of the Saxon autonomies (11,200 sq km) remained outside the comital system.

The distribution of landed property had been profoundly modified since the fourteenth century. The dissolution of the royal domain through generous grants had made the nobility the leading force among landowners. Whereas in 1382 23 per cent of the country's land belonged to the domains of the king and queen, to which should be added the free towns and the mines of precious metals and salt, this proportion had diminished to 6.5 per cent by 1439 and to 4.5 per cent by 1490. At the time of King Matthias's death the combined posses-sions of the king and queen were less extensive than the estates of the greatest landowner, Duke John Corvinus.

Since the main beneficiaries of royal grants were laymen, they profited most from the dissolution of the royal domain. Whereas in 1382 50 per cent of the land was noble property, this figure had grown to 70 per cent by 1490. The free royal towns and the districts of the Saxons of Transyl-vania were also counted among the landowners, but their share, though it also increased, remained insignificant (4.1 per cent). The lands of the Székely seats and the districts of the *Jász* and the Cumans amounted to some 6.5 per cent of the land. The latter gradually lost their original autonomy, however, and by 1500 their status had deteriorated to such an extent that they were regarded as the king's peasant tenants.

The proportion of property in the hands of the Church had grown only slightly since the time of the Angevins (from 12 to 13.5 per cent) and remained at a fairly low level by European standards. Moreover, more than one-third of this property (5.5 per cent) was concentrated in the hands of a few prelates, namely the two archbishops, the 12 bishops and the prior of the Knights Hospitallers of Vrana. A further 3.5 per cent was possessed at the end of the Middle Ages by the 15 cathedral and 31 collegiate chapters, the rest (4.4 per cent) being divided between different, chiefly monastic, orders. The territorial distribution of ecclesiastical property was likewise irregular. The bulk of it had originated from the family property of the Árpádians and was accordingly concentrated in central parts of the country. Whereas in the county of Veszprém 40.5 per cent of the holdings were owned by the Church (1488: see Map 6), in five north-eastern counties this figure was as low as four per cent (1427).

THE CHURCH

The Hungarian Church showed signs of crisis similar to those evident elsewhere in Europe. The bishops were above all barons, then statesmen and men of war. Religious duties came last among their priorities. Some of them had not even been ordained, and those who had taken holy orders normally had their pastoral activities performed by substitutes. An episcopal appointment was the reward for previous services at court or the result of intervention on their behalf by powerful kinsmen. Many of them served at the chancellery or as royal secretaries before becoming bishops, and for such men their main interest remained politics throughout their lives. Moreover, they were obliged to recruit troops in proportion to their estates and were expected to lead them in person in the event of war. At the battle of Mohács in 1526 half of the prelates – two archbishops and five bishops – fell with swords in their hands.

The process that is generally referred to as secularisation also affected the chapters. By the middle of the fourteenth century it had become customary for the simple canons, not to mention the dignitaries, to live in separate houses and to engage, above all, in the management and distribution of their revenues. The end of communal life disrupted the traditional *horarium*. In order to escape this obligation each chapter employed deacons and prebendaries whose duty was not only to pray but also to do all kinds of work that had originally been carried out by the canons themselves, such as the drafting of legal documents, which was the central function of places of authentication.

At the same time, secularisation went hand in hand with a growing appreciation of education. It is beyond doubt that it was the well-to-do clerics who represented the intellectual elite of contemporary Hungary. Half of the bishops and nearly 40 per cent of the canons had studied at various European universities. Most of them, naturally enough, went to Vienna and Cracow, but many travelled to Italy as well. The most brilliant minds among them preserved their taste for humanism and the Renaissance way of life even after returning to their homeland. They collected books, constructed buildings in the most up-to-date Italian style and spent a great deal of money on the education of talented young men. In this respect there was no difference between prelates who had been born nobly and those of common birth. However, that the education of the Hungarian prelacy was relatively advanced was to a great extent due to the fact that it had not become a predominantly aristocratic body. Unlike their counterparts in Germany, the Hungarian nobility were for some reason unwilling to give their younger sons to the Church, though it would have provided a much better living for many of them. Even in the case of families with many sons, it was rare for one of them to enter the Church and be educated therein. The Church was consequently open to practically everyone and this compensated, at least partly, for the lack of social mobility that we have already discussed. Out of the 526 members of four chapters between 1458 and 1526 only 138 were of noble birth, 247 of them being commoners; and of the 53 bishops who were appointed during this period 14 were sons of burghers or even peasants.

Unlike the clergy the monastic orders were evidently in decline. The number of monasteries in Hungary was never large by European standards and many of them had ceased to exist by the end of the Middle Ages. In 1526 the Benedictines had only 45 houses, the Premonstratensians had 11, the Cistercians and the Augustinian Canons, nine each and the canons of the Order of the Holy Sepulchre, two. The underlying reason for the decrease was the evident crisis within the orders themselves. In 1508 the visitation concerning 17 Benedictine monasteries revealed miserable conditions practically everywhere: derelict buildings, with a few drunken monks quarrelling inside, and an almost complete neglect of the Rule. The poorer communities were gradually disappearing altogether, but the wealthier ones also faced serious difficulties. One of the richest monasteries, Somogyvár, whose domain extended over 30 to 40 villages, was governed by a commendator who was even starving the few remaining monks. According to the report two of them were old, the third almost blind, while the remaining two were always on the move, performing the tasks that followed from their abbey being a place of authentication. The situation of the Cistercians was no more enviable, though most of their monasteries were richly endowed. The order 'is languishing miserably and is almost extinct' complained the king to the grand chapter in 1478,[3] and though he did try to help, it was to no avail. Seven out of the still existing 16 Cistercian monasteries had disappeared by 1510, their estates being annexed by the local bishop. That the Premonstratensians faced similar problems can be inferred from the fact that a comprehensive reform of the order took place in 1506. It was directed by Francis Fegyverneki, provost of Šahy, who could rely on the active support of Archbishop Bakócz. An attempt to reform the Benedictines was made at the same time by Matthew Tolnai, abbot of Pannonhalma, but his efforts bore no lasting results.

Completely different was the situation of the orders of hermits. The Paulines, the only order of this kind to be founded in Hungary, remained extremely popular throughout the Middle Ages. Around 1520 they had 70 houses, 15 of which had been founded during the last 50 years. Some of them were abandoned Benedictine and Premonstratensian churches, granted to the Paulines by Matthias and Wladislas II, the others having been founded by barons such as Emeric Szapolyai, Paul Kinizsi, Emeric Perényi, Bartholomew Drágfi and others. Their popularity was to a great extent due to their faultless discipline and to their studiously old-fashioned ideas. The love of science and books was as alien to them as modern mysticism, though their prior general, Gregory Gyöngyösi, who also wrote a history of the order, tried to turn them towards the *devotio moderna* around 1520. Praying was the foremost activity in their houses, which had generally been founded far from other human settlements, hidden in deep forests; but a great deal of manual labour was done as well, since most of the houses were poor, possessing but a few vineyards and mills and occasionally a handful of tenants. The Carthusians remained as strictly disciplined as the Paulines, but they had only four monasteries in Hungary.

Whereas the Paulines were supported above all by the nobility, the mendicant orders enjoyed a more general popularity. They had some 180 friaries around 1520, 107 of which belonged to the two branches of the Franciscans, 42 to the Dominicans, 26 to the Augustinians and four to the Carmelites. Most of them were established in the towns, and in Buda and Pécs all four orders were represented. None of them faced a crisis, least of all the Dominicans, who could rely on the special protection of King Matthias and created as many as ten new communities between 1458 and 1526. Their schools remained highly appreciated, especially the *studium generale* at Buda, and many members of the order went on to study at various European universities, above all in Italy. Nevertheless, the absolute dominance of the more rigorous, 'observant' branch of the Franciscans had been unquestioned since the middle of the fifteenth century. In the 1440s Cardinals

Cesarini and Carvajal handed over to them seven important friaries, among them that of Buda, which had so far been possessed by their rivals, the Conventualists. Henceforth they found unbroken sympathy among the powerful, from John Hunyadi and his son King Matthias to magnates like Nicholas Újlaki and prelates like Denis Szécsi or Thomas Bakócz. Not surprisingly, from 1449 onwards they established 46 new friaries, while the Conventualists had to content themselves with one or two. By the end of the Middle Ages the Hungarian vicariate of the Observant Friars, which comprised 70 monasteries, had become the main basis of the order outside Italy. In 1523 1,472 friars lived in Hungary, which was nearly 30 per cent of the total number to be found throughout the rest of Europe, England included. A friar of Buda, Pelbartus Temesvári (d. 1504), was one of the most popular preachers of the period; his works were each reprinted 18 to 20 times. Another Franciscan, Oswald Laskai (d. 1512), though not as well known as Temesvári, had the same profound influence on his contemporaries and his writings were also published several times in Italy and elsewhere. Unlike the other mendicant orders, the Minorites were willing to settle in the market towns and they seem to have been especially popular there, mainly because many of them were receptive to the social problems of the age. From the 1490s onwards they frequently spoke out in defence of the 'poor' against the arbitrary measures of the 'powerful' and it has been demonstrated that their ideas played a crucial role in preparing the ground for the great peasant war.

A special feature of monastic life in Hungary was that, apart from about 30 communities of the Franciscan Beguines, there were but a few convents for women, a mere 18 at the end of the Middle Ages. Two of them belonged to the Benedictines, another two to the Cistercians, the rest being shared between the Franciscan Clares (8) and the Dominicans (6). The latter, though nominally belonging to a mendicant order, were not bound by the order's vow of poverty. The convent of the Dominican nuns on Marguerite Island and the Clares nunnery of Óbuda were in fact counted among the wealthiest of ecclesiastical establishments. The fact that there were so few nuns in Hungary cannot as yet be accounted for; but it is clear that it was not customary for the surplus daughters of noble families to be sent to cloisters. The phenomenon may be linked in some way to the nobility's general unwillingness to make a career within the Church, but this is no more than conjecture.

It is worth mentioning that since the end of the fourteenth century a few Basilite monasteries had been founded on estates belonging to orthodox lords, but very little is known about their fate. The oldest seems to have been established by the Lithuanian prince, Theodore Koriatovič, lord of Mukačeve (1395–1415). Most of them lay in the southern counties, however, mainly in Srem, and must have been founded by the despots of Serbia who had extensive domains there.

In view of what has been outlined above, it is not surprising that, with the sole exception of the prelates, the political weight of the Church was small. The abbacies, provostships and other benefices like them were distributed, like the bishoprics, in the royal court as rewards for service, the only difference being that more people were involved and the rewards were less substantial. The dominant factor in society and politics was not the Church, but the nobility, within which a crucial role was played by the wealthiest families, a few dozen aristocratic kindreds that were on the way to forming an estate of their own.

THE NOBILITY

The Hungarian nobility formed a fairly populous class. According to a recent and reliable estimate it comprised at least 20,000 families (excluding Slavonia) and amounted to 3.5 to 4.5 per cent of the entire population (depending on the figure we assume for the latter). This is a very high proportion; indeed, only Poland seems to have had a higher proportion of nobles. Yet it is obvious that this mass of people cannot be regarded in the same way as the French *noblesse* or the English gentry. In view of what we have said so far it is evident that the nobility in Hungary meant neither an aristocracy nor an elite, however widely these terms might be interpreted. The word *nobilis* meant no more than a *homo possessionatus*. It referred to anyone having a 'posses-sion': a piece of land, however small, to which he had a special, 'noble' title, which meant in fact that it was free from any dependence, service and obligation. It was by virtue of this possession that he could regard himself as an absolutely free 'inhabitant of the realm', whose only lord was the king and who enjoyed privileges from which the 'non-posses-sioners' were excluded. Consequently, for each nobleman, 'possession', that is land, was of the ultimate value.

Within the class of landowners there were always enormous differ-ences, which further increased during the fifteenth century, for the royal domains that were granted away after 1387 tended to be concen-trated in the hands of a limited number of families. At the time of King Matthias's death, in 1490, 32 aristocratic families were each, on average, in possession of more than 50 villages and 1000 portae, and together they owned 27 per cent of the country's land. The greatest landowner, Duke John Corvinus, was the lord of 30 castles, 17 *castella* (manor houses), 49 market towns and about 1000 villages. It can be estimated that he had some 15,000 *portae*. A further 56 illustrious fami-lies owned another 10 per cent of the land, while 30 per cent was in the possession of the lesser nobility. The latter group included some 80 wealthy and hundreds of well-to-do families, but was overwhelmingly composed of thousands of petty nobles and over ten thousand peasant–nobles.

There were, therefore, considerable differences of wealth, but the nobility as a whole remained a relatively closed caste within Hungarian society until the middle of the fifteenth century. There were only two ways to cross the barrier that separated it from the rest of the population. The first was to obtain a noble estate from the king. This normally happened when a prelate of 'ignoble' birth – the son of a burgher or a peasant – made a fortune and transferred it to his brothers or nephews. The other way concerned only the lowest ranks of the nobility. When a noble girl married a commoner, customary law made it possible for her to receive her inheritance, called the 'daughter's quarter' (*quartalicium*), in land instead of in movable things, which was otherwise the rule. Her descendants on the male line were then regarded as nobles. Such marriages were fairly common, but obviously most usually among the petty nobility. They provided a means of access to the group of the privileged, but rarely further than to their lowest ranks.

About two-thirds of the nobility – some 12–13,000 families, excluding Slavonia – were in fact regarded as peasants and sometimes even treated as such. In the fifteenth and sixteenth centuries they were called 'noblemen with a single holding' (*nobiles unius sessionis*), for they had no tenants at all and their 'estate' consisted of the piece of land that they lived on. That they also enjoyed noble privileges was never contested, but they were subject to certain restrictions. The inferior quality of their nobility was above all reflected in the fact that from 1439 onwards they were frequently compelled to pay the *taxa portalis*, which could never happen to real nobles. Admittedly they paid less than the peasants (normally half as much), but they nevertheless did pay. Their noble land was comparable in size to a normal peasant holding, with the significant difference that the 'lord' was the noble himself. These 'peasant–nobles' were common throughout the country, but in some regions they lived in exceptionally large numbers. Eighty-one per cent of the lay landowners of the county of Veszprém in 1488 belonged to this group (see Map 6). For other counties we have later evidence, based on the tax registers of 1542 and 1554, according to which, respectively, there lived 813 such families in the county of Zala and 919 in that of Vas, most of them in villages where all the inhabitants were nobles. Although these villages were generally tiny settlements, some could be considerably larger: there were 42 noble households in Szentkirályszabadja, 58 in Szentgyörgyvölgy and 62 in Nagyváty. Differences in wealth were surprisingly great. As among the peasants, there existed nobles who lived on a half or a quarter of a normal holding, and we also have evidence of one holding being shared by more than ten families. Out of the 577 peasant nobles who lived in a district of the county of Baranya, three paid a tax of 150 pennies. They probably had servants of their own and seem to have lived in a way that came fairly close to that of some of the wealthier nobles. On the other hand, it is fairly difficult to treat as members of the privileged class those who paid a tax of two or three pence, still less those who did not pay a penny because they were considered 'poor'.

The group of true lords – those having tenants of their own – might have comprised 6,500 to 7,000 families. Those among them who owned fewer than 20 holdings (the size of an average village) would also have been poor. In five north-eastern counties in 1427 two out of three noble families belonged to this category. In 1488, 88 out of 102 landowners in the country of Veszprém remained below the 20-holding limit, and 70 per cent of them had fewer than six tenants. It is evident that the lesser nobility were hardly distinguishable socially from the peasant–nobles, and they were often treated in the same way. They did not pay tax, of course, but their political rights – attending the diet and so on – were as limited as those of the peasant–nobles.

The elite of the county nobility was composed of the 'well-to-do' (*bene possessionatus*) families: those whose wealth – ranging from 20 to hundreds of holdings – assured a decent living. The members of this group were the leading figures in the county assemblies, and it was mostly from among these men that the count's deputies, the members of the diets as well as the castellans, stewards and leading retainers of the barons were chosen. They were distinguished from the lesser nobility by the title of *egregius*. At first they were fairly numerous. In 1427 in the five counties of Šariš, Gemer, Abaúj, Ung and Turna some 90 families (excluding the barons) had a landed wealth exceeding 20 holdings. Yet the course of natural evolution, at all levels of society, led towards an ever increasing polarisation. Sooner or later every family was visited by one or other of those implacable enemies of the nobility, impoverishment or extinction, and few were able to avoid both.

Impoverishment was a natural consequence of repeated partitions, each son having the right to an equal share in the paternal inheritance. The general form of division since the middle of the fourteenth century was that the brothers were given equal parts in each of their villages, which meant in fact that the division concerned the peasant holdings only, the familial property itself, whatever its size, remaining intact. That part of a given village that was accorded to one of the brothers was called a 'portion' (*portio possessionaria*). This was not a parcel of land but a certain number of peasant holdings. The landed wealth of practically all the nobles was made up of such portions, even the poorest nobleman having one or two. Wealthier noblemen owned parts of 30 to 40 villages, while baronial fortunes were often dispersed in more than 100 settlements. The process of impoverishment due to estate partitions is perfectly illustrated by the example of the Bánffy, the most illustrious kindred in Transylvania. Their wealth originally consisted of three castle lordships, containing 68 villages altogether, and their ancestor, Stephen (d. 1459), was accordingly a leading baron in the age of John Hunyadi. But Stephen's four sons had numerous offspring, and by 1526 the family estate had been divided between 14 adult members, each of them having a tiny portion in every village. The economic unity of the estate gradually disintegrated and then disappeared altogether, and the family soon lived like, and took spouses from, the well-to-do gentry.

Landowners employed various means to thwart this process. Brothers sometimes avoided partition by allowing the eldest to administer the family estate. In families with several sons, not all of them would marry. By far the most usual practice was the restriction of the number of children, but families that adopted this method would die out sooner or later. Their landed wealth devolved upon the Crown and was generally incorporated in a greater fortune. Between 1417 and 1433 Ban John Maróti acquired the estates of four extinct families, consisting altogether of 40 villages. Out of the 36 baronial families that could be regarded as the most illustrious at the time of Sigismund's death, 11 had disappeared by 1490, a further six by 1526, and only eight existed in 1570. The same lines of development can be observed among the lesser nobility. Between 1398 and 1538, 16 out of 45 noble families in the county of Ung disappeared, most of them presumably dying out, and the inheritances of six of them were appropriated by barons. A further ten families sank into the ranks of the peasant–nobles. The latter were so prolific that the peasants gradually disappeared from the villages, their place being taken by nobles.

As a result of the repeated estate partitions both the land and the noble society of each county were gradually divided into two parts. Some of the villages consisted of a large number of portions, possessed by poor or relatively wealthier nobles, generally in the greatest entanglement, for there were very few noble villages with a single family as the lord. The remaining villages that were not Church property were owned by well-to-do families and generally formed part of a lordship. Although it was quite often the case that lords had portions in villages owned by nobles, it was by no means typical.

At the end of the fifteenth century we find 290 castles in lay hands. Most of them were centres of a domain, but naturally there were exceptions. The castle of Oponice (Appony), for instance, whose impressive ruins can still be seen near Nitra, was one of them. Its owners, the Apponyi, had only 11 villages, dispersed throughout the county, and these were shared by the three branches of the family. They lived like those nobles who lacked castles, and it would be difficult to count them among the magnates. Yet if we leave out of consideration the few similar exceptions, it is clear that the appurtenances of the castles were sharply distinguished from the villages of the nobility, and as sharp as this was the social divide that separated the small group of those possessing castles from the great mass of the common nobles.

THE MAGNATES

It was from this narrow circle of wealthy families that the class of magnates was formed. With the exception of a handful of 'perpetual counts', there were no hereditary titles in Hungary before the modern period. Membership of the new aristocracy that came into being in the fifteenth century depended not upon titles but upon a group of privileges that became attached to a limited number of families. Two of these prerogatives were exceptionally important because of their political consequences. First, the head of a magnate family had a hereditary seat on the royal council and in the diet; and, second, he had the right to his own 'banner', that is, to set up and lead a military contingent of his own. These privileges had originally been attached to the person of a 'baron'; that is, they had been exclusively enjoyed by the chief office-holders of the kingdom. The process by which a hereditary class of magnates came into being began with the gradual, and more or less informal, extension of these privileges to a number of families, and ended with the legal fixing of the list of privileged lords. It is from this time on that one can speak, in the legal sense, of a hereditary class of magnates in Hungary.

The process was naturally a long one. First the law of 1397 sought to define the group of those powerful lords who held no office, calling them 'sons of barons' (*filii baronum*), a name later replaced by *magnates* or *potentes*. Under Sigismund some of them were already invited to the royal council despite not being office holders, and after 1428 there is some evidence that they led contingents of their own, like a baron. The process was greatly accelerated by the triumph of the Estates and the consolidation of the diet. From 1439 it was customary for the most powerful lords to be invited to both the council and the parliament. In the civil war that broke out in 1440 they all took the field at the head of their own armies, and with growing frequency they were accorded the title of *magnificus*, otherwise restricted to the barons. In the Treaty of Sankt Pölten of 1487 they are enumerated as 'natural barons' (*barones naturales*) after the 'barons of office' (*barones ex officio*), that is, the chief dignitaries of the realm.[4] The process culminated in article 22 of the

law of 1498, which officially authorised the heads of the greatest families to hold military contingents of their own. It named 38 lords
(completed by the Croatian counts, Frankopan and of Corbavia), each
of whom had the right to equip his own contingent and lead it to war
under his own banner. All of these 'lords of banner' (*domini banderiati*)
also had the right to attend the sessions of the royal council. These
privileges were, in theory at least, personal, but, since they were
attached to the head of each family by virtue of his wealth, they were in
practice regarded as hereditary. Therefore, the law institutionalised the
notion of hereditary aristocracy by determining the group of families
to be counted among the barons. In 1500 the right to equip a separate
contingent was extended to ten influential members of the household,
but the *decempersonatus*, as it was called, could not be inherited and the
so-called *decemviri* were not necessarily given access to the royal
council.

The enactment of aristocratic privileges went against the interests of
the nobility, for it infringed the general principle, established in 1351,
according to which all noblemen enjoyed one and the same 'liberty',
independently of their wealth or birth. The leading ideologist of the
common nobles, Stephen Werbőczy, accordingly denied the existence
of a hereditary aristocracy. The 'real' barons of the kingdom (*veri
barones regni*), he argued, are the chief office-holders; the others, who
are generally referred to by this name, are merely 'nominal barons'
(*barones solo nomine*).[5] Yet even Werbőczy was unable to reverse the *fait
accompli*: the hereditary aristocracy had been born and its existence
legally acknowledged.

Parallel to the legal process was a profound social transformation.
The new aristocracy pursued a completely new lifestyle, radically
different from that which had characterised the barons of the Angevin
era. At that time, the normal scene of a baron's life was the court,
whence he occasionally visited his family estates. He was obliged to live
at court, which was the only source of rank and wealth, and where all
important matters were decided. From the middle of the fifteenth
century some of the court's functions were assumed by the magnate
residences. The barons now spent most of their time on their estates,
and only came to the royal court or to the diet when their presence
there was judged necessary. Naturally, their primary aim remained the
enhancement of their own family's power, but in order to achieve this it
was becoming sufficient to meet their own peers, many of the most
important decisions now being made outside the court. Their castles
were gradually transformed into aristocratic residences. From the
beginning of the fifteenth century the manor houses that had been
used in the past, which were mostly timber constructions, were
replaced by modern, relatively comfortable stone castles, built not on

inaccessible rocks far away in the mountains but near, or in the middle of, flourishing market towns, and designed to be luxurious family homes. In their castles the barons organised quasi-royal courts of their own noble retainers. Each baron had his own 'chancellor', 'marshal' (*magister curie*) and other dignitaries, sometimes even a physician, and his permanent retinue was to be the core of his private army in the event of war. The barons collected their revenues in the centre of their estates, and entrusted their administration, as King Matthias did, to a *provisor curiae*. Their treasures and charters were also generally held securely in the new residences, though some of them continued to store these precious items in one of their inaccessible eyries. It may have been from the end of the fifteenth century that the use of the written word became a normal means of domanial administration; at least the first known account books and registers (*urbarium*), listing the service dues and obligations of tenants, were drawn up at that time. Yet it would still be an exaggeration to speak about the economic activity of the aristocracy in general. Almost none of the barons had a demesne (*allodium*) of his own, and wine was the only produce in whose production they took a major interest. In some cases as much as half of their income derived from the sale of wine, the rest coming from taxing their peasants, from tolls and from the royal taxes that were usurped after 1490.

The castellans and members of the baronial following were recruited from among the lesser nobility. In this way an important part of the county nobility gravitated towards the greatest landowners of each county. The aristocratic residences became the natural centres of social and political life, and it was now there, rather than at the royal court, that the surrounding nobility sought their fortune.

Chapter 20

The Age of the Jagiellonian Kings
(1490–1526)

The death of Matthias relieved the Estates of an enormous amount of pressure. The autocratic habits that the king had assumed during the last decade of his rule irritated both his partisans and his enemies, whether prelates, barons or nobles. Their programme was formulated by Stephen Szapolyai some two weeks after the ruler's death: it was 'to relieve Hungary of the trouble and oppression from which it had suffered so far.'[1] This desire determined the choice of Matthias's successor.

KING WLADISLAS II

There were three candidates, one Habsburg and two Jagiellonians, who entered the lists alongside John Corvinus. The king of the Romans, Maximilian, who had led his father's war against Matthias, based his claim on the treaty of 1463. Wladislas, king of Bohemia, and his younger brother, John Albert, heir to the Polish throne, were rival claimants, both deriving their right from their mother, a sister of Ladislaus V. The competition was won by Wladislas. Peaceful and irresolute, of the three candidates he least fitted the traditional ideals of the Hungarian nobility; but in fact he was not expected to do so. When the diet convened on 17 May 1490, it soon became clear that he had the support of the most influential barons and prelates. Corvinus decided to take up arms. He seized the royal treasury and mobilised his partisans in Transdanubia and the southern counties, but the army of the barons, led by Stephen Bátori and Paul Kinizsi, followed suit and dispersed Corvinus's troops on 4 July near Gyönk in Tolna. On 15 July Wladislas, who was already on the way to Hungary, was elected as king by the barons. On 31 July he accepted the conditions that they presented to him and was crowned at Székesfehérvár on 21 September. Corvinus signed an agreement with the new ruler by which he handed over the royal castles that were in his custody, but he was allowed to retain his 30 castles in Hungary along with his duchies in Silesia and was honoured with the title of Duke of Slavonia. His immense wealth had been intended by his father to serve as a base upon which royal authority could be founded, but the barons' resistance prevented it from fulfilling its role.

Wladislas's victory had been helped by the fact that he had gained the support of Queen Beatrice, who, because of her considerable wealth, was still an important factor in politics. During her husband's lifetime she had done her utmost to prevent her stepson's succession. She was determined to have a word in the kingdom's government and her moment seemed now to have come. At the time of his election Wladislas had promised to marry her, and the ceremony was indeed carried out secretly by Thomas Bakócz, bishop of Győr, two weeks after the coronation. Beatrice immediately raised money on part of her estates in order to help her new husband. Only gradually did she realise that she had been deceived. Following the counsel of Bakócz himself, the king had declared before the wedding, in the presence of witnesses, that the marriage would not be valid since he was acting 'under constraint'.[2] As soon as he had consolidated his rule, he initiated the divorce, but the affair soon became an international scandal and it took no fewer than nine years for the marriage to be dissolved by Pope Alexander VI. Beatrice's domains were then confiscated and the queen returned to Naples where she passed her days in mourning until her death in 1508.

The new ruler spent a whole year in gaining ascendancy over his rivals, and in the meantime Matthias's empire fell apart. Immediately after the king's death revolt broke out in Moravia, Lausitz and Silesia and these territories returned as a matter of course to the crown of Bohemia. The Estates never managed to get the 400,000 florins that had once been stipulated as the condition for their redemption. Matthias's conquests in Austria were also lost within a couple of months. Maximilian received Vienna's homage as early as August 1490 and he soon succeeded in rallying several of Corvinus's former supporters as well. One of the latter, Jacob Székely, captain of Radkersburg, handed the Styrian castles over to him. In November Maximilian advanced as far as Buda, but lack of money soon forced him to give up his plans in Hungary. The castles that he had occupied on his march through Transdanubia were lost in no time and most of his partisans deserted him. Moreover, a new turn of events in the West – the unexpected prospect of acquiring Brittany – also prompted him to abandon his claim. Since his rival was also interested in a swift settlement of their conflict, the peace treaty was signed at Pressburg on 7 November 1491. Wladislas renounced all of Matthias's conquests in Austria and surrendered the seigneuries that had been held by the Habsburgs as a mortgage from Hungary since 1445, evacuated the castles still in Hungarian hands and acknowledged the Habsburgs' hereditary right to the Hungarian throne that had been declared in 1463. Moreover, he engaged himself to pay an indemnity of 100,000 florins. In view of the fact that Wladislas had not suffered a military defeat, the treaty was surprisingly unfavourable to the Hungarians. It is small wonder that the diet that convened in February 1492 reacted with a stormy protest, accused the authors of treachery and demanded their immediate punishment. Indeed, 'it almost came to a revolt.'[3] Only after the crowd had dispersed did the king succeed in persuading the barons and the counties to ratify the treaty in separate declarations.

After Maximilian's departure, Wladislas was finally able to concentrate his forces against John Albert, his other rival. As early as the summer of 1490 the prince of Poland occupied some border castles, marched against Pest, then turned back and laid siege to Košice. But a renewed attack, at the end of 1491, was halted by the troops withdrawn from Austria and Moravia. He was soon driven out of Hungary permanently and forced to make peace with his brother. Henceforth, Wladislas never ceased to emphasise that it was thanks to him that the long-desired restoration of order in the realm had been achieved.

At the time of his election Wladislas promised that he would reside at Buda and he did indeed regard himself, first and foremost, as king of Hungary. Out of the 26 years of his reign he spent barely more than two in Bohemia: two four-month sojourns in 1497 and 1502 were followed by two longer stays in 1509–11. When in Hungary he rarely left his capital and there were, in fact, few reasons for him to do so. He waged but a single war and was little attracted by the prospect of meetings with neighbouring rulers. He felt comfortable at home, especially if he could hunt, was well fed and was not bothered by governmental matters. He had no desire to influence the course of events, possibly because he realised that he would be unable to do so. He became somewhat more active only when his divorce was finally declared and he could remarry. His young bride soon died, however, and the king relapsed into apathy, never again to break out of it. He conscientiously attended the meetings of the royal council, but let the chancellor preside and took no part in decision-making. 'All right': that was all he would say, generally in Czech, which earned him the nickname '*dobře*' ('good'). It caused some excitement when once he added: 'Well, do it.'

THE NEW PARLIAMENTARY ERA

The bishop of Oradea, John Filipec, warned the recently elected Wladislas, and not without reason, that the Hungarians 'are bellicose and fierce' and 'need to be forced to obedience with a rod of iron'.[4] Such a coercive object not being to hand, the change of ruler had very grave consequences. A new political regime, unprecedented in the constitutional history of the kingdom, was born and was to last until 1526. Formally, it did not bring about a change: Hungary remained a monarchy as it had been before. Novelty resided in the defective functioning of central authority, which gradually broke down almost completely. The regime's measures soon provoked a serious internal crisis whose final outcome, the peasant revolt of 1514, threatened for a moment to sweep it away altogether. The Ottoman expansion presented the new political order with an even more serious menace, with which it was wholly unable to cope.

The accession of Wladislas led to only two minor modifications within the regime which, moreover, did not seem to concern constitutional principles. On the one hand political decisions were henceforth made collectively by the royal council instead of by the weak ruler, and as a consequence the government of the realm became oligarchic in nature. On the other hand, the diet, which had been forced into abeyance by Matthias, began once again to function as a regular organ of power. Between 1491 and 1526 the diet assembled no fewer than 43 times. There were six years when two sessions were held and in 1518 there were three.

Since the diet was intended to represent the 'university' of the realm, it consisted of the free landowners (who were counted among the *regnicolae*) or their representatives. One part of the diet – later known as the Upper House – was composed of the prelates, barons and a group of 'notables' (*proceres*), that is, the members of the royal council, while the other part – later to become the Lower House – represented above all the county nobility. The two estates held their assemblies separately but at the same place.

The composition of the assembly, which was therefore not entirely unlike the English parliament, had been gradually fixed during the course of the fifteenth century. Whereas the nobility were invited universally, the members of the 'Upper House' were entitled to a personal invitation. It was obvious from the beginning that the latter group should comprise the 'leading' personalities of the kingdom but, as in England, it took some time for their ranks to crystallise permanently. The barons, the highest office-holders and those magnates who were considered equal to them by virtue of their wealth could participate as a matter of course; their number, as we have seen, was determined by the law of 1498. The remaining part of the 'Upper House' consisted of the somewhat ill-defined group of 'notables': persons who were not barons in any sense but were nevertheless expected to take part in deliberations. These included the bans of the southern border castles, the deputies of the chief judges, some of the counts and a handful of distinguished nobles who had been elected by the diet to be members of the council.

The counties had long been represented (as early as 1385) by elected envoys whose number was normally four for each county. It was in 1446, when Hunyadi was elected governor, that the nobility in its entirety was for the first time invited. The diet of 1495 once again declared the nobility's obligation to appear in person, while that of 1498 threatened to punish absentees. Yet it remained normal for the counties to send envoys; it was exceptional for the nobility to assemble in great numbers and – as in 1518 at Bač – under arms. If the assembly was summoned to Buda or Pest, which was generally the case, the lords held their discussions in the castle, their retainers and the nobility camping on the other side of the Danube, on the field called Rákos near Pest, which had regularly been used for similar purposes since the reign of Andrew III. By 1500 the word 'Rákos' had come to stand for crowded assemblies to such an extent that the Estates of Poland later gave the name *rokosz* to their own institution of a similar character. It is also worthy of note that these assemblies normally represented the landowners of Hungary proper, only rarely receiving envoys from Transylvania and Slavonia. Theoretically the envoys of the royal towns also had the right to participate, but they were frequently excluded and even if present could not take part in the decision-making process. Since the Church did not form a separate estate and was represented by a handful of prelates, the diet practically became an organ of the nobility.

OLD AND NEW IDEAS

The ideology that was to determine the historical and political thinking of the nobility for centuries was born in the heat of parliamentary debate. In the definitive formulation and diffusion of this ideology, a decisive role seems to have been played by Stephen Werbőczy, a member of the lesser nobility of Ugoča. Werbőczy's career was spectacularly successful. From being a simple notary at the chancellery he rose to become one of the most distinguished personalities of the reign of Wladislas II. A talented rhetorician, he had long been a well-known figure of the diets when in 1502 he became the judge royal's protonotary. He had a unique knowledge of Hungarian common law and was well-read in history and Roman law. He was, therefore, more suited than any of his contemporaries to compile the corpus of Hungarian customary law, a work he completed in 1514. His book, consisting of three parts – concerning persons, substantial law and procedure – and referred to as the Tripartite, was a masterpiece of its genre: a logical, concise and lucid summary of contemporary Hungarian legal customs that had never before been codified. The author intended his work to become an official law-code but the court refused to sanction it and the Tripartite was never enacted. In 1517 Werbőczy had it printed at Vienna but it only became popular after his death. It has had no fewer than 51 editions since 1545 and it remained the favourite reading, if not the Bible, of the nobility until the beginning of the modern era.

Werbőczy developed his ideas from a mixture of pagan traditions and late medieval political theories. For historical facts and the basic elements of constitutional law he turned to Simon Kézai and János Thuróczy, successfully adapting their ideas to the expectations of his own age. No one was more aware than he of the kind of spiritual nourishment that the nobility needed and no one could have formulated it as simply and effectively as he did. His work contained everything that a nobleman wanted to hear, whether he was rich or poor, educated or illiterate. He accounted for the nobility's superiority over the other classes of society and explained why it was their exclusive privilege to govern the kingdom.

The nobility, in the eyes of Werbőczy, was in fact identical to the Hungarian people, the 'nation' (*gens, natio*). They had come from the land of the 'Scythians', a people of legendary prowess, where Hunor and Magor, the ancestors of the Huns and Hungarians, had lived. They were the sons of Nimrod, grandson of Ham (or, alternatively, the sons of Magog, son of Japhet), and their descendant was Attila, who had left his homeland to conquer the land of Hungary. The Magyars of Árpád were his heirs and merely recovered their own land 'at the price of their blood', a fact that gave them a title to rule over it. Thuróczy had still thought that the Huns and the Magyars were merely akin to each other, but Werbőczy suggested that they were one and the same people, and that Attila, before whose terrible power Europe had once trembled, had in fact been king of the Magyars.

The Hungarians inherited their moral values and customs from the 'Scythians', who had once defeated even Darius and Alexander the Great. Their true vocation was war, which was the only activity that was noble enough to suit them. Their prowess was unrivalled among the peoples of the world and since abandoning their pagan beliefs they had been the only 'shield and bulwark' (*clipeus et antemurale*) of Christendom. According to the 'Scythian' laws, all the members of the nation were free and equal to one another; but, since those who refused to fight were punished severely, only the courageous were able to preserve their ancient liberty. Those who had shown cowardice were condemned to death or to 'perpetual serfdom and villeinage' (*perpetua servitus et rusticitas*).[5] Their descendants were the peasants, who also belonged to the Hungarian people (*populus*) in the broader sense of the word, but who were deprived for ever of those privileges that were enjoyed by the true 'regnicoles'.

These privileges were summarised in four points, based on the Golden Bull, by the most famous chapter of the Tripartite, the so-called *Primae Nonus* (the ninth chapter of the first part). According to Werbőczy, nobles 'cannot be arrested by anyone...without a formal summons and a lawful sentence'; 'they are not subjected to the power of anyone with the sole exception of their lawful ruler'; 'they cannot be impeded in the free use of their rights and revenues that are found within the boundaries of their estate'; and, finally, they have the right to oppose the ruler without being guilty of the crime of infidelity if the latter tries to encroach upon their privileges.

The idea of the ancient 'Scythian' freedom also implied that the ultimate source of power was the 'people'. Power was conferred not by hereditary right but by the free election of the 'people'. It was by such election that both Attila and Saint Stephen had become kings of the Hungarians. The ruler's chief obligation was to govern in a way that would promote the welfare of the people, but he was free to reward the meritorious by making them nobles. While the freedom of the people dates back to ancient times, nobility had not existed before the introduction of the institution of kingship, for the only source for the noble condition was royal authority. The people and their king are bound together by the Holy Crown in a kind of mystical unity. Although the Crown is worn by the king, it is in fact a symbol of the realm and of the entire community, and every nobleman is *ipso facto* a 'member of the Holy Crown'. The right to elect a king always reverts to the community precisely because it is the real owner of the Holy Crown. According to this theory, then, the source of royal authority is the noble estate. This complicated theory – which is normally referred to as 'the doctrine of the Holy Crown' – provided the ideological foundation for a republic of nobles. On the one hand it seemed to degrade the ruler to a simple 'civil servant' in the hands of the Estates; on the other, it led to the highly practical conclusion that the nobleman owed fidelity not to the king but to the Crown, that is, to the 'realm', which was, of course, identical to the Estates.

The fact that this 'Scythian' identity became the central element of noble ideology had important consequences. It made the nobility inclined to think in terms of historical fictions and to cherish illusions. They thought that they had the right to rule their subjects without having to meet any obligations. It also involved an extreme respect for traditions, and gave birth to what was an early form of 'nationalism'. The nobility's ideology overvalued everything that was, or was thought to be, ancient, and regarded everything that seemed strange or unusual with aversion or even hostility. This attitude was entirely in keeping with the nobility's traditional xenophobia, for it had always been a habit to blame the unwanted 'foreigners' for all the sufferings of the realm, and Werbőczy knew perfectly how to drive this feeling to the extreme, something he did in the diet of 1505. The nobles also took much delight in hearing about 'Scythian' values, for they imagined that they recognised their own virtues in them. Among the petty nobility the ideal of martial simplicity must have become especially popular, for it made a virtue out of their misery and illiteracy. 'It is well known that our Hungarians had always been more willing to wield weapons or tools with which they could sow or harvest than to read Cicero, Livy, Sallust or Aulus Gellius.'[6] It must have been comforting to hear that.

It is difficult, however, to determine to what extent these values had already become part of the ideology of the nobility during Werbőczy's time. What is certain is that the lower gentry did not as yet act as a homogeneous political force. According to an often cited remark made in 1525 by the papal nuncio, Burgio, in Hungary there were three kinds of nobles: some were fighting on the borders, others lived on their estates and abstained from politics, while those who did engage in political activity were dependent on their lords. It seems, in fact, that only the upper stratum of the gentry, titled *egregii* and comprising hardly more than a few hundred families, played a continual role in public life. From among them were drawn the active members of the diets, the spokesmen of the Estates and the elected assessors of the royal council. Most of these men are known to have belonged to one of the baronial groups and some of them even became retainers of a magnate. Therefore, the political struggles that are so characteristic of the period did not involve conflict between the barons and the nobility, but were actually fought between various baronial groups and their adherents.

THE STAFF OF GOVERNMENT

The kingdom was nominally governed by the royal council, but its 60 to 70 members only rarely came together fully. Everyday affairs were dealt with by eight to twelve persons, forming something of an inner council, who took those decisions concerning domestic and foreign affairs that did not need parliamentary sanction. Its constant members were the holders of the chief governmental offices: the palatine, the judge royal, the *magister tavarnicorum*, the master of the court and some of the prelates. Especially important was the role of the chancellor, who kept the royal seals and was therefore in the best position to influence the king. Whatever the ruler continued to have a say in – such as royal grants, the principles of foreign policy and appointments to ecclesiastical benefices – was in fact decided by the chancellor.

At the beginning, when the offices of the chancellor and the palatine remained unfilled, the reins of power were in the hands of Urban Nagylucsei, bishop of Eger, who was at the same time treasurer and head of the palatine's court. He played a prominent role in the election of Wladislas. After his death in 1491 both his bishopric and his influence were transferred to Thomas Bakócz, who once again bore the title of arch- and secret chancellor. Bakócz, like his predecessor, came from a peasant family and had been appointed bishop of Győr by King Matthias. In 1498 he gave the see of Eger to the young Ippolito d'Este in return for the archbishopric of Esztergom, and obtained the cardinal's hat two years later. His intelligence and erudition were never questioned. He had studied in Vienna and at several Italian universities and his taste for Renaissance art is well illustrated by the fine chapel that he erected at Esztergom and which somehow survived the Ottoman era. Yet his opponents accused him, and not without reason, of nepotism and excessive greed. That he obtained bishoprics and other ecclesiastical benefices for several of his kinsmen can be interpreted as part of his policy. But it remains a fact that he missed not a single opportunity to increase his own lands. His favourite method was to sign treaties of inheritance with lords without a heir. His nephews, who were to inherit his enormous acquisitions, were the ancestors of the Counts Erdődy, one of the most respected magnate dynasties of modern Hungary.

Bakócz was far from popular among the Estates, who tried to restrain his power whenever they could. At the diet of 1497 they were successful in persuading the king to take the seals from the archbishop. Yet Bakócz was able to retain his title of arch-chancellor until his death in 1521 and also much of his influence until the peasant war of 1514. The only difference was that the seals were henceforth handled by his own creature, George Szatmári. Szatmári came from a family of burghers of Košice and was linked by ties of friendship and marriage to the Thurzó, the great entrepreneurs of the period. He too had studied in Italy and had been Bakócz's closest assistant as a royal secretary since 1494. In 1499 he became a bishop and from 1503 he took an active part in government as secret chancellor. No less than Bakócz, Szatmári proved able to keep political power firmly in his hands, so his promotion to chancellor did not significantly modify the nature of government. The two prelates, while occasionally disagreeing on questions of foreign policy, continued to form a united front against the aspirations of the Estates.

Nagylucsei, Bakócz and Szatmári all used their influence in order to put their relatives and protégés in key positions, whether governmental or ecclesiastical. It was, therefore, not without reason that contemporaries thought that the chancellor was the 'master of all matters'. He had a say in the distribution of dignities, and the governmental apparatus was almost wholly dependent on him. The treasurer and the Personal were generally his men, as were the royal secretaries (numbering two from 1500, four from 1502 and six from 1509), who were the chief agents of his power. The principal duty of the secretaries was to report on cases in the council, but in fact they worked under the immediate direction of the chancellor and were not controlled by the council. It was from this group that most of the prelates were recruited: 13 out of Wladislas's 17 secretaries ended their careers as bishops.

These government officials resembled a group of 'civil servants'. They came from all layers of society, from the nobility as well as from the peasantry, but what they had in common were their tastes, mentality and political orientation. Though most of them worked within the Church, they thought and acted as laymen. Most of them had been educated at Italian universities and proved to be generous patrons of art in their homeland. Nor did they lack the skill they were expected to display as leading officials. All of them were true representatives of the state, and if its machinery did not function properly, it was not because they did not know how to make it work.

In addition to these officials only a handful of lay dignitaries had a say in decision-making. The very first among them was naturally the palatine. This office was held successively by three barons of enormous wealth, Stephen Szapolyai (1492–99), Peter Geréb (1500–03) and Emeric Perényi (1504–19), all of whom were key figures of the period. While the great majority of the other barons also came from aristocratic families, the most influential ones were often drawn from a gentry background – men like the *magister tavarnicorum*, Blaise Ráskai; the seneschal, Moses Buzlai; or the future judge royal, Ambrose Sárkány. Although not all of them were consequent allies of the chancellors, they too had some affinity for Italian culture and were as willing as the clerics to block the political ambitions of the nobility.

This was not easy to achieve, however, for the king, though willing to do what was expected of him, was severely restricted in his freedom of manoeuvre. Before his election, he had to promise that he would respect the liberties of the Estates, annul the 'innovations' that King Matthias had introduced 'to their detriment and oppression', and not establish new ones, let alone levy extraordinary taxes.[7] He agreed not to confer ecclesiastical and lay dignities on anyone other than 'regnicoles', nor was he allowed to grant estates to foreigners or to take counsel with them. The Crown was to be in the custody of the prelates and the barons who entrusted it to 'crown guards', elected by them. These conditions were enacted by the diet of 1492 and completed by other articles, among which was an unprecedented one (annulled six years later), that the ruler could not grant away estates with more than 100 tenants without the council's consent.

THE DIET'S AMBITIONS

The diet was seemingly enjoying its newly won authority. It enacted hundreds of articles, with some of them being repeated several times – a sure sign that they had not been carried out. Some dispositions even contradicted each other, which seems to reflect the opposing interests that led to their enactment. Not all of them came into force, some decisions not having been sanctioned by the king, yet more laws were enacted in the course of a mere 36 years than during the previous five centuries.

The leaders of the nobility were aware that the court constituted the main obstacle to their political ambitions. One of their chief aims was therefore to have representatives in the law courts and on the royal council, at the same time enhancing the authority of these bodies. The first fruit of their efforts came in 1495, when the noble jurors (*assessor*) of the octaval courts gained predominance over the barons and prelates sitting there. In 1498 eight of these nobles were admitted onto the royal council. In 1507 it was decreed that no office could be filled without the council's consent, and in 1511 administration of the extraordinary tax was taken away from the royal treasurer and entrusted to a baron and a nobleman as elected officers of the Estates. The nobility also tried to secure a salary of 3d per *porta* for their representatives on the royal council, but their efforts were thwarted by the king. Another of their chief objectives was to widen the competence of the county elite. It was decreed in 1495 that every landowner, whatever his social status, was to be subjected to the county authorities; also, that the count should not appoint his deputy without the consent of the local nobility and should not be permitted to act without authorisation from them. The granting of the count's office 'perpetually', i.e. hereditarily, by the ruler was also repeatedly forbidden.

Some of the nobility's efforts were directed against the Church and these were fully supported by the lay barons. Laws were enacted against the jurisdiction of the Holy See and the institution of ecclesiastical attorneys was prohibited. Another important achievement was that henceforth the 'ninth' due to the lord was to be collected before the tithe, a measure that had the effect of allowing the lord to take 11 per cent of the crop and the Church only nine per cent.

That the nobility also turned against the towns was no surprise. The underlying reasons for their dislike were, firstly, that the burghers had their own laws, which were different from common law; and, secondly, that they were, as a rule, German speaking. This antipathy, mutual by its very nature, was now coloured by conflicting economic interests, as there were increasing numbers of nobles who wished to sell their produce on the market. The most irritating of the towns' privileges was that within their walls nobles had the same status as burghers and were consequently obliged to pay tax on their houses. Not surprisingly, as early as 1492 the diet decreed that the houses of the nobility and clergy in Buda should be exempted from any tax. In 1498 a further series of dispositions directed against the towns was accepted. It was decreed that no tolls should be levied on the merchandise of noblemen; that cases concerning peasants living on the domains of the towns should be tried by the county court; that the vineyards of burghers lying on noble land should be subject to the lord's court and taxed by the same 'ninth' as the vineyards of peasants. The opinion that the burghers should not be counted among the 'regnicoles' became widely accepted and it was in 1508 that their envoys were invited to the diet for the last time.

It is evident, however, that it was the peasantry that suffered most from the rule of the Estates. There had been indications that the nobility would curb the liberties of their peasants as soon as they had the means to do so. Non-nobles had been denied the right of testifying against nobles as early as 1486. In 1500 peasants were for the first time prohibited from hunting. It was also enacted that persons born from peasant parents could not become judges at the chief courts. The most important development, however, was the gradual limitation of the tenants' rights of movement. The Estates' consent to the levy of the annual subsidy had been dependent since 1458 upon the temporary suspension of that liberty. Since the tax was levied every year, freedom of movement was prohibited, in theory at least, almost continuously. Yet it is evident from the sources that peasants could move quite freely under Matthias and that they were not really prevented from doing so before 1490. In 1492 the county court was authorised to judge the grievances of tenants desiring to move to another lord. In 1495 the conditions of a tenant leaving his lord were tightened and thereafter the peasant could not take his house with him. Lords who gave shelter to runaway tenants were threatened with severe punishments. It was also enacted in 1500, and again in 1504, that no peasant could leave his lord without the mediation of the noble magistrates. It must be emphasised, however, that these measures did not bring the peasants' freedom of movement to an end. More than once, the county authorities brought judgement in favour of the tenant against his lord. Yet the nobility's willingness to restrict the liberties of their peasants was evident.

The burdens of the peasantry also became heavier than before. Favourable economic trends prompted the lords to demand taxes in kind rather than in money and to sell the crop on the market. The ninth was established as an obligatory seigneurial tax in 1492, a disposition that was reiterated in 1498 and 1500. The tax itself was not a novelty but hitherto it had only concerned the peasant's vineyards and assarts. Now, by being extended to cover the peasant holding proper, it became the most burdensome of all seigneurial services. The prohibition of the export of livestock by the kingdom's inhabitants in 1498 and 1500 was mainly directed against the peasant burghers of the market towns.

An important sign of the Estates' ambitions was a marked decline in the status of the Cumans and the Jász. In Matthias's time they had been able to preserve their ancient liberties, similar to those of the Székely, and had paid an annual tax to the king, which since 1458 had been administered by the royal provisorate of Buda. Shortly after 1490 there emerged a new idea that the Cumans ought to be regarded as simple tenants of the king, and within a couple of years it had prevailed.

DECLINE OF THE STATE

The rule of the Estates could be interpreted by contemporaries in two different ways. The barons liked to think that, being their own body presided over by the king, the royal council would now govern the kingdom, the monarchy being transformed into an oligarchy to which the diet would be no more than decoration. By contrast, the leaders of the nobility dreamed of a new state where the king ruled in concert with the 'regnicoles', important decisions being taken by the diet. Neither of these divergent interpretations prevailed for any length of time, but their combined effect was to bring about increasing governmental paralysis.

The first and most damaging symptom was the breakdown of royal finances. Wladislas inherited an empty treasury from Matthias and thereafter was unable to overcome his financial difficulties. In 1494–95 his annual revenues amounted to some 310,000 florins, which was about half of the sum that had once been at Matthias's disposal. Some of the usual resources had dried up, while others yielded only a fraction of their former output. The salt mines of Maramureş, as well as some of the silver and gold mines, remained in Beatrice's hands until their confiscation by the treasury in 1497 and 1500 respectively. From 1498 the chamber of Kremnica was rented by the Thurzó for 14,000 florins per year. As early as 1492, the whole income from the thirtieth was pawned to Szapolyai, and a good number of royal towns – Trnava, Zagreb, Sopron and Bardejov, later also Szeged, Skalica, Esztergom, Óbuda, Prešov, Sabinov and Cluj – were mortgaged to barons and prelates in order to meet their military expenses, which the king was unable to refund from other sources.

The most important source of royal revenue remained the one-florin tax, called the 'subsidy'. Despite constant protests from the Estates it was regularly levied from 1490 onwards, though it could not be collected in the first year and some tax-collectors were killed in 1494. That 74 per cent of the kingdom's revenues in 1494–95 derived from the subsidy is sufficient indication of its central importance. On the other hand the fact that only 54 per cent of the imposed sum reached the treasury indicates the innate inefficiency of the regime: 15 per cent of the sum was consumed in costs and losses and as much as 31 per cent was acquired by individuals for one reason or another. Since 1493 the greatest barons had been authorised to retain the tax on their lands in order to pay their troops. The diets of 1498 and 1500 consented to the transformation of the subsidy into an ordinary tax but the Estates made their consent dependent upon a more equitable division of its yield. It was laid down that only one part of it – 50d or 60d from each florin – should be regarded as a subsidy and thus handed over to the treasury, the rest remaining with the landholders as 'war expenses' (pecunia exercitualis), to be used to pay and equip their soldiers. The money would be collected by the barons and the prelates on their own lands and by the county authorities from all the other landholders, each county having its own army to pay.

These dispositions would have completely undermined the finances of the state had it not been possible to find other, irregular resources. No amount of money, however trifling, could be neglected. In 1500 Oswald Túz, bishop of Zagreb, bequeathed 32,000 florins for the upkeep of the border castles, left a further 10,000 to the king and cancelled a royal debt of 3,500 florins. By far the greatest help came from abroad, however. Pope Alexander VI sent 106,773 florins in all and in 1500–1 the Republic of Venice transferred 188,800.

Running parallel with the breakdown of royal finances was the collapse of the kingdom's defences. The barons were unanimous in desiring the liquidation of Matthias's mercenary army, not least because they lacked the means to pay it. After 1490 the army got out of control and was accused of heresy; but it was annihilated in 1492 by Paul Kinizsi, the captives being roasted alive 'for having dared to hold the name of Christ in contempt'.[8] On 3 January 1493 the army was officially dissolved, to be replaced by carefully worded but ineffective laws. As early as 1492 eight articles had been designed to revive the institution of the militia portalis. In 1498 they were followed by a more ambitious reform plan. On the one hand, the military obligations of the barons, lay and ecclesiastical alike, were clearly defined. Thirteen bishops (that of Bosnia enjoying exemption), two abbots and nine chapters were obliged between them to equip 7,000 heavily armoured cavalrymen, and 39 lay barons had to set up contingents of their own in proportion to the size of their estates. The *militia portalis* of the counties was to consist of mercenaries; the ratio was one man-at-arms per 36 *portae*, with the exception of the southern regions where a hussar was to be equipped by 24 *portae*. In 1500 the treasurer and ten other well-to-do members of the court (called *decempersonae* or *decemviri*) were also authorised to set up contingents of their own. Although the law did to some extent improve the dangerously inefficient defensive system, its primary effect was to legitimise the maintenance of private armies and to deprive the treasury of considerable revenues.

Frontier defence consumed enormous sums. In 1513–14 the voivode of Transylvania received 12,000 florins for the defence of the castles under his command, while the cost of equipping and supplying the 7,517 mercenaries stationed in other provinces in the south amounted to 116,000 florins. With the cost of the construction and upkeep of castles added, the maintenance of the whole defensive system would have required at least 150,000 florins per year; and because the treasury was never able to provide the necessary means, the mercenaries regularly remained unpaid and lived off plundering and the ransoming of their own prisoners.

While the lords blamed one another for the difficulties that were all too manifest, the people blamed them. The Franciscan Laskai went as far as to pronounce that 'the great and the powerful' were the adherents of the Antichrist.[9] The nobles were convinced that the barons and prelates 'were in search of their own profit instead of keeping the common good before their eyes.' Widespread discontent led to accusations that the treasurer, Ernuszt, had embezzled royal revenues and he was temporarily imprisoned in 1496. A year later the arch-chancellor, Bakócz, who was seen as the source of all the problems, was deprived of his office. In 1499 the nobles set up gallows on their way to the diet, meaning this as a warning to those in power.

FOREIGN AFFAIRS

In the meantime the threat from the south had assumed dangerous dimensions. From 1490 raids by Ottoman armies became regular events. In 1492 they laid siege to Turnu Severin, but the two cartloads of Turkish heads sent to Buda by the ban seemed to demonstrate that the defensive system was still functioning. Defeat was not long in coming, however. On 11 September 1493 Yakub, pasha of Bosnia, won a great victory near Udbina in Croatia and captured the ban, Emeric Derencsényi. In 1495 Bayezid II asked for a three-year truce in view of Charles VIII of France's advance into Italy, but war was renewed in 1498. In 1501 Wladislas signed a treaty of alliance with Venice, which had been fighting for the remnants of its Greek colonies since 1499. The Republic engaged itself to finance Hungary with an annual subsidy of 100,000 florins in the event of war and 30,000 florins in peacetime. No major clashes with the Ottomans took place, however, and a peace treaty was signed at Buda on 22 February 1503 in which Wladislas acquiesced in the loss of some castles in Bosnia. The seven-year peace was renewed in 1510 and then in 1511 for five years; but a year later it was annulled upon the accession of Bayezid's successor.

That the real scale of the danger was still not appreciated is shown by the fact that in 1495 the kingdom wasted its energies in a petty civil war. The target was Duke Lawrence Újlaki, son of King Nicholas and the most powerful lord in the south. He had insulted Wladislas, calling him an ox, and on this occasion the king, his usual patience exhausted, led a regular expedition – near the Ottoman frontier – against his insolent subject and forced him to obedience. The duke lost no more than a few of his many seigneuries, but the success of the expedition seemed to prove that the kingdom's military organisation was still functioning effectively.

In fact, Hungary continued to be counted among the leading powers of Europe, and it was only gradually that its decline became apparent. The court did its best to pursue a well-founded and moderate foreign policy. The Ottoman threat forced it to maintain peaceful relations with its neighbours, a policy greatly facilitated by the pacific character of the king. In 1492 Wladislas made an alliance with John Albert, the new king of Poland. This was strengthened at a meeting between the two kings at Levoča in 1494 and renewed once again in 1498. In August 1500 their alliance was joined by Louis XII of France, and in 1502 Wladislas, having detached himself from Beatrice, married Anne of Foix, a cousin of Louis's wife. The young queen seems to have been determined to widen the court's capacity for action, but as early as 1506 she died in childbirth, leaving her husband with a son and a daughter. Anne happened to be a niece of Ferdinand 'the Catholic' of Aragon and as such was also related to the Habsburgs. It seems to have been due to her that Hungary's relations with Maximilian I remained peaceful, since the emperor was no friend of the Valois and was also trying to defend the Teutonic Order against the ambitions of the Polish Crown. In March 1506, before Anne's death, Wladislas and Maximilian agreed on the future marriage of the emperor's grandson, Ferdinand, with Wladislas's daughter, Anne. Relations with Poland remained friendly after Sigismund I, another of Wladislas's brothers who had spent several years in Buda, acceded to the Polish throne in 1506.

On more than one occasion, however, the sober foreign policy was thwarted by the anti-German sentiments of the nobility. Since the natural target for their hatred had always been the Germans, news of an alliance with the Habsburgs led to an outburst of public anger at the diet in September 1505. Werbőczy explained to the nobility that the ruin of the realm had always been caused by its foreign rulers, who did not know its 'generic' traditions and cruelly oppressed its people. On the other hand, kings of true 'Hungarian birth', such as Louis the Great and Matthias, had enhanced the glory and fame of the nation through their deeds. Not surprisingly, Werbőczy's oration met with stormy success. The Estates, while declaring their fidelity to Wladislas, made a solemn oath never again to elect a foreign king, and went as far as to condemn to 'eternal serfdom' anyone who defied their decision.[10] This was in fact a scarcely concealed offer to Count John Szapolyai, the elder son of the late palatine. With his 30 or so castles and many other domains, John had long been the greatest landowner in the kingdom. There were counties, such as Spis, Trenčín, Turna, Orava and Liptov, which belonged almost entirely to the family – to John himself, to his younger brother, George, and to their mother, Hedwig of Masovia. John was, like Hunyadi, but perhaps with less reason, the object of adoration among the nobility, and he was the only lord whom they were willing to accept as their leader.

Though the decisions of the diet of 1505 were not ratified by the king, they surfaced now and again and even caused a brief and inglorious war against Austria in 1506. The diet of 1507 tried to set further limits on royal power, and refused to accept the succession of Wladislas's son, Louis. Although the boy was finally crowned on 4 June 1508, the question of Hungary's joining the League of Cambrai against Venice had by then led to a new political crisis. It was at that time that the well-born and educated bishop of Vác, Francis Várdai, broke out with anger: 'The people who come to the diet are completely barbarous and devoid of reason. It is impossible to argue with them.'[11]

The accession of Sultan Selim in 1512 opened a new chapter in Ottoman-Hungarian relations. In October 1512 Srebrenik, one of the pillars of the defence line created by Matthias, fell to the Ottomans and in early 1514 they laid siege to Knin, residence of the ban of Croatia. Although in the course of 1513 Stephen Bátori, Peter Beriszló and Ambrose Sárkány had won some minor victories, these by no means counterbalanced the overwhelming weight of the Ottoman Empire. Thus it was amidst a rapidly deteriorating military situation that Hungary was shaken by one of the greatest crises of its history: the peasant war of 1514.

THE PEASANT WAR

The revolt broke out unexpectedly. Though its intensity is explained by the immense hatred that had accumulated within the peasantry during the past decades, and especially in the last few years, this hatred smouldered under the ashes, and a month before the explosion no one, possibly not even the peasants themselves, anticipated that it would suddenly flare up.

The war was not unrelated to the Ottoman threat, but its immediate cause was, strange as it may seem, the papal election of 1513. After the death of Julius II, Bakócz himself entered the lists, and spent a fortune on his sumptuous march into the Eternal City in an effort to dazzle the cardinals; but in the conclave he received only eight votes. As compensation to Bakócz, the new Pope, Leo X, authorised him, as papal legate, to proclaim an anti-Ottoman crusade throughout Europe.

It was thus in a successful crusade that Bakócz hoped to find some consolation for the loss of the tiara, and after his return to Hungary he did his best to secure the consent of the royal council for the project. Although both the barons and the nobility objected to it, on 9 April Bakócz was finally able to proclaim the crusading bull. Recruiting was done mostly by priests and Franciscan friars and was unexpectedly successful. Scholars put the number of armed peasants who assembled – most it seems in a camp near Pest – at about 40,000. Of the peasants on the Great Plain, one in ten appears to have taken the field. On 24 April Bakócz appointed a Székely warrior, George Dózsa, to be commander of the army. Dózsa had served in Belgrade and had consequently fought the Ottomans several times before.

At first all seemed to go well. The bulk of the army left Pest around 9 May and began to march across the Great Plain towards the southern border. By that time, however, tension had increased throughout the land. The nobles were angry to see their peasants leave before the beginning of harvest time, and tried to retain them. This led to sporadic clashes in which there were casualties among both the peasants and the nobles. Tension was further heightened by violent acts committed by the gathering troops. Systematic plundering of villages along their route had always been a common means of provisioning noble armies, but this time plunder and requisition were mainly directed against noble residences. Moreover, the peasants seem to have refused to pay their taxes and seigneurial dues. Unable to resist the increasing pressure from the lords, Bakócz suspended recruitment on 15 May. On 24 May he and the king ordered the crusaders to disband. The nobility of several counties were gathering to bridle their disobedient subjects, and minor clashes took place in various places. The first battle was fought in Bihor on 22 May, on which occasion the peasants routed the attacking nobles.

War on a large scale broke out when the wind of resistance reached Dózsa's army. News of the suspension of recruitment had been received with such anger in the crusaders' camp that Dózsa simply ignored the order and continued on his way southwards. But after his vanguard had been dispersed on 23 May at Apátfalva near Cenad by Stephen Bátori, count of Timiş, and Nicholas Csáki, bishop of Cenad, Dózsa surprised them at Nădlac and took the bishop captive. Upon receiving the news that the crusade had been annulled, Dózsa had the bishop impaled together with other notables. From this point there was no turning back.

The rebels were joined by burghers from the market towns and also by petty nobles, but it was the *hajdú* who, apart from the peasants, played an outstanding role in the revolt. Although in the western counties the peasantry remained fairly calm, the revolt spread over an enormous area including the whole of the Great Plain. There were many camps, some of them led by parish priests and Minorite friars, but there is no evidence that the commanders co-ordinated their plans. Their military operations were as ill-defined as their vision of the future. It is unclear what they intended to do in the event of victory. There are traces of evidence suggesting that their aim was to acquire the liberties of the Székely and that they dreamed of a land without nobles and subjected peasants. That it might have been so is shown by the fact that, though many nobles fell victim to their rage, they were even more systematic in destroying records.

In June war was raging everywhere from Zemplín and Heves down to Tolna and Srem. One of the armies, which marched southwards along the left bank of the Danube, reduced some castles in Srem and laid siege to Bač, the residence of the archbishop of Kalocsa. Another contingent, led by a priest called Lawrence, occupied Oradea and went on towards Transylvania. The main army of Dózsa, having taken Lipova and Şoimoş, on either side of the River Mureş, turned against Timişoara, the main stronghold of the region, defended by its count, Bátori. The siege began on 13 June.

The ramshackle government proved impotent in the face of the danger. By the time that a general levy could be summoned the initiative in each region had already been taken by a powerful baron who was able to rally the local nobility around him. Although at first the rebels won some minor victories, the nobility slowly gained the upper hand everywhere. John Bornemissza, the castellan of Buda, routed the rebels' camp at Pest and by mid-July had pacified the region between the Danube and the Tisza. On 10 July the Transylvanian nobility halted the army of Lawrence the priest at Cluj and drove it back as far as Bihor. But the fate of the rebels was sealed by the swift action of John Szapolyai. From Transylvania, of which he had been voivode since

1510, he hurried to relieve Timişoara and defeated the peasant army under its walls on 15 July. Dózsa was captured and executed in a cruel way; he was put on a red-hot iron throne, and his companions were forced to bite into his flesh before they were put to death themselves. Six weeks after the revolt broke out peace had returned to the realm.

Retaliation followed, of course, but it was less brutal than might have been expected. Although the leaders and other prominent figures of the movement were executed, no general revenge took place. The lords were in need of manpower and were willing to forgive, especially if the crimes to be pardoned had been committed against other lords. For example, we know of a peasant who impaled his lord with his own hands and later lived quietly on the estate of another. Retaliation was directed not against individuals but against the peasantry as a whole. The diet that assembled in October 1514 deprived them of the right of free movement and condemned them and their descendants to serve their lords 'perpetually'. Their right to bear arms was restricted and the same punishment awaited the *hajdú*, the 'literates' and the priests. The peasants were also obliged to pay for the damage caused to their lords. Szapolyai was able to play the role of 'liberator of the realm', and the diet began its work by voting him the immense sum of 20d for each *porta* in reward for his outstanding merits.

The kingdom had thus overcome the crisis, although there was no longer any prospect of modernisation. Hungary like Poland could have survived in its traditional form for centuries had it not been exposed to an ever increasing external threat. During the next decade it was confronted by tasks of a magnitude that it was wholly unable to deal with.

THE STRUGGLE FOR POWER

The failure of the crusade naturally strengthened the position of the nobility. Bakócz, who was most responsible for the recent troubles, was forced to withdraw to the background, though his informal influence remained considerable. Paragraph 55 of the law of 1514 ordained that the Personal should be a skilled lawyer, and the office was given to Werbőczy in 1516. The man who profited most from the suppression of the revolt was Szapolyai. Most of the noble assessors were his own men, and the place of Chancellor Szatmári was taken, though only temporarily (1515–16), by one of his friends, Gregory Frankopan, archbishop of Kalocsa. Since the diet of 1505, Szapolyai had been regarded by many as the future ruler of the kingdom, and his prospects now continued to improve. Through the marriage of his sister in 1512 he had became the brother-in-law of Sigismund of Poland, and there were rumours of his marrying Wladislas's little daughter. The possibility that he might become king of Hungary after Wladislas' death could not be excluded.

The court, headed by Szatmári, tried to thwart the voivode's plans by promoting the succession of the Habsburgs. An important reason for doing this was that the Empire was the only power besides the Holy See from which effective help against the Ottoman menace could be expected. Recent developments in international politics now made it possible for a decisive turn in Hungarian diplomacy to be brought about. It was facilitated by Szapolyai's defeat at Žarnov in Serbia, which greatly damaged his reputation. The plan also enjoyed the active support of the Fugger, who, because of their copper mines, were much interested in the direction taken by Hungarian domestic affairs. Thus the court was successful in organising a summit meeting at Vienna involving Wladislas, Sigismund and Maximilian, where the three rulers agreed upon the main points concerning the destiny of central Europe. In the treaty that was signed on 19 July 1515 the emperor promised not to help the Teutonic Knights against Poland, an agreement that was to seal the fate of the Order. In return, and in the process turning away from his brother-in-law, Szapolyai, Sigismund engaged himself to promote the dynastic plans of the Habsburgs in Hungary and Bohemia. On 22 July Louis, heir to the Hungarian throne, was married to Maximilian's granddaughter Mary, and Wladislas's daughter Anne was handed over to the emperor for marriage to Maximilian himself or to Ferdinand, one of his grandsons. This treaty was to serve as the legal basis for the long Habsburg rule in Hungary.

The Treaty of Vienna was the last important diplomatic success – if it may be so termed – of medieval Hungary. Wladislas died on 13 March 1516, leaving his crowns together with enormous debts amounting to 400,000 florins to his ten-year-old son, Louis II. The boy's guardians were Maximilian and Sigismund, and his upbringing was entrusted to the late king's nephew, Margrave George of Brandenburg, and to John Bornemissza, castellan of Buda. The Margrave, one of the German Hohenzollern dynasty, had lived in Hungary for ten years, and had obtained the hand of the widow of John Corvinus, followed by her considerable inheritance in 1510. Bornemissza, a peasant's son, had been vice-treasurer under Matthias, and rose from this humble office to become one of the most powerful of the barons. Both Margrave George and Bornemissza were known to be fervent partisans of the Habsburgs, or at least of Hungary's Western orientation, an attitude that may explain their unpopularity among the Estates.

The coming decade displayed signs of ever increasing chaos. Internal strife became acute, but the battle lines were more confused than before. In Wladislas's lifetime two camps had still been clearly separated: the court had been opposed by the nobility and generally supported by most of the barons. Now the situation changed. Szatmári recovered his office of chancellor, and in 1517 it could still be said that 'he is the master of all issues';[12] but thereafter confusion gradually got the upper hand. Naturally, everyone wished to promote the common good of the realm, but no consensus was ever established as to how this should be achieved. Contemporary observers were increasingly aware that Hungary was no longer a major power but merely Europe's 'sick man'.

The struggle for power was mainly fought in the diets, which were convoked sixteen times during the ten years of Louis II's reign. Laws continued to be issued by the hundred, but no one ever seriously contemplated enforcing them. In 1518 three assemblies were held. The first was summoned to meet at Buda on Saint George's day (24 April). Here the barons, after being left to themselves by the leave of the noble envoys, unanimously accepted a series of articles, all aimed at strengthening their own authority at the expense of the Estates. In return the nobility assembled first at Tolna in July, then at Bač on 29 September. This time they were fully armed and ordered, among other things, the restitution of the mortgaged royal towns and revenues – an order that (unlike the others) was effectively carried out. They also elected two 'national' treasurers from among the leading nobles: Michael Szobi and John Paksi. However, they were not to prove successful in this role as it soon became clear that the kingdom's finances could not be administered without a minimum of expertise. In the meantime another chancellor, Ladislaus Szalkai, bishop of Vác, appeared at Szatmári's side. He was also of low birth and was later to follow Szatmári into the office of archbishop. After the death of Palatine Perényi in 1519 the nobility wanted Szapolyai to become his successor, but the barons were successful in enforcing the appointment of their candidate, Bátori. Yet during the next two years Bátori and Szapolyai forged a common policy, which led to some of the barons' forming a league against them in 1522.

In the midst of the growing confusion an effective foreign policy was no longer possible. In 1519 Louis's accession to the imperial throne, instead of Charles V, was considered a real possibility in Hungary, and Werbőczy was sent to Rome to influence the Pope in favour of the 13 year old boy. At the same time, the majority of the nobles tended to underestimate the Ottoman threat, and refused to accept any peace. It was, therefore, only in complete secrecy that the court dared to negotiate with the sultan. The course of Ottoman policy, together with military events, seemed for a while to justify the optimistic attitude of the nobility. Sultan Selim I (1512–20) concentrated on expansion towards the East and paid but little attention to the West. Having taken

Armenia from Shah Ismail of Iran in 1514, he destroyed the Mamluk sultanate in 1517 and added Syria and Egypt to his empire. Although at first he refused to accept the Hungarian court's peace offer, and even kept its envoy in honourable detention for some years, a three-year truce was finally signed on 28 March 1519 on the basis of the *status quo*.

THE COLLAPSE

Fighting was not suspended during 'peacetime'; indeed, it was in a minor clash with the Ottomans that Bishop Peter Beriszló, ban of Croatia, was killed on 20 May 1520. But the accession of Suleyman I, following the death of Selim on 22 September 1520, changed the situation. The new ruler was known – at least in the Hungarian court – as 'a man of peaceful nature who would not turn against the Christians.'[13] Although this belief was belied by later events, it remains true that Suleyman's envoy, Behram, arrived at Buda in December 1520 with an offer to renew the armistice of 1519. The barons were indeed willing to accept it, but the nobles objected, referring to the fact that 'no king of Hungary had ever asked for peace from the Turks.'[14] The envoy was accordingly thrown into prison and remained in custody for years.

We know nothing of the sultan's intentions had his offer been accepted. In May 1521 he took the field against Hungary. While his lieutenants took Šabac and Zemun, he himself laid siege to Belgrade. The young king left Buda at the head of 200 knights, but (as the Venetian ambassador reported) 'the prelates and the barons do not follow him, being divided by a serious discord.'[15] Louis had reached Tolna when, after 66 days of resistance, Belgrade fell on 29 August. The sultan left for home, but the heart of Hungary now lay open to a new Ottoman attack. There were no further major fortresses to obstruct the march of an invading army on Buda. The nobility assembled in early autumn with the intention of mounting a counter-attack, but they quickly dispersed when an epidemic broke out in the camp.

In the spring of 1521, on the very eve of the Ottomans' attack, the Estates had decided to devalue the currency in order to increase the revenues of the treasury. The silver content of the penny, which had remained stable since 1467, was reduced by 58.4 per cent and the penny was put into circulation with unaltered value. The device seemed to work excellently at first, yielding considerable gains to the treasury, but within two or three years it had completely ruined the economy. By then it had become a nuisance to the treasury as well, for its revenues came in at a nominal value while their real value decreased drastically. The government was obliged to devalue the 'copper money' continually and stopped minting it altogether in 1525.

With the fall of Belgrade the situation in the south became virtually hopeless. Petrovaradin now became the central pillar of southern defence, responsibility for which, since the spring of 1523, was in the hands of Paul Tomori, the new archbishop of Kalocsa. He had gained experience of fighting on the marches before joining the Friars Minor, and it was upon the expressed order of the Pope that he now accepted the archbishopric and his appointment as captain general. Though his only source of money was the papal nuncio, he did his very best to organise an effective defence. He tried to set up a new defensive line, and in August 1523 routed the army of Ferhad, pasha of Bosnia, near Sremska Mitrovica, at the price, it is true, of serious losses in his own ranks. But the Ottoman threat continued to grow, and the frontier line from the Adriatic to the Carpathians was on the verge of collapse. Klis and Jajce were relieved in 1524 and 1525 respectively, but by that time a number of important fortresses had already fallen, like Orşova (1522) and Turnu Severin (1524) in the south-east, and Skradin and Knin (1522) as well as Ostrovica (1523) in the west. The treasury was practically empty, and the ordinary revenues figuring in the budget prepared by the treasurer, Paul Várdai, on 8 December 1523 amounted to no more than 88,000 florins per year.

That Hungary, in the depth of so serious a crisis, was left to its own devices was partly due to the state of international politics but was also the consequence of the kingdom's bad reputation. The imperial Estates could justify their refusal to give aid by pointing to the hostility shown towards Germans and the base quality of the Hungarian coinage, both of which were facts well known in the Empire. As for political conditions, the Empire and Charles V were focusing their attention not only on Luther, but also on France, for the French king, Francis I, was himself seeking to make contact with the sultan. The king of Poland signed a long truce with Suleyman in 1525, and encouraged the Hungarians to do the same. The emperor's brother, Ferdinand, archduke of Austria, gave no more than empty promises, as he did in October 1523 when receiving Louis II and the Polish archchancellor, Krzysztof Szydlowiecki at Wiener Neustadt. In 1524 a rumour arose that the sultan had made a peace offer to Hungary, promising autonomy in return for the payment of a tax and the free passage of Ottoman armies through Hungarian territory to Austria. The news may have been put into circulation by the Hungarian court with the intention of causing alarm in the West, but if so, the effect proved to be minimal. The Holy See was the only European power to send financial aid regularly. This was done through the papal nuncio in Buda, Baron Burgio, who transferred these sums directly to Tomori or recruited mercenaries himself, lest the money, like the kingdom's other revenues, fell into the hands of the Estates.

Yet in Hungary the ruling elite showed few signs of being really aware of the danger. The barons were preoccupied with the augmentation of their wealth, and quarrelled over the immense Újlaki domains, which came into the Crown's possession in 1524. The nobility, while maintaining opposition to any peace treaty with the Ottomans, was irritated by the presence of foreigners, and especially by that of the Germans. Their feelings in this respect may explain the hostility with which they received the very first signs of the Reformation. Since it was well known that the young Queen Mary, George of Brandenburg and the German and Saxon burghers were in general receptive to the new ideas, the diet of 1523 ordered that the followers of Luther should be punished with the loss of their lives and property. At the same time the flames of national zeal blazed high. At the diet of 1524 it was rumoured that the nobles intended to 'elect captains in the manner of the great Attila';[16] and they demanded that all foreigners, including ambassadors and excepting only the king's Czech courtiers, should be driven from the court. One year later the kingdom was already on the verge of civil war. At the diet held in May on the plain of Rákos there were tumultuous scenes. The crowd accused Palatine Bátori of high treason, reviled Archbishop Szalkai as the 'son of a shoemaker', and emphatically demanded the expulsion of the Fugger, who 'exploit and take away the realm's treasures'.[17] The atmosphere was so strained that the prelates and the barons, led by Szalkai and the palatine, found it advisable to form a league and take radical measures to curb the nobility. In response, thousands of armed nobles assembled on 24 June 1525 at Hatvan, and a pamphlet was circulated that urged them to take arms in defence of their 'liberty'. Though a war did not break out, the entire government was removed. Werbőczy was appointed as palatine, and the judge royal, Ambrose Sárkány, who was known for his Habsburg sympathies and was denounced for his 'trading with skins and cattle and retailing wine like an innkeeper',[18] barely escaped with his life. Szalkai was replaced in the office of chancellor by Paul Várdai, who was at the same time 'elected' by the Estates as archbishop of Esztergom, something that had never occurred before.

The person most active in seeking a remedy for the chaotic state of affairs in Hungary had for some time been Queen Mary. It was in the spring of 1523 that she returned with her husband from Prague and immediately began to increase royal authority by widening her own influence. After the diet of Hatvan she somehow managed to win over a group of the leaders of the opposition, and in November 1525 a royal league was formed at Kecskemét, which rallied prestigious courtiers and equally prestigious noble politicians. At the diet that was held in April 1526, Mary, backed by the newly formed league, won a decisive victory. Werbőczy and Szobi were convicted of high treason and condemned to loss of property, and Bátori recovered the office of palatine. Moreover, for the first time under the Jagiellonians, all the laws enacted were intended to strengthen royal authority. 'If Hungary were well governed she would be the most powerful and valiant rival of the Turk': this had been Burgio's view only a year before.[19] Now it seemed for a brief moment that a more effective government was indeed possible. But it was already too late.

After several years of hesitation Suleyman finally decided on the invasion of Hungary and left Istanbul on 23 April 1526. The core of his army consisted of some 80,000 regular troops and was completed, as usual, by a crowd of irregular auxiliaries. He reached the Sava on 2 July, took Petrovaradin on 27 July after a two-week siege, and Ilok on 8 August. By 23 August his troops had crossed the Drava at Osijek without meeting resistance. On the same day King Louis arrived at Mohács, having left Buda on 20 July. His army, having in the meantime been joined by new contingents, grew from 4,000 soldiers to about 25,000 by the day of the battle. There were 10,000 infantrymen, most of them mercenaries from Bohemia, Germany and Poland, the rest being the mounted contingents of the barons and the prelates. Leadership was forced upon the reluctant Tomori, while George Szapolyai was made co-commander of the army. All the barons and lords were present, with the exception of those who had been ordered to stay elsewhere. On the eve of the battle even the ban, Francis Batthyány, arrived from Slavonia. The only major absentees were Christopher Frankopan, who was still marching with troops from Croatia, and John Szapolyai, who had been summoned too late and had only left Turda in Transylvania on 15 August.

The Hungarian army waited for the Ottomans on the plain south of Mohács on 29 August and was routed in less than two hours. Both archbishops, five bishops and some 20 barons were killed, among them the judge royal, John Drágfi, with the royal banner in his hands, the Master of the Horse, George Bátori, Count George Szapolyai, Ambrose Sárkány, Anthony Pálóci, Gabriel Perényi and many others. The infantry, left on its own as usual, was slaughtered after a fierce resistance. Some of the lords, the palatine among them, managed to escape, but the king was drowned when, in flight from the field, he tried to cross the flooding Csele creek in full armour.

EPILOGUE

Our story must come to an end at this point. That a new era in the history of Hungary had begun in the year 1526 was clear to later generations, and such a view has become a commonplace today. It has long been accepted as the profound dividing line between the ages that we call medieval and modern, and it is always kept in mind, at least in Hungary, when textbooks are compiled, university chairs and syllabuses are established, archival records are kept or monuments registered. It has also generally been considered a national tragedy, marking the end of an era of independence and greatness and the beginning of foreign rule and misery.

From our perspective, the events of 1526 may appear to form a significant watershed, but it was not so for contemporaries. Hungary did not lose her independence immediately after the battle. Suleyman pushed forward as far as Buda, which he took and plundered, but in October he withdraw without having added an inch of land to his empire, apart from a few fortresses in Srem. He returned in 1529 and also in 1532, but his aim on these occasions was to take Vienna, not to conquer Hungary. He embarked upon a purposeful conquest of Hungary only in 1541, when he seized Buda and made it the residence of an Ottoman pasha.

Until then life continued in Hungary as if nothing had happened. Immediately after the defeat, John Szapolyai was proclaimed king by the Estates, while Ferdinand of Austria was also elected by another group of lords in December 1526. In 1529 King John met the sultan at Mohács, did homage to him and accepted the status of Ottoman vassal. Werbőczy became his chancellor and through his support acquired an enormous fortune. He lost it, however, when King John died in 1540 and the Turks came in; and he spent his last days in Buda, living on a pension that Suleyman graciously allowed to him.

A bloody civil war between the two kings began, and what was left of Hungary after 1541 was finally divided between them. Ferdinand kept the western and northern parts, attaching them to his empire, while King John II, the son of Szapolyai, went on to rule in the east, in a small territory from which was to emerge the principality of Transylvania, a vassal state of the Ottomans.

Maps

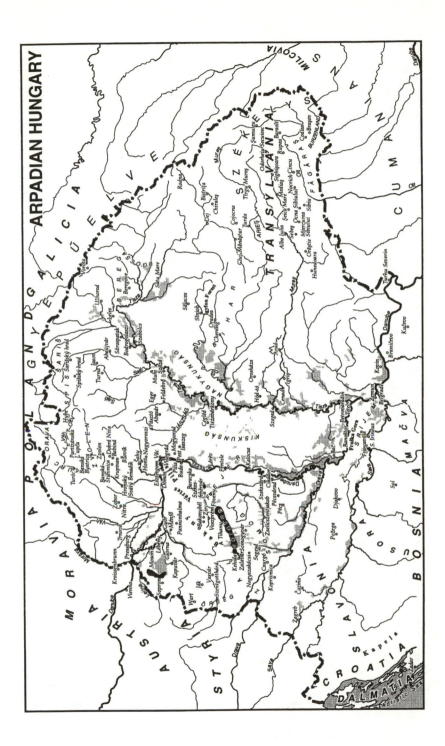

ARPADIAN HUNGARY

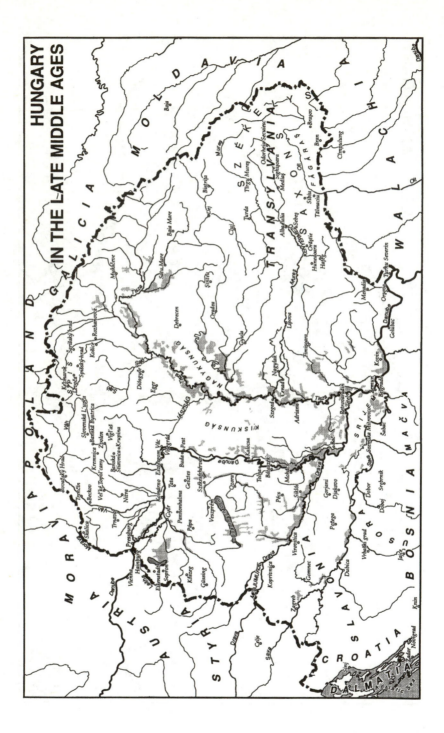

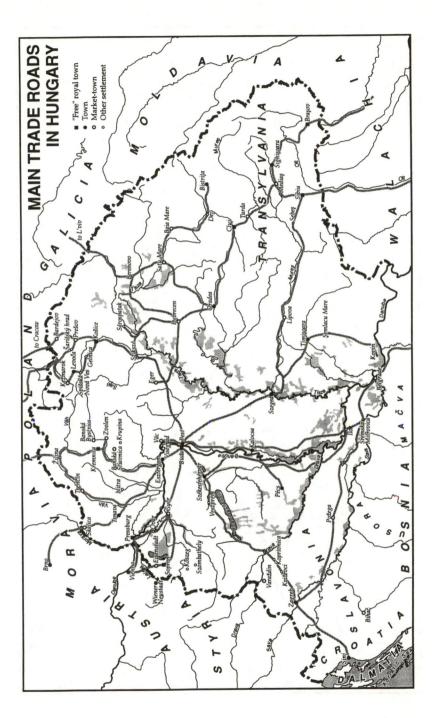

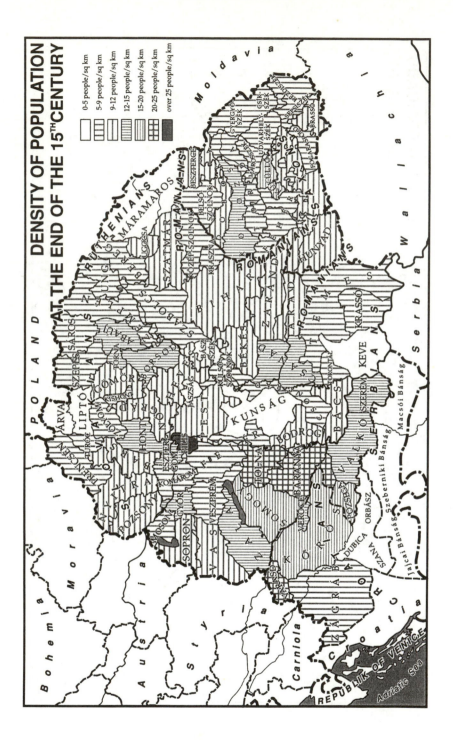

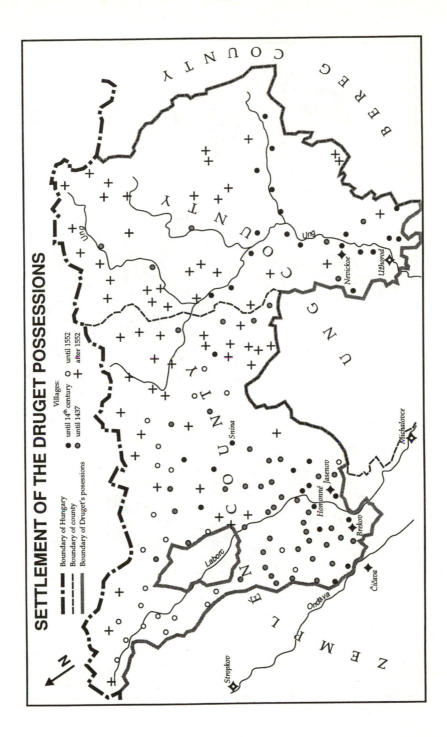

SETTLEMENT OF THE DRUGET POSSESSIONS

Boundary of Hungary
Boundary of county
Boundary of Druget's posessions

Villages:
until 14th century   ○ until 1552
until 1437   + after 1552

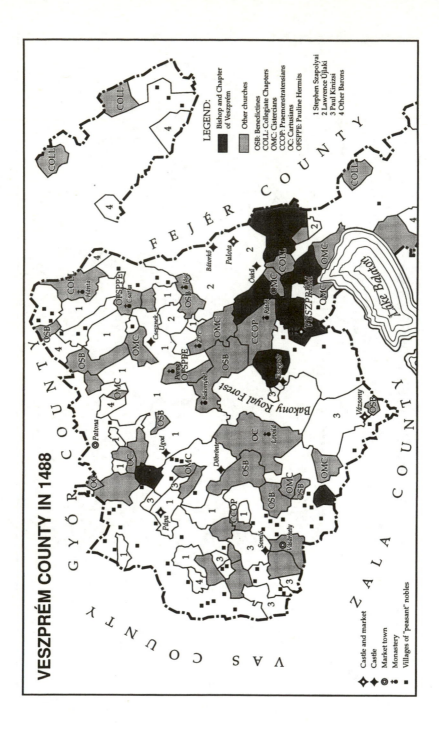

VESZPRÉM COUNTY IN 1488

LEGEND:

◼ Bishop and Chapter of Veszprém

▨ Other churches

OSB: Benedictines
COLL: Collegiate Chapters
OMC: Cistercians
CCOP: Praemonstratensians
OC: Carthusians
OFSPPE: Pauline Hermits

1 Stephen Szapolyai
2 Lawrence Újlaki
3 Paul Kinizsi
4 Other Barons

◆ Castle and market
◆ Castle
◉ Market town
✝ Monastery
▪ Villages of 'peasant' nobles

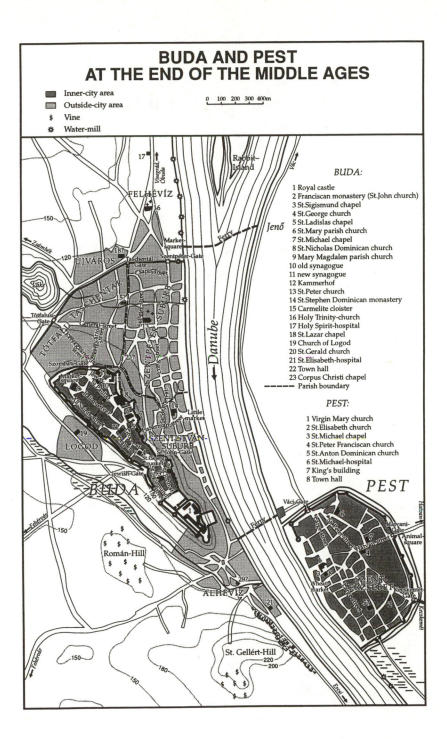

BUDA AND PEST
AT THE END OF THE MIDDLE AGES

■ Inner-city area

▨ Outside-city area

$ Vine

✿ Water-mill

0 100 200 300 400m

BUDA:

1 Royal castle
2 Franciscan monastery (St.John church)
3 St.Sigismund chapel
4 St.George church
5 St.Ladislas chapel
6 St.Mary parish church
7 St.Michael chapel
8 St.Nicholas Dominican church
9 Mary Magdalen parish church
10 old synagogue
11 new synagogue
12 Kammerhof
13 St.Peter church
14 St.Stephen Dominican monastery
15 Carmelite cloister
16 Holy Trinity-church
17 Holy Spirit-hospital
18 St.Lazar chapel
19 Church of Logod
20 St.Gerald church
21 St.Elisabeth-hospital
22 Town hall
23 Corpus Christi chapel
------- Parish boundary

PEST:

1 Virgin Mary church
2 St.Elisabeth church
3 St.Michael chapel
4 St.Peter Franciscan church
5 St.Anton Dominican church
6 St.Michael-hospital
7 King's building
8 Town hall

Genealogical Tables

Kings of Hungary I

Taksony

Géza
† 997

Michael

Basil (Vazul)

Stephen I
997-1038
◊ Gisela of Bavaria

Emery
† 1031

(daughter)
◊ Otto Orseolo
of Venice

Peter
1038-1046

(daughter)
◊ Samuel (Aba)
1041-1044

Levente
† 1046/47

Andrew I
1046-1060
◊ Anastasia of Kiev

Béla I
1060-1063
◊ Richeza of Poland

Solomon
1063-1074
† 1087
◊ Judith of Germany

David
† after 1091

Géza I
1074-1077
◊ 1. Sophia of Looz
2. N. Synadene

Ladislas I
1077-1095
◊ Adelhaid of
Rheinfelden

Lambert
† about 1095

Prisca (Irene)
† 1134
◊ John II Comnenus, Emperor

from 1.:
Álmos
† 1127
◊ Predslava of Kiev

Coloman
1095-1116
◊ 1. N. of Sicily
2. Euphemia of Kiev

Béla II
1131-1141
◊ Helena of Serbia

from 2.:
Boris
† c. 1155

from 1.:
Stephen II
1116-1131
◊ N. of Capua

Géza II
1141-1162
◊ Euphrosyna of Kiev

Ladislas II
1162-1163

Stephen IV
1163
† 1165

Stephen III
1162-1172
◊ Agnes of Austria

Béla III
1172-1196
◊ 1. Anna of Antioch, † c. 1184
2. Marguerite of France, † 1197
from 1.:

Géza
† after 1190

Elisabeth
◊ Frederick of Bohemia

Helena
◊ Leopold V of Austria

Emery
1196-1204
◊ Constance of Aragon

Andrew II
1205-1235
(see on Table II)

Marguerite
◊ 1. Isaac II Angelus, Emperor
2. Boniface of Montferrat
3. Nicholas of St Omer

Constance
† 1240
◊ Otakar Přemysl I of Bohemia

Ladislas III
1204-1205

Kings of Hungary II

Andrew II (see on Table I)
1205-1235
◊ 1. Gertrud of Andechs-Merania, † 1213
2. Yolande of Courtenay, † 1233
3. Beatrice of Este, † 1245

from 1.:	from 1.:	from 1.:	from 1.:	from 2.:	from 3.:
Béla IV **1235-1270** ◊ Maria Lascaris of Nicea, † 1270	Coloman King of Galicia † 1241	Andrew Prince of Galicia † 1234	Maria † 1237/38 ◊ Ivan Asen II of Bulgaria	Elisabeth (St.) † 1231 ◊ Louis IV of Thuringia	Yolande † 1251 ◊ James I of Aragon	Stephen † 1272 ◊ Tomasina Morosini

Stephen V **1270-1272** ◊ Elisabeth, Cuman princess

Béla Duke of Croatia † 1269

Anna † after 1270 ◊ Rostislav of Černigov Tsar of Bulgaria

Constance ◊ Leo of Galicia

Elisabeth † 1271 ◊ Henry of Bavaria

Yolande † 1298 ◊ Boleslaw of Kalisz

Marguerite (St.) nun † 1272

Andrew III **1290-1301** ◊ 1. Fennena of Cujawia 2. Agnes of Austria † 1338

Elisabeth nun † 1338

Kunigunda † 1292 ◊ Boleslaw V of Cracow

Ladislas IV **1272-1290** ◊ Isabella of Sicily † c. 1304

Andrew † 1278

Catherine ◊ Stephen Dragutin of Serbia

Maria † 1323 ◊ Charles II Anjou of Sicily (Naples) (see on Table III)

Béla Duke of Mačva † 1272

Kunigunda † 1285 ◊ Otakar Přemysl II of Bohemia

Wenceslas II King of Bohemia † 1305 ◊ Jutta of Austria

Wenceslas (III) **1301-1305** King of Bohemia 1305-1306

Otto **1305-1307** Duke of Bavaria † 1312 ◊ Catherine of Austria

382

Kings of Hungary III

Maria of Hungary (see on Table II)
† 1323
◊ Charles II of Anjou
King of Sicily (Naples)

Charles Martel
† 1295
◊ Clemence of Austria

Charles I
1301-1342
◊ 1. Maria of Galicia
2. Maria of Silesia, † 1317
3. Beatrice of Bohemia, † 1319
4. Elisabeth of Poland, † 1380
from 4.:

Ladislas
† 1329

Louis I
1342-1382
◊ 1. Marguerite of Bohemia, † 1349
2. Elisabeth of Bosnia, † 1387
from 2.:

Catherine
† 1378

Mary
1382-1395
◊ Sigismund of Luxemburg
1387-1437
(see on Table IV)

Hedwig
† 1399
◊ 1. William of Austria
2. Wladislas II Jagiello

Louis (St)
Bishop of Toulouse
† 1299

Robert
King of **Naples**
† 1343

Charles
Duke of Calabria
† 1328

Joan I
Queen of Naples
† 1382
◊ 1. Andrew of Hungary
2. Louis of Tarent
3. James III of Mallorca

Maria
◊ Charles of Durazzo

Andrew
Duke of Calabria
† 1345
◊ Joan I of Naples

Charles Martel
Duke of Calabria
† 1348

Philip
Prince of **Tarent**
† 1331

Robert
titular Emperor
† 1364

Louis
King of Naples
† 1362
◊ Joan I of Naples

Philip
titular Emperor
† 1373
◊ Elisabeth of
Hungary

Stephen
Duke of Croatia
† 1354
◊ Marguerite of Bavaria

John
Duke of Croatia
† 1360

Elisabeth
† after 1380
◊ Emperor Philip of Tarent

John
◊ Duke of **Durazzo**
† 1335

Charles
† 1348
◊ Maria
of Naples

Louis
† 1362

Robert
† 1356

Marguerite = **Charles II**
1386
King of Naples 1381-1386

Ladislas
King of Naples
† 1414

Joan II
Queen of Naples
† 1435

Kings of Hungary IV

Charles IV of Luxemburg
King of Bohemia, Emperor
† 1378
◊ 1. Blanche of Valois
2. Anne of the Palatinate
3. Anna of Schweidnitz (Silesia)
4. Elisabeth of Pomerania

from 1.:
Marguerite
† 1349
◊ Louis I of Hungary

from 2.:
Wenceslas
King of Bohemia, Emperor
† 1419

from 4.:
Sigismund
1387-1437
King of Germany and Bohemia, Emperor
◊ 1. Mary of Anjou, Queen of Hungary, † 1395
(see on Table III)
2. Barbara of Cilli, † 1451

from 4.:
John
Duke of Görlitz
† 1396

from 4.:
Marguerite
† 1410
◊ John of Hohenzollern
Burggraf of Nurenberg

from 2.:
Elisabeth
† 1442
◊ **Albert of Habsburg**
1437-1439
Duke of Austria, King of Bohemia and Germany

Wladislas II Jagiello
King of Poland
† 1434
◊ 1. Hedwig of Hungary, † 1399
2. Anne of Cilli
3. Elisabeth of Pilcza
4. Sophia of Holszany
from 4.:

Ladislas V
1440-1457
King of Bohemia, Duke of Austria

Elisabeth = Casimir IV
† 1505   King of Poland
              † 1492

John Albert
King of Poland
† 1501

Alexander
King of Poland
† 1506

Wladislas I
1440-1444
King of Poland

Sigismund I
King of Poland
† 1548
◊ 1. Barbara Szapolyai
2. Buona Sforza

Wladislas II
1490-1516
King of Bohemia 1471-1516
◊ 1. Barbara of Brandenburg
2. Beatrice of Naples (
3. Anne de Foix (Candalle), † 1506

Casimir
† 1484

Anne
† 1547
◊ **Ferdinand I** (Habsburg) of Austria
1526-1564

Louis II
1516-1526
King of Bohemia
◊ Maria of Austria, † 1558

János (John) Hunyadi
Regent, 1446-1452
† 1456
◊ Elisabeth Szilágyi

Ladislas   **Matthias "Corvinus"**
† 1457   **1458-1490**
              ◊ Beatrice of Naples, † 1504

illegitimate:
John Corvinus
Duke of Croatia
† 1504

384

Abbreviations

AEA	Gusztáv Wenzel (ed.), *Acta extera Andegavensia*, Monumenta Hungariae historica, Diplomata, 3 vols (Budapest, 1874–6)
Bak, *Königtum*	János M. Bak, *Königtum und Stände in Ungarn im 14–16 Jahrhundert* (Wiesbaden, 1973)
Bertrandon	Bertrandon de la Broquière, *Voyage d'Outremer*, ed. Charles Schefer, Recueil de voyages et de documents pour servir à l'histoire de la géographie, vol 12 (Paris, 1892)
Bonfini	Antonius de Bonfinis, *Rerum Ungaricarum decades*, ed. I. Fógel, B. Iványi et L. Juhász, 4 vols (Budapest, 1936–41)
CD	Georgius Fejér (ed.), *Codex diplomaticus Hungariae ecclesiasticus ac civilis*, tom. I–XI, 40 vols (Buda, 1829–44)
CDHA	Imre Nagy and Gyula Tasnádi Nagy (eds), *Codex diplomaticus Hungaricus Andegavensis*, Monumenta Hungariae historica, Diplomata, 7 vols (Budapest, 1878–1920)
DHA	Georgius Györffy et al. (eds), *Documenta Hungariae antiquissima*, vol 1 (1000–1131) (Budapest, 1992)
DRH 1	Franciscus Döry et al. (eds), *Decreta regni Hungariae: Gesetze und Verordnungen Ungarns 1301–1457* (Budapest, 1976)
DRH 2	Franciscus Döry et al. (eds), *Decreta regni Hungariae: Gesetze und Verordnungen Ungarns 1458–1490* (Budapest, 1989)
DV	Antonius Fekete Nagy and Ladislaus Makkai (eds), *Documenta historiam Valachorum in Hungaria illustrantia usque ad annum 1400 p. Christum* (Budapest, 1941)

Górka	Olgierd Górka (ed.), *Anonymi Descriptio Europae Orientalis anno MCCCVIII* (Cracow, 1916)
Hrbek	Ivan Hrbek, 'Ein arabischer Bericht über Ungarn (Abū Ḥāmid al-Andalusī al-Garnāṭī, 1080–1170)', *Acta Orientalia Academiae Scientiarum Hungaricae* v (1955), pp 205–30
Joachim	Erich Joachim, 'König Sigmund und der Deutsche Ritterorden in Ungarn 1429–1432', *Mitteilungen des Instituts für österreichische Geschichtsforschung* xxxiii (1912), pp 87–119
LMH	János M. Bak et al. (eds), *The Laws of the Medieval Kingdom of Hungary*, 3 vols (Salt Lake City etc, 1992–99)
Mátyás levelei	Vilmos Fraknói (ed.), *Mátyás király levelei* [The letters of King Matthias], vol 1 (Budapest, 1893)
MDCB	L. Bernardus Kumorovitz (ed.), *Monumenta diplomatica civitatis Budapest*, vol 3 (1382–1439), 2 parts (Budapest, 1987)
MES	Ferdinandus Knauz et al. (eds), *Monumenta ecclesiae Strigoniensis*, 4 vols (Esztergom, 1874–1999)
MGH SS	Monumenta Germaniae historica, Scriptores
Moravcsik	Gyula Moravcsik (ed.), *Fontes Byzantini historiae Hungaricae aevo ducum et regum ex stirpe Árpád descendentium* (Budapest, 1984)
Moravcsik-Jenkins	Constantine Porphyrogenitus, *De administrando imperio*, ed. Gy. Moravcsik, trans. R.J.H. Jenkins (Budapest, 1949)
SRH	Emericus Szentpétery et al. (eds), *Scriptores rerum Hungaricarum*, 2 vols (Budapest, 1937–38; repr. 1999)
Theiner	Augustinus Theiner (ed.), *Vetera monumenta historica Hungariam sacram illustrantia*, 2 vols (Rome, 1859–60)
Thuróczy	Johannes de Thurocz, *Chronica Hungarorum*, vol 1, Text, ed. Elisabeth Galántai and Julius Kristó, Bibliotheca scriptorum medii recentisque aevorum, Series nova, vol 7 (Budapest, 1985)
Trip	Stephanus de Werbewcz, *Tripartitum opus juris consuetudinarii inclyti regni Hungariae*, ed. Dezsö Márkus et al., Corpus Juris Hungarici (Budapest, 1897)
UGDS	Franz Zimmermann et al. (eds), *Urkundenbuch zur Geschichte der Deutschen in Siebenbürgen*, 7 vols (Hermannstadt, Bucharest, 1892–1991)
ZsO	Elemér Mályusz and Iván Borsa (eds), *Zsigmondkori oklevéltár* [Documents of the reign of Sigismund], 5 vols (Budapest, 1951–97)

Endnotes

CHAPTER 1

1. In a charter of King Louis the German (860), cited by Teréz Olajos, 'Adalék a Hungarii népnév és a késôi avarkori etnikum történetéhez' [Contribution to the history of the ethnonym 'Hungarii'], *Antik Tanulmányok* xvi (1969), p 87.

CHAPTER 2

1. A. P. Martinez, 'Gardizi's Two Chapters on the Turks' [trans. and commentary], *Archivum Eurasiae Medii Aevi* ii (1982) p 159.
2. Anonymus, c. 37 (SRH, vol 1, p 78).
3. *Annales Fuldenses* ad a. 894, MGH SS, vol 1 (Hannover, 1826), p 410.
4. Chron. s. XIV, c. 36 (SRH, vol 1, p 294).
5. Regino: *Chronicon* ad a. 889, MGH SS, vol I, p 600.
6. Leonis Imperatoris, *Tactica*, XVIII, 52; XIV, 42 (Moravcsik, pp 19, 16).
7. Martinez, 'Gardizi's Two Chapters on the Turks', p 162.
8. Ibn Rusteh, *Les autours précieux*, traduction de Gaston Wiet (Cairo, 1955), p 160.
9. Ibn Rusteh, p 160.
10. Anonymus, c. 5 (SRH, vol 1, p 40).
11. Chron. s. XIV, c. 28 (SRH, vol 1, p 287).
12. Constantine Porphyrogenitus, *De administrando imperio*, c. 38 (Moravcsik-Jenkins, p 173).
13. Constantine Porphyrogenitus, *De administrando imperio*, c. 40 (Moravcsik-Jenkins, p 179).
14. Constantine Porphyrogenitus, *De administrando imperio*, c. 39 (Moravcsik-Jenkins, p 175).
15. Johannes Scylitzes: *Chronicle* (Moravcsik, p 85).

CHAPTER 3

1. 'quia manus pollutas humane sanguino gestas': Legenda S. Stephani maior, c. 3 (SRH, vol 2, p 379); cf. Isaiah 59, 2–3.
2. Legenda S. Stephani maior, c. 2 (SRH, vol 2, p 379).
3. 'sollicitus de rebellibus domandis et ritibus sacrilegis destruendis': Legenda S. Stephani maior, c. 3 (SRH, vol 2, p 379).

4. 'Imperatoris predicti gratia et hortatu … Waic … coronam et benedictionem accepit': Thietmarus Merseburgensis: *Chronicon*, MGH SS, vol 3 (Hannover, 1839), p 784.
5. Chron. s. XIV, c. 71 (SRH, vol 1, p 323).
6. Chron. s. XIV, c. 76 (SRH, vol 1, p 332).
7. Chron. s. XIV, c. 143 (SRH, vol 1, p 421).
8. 'cum rege Ungarorum Colomanno, super reges universos suo tempore degentes litterali scientia erudito': *Chronicae Polonorum usque ad a. 1113, libri tres*, MGH SS, vol 9 (Hannover, 1851), p 456.
9. DHA, vol 1, p 357.
10. SRH, vol 2, pp 625, 626.
11. DHA, vol 1, p 150.
12. 'ingruente namque bellorum tempestate, qua inter Theotonicos et Ungaros seditio maxima excreverat': DHA, vol 1, p 39.
13. 'quatuor civitates': DHA, vol 1, p 52.
14. SRH, vol 2, p 489.
15. 'quem constituit principem domus regis et domus Achtum': SRH, vol 2, p 492.
16. Synod of Esztergom: 41 (LMH, vol 1, p 64).
17. Synod of Esztergom: 29 (LMH, vol 1, p 64).
18. 'super tulbou [goatskin] sedentes ritu paganismo transnataverunt', Anonymus c. 7 (SRH, vol 1, p 41).
19. Chron. s. XIV, c. 82 (SRH, vol 1, p 338).
20. Stephen I: 9 (LMH, vol 1, p 3).
21. Stephen I: 19 (LMH, vol 1, p 5).
22. Stephen II: 1 (LMH, vol 1, p 9).
23. Synod of Szabolcs: 11 (LMH, vol 1, p 57).
24. Synod of Szabolcs: 8 (LMH, vol 1, p 57).
25. Stephen I: 30 (LMH, vol 1, p 6).
26. Synod of Esztergom: 54 (LMH, vol 1, p 65).
27. Coloman: 57 (LMH, vol 1, p 30).
28. Coloman: 73 (LMH, vol 1, p 31).
29. Synod of Esztergom: 7 (LMH, vol 1, p 62).
30. 'literas Sancti Stephanis regis aut successorum eiusdem in quibus libertates et statuta habentur': József Teleki, *Hunyadiak kora Magyarországon* [The age of the Hunyadi in Hungary], vol 10 (Pest, 1853), p 7.

CHAPTER 4

1. Otto Frisingensis: *Gesta Friderici*, lib. I, c. 31 (MGH SS, vol 20 [Hannover, 1869], p 369).
2. Hrbek, p 210.
3. Constantinus Manasses: *Oratio* (Moravcsik, p 158).
4. SRH, vol 2, p 489.
5. Hrbek, p 210.
6. Hrbek, p 208.
7. *Géographie d'Édrisi*, trad. Pierre-Amédée Jaubert, vol 2, Recueil de voyages et de mémoires publié par la Société de Géographie, vol 6 (Paris, 1840; repr. Amsterdam, 1975), p 377.
8. 'Pannonia dicebatur etiam a panis habundantia': Górka, p 43.
9. Synod of Szabolcs: 19 (LMH, vol 1, p 58).
10. Synod of Esztergom: 85 (LMH, vol 1, p 67).
11. Otto Frisingensis: *Gesta Friderici*, lib. I, c. 31 (MGH SS, vol 20, p 369).

12. Otto Frisingensis: *Gesta Friderici*, lib. I, c. 31 (MGH SS, vol 20, p 369).
13. Hrbek, p 208.
14. Hrbek, p 208.
15. 'Bezprenensis mercati tributum, [vide]licet suam partem in cacabis et [v]ome[.r]ibus, in [y]driis, etiam in omnibus ferramentis': DHA, vol 1, p 152.

CHAPTER 5

1. Stephen I: 28 (LMH, vol 1, p 7).
2. Stephen II: 7, 15 (LMH, vol 1, p 10).
3. Stephen I: 20 (LMH, vol 1, p 5).
4. Synod of Szabolcs: 31 (LMH, vol 1, p 59).
5. Stephen I: 15 (LMH, vol 1, p 4).
6. Stephen I: 23 (LMH, vol 1, p 6).
7. SRH, vol 2, p 623.
8. 'Si quando vero exercitum rex ducere voluerit, ... coloni quidem, qui in vicis morantur, novem decimum, vel etiam septem octavum vel infra, si necesse fuerit, cum subpellectili ad bellum necessaria instruunt, caeteris pro cultura terrae domi relicta': Otto Frisingensis: *Gesta Friderici*, lib. I, c. 31 (MGH SS, vol 20, p 368).
9. 'civiles ebdomadarii', Coloman: 45 (LMH, vol 1, p 29).
10. Stephen II: 15 (LMH, vol 1, p 10).
11. Stephen II: 2 (LMH, vol 1, p 9).
12. Stephen I: 7 (LMH, vol 1, p 3).
13. 'Ministris quoque, qui serviunt cum equis, CLVI, item ministris, qui serviunt cum equis et curribus, CCCCVIIII': DHA, vol 1, pp 72–73.
14. 'de servis suis in liberos, vel de liberis in servos ... aliquos transferre': MES, vol 1, p 95.
15. DHA, vol 1, p 85.
16. 'Preterea do territorium ... in villa qui dicitur Ceda, unde ex hac die recedant, preter ecclesiasticam familiam, quicunque libertatis nomen affectant': DHA, vol 1, p 184.
17. Coloman: 19 (LMH, vol 1, p 27).
18. Ladislaus III: 1 (LMH, vol 1, p 18).
19. Coloman: 26 (LMH, vol 1, p 28).

CHAPTER 6

1. *Annales Marbacenses*, MGH SS, vol 17 (Hannover, 1861), p 173.
2. 'optima in principe donandi mensura immensitas iudicetur': Emericus Szentpétery (ed.), *Regesta regum stirpis Arpadianae critico-diplomatica*, vol 1 (Budapest, 1923), no 527 (p 75).
3. 'non Hungariam, sed tantum angariatam atque dissipatam et cunctis fisci proventibus spoliatam reperimus': Theiner, vol 1, p 20.
4. 'tanta multitudinis turba, turbata modestia rationis, ab eodem rege diffi-cilia et iniusta soleant postulare', Theiner, vol 1, p 36.
5. LMH, vol 1, p 34.
6. LMH, vol 1, pp 36–7.
7. Thomas Spalatensis: *Historia*, c. 36 (MGH SS, vol 29 [Hannover, 1892], p 585).
8. 'Hoc anno regnum Ungarie, quod 350 annis duravit, a Tartarorum gente destruitur', Hermannus Altahensis: *Annales*, MGH SS, vol 17 (Hannover, 1861), p 394.

CHAPTER 7

1. Rogerius, c. 40 (SRH, vol 2, p 586).
2. *Chronicon Austriacum*, in Adrian Rauch (ed.), *Rerum Austriacarum scriptores*, vol 2 (Vienna, 1793), p 245.
3. *Géographie d'Édrisi*, trad. Pierre-Amédée Jaubert, vol 2, Recueil de voyages et de mémoires publié par la Société de Géographie, vol 6 (Paris, 1840; repr. Amsterdam, 1975), p 377.
4. 'nos ex suscepti regiminis officio tenemur nostram donationem nequaquam minuere, set eam potius augmentare': CD, vol VII/5, p 274.
5. 'sed domus Hungarie incredibilem habet potentiam, indicibilem quidem armatorum gentem, ita quod in partibus orientis et aquilonis nullus sit pedem ausus movere, ubi triumphator, rex scilicet gloriosus, potentem exercitum suum movit: Gusztáv Wenzel (ed.), *Codex diplomaticus Arpadianus continuatus*, vol 8 (Pest, 1870), p 316.
6. 'contra flagitiosos seu pestilentes regni', UGDS, vol 1, p 131.
7. Cf. LMH, vol 1, p 67.
8. LMH, vol 1, p 69.
9. 'do verlobt er daz got, daz in mit bet noch mit gebot der babst des niht mer überkaeme, daz er deheine reise naeme uf ungerisch erden': Ottokar von Steier, *Österreichische Reimchronik*, ed. Joseph Seemüller, Monumenta Germaniae Historica, Scriptores qui vernacula lingua usi sunt, vol 5 (Hannover, 1890–1893), verse 24940 et seq.
10. 'ab archiepiscopo, inquit, Strigoniensi suffraganeisque incipiens gladiis Tartaricis amputari faciam omnem obertam usque Romam': *Századok* xliv (1910) p 7.
11. LMH, vol 1, p 48.
12. 1257: 'cum plures homines de populis nostris... exivissent, et ad aliorum predia fuissent dispersi': Richard Marsina (ed.), *Codex diplomaticus et epistolaris Slovaciae*, vol 1 (Bratislava, 1971), p 397.
13. Anonymus, c. 25–7 (SRH, vol 1, p 65–9).
14. 'universos Olacos in possessionibus nobilium vel quorumlibet aliorum residentes ad predium nostrum regale Scekes vocatum ordinassemus revocari, reduci et etiam compelli', UGDS, vol 1, p 195; also in DV, p 38.
15. LMH, vol 1, p 42.
16. Best edition in Imre Nagy (ed.), *Zala vármegye története: Oklevéltár* [History of Zala county: Records], vol 2 (Budapest, 1890), p 643; more accessible in CD, vol III/2, p 315.
17. Simon de Keza, c. 4 (SRH, vol 1, p 144).
18. Simon de Keza, c. 6 (SRH, vol 1, p 146).
19. Simon de Keza, c. 7 (SRH, vol 1, p 148).

CHAPTER 8

1. Bak, *Königtum*, p 124.
2. Chron. s. XIV, c. 189 (SRH, vol 1, p 481).
3. Chron. s. XIV, c. 190 (SRH, vol 1, p 482).
4. Chron. s. XIV, c. 194 (SRH, vol 1, p 486).
5. Chron. s. XIV, c. 196 (SRH, vol 1, p 488).
6. Chron. s. XIV, c. 206 (SRH, vol 1, p 494).

CHAPTER 9

1. CD, vol VIII/4, p 323. Yet a *generalis congregatio regnicolarum* was held in 1336: see Hungarian National Archives, Collection of Photocopies, DF 279568.

2. 1335: 'mandatis ... regis, que legis habent vigorem, obedientes ut tenemur', cited by József Gerics, 'Beiträge zur Geschichte der Gerichtsbarkeit im ungarischen königlichen Hof und der Zentralverwaltung im 14. Jahrhundert', *Annales Universitatis Scientiarum Budapestinensis, Sectio historica* vii (1965), p 7.

3. CD, vol VIII/7, p 204.

4. 1312: 'more et consuetudine nobilium regni nostri cum ipsorum propriis expensis et sumptibus, quandocumque nos exercitum habere contingat, nobiscum tenentur exercituare': Vincent Sedlák (ed.), *Regesta diplomatica nec non epistolaria Slovaciae*, vol 1 (Bratislava, 1980), p 429.

5. 'de ... bono statu regni opportunis remediis providere', MES, vol 2, p 745.

6. CD, vol VIII/4, p 323.

7. 1323:'imprimis quidem, cum adhuc regimen et regni nostri gubernaculum pleno non fuissemus adepti', CDHA, vol 2, p. 69.

8. Pál Engel, 'Die Güssinger im Kampf gegen die ungarische Krone', in Heide Dienst and Irmtraut Lindeck-Pozza (eds), *Die Güssinger* (Eisenstadt, 1989), p 108.

9. 'Gli Ungheri sono grandissimi popoli, e quasi tutti si reggono sotto baronaggi, e le baronie d'Ungheria non sono per successione ne a vita, ma tutte si danno e tolgono a volonta del signore' (Lib. VI, cap. 54): *Croniche di Giovanni, Matteo e Filippo Villani*, vol 2 (Trieste, 1858), p 202.

10. DRH, vol 1, pp 96–102.

11. 1335: 'aliquantulum ponderatiores', DRH 1, p 86.

12. 'habens secum pro expensa viginti septem millia marcarum puri argenti et decem septem millia marcarum purissimi auri. ... Lodowicus rex ... misit post eam quattuor millia marcarum auri electi. Habuit etiam secum de florenis fere cum media garleta': Thuróczy, pp 162–3.

CHAPTER 10

1. Thuróczy, p 188.

2. Thuróczy, p 160.

3. 'barones et milites sibi nimium improperabant, quod ad talia se ingessit, que non decent regiam maiestatem': Thuróczy, p 172.

4. Thuróczy, p 182.

5. 1354: 'tempore mortalitatis preterite'. Jenő Házi, *Sopron szabad királyi város története: Oklevelek* [History of the free royal town of Sopron: Records], part 1, vol 1 (Sopron, 1921), p 103.

6. AEA, vol 2, pp 547, 548.

7. AEA, vol 2, p 502.

8. AEA, vol 3, p 435.

9. *Documenta Romaniae historica*, part D, vol 1 (Bucharest, 1977), p 78.

10. Thuróczy, p 181.

11. Thuróczy, p 180.

12. Thuróczy, p 185.

13. 'genitricem meum ... vino repletus vitiosis verbis inficere stupuisses': AEA, vol 2, p 583.

14. MES, vol 3, p 644.

15. CD, vol IX/3, p 543.

16. Thuróczy, p 185.

17. Thuróczy, p 185.

18. Thuróczy, p 187.

CHAPTER 11

1. László Solymosi, 'Hospeskiváltság 1275-ből' [A privilege of hospites from 1275], *Tanulmányok Veszprém megye múltjából* iii (1984), p 67.
2. 1351: 11 (LMH, vol 2, p 11).
3. 1222: 4 (LMH, vol 1, p 34).
4. LMH, vol 2, p 9.
5. 1332: 'cui domine licet de iure naturali atque positivo hereditas deberetur paterna, tamen quia huic iuri repugnat observata ab antiquo regni nostri Hungariae consuetudo, que non nisi masculum heredem in patriam hereditatem succedi permittit': Irmtraut Lindeck-Pozza (ed), *Urkundenbuch des Burgenlandes*, vol 4 (Graz-Köln, 1985), p 135.
6. CD, vol IX/4, p 576.
7. 'cum universis Olachis aliisque populis et famulis ... tam peditibus quam equitibus': DV, p 162 (erroneously dated to 15 July). There are copies of two other documents in the Hungarian National Archives, Collectio Fekete-Nagy, while a third is referred to by Antal Pór, *Nagy Lajos* [Louis the Great] (Budapest, 1892), p 436.
8. 'castrum in Brasso fortissimum Therch vocatum circa terminos Transalpinos edificavit, gente armata briganciis et balestrariis Anglicis custodiam castri muniendo': Thuróczy, p 182.
9. 'regalem collectam quatuor florenorum': Hungarian National Archives, Medieval Records, DL 100046.
10. *Századok* xxxiii (1900), p 606 (erroneously dated to 1368).
11. Hungarian National Archives, Medieval Records, DL 47872, 47875; Remig Békefi, *A népoktatás története Magyarországon* [The history of primary schools in Hungary] (Budapest, 1906), p 228.

CHAPTER 12

1. Gyula Nagy (ed.), *A nagymihályi és sztárai gróf Sztáray család oklevéltára* [Records of the archives of the Counts Sztáray], vol 1 (Budapest, 1887), p 416.
2. Thuróczy, p 196.
3. LMH, vol 2, p 19.
4. Bak, *Königtum*, pp 132–33; also in AEA, vol 3, pp 620–23.
5. 'Ego, inquit, tibi velut scrophe Bohemicali serviturus ero nunquam': Thuróczy, p 212.
6. 1397: 6 (LMH, vol 2, p 22).
7. 1397: 63 (LMH, vol 2, p 26).
8. *Deutsche Reichstagsakten*, vol 5 (Munich, 1885), p 178.

CHAPTER 13

1. Thuróczy, p 218.
2. ZsO, vol 2/I, no 1411-12, and CD, vol X/4, pp 108, 112.
3. Propositions, c. 2 (LMH, vol 2, p 141).
4. Propositions, c. 5 (LMH, vol 2, p 143).
5. Propositions, c. 2 (LMH, vol 2, p 142).
6. Propositions, c. 16 (LMH, vol 2, p 146).
7. Sigismund, 31 August 1405: 10 (LMH, vol 2, p 48).
8. 'In Polonia autem et per totam Alemaniam et Italiam ac in toto mundo sal venditur ad pondus et mensuram': Propositions, c. 9 (LMH, vol 2, p 144).
9. DRH 1, p 91.

10. János M. Bak, 'Monarchie im Wellental', in Reinhard Schneider (ed.), *Das spätmittelalterliche Königtum im europäischen Vergleich*, Vorträge und Forschungen, vol 32 (Sigmaringen, 1987), p 382.

CHAPTER 14

1. Cf. his letter to Wladislas of Poland in January 1416: ZsO, vol 5, no 159.
2. Joachim, p 112.
3. '260 sulcher knechte, di do thun mussen alles das man sie heisset, und sien ouch weerhaftig': Joachim, p 108.
4. 'multa pulcra negotia mercimonia reperiuntur in civitate ista, sed ex quo caremus pecunia, libenter ea videre nolumus': MDCB, vol 3, part 2, p 2.
5. *Analecta Bollandiana* xxvii (1908), pp 43–59.
6. 'littere missive de amore que in dictis scripturis et alibi forte reperientur, in ignem ponere debeant ut comburantur, ... et si inter libros meos et cartas aliquis seu aliqua contra ius et animam reperiretur, comburi debeat et comburatur': Archivio di Stato di Venezia, Procuratori di San Marco di citra, Commissaria publica, pusta 120, Salgo. For the microfilm of this document I am indebted to Mrs Giustiniana Migliardi Colasanti.

CHAPTER 15

1. Bertrandon, p 233.
2. László Zolnay, 'István ifjabb király számadása 1264-ből' [The accounts of the Junior King Stephen from 1264], *Budapest Régiségei* xxi (1964), pp 80–2.
3. MDCB, vol 3, part 2, pp 271–3.
4. A. Wesselofsky, *Il Paradiso degli Alberti* (Bologna, 1876), vol 3, Testo, p IV: cited by Tibor Kardos in *Minerva* xv (1936), p 4.
5. C.R. Beazley, 'Directorium ad faciendum passagium transmarinum', *American Historical Review* xii (1906–7), p 813.
6. CDHA, vol 2, p 527.
7. Bertrandon, p 235.
8. Sigismund, 15 April 1405: 11 (LMH, vol 2, p 39).
9. MDCB, vol 3, part 2, p 284.
10. ZsO, vol 1, nos 940, 944–5.

CHAPTER 16

1. 'videtur prefatum regnum esse omnino vacuum propter magnitudinem eiusdem': Górka, p 49.
2. DV, p 74.
3. 1351: 6 (LMH, vol 2, p 10).
4. József Teleki, *Hunyadiak kora Magyarországon* [The age of the Hunyadi in Hungary], vol 10 (Pest, 1853), p 3.
5. UGDS, vol 4, p 638.

CHAPTER 17

1. 'novitates et nocivas consuetudines': Bak, *Königtum*, p 136.
2. LMH, vol 2, p 81.
3. 'semper regum coronatio a regnicolarum voluntate dependet, et efficacia et virtus corone in ipsorum approbatione consistit': Bak, *Königtum*, p 142.
4. LMH, vol 2, p 90.

5. N. Iorga, *Notes et extraits pour servir à l'histoire des croisades au XVe siècle*, vol 2 (Paris, 1899), p 407.
6. Joannis Dlugossii, *Opera omnia*, ed. Alexander Przezdziecki, vol 13 (Cracow, 1877), p 709.

CHAPTER 18

1. 'Ut domi quiete viveret, foris bellum alebat': Bonfini IV, 3, 3 (vol 4, p 40).
2. 'sive ergo in Bohemos, sive in Turcos opus est, ecce Mathias simul et Hungaria ... apostolice sedi et vestre beatitudini devote manet': *Mátyás levelei*, vol 1, p 114.
3. 'de pace mutua et bona amicitia', *Mátyás levelei*, vol 1, p 381.
4. 'nimis quippe absurdum est ... ecclesiam huiusmodi, uti etiam quamcumque aliam, puero et ipsi infanti committere': Theiner, vol 2, p 509.
5. DRH 2, p 224.
6. 'militari prestantia et armorum virtute ceteras nationes longe evadere': Thuróczy, p 23.
7. Janus Pannonius, *The Epigrams*, ed. and trans. Anthony A. Barrett (Budapest, 1985), p 105 (Ad Galeotum = To Galeotto).

CHAPTER 19

1. Trip. III, 70, 7.
2. Hungarian National Archives, Medieval Records, DL 72186.
3. Ferenc L. Hervay, *Repertorium historicum Ordinis Cisterciensis in Hungaria* (Rome, 1984), p. 37, cited from Jos. Canivez, *Statuta*, vol 5 (1478: 21).
4. József Teleki, *Hunyadiak kora Magyarországon* [The age of the Hunyadi in Hungary], vol 12 (Pest, 1857), p 375.
5. 'Si enim magnas vel baro solo nomine fuerit, et officio baronatus caruerit': Trip. I, 93, 4.

CHAPTER 20

1. 'ut a tantis angustiis et oppressionibus, quibus hactenus regnum Hungarie una nobiscum laboravit, liberaretur': Carolus Wagner (ed.), *Analecta Scepusii sacri et profani*, vol 4 (Vienna, 1778), p 22.
2. Bonfini, V, 1 (vol 4, p. 207).
3. Bonfini, V, 2 (vol 4, p. 229).
4. 'non clementia et impunitate, sed virga ferrea in obsequio retineri': Bonfini, IV, 9, 219 (vol 4, p 188).
5. Trip. I, 3, 4.
6. Trip. Conclusio.
7. 'nullas prorsus novitates, quemadmodum ... Matthias rex fecerat, in eorundem detrimentum et oppressionem ... introducamus': Bak, *Königtum*, p 152.
8. Bonfini, V, 3, (vol 4, p 237).
9. Cited by J. Szűcs, 'Die oppositionelle Strömung der Franziskaner im Hintergrund des Bauernkrieges und der Reformation in Ungarn', *Etudes historiques hongroises 1985 publiées à l'occasion du Congrès International des Sciences Historiques*, vol 1 (Budapest, 1985), p 511.
10. Bak, *Königtum*, p 158.
11. Cited by Elemér Mályusz, 'A magyar társadalom a Hunyadiak korában [Hungarian society in the age of the Hunyadi], *Mátyás király emlékkönyv*, vol 1 (Budapest, s.a. [1940]), p. 390.

12. 'penes quem est hoc tempore summa rerum': a letter of Geronimo Balbi in *Történelmi Tár*, 1882, p 658, cited by Zsuzsanna Hermann, *Az 1515. évi Habsburg-Jagelló szerződés* [The Habsburg-Jagiellonian Treaty of 1515] (Budapest, 1961), p 64.
13. Sanuto, *I Diarii*, vol 29, col. 452, cited by Zsuzsanna Hermann in *Századok* cix (1975), p 309.
14. Vienna, Haus-, Hof- und Staatsarchiv, Grosse Correspondenz, fasc. 25/a, report of Andrea da Burgo from 3 July 1523, cited by András Kubinyi in: Lajos Rúzsás and Ferenc Szakály (eds), *Mohács* (Budapest, 1986), p 65.
15. Sanuto, *I Diarii*, vol 31, col. 160, cited by Zsuzsanna Hermann in *Századok* cix (1975), p 310.
16. Vienna, Haus-, Hof- und Staatsarchiv, Grosse Correspondenz, fasc. 25/a, cited by András Kubinyi in: Pál Engel, Gyula Kristó and András Kubinyi, *Magyarország története 1301–1526* [History of Hungary, 1301–1526] (Budapest, 1998), p 383.
17. Cited by Péter Kulcsár, *A Jagelló-kor* [The age of the Jagiellonians] (Budapest, 1981), p 200.
18. Johann Christian von Engel, *Geschichte des Ungrischen Reichs und seiner Nebenländer*, vol 2 (Halle, 1798), p 44, cited by András Kubinyi, in: Lajos Rúzsás and Ferenc Szakály (eds), *Mohács* (Budapest, 1986), p 61.
19. *Relationes oratorum pontificiorum 1524–1526*, Monumenta Vaticana historiam regni Hungariae illustrantia, series II, vol 1 (Budapest, 1884), p 156.

Bibliography

This bibliography lists works in English, French, German and Italian. Relevant literature in other languages can be found in:

Bernath, M. and F. von Schroeder (eds), *Biographisches Lexikon zur Geschichte Südosteuropas*, 4 vols (Munich, 1974–81)

Engel, Pál, Gyula Kristó and András Kubinyi, *Magyarország története 1301–1526* (Budapest, 1998)

Kristó, Gyula, *Magyarország története 895–1301* (Budapest, 1998)

Seewann, Gerhard, 'Ungarn', in M. Bernath (ed.), *Historische Bücherkunde Südosteuropas*, vol 1, part 2 (Munich, 1980), pp 755–1227

GENERAL

Bak, János M., *Königtum und Stände in Ungarn im 14–16. Jahrhundert* (Wiesbaden, 1973)

——, 'The price of war and peace in late medieval Hungary', in B.P. McGuire (ed.), *War and Peace in the Middle Ages* (Copenhagen, 1987), pp 161–78

——, 'East–central Europe', in D. Hay, *Europe in the Fourteenth and Fifteenth Centuries* (2nd edn, London, 1989), pp 214–62

——, 'Roles and functions of queens in Arpádian and Angevin Hungary (1000–1386 AD)', in John Carmi Parsons (ed.), *Medieval Queenship* (New York, 1993), pp 13–24

——, '"Linguistic pluralism" in medieval Hungary', in Marc A. Meyer (ed.), *The Culture of Christendom* (London, 1993), pp 269–79

——, 'Queens as scapegoats in medieval Hungary', in A.J. Duggan, (ed.), *Queens and queenship in medieval Europe* (Woodbridge, 1997), pp 223–33

——, 'Hungary: Crown and Estates', in C. Allmand (ed.), *New Cambridge Medieval History, vol. 7: c. 1415–c. 1500* (Cambridge, 1998), pp 707–26

Bak, János M. and Béla K. Király (eds), *From Hunyadi to Rákóczi: War and Society in Medieval and Early Modern Hungary* (New York, 1982)

Barta, Gábor et al., *History of Transylvania* (Budapest, 1994)

Bérenger, Jean, *A History of the Habsburg Empire, 1273–1700* (London, 1994)

Bogyay, Thomas v., *Grundzüge der Geschichte Ungarns* (Darmstadt, 1967, 4th edn, 1981)

Domanovszky, Alexander, *Die Geschichte Ungarns* (Munich, 1923)

Eckhart, Ferenc, *A Short History of the Hungarian People* (London, 1931)

Fine, John V.A. Jr., *The Late Medieval Balkans. A Critical Survey from the Late Twelfth Century to the Ottoman Conquest* (Ann Arbor, 1987)

Fügedi, Erik, *Kings, Bishops, Nobles and Burghers in Medieval Hungary* [collected studies] (London, 1986)

——, *Castle and Society in Medieval Hungary (1000–1437)*, Studia historica, No 187 (Budapest, 1986)

——, 'Two kinds of enemies – two kinds of ideology: the Hungarian-Turkish wars of the fifteenth century', in B.P. McGuire (ed.), *War and Peace in the Middle Ages* (Copenhagen, 1987), pp 146–60

——, *The Elefánthy: The Hungarian Nobleman and his Kindred* (Budapest, 1998)

Hanák, Péter (ed.), *The Corvina History of Hungary from Earliest Times until the Present Day* (Budapest, 1991)

Hóman, Bálint, 'Hungary 1301–1490', in *The Cambridge Medieval History*, vol 7 (Cambridge, 1936), pp 587–619; bibliography: pp 961–64

——, *Geschichte des ungarischen Mittelalters*, 2 vols (Berlin, 1940–1943)

Housley, Norman, *The Later Crusades: From Lyons to Alcazar, 1274–1580* (Oxford, 1992)

Huber, Alfons, 'Studien über die Geschichte Ungarns im Zeitalter der Arpaden', *Archiv für österreichische Geschichte* lxv (1883–84), pp 153–230

Imber, Colin, *The Ottoman Empire 1300–1481* (Istanbul, 1990)

Inalcik, Halil, *The Ottoman Empire: The Classical Age 1300–1600* (London, 1973)

Káldi-Nagy, Gyula (ed.), *Hungaro-Turcica: Studies in Honor of Julius Németh* (Budapest, 1974)

Kosary, D.G., *A History of Hungary* (New York, 1971)

Krekić, Bariša, *Dubrovnik, Italy and the Balkans in the Late Middle Ages* (London, 1980)

——, *Dubrovnik. A Mediterranean Urban Society, 1300–1600* [collected studies] (Aldershot, 1997)

Kristó, Gyula, *Die Arpadendynastie. Die Geschichte Ungarns von 895 bis 1301* (Budapest, 1993)

Lübke, Christian, *Arbeit und Wirtschaft in östlichen Mitteleuropa* (Stuttgart, 1991)

Macartney, C.A., *Hungary: A Short History* (Edinburgh, 1967)

——, *Studies on Early Hungarian and Pontic History* [collected studies] (Aldershot, 1999)

Magocsi, P.R., *Historical Atlas of East-Central Europe* (Seattle, 1993)

Mályusz, Elemér, 'Hungarian nobles of medieval Transylvania', in J.M. Bak (ed.), *Nobilities in Central and Eastern Europe*, History and Society in Central Europe, vol 2 (Budapest, 1994), pp 25–53

Obolensky, D., *The Byzantine Commonwealth: Eastern Europe, 500–1453* (New York, 1971)

Ostrogorsky, George, *History of the Byzantine State* (2nd edn, transl. by Joan Hussey, Oxford, 1968)

Pach, Zsigmond Pál, *Hungary and the European Economy in Early Modern Times* [collected studies] (Aldershot, 1994)

Rhode, Gotthold, 'Ungarn vom Ende der Verbindung mit Polen bis zum Ende der Türkenherrschaft (1444–1699)', in Th. Schieder (ed.), *Handbuch der europäischen Geschichte*, vol 3 (Stuttgart, 1971), pp 1061–1117

Runciman, Stephen, *A History of the Crusades*, 3 vols (Cambridge, 1951–55)

Sedlar, Jean, *East Central Europe in the Middle Ages, 1000–1500* (Seattle and London, 1994)

Setton, Kenneth M. (ed.), *A History of the Crusades*, 6 vols (2nd edn, Madison, Wis., 1969–90)

——, *The Papacy and the Levant* (1204–1571), 4 vols (Philadelphia, 1976–84)

Sinor, Denis, *History of Hungary* (New York, 1959)

Sugar, Peter, *Southeastern Europe Under Ottoman Rule, 1354–1804* (Seattle, 1993)

Sugar, Peter and Peter Hanák (eds), *A History of Hungary* (Bloomington, 1989)

Szögi, László and Julia Varga (eds), *Universitas Budensis 1395–1995* (Budapest, 1997)

Szűcs, Jenő, *Nation und Geschichte. Studien* (Budapest, 1981)

——, 'The three regions of Europe: an outline', *Acta Historica Academiae Scientiarum Hungaricae* xxix (1983), pp 131–84

Werner, Ernst, *Die Geburt einer Grossmacht – die Osmanen (1300–1481)*, (2nd rev. edn, Berlin, 1972)

SOURCES

Bak, János M. et al. (eds), *The Laws of the Medieval Kingdom of Hungary,* vols 1–3 (Salt Lake City, 1989–96): vol 1 (1000–1301); 2 (1301–1457); 3 (1458–1490)

Balázs, Péter (ed.), *Guide to the Archives of Hungary* (Budapest, 1976)

Bedo, A.K., et al. (eds), *The Legal Sources and Bibliography of Hungary* (New York, 1956)

Döry, Ferenc et al. (eds), *Decreta regni Hungariae. Gesetze und Verordnungen Ungarns 1301–1457* (Budapest, 1976)

Galántai, Elisabeth, and Julius Kristó (eds), *Johannes de Thurocz: Chronica Hungarorum* (Budapest, 1985)

Györffy, Georgius (ed.), *Diplomata Hungariae Antiquissima Accedunt epistolae et acta ad historian Hungariae pertinentia*, vol 1 (1000–1131) (Budapest, 1992)

Helbig, Helmut and Lorenz Weinrich (eds), *Diplomata et chronica locationis Teutonicorum illustrantia*, Part 2 (Darmstadt, 1970)

Iorga, N., *Notes et extraits pour servir à l'histoire des croisades au XVe siècle* (six series, Paris and Bucharest, 1899–1916)

Kaindl, Raimund Friedrich, 'Studien zu den ungarischen Geschichtsquellen, I–XVI', *Archiv für österreichische Geschichte* lxxxi (1894), pp 323–46; lxxxii (1895), pp 575–638; lxxxiv (1898), pp 503–43; lxxxv (1898), pp 431–507; lxxxviii (1900), pp 203–312, 367–472; xci (1902), pp 1–5

Kardos, Tibor et al. (eds), *Die ungarische Bilderchronik* (Berlin, 1961)

Macartney, C.A., *Studies on the Earliest Hungarian Historical Sources*, 7 parts (Budapest-Oxford, 1938–51); reprinted in Macartney, *Studies on early Hungarian and Pontic history*

——, *The Medieval Hungarian Historians: A Critical and Analytical Guide* (Cambridge, 1953)

Mantello, Frank (transl.) and Pál Engel (foreword and commentary), *János Thuróczy: Chronicle of the Hungarians* (Bloomington, 1991)

Michael, Maurice (trans. and ed.), *The Annals of Jan Długosz* (Chichester, 1997)

Veszprémy, László and Frank Schaer (trans. and eds), *Simon of Keza: The Deeds of the Hungarians* (Budapest, 1999)

Wolf, A., 'Die Gesetzgebung der entstehenden Territorialstaaten …', in H. Coing (ed.), *Handbuch der Quellen und Literatur der neueren europäischen Privatrechtsgeschichte*, vol 1 (München, 1973), pp 721–62

CHAPTER 1: THE CARPATHIAN BASIN BEFORE THE HUNGARIANS

Alföldi, András, *Der Untergang der Römerherrschaft in Pannonien* (Berlin-Leipzig, 1924)

Altheim, Franz (ed.), *Attila und die Hunnen* (Baden-Baden, 1951)

——, *Geschichte der Hunnen*, 5 vols (Berlin, 1959–1962)

Bona, Istvan, *The Dawn of the Dark Ages: The Gepids and the Lombards in the Carpathian Basin* (Budapest, 1976)

——, *Das Hunnenreich* (Budapest, 1991)

Cs. Sós, Ágnes, *Die slawische Bevölkerung Westungarns im 9. Jahrhundert* (München, 1973)

Czeglédy, Károly, 'From east to west: the age of nomadic migrations in Europe', *Archivum Eurasiae Medii Aevi* iii (1983), pp 25–126

Daim, Folko (ed.), *Awarenforschungen*, 2 vols (Vienna, 1992)

Dobó, Árpád, *Die Verwaltung der römischen Provinz Pannonien von Augustus bis Diocletianus* (Budapest-Amsterdam, 1968)

Fülöp, Gyula, 'New research on finds of Avar chieftain burials at Igar, Hungary', in David Austin and Leslie Alcock (eds), *From the Baltic to the Black Sea: Studies in Medieval Archaeology* (London and New York, 1990), pp 138–46

Harmatta, János, 'La société des huns à l'époque d'Attila', *Recherches internationales à la lumière du marxisme*, vol 2 (Paris, 1957), pp 179–238

Lindner, R.P., 'Nomadism, horses and Huns', *Past and Present* xcii (1981), pp 3–19

Maenchen-Helfen, O.J., *The World of the Huns: Studies of their History and Culture*, ed. Max Knight (Berkeley-Los Angeles-London, 1973)

Mócsy, András, *Die Bevölkerung Pannoniens bis zu den Markomannenkriegen* (Budapest, 1959)

Pohl, W., *Die Awaren: Ein Steppenvolk in Mitteleuropa 576–822 n. Chr.* (München, 1988)

Popoli delle steppe: Unni, Avari, Ungari (Spoleto, 1988)

Simonyi, Dezső, 'Die Kontinuitätsfrage und das Erscheinen der Slawen in Pannonien', *Studia Slavica Academiae Scientiarum Hungaricae* i (1955), pp 333–61

Soproni, Sándor, *Die letzten Jahrzehnte des pannonischen Limes*, Münchner Beiträge zur Vor- und Frühgeschichte, vol 38 (Munich, 1985)

Thompson, E.A., *A History of Attila and the Huns* (Oxford, 1948)

Várady, László, *Das letzte Jahrhundert Pannoniens 376–476* (Budapest, 1969)

Wolfram, Herwig, *Conversio Bagoariorum et Carantanorum* (Wien etc., 1979)

CHAPTER 2: THE PAGAN HUNGARIANS

Bálint, Csanád, *Südungarn im 10. Jahrhundert*, Studia archaeologica, vol 11 (Budapest, 1991)

Bárczi, Géza, 'La toponymie hongroise du moyen âge', *Annales Universitatis Scientiarum Budapestinensis, Sectio philologica* ii (1960), pp 25–43

Bartha, Antal, *Hungarian Society in the Ninth and Tenth Centuries* (Budapest, 1975)

Benkő, Loránd, 'Zur Geschichte des Ungartums vor der Landnahme im Zusammenhang mit Leved und Etelköz', *Acta Linguistica Academiae Scientiarum Hungaricae* xxxiv (1984), pp 153–95

Bogyay, Thomas von, *Lechfeld: Ende und Anfang* (Munich, 1955)
——, 'Forschungen zur Urgeschichte der Ungarn nach dem 2. Welt-krieg', *Ural-altaische Jahrbücher* xxix (1957), pp 93–114
——, 'Bemerkungen zum Problem der ersten byzantinisch-ungarischen Berührungen', in J.G. Farkas (ed.), *Überlieferung und Auftrag: Festschrift für Michael de Ferdinandy zum 60. Geburtstag* (Wies-baden, 1972)
Bowlus, Charles R., *Franks, Moravians and Magyars. The Struggle for the Middle Danube, 788–907* (Philadelphia, 1995)
Dienes, István, *The Hungarians Cross the Carpathians* (Budapest, 1972)
Eberl, Barthel, *Die Ungarnschlacht auf dem Lechfeld im Jahre 955* (Augs-burg, 1955)
Fasoli, Gina, *Le incursione ungare in Europa nel secolo X* (Florence, 1945)
Fehér, Géza, 'Die landnehmenden Ungarn und ihr Verhältnis zu den Slawen des mittleren Donaubeckens', *Studia Slavica Academiae Scien-tiarum Hungaricae* iii (1957), pp 7–58
Fodor, István, *In Search of a New Homeland: The Prehistory of the Hungarian People and the Conquest* (Budapest, 1982)
Göckenjan, Hansgerd, *Hilfsvölker und Grenzwächter im mittealterlichen Ungarn* (Wiesbaden, 1972)
Györffy, György, 'Formations d'états au IXe siècle suivant les "Gesta Hungarorum" du Notaire Anonyme', *Nouvelles études historiques publiées à l'occasion du XIIe Congrès International des Sciences Historiques*, vol 2 (Budapest, 1965), pp 27–53
——, *Autour de l'Etat des semi-nomades: le cas de la Hongrie*, Studia historica, No 95 (Budapest, 1975); also in: *Etudes historiques hongroises 1975 publiées à l'occasion du XIVe Congrès International des Sciences Historiques*, vol 1 (Budapest, 1975), pp 221–38
——, *Wirtschaft und Gesellschaft der Ungarn um die Jahrtausendwende*, Studia historica, No 186 (Budapest, 1983)
——, 'Landnahme, Ansiedlung und Streifzüge der Ungarn', *Acta Historica Academiae Scientiarum Hungaricae* xxxi (1985), pp 231–70
——, 'Die Anfänge der ungarsich-slawischen Berührungen', *Studia Slavica Academiae Scientiarum Hungaricae* xxxvi (1990), pp 159–86
Kniezsa, István, *Ungarns Völkerschaften im XI. Jahrhundert* (Budapest, 1938); also in: *Archivum Europae Centro-Orientalis* iv (1938), pp 241–412
Kristó, Gyula, 'Konstantinos Porphyrogennetos und die Herausbildung des ungarischen Stämmebundes', *Opuscula Byzantina* vii (1981), pp 77–89
——, *Hungarian History in the Ninth Century* (Szeged, 1996)
László, Gyula, *The Magyars: Their Life and Civilisation* (Budapest, 1996)
Leyser, Karl, 'The battle of the Lech, 955 – a study in tenth-century warfare', *History* l (1965), pp 1–25

Macartney, C.A., *The Magyars in the Ninth Century* (Cambridge, 1930; repr. 1968).

——, *Studies on Early Hungarian and Pontic History* (Aldershot, 1999)

Moór, Elemér, 'Studien zur Früh- und Urgeschichte des ungarischen Volkes', *Acta Ethnographica Academiae Scientiarum Hungaricae* ii (1951), pp 25–138

——, 'Die Ausbildung des ungarischen Volkes im Lichte der Laut- und Wortgeschichte', *Acta Ethnographica Academiae Scientiarum Hungaricae* vi (1956), pp 279–341

Moravcsik, Gyula, 'Byzantine Christianity and the Magyars in the period of their migration', *American Slavic and East European Review* xiv (1946), pp 29–45

Róna-Tas, András, *Hungarians and Europe in the Early Middle Ages* (Budapest, 1999)

Siklódi, Csilla, *Between East and West: Everyday Life in the Hungarian Conquest Period* (Budapest, 1996)

Silagi, Gabriel and László Veszprémy (eds), *Die 'Gesta Hungarorum' des anonymen Notars. Die älteste Darstellung der ungarischen Geschichte*, Ungarns Geschichtsschreiber, vol 4 (Sigmaringen, 1991)

Székely, György, 'La Hongrie et Byzance aux Xe-XIIe siècles', *Acta Historica Academiae Scientiarum Hungaricae* xiii (1967), pp 291–311

Takács, Miklós, *Die Arpadenzeitlichen Tonkessel im Karpatenbecken* (Budapest, 1986)

Vajay, Szabolcs de, *Der Eintritt des ungarischen Stämmebundes in die europäische Geschichte 862–933* (Mainz, 1968)

Vernadsky, George, and Michael de Ferdinandy, *Studien zur ungarischen Frühgeschichte*, 2 parts (Munich, 1957)

Veszprémy, László and Frank Schaer (trans. and eds), *Simon of Keza: The Deeds of the Hungarians* (Budapest, 1999)

CHAPTER 3: THE FIRST CENTURY OF THE CHRISTIAN KINGDOM

Adriányi, Gabriel, 'Der Eintritt Ungarns in die christlich-abendländische Volksgemeinschaft', *Ungarn-Jahrbuch* vi (1974–75), pp 24–37

Bakay, Kornél, 'Archäologische Studien zur Frage der ungarischen Staatsgründung', *Acta Archaeologica Academiae Scientiarum Hungaricae* xix (1967), pp 105–73

Bogyay, Thomas von, *Stephanus rex* (Vienna, 1975)

Bogyay, Thomas von, Gábor Silagi and János Bak (eds) *Die heiligen Könige*, Ungarns Geschichtsschreiber, vol 1 (Graz, 1976)

Brackmann, A., *Zur Entstehung des ungarischen Staates* (Berlin, 1940)

Csizmadia, Andor, 'Die rechtliche Entwicklung des Zehnten (Decima) in Ungarn', *Zeitschrift der Savigny-Stiftung für Rechtsgeschichte, Kanonistische Abteilung* lxi (1975), pp 228–57

Deér, József, *Die Anfänge der ungarisch-kroatischen Staatsgemeinschaft* (Leipzig, 1936)

——, *Die Entstehung des ungarischen Königtums* (Budapest-Leipzig, 1942)

——, 'Die Ansprüche der Herrscher des 12. Jahrhunderts auf die apostolische Legation', *Archivum historiae ponticifiae* ii (1964), pp 117–86

——, *Die Heilige Krone Ungarns* (Graz, 1966)

——, *Heidnisches und Christiches in der altungarischen Monarchie* (2nd edn, Darmstadt, 1969)

Gábriel, Asztrik, *Les Hongrois et la Sorbonne médiévale* (Budapest, 1940)

Gerics, József, 'Die Kirchenpolitik des Königs Peter und deren Folgen', *Annales Universitatis Scientiarum Budapestinensis, Sectio historica* xxiv (1986), pp 269–75

Gombos, Albin F., *Saint Étienne dans l'historiographie européenne du moyen âge* (Leipzig, 1938)

Györffy, György, 'Das Güterverzeichnis des griechischen Klosters zu Szavaszentdemeter aus dem 12. Jahrhundert', *Studia Slavica Academiae Scientiarum Hungaricae* v (1959), pp 9–74

——, 'Zu den Anfängen der ungarischen Kirchenorganisation auf Grund neuer quellenkritischer Ergebnisse', *Archivum historiae pontificiae* vii (1969), pp 79–113

——, 'Die Nordwestgrenze des byzantinischen Reiches im 11. Jahrhundert und die Ausbildung des "ducatus Sclavoniae"', in P. Brière (ed.), *Mélanges offerts à Szabolcs de Vajay* (Braga, 1971), pp 295–314

——, 'Civitas, castrum, castellum', *Acta Antiqua Academiae Scientiarum Hungaricae* xxiii (1975), pp 331–4

——, 'Die Entstehung der ungarischen Burgorganisation', *Acta Archaeologica Academiae Scientiarum Hungaricae* xxviii (1976), pp 323–58

——, *King Saint Stephen of Hungary* (New York, 1994); previously published in German: *König Stephan der Heilige* (Budapest, 1988)

Hóman, Bálint, *King Stephen the Saint* (Budapest, 1938)

Karpat, Josef, 'Corona regni Hungariae im Zeitalter des Arpáden', in Manfred Hellmann (ed.), *Corona regni. Studien über die Krone als Symbol des Staates im späteren Mittelalter* (Weimar, 1961), pp 263–332

Kerbl, R., *Byzantinische Prinzessinnen in Ungarn zwischen 1050–1200 und ihr Einfluß auf das Arpaden-Königreich* (Vienna, 1979)

Klaniczay, Gábor, 'Rex iustus: le saint fondateur de la royauté chrétienne', *Cahiers d'Etudes Hongroises* viii (1996), pp 34–58

Komjáthy, Miklós, *Quelques problèmes concernant la charte de fondation de l'abbaye de Tihany* (Budapest, 1960); also in: *Etudes historiques publiées par la Commission Nationale des Historiens Hongrois*, vol 1 (Budapest, 1960), pp 219–52

——, 'Quelques problèmes relatifs à la charte de fondation du couvent des religieuses de Veszprémvölgy', in P. Brière (ed.), *Mélanges offerts à Szabolcs de Vajay* (Braga, 1971), pp 369–80

Koszta, László, 'Die Domkapitel und ihre Domherren bis Anfang des 12. Jahrhunderts in Ungarn', in Balázs Nagy and Marcell Sebők (eds), *The Man of Many Devices, Who Wandered Full Many Ways* (Budapest, 1999), pp 478–91

Kosztolnyik, Zoltán J. 'The importance of Gerard of Csanád as the first author in Hungary', *Traditio* xxv (1969), pp 376–85

——, 'The negative results of the enforced missionary policy of King Saint Stephen of Hungary: the uprising of 1046', *The Catholic Historical Review* lix (1974), pp 569–86

——, *Five Eleventh-Century Hungarian Kings* (Boulder, 1981)

——, 'The Church and the Hungarian court under Coloman the Learned', *East European Quarterly* xviii/2 (1984), pp 130–41

——, *From Coloman the Learned to Béla III (1095–1196)* (Boulder, 1987)

——, 'Early twelfth-century German politics in the background of Hungary', in S.B. Várdy and A.H. Vardy (eds), *Triumph in Adversity: Studies in Hungarian Civilization in Honor of Professor Ferenc Somogyi* (Boulder, 1988), pp 61–76

Kovács, Éva, and Zsuzsa Lovag, *The Hungarian Crown and other Regalia* (Budapest, 1988)

Kristó, Gyula, 'Ajtony and Vidin', *Studia Turco-Hungarica*, vol 5 (Budapest, 1981) pp 129–35

——, 'Die Entstehung der Komitatsorganisation unter Stephan dem Heiligen', in Ferenc Glatz (ed.), *Etudes historiques hongroises 1990*, vol 1 (Budapest, 1990), pp 13–25

——, 'Les Kean dans le bassin carpathique', *Hungaro-Bulgarica*, vol 5 (Szeged, 1994) pp 11–24

Mályusz, Elemér, 'Die Eigenkirche un Ungarn', *Studien zur Geschichte Osteuropas* iii (1966), pp 76–95

Mezey, László, 'Ungarn und Europa im 12. Jahrhundert: Kirche und Kultur zwischen Ost und West', *Vorträge und Forschungen* xii (1968), pp 255–2

Moravcsik, Gyula, 'The role of the Byzantine Church in medieval Hungary', *American Slavic and East European Review* xviii–xix (1947), pp 134–51

——, *Byzantium and the Magyars* (Amsterdam, 1970)

Pražák, Richard, 'The legends of King Stephen', *Hungarian Studies* i (1985), pp 163–78

Ripoche, J.P., 'La Hongrie entre Byzance et Rome: problème de choix religieux', *Ungarn-Jahrbuch* vi (1974–75), pp 9–23

Sawicki, J. von, 'Zur Textkritik und Entstehungsgeschichte der Gesetze König Stefans des Heiligen', *Ungarische Jahrbücher* ix (1929), pp 395–425

Szabó, Csaba, 'Die militärischen Aspekte der deutsch-ungarischen Beziehungen während der Salierzeit', *Ungarn-Jahrbuch*, xxi (1995 for 1993–94), pp 1–18

Székely, György, 'Gemeinsame Züge der ungarischen und polnischen Kirchengeschichte im XI. Jahrhundert', *Annales Universitatis Scientiarum Budapestinensis, Sectio historica* iv (1962), pp 55–80

——, 'La Hongrie et Byzance aux Xe-XIIe siècles', *Acta Historica Academiae Scientiarum Hungaricae* xiii (1967), pp 291–311

Szentirmai, A., 'Der Ursprung des Archidiakonats in Ungarn', *Österreichisches Archiv für Kirchenrecht* vii (1956), pp 231–44

——, 'Das Recht des Erzdechanten (Archidiakon) in Ungarn während des Mittelalters', *Zeitschrift der Savigny-Stiftung für Rechtsgeschichte, Kanonistische Abteilung* xliii (1957), pp 132–201

——, 'Die Anfänge der Rechts der Pfarrei in Ungarn', *Österreichisches Archiv für Kirchenrecht* x (1959), pp 31–35

——, 'Der Einfluss des byzantinischen Kirchenrechts auf die Gesetzgebung Ungarns im XI.-XII. Jahrhundert', *Jahrbuch der österreichischen byzantinischen Gesellschaft* x (1961), pp 73–83

Szűcs, Jenő, 'König Stephan in der Sicht der modernen ungarischen Geschichtsforschung', *Südost-Forschungen* xxxi (1972), pp 17–40

——, 'King Stephen's exhortations and his state', *The New Hungarian Quarterly* cxii (1988), pp 89–97

Urbansky, A., *Byzantium and the Danube Frontier* (New York, 1968)

Váczy, Péter von, *Die erste Epoche des ungarischen Königtums* (Pécs, 1935)

CHAPTER 4: THE TWELFTH CENTURY

Ammann, Hektor, 'Die französische Südostwanderung im Rahmen der mittelalterlichen französischen Wanderungen', *Südost-Forschungen* xiv (1955), pp 406–28

Barta, Gábor, and János Barta, 'Royal finance in medieval Hungary: the revenues of King Béla III', in W.M. Ormrod, M.M. Bonney and R.J. Bonney (eds), *Crises, Revolutions and Self-Sustained Growth: Essays in European Fiscal History, c. 1130–1830* (Stamford, 1999), pp. 24–40.

Deér, József, 'Ungarn in der Descriptio Europae Orientalis', *Mitteilungen des Instituts für österreichische Geschichtsforschung* xlv (1931), pp 1–22

Dölger, Franz, 'Ungarn in der byzantinischen Reichspolitik', *Archivum Europae Centro-Orientalis* viii (1942), pp 315–412

d'Eszlary, C., 'Un état des revenus hongrois au XIIe siècle', *Annales* xvii (1962), pp 1117–24

Fügedi, Erik, 'Die Entstehung des Städtewesens in Ungarn', *Alba Regia* x (1969), pp 101–18; reprinted in Fügedi, *Kings*, chapter IX

Górka, Olgierd (ed.), *Anonymi Descriptio Europae Orientalis anno MCCCVIII* (Cracow, 1916)

Györffy, György, 'Les débuts de l'évolution urbaine en Hongrie', *Cahiers de civilisation médiévale* xii (1969), pp 127–46, 253–64

Hrbek, Ivan, 'Ein arabischer Bericht über Ungarn (Abu Ḥāmid al-Andalusī al-Garnāṭī, 1080–1170)', *Acta Orientalia Academiae Scientiarum Hungaricae* v (1955), pp 205–30

Kosztolnyik, Z.J., 'The church and Béla III of Hungary (1172–1196): the role of Archbishop Lukács of Esztergom', *Church History* xlix (1980)

——, *From Coloman the Learned to Béla III (1095–1196)* (Boulder, 1987)

Kubinyi, András, 'Die Anfänge des städtischen Handwerks in Ungarn', in László Gerevich and Ágnes Salamon (eds), *La formation et le développement des métiers au Moyen Age (Ve-XVe siècles)* (Budapest, 1977), pp 139–153

Kumorovitz, Bernát. L., 'Die erste Epoche der ungarischen privatrechtlichen Schriftlichkeit im Mittelalter (XI-XII. Jahrhundert)', *Etudes historiques publiées par la Commission Nationale des Historiens Hongrois*, vol 1 (Budapest, 1960), pp 253–90

Laszlovszky, József, 'Einzelsiedlungen in der Arpadenzeit', *Acta Archaeologica Academiae Scientiarum Hungaricae* xxxviii (1986), pp 227–55

——, 'Nicholaus clericus: a Hungarian student at Oxford University in the twelfth century', *Journal of Medieval History* xiv (1988), pp 217–31

Makk, Ferenc, *The Árpáds and the Comneni* (Budapest, 1989)

Makkai, László, 'Östliches Erbe und westliche Leihe in der ungarischen Landwirtschaft der frühfeudalen Zeit (10.–13. Jahrhundert)', *Agrártörténeti Szemle* xvi (1974) Supplement, pp 2–53

Otto of Freising, *The Deeds of Frederick Barbarossa*, ed. C.C. Mierow and R. Emery (New York, 1953)

Romhányi, Beatrix, 'The role of the Cistercians in medieval Hungary: political activity or internal colonization?', *Annual of Medieval Studies at the CEU, 1993–94* (Budapest, 1995), pp 180–204

Stephenson, Paul, 'Manuel I. Comnenus and Géza II: A revised context and chronology for Hungaro-Byzantine relations, 1148–1155', *Byzantinoslavica* lv (1994), pp 251–78

Székely, György, 'Wallons et Italiens en Europe centrale aux XIe-XVIe siècles', *Annales Universitatis Scientiarum Budapestinensis, Sectio historica* vi (1964), pp 3–71

Szovák, Kornél, 'The transformations of the image of the ideal king in twelfth-century Hungary', in Anne J. Duggan (ed.), *Kings and Kingship in Medieval Europe* (London, 1993), pp 241–64

Szűcs, Jenő, 'The peoples of medieval Hungary', in Ferenc Glatz (ed.), *Etudes historiques hongroises*, vol 2 (Budapest, 1990), pp 11–20

Váczy, Péter, 'Some questions of early Hungarian history and material culture', *Antaeus* xix–xx (1990–91), pp 257–329

CHAPTER 5: EARLY HUNGARIAN SOCIETY

Bolla, Ilona, and Pál Horváth, 'La rôle de la liberté commune dans le développement de la société hongroise médiévale', *Annales Universitatis Scientiarum Budapestinensis, Sectio iuridica* xxiii (1981), pp 9–25

Györffy, György, 'Zur Herkunft der ungarländischen Dienstleute', *Studia Slavica Academiae Scientiarum Hungaricae* xxii (1976), pp 40–83, 311–37

——, *Wirtschaft und Gesellschaft der Ungarn um die Jahrtausendwende*, Studia historica, No 186 (Budapest, 1983)

Kucera, M., 'Anmerkungen zur Dienstorganisation im frühmittelalterlichen Ungarn', *Zborník filozofickej fakulty Univerzity Komenského, Historica* xxi (1970)

Lederer, Emma, *La structure de la société hongroise du début du moyen-âge* (Budapest, 1960); also in: *Etudes historiques publiées par la Commission Nationale des Historiens Hongrois*, vol 1 (Budapest, 1960), pp 195–217

CHAPTER 6: THE AGE OF THE GOLDEN BULLS

Adriányi, Gabriel, 'Zur Geschichte des Deutschen Ritterordens im Burzenland', *Ungarn-Jahrbuch* iii (1971), pp 9–22

Baliç, S., 'Der Islam im mittelalterlichen Ungarn', *Südost-Forschungen* xxiii (1964), pp 19–35

Chalikow, A.H., 'Auf der Suche nach "Magna Hungaria"', *Hungarian Studies* ii (1986), pp 189–215

Deér, Josef, 'Der Weg zur Goldenen Bulle Andreas II.', *Schweizer Beiträge zur allgemeinen Geschichte* x (1952), pp 104–38

Fügedi, Erik, *Castle and Society in Medieval Hungary (1000–1437)*, Studia historica, No 187 (Budapest, 1986): chapter 2

Glassl, Horst, 'Der Deutsche Orden im Burzenland und in Kumanien', *Ungarn-Jahrbuch* iii (1971), pp 23–49

Göckenjan, Hansgerd, and J.R. Sweeney (eds), *Der Mongolensturm. Berichte von Augenzeugen und Zeitgenossen, 1235–1250* (Graz, Vienna and Köln, 1985)

Koszta, László, 'Un prélat français en Hongrie: Bertalan, évêque de Pécs (1219–1251)', *Cahiers d'études hongroises* viii (1996), pp 71–96

Kosztolnyik, Zoltán J., 'De facultate resistendi: two essential characteristics of the Hungarian Golden Bull of 1222', *Studies in Medieval Culture* v (1975), pp 97–104

——, *Hungary in the Thirteenth Century* (New York, 1996)

Kubinyi, András, 'Königliche Kanzlei und Hofkapelle in Ungarn um die Mitte des 12. Jahrhunderts', in Herwig Ebner (ed.), *Festschrift Friedrich Hausmann* (Graz, 1977), pp 299–324

Maksay, Ferenc, 'Umwandlung der ungarischen Siedlungs- und Agrarstruktur (11.–14. Jh.)', *Zeitschrift für Agrargeschichte und Agrarsoziologie* xxiii (1975), pp 154–64

Pálóczi Horváth, A., *Pechenegs, Cumans, Iasians. Steppe Peoples in Medieval Hungary* (Budapest, 1989)

Strakosch-Grassmann, Gustav, *Der Einfall der Mongolen in Mitteleuropa in den Jahren 1241 und 1242* (Innsbruck, 1893)

Sweeney, James Ross, 'The Decretal Intellecto and the Hungarian Golden Bull of 1222', *Album Elemér Mályusz* (Brussels, 1976), pp 89–96

——, 'Hungary in the Crusades, 1169–1218', *International History Review* iii (1981), pp 468–81

——, 'Innocent III, canon law and papal judges delegate in Hungary', in J.R. Sweeney and S. Chodorow (eds), *Popes, Teachers and Canon Law in the Middle Ages* (Ithaca and London, 1989), pp 26–52

——, 'Identifying the medieval refugee: Hungarians in flight during the Mongol invasion', in L. Löb et al. (eds), *Forms of identity* (Szeged, 1994), pp 63–76

——, '*Summa potestas post Deum* – *Papal dilectio* and Hungarian *devotio* in the reign of Innocent III', in Balázs Nagy and Marcell Sebök (eds), *The Man of Many Devices, Who Wandered Full Many Ways* (Budapest, 1999), pp 492–98

Szabó, István, 'The praedium: studies on the economic history and the history of settlement of early Hungary', *Agrártörténeti Szemle* v (1963) Supplementum, pp 1–24

Wertner, Moritz, 'Ungarns Hofwürdenträger bis 1301', *Jahrbuch des k[aiserlichen und] k[öniglichen] heraldischen Gesellschaft 'Adler'*, NF v–vi (1895), pp 83–112

Zimmermann, Harald, *Im Bann des Mittelalters* (Sigmaringen, 1986), pp 152–183 (chapter: 'Der deutsche Ritterorden in Siebenbürgen')

CHAPTER 7: THE LAST ÁRPÁDIANS

Bónis, György, 'Les autorités de "foi publique" et les archives des "loci credibiles" en Hongrie', *Archivum* xii (1962), pp 87–104

Darkó, Eugen, *Byzantinisch-ungarische Beziehungen in der zweiten Hälfte des XIII. Jahrhunderts* (Weimar, 1933)

Dienst, Heide, *Die Schlacht an der Leitha 1246* (Vienna, 1971)

Eckhart, Franz, 'Die glaubwürdigen Orte Ungarns im Mittelalter', *Mitteilungen des Instituts für österreichische Geschichtsforschung, Ergänzungsband* ix (1913/15), pp 395–558

Fügedi, Erik, 'Kirchliche Topographie und Siedlungsgeschichte im Mittelalter in der Slowakei', *Studia Slavica Academiae Scientiarum Hungaricae* v (1959) pp 363–400

——, 'Das mittelalterliche Königreich Ungarn als Gastland', in Walter Schlesinger (ed.), *Die deutsche Ostsiedlung des Mittelalters als Problem der europäischen Geschichte*, Vorträge und Forschungen, vol 18 (Sigmaringen, 1975), pp 471–507; reprinted in Fügedi, *Kings*, chapter VIII

——, *Castle and Society in Medieval Hungary (1000–1437)*, Studia historica, No 187 (Budapest, 1986): chapters 3 and 4

Gerics, József, 'Über das Rechtsleben Ungarns um die Wende des 13.–14. Jahrhunderts', *Annales Universitatis Scientiarum Budapestinensis, Sectio historica* xvii (1976), pp 45–80

——, 'Das Gericht *prasentia regia* in Ungarn am Ende des 13. Jahrhunderts', *Annales Universitatis Scientiarum Budapestinensis, Sectio historica* xix (1978), pp 33–46

——, 'Das frühe Ständewesen in Ungarn und sein europäischer Hintergrund: Das Patriarchat von Aquileja und Ungarn am Ende des 13. Jahrhunderts', in Ferenc Glatz and Ervin Pamlényi (eds), *Etudes historiques hongroises 1985 publiées à l'occasion du Congrès International des Sciences Historiques*, vol 1 (Budapest, 1985), pp 285–303

Göckenjan, Hansgerd, *Hilfsvölker und Grenzwächter im mittealterlichen Ungarn* (Wiesbaden, 1972)

Grothusen, K.-D., *Entstehung und Geschichte Zagrebs bis zum Ausgang des 14. Jahrhunderts* (Wiesbaden, 1971)

Györffy, György, *Einwohnerzahl und Bevölkerungsdichte in Ungarn bis zum Anfang des 14. Jahrhunderts*, Studia historica, No 42 (Budapest, 1960); also in: *Etudes historiques publiées par la Commission Nationale des Historiens Hongrois*, vol 1 (Budapest, 1960), pp 163–193

Hajnal, István, 'Die Kanzlei König Bélas IV.', *Ungarische Rundschau für historische und soziale Wissenschaften* v (1916/17), pp 26–62

Honemann, V., 'A medieval queen and her stepdaughter: Agnes and Elisabeth of Hungary', in A.J. Duggan, ed., *Queens and queenship in medieval Europe* (Woodbridge, 1997), pp 109–19

Horedt, Kurt, *Siebenbürgen im Frühmittelalter* (Bonn, 1986)

Hunyadi, Zsolt, 'The Knights of St John and the Hungarian private legal literacy up to the mid-fourteenth century', in Balázs Nagy and Marcell Sebők (eds), *The Man of Many Devices, Who Wandered Full Many Ways* (Budapest, 1999), pp 507–19

Kaindl, Raimund Friedrich, 'Studien zur Geschichte des deutschen Rechtes in Ungarn und dessen Nebenländern', *Archiv für österreichische Geschichte* xcviii (1909), pp 383–470

Kaufmann, Jacques, *Eine Studie über die Beziehungen der Habsburger zum Königreiche Ungarn in den Jahren 1278 bis 1366*, Burgenländische Forschungen, 59 (Eisenstadt, 1970)

Kordé, Zoltán, 'Problems of medieval and modern identity: the case of the Székelys', in Ladislaus Löb et al. (eds), *Forms of identity: Definitions and Changes* (Szeged, 1994), pp 37–44

Kosztolnyik, Z.J., 'Did the Curia intervene in the struggle for the Hungarian throne during the 1290s', in Imre Békési et al. (eds), *Régi és új peregrináció Magyarok külföldön külföldiek Magyarországon*, 3 vols (Budapest, 1993), vol. 1, pp. 140–58

——, 'In the European mainstream: Hungarian churchmen and thirteenth-century synods', *Catholic Historical Review* lxxix (1993), pp 413–33

——, 'Remarks on Andrew III of Hungary', in László Koszta (ed.), *Kelet és Nyugat között* (Szeged, 1995), pp 273–90

——, *Hungary in the Thirteenth Century* (New York, 1996)

Kovách, A., 'Der "Mongolenbrief" Bélas IV. an Papst Innozenz IV.', in J.G. Farkas (ed.), *Überlieferung und Auftrag: Festschrift für Michael de Ferdinandy zum 60. Geburtstag* (Wiesbaden, 1972)

Kristó, Gyula, 'Über die Hunnentradition der Ungarn', *Varia Eurasiatica. Festschrift für Professor András Róna-Tas* (Szeged, 1991), pp 117–25

Kurcz, Ágnes, 'Arenga und Narratio ungarischer Urkunden des 13. Jahrhunderts', *Mitteilungen des Instituts für österreichische Geschichtsforschung* lxx (1962), pp 323–54

Mályusz, Elemér, 'La chancellerie royale et la rédaction des chroniques dans la Hongrie médiévale', *Le Moyen Age* lxxv (1969), pp 51–86, 219–54

Mezey, László, 'Anfänge der Privaturkunde in Ungarn und der glaubwürdigen Orte', *Archiv für Diplomatik* xviii (1972) pp 209–302

Nägler, Thomas, *Die Ansiedlung der Siebenbürger Sachsen* (Bukarest, 1992)

Pálóczi Horváth, A., *Pechenegs, Cumans, Iasians. Steppe Peoples in Medieval Hungary* (Budapest, 1989)

Pop, Ioan-Aurel, *Romanians and Hungarians from the 9th to the 14th Century: The Genesis of the Transylvanian Medieval State* (Cluj-Napoca, 1996)

Schlesinger, W. (ed.), *Die deutsche Ostsiedlung des Mittelalters als Problem der eupäischen Geschichte* (Sigmaringen, 1975)

Schramm, Gottfried, 'Frühe Schicksale der Rumänen. Acht Thesen zur Lokalisierung der lateinischen Kontinuität in Südosteuropa', *Zeitschrift für Balkanologie* xxi (1985), pp 223–41; xxii (1986), pp 104–25; xxiii (1987), pp 78–94

Schünemann, K., *Die Entstehung des Städtewesens in Südosteuropa* (Bresslau-Oppeln, 1928)

Szűcs, Jenő, *Theoretical Elements in Master Simon of Kéza's Gesta Hungarorum: 1282–1285 A.D.*, Studia historica, No 96 (Budapest, 1975); also in: *Etudes historiques hongroises 1975 publiées à l'occasion du XIVe Congrès International des Sciences Historiques*, vol 1 (Budapest, 1975), pp 239–81

Veszprémy, László and Frank Schaer (trans. and eds), *Simon of Keza: The Deeds of the Hungarians* (Budapest, 1999)

Zajtay, I., 'Le registre de Várad: Un document judiciaire du XIIIe siècle', *Revue d'histoire du droit* iv/32 (1954), pp 527–562

CHAPTER 8: CHARLES I OF ANJOU (1301–1342)

Angioini: Colloquio italo-ungherese sul tema "Gli Angioini d Napoli e di Ungheria" (Rome, 1974)

Bak, János M., 'Sankt Stefans Armreliquie im Ornat König Wenzels von Ungarn', *Festschrift Percy Ernst Schramm zu seinem 70. Geburtstag ... zugeeignet* (Wiesbaden, 1964), pp 175–188

Engel, Pál, 'Die Güssinger im Kampf gegen die ungarische Krone', in Heide Dienst and Irmtraut Lindeck-Pozza (eds), *Die Güssinger. Beiträge zur Geschichte der Herren von Güns/Güssing und ihrer Zeit (13./14. Jahrhundert)* (Eisenstadt, 1989), pp 85–113

Karpat, Josef, 'Die Idee der Heiligen Krone Ungarns in neuer Beleuchtung', in Manfred Hellmann (ed.), *Corona regni. Studien über die Krone als Symbol des Staates im späteren Mittelalter* (Weimar, 1961), pp 349–98

Knoll, P., *The Rise of the Polish Monarchy: Piast Poland in East Central Europe, 1320–1370* (Chicago–London, 1972)

Kristó, Gyula, 'Die Macht der Territorialherren in Ungarn am Anfang des 14. Jahrhunderts', *Etudes historiques hongroises 1985 publiées à l'occasion du Congrès International des Sciences Historiques*, vol 1 (Budapest, 1985), pp 597–614

Léonard, Émile G., *Les Angevins de Naples* (Paris, 1954)

Rowell, S.C., *Lithuania Ascending. A Pagan Empire Within East-Central Europe, 1295–1345* (Cambridge, 1994)

Szekfý, Julius, 'Die Servienten und Familiaren im ungarischen Mittelalter', *Ungarische Rundschau*, ii (1912), pp 524–57

CHAPTER 9: THE NEW MONARCHY

Bónis, György, *Einflüsse des römischen Rechts in Ungarn*, Jus Romanum Medii Aevi, part 5, no 10 (Milan, 1964)

Boulton, D'A.J.D., *The Knights of the Crown: the Monarchical Orders of Knighthood in Later Medieval Europe, 1325–1520* (Woodbridge, 1987): chapter 2 on the 'Fraternal Society of Knighthood of St George'

Engel, Pál, 'Die Grafschaft (Gespanschaft) Eisenburg im 14. Jahrhundert', in Heide Dienst and Irmtraut Lindeck-Pozza (eds), *Die Güssinger. Beiträge zur Geschichte der Herren von Güns/Güssing und ihrer Zeit (13./14. Jahrhundert)* (Eisenstadt, 1989), pp 115–26

——, 'Honor, castrum, comitatus. Studies in the Government System of the Angevin Kingdom', *Quaestiones Medii Aevi Novae*, i (1996), pp 91–100

Fügedi, Erik, *Castle and Society in Medieval Hungary (1000–1437)*, Studia historica, No 187 (Budapest, 1986)

——, 'Turniere im mittelalterlichen Ungarn', in Josef Fleckenstein (ed.), *Das ritterliche Turnier im Mittelalter* (Göttingen, 1985), pp 390–400

Györffy, György, 'Zur demographischen Wertung der päpstlichen Zehntlisten', *Etudes historiques hongroises 1980 publiées à l'occasion du*

XVe Congrès International des Sciences Historiques, vol 1 (Budapest, 1980), pp 61–84

Holub, József, 'Ordinaria potentia – absoluta potentia', *Revue historique de droit français et étranger* xxvii (1950), pp 92–9

Laszlovszky, József (ed.), *Medieval Visegrád* (Budapest, 1995)

Prokopp, M., *Italian Trecento Influence on Murals in East-Central Europe, Particularly Hungary* (Budapest, 1983)

CHAPTER 10: LOUIS THE GREAT (1342–1382)

Cox, E.L., *The Green Count of Savoy: Amadeus VI and Transalpine Savoy in the Fourteenth Century* (Princeton, 1967)

Davies, Norman, *God's Playground. A History of Poland*, 2 vols (Oxford, 1981): vol 1, chapter 4

Deletant, Dennis, 'Moldavia between Hungary and Poland, 1347–1412', *The Slavonic and East European Review* lxiv (1986), pp 189–211

Engel, Pál, 'Zur Frage der bosnisch-ungarischen Beziehungen im 14–15. Jahrhundert', *Südost-Forschungen* lviii (1997), pp 27–42

Ferdinandy, Michael de, 'Ludwig I. von Ungarn (1342–1382)', *Südost-Forschungen* xxxi (1972), pp 41–80; also in: Vardy et al., *Louis the Great*, pp 3–48

Gill, J. 'John V Palaeologus at the court of Louis I of Hungary (1366)', *Byzantinoslavica* xxxviii (1977), pp 31–8

Gjuzelev, Vasil, 'La guerre bulgaro-hongroise au printemps de 1365 et des documents nouveaux sur la domination hongroise du royaume de Vidin (1365–1369), *Byzantinobulgarica* vi (1980), pp 153–72

Halecki, O., *Un empereur de Byzance à Rome. Vingt ans de travail pour l'union des églises et pour la défense de l'Empire d'Orient: 1355–75* (Warsaw, 1930)

Housley, Norman, 'King Louis the Great of Hungary and the Crusades, 1342–1382', *Slavonic and East European Review* lxxii (1984), pp 192–208

——, *The Avignon Papacy and the Crusades, 1305–78* (Oxford, 1986)

Huber, Alfons, 'Ludwig I. von Ungarn und die ungarischen Vasallenländer', *Archiv für österreichische Geschichte* lxvi (1885), pp 1–44

Karbić, Damir, 'Defining the position of Croatia during the restoration of royal power (1345–1361): an outline', in Balázs Nagy and Marcell Sebök (eds), *The Man of Many Devices, Who Wandered Full Many Ways* (Budapest, 1999), pp 520–6

Kardos, Tibor et al. (eds), *Die ungarische Bilderchronik* (Berlin, 1961)

Klaniczay, Gábor, 'The cult of dynastic saints in central Europe (fourteenth-century Angevins and Luxemburgs)', in K. Margolis (ed.), *The Uses of Supernatural Power: The Transformation of Popular Religion in Medieval and Early Modern Europe* (Cambridge, 1990), pp 111–28

Steinherz, S., 'Die Beziehungen Ludwigs I. von Ungarn zu Karl IV.', *Mitteilungen des Instituts für österreichische Geschichtsforschung* viii (1887), pp 219–57; ix (1888), pp 529–637

Valois, N., 'Le projet de mariage entre Louis de France et Cathérine de Hongrie et le voyage de l'empereur Charles IV à Paris', *Annuaire Bulletin de la Société de l'Histoire de France*, 1893

Vardy, S.B., Géza Goldschmidt and Leslie S. Domonkos (eds), *Louis the Great, King of Hungary and Poland* (New York, 1986)

CHAPTER 11: THE MONARCHY OF LOUIS THE GREAT

Bónis, György, 'Men learned in the law in medieval Hungary', *East Central Europe* iv/1 (1977), pp 181–91

Domonkos, L.S., 'The problems of Hungarian university foundations in the Middle Ages', in S.B. Vardy and A.H. Vardy (eds), *Society in Change: Studies in Honour of Béla K. Király* (New York, 1983), pp 371–90

Engel, Pál, 'Erbteilung und Familienbildung', in Balázs Nagy and Marcell Sebök (eds), *The Man of Many Devices, Who Wandered Full Many Ways* (Budapest, 1999), pp 411–21

Fügedi, Erik, 'The avus in the medieval conceptual framework of kinship in Hungary', *Studia Slavica Academiae Scientiarum Hungaricae* xxv (1979), pp 137–42; reprinted in Fügedi, *Kings*, chapter IV

——, '*Verba volant*… Oral culture and literacy among the medieval Hungarian nobility', in Fügedi, *Kings*, chapter VI

Gabriel, Astrik L., *The Medieval Universities of Pécs and Pozsony* (Frankfurt a. M., 1969)

Gerics, József, 'Beiträge zur Geschichte der Gerichtsbarkeit im ungarischen königlichen Hof und der Zentralverwaltung im 14. Jahrhundert', *Annales Universitatis Scientiarum Budapestinensis, Sectio historica* vii (1965), pp 3–28

Holub, József, 'La "quarta puellaris" dans l'ancien droit hongrois', *Studi in memoria di Adelo Albertoni*, vol 3 (Padova, 1935), pp 277–97

Rady, Martyn, 'The filial quarter and female inheritance in medieval Hungarian law', in Balázs Nagy and Marcell Sebök (eds), *The Man of Many Devices, Who Wandered Full Many Ways* (Budapest, 1999), pp 422–31

Sroka, Stanisław, 'Herzog Ladislaus von Oppeln als ungarischer Palatin (1367–1372)', *Zeitschrift für Ostmitteleuropa-Forschung* xlvi (1997), pp 224–34

Székely, György, 'Die Einheit und Gleichheit des Adels: Bestrebungen in Ungarn des 14. Jahrhunderts', *Annales Universitatis Budapestinensis, Sectio historica* xxvi (1993), pp 113–39

Vardy, S.B., Géza Goldschmidt and Leslie S. Domonkos (eds), *Louis the Great, King of Hungary and Poland* (New York, 1986)

Virágos, Gábor, 'A history of the Cyko family of Pomáz', in Balázs Nagy and Marcell Sebök (eds), *The Man of Many Devices, Who Wandered Full Many Ways* (Budapest, 1999), pp. 539–49

CHAPTER 12: THE YEARS OF CRISES (1382–1403)

Atiya, Aziz Suryal, *The Crusade of Nicopolis* (London, 1934, reprinted 1978)

Bartl, Július, 'Political and social situation in Slovakia at the turning point of the 14th and 15th centuries and the reign of Sigismund of Luxemburg', *Studia Historica Slovaca* ix (1979), pp 41–84

Beckmann, Gustav, *Der Kampf Kaiser Sigismunds gegen die werdende Groß-macht der Osmanen (1392–1437)* (Gotha, 1902)

Borosy, András, 'The militia portalis in Hungary before 1526', in János M. Bak and Béla K. Király (eds), *From Hunyadi to Rákóczi: War and Society in Medieval and Early Modern Hungary* (New York, 1982), pp 63–80

Cutolo, Alessandro, *Re Ladislao d'Angiò-Durazzo*, 2 vols (Milan, 1936)

Gündisch, Gustav, 'Die Türkeneinfälle in Siebenbürgen bis zur Mitte des 15. Jahrhunderts', *Jahrbücher für Geschichte Osteuropas* ii (1937), pp 393–412

——, 'Siebenbürgen in der Türkenabwehr, 1395–1526', *Revue Roumaine d'Histoire* xiii (1974), pp 415–43

Emmert, T.A., *Serbian Golgotha: Kosovo, 1389* (Boulder, 1990)

Halecki, O., *Jadwiga of Anjou and the Rise of East Central Europe* (Boulder, 1991)

Hoensch, Jörg K. (ed.), *Itinerar König und Kaiser Sigismunds von Luxem-burg 1368–1437* (Warendorf, 1995)

——, *Kaiser Sigismund. Herrscher an der Schwelle zur Neuzeit 1368–1437* (München, 1996; bibliography on pp 527–47)

Huber, Alfons, 'Die Gefangennehmung der Königinnen Elisabeth und Maria von Ungarn und die Kämpfe König Sigismunds gegen die neapolitanische Partei und die übrigen Reichsfeinde in den Jahren 1386–1395', *Archiv für österreichische Geschichte* lxvi (1885), pp 509–46

Inalcik, Halil, 'An Ottoman document on Bayezid I's expedition into Hungary and Wallachia', *Actes du Xe Congrès International d'Etudes Byzantines* (Istanbul, 1957) pp 220–222

Kintzinger, Martin, 'Sigismond, roi de Hongrie et la croisade', *Annales de Bourgogne*, lxviii/3 (1996), pp 23–33

Kupelwieser, Leopold, *Die Kämpfe Ungarns mit den Osmanen bis zur Schlacht bei Mohács* (Vienna, 1895)

Macek, Josef, Ernö Marosi and Ferdinand Seibt (eds), *Sigismund von Luxemburg, Kaiser und König in Mitteleuropa 1387–1437* (Warendorf, 1994)

Mályusz, Elemér, *Kaiser Sigismund in Ungarn 1387–1437* (Budapest, 1990); bibliography: pp 378–98.

Nowak, Zenon Hubert, 'Kaiser Siegmund und die polnische Monarchie (1387–1437)', *Zeitschift für Historische Forschung* xv (1988), pp 423–36

Pfotenhauer, P., 'Eine schlesische Prinzessin als ungarische Königsbraut', *Zeitschrift des Vereins für Geschichte und Altertum Schlesiens* xxv (1891), pp 331–40

Sághy, Marianne, 'Aspects of female rulership in late medieval literature: the queens' reign in Angevin Hungary', *East Central Europe/ L'Europe du Centre Est* xx–xxiii/1 (1993–6), pp 69–86

Szakály, Ferenc, 'Phases of Turco-Hungarian Warfare before the battle of Mohács (1365–1526)', *Acta Orientalia Academiae Scientiarum Hungaricae* xxxiii (1979), pp 65–111

CHAPTER 13: SIGISMUND'S CONSOLIDATION

Bak, János M., 'Monarchie im Wellental: Materielle Grundlagen des ungarischen Königtums im späteren Mittelalter', in R. Schneider (ed.), *Das spätmittelalterliche Königtum im europäischen Vergleich* (Sigmaringen, 1987), pp 347–87

Bard, I.N., 'The Break of 1404 between the Hungarian Church and Rome', *Ungarn-Jahrbuch* x (1979), pp 59–69

Dopsch, Heinz, 'Die Grafen von Cilli – ein Forschungsproblem', *Südostdeutsches Archiv* xvii/xviii (1974/75), pp 9–49

Draskóczy, István, 'Zur Frage des ungarischen Salzwesens unter König Sigismund', in Josef Macek, Ernö Marosi and Ferdinand Seibt (eds), *Sigismund von Luxemburg, Kaiser und König in Mitteleuropa 1387–1437* (Warendorf, 1994), pp 184–91

'Due vite di Filippo Scolari detto Pippo Spano', *Archivio Storico Italiano* iv (1843), pp 117–232

Engel, Pál, 'Die Einkünfte Kaiser Sigismunds in Ungarn', Josef Macek, Ernö Marosi and Ferdinand Seibt (eds), *Sigismund von Luxemburg, Kaiser und König in Mitteleuropa 1387–1437* (Warendorf, 1994), pp 179–82

Fahlbusch, Friedrich Bernward, 'König Sigmunds Dekret von 1405 April 15', *Zeitschrift für Siebenbürgische Landeskunde* iv (1981), pp 61–74

——, *Städte und Königtum im frühen 15. Jahrhundert. Ein Beitrag zur Geschichte Sigismunds von Luxemburg* (Köln-Wien, 1983)

Held, Joseph, 'Military reform in early 15th-century Hungary', *East European Quarterly* xi/2 (1977), pp 129–39

Isenmann, Eberhard, 'Reichsfinanzen und Reichssteuern im 15. Jahrhundert', *Zeitschrift für Historische Forschung* vii (1980), pp 1–76, 129–218

Krzenck, Thomas, 'Barbara von Cilli – eine "deutsche Messalina"?', *Mitteilungen der Gesellschaft für Salzburger Landeskunde* cxxxi (1991), pp 45–67

Kubinyi, András, 'Der ungarische König und seine Städte im 14. und am Beginn des 15. Jahrhunderts', in Wilhelm Rausch (ed.), *Stadt und Stadtherr im 14. Jahrhundert* (Linz, 1972), pp 193–228

Mályusz, Elemér, *Das Konstanzer Konzil und das königliche Patronatsrecht in Ungarn*, Studia historica, No 18 (Budapest, 1959)

——, *Die Zentralisationsbestrebungen König Sigismunds in Ungarn*, Studia historica, No 50 (Budapest, 1960); also in: *Etudes historiques publiées par la Commission Nationale des Historiens Hongrois*, vol 1 (Budapest, 1960), pp 317–358

Pirchegger, Hans, 'Die Grafen von Cilli, ihre Grafschaft und ihre unter-steirischen Herrschaften', *Ostdeutsche Wissenschaft* ii (1955), pp 157–200

Süttö, Szilárd, and Pál Engel, 'Beiträge zur Herkunft und zur Tätigkeit der Familie von Alben in Ungarn', *Südost-Forschungen* liv (1995), pp 23–48

Szilágyi, Loránd, 'Die Personalunion des deutschen Reiches mit Ungarn in den Jahren 1410–1439', *Ungarische Jahrbücher* xvi (1936), pp 145–89

CHAPTER 14: SIGISMUND'S FOREIGN POLICY (1403–1437)

Altmann, Wilhelm (ed.), *Eberhart Windeckes Denkwürdigkeiten zur Geschichte des Zeitalters Kaiser Sigismunds* (Berlin, 1893)

Delehaye, H., 'Le pélerinage de Laurent de Pasztho au purgatoire de S. Patrice', *Analecta Bollandiana*, xxvii (Brussels, 1908), pp 35–60

Domonkos, Leslie S., 'The History of the Sigismundean Foundation of the University of Óbuda', *Studium Generale: Studies Offred to A.L. Gabriel* (Notre Dame, 1967), pp 1–28

Ducellier, Alain, 'Deux projets vénitiens d'assasinat du roi Zsigmond (1415–1419)', *Études Finno-Ougriennes* viii (1975), pp 61–6

Joachim, Ernst, 'König Siegmund und der Deutsche Ritterorden in Ungarn 1429–1432, *Mitteilungen des Instituts für österreichische Geschichtsforschung* xxxiii (1912), pp 87–119

Mályusz, Elemér, 'Die vier Gebrüder Tallóci', *Studia Slavica Academiae Scientiarum Hungaricae* xxviii (1982), pp 1–66

——, 'Die gesellschaftlichen Grundlagen der ungarischen geistlichen Intelligenz im Mittelalter. Zur Geschichte der Ofner Universität', *Acta Historica Academiae Scientiarum Hungaricae* xxxii (1986), pp 243–70

Stromer, Wolfgang von, 'Diplomatische Kontakte des Herrschers vom Weissen Hammel, Uthman genannt Qara-Yuluq, mit dem deutschen König Sigismund', *Südost-Forschungen* xx (1961), pp 267–72

——, 'Eine Botschaft des Turkmenenfürsten Qara Yuluq an König Sigismund auf dem Nürnberger Reichstag im März 1431', *Jahrbuch für Fränkische Landesforschung* xxii (1962), pp 433–41

——, 'König Siegmunds Gesandte in den Orient', *Festschrift für Hermann Heimpel zum 70. Geburtstag*, vol 2 (Göttingen, 1972), pp 591–609

——, 'Landmacht gegen Seemacht. Kaiser Sigismunds Kontinentalsperre gegen Venedig 1412–1433', *Zeitschrift für Historische Forschung* xxii (1995), pp 145–89

Székely, György, 'Sigismund von Luxemburg und das Universitätsleben', in Josef Macek, Ernö Marosi and Ferdinand Seibt (eds), *Sigismund von Luxemburg, Kaiser und König in Mitteleuropa 1387–1437* (Warendorf, 1994), pp 132–43

Tardy, Lajos, 'Ungarns antiosmanische Bündnisse mit Staaten des Nahen Ostens und deren Vorgeschichte', *Anatolica* iv (1971/72), pp 139–56

Tenenti, Alberto, 'La politica veneziana e l'Ungheria all' epoca di Sigismondo', in Tibor Klaniczay (ed.), *Rapporti veneto-ungheresi all' epoca del Rinascimento* (Budapest, 1975), pp 219–29

Wakounig, Marija, *Dalmatien und Friaul. Die Auseinandersetzungen zwischen Sigismund von Luxemburg und der Republik von Venedig um die Vorherrschaft im adriatischen Raum* (Vienna, 1990)

CHAPTER 15: TRADE AND TOWNS

Barta, Étienne, 'L'Université Charles de Prague et la Hongrie', *Revue d'Histoire Comparée* xxvi (1948), pp 213–31

Bartosiewicz, László, *Animals in the Urban Landscape in the Wake of the Middle Ages: a Case Study from Vác*, Hungary, BAR International Series, 609 (Oxford, 1995)

Bertényi, Iván, 'Die städtischen Bürger und das Gericht der königlichen Anwesenheit im 14. Jahrhundert', *Annales Universitatis Scientiarum Budapestinensis, Sectio historica* xi (1970), pp 3–31

Biegel, Gerd (ed.), *Budapest im Mittelalter* (Braunschweig, 1991)

Birnbaum, M.D., 'Buda between Tartars and Turks', in B. Krekiç (ed.), *Urban Society of Eastern Europe in Premodern Times* (London, 1987), pp 137–57

Fügedi, Erik, 'Die Verflechtung des Bürgertums und Adels in Ungarn am Ende des XIV. Jahrhunderts: Die Familie Vincze von Szentgyörgy', in P. Brière (ed.), *Mélanges offerts à Szabolcs de Vajay* (Braga, 1971), pp 231–46

——, 'Die Ausbreitung der städtischen Lebensform: Ungarns oppida im XIV. Jahrhundert', in Wilhelm Rausch (ed.), *Stadt und Stadtherr im XIV. Jahrhundert* (Linz, 1972), pp 165–92; reprinted in Fügedi, *Kings*, chapter XIII

Gerevich, László, *The Art of Buda and Pest in the Middle Ages* (Budapest, 1971)

—— (ed.), *Towns in Medieval Hungary* (Budapest, 1990)

Gündisch, Konrad G., *Das Patriziat siebenbürgischer Städte im Mittelalter* (Cologne, 1993)

Halaga, Ondrej R., 'Kaufleute und Handelsgüter der Hanse im Karpatengebiet', *Hansische Geschichtsblätter* lxxxv (1967), pp 59–84

——, 'Kaschaus Rolle in der Ostpolitik Siegmunds von Luxemburg', in Uwe Bestmann et al. (eds), *Hochfinanz, Wirtschaftsräume, Innovationen. Festschrift für Wolfgang von Stromer*, vol 1 (Trier, 1987), pp 384–411

Heckenast, Gusztáv, 'Die Verbreitung des Wasserradantriebs im Eisenhüttenwesen in Ungarn', *Nouvelles études historiques publiées à l'occasion du XIIe Congrès International des Sciences Historiques*, vol 1 (Budapest, 1965) pp 159–79

——, 'Das Eisenwesen im mittelalterlichen Ungarn: Die Produktions – und Eigentumsverhältnisse', *Der Anschnitt* xxxv (1983), pp 2–11

——, 'Der Anteil des Deutschtums in der technischen Entwicklung des oberungarischen Eisenhüttenwesens vom 13. bis Ende des 18. Jahrhunderts', *Südostdeutsches Archiv* xxxii–xxxiii (1989–90), pp 112–21

——, 'Zur Geschichte des Technologietransfers von Deutschland nach Ungarn im Eisenhüttenwesen (14. bis 18. Jahrhundert)', H. Fischer and F. Szabadváry (eds), *Technologietransfer und Wissenschaftsaustausch zwischen Ungarn und Deutschland* (Munich, 1995), pp 59–69

Holl, Imre, 'Sopron (Ödenburg) im Mittelalter, *Acta Archaeologica Academiae Scientiarum Hungaricae* xxxi (1979), pp 105–49

Hóman, Bálint, 'La circolazione delle monete d'oro in Ungheria dal X al XIV secolo e la crisi europea dell'oro nel secolo XIV', *Rivista Italiana di Numismatica* xxxv (1922), pp 109–56

Huszár, Lajos, 'Der ungarische Goldgulden im mittelalterlichen Münzverkehr', *Hamburger Beiträge zur Numismatik*, xxiv–xxvi (1970/72), pp 71–88

Kováts, Ferenc, 'Handelsverbindungen zwischen Köln und Preßburg im Spätmittelalter', *Mitteilungen aus dem Stadtarchiv von Köln* xiv (1912–14), pp 1–31

Kubinyi, András, 'Topographic growth of Buda up to 1541', *Nouvelles études historiques publiées à l'occasion du XIIe Congrès International des Sciences Historiques*, vol 1 (Budapest, 1965), pp 133–58

——, 'Soziale Stellung und Familienverbindungen des deutschen Patriziats von Ofen in der ersten Hälfte des 14. Jahrhunderts', *Archiv für Sippenforschung* xxxvi (1970), pp 446–54

——, *Die Anfänge Ofens* (Giessen, 1972)

——, 'Zur Frage der deutschen Siedlungen im mittleren Teil des Königreichs Ungarn (1200–1541)', Walter Schlesinger (ed.), *Die deutsche*

Ostsiedlung des Mittelalters als Problem der europäischen Geschichte, Vorträge und Forschungen, vol 18 (Sigmaringen, 1975), pp 527–66

——, 'Einige Fragen zur Entwicklung des Städtenetzes in Ungarn im 14–15. Jahrhundert', in Heinz Stoob (ed.), *Die mittelalterliche Städtebildung im südöstlichen Europa* (Cologne–Vienna, 1977), pp 163–83

——, 'Handel und Entwicklung der Städte in der ungarischen Tiefebene im Mittelalter', in Klaus-Detlev Grothusen and Klaus Zernack (eds), *Europa Slavica – Europa Orientalis* (Berlin, 1980), pp 423–44

——, 'Ethnische Minderheiten in den ungarischen Städten des Mittelalters', in Bernhard Kirchgässner and Fritz Reuter (eds), *Städtische Randgruppen und Minderheiten* (Sigmaringen, 1986), pp 183–99

——, 'Horizontale Mobilität im spätmittelalterlichen Königreich Ungarn', in G. Jaritz and A. Müller (eds), *Migration in der Feudalgesellschaft* (Frankfurt–New York, 1988), pp 113–39

——, 'Königliches Salzmonopol und die Städte des Königreichs Ungarn im Mittelalter', in Wilhelm Rausch (ed.), *Stadt und Salz* (Linz, 1988), pp 213–32

——, 'Die Zusammensetzung des städtischen Rates im mittelalterlichen Königreich Ungarn', *Südostdeutsches Archiv* xxxiv–xxxv (1991–92), pp 23–42

——, 'Das ungarische Städtewesen in der Sigismund-Zeit', in Josef Macek, Ernö Marosi and Ferdinand Seibt (eds), *Sigismund von Luxemburg, Kaiser und König in Mitteleuropa 1387–1437* (Warendorf, 1994), pp 171–78

——, 'Stadt und Kirche in Ungarn im Mittelalter', in Franz-Heinz Hye (ed.), *Stadt und Kirche* (Linz, 1995), pp 179–97

——, *König und Volk im spätmittelalterlichen Ungarn* (Herne, 1998)

Ladányi, Erzsébet, 'Libera villa, civitas, oppidum: Terminologische Fragen in der ungarischen Städteentwicklung', *Annales Universitatis Scientiarum Budapestinensis, Sectio historica* xviii (1977), pp 6–14

Mályusz, Elemér, 'Geschichte des Bürgertums in Ungarn', *Vierteljahrschrift für Sozial- und Wirtschaftsgeschichte* xx (1928), pp 357–407

——, 'Der ungarische Goldgulden in Mitteleuropa zu Beginn des 15. Jahrhunderts', in Ferenc Glatz and Ervin Pamlényi (eds), *Etudes historiques hongroises 1985 publiées à l'occasion du Congrès International des Sciences Historiques*, vol 2 (Budapest, 1985), pp 21–35

Marsina, Richard (ed.), *Städte im Donauraum: Bratislava–Preßburg 1291–1991* (Bratislava, 1993)

Mollay, Károly (ed.), *Das Ofner Stadtrecht. Eine deutschsprachige Rechtssammlung des 15. Jahrhunderts aus Ungarn* (Budapest, 1959)

Nagy, Balázs, 'Transcontinental trade from east-central Europe to western Europe (fourteenth and fifteenth centuries)', in Balázs Nagy and Marcell Sebök (eds), *The Man of Many Devices, Who Wandered Full Many Ways* (Budapest, 1999), pp 347–56

Pach, Zsigmond Pál, 'Levantine trade and Hungary in the Middle Ages (theses, controversies, arguments)', *Etudes historiques hongroises 1975 publiées à l'occasion du XIVe Congrès International des Sciences Historiques*, vol 1 (Budapest, 1975), pp 283–307; reprinted in Pach, *Hungary and the European Economy*, ch. VI

——, 'The Transylvanian route of Levantine trade at the turn of the 15th and 16th centuries', *Etudes historiques hongroises 1980 publiées à l'occasion du XVe Congrès International des Sciences Historiques*, vol 1 (Budapest, 1980), pp 133–66; reprinted in Pach, *Hungary and the European Economy*, ch. VII

Paulinyi, Oszkár, 'The Crown monopoly of the refining metallurgy of precious metals and the technology of the cameral refineries in Hungary and Transylvania in the period of advanced and late feudalism (1325–1700), with data on the output', H. Kellenbenz (ed.), *Precious Metals in the Age of Expansion* (Stuttgart, 1981)

Petrovics, István, 'The role of towns in the defence system of medieval Hungary', in P. Contamine and O. Guyotjeannin (eds), *La guerre, la violence et les gens au moyen age*, 2 vols (Paris, 1996), vol. 1, pp 263–71

——, 'The fading glory of a former royal seat: the case of medieval Temesvár', in Balázs Nagy and Marcell Sebök (eds), *The Man of Many Devices, Who Wandered Full Many Ways* (Budapest, 1999), pp 527–38

Pohl, Artur, *Die Grenzlandprägung. Münzprägung in Österreich und Ungarn im fünfzehnten Jahrhundert* (Graz, 1972)

——, *Ungarische Goldgulden des Mittelalters (1325–1526)* (Graz, 1974)

Probszt, Günther, 'Die Rolle des ungarischen Goldguldens in der österreichischen Wirtschaft des Mittelalters', *Südost-Forschungen* xxii (1963), pp 234–58

Rady, Martyn C., *Medieval Buda: A Study in Municipal Government and Jurisdiction in the Kingdom of Hungary* (Boulder, 1985)

——, 'The Hungarian Copper Trade and Industry in the Later Middle Ages', in M. McCauley and J.E.O. Screen (eds), *Trade and Transport in Russia and Eastern Europe* (London, 1985)

Stromer, Wolfgang von, *Oberdeutsche Hochfinanz 1350–1450*, Vierteljahrschrift für Sozial- und Wirtschaftsgeschichte, Beihefte 55–57, 3 vols (Wiesbaden, 1970)

——, 'Medici-Unternehmen in den Karpatenländern: Versuche zur Beherrschung des Weltmarkts für Buntmetalle', in Bruno Dini (ed.), *Aspetti della vita economica medievale* (Florence, 1985), pp 370–97

——, 'Die Saigerhütte', in H. Fischer and F. Szabadváry (eds), *Technologietransfer und Wissenschaftsaustausch zwischen Ungarn und Deutschland* (Munich, 1995), pp 27–57

Székely, György, 'Les facteurs économiques et politiques dans les rapports de la Hongrie et de Venise à l'époque de Sigismond', in

Vittore Branca (ed.), *Venezia e Ungheria nel Rinascimento* (Florence, 1973), pp 37–51

Szende, K., 'Some aspects of urban landownership in western Hungary', in Finn-Einar Eliassen and Geir Atle Ersland (eds), *Power, Profit and Urban Land* (Aldershot, 1996), pp 141–66

——, 'Was there a bourgeoisie in medieval Hungary?', in Balázs Nagy and Marcell Sebök (eds), *The Man of Many Devices, Who Wandered Full Many Ways* (Budapest, 1999), pp 445–59

Szűcs, Jenő, *Das Städtewesen in Ungarn im 15.–17. Jahrhundert*, Studia historica, No 53 (Budapest, 1963); also in: György Székely et al. (eds), *Renaissance und Reformation in Polen und in Ungarn 1450–1650* (Budapest, 1963), pp 97–164

CHAPTER 16: THE RURAL LANDSCAPE

Belényesy, Márta, 'Der Ackerbau und seine Produkte in Ungarn im XIV. Jahrhundert', *Acta Ethnographica Academiae Scientiarum Hungaricae* vi (1958), pp 256–321

——, 'Hufengröße und Zugtierbestand der bäuerlichen Betriebe in Ungarn im 14-15. Jh.', in L. Földes (ed.), *Viehwirtschaft und Hirtenkultur* (Budapest, 1969), pp 460–502

Held, Joseph, 'The peasant revolt of Bábolna, 1437–1438', *Slavic Review* xxxvi (1977), pp 25–38

——, 'Peasants in arms, 1437–1438 and 1456', in János M. Bak and Béla K. Király (eds), *From Hunyadi to Rákóczi: War and Society in Medieval and Early Modern Hungary* (New York, 1982), pp 81–102

——, 'Fifteenth-century peasant life in Hungary', in Ferenc Glatz (ed.), *Modern Age – Modern Historian: In Memoriam György Ránki* (Budapest, 1990), pp 19–39

Ila, Bálint, 'Beiträge zur Geschichte der Rechtsprechung über die Hörigen in Ungarn im 15. Jahrhundert', P. Brière (ed.), *Mélanges offerts à Szabolcs de Vajay* (Braga, 1971), pp 337–54

Komjáthy, Anthony, 'Hungarian *jobbágyság* in the fifteenth century', *East European Quarterly* X/1 (1976), pp 77–111

Kubinyi, András, 'Bäuerlicher Alltag im spätmittelalterlichen Ungarn', *Bäuerliche Sachkultur des Spätmittelalters* (Vienna, 1984), pp 235–64

——, 'Die Rolle der Archäologie und der Urkunden bei der Erforschung des Alltagslebens im Spätmittelalter', in Ferenc Glatz and Ervin Pamlényi (eds) *Etudes historiques hongroises 1985 publiées à l'occasion du Congrès International des Sciences Historiques*, vol 1 (Budapest, 1985), pp 615–44

——, 'Mittelalterliche Siedlungsformen in Westungarn', in Helmuth Feigl (ed.), *Siedlungsnamen und Siedlungsformen als Quellen zur Besiedlungsgeschichte Niederösterreichs* (Vienna, 1986), pp 151–70

——, *König und Volk im spätmittelalterlichen Ungarn* (Herne, 1998)

Kubinyi, András and József Laszlovszky (eds), *Alltag und materielle Kultur im mittelalterlichen Ungarn*, Medium aevum quotidianum, vol 22 (Krems, 1991)

Laszlovszky, József, 'Field systems in medieval Hungary', in Balázs Nagy and Marcell Sebök (eds), *The Man of Many Devices, Who Wandered Full Many Ways* (Budapest, 1999), pp. 423–44

Makkai, László, 'Agrarian landscapes of historical Hungary in feudal times', *Etudes historiques hongroises 1980 publiées à l'occasion du XVe Congrès International des Sciences Historiques*, vol 1 (Budapest, 1980), pp 193–208

Maksay, F., 'Das Agrarsiedlungssystem des mittelalterlichen Ungarns', *Acta Historica Academiae Scientiarum Hungaricae* xxiv (1978), pp 83–108

Pascu, Stefan, *Der transsilvanische Volksaufstand* (Bukarest, 1964)

Székely, György, 'Antal Budai Nagy et la guerre paysanne de Transylvanie', *Etudes historiques hongroises 1980 publiées à l'occasion du XVe Congrès International des Sciences Historiques*, vol 1 (Budapest, 1980), pp 85–100

CHAPTER 17: THE AGE OF JOHN HUNYADI (1437–1457)

Babinger, Franz, 'Von Amurath zu Amurath: Vor- und Nachspiel der Schlacht bei Varna (1444)', *Oriens* iii (1950), pp 229–65

——, *Mehmed the Conqueror and his time* (Princeton, 1978)

Bertényi, Iván, 'Les sceaux comme sources de la préhistoire des droits des Ordres (Etats) Hongrois dans la conservation de la Sainte Couronne', *Parliaments, Estates and Representation* xv (1995), pp 73–9

Cvetkova, Bistra, *La bataille mémorable des peuples: Le sudest européen et la conquete ottomane* (Sofia, 1971)

Engel, Pál 'János Hunyadi: The decisive years of his career, 1440–1444', in János M. Bak and Béla K. Király (eds), *From Hunyadi to Rákóczi: War and Society in Medieval and Early Modern Hungary* (New York, 1982), pp 103–23

——, 'János Hunyadi and the peace "of Szeged"', *Acta Orientalia Academiae Scientiarum Hungaricae* xlvii (1994), pp 241–57

Fine, John V.A., 'A tale of three fortresses: controversies surrounding the Turkish conquest of Smederevo, of an unnamed fortress at the junction of the Sava and Bosna, and of Bobovac', in Timothy S. Miller and John Nesbitt (eds), *Peace and War in Byzantium* (Washington, 1995), pp 181–96

Halecki, Ottokar, *The Crusade of Varna. A Discussion of Controversial Problems* (New York, 1943)

Held, Joseph, 'The defense of Nándorfehérvár (Belgrade) in 1456: a discussion of controversial issues', in S.B. Vardy and A.H. Vardy (eds),

Society in Change: Studies in Honor of Béla K. Király (New York, 1983), pp 25–37

——, *Hunyadi: Legend and Reality* (New York, 1985)

Kritovoulos, *History of Mehmed the Conqueror*, trans. C.T. Riggs (Princeton, 1964)

Mollay, K. (ed.), *Die Denkwürdigkeiten der Helene Kottanerin* (Vienna, 1971)

Pall, Francis, 'Scanderbeg et Janco de Hunedoara', *Studia Albanica* v (1968), pp 103–17

Sweeney, James R., 'The tricky queen and her clever lady-in-waiting: stealing the crown to secure succession, Visegrád, 1440', *East Central Europe/L'Europe du Centre Est* xx–xxiii/1 (1993–96), pp 87–100

Székely, György, 'The court party versus the Hunyadi party – structural changes in the government of the Hungarian state', in Ferenc Glatz and Ervin Pamlényi (eds), *Etudes historiques hongroises 1985 publiées à l'occasion du Congrès International des Sciences Historiques*, vol 2 (Budapest, 1985), pp 461–82

Tursun Beg, *The History of Mehmed the Conqueror*, ed. H. Inalcik and R. Murphey (Minneapolis, 1978)

Williamson, Maya B. (trans), *The Memoirs of Helene Kottanner* (Woodbridge, 1998)

Wostry, Wilhelm, *König Albrecht II (1437–1439)*, 2 vols (Prague, 1906–7)

Zsolnay, Vilmos von, *Vereinigungsversuche Südosteuropas im 15. Jahrhundert. Johann von Hunyadi* (Frankfurt, 1967)

CHAPTER 18: KING MATTHIAS CORVINUS (1458–1490)

Andreescu, Ştefan and Raymond T. McNally, 'Exactly where was Dracula captured in 1462?', *East European Quarterly*, xxiii (1989), pp 269–81

Antonius de Bonfinis, *Rerum Ungaricarum decades*, ed. I. Fógel, B. Iványi et L. Juhász, 4 vols (Budapest, 1936–41)

Bak, János M., 'Janus Pannonius (1434–1472): The historical background', in A. Barrett (ed.), *Janus Pannonius: The Epigrams* (Budapest, 1985), pp 29–45

——, 'The Hungary of Matthias Corvinus: a state in "central Europe" on the threshold of modernity', *Bohemia* xxxi (1990), pp 339–49

Berzeviczy, Albert., *Béatrice d'Aragon, reine de Hongrie*, 2 vols (Paris, 1911–12)

Białostocki, Jan, 'Borrowing and originality in the east-central European Renaissance', in Antoni Mączak, Henryk Samsonowicz and Peter Burke (eds), *East-Central Europe in Transition: From the Fourteenth to the Seventeenth Century* (Cambridge, 1985), pp 153–66

Birnbaum, Marianna, *Janus Pannonius: Poet and Politician* (Zagreb, 1981)

Bónis, György, 'King Matthias the legislator', *The Hungarian Quarterly* vi (1940), pp 699–710

Branca, Vittore (ed.), *Venezia e Ungheria nel Rinascimento* (Florence, 1973)

Csapodi, Csaba, *The Corvinian Library: History and Stock* (Budapest, 1973)

Csapodi, Csaba, and Klára Csapodi-Gárdonyi (eds) *Bibliotheca Corviniana: The Library of King Matthias Corvinus of Hungary* (Budapest, 1969)

Domonkos, Leslie S., 'The origins of the University of Pozsony in the fifteenth century', *The New Review: Journal of East European History* 9 (1969) pp 270–89

——, 'János Vitéz, the father of Hungarian humanism', *The New Hungarian Quarterly* xx (1979), pp 142–50

——, 'The problems of Hungarian university foundations in the Middle Ages', in S.B. Vardy and A.H. Vardy (eds), *Society in Change: Studies in Honor of Béla K. Király* (New York, 1983), pp 371–90

——, 'The Hungarian royal chancery, 1458–1490: was it a center of humanism?', in S.B. Várdy and A.H. Vardy (eds), *Triumph in Adversity: Studies in Hungarian Civilization in Honor of Professor Ferenc Somogyi* (Boulder, 1988), pp 97–111

Döry, Ferenc et al. (eds), *Decreta regni Hungariae. Gesetze und Verordnungen Ungarns 1458–1490* (Budapest, 1989)

Feuer-Tóth, Rózsa, *Art and Humanism in the Age of Matthias Corvinus* (Budapest, 1990)

Fraknói, Vilmos, *Matthias Corvinus, König von Ungarn (1458–1490)* (Freiburg i. Brsg., 1891)

Glassl, Horst, 'Ungarn im Mächtedreieck Osteuropa und der Kampf um das Zwischenland Schlesien', *Ungarn-Jahrbuch* v (1973), pp 16–49

Gragg, Florence A. (trans.), *The Commentaries of Pius II*, Smith College Studies in History, vols 22, 25, 30, 35, 43 (Northampton, Mass., 1936–57)

Grieger, Rudolf, *Filipecz. Johann, Bischof von Wardein, Diplomat der Könige Matthias und Wladislaw*, Studia Hungarica 20 (München: Trofenik, 1982)

Hoensch, Jörg K., *Matthias Corvinus: Diplomat, Feldherr und Mäzen* (Graz, 1998)

Kadić, Ante, 'Croatian humanists at the Hungarian court', *East European Quarterly* xxii (1988), pp 129–46

Kaufmann, Thomas D., *Court, Cloister and City: the Art and Culture of Central Europe, 1450–1800* (London, 1995)

Klaniczay, Tibor (ed.), *Rapporti veneto-ungheresi all'epoca del Rinascimento* (Budapest, 1975)

Klaniczay, Tibor and J. Jankovics (eds), *Matthias Corvinus and the Humanism in Central Europe* (Budapest, 1994)

Kubinyi, András, 'Die Frage des bosnischen Königtums von Nikolaus Újlaky', *Studia Slavica Academiae Scientiarum Hungaricae* iv (1958), pp 373–84

——, *Matthias Corvinus* (Herne, 1999)

Laszlovszky, József (ed.), *Medieval Visegrád* (Budapest, 1995)

Nehring, Karl, *Matthias Corvinus, Kaiser Friedrich III. und das Reich* (Munich, 1975; 2nd edn 1989)

Rázsó, Gyula, *Die Feldzüge Königs Matthias Corvinus in Niederösterreich, 1477–1490* (Vienna, 1973)

——, 'Una strana alleanza', in Vittore Branca (ed.), *Venezia e Ungheria nel Rinascimento* (Florence, 1973), pp 79–100

——, 'The mercenary army of King Matthias Corvinus', in János M. Bak and Béla K. Király (eds), *From Hunyadi to Rákóczi: War and Society in Medieval and Early Modern Hungary* (New York, 1982), pp 125–40

——, 'Die Türkenpolitik Matthias Corvinus', *Acta Historica Academiae Scientiarum Hungaricae* xxxii (1986), pp 3–50

Rees, Valery, 'Pre-reformation changes in Hungary at the end of the fifteenth century', in Karin Maag (ed.), *The Reformation in Eastern and Central Europe* (Aldershot, 1997), pp 19–35

Stangler, Gottfried et al. (eds), *Schallaburg '82. Matthias Corvinus und die Renaissance in Ungarn 1458–1541*, Katalog des Niederösterreichischen Landesmuseums, Neue Folge, no 118 (Vienna, 1982)

Stoicescu, Nicolae, *Vlad Țepeș, Prince of Walachia* (Bucharest, 1978)

Székely, György, 'Oligarchie, Adelige, Bürger: Ungarn in den Jahren 1458–60', *Parliaments, Estates and Representation* xv (1995), pp 82–89

Székely, György, and E. Fügedi (eds), *La renaissance et la réformation en Pologne et en Hongrie 1450–1650* (Budapest, 1963)

Vajay, Szabolcs de, 'Un ambassadeur bien choisi: Bernardinus de Frangipanus et sa mission à Naples, en 1476', in Balázs Nagy and Marcell Sebök (eds), *The Man of Many Devices, Who Wandered Full Many Ways* (Budapest, 1999), pp 550–57

V. Kovács, Sándor, 'Die Sodalitas Litteraria Danubiana und das ungarische geistige Leben', *Studien zur Geschichte der deutsch-ungarischen literarischen Beziehungen* (Berlin, 1969), pp 44–51

CHAPTER 19: HUNGARY AT THE END OF THE MIDDLE AGES

Bónis, György, 'Die Entwicklung der geistlichen Gerichtsbarkeit in Ungarn vor 1526', *Zeitschrift der Savigny-Stiftung für Rechtsgeschichte, Kanonistische Abteilung* xlix (1963), pp 174–235

Csizmadia, Andor, 'Die Entwicklung des Patronatrechts in Ungarn', *Österreichisches Archiv für Kirchenrecht*, xxv (1974), pp 308–27

Domonkos, L.S., 'The multiethnic character of the late medieval Hungarian state', in J.F. Cadzow, A. Ludanyi, J.L. Éltetö (eds),

Transylvania: The Roots of Ethnic Conflict (Kent, Ohio, 1983), pp 41–60

Engel, Pál, 'Der Adel Nordostungarns zur Zeit König Sigismunds (1387–1437)', in Ferenc Glatz (ed.), *Études historiques hongroises 1990*, vol 1 (Budapest, 1990), pp 27–47

Fügedi, Erik, 'Hungarian bishops in the fifteenth century', *Acta Historica Academiae Scientiarum Hungaricae* xi (1965), pp 375–91; reprinted in Fügedi, *Kings*, chapter II

——, 'Der Außenhandel Ungarns am Anfang des 16. Jahrhunderts', Der Außenhandel Ostmitteleuropas 1450–1650 (Cologne–Vienna, 1971), pp 56–85

Hervay, Franciscus L., *Repertorium historicum Ordinis Cisterciensis in Hungaria* (Rome, 1984)

——, (ed.), *Gyögyösi Gergely: Vitae fratrum eremitarum ordinis sancti Pauli primi eremitae* (Budapest, 1988)

Kubinyi, András, 'Die Nürnberger Haller in Ofen. Ein Beitrag zur Geschichte des Südosthandels im Spätmittelalter', *Mitteilungen des Vereines für Geschichte der Stadt Nürnberg* lii (1963–64), pp 80–128

——, 'Die Städte Ofen und Pest und der Fernhandel am Ende des 15. und am Anfang des 16. Jahrhunderts', in Ingomar Bog (ed.), *Der Aussenhandel Ostmitteleuropas 1450–1650* (Cologne–Vienna, 1971), pp 342–433

——, 'Les Cotta de Tolède et la colonie espagnole à Bude aux 15e et 16e siècles', in P. Brière (ed.), *Mélanges offerts à Szabolcs de Vajay* (Braga, 1971), pp 381–90

——, 'Die Auswirkungen der Türkenkriege auf die zentralen Städte Ungarns bis 1541', in Othmar Pickl (ed.), *Die wirtschaftlichen Auswirkungen der Türkenkriege* (Graz, 1971), pp 201–19

——, 'Wüstungen, Zersplitterung der Bauernhufen und Wirtschaft in den Besitzungen der Magnatenfamilie Garai in Ungarn', in *Festschrift Othmar Pickl* (Graz–Vienna, 1987), pp 367–77

——, 'Residenz und Herrschaftsbildung in Ungarn in der zweiten Hälfte des 15. Jahrhundert und am Beginn des 16. Jahrhunderts', in Hans Patze and Werner Paravicini (eds), *Fürstliche Residenzen im spätmittelalterlichen Europa*, Vorträge und Forschungen, vol 36 (Sigmaringen, 1991), pp 421–62

——, 'Wirtschaftsgeschichtliche Probleme in den Beziehungen Ungarns zum Westen am Ende des Mittelalters', in *Westmitteleuropa-Ostmitteleuropa, Festschrift für Ferdinand Seibt zum 65. Geburtstag* (München, 1992), pp 165–174

——, 'Der Eisenhandel in den ungarischen Städten des Mittelalters', in Ferdinand Oppl (ed.), *Stadt und Eisen* (Linz, 1992), pp 197–206

——, 'Der königliche Hof als Integrationszentrum Ungarns von der Mitte des 15. bis zum ersten Drittel des 16. Jahrhunderts und sein

Einfluss auf die städtische Entwicklung Ungarns', in Evamaria Engel (ed.), *Metropolen im Wandel. Zentralität in Ostmitteleuropa an der Wende vom Mittelalter zur Neuzeit* (Berlin, 1995), pp 145–62

——, *König und Volk im spätmittelalterlichen Ungarn* (Herne, 1998)

Maksay, F., *Le pays de la noblesse nombreuse*, Studia historica, No 139 (Budapest, 1980); also in: *Etudes historiques hongroises 1980 publiées à l'occasion du XVe Congrès International des Sciences Historiques*, vol 1 (Budapest, 1980), pp 167–92

Mályusz, Elemér, *Die Entstehung der ständischen Schichten im mittelalterlichen Ungarn*, Studia historica, No 137 (Budapest, 1980); also in: *Etudes historiques hongroises 1980 publiées à l'occasion du XVe Congrès International des Sciences Historiques*, vol 1 (Budapest, 1980), pp 101–32

Pach, Zsigmond Pál, 'Das Entwicklungsniveau der feudalen Agrarverhältnisse in Ungarn in der zweiten Hälfte des XV. Jahrhunderts', *Etudes historiques publiées par la Commission Nationale des Historiens Hongrois*, vol 1 (Budapest, 1960), pp 387–435

——, 'The development of feudal rent in Hungary in the fifteenth century', *Economic History Review*, 2nd series, xix (1966), pp 1–14; reprinted in Pach, *Hungary and the European Economy*, chapter I

——, 'Sixteenth-century Hungary: commercial activity and market production by the nobles', in Pach, *Hungary and the European Economy*, chapter III

Skladaný, Marian, 'Europäische Bedeutung des Kupferwesens in Banská Bystrica im 15. Jahrhundert', *Historický časopís* 31 (1983), pp 345–70

Szabó, István, 'La répartition de la population de Hongrie entre les bourgades et les villages dans les années 1449–1526', *Etudes historiques publiées par la Commission Nationale des Historiens Hongrois*, vol 1 (Budapest, 1960), pp 359–85

Székely, György, 'Landwirtschaft und Gewerbe in der ungarischen ländlichen Gesellschaft um 1500', *Etudes historiques publiées par la Commission Nationale des Historiens Hongrois*, vol 1 (Budapest, 1960), pp 469–503

CHAPTER 20: THE AGE OF THE JAGIELLONIAN KINGS (1490–1526)

Alföldi, László M., 'The Battle of Mohács, 1526', János M. Bak and Béla K. Király (eds), *From Hunyadi to Rákóczi: War and Society in Medieval and Early Modern Hungary* (New York, 1982), pp 189–201

Bak, J.M., 'Delinquent lords and forsaken serfs: thoughts on war and society during the crisis of feudalism', in S.B. Vardy and A.H. Vardy (eds), *Society in Change: Studies in Honor of Béla K. Király* (New York, 1983), pp 291–304

Bónis, György, 'Ständisches Finanzwesen in Ungarn im frühen 16. Jahrhundert', *Nouvelles études historiques publiées à l'occasion du XIIe Congrès International des Sciences Historiques*, vol 1 (Budapest, 1965), pp 83–103

——, 'The Hungarian feudal Diet (13th to 18th centuries)', *Recueils de la Société Jean Bodin* xxv (1965), pp 287–307

Deér, J., 'Le sentiment national hongrois au moyen âge', *Nouvelle Revue de Hongrie* lv (1936), pp 411–19

Domonkos, Leslie S., 'Ecclesiastical patrons as a factor in the Hungarian Renaissance', *New Review of East European History* xiv (1974), pp 100–16

——, 'The battle of Mohács as a cultural watershed', in János M. Bak and Béla K. Király (eds), *From Hunyadi to Rákóczi: War and Society in Medieval and Early Modern Hungary* (New York, 1982), pp 203–24

Holub, József, 'Quod omnes tangit', *Revue historique de droit français et étranger* iv/28 (1951), pp 97–102

——, 'La représentation politique en Hongrie au Moyen Age', *Etudes présentées à la Commission Internationale pour l'Histoire des Assemblées d'États* xviii (Louvain–Paris, 1958), pp 79–121

Housley, Norman, 'Crusading and social revolt: the Hungarian peasant rising of 1514', *Journal of Ecclesiastical History* xlix (1998), pp 1–29

Klaniczay, Gábor, 'Images and designations for rebellious peasants in late medieval Hungary', in Balázs Nagy and Marcell Sebök (eds), *The Man of Many Devices, Who Wandered Full Many Ways* (Budapest, 1999), pp 115–27

Kubinyi, András, 'Die Wahlkapitulationen Wladislaws II. in Ungarn (1490)', in Rudolf Vierhaus (ed.), *Herrschaftsverträge, Wahlkapitulationen, Fundamentalgesetze* (Göttingen, 1977), pp 140–62

——, 'Zur Frage der Vertretung der Städte im ungarischen Reichstag bis 1526', in Bernhard Töpfer (ed.), *Städte und Ständestaat* (Berlin, 1980), pp 215–46

——, 'The road to defeat: Hungarian politics and defense in the Jagiellonian period', in János M. Bak and Béla K. Király (eds), *From Hunyadi to Rákóczi: War and Society in Medieval and Early Modern Hungary* (New York, 1982), pp 159–78

——, 'Stände und Staat in Ungarn in der zweiten Hälfte des 15. Jahrhunderts', *Bohemia* xxxi (1990), pp 312–25

——, 'Alltag und Fest am ungarischen Königshof der Jagellonen 1490–1526', in Werner Paravicini (ed.), *Residenzforschung*, vol 5 (Sigmaringen, 1995), pp 197–215

——, 'István Werbőczy als Politiker vor Mohács (1526)', in Balázs Nagy and Marcell Sebök (eds), *The Man of Many Devices, Who Wandered Full Many Ways* (Budapest, 1999), pp 558–82

Kulcsár, Péter (ed.), *Stephanus Brodericus: De conflictu Hungarorum cum Solymano Turcarum imperatore ad Mahach historia verissima* (Budapest, 1985)

Kunt, M. and C. Woodhead (eds), *Suleyman the Magnificent and his Age* (London, 1995)

Mályusz, Elemér, 'Les débuts du vote de la taxe par les ordres dans la Hongrie féodale', *Nouvelles études historiques publiées à l'occasion du XIIe Congrès International des Sciences Historiques*, vol 1 (Budapest, 1965), pp 55–82

Pellathy, G.S., 'The Dozsa revolt: prelude and aftermath', *East European Quarterly* xxi (1987), pp 275–95

Perjés, G., *The Fall of the Medieval Kingdom of Hungary: Mohács, 1526 Buda, 1541* (Boulder, 1989)

Szakály, Ferenc, 'The 1526 Mohács disaster', *The New Hungarian Quarterly* xviii (1977), pp 43–63

——, 'The Hungarian-Croatian border defense system and its collapse', in János M. Bak and Béla K. Király (eds), *From Hunyadi to Rákóczi: War and Society in Medieval and Early Modern Hungary* (New York, 1982), pp 141–58

Szűcs, Jenő, '"Nationalität" und "Nationalbewusstsein" im Mittelalter: Versuch einer einheitlichen Begriffssprache', *Acta Historica Academiae Scientiarum Hungaricae* xviii (1972), pp 1–38, 245–66

——, 'Die Ideologie des ungarischen Bauernkrieges', in Gusztáv Heckenast (ed.), *Aus der Geschichte der ostmitteleuropäischen Bauernbewegungen im 16–17. Jahrhundert* (Budapest, 1977), pp 157–87

——, 'Die oppositionelle Strömung der Franziskaner im Hintergrund des Bauernkrieges und der Reformation in Ungarn', in Ferenc Glatz and Ervin Pamlényi (eds), *Etudes historiques hongroises 1985 publiées à l'occasion du Congrès International des Sciences Historiques*, vol 2 (Budapest, 1985), pp 483–513

Index

431

Carleton College Library
One North College Street
Northfield, MN 55057-4097

WITHDRAWN